CAMBRIDGE TEXTS IN THE
HISTORY OF POLITICAL THOUGHT

———

G. W. F. HEGEL
Elements of the Philosophy of Right

CAMBRIDGE TEXTS IN THE
HISTORY OF POLITICAL THOUGHT

Series editors

RAYMOND GEUSS *Professor of Philosophy, Columbia University*
QUENTIN SKINNER *Professor of Political Science in the University of Cambridge*

This series will make available to students the most important texts required for an understanding of the history of political thought. The scholarship of the present generation has greatly expanded our sense of the range of authors indispensable for such an understanding, and the series will reflect those developments. It will also include a number of less well-known works, in particular those needed to establish the intellectual contexts that in turn help to make sense of the major texts. The principal aim, however, will be to produce new versions of the major texts themselves, based on the most up-to-date scholarship. The preference will always be for complete texts, and a special feature of the series will be to complement individual texts, within the compass of a single volume, with subsidiary contextual material. Each volume will contain an introduction on the historical identity and contemporary significance of the text concerned, as well as such student aids as notes for further reading and chronologies of the principal events in a thinker's life.

For a complete list of titles published in the series, see end of book.

G. W. F. HEGEL

Elements of the Philosophy of Right

EDITED BY

ALLEN W. WOOD
Professor of Philosophy, Cornell University

TRANSLATED BY

H. B. NISBET
Professor of Modern Languages,
University of Cambridge
and
Fellow of Sidney Sussex College

The right of the
University of Cambridge
to print and sell
all manner of books
was granted by
Henry VIII in 1534.
The University has printed
and published continuously
since 1584.

CAMBRIDGE UNIVERSITY PRESS
CAMBRIDGE
NEW YORK   PORT CHESTER
MELBOURNE   SYDNEY

Published by the Press Syndicate of the University of Cambridge
The Pitt Building, Trumpington Street, Cambridge CB2 1RP
40 West 20th Street, New York, NY 10011–4211, USA
10 Stamford Road, Oakleigh, Melbourne 3166, Australia

© Cambridge University Press 1991

First published 1991

Printed in Great Britain by The Bath Press, Avon

British Library cataloguing in publication data
Hegel, Georg Wilhelm Friedrich 1770–1831
Elements of the philosophy of right – (Cambridge texts in
the history of political thought).
1. State. Theories
I. Title II. Wood, Allen W. III. Nisbet, H. B. (Hugh
Barr) *1940–* IV. [Grundlinien der Philosophie des Rechts.
English]
320.101

Library of Congress cataloguing in publication data

Hegel, Georg Wilhelm Friedrich, 1770–1831
[Grundlinien der Philosophie des Rechts. English]
Elements of the philosophy of right/G.W.F. Hegel; edited by Allen W. Wood;
translated by H. B. Nisbet.
p. cm. – (Cambridge texts in the history of political thought)
Translation of: Grundlinien der Philosophie des Rechts.
ISBN 0–521–34438–7. – ISBN 0–521–34889–9 (pbk.)
1. Law–Philosophy. 2. Natural law. 3. State, The.
4. Political science. 5. Ethics.
I. Wood, Allen W. II. Nisbet, Hugh Barr. III. Title. IV. Series.
K230.H43G7813 1991
340′. 1–dc20 90–21617 CIP

ISBN 0 521 34438 7 hardback
ISBN 0 521 348889 paperback

BS
WV

Contents

Editor's introduction

Hegel was born on 27 August 1770 in Stuttgart, in the south German state of Württemberg, son of a middle-class civil servant. His professional career, pursued entirely outside his home state, did not begin until he was over thirty, and was interrupted between 1806 and 1816. His eventual rise to prominence was meteoric: Hegel was offered a professorship at the University of Heidelberg in 1816, followed by an appointment two years later to the prestigious chair in philosophy at the University of Berlin which had had Fichte as its only previous occupant. Hegel occupied this position until his death from cholera on 14 November 1831. The influence of his philosophy began to decline even before his death, but its impact on Prussian academic life was perpetuated through the activity of some of his students, especially Johannes Schulze, who was Privy Councillor in charge of education from 1823 until the 1840s.[1]

Hegel's first lectures on right, ethics and the state were delivered in 1817, during his first autumn at Heidelberg. As his text he used the paragraphs on 'objective spirit' from his newly published *Encyclopaedia of the Philosophical Sciences* (1816) (EH §§ 400–452).[2] His second series of lectures came a year later in Berlin. He soon formed the intention of expanding his treatment of this part of the system in a longer text, which probably existed in draft well before his third series of lectures on right and the state were delivered in 1819–1820.

A fateful turn of political events in Prussia forced him to delay publication of this new work. Since the defeat of Prussia by Napoleon in 1806–1807, a reform movement within the government had been taking the country away from absolutism and toward constitutionalism.

After the defeat of Napoleon in 1815, this made Prussia an object of suspicion and alarm throughout the relatively less progressive continental states, especially Austria and Russia. In the summer of 1819, the cause of reform was decisively defeated by its opponents within the feudal nobility (see Preface, note 18). In September there was a conference of German states in Carlsbad. It imposed censorship on all academic publications and set forth guidelines for the removal of 'demagogues' from the universities. This resulted in the dismissal of several prominent academics, including Hegel's old personal enemy J. F. Fries, but also in the arrest of some of Hegel's own students and assistants (see Preface, notes 6, 8, 11, 12, 15, 18). In the light of the new situation, Hegel revised his textbook on right, composing a new preface in June, 1820. Published early in 1821, it was to be his last major work.

Images of Hegel's political thought

From the beginning the *Philosophy of Right* was an object of controversy. The earliest reviews, even those written by men Hegel had counted among his friends, were almost uniformly negative.[3] Hegel's attack on Fries in the Preface was interpreted as showing unqualified approval of the academic repression. His declaration: 'What is rational is actual; and what is actual is rational' was read as bestowing an unqualified blessing on the political status quo (see Preface, note 22). Many could see nothing in Hegel's book except an attempt to ingratiate himself with the authorities. As Fries himself put it: 'Hegel's metaphysical mushroom has grown not in the gardens of science but on the dunghill of servility.'[4]

The earliest attacks on the *Philosophy of Right* viewed it solely in relation to the immediate political situation. Later critics in the liberal tradition followed their interpretation, but gave to the image of Hegel as conservative sycophant a broader philosophical significance.[5] Right-Hegelian interpretations of Hegel's political thought under Friedrich Wilhelm IV and German nationalist and statist interpretations during the Bismarck period tended only to confirm the idea that Hegel's political thought consorts well with the spirit of absolutism and the Prussian *Machtstaat*.[6] In the first half of our century the same image of Hegel naturally led critics to see him as a forerunner of German imperialism and National Socialism.[7] Together with the thought that the roots of Marxism lie in Hegel's philosophy, this secured for Hegel a prominent if unenviable place in the popular demonology of totalitarianism.[8]

There were always those, however, who insisted that Hegel was fundamentally a theorist of the modern constitutional state, emphasizing in the state most of the same features which win the approval of Hegel's liberal critics. This was always the position of the Hegelian 'centre', including Hegel's own students and most direct nineteenth-century followers.[9] This more sympathetic tradition in Hegel scholarship has reasserted itself decisively since the middle of this century, to such an extent that there is now a virtual consensus among knowledgeable scholars that the earlier images of Hegel, as philosopher of the reactionary Prussian restoration and forerunner of modern totalitarianism, are simply wrong, whether they are viewed as accounts of Hegel's attitude toward Prussian politics or as broader philosophical interpretations of his theory of the state.[10]

Hegel and the Prussian state

Hegel's political thought needs to be understood in relation to the institutions and issues of its own time. Yet this is something even Hegel's contemporaries themselves were often unable to do. The difficulty and obscurity of Hegel's writings posed problems for them, just as they have for subsequent readers. The Preface of the *Philosophy of Right*, with its immediate relation to events of the day, provided the earliest critics with an easy and obvious way of grasping, labelling, and categorizing its contents. From Hegel's attacks on Fries and his evident attempt to placate the censors, they inferred that he was an opponent of the Prussian reform movement, siding with the reaction's repressive policies toward intellectual life generally and the universities in particular. In the light of these conclusions, they judged (or prejudged) the political theory presented in the rest of the book. Had the critics studied the actual contents of the *Philosophy of Right* more closely, however, they could not have reconciled them with the idea that Hegel's defence of the state is an apology either for the conservative position or for the Prussian state as it existed in 1820.

In 1815, under the reform administration of Chancellor Hardenberg, King Friedrich Wilhelm III solemnly promised to give his people a written constitution. The political victory of the conservatives in the summer of 1819 ensured that the promise would never be kept, and it was a firm tenet of the conservative position that it never should be kept, that it never should have been given in the first place. Yet earlier in the year both Hardenberg and the progressive Interior Minister Wilhelm von Humboldt drew up constitutional plans, providing for representative institutions, in the shape of a bicameral estates assembly. These plans are strikingly similar to the Estates as described by Hegel in PR §§ 298–314 (see § 300, note 1; § 303, note 1; § 312, note 1).

The Prussian officer corps and the higher levels of the civil service were open only to the hereditary nobility. Reformers under the administration of Chancellor Karl Freiherr vom Stein (1808–1810) had attempted without success to open them to the bourgeoisie. In Hegel's rational state, all citizens are eligible for military command and the civil service (PR § 271, note 2; § 277, note 1; § 291 and note 1). Hegel advocates public criminal trials and trial by jury, neither of which existed in Prussia during his lifetime (PR § 228 and note 1).

Hegel's rational state does strongly resemble Prussia, not as it ever was, but Prussia as it was to have become under the reform administrations of Stein and Hardenberg, if only they had been victorious. Where Hegel's state does resemble the Prussia of 1820, it provides for the liberalizing reforms which had been achieved between 1808 and 1819 (PR § 206 and note 1; § 219 and note 2; § 288 and note 1; § 289 and note 1).

Hegel was no radical, and certainly no subversive. In relation to the Prussian state of 1820 he represented the tendency toward moderate, liberalizing reform, in the spirit of Stein, Hardenberg, Humboldt and Altenstein (who had arranged for his appointment to his chair in Berlin). Hegel did not have to be ashamed of publishing his views (until the middle of 1819, most of them were even the official position of the monarch and his chief ministers). But they were diametrically opposed to the views of Prussian conservatives on some of the largest and most sensitive political issues of the day.

If Hegel was not a conservative, does that mean that he was a 'liberal'? It does mean that Hegel was a proponent (usually a cautious and moderate one) of many social and political policies and tendencies that we now recognize as part of the liberal tradition. But the term 'liberalism' normally connotes not only these policies, but also a deeper philosophical rationale for them, or rather a plurality of rationales which to some degree share a common spirit and social vision. The vision is individualistic, conceiving society as nothing but the outcome of the actions and interactions of human individuals pursuing their individual ends. The spirit is one which tends to be suspicious of grand theories of human destiny or the good, preferring instead to protect individual rights and freedoms, and living by the faith that human progress is most likely if individuals are left to find their own way toward whatever they happen to conceive of as the good. In line with what has just been said, it is also a moralistic spirit, for which individual conscience, responsibility and decency are paramount values. The power of this vision and this spirit in modern society can perhaps best be measured by the fact that 'liberalism' in this sense is the common basis of both 'liberalism' and 'conservatism' as those terms are now used in everyday political parlance, and by the fact that liberalism's principles sound to most of us like platitudes, which no decent person could think of denying.

Hegel does not see liberalism in this sense as a foe, since he sees its standpoint as expressing something distinctive and valuable about the modern world. But he does regard its standpoint as limited, and for this reason potentially destructive of the very values it most wants to promote. He regards this standpoint as salvageable only when placed in the context of a larger vision, which measures the subjective goals of individuals by a larger objective and collective good, and assigns to moral values a determinate, limited place in the total scheme of things. In this sense, Hegel is a critic of liberalism, even its deepest and most troubling modern critic. This is what gives the greatest continuing interest to Hegel's ethical thought and social theory.

Freedom

The *Philosophy of Right* is founded on an ethical theory which identi-fies the human good with the self-actualization of the human spirit. Hegel's name for the essence of this spirit is *freedom* (PR § 4). But Hegel does not mean by 'freedom' what most people mean by it. Most people, according to Hegel, think that freedom consists in *possibilities* of acting, but freedom is really a kind of *action*, namely one in which I am determined entirely through myself, and not at all by anything external (PR § 23). Even in the case of free action, Hegel thinks that most people identify it with 'arbitrariness' (*Willkür*), with doing whatever we please (PR § 15,R) or with venting our particularity and idiosyncrasy (PR § 15A). Hegel regards this view as shallow and immature; he insists that we are free only when we overcome 'particularity' and act 'universally' or 'objectively', according to the 'concept' of the will (PR § 23).

Free action is action in which we deal with nothing that is external to our own objective nature. That does not mean that freedom consists in withdrawing from what is other than ourselves. On the contrary, Hegel insists that 'absence of dependence on an other is won not outside the other but in it, it attains actuality not by fleeing the other but by overcoming it' (EG § 382A). Thus Hegel describes freedom as 'being with oneself in an other', that is, actively relating to something other than oneself in such a way that this other becomes integrated into one's projects, completing and fulfilling them so that it counts as belonging to one's own action rather than standing over against it. This means that freedom is possible only to the extent that we act rationally, and in circumstances where the objects of our action are in harmony with our reason. The most spiritual of such objects is the social order in which we live: just as Hegel's treatment of individual human psychology falls under the heading of 'subjective spirit', so his treatment of the rational society, in the *Philosophy of Right*, constitutes the sphere of 'objective spirit' (EG § 385). Freedom is actual, therefore, only in a rational society whose institutions can be felt and known as rational by individuals who are 'with themselves' in those institutions.

Hegel's name for a rational system of social institutions is 'ethical life' (*Sittlichkeit*) (PR §§ 144–145). Corresponding to 'objective' ethical life (the system of rational institutions) is a 'subjective' ethical life, an individual character which disposes the individual to do what the institutions require (PR §§ 146–148). The ethical disposition is Hegel's answer to the Kantian separation of duty from inclination, and more generally to the moralistic psychology which supposes that unless we are moved by impartial reason to follow moral principles adopted from a universalistic standpoint, we will inevitably adopt the utterly selfish policy of maximizing our own interests. On the contrary, Hegel is convinced that the most potent, as well as the most admirable, human dispositions follow neither of these two patterns. A rational society is one where the demands of social life do not frustrate the needs of individuals, where duty fulfils individuality rather than suppressing it. In such a society rational individuals can promote their self-interest to a satisfactory degree without having to maximize it, and they need not make great sacrifices in order to give priority to right and duty or to show concern for the good of others. Because our social life is in harmony with our individuality, the duties of ethical life do not limit our freedom but actualize it. When we become conscious of this, we come to be 'with ourselves' in our ethical duties. Such duties, Hegel insists, do not restrict us, but liberate us (PR § 149).

We might put the point by saying that for Hegel I am free when I 'identify' myself with the institutions of my community, feeling myself to be a part of them, and feeling them to be a part of me. But Hegel would deny that such feelings constitute freedom unless they are a 'certainty based on *truth*' (PR § 268). That is, the institutions of the community must *truly* harmonize the state's universal or collective interest with the true, objective good of individuals; and individuals must be *conscious* of this harmony. Of course there is no freedom at all in a society whose members 'identify' themselves with it only because they are victims of illusion, deception, or ideology.[11]

Personhood and subjectivity

Liberals are usually proud of the fact that they mean by freedom what most people mean by it, not what Hegel means. They usually think freedom is the absence of obstacles to doing as we like, whether our choices are good or bad, rational or arbitrary. Confronted with Hegel's doctrines, they often think that his praise of freedom is a dangerous deception; they fear that he wants to restrict freedom as they mean it in the name of freedom as he means it. Such fears are largely unfounded. Hegel's ethical theory is not based on freedom in the ordinary sense, but it does not follow from this that Hegel's theory is hostile or even indifferent to freedom in the ordinary sense. On the contrary, Hegel thinks that in the modern world, people cannot be free in his sense unless social institutions provide considerable scope and protection for arbitrary freedom.

This is because Hegel thinks that, in the modern world, we are conscious of ourselves in new ways, and that we cannot be 'with ourselves' in social institutions unless they provide for the actualization of our self-image in these respects. First, we think of ourselves as *persons*, indeterminate choosers, capable of abstracting from all our desires and qualities (PR § 5), and demanding an external sphere for the exercise of our arbitrary freedom (PR § 41). This sphere begins with the person's external body and extends to all the person's property (PR §§ 45–47). The category of 'abstract right' applies to such a sphere of arbitrary freedom. It is called 'abstract right' because in protecting the rights of persons we must abstract from the particular use they make of these rights, even from its bearing on the person's own interests (PR § 37). Abstract right is a variety of freedom in the Hegelian sense because it involves 'being with oneself' in the external objects which one owns. The rationality of the modern state requires that the abstract right of persons be safeguarded; this is the primary function of legal institutions (PR § 209,R).

Modern individuals not only regard themselves as arbitrarily free choosers, but they also see themselves as giving meaning to their lives through the particular choices they make. So regarded, individuals are *subjects* (PR §§ 105–106). Subjects derive what Hegel calls 'self-satisfaction' from their role in determining for themselves what will count as their own particular good or happiness (PR §§ 121–123). Their sense of self-worth is bound up with the fact that they are aware of leading a reflective life, shaped through their own deeds. Subjectivity is also the sphere of morality, in which individuals measure their choices by universal standards and reflect on their actions from the standpoint of conscience.

Hegel gives the name 'subjective freedom' to the variety of 'being with oneself in an other' in which the 'other' is the individual's own actions and choices. Modern individuals cannot be free in the Hegelian sense unless social institutions provide for subjective freedom in several ways. Modern ethical life must provide for individual self-satisfaction by enabling people to shape and actualize their own determinate individualities (PR § 187). Thus the state must respect my right as an individual self to direct my own life, and provide for this right in the form of its institutions (PR §§ 185R, 206R). It must also honour moral conscience (PR § 137R) and hold me responsible for my actions only in so far as they are the expression of my subjectivity (PR §§ 115–120). A state which fails to do these things is to that extent a state in which individuals cannot be free or 'with themselves'.

For modern individuals, Hegelian freedom cannot exist unless there is room for freedom in the ordinary sense. Hegel wants to replace the ordinary concept of freedom with his concept not because he is opposed to freedom in the ordinary sense, but because he thinks that starting with his concept of freedom enables us to see *why* freedom in the ordinary sense is objectively a good thing for people to have. In that way, Hegel's view is not at odds with those who value freedom in the sense of the unhindered ability to do as we please. On the contrary, Hegel's ethical theory shows how their position can be justified.

At the same time, Hegel's view also proposes to tell us something about *when* freedom in the ordinary sense is objectively valuable, and when it is not. Like John Stuart Mill, Hegel thinks the ability to do as we please is good not in itself but because it is required for the achievement of other vital human goods. The chance to do as we please is valuable when it is necessary for or conducive to freedom in the Hegelian sense; otherwise, it may be worthless or even harmful. Hegel's view implies that freedom in the ordinary sense should be protected when it belongs to the rightful sphere of some person or when it is conducive to a subject's self-satisfaction or to the actualization of that subject's individuality. It also implies that in a case where doing as we please is not conducive to these goods, there is no reason to value such freedom at all.

Hegel does not believe that we can decide in the abstract and irrespective of a structured social context when freedom in the ordinary sense falls within our right and serves to actualize our individuality. He does name certain things which are central to our personality, and hence belong without exception to our inalienable and imprescriptible rights: the right to our own body and free status (PR § 57); the right to hold private property (PR §§ 45–49); and the right over one's own ethical life, religion, and conscience (PR § 66). But he does not agree with Kant that we should try to construct our social institutions so that they maximize the amount of personal freedom which everyone can enjoy according to a universal law.[12] Instead, Hegel thinks that the precise content of our right as persons and subjects depends on a system of rational institutions, apart from which we cannot even be sure what 'maximal personal freedom' might mean, much less determine how it might be achieved.

It is the function of positive law, for example, to make right determinate. Our rights as persons have validity only when they are expressed in law. Conversely, however, Hegel holds that positive laws are obligatory only to the extent that they agree in content with what is in itself right (PR §§ 209–213). Although personal rights are not determinate except within a system of law, Hegel does think that some laws (e.g. those establishing slavery or forbidding persons to hold private property) are plainly unjust in the context of any system of law. In such cases, he agrees with the natural law tradition that those laws do not obligate us.

Hegel's liberal critics are in the habit of saying that he does not believe in founding a social order on the conception of individual rights. The element of truth in this assertion is that Hegel thinks personal right, apart from a developed system of ethical life, is an empty abstraction; he believes that a social order founded (as in liberal political theory) on such abstractions will be unable even to protect individual rights, much less to actualize the whole of concrete freedom. In fact, Hegel thinks that the greatest enemy of personal and subjective freedom is a 'mechanistic' conception of the state, which views the state solely as an instrument for the enforcement of abstract rights; for this sets the state up as an abstraction in opposition to individuals. In Fichte's theory, for example, Hegel sees the state as a police power whose only function is to supervise and regulate the actions of individuals through coercive force (NR 519/124). The only real guarantee of freedom is a well-constituted ethical life, which integrates the rights of persons and subjects into an organic system of customs and institutions providing individuals with concretely fulfilling lives.

Hegel is not an enemy of what liberals value in the name of freedom, but his agenda regarding freedom is not the liberal one. He believes there are limits to the state's legitimate power to interfere in the conduct of individuals, but he insists that these limits cannot be drawn precisely (PR § 234). This does not bother him because he does not share the liberals' fear that the state will inevitably trespass into the rightful territory of individual freedom unless we guard the boundaries jealously. On the contrary, Hegel maintains that the 'enormous strength' of the modern state lies in the fact that the state's 'substantive unity' rests on the principles of 'subjectivity' and 'personal particularity' (PR § 260). An inevitable tendency to violate these principles could belong only to a state which is inherently self-destructive, out to destroy the source of its own power.

From Hegel's point of view, a more serious threat to freedom in modern society is what he calls the 'principle of atomicity', the tendency in modern life for individuals to be only abstract persons and subjects, who fail to actualize their personality and subjectivity in a fulfilling social context. If people insist too stubbornly on their rights or withdraw too far into their subjectivity, Hegel believes that they become alienated from the common social life, without which nothing they do has any significance for them. This is a threat to people's freedom because it means that they cannot be 'with themselves' in their social life; it renders them powerless to make their lives their own. Where this is so, people's options, however vast and unhindered they may be, are all alike hollow and meaningless to them; wider choices only confront them with an emptiness more vast and appalling.

Hegel's primary aim in the *Philosophy of Right* is to show how personal right and subjective freedom can receive real content through the institutions of the modern state. In other words, it is to show us how the modern state is after all the actuality of concrete freedom (PR § 258). This state as Hegel describes it differs little from the state which liberal theories try to justify, but Hegel's state is not the same as theirs because his justification is different. Hegel's state is about different things, serves different human needs, sets itself different ends.

Civil society

Human beings have not always known themselves as persons and subjects. These conceptions, according to Hegel, are historically quite recent, and are still geographically restricted. They are products of European culture, deriving from the tradition of Greek ethical life and Christian spirituality. But they did not become actual even in European culture as long as there was slavery or serfdom, or property and economic relationships were bound by feudal fetters and encumbrances, or states were subject to ecclesiastical authorities or treated as the private property of an individual or a family. Personality and subjectivity were not actual in the democratic Greek polis, or the medieval Church, or the feudal state of the early modern era. They have become actual only in the modern state which arose out of the Lutheran Reformation and the French Revolution.

The modern state contains one specific institution which separates it decisively from earlier and less developed social orders: Hegel's name for it is 'civil society'. Prior to Hegel, the term 'civil society' (*bürgerliche Gesellschaft*, and its cognates in Latin, French, and other languages) was generally interchangeable with the term 'state'. 'Civil' society was the realm of citizens (*Bürger, cives, citoyens*), in contrast to 'natural' society or the family.[13] Hegel, however, distinguishes civil society from both the family, the private society based on love (PR § 158), and from the state, i.e. the public community based explicitly on reason and aiming at collective or universal ends. Civil society is the realm in which individuals exist as persons **and** subjects, as owners and disposers of private property, and as choosers of their own life-activity in the light of their contingent and subjective needs and interests. In civil society, people's ends are in the first instance purely private, particular and contingent (PR § 185), not communal ends shared with others through feeling (as in the family) or through reason (as in the state).

In other words, civil society is the realm of the market economy. Hegel holds that individuals are given their due as free persons, and achieve actuality as subjects, only when they depend on themselves for their own livelihood and welfare (PR § 182). He is a strong partisan of the view that the collectivized or state-run economy is a pre-modern institution, incompatible with the modern principle of individual freedom.

At the same time, civil society is not simply identical with the market economy. As a member of civil society, the individual has a determinate social identity signified by the term *Bürger*, not in the sense of the French word *citoyen* but in the sense of the French word *bourgeois* (PR § 190R). A *bourgeois* for Hegel is much more than a self-interested, calculating *homo economicus*. Hegel's study of the science of political economy (in the writings of people such as Adam Smith, Say and Ricardo) convinces him that people's collective market behaviour possesses a kind of collective rationality, which is none the less real for being unintended (PR § 189R). This 'inner necessity' forms the unconscious basis of genuine social relationships between people, and gives rise to a 'principle of universality' within civil society, harmonizing with the principle of free individuality (PR §§ 182–184). Civil society is not merely the natural result of people's free and self-interested behaviour (a conception Hegel had earlier satirized under the title 'the spiritual animal kingdom' (PhG ¶ 397)). It is a genuine form of society, a 'universal family' which makes collective demands on its members and has collective responsibilities toward them (PR § 239).

As members of this society, individuals have the duty to support themselves through labour which benefits the whole, while civil society as a whole owes each individual the opportunity to labour in a way which provides a secure, respected and self-fulfilling mode of life (PR § 238). This means that civil society is charged with the education of individuals for membership in it (PR § 239), and also collectively responsible for preventing them from falling into poverty, whether through their own improvidence (PR § 240) or through the contingencies of the market system. The poor in civil society are victims not of some natural misfortune, but of a social *wrong* (PR § 241).

Though the market economy has a tendency toward rationality, Hegel sees that it is the scene of systematic conflicts of interest between producers and consumers, and also of occasional imbalances which adversely affect everyone; the activities of civil society must be consciously supervised if it is to remain just and stable (PR §§ 235–236). Thus he regards state-run economy and complete freedom of trade and commerce as extremes; the health of civil society requires a middle course (PR § 236R). The responsibility for overseeing and regulating civil society's economic activities belongs to what Hegel calls the state's 'police' function (see PR § 231, note 1).

Estates and corporations

Individual freedom in civil society involves much more than simply being left alone to find our way through life in a market system. If we are to be 'with ourselves' as members of civil society, we must also achieve a determinate social identity, a specific trade or profession (*Gewerbe*), conferring upon us a determinate social estate, standing or status (*Stand*) (PR § 207). Through membership in an estate, our economic activity ceases to be mere individual self-seeking. It becomes a determinate kind of contribution to the welfare of civil society as a whole, recognized for what it is by others.

In the case of the urban trades and professions, Hegel thinks this calls for the organization of civil society into 'corporations' –

professional associations or guilds, recognized by the state. A corporation provides its members with a collective responsibility and aim within civil society: to look after the special business of their profession, to train new people to work in it, and to set standards for the work it does. Corporations also look after their own interests, providing assistance to members who are out of work, without undermining their dignity as tends to happen when they depend on either private charity or public assistance (PR § 253R). In Hegel's state, as in the constitutional proposals of Humboldt and Hardenberg, corporations are also the chief vehicles for popular political representation (see PR § 303, note 1). Probably the only reform of the Stein or Hardenberg administrations about which Hegel had serious reservations was the abolition of guild monopolies, which were terminated in the interests of free trade (see PR § 255, note 2).

Above all, corporation membership provides individuals with a sense of concrete social identity. Civil society provides for subjective freedom by offering individuals a wide variety of different lifestyles between which to choose. But Hegel does not sympathize with Mill's notion that society should encourage individuals to engage in all sorts of eccentric experiments with their lives, in the hope that by trial and error they may occasionally find something worth imitating.[14] He thinks their choices must be between recognized ways of life, systematically integrated into the organic system of modern ethical life; the various ways of life should be known to provide dignity and fulfilment to those who lead them. Corporation membership helps individuals to achieve a recognized estate or status (*Stand*) of this kind. Without this, individuals will be isolated from others, alienated from civil society, and lacking in any determinate standards for success in life. They will gauge their self-worth in civil society not by ethical standards, but only by the selfish pursuit of wealth, which can never satisfy them because it has no determinate measure (PR § 253).

In Hegel's state, however, corporation membership is open mainly to the male urban middle class. Hegel argues that civil servants do not need corporations since the place of corporations for them is taken by the organization of the government service; he also thinks that the unreflective ethical disposition of the rural population is unsuited to the corporate spirit (PR § 250). But he also recognizes that wage-labourers are not eligible for corporation membership (PR § 252R).

Hegel is disturbed by civil society's systematic tendency toward extremes of wealth and poverty. He notes that the economic processes of civil society themselves produce a class which is systematically excluded from civil society's wealth, its spiritual benefits, and consequently even from its ethical life (PR §§ 243–244). Hegel's treatment of this topic is characteristically hard-headed, perceptive and unsentimental. His main concern is with the social causes of poverty and with its consequences for the ethical health of civil society. He sees the fundamental cause of poverty as the process of 'universalization' applied both to people's needs (through the standardization and mass-marketing of commodities) and to their labour (through mass-production). The greatest profits come as a result of employing cheap mass-labour, so that the wealthy have an interest in the existence of a poor class, whose bargaining power is weak in relation to capital (PR § 243). 'When there is great poverty, the capitalist finds many people who work for small wages, which increases his earnings; and this has the further consequence that smaller capitalists fall into poverty' (VPR IV, 610). For Hegel, poverty in civil society is not an accident, or a misfortune or the result of human error or vice; rather, 'the complications of civil society itself produce poverty' (VPR17 138), which (along with personal right and subjective freedom) is a special characteristic of modern civil society. 'The emergence of poverty is in general a consequence of civil society; from which on the whole poverty arises necessarily' (VPR19 193).

Hegel refuses to blame either the wealthy or the poor, as individuals, for the fact of poverty. But he does regard poverty as a cause of moral degradation, turning those subject to it into a 'rabble' (*Pöbel*). Since Hegel thinks every member of civil society has a right to earn an adequate living as a member of a recognized estate, he regards the poor as victims of *wrong* at society's hands. The basis of the 'rabble mentality' (*Pöbelhaftigkeit*) is the outrage of the poor (against the rich, civil society, and the state) at the wrong they suffer (PR § 241). Under the conditions of life to which the poor are subject, however, the effect of this justified outrage is to produce a disposition which is fundamentally at odds with the ethical principles of civil society. Because they have no chance of the dignity and self-sufficiency afforded by recognized labour in civil society, the rabble lose both a sense of self-respect and a sense of right and wrong as applied to their own actions. They cease to recognize the rights of others, and the only right they are interested in is their own imagined right to live at civil society's expense without working at all.

Thus the rabble mentality becomes a criminal mentality. Hegel suggests that a similar attitude may also develop among the wealthy. The rich find that they can buy anything, that they do not need to work, that no one's personality or subjectivity is immune to the power of their wealth. The rich and the poor equally come to regard the ethical principles of civil society with scorn (see PR § 244, note 1). 'Hence wealth can lead to the same mockery and shamelessness as we find among the rabble. The disposition of the master over the slave is the same as that of the slave' (VPR19 196).

For Hegel's student and colleague Eduard Gans (to whom Hegel left the task of lecturing on the *Philosophy of Right* in Berlin during the last half of the 1820s), the philosophical proposition that the modern state is rational entails the conclusion that the problem of poverty must be soluble, that it must be possible to prevent the formation of a rabble. 'Hence the police must be able to bring it about that there is no rabble. [The rabble] is a fact, not a right. We must be able to go to the basis of this fact and abolish it.'[15] Hegel's own reflections on the problem of poverty are less aprioristic, and less optimistic. Poverty provides plenty of occasion for exercise of morally good intentions, but Hegel thinks that private charity is no solution to the problem of poverty, and often even makes it worse (see PR § 242, note 1). The state, in its action on civil society (which Hegel calls the state's 'police power') is the agency responsible for preventing poverty; but Hegel considers the various means at its disposal for doing so, and argues that none of them can solve the underlying social problems (PR § 245). Hegel holds that poverty and the rabble mentality are systematic products of civil society, but he does not pretend that civil society has any remedy for the ills it creates.

The political state

As the distinctively modern social institution, civil society is decisive for the form of the other institutions of modern ethical life. Because modern individuals are persons with rights of property, there is no longer a place for the extended family as an economic organization. In modern society, 'family' can refer only to the patriarchal bourgeois nuclear family; the feudal family, the 'clan' or wider kinship group (*Stamm*) – celebrated by some of Hegel's Romantic contemporaries as the model for all social relations – no longer has any legitimacy (PR §§ 172, 177).

The family's sole remaining function is to enable individuals to find a haven from the harsh interaction of independent persons in civil society, by participating in bonds of substantial unity on the level of immediate feeling. For this reason, Hegel argues that property within the family should be held in common, administered by the husband and father. He alone, under normal circumstances, exercises the rights of personality in the sphere of civil society (PR §§ 170–171); the wife and mother is naturally confined to the sphere of the family, as the guardian of its principle (PR § 166). She and the children exercise their personal rights in their own name only at those points where the family reaches its limit and dissolution: when a marriage ends in divorce (PR § 176), when the children leave the family to found new families of their own (PR § 177), or when the father dies (PR § 178).

Civil society in Hegel's theory also determines the political form of the modern state. Hegel argues that the form most suited to the modern state is constitutional monarchy (PR § 273). Only there does a political system which is explicit and rational come to be personified in an individual, who thus gives the state the form of subjective freedom (PR § 279). The offices of the state must no longer be (as in the feudal state, and in the Prussia of Hegel's time) the property or the personal prerogatives of individuals or families; the civil service must be a body of qualified professionals, open to all members of society irrespective of birth (PR § 291).

In a society which emphasizes the dignity of free subjectivity, individuals are naturally interested in the conduct of the state's affairs, and they want a voice in determining its policies. Consequently, the modern state must have representative institutions (PR § 301). Hegel argues that deputies to the Estates (*Stände*) should be chosen not by popular election from geographical districts but (as their name implies) they should represent determinate groups (corporations) within civil society. Otherwise, individuals, who are connected to the political process only through the casting of one vote in an immense multitude, will be alienated from the state by the very process whose function is to connect them to it (PR § 311R).

In a Hegelian constitutional monarchy, the hereditary prince or sovereign represents the 'moment of ultimate decision' (PR § 275). But Hegel intends this only in a 'formal' or 'subjective' sense; 'objectively', he says, the sovereign is bound by his ministers, so that in a well-constituted state the individual qualities of the sovereign will be of no consequence (PR §§ 279A, 280A). Hegel plainly intends real political power to be in the hands neither of the prince nor of the people, but of an educated class of professional civil servants.

For Hegel, as for Mill, the function of representative institutions is not to govern, but to advise those who govern, and to determine who it is that governs.[16] Hegel expects deputies to the Estates to be ordinary citizens, not professional politicians. One evident reason for this is that he wants the Estates to be close to the people, and to represent its true sentiments; another reason (unstated, but quite evident) is that he does not want the Estates to be politically strong enough to challenge the power of the professionals who actually govern. But he does not intend the Estates to be powerless either. In his lectures, Hegel describes a multi-party system in the Estates, and he insists that the government's ministry must always represent the 'majority party'; when it ceases to do so, he says, it must resign and a new ministry, representing the majority in the Estates, must take its place (see PR § 301, note 2). This idea takes the Hegelian constitutional monarchy most of the way toward presently existing parliamentary systems with a nominal hereditary monarch (as in Britain, Holland, Belgium, or Sweden).

The state and the individual

To be absolutely and substantively free, individuals must be 'with themselves' in their social life. One aspect of this is the satisfaction of their subjectivity, in that ample scope is allowed for arbitrary choice and the satisfaction of individual welfare. As rational and thinking beings, however, we relate ourselves universally to the whole of the social world. Our freedom is not fully actual until we are with ourselves in ends which are universal in scope. We cannot be free (in Hegel's sense) unless we successfully pursue ends larger than our own private good, indeed larger than anyone's private good.

Through corporations, individuals in civil society acquire ethical ends which go beyond their self-interest. These ends, Hegel says, pass over in turn into the absolutely universal end: the state (PR § 256). Hegel distinguishes 'the political state proper' from the state in a broader sense, the community as a whole with all its institutions (PR § 267). He regards the state in the latter sense as the individual's final end.

Hegel asserts that the individual's highest freedom consists in membership in the state (PR § 258). Accordingly, the highest consciousness of freedom is the consciousness of this membership, in what he calls the 'political disposition' or 'patriotism'. Hegel denies, however, that true patriotism consists in the willingness to do heroic deeds and make extraordinary sacrifices for the sake of one's country. Instead, he says patriotism is nothing more than a habit of leading one's normal life and doing one's ethical duty, while taking the state as one's 'substantial basis and end' (PR § 268).

Hegel locates the absolutely universal end in the state because it alone is a self-sufficient individuality, not part of any larger whole. To those who would relate their actions to some still larger entity ('humanity at large', a 'cosmopolitan world society' or 'all sentient creation') Hegel points out that such entities are not real, but only abstractions. We do not actualize our freedom by entertaining the empty imaginings of moralists, but only by relating ourselves to something real which truly actualizes the power of reason in the world. The state, Hegel says, is 'the absolute power on *earth*' (PR § 331).

For the same reason, the state is also the fundamental vehicle of world history. Human history for Hegel is a progressive succession of spiritual principles, which actualize themselves successively in the political constitution and spiritual culture of nation states (PR § 344). Thus human actions gain universal, cosmopolitan significance not through their relation to abstract moral principles, but only in so far as they are the actions of someone culturally and historically situated, and give existence to the ethical life of a determinate people at a given stage of its history. If I want to see my actions in their universal historical significance, I must regard myself as the child of my age and people, and my deeds as the expression of the principle embodied in my state and my time.

The state, for Hegel, is an 'absolute end'; individuals should place it above their own private interests. '[The state has] the highest right in relation to individuals, whose *highest duty* is to be members of the state' (PR § 258). But the state is an absolute end only because it is *rational*; Hegel describes 'rationality' as the 'unity and interpenetration of universality and individuality' (PR § 258R). In other words, what makes the state an end in itself is the way in which it systematically harmonizes the personal right, subjective freedom and happiness of its individual members. The state is an 'infinite' end distinct from and higher than its members' rights and happiness only because it systematically unifies these finite ends.

This is why patriotism, for Hegel, is not a disposition to do extraordinary deeds on the state's behalf, but only the 'certainty, based on truth' that in pursuing all my other ends (in my personal, family or professional life) I thereby always relate myself at the same time to the state as my universal and ultimate end. That consciousness is what makes the state 'the actuality of concrete freedom' (PR § 260).

> [Patriotism is] the consciousness that my substantial and particular interest is preserved and contained in the interest and end of an other (in this case, the state), and in the latter's relation to me as an individual. As a result, this other immediately ceases to be an other for me, and in my consciousness of this, I am free.
>
> (PR § 268)

This makes it a gross distortion to associate Hegel's view with the image of individuals having to sacrifice themselves to the ends of the state. Such sacrifices may be required in some circumstances, but it is precisely the *abnormality* of such circumstances which makes the state an end in itself.

The principal such circumstance for Hegel is *war*. It is mainly here, Hegel thinks, that the universal interest of the state can for once be clearly distinguished from the lesser interests of individuals. Although war is an abnormal condition in the life of nations, Hegel thinks that occasional wars are inevitable, even that they are necessary to preserve the ethical health of peoples (PR § 324R).

We badly misunderstand Hegel's view if we think it implies that wars are a good thing, or that we should not try our best to avoid them. Even during war, Hegel says, war always has the character of something that ought to cease (PR § 338). It may help us to understand Hegel's view of war if we realize that what he believes about war is closely analogous to what we all believe about human mortality generally. We know we cannot live forever, and we realize that if we all could, then this would eventually have disastrous consequences for the human race as a whole. Hegel's views about war no more imply that wars are a good thing, which we should not try our best to avoid, than our views about human mortality imply that our own death is a good thing, which we should not try our best to avoid.

Hegel's legacy

Hegel is an important philosopher; his penetrating analysis of the human predicament in modern society is perhaps unsurpassed among social observers of the past two centuries. At the same time, his thought is subtle and complex; his writings are difficult, even infuriating – laden with impenetrable and pretentious jargon from which his meaning can be separated only with skilled and careful surgery, even then usually not without risk of mortal injury.

The inevitable result is that Hegel is cited much more frequently than he is read, and discussed far oftener than he is understood. Some of those who discourse on Hegel with the greatest sophistication know him only through warped, inaccurate or bowdlerized second-hand accounts (for instance, accounts of the Hegelian dialectic as 'thesis–antithesis–synthesis').[17] The 'Hegelian' ideas which capture the popular imagination are often not present in Hegel at all, or have only the most tenuous and dubious connection with what Hegel actually thought or wrote. Before it gains currency, a fact about Hegelian doctrine has often been so distorted by oversimplification and misunderstanding that the truth from which it started is almost impossible to recognize.

This is the case with the traditional images of Hegel as reactionary, absolutist, totalitarian. Taken literally, of course, these images have been long discredited. Yet in our liberal culture they nevertheless possess a kind of symbolic truth, because they represent this culture's self-doubts projected with righteous venom into its iconography of the enemy. Hegel is especially unappealing to that dogmatic kind of liberal who judges past social and political thinkers by the degree to which they articulate the views which (it has been decided beforehand) all people of good will must share. The value of Hegel's social thought will be better appreciated by those who are willing to question received views, and take a deeper look at the philosophical problems posed by modern social life.

Hegel leaves the liberal's state pretty much intact, but his social theory is mercilessly critical of the ahistorical, individualistic and moralistic rationale which liberalism provides for it. In its place, Hegel gives us an alternative interpretation of modern social life, of modern economic and political institutions, of modern humanity's conception of the human good, of the meaning of its fundamental and insatiable drive for freedom.

This means that although Hegel's theory was put forward as a rational *defence* of the modern state, his true legacy belongs rather to the *critics* of modern society. The basic tendency of Hegel's social thought is to undermine modern society's liberal self-interpretation; to the extent that its institutions have been shaped by this interpretation, its tendency is even to criticize those institutions themselves. He presents a communitarian rather than an individualistic rationale for modern economic and political institutions and of the freedom they seek to actualize. This provides the basis for an indictment of any society which tries to call itself 'free' even though it fails to offer its members any rationally credible sense of collective purpose, leaves them cynically discontented with and alienated from its political institutions, deprives them of a socially structured sense of self-identity, and condemns many of them to lives of poverty, frustration and alienation. It leads us to question the value of the formalisms – representative democracy, the market economy, the protection of individual liberties – with which liberals wish to identify 'freedom', and to emphasize instead the social contents and consequences which liberals would usually prefer to leave 'open' by excluding them from the domain of collective concern and control.

Once we realize this, we can understand why it is that Hegel's most bitter twentieth-century foes have been those who want to save the liberal state from its radical opponents on the right or the left. We can also see through the ironic deception they perpetrate when they avail themselves of the distorted nineteenth-century image of Hegel as quietist and conservative apologist. What *they* fear in Hegel's thought is not quietism, but the very opposite – subversion of the liberal status quo.

Clearly, Hegel's social thought is now outdated in important respects. As Hegel writes about them, the family, civil society, and the state are clearly institutions of the early nineteenth century. Hegel insists on the one hand that all human individuals are persons and subjects who must be treated universally as such; on the other hand, he defends a state which excludes women from public life entirely, and large segments of the population from all political participation. With hindsight, it is easy for us to perceive an irreconcilable antagonism between these two positions. We are just as unlikely to be persuaded by Hegel's defence of hereditary monarchy, or his version of a representative legislature. Even more fundamentally, the nation state itself was probably never able to play the lofty role in human life which Hegel assigned it.

Yet at a deeper level, Hegel's philosophy may not be dated at all. It is not clear that we have in any way surpassed Hegel's conception of modern human beings, their history, their needs and aspirations, and the general social conditions required for their self-actualization. Without denying the right of persons and subjects, Hegel asserts against liberal orthodoxy the vital necessity for modern humanity of concrete social situatedness and integration. He reminds us that without this, the formal freedom to make arbitrary choices and express our subjectivity leads in the direction of alienation rather than self-actualization. He stresses the point that we cannot be free unless our social life is self-transparent. We must be able to gain rational insight into it, and live consciously in the light of this self-awareness.

Hegel remains an important social thinker largely because these ideas, products of the age of German idealism, are still central to our aspirations as reflective social beings. Hegel is also current because these same aspirations are still radically unfulfilled. This can add only urgency to Hegel's idea that the value of those freedoms liberals most prize, though real and important, is nevertheless only conditional, since it casts serious doubt on the extent to which the conditions are really satisfied. Hegel meant the *Philosophy of Right* to afford its readers a joyous reconciliation with the social world around them. But for us the actual effects of studying Hegel's book may be very different from what its author intended.

Some information used in the editorial notes was given to me by Terence Irwin, Allen Rosen, and Rega Wood. Professor H. B. Nisbet provided detailed, informative advice on the introduction and editorial notes. Professor Raymond Geuss provided advice on the content and structure of the introduction. In preparing the notes, I was also aided by the informative editorial apparatus in Hermann Klenner's excellent edition of *Grundlinien der Philosophie des Rechts* (Berlin: Akademie Verlag der DDR, 1981).

Ithaca, June 1990   Allen W. Wood

Notes to editor's introduction

1 See John Edward Toews, *Hegelianism* (Cambridge: Cambridge University Press, 1980), p. 113; cf. C. Varrentrapp, *Johannes Schulze und das höhere preußische Unterrichtswesen in seiner Zeit* (Leipzig, 1889).

2 See pp. xlv–xlix for key to abbreviations of the titles of Hegel's writings.

3 See Manfred Riedel (ed.), *Materialien zu Hegels Rechtsphilosophie* (Frankfurt: Suhrkamp, 1975), I, pp. 53–208.

4 J. F. Fries, Letter of 6 January 1821, in Günther Nicolin, *Hegel in Berichten seiner Zeitgenossen* (Hamburg: Felix Meiner, 1970), p. 221.

5 In his highly influential book *Hegel und seine Zeit* (1857), Rudolf Haym not only depicted Hegel's philosophy as 'the scientific domicile of the spirit of Prussian reaction', but also concluded that Hegelian speculative idealism, rightly understood, leads to 'the absolute formula of political conservatism':

> As far as I can see, in comparison with the famous saying about the rationality of the actual in the sense of Hegel's Preface, everything Hobbes and Filmer, Haller or Stahl have taught is relatively liberal doctrine. The theory of God's grace and the theory of absolute obedience are innocent and harmless in comparison with that frightful dogma *pronouncing the existing as existing to be holy.*

> (Rudolf Haym, *Hegel und seine Zeit* (Berlin: Rudolf Gaertner, 1857), pp. 367–368)

6 For instance, in: J. E. Erdmann, *Philosophische Vorlesungen über den Staat* (1851); C. Rössler, *System der Staatslehre* (1857); A. Lasson, *System der Rechtsphilosophie* (1882). For a recent account of their views, see Henning Ottmann, *Individuum und Gemeinschaft bei Hegel, Band I: Hegel im Spiegel der Interpretationen* (Berlin: de Gruyter, 1977), pp. 124–152.

7 See Ottmann's account of Hegel interpretation under the Third Reich: *Individuum und Gemeinschaft*, pp. 152–182. It is noteworthy, however, that Hegel was seldom cited in Nazi literature itself, and mention of him there was almost uniformly negative. Alfred Rosenberg, the 'official philosopher' of National Socialism, was well

aware of Hegel's admiration for the French Revolution, and denounced the Hegelian *Volksstaat* as a conception 'alien to our blood' (Rosenberg, *The Myth of the Twentieth Century*, tr. V. Bird (Torrance, CA: Noontide, 1982), p. 328). Hegel has usually been associated with twentieth-century fascism by those who hate both Hegel and fascism, and most often by those whose real target is not so much fascism as Marxism.

8 See John Dewey, *German Philosophy and Politics* (1915); Karl Popper, *The Open Society and Its Enemies, Volume II; The High Tide of Prophecy: Hegel, Marx and the Aftermath* (1945). For a broader account of this tradition, see Ottmann, *Individuum und Gemeinschaft*, pp. 192–223.

9 These included Eduard Gans, Karl Ludwig Michelet, Karl Rosenkranz, and the Education Minister Johannes Schulze. See John Edward Toews, *Hegelianism*, especially pp. 71–154, 203–242.

10 In the early twentieth century, this position was represented by scholars such as Franz Rosenzweig and Hans Heimsöth (Franz Rosenzweig, *Hegel und der Staat* (1920); Hans Heimsöth, *Politik und Moral in Hegels Geschichtsphilosophie* (1935)). After the Second World War, the 'centrist-reformist' image of Hegel's political philosophy was powerfully defended by three influential scholars: Joachim Ritter, Eric Weil, and T. M. Knox. See Knox, 'Hegel and Prussianism' (1935) (reprinted in Walter Kaufmann (ed.), *Hegel's Political Philosophy* (New York: Atherton, 1970)), and also the editorial material in Knox's 1942 translation of *The Philosophy of Right* (Oxford University Press, 1967); Eric Weil, *Hegel et l'état* (1950); and Joachim Ritter, *Hegel and the French Revolution* (1957), tr. R. D. Winfield (Cambridge, MA: MIT Press, 1982). A list of prominent Hegel scholars since the 1950s who share the basic view of Knox, Weil, and Ritter would have to include virtually every responsible scholar of Hegel's thought in the past two generations. See especially: Shlomo Avineri, *Hegel's Theory of the Modern State* (Cambridge University Press, 1972); Jacques d'Hondt, *Hegel in His Time* (1973), translated by John Burbidge (Lewiston, NY: Broadview, 1988). Once again, for a reliable account of the tradition which views Hegel as part of the 'mainstream of Western political theory' see Ottmann, *Individuum und Gesellschaft*, pp. 224–378. A debate between proponents of the new consensus and the older tradition of liberal criticism can be found in Walter Kaufmann (ed.), *Hegel's Political Philosophy*. The recent publication of transcriptions of Hegel's lectures between 1817 and 1831 has further confirmed such interpretations. See the editors' introductions to these texts by Karl-Heinz Ilting (VPR 1, 25–126, VPR17 17–34) and Dieter Henrich (VPR19 9–39).

11 There are some who deny there is any such thing as a community's 'common interest' and some who think there are no objective individual interests, that individual interests are nothing but what individuals happen to enjoy, want or prefer. If such people are right, of course, then there cannot be any such thing as (Hegelian) freedom; freedom itself will be only an illusion.

12 Kant, A316/B373; TP 289–290/73; RL 230/35. (For key to abbreviations see pp. xlix–l.)

13 See Manfred Riedel, *Between Tradition and Revolution*, tr. Walter Wright (Cambridge: Cambridge University Press, 1984), Chapter 6, pp. 132–137.

14 See Mill, *On Liberty*, ed. Elizabeth Rapaport (Indianapolis: Hackett, 1978), pp. 61–65, 108.

15 Eduard Gans, *Naturrecht und Universalrechtsgeschichte*, ed. Manfred Riedel (Stuttgart: Klett-Cotta, 1981), p. 92.

16 Mill, *On Representative Government*, ed. Currin Shields (Indianapolis: Bobbs-Merrill, 1958), pp. 74–76, 81–82.

17 This particular triadic piece of jargon was actually used by both Fichte and Schelling (each for his own purposes), but to my knowledge it was never used, not even once, by Hegel. We owe this way of presenting the Hegelian dialectic to Heinrich Moritz Chalybäus, a bowdlerizer of German idealist philosophy (see G. E. Mueller, 'The Hegel Legend of "Thesis–Antithesis–Synthesis"', *Journal of the History of Ideas* 19 (1958), pp. 411–414. To use this jargon in expounding Hegel is almost always an unwitting confession that the expositor has little or no first-hand knowledge of Hegel.

Chronology

1817	Lectures for the first time on the system of ideas later presented in the *Philosophy of Right* during the academic year 1817–1818.
1818	Invited to succeed Fichte (d. 1814) at the prestigious chair of philosophy at the University of Berlin. At Berlin, lectures for a second time (1818–1819) on the *Philosophy of Right*, which by now probably exists complete in draft.
1819	Political upheavals and the institution of academic censorship lead to withdrawal and revision of the *Philosophy of Right*. Lectures on these topics for a third time 1819–1820.
1820	Completes the *Philosophy of Right*.
1821	Publication of the *Philosophy of Right* in January. Lectures on its subject a fourth time 1821–1822.
1822	Lectures on the philosophy of right a fifth time 1822–1823.
1824	Lectures on the philosophy of right a sixth time 1824–1825.
1827	*Encyclopaedia of the Philosophical Sciences* revised and expanded to three volumes.
1830	Third edition of *Encyclopaedia of the Philosophical Sciences*.
1831	Begins lecturing a seventh time on the philosophy of right. After a month, is stricken with cholera and dies 14 November.

Translator's preface

This translation is based on the text of the first edition of the *Rechts-philosophie* (1820), as reproduced in Volume VII of Hegel's *Werke*, edited by Eva Moldenhauer and Karl Markus Michel and published by the Suhrkamp Verlag (Frankfurt am Main, 1970). I have compared the text throughout with the variorum edition of the work in Volume II of Karl-Heinz Ilting's edition of Hegel's *Vorlesungen über Rechts-philosophie 1818–1831* (referred to as VPR II, see key to abbreviations, p. xlviii), whose readings I have at times adopted in preference to those of the Suhrkamp edition; in all such cases, and on those occasions when I have encountered errors in the Suhrkamp text, I have supplied explanatory footnotes.

To the main numbered paragraphs of his text, Hegel frequently adds elucidatory comments, often of considerable length, which he describes as *Anmerkungen* – a term which I have translated (both in the singular and in the plural) as 'Remarks'. These Remarks are indented throughout the translated text, as they are in the German original, to distinguish them from the main text of the numbered paragraphs to which they are appended. Many of these paragraphs are further augmented by 'Additions' (*Zusätze*) consisting of additional material from lectures on the *Rechtsphilosophie* delivered by Hegel after the first edition of the work had appeared. These Additions are not indented, but printed in smaller type and prefixed in each case by the word 'Addition' in order to distinguish them from Hegel's basic text and Remarks. The Additions were not in fact compiled by Hegel, but by his pupil Eduard Gans, who incorporated them in his own edition of the *Rechtsphilosophie*, first published in 1833 and reissued in

1840; they have also been included in more recent editions such as those of Bolland (1902) and Lasson (1911), as well as that of the Suhrkamp Verlag (1970). Gans derived the Additions not from manuscripts of Hegel himself, but from the lecture notes of two other pupils, namely H. G. Hotho, who attended Hegel's lectures of 1822–1823, and K. G. von Griesheim, who attended the lectures of 1824–1825. They are included in this translation rather because of their long traditional association with Hegel's text than because of any claim they might have to scrupulous philological accuracy. They should, in fact, be treated with caution, not so much because they are based on the notes of students (which actually seem to be conscientious and reasonably accurate in this case), but because Gans's extracts are highly selective, combining material from two distinct lecture series and consisting largely of paraphrase rather than verbatim quotation. The complete original texts of Hotho's and Griesheim's notes have been available since 1974 in Volumes III and IV respectively of Ilting's edition of the *Vorlesungen über Rechtsphilosophie* (VPR), in which Ilting helpfully encloses in curly brackets those sections drawn upon by Gans for the Additions. To facilitate comparison between Gans's versions and the original lecture notes as published by Ilting, I have identified the source of each Addition by prefixing to it the letter H (Hotho; see VPR III), G (Griesheim; see VPR IV), or both. I have checked Gans's Additions against their sources throughout, and while I have made no attempt to indicate the content of those large sections of Hotho's and Griesheim's notes which Gans has simply ignored, or to record the numerous modifications of phrasing and terminology which he has himself introduced, I have drawn attention in footnotes to those occasions on which he appears to have misread or seriously misrepresented the text of Hotho's and/or Griesheim's notes, or added comments of his own for which there is no precedent in the sources.

Gans also had at his disposal Hegel's own manuscript annotations to §§ 1–180 of the first edition of the *Rechtsphilosophie*. These annotations, which are reproduced in Hoffmeister's (1955) and Ilting's editions of the work and in that of the Suhrkamp Verlag, are not included here, because they consist for the most part not of continuous prose but of highly condensed jottings whose value for an understanding of the text is limited; besides, they are frequently cryptic, so that any translation of them would have to rely heavily on conjecture.

In those sections of the text for which he was himself responsible, Hegel uses two distinct means in order to indicate paragraph divisions, and I have retained this distinction in my translation. Major divisions – of which there are relatively few – are indicated by the conventional device of starting a new line and indenting the beginning of the new paragraph. Less important divisions are marked only by a dash before the beginning of the next sentence (or group of sentences).

I have also attempted to reproduce, in the English translation, Hegel's frequent use of italics for emphasis. These italics are an important pointer not only to those terms or ideas on which Hegel wished to lay particular stress, but even at times to his meaning (see, for example, the first sentence of § 167, in which the italics make it clear that the words in parenthesis refer only to the noun 'inwardness', and not to the noun 'truth' as well). Hegel's use of italics for titles of books is likewise retained, although I have not followed his (by no means consistent) practice, in which he was influenced by printing conventions of his day, of italicizing personal names and both real and hypothetical quotations; in keeping with modern usage, names are set in normal type and quotations are identified as such by quotation-marks alone. Only on very rare occasions (for example, on two occurrences of the word 'this' in the Addition to § 70) have I introduced italics of my own to indicate necessary emphasis in English.

A word must now be said concerning the principles underlying this translation, and about the ways in which it differs from the well-known version by T. M. Knox (Oxford, 1942).

The *Rechtsphilosophie* is characterized by a high level of abstraction and density of expression, and makes frequent use of technical terms and phrases of uniquely Hegelian significance. I could not therefore hope to attain that degree of readability and naturalness of English expression at which I aimed in my translation of Hegel's *Lectures on the Philosophy of World History (Introduction)* (Cambridge, 1975), for the latter work is for the most part considerably less abstract and technical in character than the *Rechtsphilosophie*. But I have attempted, as in the previous translation, to achieve a high degree of literalness, especially in conveying the conceptual basis of Hegel's thought; on the present occasion, however, I have been more conscious of the need to maintain consistency in translating technical terms and words which Hegel uses particularly frequently, or which have a particular significance within his thought. To cite two examples, I translate terms such as *an und für sich* ('in and for itself') literally throughout, and render Hegel's much-used term *Bestimmung* as 'determination' wherever possible, supplying the original in brackets in cases where sense and usage call for alternative renderings. I considered it less essential, on the other hand, to try to reproduce Hegel's sentence structure exactly where this would have made for unduly cumbersome or unidiomatic English.

The term *Recht*, which occurs in the title of Hegel's work and on numerous occasions throughout the text, also calls for comment. Its range of meaning, which is closely akin to that of the Latin term *ius*, is much wider than that of the English word 'right', for it encompasses not only the rights of specific individuals and groups of people, but also the entire realm of law and justice, both as philosophical concepts (cf. *Naturrecht*, English 'natural law') and actual institutions (cf. *römisches Recht*, English 'Roman law'). For the sake of consistency, I have translated it as 'right' whenever possible, and on those (relatively infrequent) occasions when I have had to translate the word *Recht* – as distinct from its compounds – as 'law' or 'justice', I have added the original in square brackets.

T. M. Knox's translation has been of considerable assistance to me. On many occasions, I found myself indebted to his solutions to daunting problems which confront the reader and translator of Hegel's text. Where Knox's renderings seemed incapable of significant improvement – as was not infrequently the case – I made no attempt to look for alternatives simply for the sake of being different. On the other hand, Knox's language is often excessively formal by today's standards, and even at times archaic (which is scarcely surprising after almost half a century); in such cases, I have tried to adopt a less stilted idiom.

The main difference between my translation and Knox's, however, is that his general strategy is almost the reverse of my own as described at the top of this page. Knox declares in his preface (pp. xi–xii) that he has aimed at a literal translation. This literalness is more conspicuous, however, in his attempts to reproduce Hegel's sentence-structure and turns of phrase, even at the expense of English idiom, than in his treatment of Hegel's network of concepts. He tends to paraphrase technical expressions (for example, by rendering *an und für sich* as 'absolute(ly)'), and to translate the same conceptual term in numerous different ways according to context (for example, by employing over twenty-five different translations for the term *Bestimmung* – admittedly an extreme and problematic case); and in particularly abstract passages, he tends to abandon even his customary adherence to Hegel's sentence-structure in favour of free paraphrase (comparison of our respective renderings of § 183, for example, or of the first sentence of § 173 should make the latter difference apparent). In view of these differences of approach, Knox's renderings have on many occasions struck me as too loose or imprecise, and I have duly endeavoured to improve on them. But I must again acknowledge with gratitude that Knox's general understanding of Hegel's German is of a high order, with the result that the number of outright errors I have been able to identify in his translation (around seventy-five) is remarkably small for a work as long and complex as the *Rechtsphilosophie*.

Some of Knox's solutions to problems posed by Hegel's technical terminology are now so well established in English-speaking Hegel scholarship that I have simply taken them over, as I did in my previous translation. These include his translations of *real* and *wirklich* as 'real' and 'actual', and of *moralisch* and *sittlich* as 'moral' and 'ethical'. (The latter translation, incidentally, is sanctioned by a manuscript gloss of Hegel's on the expression *ethische Pflichtenlehre* ('ethical theory of duties') in § 148: the gloss reads '*Ethisch* – statt moralisch – sittlich' (i.e. 'not moral, but ethical or *sittlich*') – see V P R II, 557.)

The pairs of words just cited are, however, only two instances of a phenomenon which occurs with bewildering frequency in Hegel's writings and which confronts the translator with formidable difficulties – namely his tendency to employ pairs, or even triads, of terms which were virtually synonymous in the German of his day and to invest them at times – but by no means invariably – with nuances of difference or even with contrasting meanings; some of these differences of meaning will indeed be apparent only to those who are familiar with the connotations of the terms in question in other parts of Hegel's philosophical system. Examples of such couplings (in addition to the two already mentioned) include *Dasein* and *Existenz, Ding* and *Sache*, *Objekt* and *Gegenstand*, *Beziehung* and *Relation* (also *Verhältnis*), *Grenze* and *Schranke*, *Gefühl* and *Empfindung*, and *Nation* and *Volk*. It is sometimes possible to find equivalent (if at times somewhat arbitrarily chosen) pairs of words in English, such as 'reference' and 'relation' for *Beziehung* and *Verhältnis*, or 'boundary' and 'limit' for *Grenze* and *Schranke*. But on many occasions, the only natural translation for both German words will be the same English word, as with 'existence' for both *Dasein* (very awkwardly rendered by some earlier translators as 'determinate being') and *Existenz*, 'thing' for *Ding* and *Sache*, and 'object' for *Objekt* and *Gegenstand*. My solution in such cases has usually been to employ the same English word for both, adding the German originals in square brackets; the wider associations and range of meaning of such terms, as used by Hegel, can then be followed up in the glossary at the end of the volume.

When both of the words in such a coupling occur with great frequency, I have supplied the originals of both (as with *Dasein* and *Existenz*, *Ding* and *Sache*). But where one of the two is used with greater frequency, or adheres consistently to a shared meaning from which its partner at times deviates, I have supplied the original only of the less frequent or more variable term, as with the adjectives *besonder* (frequently used) and *partikular* (less frequently used) for 'particular', and the nouns *Objekt* (consistent meaning) and *Gegenstand* (more variable meaning) for 'object'. This arrangement has the advantage of reducing the number of German interpolations needed in the text. To the same end, I have normally supplied such words, where they are required, only on their first occurrence within each of Hegel's numbered paragraphs (including any subsequent Remarks or Addition), except where the interval between successive occurrences is so long as to justify a repetition; later occurrences of the relevant English term within the same paragraph and its appendages can normally be assumed to translate the German term already supplied on the previous occasion. When the near-synonym of the German term in question also occurs within a given paragraph and its appendages, I have continued to supply the German originals of both in all instances where the two might otherwise be confused. In a few cases where I have been unable to detect any semantic difference between such terms – as with the pairings *Grundsatz* and *Prinzip* ('principle') or *Jurist* and *Rechtsgelehrter* ('jurist'), for example, and on some occasions with *Berechtigung* and *Rechtfertigung* ('justification') – I have used the same English word for both without supplying the original of either. But in all cases where significant distinctions might otherwise be missed, or where conceptually significant German terms are translated in an unconventional or anomalous manner, I have added the original in brackets. The obvious disadvantage of interrupting the English text with parentheses of this kind is, to my mind, outweighed by the greater precision and insight into Hegel's usage which this procedure makes possible.

All of the German terms so far mentioned are to be found, with their English translations, in the glossary. In this glossary, those English renderings which, in the text, are normally accompanied by the German original are identified by an asterisk, and cross-references to their synonyms, near synonyms, and apparent synonyms are also supplied. The glossary makes no claim to comprehensiveness; it includes only key terms, and in particular those which present difficulties of translation. Its chief purpose, apart from listing the standard translations employed, is to elucidate, by means of cross-references to related terms and by including most secondary as well as primary English renderings of the German words listed, those clusters of concepts which are of vital importance to an understanding of Hegel's thought. It is, of course, impossible to apply a list of standard English equivalents mechanically in translating a work as complex as the *Rechtsphilosophie*, or to use the glossary in reverse as a key to the German originals of every English term listed in it. Two examples may illustrate the difficulties involved. First, two or more completely different German words, which are in no way synonyms, may have to be translated by the same English term which happens to have two or more distinct meanings. Thus, the words *Subjekt, Gegenstand* (in certain contexts), and *Untertan*, may all be translated as 'subject', as applied respectively to mind as distinct from its object, to the topic of a treatise or discourse, and to one who owes allegiance to a sovereign or state. But in the absence of full dictionary-style definitions of each distinct usage – and such definitions are beyond the scope of a glossary of translations – only the context within the work itself can make the different senses intelligible. And secondly, in cases where literal translation is impossible – as with many of Hegel's adjectival nouns, whose English translation requires a noun to be added to the adjective in question (for example, in the second sentence of § 170, where *ein Gemeinsames* is translated 'a common purpose', or in the third sentence of § 118, where *ganz anderes* is translated as 'things quite different') – words may be generated ('purpose' and 'things' in the examples just cited) for which no precise equivalent is present in the original. In those (relatively few) instances of this kind where confusion or serious ambiguity seemed likely to result, I have supplied the original German in brackets. It must, however, be emphasized that, in any systematic study of Hegel's linguistic usage, there is no substitute for consulting the original text.

Another class of terms which present the translator with difficulties are those which Hegel on some occasions invests with a sense peculiar to his own system, but on other occasions continues to use in one or more of the senses which they possess in everyday usage. The most familiar of these is perhaps the verb *aufheben*, which I have normally translated as 'to supersede' when it is used in its technical sense (which itself encompasses the meanings 'to remove (or cancel)', 'to raise', and 'to preserve'); when translating it in other ways (for example, as 'to overcome'), I have added the original in brackets. Similarly, *Vorstellung* often denotes that mode of 'representational thought' or 'representational thinking' which, for Hegel, deals not in concepts but in images raised to the form of universality; but on other occasions, it signifies no more than a 'notion' or 'idea' in the everyday senses of these words. The range of this particular term – like the term *Bestimmung* – is exceptionally wide and variable in Hegel's writings, and I have supplied the original in brackets on those occasions where translations other than 'representational thought' or 'representational thinking' are required. Hegel's use of the term *Idee*, however, is more consistent. He uses it almost invariably in its technical sense, to denote the full development (or 'truth') of the *Begriff* or concept. To indicate this special significance, I have translated it throughout with a capital, as 'Idea'.

Certain other terms cause difficulties because the institutions to which they refer do not have precise counterparts in present-day society, or because the German term in question has no precise equivalent in English. Thus, Hegel's *Polizei* has a much wider sense than the English 'police', since it refers to an authority whose responsibility extends beyond the upholding of law and order to such matters as price control, public works, and welfare provisions; for this reason, Knox and others have translated it as 'public authority'. To this I would object that Hegel's *Polizei* is just as alien to modern

German-speakers as the translation 'police' is to modern English-speakers, because the word *Polizei* in modern German has much the same range of meaning as 'police' has in modern English. I have accordingly used the translation 'police' throughout. The term *Stände* poses two distinct problems, first because the institutions to which it refers have changed in character since Hegel's day, and secondly because it has not just one but two (albeit closely related) meanings. The *Stände* were, in the first place, the Estates (or *Etats*) of feudal and absolutist society, whose representatives might constitute a formal assembly or parliament. The identity of these Estates was grounded in supposedly natural divisions within society (such as nobility, clergy, and commoners), and the term could accordingly be used in a wider sense (as the singular *Stand* regularly was) to denote other naturally distinct social groups such as the practitioners of different trades or professions. In the former, predominantly political sense, I have translated *Stände* as 'Estates' (with a capital). And in the latter, wider sense, I have translated it as 'estates' (with a small letter), in order to distinguish it from Hegel's term *Klasse*, which I have in turn translated as 'class' and which corresponds more closely to the modern concept of class as a socio-economic category. The term *Wissenschaft*, in Hegel's day as in the present, has no precise equivalent in English, the nearest approximation being the term 'science', which I have accordingly used to translate it. *Wissenschaft* in German denotes any branch of knowledge or scholarly activity which is pursued and cultivated in a systematic manner, and in Hegel's case, it is associated in particular with philosophy as he himself understood it. The English term 'science', on the other hand, at least since the first half of the nineteenth century, has carried a more circumscribed meaning, being associated first and foremost with the explanation of natural phenomena.

Even the commonest of German verbs, the verb *sein* ('to be'), can cause considerable problems, chiefly because Hegel often uses it in an absolute sense (i.e. without a predicate). Such usage (as in 'To be, or not to be') is rare in English, so that literal translation is not always possible. Where *sein* in the absolute sense is coupled with *an sich* ('in itself'), *für sich* ('for itself'), etc., I have translated it as 'to have being' (for example, 'to have being in and for itself' for Hegel's *an und für sich sein*). Where it means 'to exist', I have at times rendered it as 'to be present' in order to avoid confusion with 'to exist' as a translation of Hegel's *existieren*, although 'to exist' is sometimes feasible where no confusion with *existieren* is possible.

A word must be said in conclusion on the issue of gender-specific language. By present-day standards, Hegel's views on women, like those of many of his contemporaries, are highly discriminatory and even offensive (see, for example, § 166 of the *Rechtsphilosophie*). Accordingly, he regularly uses masculine pronouns, adjectival forms, etc. either to include the feminine, or to exclude it altogether because he considers the female sex irrelevant to whatever political or social institution he is discussing. In the interests of accuracy, I have wherever possible translated such forms literally. I have, however, in most cases translated the word *Mensch* as 'human being', although in a minority of contexts where this would have sounded unduly awkward or necessitated a misleading use of the plural, I have translated it as 'man' or 'mankind' (see, for example, § 18 and the Addition to § 139).

Square brackets are used throughout to indicate material interpolated by the editor or translator. Such material includes both original German terms where these are supplied, and words or phrases which I have added for ease of reading or comprehension, but which have no equivalents in the original. Works frequently cited in the footnotes are referred to by short title or abbreviation, followed (where applicable) by volume-number in Roman numerals and page-number: e.g. VPR III, 100; *Werke*, VII, 200.

Finally, I wish to express my gratitude to Professor Allen Wood for his scrutiny of my translation and for many helpful suggestions, and to Mrs Erna Smith for fitting into an already busy schedule the time-consuming task of typing the manuscript.

Cambridge, June 1990   H. B. Nisbet

Key to abbreviations

In the editorial notes, writings of Hegel, Kant, Fichte, and Fries will be cited according to the following system of abbreviations. All translations occurring in the notes are by the editor, but standard English translations (where they exist) will normally be cited, with English pagination following German pagination, separated by a slash (/).

Writings of Hegel

Werke   *Hegel: Werke: Theorie Werkausgabe.* Frankfurt: Suhrkamp Verlag, 1970. Cited by volume and page number.

B   *Hegels Briefe*, edited by Johannes Hoffmeister and Friedhelm Nicolin. Hamburg: Felix Meiner Verlag, 1981. Cited by volume and page number.
Hegel: The Letters, translated by Clark Butler and Christiane Seiler. Bloomington: Indiana University Press, 1984. Cited by page number.

D   *Differenz des Fichte'schen und Schelling'schen Systems der Philosophie* (1801), *Werke* II.
The Difference Between Fichte's and Schelling's System of Philosophy, translated by H. S. Harris and Walter Cerf. Albany: SUNY Press, 1977.

DV   *Die Verfassung Deutschlands, Werke* I.
'The German Constitution', translated by T. M. Knox,

in Z. Pelczynski (ed.) *Hegel's Political Writings*, Oxford: Clarendon Press, 1964.

EH   *Enzyklopädie der philosophischen Wissenschaften* (1817 Heidelberg version). *Hegels sämtliche Werke*, IV. Auflage der Jubiläumsausgabe, edited by Hermann Glockner. Stuttgart: Friedrich Frommann Verlag, 1968. Volume VI. Cited by paragraph (§) number.

EL   *Enzyklopädie der philosophischen Wissenschaften* I (1817, rev. 1827, 1830), *Werke* VIII.
Hegel's Logic, translated by William Wallace. Oxford University Press, 1975. Cited by paragraph (§) number. Additions are indicated by an 'A'.

EN   *Enzyklopädie der philosophischen Wissenschaften* II (1817, rev. 1827, 1830), *Werke* IX.
Hegel's Philosophy of Nature, edited by M. J. Petry. New York: Humanities Press, 1970. Cited by paragraph (§) number.

EG   *Enzyklopädie der philosophischen Wissenschaften* III (1817, rev. 1827, 1830), *Werke* X.
Hegel's Philosophy of Mind, translated by William Wallace and A. V. Miller. Oxford University Press, 1971. Cited by paragraph (§) number. Additions are indicated by an 'A'.

GW   *Glauben und Wissen* (1802), *Werke* II.
Faith and Knowledge, translated by Walter Cerf and H. S. Harris. Albany: SUNY Press, 1977.

JR   *Jenaer Realphilosophie* (1805–1806) (previous title: *Jenenser Realphilosophie* II), edited by J. Hoffmeister. Hamburg: Felix Meiner Verlag, 1969.
Hegel and the Human Spirit, translated by Leo Rauch. Detroit: Wayne State University Press, 1983. Cited by page number.

JR I   *Jenenser Realphilosophie* I (1803–1804), edited by J. Hoffmeister. Hamburg: Felix Meiner Verlag, 1930. Cited by page number.

LW   *[Beurteilung der] Verhandlungen in der Versammlung der Landstände des Königreichs Württemberg im Jahr 1815 und 1816, Werke* IV.
'Proceedings of the Estates Assembly in the Kingdom of Württemberg, 1815–1816', *Hegel's Political Writings.*

NP   *Nürnberger Propädeutik* (1808–1811), *Werke* IV.

NR   *Über die wissenschaftlichen Behandlungsarten des Naturrechts* (1802), *Werke* II.
Natural Law, translated by T. M. Knox. Philadelphia: University of Pennsylvania Press, 1975. Cited by page number.

PhG   *Phänomenologie des Geistes* (1807), *Werke* III.
Phenomenology of Spirit, translated by A. V. Miller. Oxford University Press, 1977. Cited by paragraph (¶) number.

PR   *Philosophie des Rechts* (1821), *Werke* VII.
Hegel's Philosophy of Right, the present translation. Cited by paragraph (§) number. Remarks are indicated by an 'R', Additions by an 'A'.

RB   *Über die englische Reformbill* (1831), *Werke* XI.
'The English Reform Bill', *Hegel's Political Writings.*

SP   *Verhältnis des Skeptizismus zur Philosophie. Darstellung seiner verschiedenen Modifikationen und Vergleichung des neuesten mit dem alten, Werke* II.
'Relationship of Skepticism to Philosophy, Exposition of its Different Modifications and Comparison of the Latest Form with the Ancient One', in George di Giovanni and H. S. Harris, *Between Kant and Hegel.* Albany: SUNY Press, 1985, pp. 311–362.

SS   *System der Sittlichkeit* (1802), edited by G. Lasson. Hamburg: Felix Meiner Verlag, 1967.
System of Ethical Life and First Philosophy of Spirit, translated by H. S. Harris. Albany, 1979. Cited by page number.

TJ   *Theologische Jugendschriften* (1793–1800), *Werke* I.

TE   *Hegel: Three Essays, 1793–1795*, translated by Peter Fuss and John Dobbins. University of Notre Dame Press, 1984.

ETW   *Early Theological Writings*, translated by T. M. Knox. Philadelphia: University of Pennsylvania Press, 1971. Cited by page number.

VA   *Vorlesungen über die Ästhetik*, 3 vols. *Werke* XIII–XV. *The Philosophy of Fine Art*, translated by F. B. P. Osmaston. New York: Hacker, 1975. 4 vols. Cited by volume and page number.

VG   *Die Vernunft in der Geschichte*, edited by J. Hoffmeister. Hamburg, 1955. *Lectures on the Philosophy of World History: Introduction*, translated by H. B. Nisbet. Cambridge, 1975. Cited by page number.

VGP   *Vorlesungen über die Geschichte der Philosophie* I–III, *Werke* XVIII–XX. *Lectures on the History of Philosophy*, translated by Elizabeth Haldane. New York: Humanities Press, 1968. Cited by volume and page number.

VPG   *Vorlesungen über die Philosophie der Geschichte, Werke* XII. *The Philosophy of History*, translated by J. Sibree. New York: Dover, 1956. Cited by page number.

VPR   *Vorlesungen über Rechtsphilosophie*, edited by K.-H. Ilting. Stuttgart: Frommann Verlag, 1974. Including notes and transcriptions from Hegel's lectures of 1818–1819 (transcription by C. G. Homeyer), 1821–1822, 1822–1823 (transcription by H. G. Hotho), 1824–1825 (transcription by K. G. von Griesheim), 1831 (transcription by D. F. Strauß). Cited by volume and page number.

VPR17   *Die Philosophie des Rechts: Die Mitschriften Wannenmann (Heidelberg 1817–1818) und Homeyer (Berlin*

    1818–1819), edited by K.-H. Ilting. Stuttgart: Klett-Cotta Verlag, 1983. Cited by page number.

VPR19 *Philosophie des Rechts: Die Vorlesung von 1819/1820*, anonymous transcription or transcriptions edited by Dieter Henrich. Frankfurt: Suhrkamp Verlag, 1983. Cited by page number.

VR   *Vorlesungen über die Philosophie der Religion, Werke* XVI–XVII.
    Lectures on the Philosophy of Religion, 3 volumes, translated by E. B. Speirs and J. B. Sanderson. London: Routledge & Kegan Paul Ltd., 1895. Cited by volume and page number.

WL   *Wissenschaft der Logik* (1812, 1816), *Werke* V–VI. Cited by volume and page number.
    Hegel's Science of Logic, translated by A. V. Miller. London: George Allen & Unwin, 1969. Cited by page number.

In writings cited by paragraph (§), a comma used before 'R' or 'A' means 'and'. Thus: 'PR § 33,A' means 'PR § 33 and the addition to § 33'; 'PR § 270,R,A' means: 'PR § 270 and the Remarks to § 270 and the Addition to § 270'.

Writings of Kant

GS   *Kants Gesammelte Schriften*. Berlin: Ausgabe der königlich preussischen Akademie der Wissenschaften, 1910– . Cited by volume and page number.

A/B   *Kritik der reinen Vernunft*, edited by Raymund Schmidt. Hamburg: Meiner, 1956.
    Immanuel Kant's Critique of Pure Reason, translated by Norman Kemp Smith. New York: St Martin's, 1963. Cited by first (A) and second (B) edition pagination, separated by a slash (e.g. A84/B116).

EF   *Zum ewigen Frieden*, GS VIII.
    'Perpetual Peace', translated by H. B. Nisbet, in Hans Reiss (ed.) *Kant's Political Writings*. Cambridge: Cambridge University Press, 1970. Cited by page number.

G	*Grundlegung der Metaphysik der Sitten*, GS IV. *Foundations of the Metaphysics of Morals*, translated by Lewis White Beck. Indianapolis: Bobbs-Merrill, 1959. Cited by page number.
KpV	*Kritik der praktischen Vernunft*, GS V. *Critique of Practical Reason*, translated by Lewis White Beck. Indianapolis: Bobbs-Merrill, 1956. Cited by page number.
R	*Religion innerhalb der Grenzen der bloßen Vernunft*, GS VI. *Religion Within the Limits of Reason Alone*, translated by Theodore M. Greene and Hoyt H. Hudson. New York: Harper & Row, 1960. Cited by page number.
RL	*Metaphysik der Sitten*: Rechtslehre, GS VI. *Metaphysical Elements of Justice*, translated by John Ladd. Indianapolis: Bobbs-Merrill. Cited by page number, but occasionally by section (§) number, especially passages not translated into English.
TL	*Metaphysik der Sitten*: Tugendlehre, GS VI. *The Doctrine of Virtue*, translated by Mary J. Gregor. New York: Harper & Row, 1964. Cited by page number.
TP	*Über den Gemeinspruch: Das mag in der Theorie richtig sein, taugt aber nicht für die Praxis*, GS VIII. 'On the Common Saying: 'This May Be True In Theory, But It Does Not Apply In Practice', translated by H. B. Nisbet, in Hans Reiss (ed.) *Kant's Political Writings*. Cited by page number.
VE	*Eine Vorlesung Kants über Ethik*, edited by P. Menzer (Berlin: Pan Verlag Rolf Heise, 1924). *Lectures on Ethics*, translated by L. Infield. New York: Harper, 1963. Cited by original German and English page number.

Writings of Fichte

FW   *Fichtes Werke*, edited by I. H. Fichte. Berlin: W. de Gruyter & Co., 1971. Cited by volume and page number.

FR   *Beitrag zur Berichtigung der Urteile des Publikums über die französische Revolution* (*An Attempt to Correct the Public's Judgments Concerning the French Revolution*) (1793), FW VI.

GNR   *Grundlagen des Naturrechts* (1796), FW III.
       Science of Rights, translated by A. E. Kroeger. London: Trubner & Co., 1889.

SL   *System der Sittenlehre* (1798), FW IV.
       The Science of Ethics, translated by A. E. Kroeger. London: Kegan Paul, Trench, Trubner & Co. Ltd., 1897.

W   *Wissenschaftslehre* (1794), including the two introductions (1797), FW I.
       The Science of Knowledge, translated by Peter Heath and John Lachs. Cambridge University Press, 1983.

Writings of Fries

AKV   *Anthropologische Kritik der Vernunft* (*Anthropological Critique of Reason*). Heidelberg: Winter, 1838. Cited by volume and page number, sometimes also by section (§) number.

NKV   First edition (1807) of AKV, entitled *Neue Kritik der Vernunft* (*New Critique of Reason*). Cited by volume and page number, sometimes also by section (§) number.

DBS   *Von deutschem Bund und deutscher Staatsverfassung; allgemeine staatsrechtliche Ansichten* (*The German Federation and German Constitution*). Heidelberg: Mohr & Winter, 1816. Cited by part and page number; dedication cited by page number only.

FDB	'Feierrede an die teutschen Burschen' ('Address to the German Fraternities') *Oppositionsblatt oder Weimarische Zeitung* 30 October 1817.
GDJ	*Über die Gefährdung des Wohlstandes und Characters der Deutschen durch die Juden* (*The Danger Posed by the Jews to German Well-Being and Character*). Heidelberg: Mohr & Winter, 1816. Cited by page number.
HPP	*Handbuch der praktischen Philosophie.* Heidelberg: Mohr & Winter, 1818.
JE	*Julius und Evagoras: oder, Schönheit der Seele. Ein philosophischer Roman.* (1813); 2nd expanded edn., Heidelberg: Christian Friedrich Winter, 1822. *Dialogues on Morality and Religion,* translated by David Walford. Totowa, NJ: Barnes and Noble, 1982. Cited by page number.

G. W. F. Hegel
Elements of the
PHILOSOPHY OF RIGHT
Or
Natural Law and Political Science in Outline

Table of Contents

4

Table of Contents

Preface

The immediate occasion for me to publish this outline is the need to provide my audience with an introduction to the lectures on the *Philosophy of Right* which I deliver in the course of my official duties.[1] This textbook is a more extensive, and in particular a more systematic, exposition of the same basic concepts which, in relation to this part of philosophy, are already contained in a previous work designed to accompany my lectures, namely my *Encyclopaedia of the Philosophical Sciences* (Heidelberg, 1817).[2]

The fact that this outline was due to appear in print and thus to come before a wider public gave me the opportunity to amplify in it some of those *Remarks* whose primary purpose was to comment briefly on ideas [*Vorstellungen*] akin to or divergent from my own, on further consequences of my argument, and on other such matters as would be properly elucidated in the lectures themselves. I have amplified them here so as to clarify on occasion the more abstract contents of the text and to take fuller account of related ideas [*Vorstellungen*] which are current at the present time. As a result, some of these Remarks have become more extensive than the aim and style of a compendium would normally lead one to expect. A genuine compendium, however, has as its subject-matter what is considered to be the entire compass of a science; and what distinguishes it – apart, perhaps, from a minor addition here or there – is above all the way in which it arranges and orders the essential elements [*Momente*] of a content which has long been familiar and accepted, just as the form in which it is presented has its rules and conventions which have long been agreed. But a philosophical outline is not expected to conform to this pattern, if only because it is imagined that what philosophy puts forward is as ephemeral a product as Penelope's weaving, which is begun afresh every day.[3]

It is certainly true that the primary difference between the present outline and an ordinary compendium is the method which constitutes its guiding principle. But I am here presupposing that the philosophical manner of progressing from one topic to another and of conducting a scientific proof – this entire speculative mode of cognition – is essentially different from other modes of cognition.[4] The realization that such a difference is a necessary one is the only thing which can save philosophy from the shameful decline into which it has fallen in our times. It has indeed been recognized that the forms and rules of the older logic – of definition, classification, and inference – which include the rules of the understanding's cognition [*Verstandeserkenntnis*], are inadequate for speculative science. Or rather, their inadequacy has not so much been recognized as merely felt, and then the rules in question have been cast aside, as if they were simply fetters, to make way for the arbitrary pronouncements of the heart, of fantasy, and of contingent intuition; and since, in spite of this, reflection and relations of thought inevitably also come into play, the despised method of commonplace deduction and ratiocination is unconsciously adopted. – Since I have fully developed the nature of speculative knowledge in my *Science of Logic*,[5] I have only occasionally added an explanatory comment on procedure and method in the present outline. Given that the subject-matter is concrete and inherently of so varied a nature, I have of course omitted to demonstrate and bring out the logical progression in each and every detail. But on the one hand, it might have been considered superfluous to do so in view of the fact that I have presupposed a familiarity with scientific method; and on the other, it will readily be noticed that the work as a whole, like the construction [*Ausbildung*] of its parts, is based on the logical spirit. It is also chiefly from this point of view that I would wish this treatise to be understood and judged. For what it deals with is *science*, and in science, the content is essentially inseparable from the *form*.

It is true that we may hear it said by those who seem to adopt the most thorough approach that form is a purely external quality, indifferent to the matter [*Sache*] itself, which is alone of consequence; furthermore, the task of the writer, especially the philosophical writer, may be said to consist in the discovery of *truths*, the statement of *truths*, and the dissemination of *truths* and correct concepts.[6] But if we consider how this task is actually performed, we see on the one hand how the same old brew is reheated again and again and served up to all and sundry – a task that may not be without its merits in educating and arousing the emotions, though it might sooner be regarded as the superfluous product of over-zealous activity – 'for they have Moses and the prophets; let them hear them'.[7] Above all, we have ample opportunity to wonder at the tone and pretentiousness that can be detected in such writers, as if all that the world had hitherto lacked was these zealous disseminators of truths, and as if their reheated brew contained new and unheard-of truths which ought, as they always claim, to be taken particularly to heart, above all 'at the present time'. But on the other hand, we can see how whatever truths of this kind are handed out by one party are displaced and swept away by truths of precisely the same kind dispensed by other parties. And if, amidst this jumble of truths, there is something that is neither old nor new but enduring, how can it be extracted from these formlessly fluctuating reflections – how can it be distinguished and verified other than by *scientific* means?

The *truth* concerning *right, ethics, and the state* is at any rate *as old* as its *exposition and promulgation* in *public laws and in public morality and religion*. What more does this truth require, inasmuch as the thinking mind [*Geist*] is not content to possess it in this proximate manner? What it needs is to be *comprehended* as well, so that the content which is already rational in itself may also gain a rational form and thereby appear justified to free thinking. For such thinking does not stop at what is *given*, whether the latter is supported by the external positive authority of the state or of mutual agreement among human beings, or by the authority of inner feeling and the heart and by the testimony of the spirit which immediately concurs with this, but starts out from itself and thereby demands to know itself as united in its innermost being with the truth.

The simple reaction [*Verhalten*] of ingenuous emotion is to adhere with trusting conviction to the publicly recognized truth and to base one's conduct and fixed position in life on this firm foundation. But this simple reaction may well encounter the supposed difficulty of how to distinguish and discover, among the *infinite variety of opinions*, what is universally acknowledged and valid in them; and this perplexity may easily be taken for a just and genuine concern with the matter [*Sache*] itself. But in fact, those who pride themselves on this perplexity are in the position of not being able to see the wood for the trees, and the only perplexity and difficulty that is present is the one they have themselves created; indeed, this perplexity and difficulty is rather a proof that they want something other than what is universally acknowledged and valid, something other than the substance of the right and the ethical. For if they were genuinely concerned with the latter and not with the *vanity* and *particularity* of opinions and being, they would adhere to the substantial right, namely to the commandments of ethics and of the state, and regulate their lives accordingly. – A further difficulty arises, however, from the fact that human beings *think* and look for their freedom and the basis of ethics in [the realm of] thought. But however exalted, however divine this right may be, it is nevertheless transformed into wrong if the only criterion of thought and the only way in which thought can know itself to be free is the extent to which it *diverges from what is universally acknowledged and valid* and manages to invent something *particular* for itself.

The notion [*Vorstellung*] that freedom of thought, and of spirit in general, can be demonstrated only by divergence from, and even hostility towards, what is publicly acknowledged might seem to be most firmly rooted nowadays in *relation* [*Beziehung*] *to the state*; for this very reason, it might seem to be the essential task of a philosophy of the state to invent and propound *yet another theory*, and specifically a new and particular theory. If we examine this notion [*Vorstellung*] and the activity that is associated with it, we might well imagine that no state or constitution had ever previously existed or were in existence today, but that we had *now* (and this 'now' is of indefinite duration) to start right from the beginning, and that the ethical world had been waiting only for such intellectual constructions, discoveries, and proofs as are *now* available. As far as *nature* is concerned, it is readily admitted that philosophy must recognize it *as it is*, that the philosopher's stone lies hidden *somewhere*, but *within nature itself*, that nature is *rational within itself*, and that it is this *actual* reason present within it which knowledge must investigate and grasp conceptually – not the shapes and contingencies which are visible on the surface, but nature's eternal harmony, conceived, however, as the law and essence *immanent* within it. *The ethical world*, on the other hand, the state, or reason as it actualizes itself in the element of self-consciousness, is not supposed to be happy in the knowledge that it is reason itself which has in fact gained power and authority [*Gewalt*] within this element, and which asserts itself there and remains inherent within it.*

*Addition (H). There are two kinds of laws, laws of nature and laws of right: the laws of nature are simply there and are valid as they stand: they suffer no diminution, although they may be infringed in individual cases. To know what the law of nature is, we must familiarize ourselves with nature, for these laws are correct and it is only our notions [*Vorstellungen*] concerning them which may be false. The measure of these laws is external to us, and our cognition adds nothing to them and does not advance them: it is only our cognition of them which can expand. Knowledge [*Kenntnis*] of right is in one respect similar to this and in another respect different. We get to know the laws of right in just the same way, simply as they are; the citizen knows them more or less in this way, and the positive jurist also stops short at what is given. But the difference is that, with the laws of right, the spirit of reflection*ᵃ* comes into play and their very diversity draws attention to the fact that they are not absolute. The laws of right are something *laid down,ᵇ* something *derived from* human beings. It necessarily follows that our inner voice may either come into collision with them or concur with them. The human being does not stop short at the existent [*dem Daseienden*], but claims to have within himself the measure of what is right; he may be subjected to the necessity and power of external authority, but never in the same way as to natural necessity, for his inner self always tells him how things ought to be, and he finds within himself the confirmation or repudiation of what is accepted as valid. In nature, the highest truth is that a law *exists at all*; in laws of right, however, the thing [*Sache*] is not valid because it exists; on the contrary, everyone demands that it should match his own criterion. Thus a conflict may arise between what is and what ought to be, between the right which has being in and for itself, which remains unaltered, and the arbitrary determination of what is supposed to be accepted as right. A disjunction and conflict of this kind is found only in the sphere [*Boden*] of the spirit, and since the prerogative of the spirit thus seems to lead to discord and unhappiness, we often turn away from the arbitrariness of life to the contemplation of nature and are inclined to take the latter as a model. But these very discrepancies [*Gegensätze*] between that right which has being in and for itself and what arbitrariness proclaims as right make it imperative for us to learn to recognize precisely what right is. In right,

ᵃTranslator's note: Geist der Betrachtung; Hotho's notes, on which Gans based this Addition, simply read *Geist* ('spirit'): see VPR III, 93.
ᵇTranslator's note: 'Die Rechtsgesetze sind *Gesetztes*': Hegel plays on the similarity of the word *Gesetz* (law) and *Gesetztes* (something laid down or posited).

The spiritual universe is supposed rather to be at the mercy of contingency and arbitrariness, to be *god-forsaken*, so that, according to this atheism of the ethical world, *truth* lies *outside* it, and at the same time, since reason is nevertheless *also* supposed to be present in it, truth is nothing but a problem. But, we are told, this very circumstance justifies, indeed obliges, every thinker to take his own initiative, though not *in search of* the philosopher's stone, for this search is made superfluous by the philosophizing of our times and everyone, whatever his condition, can be assured that he has this stone in his grasp. Now it does admittedly happen that those who live within the actuality of the state and are able to satisfy their knowledge and volition within it – and there are many of them, more in fact than think or know it, for *basically* this includes *everyone* – or at least those who *consciously* find satisfaction within the state, laugh at such initiatives and assurances and regard them as an empty game, now more amusing, now more serious, now pleasing, now dangerous. This restless activity of vain reflection, along with the reception and response it

the human being must encounter his own reason; he must therefore consider the rationality of right, and this is the business of our science, in contrast with positive jurisprudence, which is often concerned only with contradictions. Besides, the present-day world has a more urgent need of such an investigation, for in olden times there was still respect and veneration for the existing [*bestehenden*] law, whereas the culture [*Bildung*] of the present age has taken a new direction, and thought has adopted a leading role in the formation of values. Theories are put forward in opposition to what already exists [*dem Daseienden*], theories which seek to appear correct and necessary in and for themselves. From now on, there is a more special need to recognize and comprehend the thoughts of right. Since thought has set itself up as the essential form, we must attempt to grasp right, too, in terms of thought. If thought is to take precedence over right, this would seem to throw open the door to contingent opinions; but genuine thought is not an opinion about something [*die Sache*], but the concept of the thing [*Sache*] itself. The concept of the thing does not come to us by nature. Everyone has fingers and can take a brush and paint, but that does not make him a painter. It is precisely the same with thinking. The thought of right is not, for example, what everybody knows at first hand; on the contrary, correct thinking is knowing [*das Kennen*] and recognizing the thing, and our cognition should therefore be scientific.

encounters, might be regarded as a separate issue [*Sache*], developing independently in its own distinct way, were it not that *philosophy* in general has incurred all kinds of contempt and discredit as a result of such behaviour. The worst kind of contempt it has met with is, as already mentioned, that everyone, whatever his condition, is convinced that he knows all about philosophy in general and can pass judgement upon it. No other art or science is treated with this ultimate degree of contempt, namely the assumption that one can take possession of it outright.

In fact, what we have seen the philosophy of recent times proclaiming with the utmost pretension in relation to the state has no doubt entitled anyone who wishes to have a say in such matters to the belief that he could just as well do the same thing on his own account, and thereby prove to himself that he was in possession of philosophy. In any case, this self-styled philosophy has expressly stated that *truth itself cannot be known* [*erkannt*], but that truth consists in what *wells up from each individual's heart, emotion, and enthusiasm* in relation to ethical subjects, particularly in relation to the state, government, and constitution. What has not been said in this connection to flatter the young in particular?[8] And the young have certainly taken note of it. The saying 'for he giveth to his own in sleep' has been applied to science, so that all sleepers have counted themselves among the *chosen*; but the concepts they have acquired in their sleep have of course borne the marks of their origin.[9] – A leader of this superficial brigade of so-called philosophers, Herr Fries,† had the temerity, at a solemn public occasion which has since become notorious,[11] to put forward the following idea [*Vorstellung*] in an address on the subject of the state and constitution: 'In a people among whom a genuine communal spirit prevails, all business relating to public affairs would gain its *life from below, from the people itself; living* societies, steadfastly united *by the sacred bond of friendship*, would dedicate themselves to every single project of popular education and popular service'; and so on. – The chief tendency of this superficial philosophy is to base science not on the development of thought and the concept, but on immediate perception and contingent imagination; and likewise, to reduce the complex inner articulation of the ethical, i.e. the state, the architectonics of its rationality – which, through determinate distinc-

---

†*Hegel's note:* I have testified elsewhere to the superficiality of his science: see my *Science of Logic* (Nürnberg, 1812), Introduction, p. XVII.[10]

tions between the various spheres of public life and the rights [*Berech-tigungen*] they are based on, and through the strict proportions in which every pillar, arch, and buttress is held together, produces the strength of the whole from the harmony of its parts – to reduce this refined [*gebildeten*] structure to a mush of 'heart, friendship, and enthusiasm'.[12] According to this notion [*Vorstellung*], the ethical world, like the universe of Epicurus, should be given over to the subjective contingency of opinions and arbitrariness; but of course this *is* not the case.[13] By the simple household remedy of attributing to *feeling* what reason and its understanding have laboured to produce over several thousand years, all the trouble involved in rational insight and cognition, guided by the thinking concept, can of course be avoided. Goethe's Mephistopheles – a good authority – says much the same thing in lines which I have also quoted elsewhere:

> Do but despise reason and science,
> The highest of all human gifts –
> Then you have surrendered to the devil
> And must surely perish.[14]

The next step is for this view to assume the guise of *piety* as well; for what lengths has such behaviour not gone to in order to lend itself authority! By means of godliness and the Bible, however, it has presumed to gain the supreme justification for despising the ethical order and the objectivity of the laws. For it is surely also piety which envelops in the simpler intuition of feeling that truth which, in the world itself, is diversified into an organic realm. But if it is the right kind of piety, it abandons the form of this [emotional] region as soon as it emerges from [the condition of] inwardness into the daylight of the Idea's full development [*Entfaltung*] and manifest abundance, and it brings with it, from its inner worship of God, a reverence for the laws and for a truth which has being in and for itself and is exalted above the subjective form of feeling.

The particular form of bad conscience which betrays itself in the vainglorious eloquence of this superficial philosophy may be remarked on here; for in the first place, it is precisely where it is at its *most spiritless* that it has most to say about *spirit*, where its talk is driest and most lifeless that it is freest with the words 'life' and 'enliven', and where it shows the utmost selfishness of empty arrogance that it most often refers to the 'people'. But the distinctive mark which it carries on its brow is its hatred of law. That right and ethics, and the actual world of right and the ethical, are grasped by means of *thoughts* and give themselves the form of rationality – namely universality and determinacy – by means of thoughts, is what constitutes *the law*; and it is this which is justifiably regarded as the main enemy by that feeling which reserves the right to do as it pleases, by that conscience which identifies right with subjective conviction. The form of right as a *duty* and a *law* is felt by it to be a *dead, cold letter* and a *shackle*; for it does not recognize itself in the law and thereby recognize its own freedom in it, because the law is the reason of the thing [*Sache*] and reason does not allow feeling to warm itself in the glow of its own particularity [*Partikularität*]. The *law* is therefore, as I have remarked elsewhere in the course of this textbook,[15] the chief shibboleth by which the false brethren and friends of the so-called 'people' give themselves away.

Since this arbitrary sophistry has usurped the name of *philosophy* and persuaded a wide public that such activities are philosophy, it has almost become dishonourable to continue to speak philosophically about the nature of the state; and right-minded [*rechtliche*] men cannot be blamed if they grow impatient as soon as they hear talk of a philosophical science of the state. There is even less cause for surprise that governments have at last directed their attention to such philosophizing, for philosophy with us is not in any case practised as a private art, as it was with the Greeks, for example, but has a public existence [*Existenz*], impinging upon the public, especially – or solely – in the service of the state. Governments have had enough confidence in those of their scholars who have devoted themselves to this subject to leave the development [*Ausbildung*] and import of philosophy entirely to them – granted that here and there, they may have done so not so much out of confidence in science as out of indifference towards it, retaining teaching posts in philosophy only for reasons of tradition (just as in France, to the best of my knowledge, chairs of metaphysics at least have been allowed to lapse). But their confidence has frequently been ill repaid, or alternatively, if they are thought to be motivated by indifference, the resultant decay of thorough knowledge [*Erkenntnis*] should be regarded as the penalty for this indifference. It may initially appear that this superficial philosophy is eminently compatible at least with outward peace and order, in that it never manages to touch the substance of things [*Sachen*], or even to suspect its existence; it would thus have no cause to fear police intervention, at least initially, if it were not that the state also contained the need for a deeper education and insight, and demanded that this need be satisfied by science. But superficial philosophy leads automatically, as far as the ethical [world] and right and duty in general are concerned, to those principles which constitute superficiality in this sphere, namely the principles of the *Sophists* as we find them so clearly described by Plato.[16] These principles identify what is right with *subjective ends and opinions*, with *subjective feeling and particular [partikuläre] conviction*, and they lead to the destruction of inner ethics and the upright conscience, of love and right among private persons, as well as the destruction of public order and the laws of the state. The significance which such phenomena [*Erscheinungen*] must acquire for governments can scarcely be reduced, for example, by the claim that the very confidence shown by the state and the authority of an official position are enough to warrant the demand that the state should accept and give free rein to what corrupts the substantial source of all deeds, namely universal principles, and should even allow itself to be defied, as if such defiance were entirely proper. 'If God gives someone an office, he also gives him sense [*Verstand*]',[17] is an old chestnut which will scarcely be taken seriously by anyone nowadays.

In the importance which circumstances have again led governments to attach to the way in which philosophers conduct their business, there is no mistaking the fact that the study of philosophy now seems in many other respects to require an element [*Moment*] of protection and encouragement. For in so many publications in the field of the positive sciences, as well as in works of religious edification and other indeterminate literature, the reader encounters not only that contempt for philosophy which I have already referred to, in that the very people who reveal that their intellectual development [*Gedankenbildung*] is extremely retarded and that philosophy is completely alien to them also treat it as something they have finished and done with; beyond this, we also find that such writers expressly impugn philosophy and declare its content, the *conceptual cognition of God* and of physical and spiritual nature, the *cognition of truth*, to be a foolish, indeed sinful presumption, and that *reason*, and again *reason*, and in endless repetition *reason* is arraigned, belittled, and condemned. Or at the very least, they let us see how, for a large proportion of those engaged in supposedly scientific study, the claims of the concept constitute an embarrassment from which they are nevertheless unable to escape. If, I say, one is confronted with such phenomena [*Erscheinungen*], one might almost begin to suspect that tradition is *from this point of view* no longer worthy of respect nor sufficient to guarantee *tolerance* and a continued public existence [*Existenz*] to the study of philosophy.*†18* – The declamations and presumptuous outbursts against philosophy which are so common in our time afford the peculiar spectacle on the one hand of being in the right, by virtue of that superficiality to which philosophical science has been degraded, and on the other of themselves being rooted in the very element against which they so ungratefully turn. For by declaring the cognition of truth to be a futile endeavour, this self-styled philosophizing has reduced all thoughts and all topics *to the same level*, just as the despotism of the Roman emperors *removed all distinctions* between patricians and slaves, virtue and vice, honour and dishonour, and knowledge [*Kenntnis*] and ignorance.*20* As a result, the concepts of truth and the laws of ethics are reduced to mere opinions and subjective convictions, and the most criminal principles – since they, too, are *convictions* – are accorded the same status as those laws; and in the same way, all objects, however barren and particular [*partikular*], and all materials, however arid, are accorded the same status as what constitutes the interest of all thinking people and the bonds of the ethical world.

It should therefore be considered a stroke of *good fortune* for science – although in fact, as I have already mentioned,*21* it is a *necessary consequence* of the *thing* [*Sache*] itself – that this philosophizing, which could well have continued to spin itself into its own web of *scholastic wisdom*, has come into closer contact with actuality, in which the principles of rights and duties are a serious matter, and which lives in

---

†Hegel's note: I was reminded of such views on reading a letter of Johannes von Müller (*Werke* [Tübingen, 1810–19], Part VIII, p. 56), where he says of the condition of *Rome* in 1803 when the city was under French rule: 'Asked how the public educational institutions were faring, a professor replied: "On les tolère comme les bordels." '*ᵃ19* One can still even hear people *recommending* so-called 'rational theory' [*Vernunftlehre*], i.e. *logic*, perhaps in the belief that no one in any case bothers about it any longer as a dry and unfruitful science, or that, if this does happen now and again, those who study it will find only vacuous formulae, neither beneficial nor detrimental, so that the recommendation cannot possibly do any harm, even if it does no good either.

ᵃTranslator's note: 'They are tolerated, like the brothels.'

the light of its consciousness of these principles, and that a *public* split has consequently resulted between the two. It is *this very relation of philosophy to actuality* which is the subject of misunderstandings, and I accordingly come back to my earlier observation that, since philosophy is *exploration of the rational*, it is for that very reason the *comprehension of the present and the actual*, not the setting up of a *world beyond* which exists God knows where – or rather, of which we can very well say that we know where it exists, namely in the errors of a one-sided and empty ratiocination. In the course of the following treatise, I have remarked that even Plato's *Republic*, a proverbial example of an *empty ideal*, is essentially the embodiment of nothing other than the nature of Greek ethics; and Plato, aware that the ethics of his time were being penetrated by a deeper principle which, within this context, could appear immediately only as an as yet unsatisfied longing and hence only as a destructive force, was obliged, in order to counteract it, to seek the help of that very longing itself. But the help he required had to come from above, and he could seek it at first only in a particular *external* form of Greek ethics. By this means, he imagined he could overcome the destructive force, and he thereby inflicted the gravest damage on the deeper drive behind it, namely free infinite personality. But he proved his greatness of spirit by the fact that the very principle on which the distinctive character of his Idea turns is the pivot on which the impending world revolution turned.

> What is rational is actual;
> and what is actual is rational.[22]

This conviction is shared by every ingenuous consciousness as well as by philosophy, and the latter takes it as its point of departure in considering both the *spiritual* and the *natural* universe. If reflection, feeling, or whatever form the subjective consciousness may assume regards the *present* as *vain* and looks beyond it in a spirit of superior knowledge, it finds itself in a vain position; and since it has actuality only in the present, it is itself mere vanity. Conversely, if the *Idea* is seen as 'only an idea', a representation [*Vorstellung*] in the realm of opinion, philosophy affords the opposite insight that nothing is actual except the Idea. For what matters is to recognize in the semblance of the temporal and transient the substance which is immanent and the eternal which is present. For since the rational, which is synonymous with the Idea, becomes actual by entering into external existence

[*Existenz*], it emerges in an infinite wealth of forms, appearances, and shapes and surrounds its core with a brightly coloured covering in which consciousness at first resides, but which only the concept can penetrate in order to find the inner pulse, and detect its continued beat even within the external shapes. But the infinitely varied circumstances which take shape within this externality as the essence manifests itself within it, this infinite material and its organization, are not the subject-matter of philosophy. To deal with them would be to interfere in things [*Dinge*] with which philosophy has no concern, and it can save itself the trouble of giving good advice on the subject. Plato could well have refrained from recommending nurses never to stand still with children but to keep rocking them in their arms; and Fichte likewise need not have perfected his *passport regulations* to the point of 'constructing', as the expression ran, the requirement that the passports of suspect persons should carry not only their personal description but also their painted likeness.[23] In deliberations of this kind, no trace of philosophy remains, and it can the more readily abstain from such ultra-wisdom because it is precisely in relation to this infinite multitude of subjects that it should appear at its most liberal. In this way, philosophical science will also show itself furthest removed from the hatred which the vanity of superior wisdom displays towards a multitude of circumstances and institutions – a hatred in which pettiness takes the greatest of pleasure, because this is the only way in which it can attain self-esteem [*Selbstgefühl*].

This treatise, therefore, in so far as it deals with political science, shall be nothing other than an attempt *to comprehend and portray the state as an inherently rational entity*. As a philosophical composition, it must distance itself as far as possible from the obligation to construct a *state as it ought to be*; such instruction as it may contain cannot be aimed at instructing the state on how it ought to be, but rather at showing how the state, as the ethical universe, should be recognized.

>Ἰδοὺ Ῥόδος, ἰδοὺ καὶ τὸ πήδημα.
>*Hic* Rhodus, *hic* saltus.[24]

To comprehend *what is* is the task of philosophy, for *what is* is reason. As far as the individual is concerned, each individual is in any case a *child of his time*; thus philosophy, too, is *its own time comprehended in thoughts*. It is just as foolish to imagine that any philosophy can transcend its contemporary world as that an individual can overleap his own time or leap over Rhodes.[25] If his theory does indeed transcend his own time, if it builds itself a world *as it ought to be*, then it certainly has an existence, but only within his opinions – a pliant medium in which the imagination can construct anything it pleases.

With little alteration, the saying just quoted would read:

Here is the rose, dance *here.*[26]

What lies between reason as self-conscious spirit and reason as present actuality, what separates the former from the latter and prevents it from finding satisfaction in it, is the fetter of some abstraction or other which has not been liberated into [the form of] the concept. To recognize reason as the rose in the cross of the present[27] and thereby to delight in the present – this rational insight is the *reconciliation* with actuality which philosophy grants to those who have received the inner call *to comprehend*, to preserve their subjective freedom in the realm of the substantial, and at the same time to stand with their subjective freedom not in a particular and contingent situation, but in what has being in and for itself.

This is also what constitutes the more concrete sense of what was described above in more abstract terms as the *unity of form and content.* For *form* in its most concrete significance is reason as conceptual cognition, and *content* is reason as the substantial essence of both ethical and natural actuality; the conscious identity of the two is the philosophical Idea. – It is a great obstinacy, the kind of obstinacy which does honour to human beings, that they are unwilling to acknowledge in their attitudes [*Gesinnung*] anything which has not been justified by thought – and this obstinacy is the characteristic property of the modern age, as well as being the distinctive principle of Protestantism. What Luther inaugurated as faith in feeling and in the testimony of the spirit is the same thing that the spirit, at a more mature stage of its development, endeavours to grasp in the *concept* so as to free itself in the present and thus find itself therein. It has become a famous saying that 'a half-philosophy leads away from God' – and it is the same half-measure which defines cognition as an *approximation* to the truth – 'whereas true philosophy leads to God';[28] the same applies to philosophy and the state. Reason is not content with an approximation which, as something 'neither cold nor hot', it 'spews out of its mouth';[29] and it is as little content with that cold despair which confesses that, in this temporal world, things are bad or at best indifferent, but that nothing better can be expected here, so that for this reason alone we should live at peace with actuality. The peace which cognition establishes with the actual world has more warmth in it than this.

A further word on the subject of *issuing instructions* on how the world ought to be: philosophy, at any rate, always comes too late to perform this function. As the *thought* of the world, it appears only at a time when actuality has gone through its formative process and attained its completed state. This lesson of the concept is necessarily also apparent from history, namely that it is only when actuality has reached maturity that the ideal appears opposite the real and reconstructs this real world, which it has grasped in its substance, in the shape of an intellectual realm.[30] When philosophy paints its grey in grey, a shape of life has grown old, and it cannot be rejuvenated, but only recognized, by the grey in grey of philosophy; the owl of Minerva begins its flight only with the onset of dusk.[31]

But it is time to conclude this foreword; as a foreword, its function was in any case merely to make external and subjective comments on the point of view of the work to which it is prefaced. If a content is to be discussed philosophically, it will bear only scientific and objective treatment; in the same way, the author will regard any criticism expressed in a form other than that of scientific discussion of the matter [*Sache*] itself merely as a subjective postscript and random assertion, and will treat it with indifference.

Berlin, 25 June 1820

Introduction

§ 1

The subject-matter of *the philosophical science of right* is the *Idea of right* – the concept of right and its actualization.[1]

Philosophy has to do with Ideas and therefore not with what are commonly described as *mere concepts*. On the contrary, it shows that the latter are one-sided and lacking in truth, and that it is the *concept* alone (not what is so often called by that name, but which is merely an abstract determination of the understanding) which has *actuality*, and in such a way that it gives actuality to itself. Everything other than this actuality which is posited by the concept itself is transitory *existence* [*Dasein*], external contingency, opinion, appearance without essence, untruth, deception, etc. The *shape* which the concept assumes in its actualization, and which is essential for cognition of the *concept* itself, is different from its *form* of being purely as concept, and is the other essential moment of the Idea.

Addition (H). The concept and its existence [*Existenz*] are two aspects [of the same thing], separate and united, like soul and body. The body is the same life as the soul, and yet the two can be said to lie outside one another. A soul without a body would not be a living thing, and vice versa. Thus the existence [*Dasein*] of the concept is its body, just as the latter obeys the soul which produced it. The buds have the tree within them and contain its entire strength, although they are not yet the tree itself. The tree corresponds entirely to the simple image of the bud. If the body does

25

not correspond to the soul, it is a wretched thing indeed. The unity of existence [*Dasein*] and the concept, of body and soul, is the Idea. It is not just a harmony, but a complete interpenetration. Nothing lives which is not in some way Idea. The Idea of right is freedom, and in order to be truly apprehended, it must be recognizable in its concept and in the concept's existence [*Dasein*].

§ 2

The science of right is *a part of philosophy*. It has therefore to develop the *Idea*, which is the reason within an object [*Gegenstand*], out of the concept; or what comes to the same thing, it must observe the proper immanent development of the thing [*Sache*] itself. As a part [of philosophy], it has a determinate *starting point*, which is the *result* and truth of what *preceded* it, and what preceded it is the so-called *proof* of that result. Hence the concept of right, so far as its *coming into being* is concerned, falls outside the science of right; its deduction is presupposed here and is to be taken as *given.*[1]

Addition (G). Philosophy forms a circle.[2] It has an initial or immediate point – for it must begin somewhere – a point which is not demonstrated and is not a result. But the starting point of philosophy is immediately relative, for it must appear at another end-point as a result. Philosophy is a sequence which is not suspended in mid-air; it does not begin immediately, but is rounded off within itself.

> According to the formal, non-philosophical method of the sciences, the first thing which is sought and required, at least for the sake of external scientific form, is the *definition*. The positive science of right cannot be much concerned with this, however, since its chief aim is to state *what* is right and legal [*Rechtens*], i.e. what the particular legal determinations are. This is the reason for the warning: 'omnis definitio in iure civili periculosa.'[a3] And in fact, the more incoherent and internally contradictory the determinations of a [system of] right are, the less possible it will be to make definitions within it; for definitions should contain universal determinations, but in the present context, these would immediately make the contradictory element – in this case, what is unjust [*das Unrechtliche*] –

---

[a]*Translator's note:* 'In civil law all definitions are hazardous.'

26

visible in all its nakedness. Thus, in Roman law [*das römische Recht*], for example, no definition of a *human being* would be possible, for the slave could not be subsumed under it; indeed, the status [*Stand*] of the slave does violence to that concept. The definitions of 'property' and 'proprietor' would seem equally hazardous in many situations. – But the deduction of the definition may perhaps be reached by means of etymology, or chiefly by abstraction from particular cases, so that it is ultimately based on the feelings and ideas [*Vorstellung*] of human beings. The correctness of the definition is then made to depend on its agreement with prevailing ideas [*Vorstellungen*]. This method leaves out of account what is alone essential to science – with regard to content, the *necessity of the thing* [*Sache*] in and for itself (in this case, of right), and with regard to form, the nature of the concept. In philosophical cognition, on the other hand, the chief concern is the *necessity* of a concept, and the route by which it has become a *result* [is] its proof and deduction. Thus, given that its *content* is necessary *for itself*, the second step is to look around for what corresponds to it in our ideas [*Vorstellungen*] and language. But this concept as it is for itself in its *truth* may not only be different from our *representation* [*Vorstellung*] of it: the two must also differ in their form and shape. If, however, the representation is not also false in its content, the concept may well be shown to be contained in it and present in essence within it; that is, the representation may be raised to the form of the concept. But it is so far from being the measure and criterion of the concept which is necessary and true for itself that it must rather derive its truth from the concept, and recognize and correct itself with the help of the latter. – But if, on the other hand, the former manner of cognition with its formal definitions, inferences, proofs, and the like has now virtually disappeared, the other mode which has replaced it is a bad substitute: that is, Ideas in general, and hence also the Idea of right and its further determinations, are taken up and asserted in immediate fashion as *facts of consciousness*, and our natural or intensified feelings, our *own heart* and *enthusiasm*, are made the source of right.[4] If this is the most convenient method of all, it is also the least philosophical – not to mention here other aspects of this view, which has immediate relevance [*Beziehung*] to action and not just to cognition. Whereas the first – admittedly formal – method does at least require the *form* of the concept in its definitions and the *form* of *necessary* cognition in its proofs, the mode of immediate consciousness and feeling makes the subjectivity, contingency, and arbitrariness of knowledge into its principle. – A familiarity with the nature of scientific procedure in philosophy, as expounded in philosophical logic, is here presupposed.

§ 3

Right is in general *positive* (a) through its *form* of having validity within a [particular] state; and this legal authority is the principle which underlies knowledge [*Kenntnis*] of right, i.e. *the positive science of right.* (b) In terms of *content*, this right acquires a positive element (α) through the particular *national character* of a people, its stage of *historical* development, and the whole context of relations governed by *natural necessity;[1]* (β) through the necessity whereby a system of legal right must contain the *application* of the universal concept to the particular and *externally* given characteristics of objects [*Gegenstände*] and instances – an application which is no longer [a matter of] speculative thought and the development of the concept, but [of] subsumption by the understanding; (γ) through the *final* determinations required for *making decisions* in actuality.

If the feelings of the heart, [personal] inclinations, and arbitrariness are set up in opposition to positive right and laws, philosophy at least cannot recognize such authorities. That force and tyranny may be an element in positive right is contingent to the latter, and has nothing to do with its nature. Later in this work (§§ 211–214), it will be shown at what point right must become positive. The determinations which will be discussed in that context are mentioned here only in order to indicate the limits [*Grenze*] of philosophical right and at the same time to rule out any possible idea [*Vorstellung*], let alone expectation, that its systematic development should give rise to a positive code of laws such as is required by an actual state. – Natural law or philosophical right is different from positive right, but it would be a grave misunderstanding to distort this difference into an opposition or antagonism; on the contrary, their relation is like that between Institutes and Pandects.[2] – With regard to the historical element in positive right (first referred to in § 3 above), Montesquieu stated the true historical view, the genuinely philosophical viewpoint, that legislation in general and its particular determinations should not be considered in isolation and in the abstract, but rather as a dependent moment within *one* totality, in the context of all the other determinations which constitute the character of a nation and age; within this context they gain their genuine significance, and hence also their justification.[3] – To consider the emergence and development of determinations of right *as they appear in time* is a *purely historical* task. This task, like that of recognizing the logical consistency of such determinations by comparing them with previously existing legal relations, is meritorious and praiseworthy within its own sphere, and bears no relation to the philosophical approach – unless, that is to say, development from historical grounds is confused with development from the concept, and the significance of historical explanation and justification is extended to include a justification which is *valid in and for itself.*[4] This distinction, which is very important and should be firmly borne in mind, is at the same time a very obvious one; a determination of right may be shown to be entirely *grounded in* and *consistent with* the prevailing *circumstances* and *existing* legal institutions, yet it may be contrary to right [*unrechtlich*] and irrational in and for itself, like numerous determinations of Roman civil law [*Privatrecht*] which followed quite consistently from such institutions as Roman paternal authority and Roman matrimony. But even if the determinations of right are rightful and rational, it is one thing to demonstrate that this is so – and this cannot truly be done except by means of the concept – and another to depict their historical emergence and the circumstances, eventualities, needs, and incidents which led to their introduction. This kind of demonstration and (pragmatic) cognition in terms of proximate or remote historical causes is often called 'explanation', or even more commonly 'comprehension', in the belief [*Meinung*] that this kind of historical demonstration is all – or rather, the one essential thing – that needs to be done in order to *comprehend* the law or a legal institution, whereas in fact the truly essential issue, the concept of the thing [*Sache*], has not even been mentioned. – Similarly, we often hear talk of Roman or Germanic '*concepts of right*', or of such '*concepts* of right' as are defined in this or that legal code, although these codes contain no reference to concepts, but only to general *determinations of right*, propositions of the understanding, principles, laws, and the like. – By disregarding the difference in question, it becomes possible to shift the point of view and to turn the request for a true justification into a justification by circumstances, a logical deduction from premises which may in themselves [*für sich*] be as valueless as the conclusions derived from them, etc.; in short, the relative is put in place of the absolute, and the external appearance in place of the nature of the thing [*Sache*] itself. When a historical justification confuses an origin in external factors with an origin in the concept, it unconsciously achieves the opposite of what it intends. If it can be shown that the origin of an institution was entirely expedient and necessary under the specific circumstances of the time, the requirements of the historical viewpoint are fulfilled. But if this is supposed to amount to a general justification of the thing itself, the result is precisely the opposite; for since the original circumstances are no longer present, the institution has thereby lost its meaning and its right [to exist]. Thus if, for example, the *monasteries* are justified by an appeal to their services in cultivating and populating areas of wilderness and in preserving scholarship through instruction, copying of manuscripts, etc., and these services are regarded as the reason [*Grund*] and purpose [*Bestimmung*] of their continued existence, what in fact follows from these past services is that, since the circumstances have now changed completely, the monasteries have, at least in this respect, become superfluous and inappropriate. – Since it has now been shown that the historical significance of origins, along with their historical demonstration and exposition, belongs to a different sphere from the philosophical view of the same origins and of the concept of the thing, the two approaches can to that extent remain indifferent to one another. But since they do not always maintain such peaceful relations, even in scientific matters, I shall quote something relating to their mutual contact which appears in Herr [Gustav] Hugo's *Textbook of the History of Roman Law* [*Lehrbuch der Geschichte des römischen Rechts*, 1790], and which will also further elucidate their supposed mode of opposition.[5] Herr Hugo points out in the passage in question (fifth edition [1818], § 53) 'that Cicero praises the Twelve Tables, while *looking askance* at the philosophers',[6] whereas 'the philosopher Favorinus treats them just as many a great philosopher has subsequently treated positive right'. In the same context, Herr Hugo replies once and for all to such treatment with the explanation that 'Favorinus *understood* the Twelve Tables *just as little* as the philosophers have understood positive right'. – As to the correction of the philosopher Favorinus by the jurist Sextus Caecilius in [Aulus] Gellius' *Noctes Atticae*, xx, 1, it is primarily a statement of the true and lasting principle which must underlie the justification of anything whose impact is merely positive.[7] 'Non ignoras', says Caecilius very aptly to Favorinus, 'legum *opportunitates* et medelas pro *temporum* moribus et pro rerum publicarum *generibus*, ac pro utilitatum *praesentium* rationibus, proque *vitiorum*, quibus medendum est, *fervoribus, mutari* ac *flecti, neque uno statu consistere*, quin, ut facies coeli et maris, ita *rerum* atque *fortunae* tempestatibus *varientur*. Quid salubrius visum est rogatione illa Stolonis ... quid utilius plebiscito Voconio ... quid tam necessarium existimatum est ... quam lex Licinia ... ? Omnia *tamen* haec *obliterata* et *operta* sunt civitatis opulentia ...'[a] These laws are positive in so far as their significance and appropriateness are *circumstantial* and

[a] *Translator's note:* 'You know very well that the advantages and remedies afforded by the laws change and vary in accordance with the customs of the age and types of constitution, with considerations of present advantage and of deficiencies to be remedied, and that they do not persist in a constant state. On the contrary, they are changed by the storms of chance and circumstance, just as storms change the face of the sea and sky. What could be more salutary than the legal proposal of Stolo[8]..., what more useful than the popular decree of Voconius,[9]..., and what has been deemed as necessary... as the Licinian law...? And yet they have all been obliterated and obscured by the opulence of the present state[10]...'

their value is therefore entirely historical; they are accordingly of a transient nature. The wisdom of what legislators and governments have done for the circumstances of their time and laid down for the conditions under which they lived is a distinct issue [*eine Sache für sich*] which should be assessed by history, whose recognition of it will be all the more profound if such an assessment is supported by philosophical insights. I shall, however, cite an example of Caecilius' further attempts to justify the Twelve Tables against Favorinus, because in so doing, he employs the eternally deceptive method of the understanding and its mode of ratiocination, namely by *supplying a good reason* [*Grund*] *for a bad thing* [*Sache*] and believing that the latter has thereby been justified. He mentions the abominable law which, after a specified interval had elapsed, gave the creditor the right to kill the debtor or to sell him into slavery, or even, if there were several creditors, *to cut pieces off him and so divide him between them* that, *if anyone had cut off too much or too little, he should incur no consequent legal disadvantage*[a] (a clause which would have benefited Shakespeare's Shylock in *The Merchant of Venice* and which he would most gratefully have accepted).[11] In support of this law, Caecilius puts forward the *good reason* that it provided an additional guarantee of good faith and that, given the abominable nature of the law, it was never intended that it should be enforced.[12] In his thoughtlessness, he not only fails to reflect that this latter provision [*Bestimmung*] frustrates the former intention, namely that the law should guarantee good faith, but also overlooks the fact that he himself cites an example immediately afterwards of how the law on false witness was rendered ineffectual by its excessive severity. – But it is not clear what Herr Hugo means when he says that Favorinus did not *understand* the law; any schoolboy is capable of understanding it, and Shylock would have understood better than anyone else the clause in question, which would have been of so much advantage to him; by '*understanding*', Herr Hugo must have meant only that degree [*Bildung*] of understanding which is satisfied

---

[a] *Translator's note:* The text in the Suhrkamp edition of Hegel's *Werke* VII reads *Rechtsanteil* ('legal share'). This is clearly an error for *Rechtsnachteil*, the correct reading as in Ilting's edition (VPR II, 102).

if a *good reason* can be found for such a law. – Incidentally, a further misunderstanding of which Caecilius convicts Favorinus in the same context is one to which a philosopher may readily confess without blushing – namely his failure to realize that *iumentum*, which the law specified, 'as distinct from *arcera*', as the only mode of transport to be provided to bring a sick man as witness to the court, should be understood to signify not only a horse but also a coach or wagon.[13] Caecilius was able to derive from this legal determination a further proof of the excellence and precision of the old laws, for in determining how a sick witness was to be summoned to testify in court, they even went so far as to distinguish not just between a horse and a wagon, but even between different kinds of wagon – between a covered and upholstered wagon, as Caecilius explains, and a less comfortable one. We would thus be left with a choice between the severity of the original law and the triviality of such determinations; but to describe such things, let alone learned expositions of them, as 'trivial', would be among the greatest possible affronts to scholarship of this and other kinds.

But in the textbook cited above, Herr Hugo also has occasion to speak of *rationality* in connection with Roman law, and I was particularly struck by the following points. In his treatment of *the period from the origin of the state to the Twelve Tables* (§§ 38 and 39), he says that 'people (in Rome) had many needs and were obliged to work, requiring the *assistance* of draught animals and beasts of burden *such as we ourselves* possess, that the territory of Rome consisted of alternate hills and valleys, that the city stood on a hill, etc. – allusions which were perhaps meant to fulfil the intentions of Montesquieu, but which will scarcely be found to have captured the latter's spirit. He then points out (§ 40) 'that the position with regard to *right* was still very far from satisfying the *highest* demands of *reason*'. (This is quite correct; Roman family law [*Familienrecht*], slavery, etc. do not satisfy even the most modest demands of reason.) But in dealing with later periods, Herr Hugo forgets to tell us in which of them, if any, Roman law *satisfied the highest demands of reason*. In § 289, however, Herr Hugo says of the classical jurists in the period *of the highest development [Ausbildung] of Roman law as a science* 'that it has long since been noticed that the classical jurists had a philosophical education'; but 'few people are aware' (although the many editions of Herr Hugo's textbook have ensured that more people are now aware) 'that no category of writers is so eminently deserving as these same Roman jurists *to be likened* to the mathematicians in respect of logical deduction from first principles or to the new founder of metaphysics in respect of the strikingly distinctive way in which they develop their concepts – the latter being confirmed by the *remarkable* fact that there are nowhere so many *trichotomies* as in the classical jurists and in Kant'. – That logical consistency which Leibniz praises is certainly an essential characteristic of the science of right, as of mathematics and every other science of the understanding; but this logical consistency of the understanding has nothing to do with the satisfaction of the demands of reason and with philosophical science.[14] Apart from this, however, the very *inconsistency* of the Roman jurists and praetors should be regarded as one of their greatest virtues, for it enabled them to dissociate themselves from unjust and abominable institutions, although they were at the same time compelled to invent verbal distinctions on the sly[a] (as when they called *bonorum possessio* what nevertheless amounted to an inheritance)[15] and even silly excuses (and silliness is equally an inconsistency) in order to preserve the letter of the Twelve Tables, for example by the fiction or pretence[b] that a daughter was a son[c] (see [J. G.] Heineccius, *Antiquitatum Romanarum . . . liber* I [Frankfurt, 1771], tit. II, § 24).[16] – But it is ludicrous to see the classical jurists lumped together with Kant because of a few *trichotomous* divisions – particularly those cited in Note 5 to Herr Hugo's remarks – and to see this kind of thing called 'development of concepts'.

---

[a]*Translator's note:* Hegel uses here the Latin adverb *callide.*
[b]*Translator's note:* Hegel uses the Latin and Greek terms *fictio* and ὑπόϰρισις.
[c]*Translator's note:* Hegel uses the Latin terms *filia* and *filius.*

§ 4

The basis [*Boden*] of right is the *realm of spirit* in general and its precise location and point of departure is the *will*; the will is *free*, so that freedom constitutes its substance and destiny [*Bestimmung*] and the system of right is the realm of actualized freedom, the world of spirit produced from within itself as a second nature.

Addition (H,G). The freedom of the will can best be explained by reference to physical nature. For freedom is just as much a basic determination of the will as weight is a basic determination of bodies. If matter is described as heavy, one might think that this predicate is merely contingent; but this is not so, for nothing in matter is weightless: on the contrary, matter is weight itself. Heaviness constitutes the body and is the body. It is just the same with freedom and the will, for that which is free is the will. Will without freedom is an empty word, just as freedom is actual only as will or as subject. But as for the connection between the will and thought, the following remarks are necessary. Spirit is thought in general, and the human being is distinguished from the animal by thought. But it must not be imagined [*sich vorstellen*] that a human being thinks on the one hand and wills on the other, and that he has thought in one pocket and volition in the other, for this would be an empty representation [*Vorstellung*]. The distinction between thought and will is simply that between theoretical and practical attitudes. But they are not two separate faculties; on the contrary, the will is a particular way of thinking – thinking translating itself into existence [*Dasein*], thinking as the drive to give itself existence. This distinction between thought and will can be expressed as follows. When I think of an object [*Gegenstand*], I make it into a thought and deprive it of its sensuous quality; I make it into something which is essentially and immediately mine. For it is only when I think that I am with myself [*bei mir*], and it is only by comprehending it that I can penetrate an object; it then no longer stands opposed to me, and I have deprived it of that quality of its own which it had for itself in opposition to me. Just as Adam says to Eve: 'You are flesh of my flesh and bone of my bone',[1] so does spirit say: 'This is spirit of my spirit, and its alien character has disappeared.' Every representation [*Vorstellung*] is a generalization, and this is inherent in thought. To generalize something means to think it. 'I' is thought and likewise the universal. When I say 'I', I leave out of account every particularity such as my character, temperament, knowledge [*Kenntnisse*], and age. 'I' is totally empty; it is merely a point – simple, yet active in this simplicity. The colourful canvas of the world is before me; I stand opposed to it and in this [theoretical] attitude I overcome

35

[*aufhebe*] its opposition and make its content my own. 'I' is at home in the world when it knows it, and even more so when it has comprehended it. So much for the theoretical attitude. The practical attitude, on the other hand, begins with thought, with the 'I' itself, and seems at first to be opposed [to the world] because it immediately sets up a separation. In so far as I am practical or active, i.e. in so far as I act, I determine myself, and to determine myself means precisely to posit a difference. But these differences which I posit are nevertheless also mine, the determinations apply to me, and the ends to which I am impelled belong to me. Now even if I let go of these determinations and differences, i.e. if I posit them in the so-called external world, they still remain mine: they are what I have done or made, and they bear the imprint of my mind [*Geist*]. This, then, is the distinction between theoretical and practical attitudes; the relationship between them must now be described. The theoretical is essentially contained within the practical; the idea [*Vorstellung*] that the two are separate must be rejected, for one cannot have a will without intelligence. On the contrary, the will contains the theoretical within itself. The will determines itself, and this determination is primarily of an inward nature, for what I will I represent to myself as my object [*Gegenstand*]. The animal acts by instinct, it is impelled by something inward and is therefore also practical; but it has no will, because it does not represent to itself what it desires. It is equally impossible to adopt a theoretical attitude or to think without a will, for in thinking we are necessarily active. The content of what is thought certainly takes on the form of being; but this being is something mediated, something posited by our activity. These distinct attitudes are therefore inseparable: they are one and the same thing, and both moments can be found in every activity, of thinking and willing alike.

With regard to the freedom of the will, we may recollect the older method of cognition. It simply presupposed the *representation* [*Vorstellung*] of the will and attempted to set up a definition of the will by extracting it from this representation; then, in the manner of the older empirical psychology, the so-called *proof* of the will's freedom was derived from the various feelings and phenomena [*Empfindungen und Erscheinungen*] of ordinary consciousness, such as remorse, guilt, and the like, which could allegedly be *explained* only in terms of a *free* will. But it is more convenient simply to adhere to the notion that freedom is *given* as a *fact* of consciousness in which we must simply *believe*.[2] The deduction *that* the will is free and of *what* the will and freedom are – as already remarked in § 2 above –

36

is possible only within the context of the whole [of philosophy]. The basic features of this premise are that *spirit* is initially *intelligence* and that the determinations through which it proceeds in its development, from *feeling* to *representational thinking* [*Vorstellen*] to *thought*, are the way by which it produces itself as *will* – which, as practical spirit in general, is the proximate truth of intelligence. I have given an account of these matters in my *Encyclopaedia of the Philosophical Sciences* (Heidelberg, 1817), §§ 363–399, and hope to deal with them in greater detail on a future occasion.[3] It is all the more necessary for me to contribute in this way to what I hope will be a more thorough cognition of the nature of spirit, because, as I pointed out in the *Encyclopaedia* (Remarks to § 367), it is hard to imagine that any philosophical science can be in so bad and neglected a condition as that *doctrine of spirit* which is usually called 'psychology'.[4] – And as for those elements [*Momente*] of the concept of the will which are mentioned in this and the following paragraphs of the Introduction and which result from the premise referred to above, it is possible to form an idea [*Vorstellen*] of them by consulting the self-consciousness of any individual. In the first place, anyone can discover in himself an ability to abstract from anything whatsoever, and likewise to determine himself, to posit any content in himself by his own agency; and he will likewise have examples of the further determinations [of the will] within his self-consciousness.

§ 5

The will contains (α) the element of *pure indeterminacy* or of the 'I''s pure reflection into itself, in which every limitation, every content, whether present immediately through nature, through needs, desires, and drives, or given and determined in some other way, is dissolved; this is the limitless infinity of *absolute abstraction* or *universality*, the pure thinking of oneself.

Those who regard thinking as a particular and distinct *faculty*, divorced from the will as an equally distinct *faculty*, and who in addition even consider that thinking is prejudicial to the will –

especially the good will – show from the very outset that they are totally ignorant of the nature of the will (a remark which we shall often have occasion to make on this same subject).[1] – Only *one aspect* of the will is defined here – namely this *absolute possibility* of *abstracting* from every determination in which I find myself or which I have posited in myself, the flight from every content as a limitation. If the will determines itself in this way, or if representational thought [*die Vorstellung*] considers this aspect in itself [*für sich*] as freedom and holds fast to it, this is *negative* freedom or the freedom of the understanding. – This is the freedom of the void, which is raised to the status of an actual shape and passion. If it remains purely theoretical, it becomes in the religious realm the Hindu fanaticism of pure contemplation;[2] but if it turns to actuality, it becomes in the realm of both politics and religion the fanaticism of destruction, demolishing the whole existing social order, eliminating all individuals regarded as suspect by a given order, and annihilating any organization which attempts to rise up anew.[3] Only in destroying something does this negative will have a feeling of its own existence [*Dasein*]. It may well believe that it wills some positive condition, for instance the condition of universal equality or of universal religious life, but it does not in fact will the positive actuality of this condition, for this at once gives rise to some kind of order, a particularization both of institutions and of individuals; but it is precisely through the annihilation of particularity and of objective determination that the self-consciousness of this negative freedom arises. Thus, whatever such freedom believes [*meint*] that it wills can in itself [*für sich*] be no more than an abstract representation [*Vorstellung*], and its actualization can only be the fury of destruction.

Addition (H,G). It is inherent in this element of the will that I am able to free myself from everything, to renounce all ends, and to abstract from everything.[4] The human being alone is able to abandon all things, even his own life: he can commit suicide. The animal cannot do this; it always remains only negative, in a determination which is alien to it and to which it merely grows accustomed. The human being is pure thinking of himself, and only in thinking is he this power to give himself universality, that is, to extinguish all particularity, all determinacy. This negative freedom or freedom of the understanding is one-sided, but this one-sidedness always contains within itself an essential determination and should therefore not be dismissed; but the defect of the understanding is that it treats a one-sided determination as unique and elevates it to supreme status. This form of freedom occurs frequently in history. The Hindus, for example, place the highest value on mere persistence in the knowledge of one's simple identity with oneself, on remaining within this empty space of one's inwardness like colourless light in pure intuition, and on renouncing every activity of life, every end, and every representation [*Vorstellung*]. In this way, the human being becomes *Brahman*. There is no longer any distinction between the finite human being and Brahman; instead, every difference [*Differenz*] has disappeared in this universality. This form [of freedom] appears more concretely in the active fanaticism of both political and religious life. An example of this was the Reign of Terror in the French Revolution, during which all differences of talents and authority were supposed to be cancelled out [*aufgehoben*]. This was a time of trembling and quaking and of intolerance towards everything particular. For fanaticism wills only what is abstract, not what is articulated, so that whenever differences emerge, it finds them incompatible with its own indeterminacy and cancels them [*hebt sie auf*]. This is why the people, during the French Revolution, destroyed once more the institutions they had themselves created, because all institutions are incompatible with the abstract self-consciousness of equality.

§ 6

(β) In the same way, '*I*' is the transition from undifferentiated indeterminacy to *differentiation*, *determination*, and the *positing* of a determinacy as a content and object. – This content may further be given by nature, or generated by the concept of spirit. Through this positing of itself as something *determinate*, '*I*' steps into existence [*Dasein*] in general – the absolute moment of the *finitude* or *particularization* of the '*I*'.

> This second moment of *determination* is just as much *negativity* and cancellation [*Aufheben*] as the first – for it is the cancellation of the first abstract negativity. – Just as the particular is in general contained within the universal, so in consequence is this second moment already contained within the first and is merely a *positing* of what the first already is *in itself*. The first moment – that is, the first as it is for itself – is not true infinity

or the *concrete* universality of the concept, but only something *determinate* and one-sided. For since it is abstraction from all determinacy, it is itself not *without* determinacy; and the fact that it is abstract and one-sided constitutes its determinacy, deficiency, and finitude. – The differentiation and determination of the two moments referred to is to be found in the philosophy of Fichte and likewise in that of Kant etc., except that in Fichte – to confine ourselves to his presentation – 'I', as the unbounded (in the first proposition of his *Theory of Knowledge* [*Wissenschaftslehre*]), is taken purely and simply as something *positive* (and thus as the universality and identity of the understanding). Consequently, this abstract 'I' *for itself* is supposed to be *the truth*; and *limitation* – i.e. the *negative* in general, whether as a given external limit or as an activity of the 'I' itself – is therefore something *added* to it (in the second proposition).[1] – The further step which speculative philosophy had to take was to apprehend the *negativity* which is immanent within the universal or the identical, as in the 'I' – a step the need for which is not perceived by those who fail to apprehend the *dualism* of *infinity* and *finitude*, even in that immanent and abstract form in which Fichte understood it.

Addition (H,G). This second moment appears as the opposing one. It is to be apprehended in its universal mode: it belongs to freedom, but does not constitute the whole of freedom. The 'I' here emerges from undifferentiated indeterminacy to become differentiated, to posit something determinate as its content and object [*Gegenstand*]. I do not merely will – I will *something*. A will which, as described in the previous paragraph, wills only the abstract universal, wills *nothing* and is therefore not a will at all. The particular [thing] which the will wills is a limitation, for the will, in order to be a will, must in some way limit itself. The fact that the will wills *something* is the limit or negation. Thus particularization is what as a rule is called finitude. Reflective thought usually regards the first moment, namely the indeterminate, as the absolute and higher moment, and conversely regards the limited as a mere negation of this indeterminacy. But this indeterminacy is itself merely a negation with regard to the determinate, to finitude: 'I' is this solitude and absolute negation. The indeterminate will is to this extent just as one-sided as that which exists in mere determinacy.

§ 7

(γ) The will is the unity of both these moments – *particularity* reflected *into itself* and thereby restored to *universality*. It is *individuality* [*Einzelheit*], the *self-determination* of the 'I', in that it posits itself as the negative of itself, that is, as *determinate* and *limited*, and at the same time remains with itself [*bei sich*], that is, in its *identity with itself* and universality; and in this determination, it joins together with itself alone. – 'I' determines itself in so far as it is the self-reference of negativity. As this *reference to itself*, it is likewise indifferent to this determinacy; it knows the latter as its own and as *ideal*, as a mere *possibility* by which it is not restricted but in which it finds itself merely because it posits itself in it. – This is the *freedom* of the will, which constitutes the concept or substantiality of the will, its gravity, just as gravity constitutes the substantiality of a body.

> Every self-consciousness knows itself as universal, as the possibility of abstracting from everything determinate, and as particular, with a determinate object [*Gegenstand*], content, and end. But these two moments are only abstractions; what is concrete and true (and everything true is concrete) is the universality which has the particular as its opposite, but this particular, through its reflection into itself, has been reconciled [*ausgeglichen*] with the universal. This unity is *individuality*, but not in its immediacy as a single unit – as in our common idea [*Vorstellung*] of individuality – but rather in accordance with the concept of individuality (see *Encyclopaedia of the Philosophical Sciences*, §§ 112–114);[1] in other words, this individuality is in fact none other than the concept itself. The first two moments – that the will can abstract from everything and that it is *also* determined (by itself or by something else) – are easy to accept and grasp, because they are, in themselves [*für sich*], moments of the understanding and devoid of truth. But it is the third moment, the true and speculative (and everything true, in so far as it is comprehended, can be thought of only speculatively), which the understanding refuses to enter into, because the concept is precisely what the understanding always describes as incomprehensible. The task of proving and explaining in more detail this innermost insight of speculation – that is, infinity as self-referring

41

negativity, this ultimate source of all activity, life, and consciousness – belongs to *logic* as purely speculative philosophy. – The only thing which remains to be noted here is that, when we say that *the will is* universal and that *the will* determines itself, we speak as if the will were already assumed to be a *subject* or *substratum*. But the will is not complete and universal until it is determined, and until this determination is superseded and idealized; it does not become will until it is this self-mediating activity and this return into itself.

Addition (H). What is properly called the will contains both the preceding moments. 'I' as such is primarily pure activity, the universal which is with itself [*bei sich*]; but this universal determines itself, and to that extent is no longer with itself but posits itself as an other and ceases to be the universal. Then the third moment is that 'I' is with itself in its limitation, in this other; as it determines itself, it nevertheless still remains with itself and does not cease to hold fast to the universal. This, then, is the concrete concept of freedom, whereas the two previous moments have been found to be thoroughly abstract and one-sided. But we already possess this freedom in the form of feeling [*Empfindung*], for example in friendship and love.[2] Here, we are not one-sidedly within ourselves, but willingly limit ourselves with reference to an other, even while knowing ourselves in this limitation as ourselves. In this determinacy, the human being should not feel determined; on the contrary, he attains his self-awareness only by regarding the other as other. Thus, freedom lies neither in indeterminacy nor in determinacy, but is both at once. The will which limits itself exclusively to a *this* is the will of the stubborn person who considers himself unfree unless he has *this* will. But the will is not tied to something limited; on the contrary, it must proceed further, for the nature of the will is not this one-sidedness and restriction. Freedom is to will something determinate, yet to be with oneself [*bei sich*] in this determinacy and to return once more to the universal.

§ 8

The further determination of *particularization* (see § 6 above) constitutes the difference between the forms of the will: (a) in so far as determinacy is the *formal* [*formelle*] opposition between the *subjective* on the one hand and the *objective* as external immediate existence

[*Existenz*] on the other, this is the *formal* [*formale*]ᵃ will as self-consciousness, which *finds* an external world outside itself. As individuality [*Einzelheit*] returning in determinacy into itself, it is the process of *translating* the *subjective end* into *objectivity* through the mediation of activity and of a[n external] means. In the spirit as it is in and for itself, whereby its determinacy is absolutely true and *its own* (see *Encyclopaedia*, § 363),[1] the relation of consciousness constitutes no more than *the aspect of* the will's *appearance*. This aspect will not be separately [*für sich*] considered any further here.

Addition (H). The consideration of the will's determinacy is the task of the understanding and is not primarily speculative. The will is determined by no means only in the sense of content, but also in the sense of form. Its determinacy with regard to form is its end and the accomplishment of its end. At first this end is only *subjective* and internal to me, but it should also become *objective* and throw off the deficiency of mere subjectivity. One may ask here why it has this deficiency. If that which is deficient does not at the same time stand above its deficiency, then its deficiency does not exist for it. For us an animal is deficient, but not for itself. In so far as an end is still only ours, it is for us a deficiency, for to us, freedom and will are the unity of the subjective and the objective. Hence the end must be posited objectively, and it thereby attains not a new one-sided determination but only its realization.

ᵃ*Translator's note:* The distinction between the adjective *formal* and the preceding *formell* appears to carry no particular significance. On subsequent occasions in the *Rechtsphilosophie* (for example, § 123 and Hegel's Remarks to §§ 13, 15, 115, 135, 139, 261, etc.), Hegel uses only *formell*.

§ 9

(b) In so far as the will's determinations are *its own* – that is, its *internally* reflected particularization in general – they are its *content*. This content, as the content of the will, is its end in accordance with the form specified under (a) above – either its inner or subjective end as represented in the act of willing, or its end as actualized and accomplished through the mediation of its activity as it translates the subjective into objectivity.

§ 10

This content, or the distinct determination of the will, is primarily *immediate*. Thus, the will is *free* only *in itself* or *for us*, or it is in general the will in *its concept*. Only when the will has itself as its object [*Gegenstand*] is it *for itself* what it is *in itself*.

Finitude, according to this determination, consists in the fact that what something is *in itself* or in accordance with its concept is different in its existence [*Existenz*] or appearance from what it is *for itself*; thus, for example, *in itself* the abstract mutual externality of nature is space, but *for itself* it is time. Two points should be noted in this connection: first that, because the true is simply the Idea, we do not yet possess an object or determination in its truth if we grasp it only as it is *in itself* or in its concept; and secondly, that something *as concept* or *in itself* likewise exists, and this existence [*Existenz*] is a shape proper to the object (as with space in the above example). The separation which is present in the finite world between being-in-itself and being-for-itself at the same time constitutes the finite world's mere *existence* [*Dasein*] or *appearance* (immediate examples of this will arise in connection with the natural will and then with formal right, etc.). The understanding stops at mere *being-in-itself* and therefore calls freedom in accordance with this being-in-itself a *faculty* [*Vermögen*], since it is indeed in this case a mere *potentiality* [*Möglichkeit*]. But the understanding regards this determination as absolute and perennial, and takes the relationship [*Beziehung*] of freedom to what it wills, or in general to its reality, merely as its *application* to a given material, an application which does not belong to the essence of freedom itself. In this way, the understanding has to do with the abstract alone, not with the Idea and truth of freedom.[1]

Addition (G). The will which is a will only in accordance with its concept is free in itself but at the same time unfree, for it would be truly free only as a truly determinate content; in the latter case, it is free for itself, has freedom as its object, and *is* freedom. Whatever is still only in accordance with its concept, whatever is merely in itself, is only immediate, only natural. We are also familiar with this in representational thought [*in der*

Vorstellung]. The child is *in itself* a human being; it has reason only *in itself*, it is only the potentiality of reason and freedom, and is therefore free only in accordance with its concept. Now what exists as yet only in itself does not exist in its actuality. The human being who is rational *in himself* must work through the process of self-production both by going out of himself and by educating himself inwardly, in order that he may also become rational *for himself*.

§ 11

The will which is free as yet only *in itself* is the *immediate* or *natural* will. The determinations of the difference which is posited within the will by the self-determining concept appear within the immediate will as an *immediately* present content: these are the *drives, desires, and inclinations* by which the will finds itself naturally determined. This content, along with the determinations developed within it, does indeed originate in the will's rationality and it is thus rational in itself; but expressed in so immediate a form, it does not yet have the form of rationality.[1] *For me*, this content is admittedly entirely *mine*; but this form and that content are still different, so that the will is *a finite* will *within itself*.

> Empirical psychology relates and describes these drives and inclinations and the needs derived from them as it encounters them, or believes it encounters them, in experience, and attempts to classify this given material in the usual way. We shall discuss below what the *objective* element of these drives is, what shape this element assumes in its truth (without the form of irrationality which it possesses as drive), and also what shape it assumes in its existence [*Existenz*].

Addition (H). The animal, too, has drives, desires, and inclinations, but it has no will and must obey its drive if nothing external prevents it. But the human being, as wholly indeterminate, stands above his drives and can determine and posit them as his own. The drive is part of nature, but to posit it in this 'I' depends upon my will, which therefore cannot appeal to the fact that the drive is grounded in nature.

§ 12

The system of this content as it is *already present* in its immediacy in the will exists only as a multitude of varied drives, each of which is mine *in general* along with others, and at the same time something universal and indeterminate which has all kinds of objects [*Gegenstände*] and can be satisfied in all kinds of ways. Inasmuch as the will, in this double indeterminacy, gives itself the form of *individuality* [*Einzelheit*] (see § 7), it is a resolving will, and only in so far as it makes any resolutions at all is it an actual will.

> To resolve on something [*etwas beschließen*]^a is to cancel [*aufheben*] that indeterminacy in which each and every content is initially no more than a possibility. But our language also contains the alternative expression *sich entschließen* ['to decide'],^{b} which indicates that the indeterminacy of the will itself, as something neutral yet infinitely fruitful, the original seed of all existence [*Dasein*], contains its determinations and ends within itself, and merely brings them forth from within.

> ^{a}*Translator's note:* Literally, 'to close something'.
> ^{b}*Translator's note:* Literally, 'to unclose oneself'.

§ 13

By resolving, the will posits itself as the will of a specific individual and as a will which distinguishes itself from everything else. But apart from this *finitude* as consciousness (see § 8), the immediate will, because of the difference between its form and its content (see § 11), is purely *formal*; its only appropriate function is that of *abstract resolution*, and its content is not yet the content and product of its freedom.

> In so far as intelligence is a *thinking* power, its object [*Gegenstand*] and content remain *universal* and the intelligence itself behaves as a universal activity. In the will, the universal also means essentially 'that which is mine', as *individuality* [*Einzelheit*]; and in the immediate, i.e. formal will, it signifies abstract individuality which is not yet filled with its free universality. It is therefore in the will that the *proper* [*eigene*] *finitude* of intelligence begins, and it is only by raising itself

once more to the level of thought and by conferring immanent universality upon its ends that the will cancels [*aufhebt*] the difference of form and content and makes itself objective, infinite will. Thus those who believe that the human being is infinite in the realm of the will in general, but that he – or reason itself – is limited in the realm of thought, have little understanding of the nature of thinking and willing.[1] In so far as thinking and willing are still distinct, it is rather the converse which is true, and thinking reason, as will, is [reason] deciding [*sich entschließen*] on its own *finitude*.

Addition (H). A will which resolves on nothing is not an actual will; the characterless man can never resolve on anything. The reason [*Grund*] for such indecision may also lie in an over-refined sensibility which knows that, in determining something, it enters the realm of finitude, imposing a limit on itself and relinquishing infinity; yet it does not wish to renounce the totality which it intends. Such a disposition [*Gemüt*] is dead, even if its aspiration is to be beautiful.[2] 'Whoever aspires to great things', says Goethe, 'must be able to limit himself'.[3] Only by making resolutions can the human being enter actuality, however painful the process may be; for inertia would rather not emerge from that inward brooding in which[a] it reserves a universal possibility for itself. But possibility is not yet actuality. The will which is sure of itself does not therefore lose itself in what it determines.

[a]*Translator's note:* As T. M. Knox (Knox, p. 230, note) surmises, the *der* of the original must surely read *dem*. Gans, who compiled the 'Additions', has simply taken this error over from Hotho's transcription of Hegel's lectures (cf. VPR III, 131).

§ 14

The finite will, purely with regard to its form, is the self-reflecting *infinite 'I'* which is with itself [*bei sich selbst*] (see § 5). As such, it *stands above* its content, i.e. its various drives, and also above the further individual ways in which these are actualized and satisfied. At the same time, since it is only formally infinite, it is *tied* to this content as to the determinations of its nature and of its external actuality (see §§ 6 and 11); but since it is indeterminate, it is not restricted to this or that content in particular. To this extent, this content is only a possible one for the reflection of the 'I' into itself; it may or may not be mine; and 'I' is the *possibility* of determining myself to this or to

something else, of *choosing* between these determinations which the 'I'
must in this respect regard as external.[1]

§ 15

The freedom of the will, according to this determination, is *arbitrariness*, in which the following two factors are contained: free reflection,
which abstracts from everything, and dependence on an inwardly or
externally given content and material. Since this content, which is
necessary *in itself* as an end, is at the same time determined as a
possible content in opposition to free reflection, it follows that
arbitrariness is *contingency* in the shape of will.

> The commonest idea [*Vorstellung*] we have of freedom is that
> of *arbitrariness* – the mean position of reflection between the
> will as determined solely by natural drives and the will which
> is free in and for itself. When we hear it said that freedom in
> general consists in *being able to do as one pleases*, such an idea
> [*Vorstellung*] can only be taken to indicate a complete lack of
> intellectual culture [*Bildung des Gedankens*]; for it shows not
> the least awareness of what constitutes the will which is free in
> and for itself, or right, or ethics, etc. Reflection, the *formal*
> universality and unity of self-consciousness, is the will's
> *abstract* certainty of its freedom, but it is not yet the *truth* of
> this freedom, because it does not yet have itself as its content
> and end, so that the subjective side is still something other
> than the objective [*die gegenständliche*]; the content of this self-
> determination therefore also remains purely and simply finite.
> Instead of being the will in its truth, arbitrariness is rather the
> will as *contradiction*. – In the controversy which arose chiefly at
> the time of Wolff's metaphysics as to whether the will is
> actually free or whether our knowledge of its freedom is
> merely a delusion, it was arbitrariness which people had in
> mind.[1] To the certainty of this abstract self-determination,
> *determinism* rightly opposed the *content*, which, as something
> *encountered*, is not contained in that certainty and therefore
> *comes to it from outside* – although 'outside' here denotes drive
> or representation [*Vorstellung*], or simply the fact that the con-
> sciousness is filled in such a way that its content is not derived

from its own self-determining activity as such. Accordingly, since only the formal element of free self-determination is immanent within arbitrariness, whereas the other element is something given to it, arbitrariness may indeed be called a delusion if it is supposed to be equivalent to freedom. In all reflective philosophy, as in that of Kant and subsequently in Fries's utterly superficial revision of it, freedom is nothing other than this formal self-activity.[2]

Addition (H). Since I have the possibility of determining myself in this or that direction – that is, since I am able to choose – I possess an arbitrary will, and this is what is usually called freedom. The choice which I have lies in the universality of the will, whereby I can make this or that [thing] mine. This [thing] which is mine is a particular content and is therefore incompatible with me; thus it is separate from me and is only potentially mine, just as I am only the potentiality of uniting with it. The choice therefore lies in the indeterminacy of the 'I' and the determinacy of the content. Because of this content, the will is consequently not free, although it has in itself the aspect of infinity in a formal sense. None of these contents is in keeping with it, and it does not truly have itself in any of them. It is inherent in arbitrariness that the content is not determined as mine by the nature of my will, but by *contingency*; thus I am also dependent on this content, and this is the contradiction which underlies arbitrariness. The common man thinks that he is free when he is allowed to act arbitrarily, but this very arbitrariness implies that he is not free. When I will what is rational, I act not as a particular [*partikulares*] individual, but in accordance with the concepts of ethics in general: in an ethical act, I vindicate not myself but the thing [*die Sache*]. But a person who does something perverse gives the greatest prominence to his particularity [*Partikularität*]. The rational is the high road which everyone follows and where no one stands out from the rest. When great artists complete a work, we can say that it *had* to be so; that is, the artist's particularity has completely disappeared and no *mannerism* is apparent in it. Phidias has no mannerisms; the shape itself lives and stands out. But the poorer the artist is, the more we see of himself, of his particularity and arbitrariness.[3] If we stop our enquiry at arbitrariness, at the human being's ability to will this or that, this does indeed constitute his freedom; but if we bear firmly in mind that the content of what he wills is a given one, it follows that he is determined by it and is in this very respect no longer free.

§ 16

Whatever the will has decided to choose (see § 14), it can likewise relinquish (see § 5). But with this possibility of proceeding in turn beyond any other content which it may substitute for the previous one, and so on *ad infinitum*, it does not escape from finitude, because every such content is different from the form [of the will] and therefore finite; and the opposite of determinacy – namely indeterminacy, indecision, or abstraction – is only the other, equally one-sided moment.

§ 17

That contradiction which is the arbitrary will (see § 15) makes its *appearance* as a *dialectic* of drives and inclinations which conflict with each other in such a way that the satisfaction of one demands that the satisfaction of the other be subordinated or sacrificed, and so on; and since a drive is merely the simple direction of its own determinacy and therefore has no yardstick within itself, this determination that it should be subordinated or sacrificed is the contingent decision of arbitrariness – whether the latter is guided by calculations of the understanding as to which drive will afford the greater satisfaction, or by any other consideration one cares to name.

Addition (H). Drives or inclinations are primarily a content of the will, and only reflection stands above them; but these drives [*Triebe*] themselves become impelling [*treibend*], press upon each other, and conflict with each other, and all of them wish to be satisfied. If, then, I put all the others aside and commit myself to only one of them, I find myself in a destructive limitation, for by my very act I have relinquished my universality, which is a system of all drives. But it is of just as little help merely to subordinate certain drives [to others] – the course of action to which the understanding usually resorts – because no yardstick by which they might be arranged in order is available here; the demand for such an order therefore usually ends in tedious platitudes.[1]

§ 18

With regard to the *judgement* of drives the appearance of the dialectic is such that, as *immanent* and hence also *positive*, the determinations of the immediate will are *good*; thus *man* is said to be *by nature good*. But in so far as they are *determinations of nature*, opposed to freedom and to the concept of the spirit in general and therefore *negative*, they must be *eradicated*; thus *man* is said to be *by nature evil*. In this situation, the decision in favour of one assertion or the other likewise depends on subjective arbitrariness.¹

Addition (H). The Christian doctrine that man is by nature evil is superior to the other according to which he is good. Interpreted philosophically, this doctrine should be understood as follows. As spirit, man is a free being [*Wesen*] who is in a position not to let himself be determined by natural drives. When he exists in an immediate and uncivilized [*ungebildeten*] condition, he is therefore in a situation in which he ought not to be, and from which he must liberate himself. This is the meaning of the doctrine of original sin, without which Christianity would not be the religion of freedom.

§ 19

Underlying the demand for the *purification of the drives* is the general idea [*Vorstellung*] that they should be freed from the *form* of their immediate natural determinacy and from the subjectivity and contingency of their *content*, and restored to their substantial essence. The truth behind this indeterminate demand is that the drives should become the rational system of the will's determination; to grasp them thus in terms of the concept is the content of the science of right.

The content of this science can be expounded, with reference to all its individual moments such as right, property, morality, family, the state, etc., in the following form: man *has* by nature a drive towards right, *and also* a drive towards property and morality, *and also* a drive towards sexual love, a drive towards sociability, etc.¹ If one prefers to accord the dignity of a philosophical shape to this form of empirical psychology, then this, in the light of what has passed in recent times for philosophy (as was earlier noted) and continues to pass for it, can be achieved *at low cost* simply by declaring that man finds within himself, as a *fact of his consciousness*, that he wills right, property, the state, etc. This same content, which appears here in the shape of drives, will recur later in another form, namely that of *duties*.²

51

§ 20

When reflection applies itself to the drives, representing them, estimating them, and comparing them with one another and then with the means they employ, their consequences etc., and with a sum total of satisfaction – i.e. with *happiness¹* – it confers *formal universality* upon this material and purifies it, in this external manner, of its crudity and barbarity. This cultivation of the universality of thought is the absolute value of *education* (cf. § 187).²

Addition (H). In happiness, thought already has some power over the natural force of the drives, for it is not content with the instantaneous, but requires a whole of happiness. This is connected with education to the extent that education likewise implements a universal. But two moments are present in the ideal of happiness: the first is a universal which is superior to all particularities; but secondly, since the content of this universal is in turn merely universal pleasure, the individual and particular, i.e. a finite quantity, reappears at this point, and we are compelled to return to the drive. Since the content of happiness lies in the subjectivity and feeling [*Empfindung*] of everyone, this universal end is itself particular [*partikular*], so that no true unity of content and form is yet present within it.

§ 21

The truth, however, of this formal universality, which is indeterminate for itself and encounters its determinacy in the material already mentioned, is *self-determining universality, the will, or freedom*. When the will has universality, or itself as infinite form, as its content, object [*Gegenstand*], and end, it is free not only *in itself* but also *for itself* – it is the Idea in its truth.¹

> The self-consciousness of the will, as desire and drive, is *sensuous*, just as the realm of the senses in general denotes externality and hence that condition in which self-consciousness is external to itself. The *reflective* will has two elements – this sensuous element and that of thinking universality; the will which *has being in and for itself* has as its object the will itself as such, and hence itself in its pure universality. This universality is such that the *immediacy* of the natural and the *particularity* [*Partikularität*] with which the natural is likewise

invested when it is produced by reflection are superseded within it. But this process whereby the particular is superseded and raised to the universal is what is called the activity of *thought*. The self-consciousness which purifies and raises its object, content, and end to this universality does so as *thought asserting itself* in the will. Here is the *point at which it becomes clear* that it is only as *thinking* intelligence that the will is truly itself and free. The slave does not know his essence, his infinity and freedom; he does not know himself as an essence – he does not know himself as such, for he does not *think* himself. This self-consciousness which comprehends itself as essence through thought and thereby divests itself of the contingent and the untrue constitutes the principle of right, of morality, and of all ethics. Those who speak philosophically of right, morality, and ethics and at the same time seek to exclude thought, appealing instead to feeling, heart, emotion, and inspiration, bear witness to the profound contempt into which thought and science have fallen; for in their case, science itself, having sunk into despair and total lassitude, even adopts barbarism and thoughtlessness as its principle and does everything it can to rob mankind of all truth, worth, and dignity.

Addition (H). Truth in philosophy means that the concept corresponds to reality. A body, for example, is reality, and the soul is the concept. But soul and body ought to match one another; a dead body therefore still has an existence [*Existenz*], but no longer a true one, for it is a conceptless existence [*Dasein*]: that is why the dead body decomposes. The will in its truth is such that what it wills, i.e. its content, is identical with the will itself, so that freedom is willed by freedom.

§ 22

The will which has being in and for itself is *truly infinite*, because its object [*Gegenstand*] is itself, and therefore not something which it sees as *other* or as a *limitation*; on the contrary, it has merely returned into itself in its object. Furthermore, it is not just a possibility, predisposition, or *capacity* (*potentia*), but the *infinite in actuality* (*infinitum actu*), because the concept's existence [*Dasein*] or objective [*gegenständliche*] externality is inwardness itself.

If one therefore speaks only of the free will as such, without specifying that it is the will which is free in and *for itself*, one is speaking only of the *predisposition* towards freedom or of the natural and finite will (see § 11), and therefore not – whatever one may say and believe – of the free will. – When the understanding regards the infinite merely as something negative and hence as *beyond its sphere*, it believes that it is doing the infinite all the more honour by pushing it ever further away and distancing it as something alien. In the free will, the truly infinite has actuality and presence – the will itself is the idea which is present within itself.[1]

Addition (H). Infinity has rightly been represented by the image of the circle, because a straight line runs on indefinitely and denotes that merely negative and false infinity which, unlike true infinity, does not return into itself. The free will is truly infinite, for it is not just a possibility and predisposition; on the contrary, its external existence is its inwardness, its own self.

§ 23

Only in this freedom is the will completely *with itself* [*bei sich*],[1] because it has reference to nothing but itself, so that every relationship of *dependence* on something *other* than itself is thereby eliminated. – It is *true*, or rather it is *truth* itself, because its determination consists in being in its *existence* [*Dasein*] – i.e. as something opposed to itself – what it is in its concept; that is, the pure concept has the intuition of itself as its end and reality.

§ 24

It [the will] is *universal*, because all limitation and particular individuality [*Einzelheit*] are superseded within it. For these lie solely in the difference between the concept and its object [*Gegenstand*] or content, or, expressed in another form, in the difference between the will's subjective being-for-itself and its being-in-itself, or between its *exclusive* and resolving individuality [on the one hand] and its universality itself [on the other].

The various determinations of *universality* are given in logic (see *Encyclopaedia of the Philosophical Sciences*, §§ 118–126).[1]

54

The first thing which the expression 'universality' suggests to representational thought [*dem Vorstellen*] is an abstract and external universality; but in the case of that universality which has being in and for itself, as defined here, we should think neither of the universality of reflection – i.e. *communality* or *totality* – nor of that *abstract* universality which stands outside and in opposition to the individual – i.e. the abstract identity of the understanding (see Remarks to § 6). The universality in question is *concrete* within itself and consequently has being for itself, and it is the substance of the self-consciousness, its immanent generic character [*Gattung*] or immanent idea; it is the concept of the free will as the *universal which extends beyond* its object, which *permeates its determination* and is identical with itself in this determination. – The universal which has being in and for itself is in general what is called the *rational*, and it can be understood only in this speculative way.

§ 25

The *subjective*, as far as the will in general is concerned, denotes the will's self-conscious aspect, its individuality [*Einzelheit*] (see § 7) *as distinct from* its concept which has being *in itself*. The subjectivity of the will therefore denotes (α) *pure form*, the *absolute unity* of the self-consciousness with itself, in which the self-consciousness, as 'I' = 'I', is totally inward and *abstractly* dependent upon itself – i.e. the pure *certainty* of itself, as distinct from truth; (β) the *particularity* of the will as arbitrariness and as the contingent content of whatever ends the will may pursue; (γ) one-sided form in general (see § 8), in so far as that which is willed, whatever its content, is still only a content belonging to the self-consciousness, an unaccomplished end.

§ 26

(α) The will, in so far as it has itself as its determination and is thus in conformity with its concept and truly itself, is the *totally objective will*; (β) but the *objective* will, inasmuch as it *lacks the infinite form* of self-consciousness, is the will immersed in its object or condition, whatever the content of the latter may be – it is the will of the child, the ethical will,[1] or the will of the slave, the superstitious will, etc.;

(γ) finally, *objectivity* is the one-sided form opposed to the subjective determination of the will, and is thus the immediacy of existence [*Dasein*] as *external* existence [*Existenz*]; the will does not become *objective* to itself in this sense until its ends are fulfilled.

These logical determinations of subjectivity and objectivity have been listed here in order that we may expressly note in relation to them – since they will often be employed in what follows – that, like other distinctions and antithetical determinations of reflection, they pass over into their opposites on account of their finitude and hence of their dialectical nature. Other such antithetical determinations, however, retain a fixed significance for representational thought [*Vorstellung*] and for the understanding, because their identity is still only of an *inward* kind. In the will, on the other hand, such antitheses – which are supposed to be abstract, yet at the same time determinations *of the will* which can be known only *as the concrete* – lead by themselves to their own identity and to a confusion of their meanings, a confusion into which the understanding quite unwittingly falls. – Thus the will, as freedom *with inward being*, is subjectivity itself; subjectivity is accordingly the will's concept and hence its objectivity; but its subjectivity, as opposed to objectivity, is finitude; yet in this very opposition, the will is not with itself but involved with the object, and its finitude consists just as much in the fact that it is not subjective, etc. – Thus, the significance to be attached in what follows to the subjective or objective aspects of the will should in each case be apparent from the context, which defines their position with reference to the totality.

Addition (H). It is usually believed that the subjective and objective are *firmly* opposed to one another. But this is not the case; they in fact pass over into one another, for they are not abstract determinations like positive and negative, but already have a more concrete significance. If we first consider the term 'subjective', this may denote an end peculiar to a specific subject. In this sense, a very bad work of art which does not fulfil its purpose [*Sache*] is purely subjective. But the same term may also be applied to the content of the will, and it is then roughly synonymous with 'arbitrary': a subjective content is one which belongs only to the subject. Thus bad actions, for example, are merely subjective. – But in addition, we may also describe as subjective that pure empty 'I' which has only itself

as its object [*Gegenstand*] and which possesses the power to abstract from
any further content. Thus, subjectivity may have a wholly particular
[*partikulare*] significance, or it may mean something eminently justified,
since everything which I am to recognize also has the task of becoming
mine and gaining its validity in me. Such is the infinite greed of subjectivity, which collects and consumes everything within this simple source
of the pure 'I'. The objective may be understood in no less varied ways.
We may understand by it everything which we make our object [*uns
gegenständlich*], whether such objects are actual existences [*Existenzen*] or
are mere thoughts which we set up in opposition to ourselves. But we also
comprehend [under objectivity] the immediacy of existence [*Dasein*] in
which the end is to be realized: even if the end is itself wholly particular
[*partikular*] and subjective, we nevertheless call it objective as soon as it
makes its appearance. But the objective will is also that in which truth is
present. Thus the will of God, the ethical will, is objective. Finally, we
may also describe as objective the will which is completely immersed in its
object [*Objekt*], such as the will of the child, which is founded on trust and
lacks subjective freedom, and the will of the slave, which does not yet
know itself as free and is consequently a will with no will of its own. In this
sense, every will whose actions are guided by an alien authority and which
has not yet completed its infinite return into itself is objective.

§ 27

The absolute determination or, if one prefers, the absolute drive, of
the free spirit (see § 21) is to make its freedom into its object [*Gegenstand*] – to make it objective both in the sense that it becomes the
rational system of the spirit itself, and in the sense that this system
becomes immediate actuality (see § 26). This enables the spirit to be
for itself, as Idea, what the will is in itself. The abstract concept of the
Idea of the will is in general *the free will which wills the free will*.[1]

§ 28

The activity of the will consists in cancelling [*aufzuheben*] the contradiction between subjectivity and objectivity and in translating its
ends from their subjective determination into an objective one, while
at the same time remaining *with itself* in this objectivity. Apart from
the formal mode of consciousness (see § 8) in which objectivity is
present only as immediate actuality, this activity is the *essential development* of the substantial content of the Idea (see § 21), a development

in which the concept determines the *Idea*, which is *itself* at first *abstract*, to [produce] the totality of its system. This totality, as the substantial element, is independent of the opposition between a merely subjective end and its realization, and is *the same* in both of these forms.

§ 29

Right is any existence [*Dasein*] in general which is the *existence* of the *free will.*[1] Right is therefore in general freedom, as Idea.

> In the Kantian definition [*Bestimmung*] of right (see the introduction to Kant's *Theory of Right* [*Metaphysische Anfangs-gründe der Rechtslehre*, 1797]), which is also more widely accepted, the essential element [*Moment*] is 'the *limitation* of my freedom or *arbitrary will* in such a way that it may coexist with the arbitrary will of everyone else in accordance with a universal law'.[2] On the one hand, this definition contains only a *negative* determination – that of limitation; and on the other hand, the positive [element] – the universal law or so-called 'law of reason', the consonance of the arbitrary will of one individual with that of the other – amounts simply to the familiar [principle of] formal identity and the law of contradiction. The definition of right in question embodies the view, especially prevalent since Rousseau, according to which the substantial basis and primary factor is supposed to be not the will as rational will which has being in and for itself or the spirit as *true* spirit, but will and spirit as the *particular* individual, as the will of the single person [*des Einzelnen*] in his distinctive arbitrariness.[3] Once this principle is accepted, the rational can of course appear only as a limitation on the freedom in question, and not as an immanent rationality, but only as an external and formal universal. This view is devoid of any speculative thought and is refuted by the philosophical concept, and has at the same time produced phenomena [*Er-scheinungen*] in people's minds and in the actual world whose terrifying nature is matched only by the shallowness of the thoughts on which they are based.[4]

§ 30

Right is something *utterly sacred*, for the simple reason that it is the existence [*Dasein*] of the absolute concept, of self-conscious freedom. – But the *formalism* of right – and also of duty[1] – arises out of the different stages in the development of the concept of freedom. In opposition to the more formal, i.e. *more abstract* and hence more limited kind of right, that sphere and stage of the spirit in which the spirit has determined and actualized within itself the further moments contained in its Idea possesses a higher right, for it is the *more concrete* sphere, richer within itself and more truly universal.

> Each stage in the development of the Idea of freedom has its distinctive right, because it is the existence of freedom in one of its own determinations. When we speak of the opposition between morality or ethics and *right*, the right in question is merely the initial and formal right of abstract personality. Morality, ethics, and the interest of the state – each of these is a distinct variety of right, because each of them gives determinate shape and existence to *freedom*. They can come into *collision* only in so far as they are all in equal measure rights; if the moral point of view of the spirit were not also a right – i.e. freedom in one of its forms – it could not possibly come into collision with the right of personality or with any other right, because every right embodies the concept of freedom, the highest determination of spirit, in relation to which everything else is without substance. But a collision also contains this further moment: it imposes a limitation whereby one right is subordinated to another; only the right of the world spirit is absolute in an unlimited sense.

§ 31

The method whereby the concept, in science, develops out of itself and is merely an *immanent* progression and production of its own determinations is likewise assumed to be familiar from logic. Its progress does not depend on the assertion that various circumstances *are present* or on the subsequent *application* of the universal to such material of extraneous origin.

The moving principle of the concept, which not only dissolves the particularizations of the universal but also produces them, is what I call *dialectic*. I consequently do not mean that kind of dialectic which takes an object [*Gegenstand*], proposition, etc. given to feeling or to the immediate consciousness in general, and dissolves it, confuses it, develops it this way and that, and is solely concerned with deducing its opposite – a negative mode which frequently appears even in Plato.[1] Such dialectic may regard as its final result the opposite of a given idea [*Vorstellung*], or, as in the uncompromising manner of ancient scepticism, its contradiction, or, in a lame fashion, an *approximation* to the truth, which is a modern half-measure.[2] The higher dialectic of the concept consists not merely in producing and apprehending the determination as an opposite and limiting factor, but in producing and apprehending the *positive* content and result which it contains; and it is this alone which makes it a *development* and immanent progression. This dialectic, then, is not an *external* activity of subjective thought, but the *very soul* of the content which puts forth its branches and fruit organically. This development of the Idea as the activity of its own rationality is something which thought, since it is subjective, merely observes, without for its part adding anything extra to it. To consider something rationally means not to bring reason to bear on the object from outside in order to work upon it, for the object is itself rational for itself; it is the spirit in its freedom, the highest apex of self-conscious reason, which here gives itself actuality and engenders itself as an existing world; and the sole business of science is to make conscious this work which is accomplished by the reason of the thing [*Sache*] itself.

§ 32

The *determinations* in the development of the concept are on the one hand themselves concepts, but on the other hand, since the concept is essentially Idea, they have the form of existence [*Dasein*], and the series of concepts which results is therefore at the same time a series of *shapes*; this is how science should regard them.

In the more speculative sense, the *mode of existence* of a concept and its *determinacy* are one and the same thing. But it should be noted that the moments, whose result is a further-determined form [of the concept], precede it as determinations of the concept in the scientific development of the Idea, but do not come before it as shapes in its temporal development. Thus the Idea, in its determination as the family, presupposes those determinations of the concept from which, in a later section of this work, it [i.e. the Idea] will be shown to result. But the other side of this development is that these inner presuppositions should also be present for themselves as *shapes*, such as the right of property, contract, morality, etc., and it is only at a more advanced stage of culture [*Bildung*] that the moments of development attain this distinctive shape of existence.

Addition (H). The Idea must continually determine itself further within itself, for it is initially no more than an abstract concept. But this initial abstract concept is never abandoned. On the contrary, it merely becomes continually richer in itself, so that the last determination is also the richest. Those determinations which previously existed only in themselves thereby attain their free self-sufficiency, but in such a way that the concept remains the soul which holds everything together and which arrives at its own differentiation only through an immanent process. One cannot therefore say that the concept arrives at anything new; on the contrary, the last determination coincides in unity with the first. Thus, even if the concept appears to have become fragmented in its existence, this is merely a semblance, as is subsequently confirmed when all its details finally return in the concept of the universal. In the empirical sciences, it is customary to analyse what is found in representational thought [*Vorstellung*], and when the individual instance has been reduced to the common quality, this common quality is then called the concept. This is not how we proceed, for we merely wish to observe how the concept determines itself, and we force ourselves not to add anything of our own thoughts and opinions. What we obtain in this way, however, is a series of thoughts and another series of existent shapes, in which it may happen that the temporal sequence of their actual appearance is to some extent different from the conceptual sequence. Thus, we cannot say, for example, that property existed before the family, although property is nevertheless dealt with first. One might accordingly ask at this point why we do not begin with the highest instance, that is, with the concretely true. The answer will be that we wish to see the truth precisely in the form of a result, and it is essential for this purpose that we should first comprehend the abstract concept itself. What is actual, the shape which the concept assumes, is therefore from our point of view only the subsequent and further stage, even if it should itself come first in actuality. The course we follow is that whereby the abstract forms reveal themselves not as existing for themselves, but as untrue.

SUBDIVISIONS

§ 33

In accordance with the stages in the development of the Idea of the will which is free in and for itself, the will is

A. *immediate*; its concept is therefore abstract, as that of *personality*, and its *existence* [*Dasein*] is an immediate external thing [*Sache*]; – the sphere of *abstract* or *formal right*;
B. reflected from its external existence *into itself*, determined as *subjective individuality* [*Einzelheit*] in opposition to the *universal* – the universal partly as something internal, the *good*, and partly as something external, an *existent world*, with these two aspects of the Idea *mediated* only *through each other*; the Idea in its division or *particular* existence [*Existenz*], *the right of the subjective will* in relation to the right of the world and to the *right* of the Idea – which, however, *has being* only *in itself*; – *the sphere of morality*;
C. the *unity* and *truth* of these two abstract moments – the thought Idea of the good realized in the internally *reflected will* and in the *external world*; – so that freedom, as the *substance*, exists no less as *actuality* and *necessity* than as *subjective* will; – the *Idea* in its universal existence [*Existenz*] in and for itself; [the sphere of] *ethical life*.

But the ethical substance is likewise

(a) *natural* spirit; – the *family*,
(b) in its *division* and *appearance*; – *civil society*,
(c) the *state* as freedom, which is equally universal and objective in the free self-sufficiency of the particular will; this actual and organic spirit (α) of a people (β) actualizes and reveals itself through the relationship between the particular national spirits (γ)

and in world history as the universal world spirit whose *right* is *supreme.*

That a thing [*Sache*] or content which is posited only in accordance with its *concept* or as it is *in itself,* has the shape of *immediacy* or of *being,* is presupposed from speculative logic; the concept which exists for itself in the *form of the concept* is something different, and is no longer immediate. – The principle which determines the above subdivisions is likewise presupposed.[1] The subdivisions may also be regarded as a *historical* preview of the parts [of the book], for the various stages must generate themselves from the nature of the content itself as moments in the development of the Idea. Philosophical subdivisions are certainly not an external classification – i.e. an outward classification of a given material based on one or more extraneous principles of organization – but the immanent differentiation of the concept itself. – *Morality* and *ethics,* which are usually regarded as roughly synonymous, are taken here in essentially distinct senses.[2] Yet even representational thought [*Vorstellung*] seems to distinguish them; Kantian usage prefers the expression *morality,* as indeed the practical principles of Kant's philosophy are confined throughout to this concept, even rendering the point of view of *ethics* impossible and in fact expressly infringing and destroying it. But even if morality and ethics were etymologically synonymous, this would not prevent them, since they are now different words, from being used for different concepts.

Addition (H). When we speak here of right, we mean not merely civil right, which is what is usually understood by this term, but also morality, ethics, and world history. These likewise belong here, because the concept brings thoughts together in their true relationship. If it is not to remain abstract, the free will must first give itself an existence [*Dasein*], and the primary sensuous constituents of this existence are things [*Sachen*], i.e. external objects [*Dinge*]. This first mode of freedom is the one which we should know as *property,* the sphere of formal and abstract right; property in its mediated shape as *contract,* and right in its infringement as *crime* and *punishment,* are no less a part of this sphere. The freedom which we have here is what we call the person, that is, the subject which is free, and indeed free for itself, and which gives itself an existence [*Dasein*] in the realm of things [*Sachen*]. But this mere immediacy of existence is not in keeping with freedom, and the negation of this determination is the sphere of *morality*. I am then free no longer merely in this immediate thing [*Sache*], but also in a superseded immediacy – that is, I am free in myself, in the subjective realm. In this sphere, everything depends on my insight, my intention, and the end I pursue, because externality is now regarded as indifferent. But the good, which is here the universal end, should not simply remain with me; on the contrary, it should be realized. For the subjective will demands that what is internal to it – that is, its end – should attain an external existence [*Dasein*], and hence that the good should be accomplished in external existence [*Existenz*]. Morality and the earlier moment of formal right are both abstractions whose truth is attained only in *ethical life*. Thus, ethical life is the unity of the will in its concept and the will of the individual [*des Einzelnen*], that is, of the subject. Its initial existence [*Dasein*] is again something natural, in the form of love and feeling [*Empfindung*] – the *family*; here, the individual [*das Individuum*] has overcome [*aufgehoben*] his personal aloofness and finds himself and his consciousness within a whole. But at the next stage, we witness the disappearance of ethical life in its proper sense and of substantial unity: the family becomes fragmented and its members behave towards each other as self-sufficient individuals, for they are held together only by the bond of mutual need. This stage of *civil society* has often been equated with the state. But the *state* emerges only at the third stage, that of ethical life and spirit, at which the momentous unification of self-sufficient individuality with universal substantiality takes place. The right of the state is therefore superior to the other stages: it is freedom in its most concrete shape, which is subordinate only to the supreme absolute truth of the world spirit.

Abstract Right

§ 34

The will which is free in and for itself, as it is in its *abstract* concept, is in the determinate condition of *immediacy*. Accordingly, in contrast with reality, it is its own negative actuality, whose reference to itself is purely abstract – the *inherently individual* [*in sich einzelner*] will of a *subject*. In accordance with the moment of *particularity* of the will, it has in addition a content consisting of determinate ends, and as *exclusive individuality* [*Einzelheit*], it simultaneously encounters this content as an external world immediately confronting it.

Addition (H). When I say that the will which is free in and for itself, as it is in its abstract concept, is in the determinate condition of immediacy, this should be understood as follows. The completed Idea of the will is that condition in which the concept has fully realized itself and in which its existence [*Dasein*] is nothing but the concept's own development. Initially, however, the concept is abstract – that is, although all its determinations are contained within it, they are no more than contained in it: they have being only in themselves and have not yet developed into a totality in their own right. If I say that I am free, 'I' is still this being-within-itself [*Insichsein*] without any opposition. In morality, on the other hand, there is already an opposition; for in this sphere, I am present as an individual will, whereas the good is the universal, even though it is within me. Thus, the will already has here the distinct factors of individuality and universality within itself, and is consequently determinate. But such a distinction is not present initially, for there is no progression or mediation at the first stage of abstract unity, where the will has the form of immediacy, of being. The essential insight to be gained here, then, is that this initial indeterminacy is itself a determinacy. For indeterminacy consists in there being no distinction as yet between the will and its content; but indeterminacy itself, when opposed to the determinate, takes on the determination of being something determinate; it is abstract identity which here constitutes its determinacy; the will thereby becomes an individual will – the *person*.

§ 35

The *universality* of this will which is free for itself is formal universality, i.e. the will's self-conscious (but otherwise contentless) and *simple* reference to itself in its individuality [*Einzelheit*];[1] to this extent, the subject is a *person*. It is inherent in *personality* that, as *this* person, I am completely determined in all respects (in my inner arbitrary will, drive, and desire, as well as in relation to my immediate external existence [*Dasein*]), and that I am finite, yet totally pure self-reference, and thus know myself in my finitude as *infinite, universal,* and *free.*

> Personality begins only at that point where the subject has not merely a consciousness of itself in general as concrete and in some way determined, but a consciousness of itself as a completely abstract 'I' in which all concrete limitation and validity are negated and invalidated. In the personality, therefore, there is knowledge of the *self* as an *object* [*Gegenstand*], but as an object raised by thought to simple infinity and hence purely identical with itself. In so far as they have not yet arrived at this pure thought and knowledge of themselves, individuals and peoples do not yet have a personality. The spirit which has being in and for itself differs in this respect from spirit in its appearance, for in the same determination in which the latter is only *self-consciousness* – consciousness *of itself,* but only in accordance with the natural will and its as yet external oppositions (see *Phenomenology of Spirit,* Bamberg and Würzburg, 1807, pp. 101ff. and *Encyclopaedia of the Philosophical Sciences,* § 344)[2] – the former has itself, as abstract and free 'I', as its object and end and is consequently a *person.*

Addition (H). The will which has being for itself, or the abstract will, is the person. The highest achievement of a human being is to be a person; yet in spite of this, the simple abstraction 'person' has something contemptuous about it, even as an expression.[3] The person is essentially different from the subject, for the subject is only the possibility of personality, since any living thing whatever is a subject. A person is therefore a subject which is aware of this subjectivity, for as a person, I am completely for myself: the person is the individuality of freedom in pure being-for-itself. As *this* person, I know myself as free in myself, and I can abstract from everything, since nothing confronts me but pure personality. And yet as *this* person I am something wholly determinate: I am of such an age, of such a height, in this room, and whatever other particular things [*Partikularitäten*] I happen to be. Personality is thus at the same time the sublime and the wholly ordinary; it contains this unity of the infinite and the utterly finite, of the determinate boundary and the completely unbounded. The supreme achievement of the person is to support this contradiction, which nothing in the natural realm contains or could endure.

§ 36

1. Personality contains in general the capacity for right and constitutes the concept and the (itself abstract) basis of abstract and hence *formal* right. The commandment of right is therefore: *be a person and respect others as persons.*[1]

§ 37

2. The *particularity* of the will is indeed a moment within the entire consciousness of the will (see § 34), but it is not yet contained in the abstract personality as such. Thus, although it is present – as desire, need, drives, contingent preference, etc. – it is still different from personality, from the determination of freedom. – In formal right, therefore, it is not a question of particular interests, of my advantage or welfare, and just as little of the particular ground by which my will is determined, i.e. of my insight and intention.[1]

Addition (H). Since particularity, in the person, is not yet present as freedom, everything which depends on particularity is here a *matter of indifference*. If someone is interested only in his formal right, this may be pure stubbornness, such as is often encountered in emotionally limited people [*einem beschränkten Herzen und Gemüte*]; for uncultured people insist most strongly on their rights, whereas those of nobler mind seek to discover what other aspects there are to the matter [*Sache*] in question. Thus abstract right is initially a mere possibility, and in that respect is formal in character as compared with the whole extent of the relationship. Consequently, a determination of right gives me a warrant, but it is not absolutely necessary that I should pursue my rights, because this is only one aspect of the whole relationship. For possibility is being, which also has the significance of not being.

§ 38

With reference to *concrete* action and to moral and ethical relations, abstract right is only a *possibility* as compared with the rest of their content, and the determination of right is therefore only a *permission* or *warrant.*[1] For the same reason [*Grund*] of its abstractness, the necessity of this right is limited to the negative – *not to violate* personality and what ensues from personality. Hence there are only *prohibitions of right*, and the positive form of commandments of right is, in its ultimate content, based on prohibition.[2]

§ 39

3. The resolving and *immediate* individuality [*Einzelheit*] of the person relates itself to a nature which it encounters before it. Hence the personality of the will stands in opposition to nature as *subjective*. But since personality within itself is infinite and universal, the limitation of being merely subjective is in contradiction with it and is *null and void*. Personality is that which acts to overcome [*aufzuheben*] this limitation and to give itself reality – or, what amounts to the same thing, to posit that existence [*Dasein*] as its own.

§ 40

Right is primarily that immediate existence [*Dasein*] which freedom gives itself in an immediate way,

(a) as *possession*, which is *property*; freedom is here the freedom of the abstract will *in general*, or, by the same token, the freedom *of an individual* person who relates only to himself.
(b) A person, in distinguishing himself from himself, relates himself to *another person*, and indeed it is only as owners of property that the two have existence [*Dasein*] for each other.[1] Their identity *in themselves* acquires existence [*Existenz*] through the transference of the property of the one to the other by common will and with due respect of the rights of both – that is, by *contract*.
(c) The will which, as in (a), is differentiated within itself in its self-reference rather than distinguished from another person as in (b), is, as a *particular* will, different from and opposed to itself as the will *which has being in and for itself*. This constitutes *wrong* and *crime*.

The division of right into the right of *persons and things* [*Sachen*] and the right of *actions* [*Aktionen*], like the many other divisions of this kind, aims primarily to impose an external order upon the mass of disorganized material before us. The chief characteristic of this division is the confused way in which it jumbles together rights which presuppose substantial relations, such as family and state, with those which refer only to abstract personality. Kant's division of rights, which has since found favour with others, into the *right of things*, the *right of persons*, and *personal right of a real [dinglich] kind²* is an example of this confusion. To enlarge upon the lop-sidedness and conceptual poverty of the division into the *right of persons* and the *right of things*, which is fundamental to Roman law (the right of actions concerns the administration of justice and has no place in this classification), would take us too far. Here, it is clear at least that *personality* alone confers a right to *things*, and consequently that personal right is in essence a *right of things* – 'thing' [*Sache*] being understood in its general sense as everything external to my freedom, including even my body and my life. This right of things is the right of *personality* as *such*. But as for what is called the *right of persons* in Roman law, it regards a human being as a person only if he enjoys a certain *status* (see Heineccius, *Elementa iuris civilis* [1728], § 75); hence in Roman law even personality itself, as opposed to slavery, is merely an *estate* [*Stand*] or condition [*Zustand*].³ Apart from the right concerning *slaves* (among whom children may virtually be included) and the condition of *rightlessness* (*capitis diminutio*),⁴ the content of the so-called right of persons in Roman law is concerned with *family relationships*.⁵ In Kant, moreover, family relationships belong to *personal rights of a real kind*.⁶ The right of persons in Roman law is therefore not the right of the person as such, but no more than the right of the *particular* person; it will later be shown that the substantial basis of family relationships is rather the surrender of personality. It must, then, inevitably seem perverse to discuss the right of the person in his *particular determinacy* before the universal right of personality. – For Kant, *personal rights* are those rights which arise out of a contract whereby I give something or perform a service – in Roman law, the *ius ad rem* which arises out of an *obligatio*.⁷ Admittedly, only a person is obliged to implement the provisions of a contract, just as it is only a person who acquires the right to have them implemented. But such a right cannot therefore be called a personal right; rights of *every* kind can belong only to a person, and seen objectively, a right based on contract is not a right over a person, but only over something external to the person or something which the person can dispose of, i.e. always a thing.

SECTION I

Property

§ 41

The person must give himself an external *sphere of freedom* in order to have being as Idea.[1] The person is the infinite will, the will which has being in and for itself, in this first and as yet wholly abstract determination. Consequently, this sphere distinct from the will, which may constitute the sphere of its freedom, is likewise determined as *immediately different* and *separable* from it.

Addition (H). The rational aspect of property is to be found not in the satisfaction of needs but in the superseding of mere subjectivity of personality. Not until he has property does the person exist as reason. Even if this first reality of my freedom is in an external thing [*Sache*] and is thus a poor kind of reality, the abstract personality in its very immediacy can have no other existence [*Dasein*] than in the determination of immediacy.

§ 42

What is immediately different from the free spirit is, for the latter and in itself, the external in general – a *thing* [*Sache*], something unfree, impersonal, and without rights.

> The word '*thing*' [*Sache*], like the word 'objective', has two opposite meanings.[1] On the one hand, when we say '*that's the thing*', or '*the thing*, not the person, is what matters', it signifies what is *substantial*. On the other hand, when contrasted with the person (as distinct from the particular subject), the thing is the *opposite of the substantial*: it is that which, by definition

73

[*seiner Bestimmung nach*], is purely external. – What is external for the free spirit (which must be clearly distinguished from mere consciousness) is external in and for itself; and for this reason, the definition [*Begriffsbestimmung*] of the concept of *nature* is that it is the *external in itself.*

Addition (H). Since a thing [*Sache*] has no subjectivity, it is external not only to the subject, but also to itself. Space and time are external in this way. As an object of the senses, I am myself external, spatial, and temporal. In so far as I have sensuous intuitions, I have them of something which is external to itself. An animal can intuit, but the soul of the animal does not have the soul, or itself, as its object [*Gegenstand*], but something external.

§ 43

As the *immediate* concept and hence also [as] essentially individual, a person has a *natural* existence [*Existenz*] partly within himself and partly as something to which he relates as to an external world. – It is only these things [*Sachen*] in their immediate quality, not those determinations they are capable of taking on through the mediation of the will, which are at issue here in connection with personality, which is itself still in its initial immediacy.

> Intellectual [*geistige*] accomplishments, sciences, arts, even religious observances (such as sermons, masses, prayers, and blessings at consecrations), inventions, and the like, become objects [*Gegenstände*] of contract; in the way in which they are bought and sold, etc., they are treated as equivalent to acknowledged *things*. It may be asked whether the artist, scholar, etc. is in legal possession of his art, science, ability to preach a sermon, hold a mass, etc. – that is, whether such objects are *things*. We hesitate to call such accomplishments, knowledge [*Kenntnisse*], abilities, etc. *things*; for on the one hand, such possessions are the object of commercial negotiations and agreements, yet on the other, they are of an inward and spiritual nature. Consequently, the understanding may find it difficult to define their legal status, for it thinks only in terms of the alternative that something is *either* a thing *or* not a thing (just as it must be *either* infinite *or* finite).[1] Knowledge,

sciences, talents, etc. are of course attributes of the free spirit, and are internal rather than external to it; but the spirit is equally capable, through expressing them, of giving them an external existence [*Dasein*] and *disposing* of them (see below), so that they come under the definition [*Bestimmung*] of *things*. Thus, they are not primarily immediate in character, but become so only through the mediation of the spirit, which reduces its inner attributes to immediacy and externality. – In accordance with the unjust [*unrechtlichen*] and unethical determination of Roman law, children were, from the father's point of view, *things*. The father was consequently in legal possession of his children, although he also stood in the ethical relation of love to them (which must, of course, have been greatly weakened by the wrong referred to above). Thus, there was in this case a union – albeit a totally unjust one – of the two determinations of being a thing and not being a thing. – Abstract right is concerned only with the person as such, and hence also with the particular, which belongs to the existence [*Dasein*] and sphere of the person's freedom. But it is concerned with the particular only in so far as it is separable and immediately different from the person – whether this separation constitutes its essential determination, or whether it receives it only by means of the subjective will. Thus, intellectual accomplishments, sciences, etc. are relevant here only in their character as legal possessions; that possession of body and spirit which is acquired through education, study, habituation, etc. and which constitutes an *inner property* of the spirit will not be dealt with here. But the *transition* of such intellectual property into externality, in which it falls within the definition [*Bestimmung*] of legal and rightful property, will be discussed only when we come to the *disposal* of property.

§ 44

A person has the right to place his will in any thing [*Sache*]. The thing thereby becomes *mine* and acquires my will as its substantial end (since it has no such end within itself), its determination, and its soul – the absolute *right of appropriation* which human beings have over all things [*Sachen*].

75

That so-called philosophy which ascribes reality – in the sense of self-sufficiency and genuine being-for-and-in-itself – to immediate individual things [*Dingen*], to the non-personal realm, as well as that philosophy which assures us that spirit cannot recognize truth or know what the *thing-in-itself* is,[1] is immediately refuted by the attitude of the free will towards these things [*Dinge*]. If so-called *external things* have a semblance of self-sufficiency for consciousness, for intuition and representational thought, the free will, in contrast, is the idealism and truth of such actuality.

Addition (H). All things [*Dinge*] can become the property of human beings, because the human being is free will and, as such, exists in and for himself, whereas that which confronts him does not have this quality. Hence everyone has the right to make his will a thing [*Sache*] or to make the thing his will, or, in other words, to supersede the thing and transform it into his own; for the thing, as externality, has no end in itself, and is not infinite self-reference but something external to itself. A living creature (the animal) is also external in this way and is to that extent itself a thing [*Sache*]. The will alone is infinite, *absolute* in relation to everything else, whereas the other, for its part, is merely *relative*. Thus to appropriate something means basically only to manifest the supremacy of my will in relation to the thing [*Sache*] and to demonstrate that the latter does not have being in and for itself and is not an end in itself. This manifestation occurs through my conferring upon the thing an end other than that which it immediately possessed; I give the living creature, as my property, a soul other than that which it previously had; I give it my soul. The free will is consequently that idealism which does not consider things [*Dinge*], as they are, to be in and for themselves, whereas realism declares them to be absolute, even if they are found only in the form of finitude. Even the animal has gone beyond this realist philosophy, for it consumes things [*Dinge*] and thereby proves that they are not absolutely self-sufficient.[2]

§ 45

To have even external power over something constitutes *possession*, just as the particular circumstance that I make something my own out of natural need, drive, and arbitrary will is the particular interest of possession. But the circumstance that I, as free will, am an object [*gegenständlich*] to myself in what I possess and only become an actual will by this means constitutes the genuine and rightful element in possession, the determination of *property*.[1]

In relation to needs – if these are taken as primary – the possession of property appears as a means; but the true position is that, from the point of view of freedom, property, as the first *existence* [*Dasein*] of freedom, is an essential end for itself.

§ 46

Since my will, as personal and hence as the will of an individual [*des Einzelnen*], becomes objective in property, the latter takes on the character of *private property*; and common property, which may by its nature be owned by separate individuals, takes on the determination of an *inherently* [*an sich*] *dissolvable* community in which it is in itself [*für sich*] a matter [*Sache*] for the arbitrary will whether or not I retain my share in it.

The utilization of *elementary* objects is, by its nature, incapable of being particularized in the form of private possession. – The *agrarian laws* of Rome embody a conflict between community and private ownership of land; the latter, as the more rational moment, had to retain its supremacy, albeit at the expense of other rights.[1] – *Entailed family property* contains a moment which is opposed to the right of personality and hence of private property.[2] But those determinations which concern private property may have to be subordinated to higher spheres of right, such as a community or the state, as is the case with private property when it becomes the property of a so-called corporate person [*moralische Person*] or property in mortmain. Nevertheless, such exceptions cannot be grounded in contingency, private arbitrariness, or private utility, but only in the rational organism of the state. – The Idea of Plato's republic contains as a universal principle a wrong against the person, inasmuch as the person is forbidden to own private property.[3] The idea [*Vorstellung*] of a pious or friendly or even compulsory brotherhood of men with *communal property* and a ban on the principle of private property may easily suggest itself to that disposition which misjudges the nature of the freedom of spirit and right and does not comprehend it in its determinate moments. As for the moral or religious dimension, when Epicurus' friends planned to establish such an association with communal property, he prevented them from doing so for the simple reason [*Grund*] that their plan displayed distrust, and that those who distrust one another are not friends (Diogenes Laertius, I.X.6).

Addition (H). In property, my will is personal, but the person is a specific entity [*ein Dieses*]; thus, property becomes the personal aspect of this specific will. Since I give my will existence [*Dasein*] through property, property must also have the determination of being this specific entity, of being mine. This is the important doctrine of the necessity of *private property*. Even if exceptions may be made by the state, it is nevertheless the state alone which can make them; but frequently, especially in our own times, private property has been restored by the state. Thus, for example, many states have rightly dissolved [*aufgehoben*] the monasteries, because a community does not ultimately have the same right to property as a person does.

§ 47

As a person, I am myself an *immediate individual* [*Einzelner*]; in its further determination, this means in the first place that I am *alive* in this *organic body*, which is my undivided external existence [*Dasein*], *universal* in content, the real potentiality of all further-determined existence. But as a person, I at the same time possess *my life and body*, like other things [*Sachen*], only *in so far as I so will it*.

> The fact that, from the point of view that I exist not as the concept which has being for itself but as the immediate concept, that I am *alive* and have an organic body, depends on the concept of life and on the concept of the spirit as soul – moments which are taken over from the philosophy of nature (*Encyclopaedia of the Philosophical Sciences*, §§ 259ff.; cf. §§ 161, 164, and 298) and from anthropology (*ibid.*, § 318).[1]
>
> I have these limbs and my life only *in so far as I so will it*; the animal cannot mutilate or destroy itself, but the human being can.

Addition (G). Animals are indeed in possession of themselves: their soul is in possession of their body. But they have no right to their life, because they do not will it.

§ 48

In so far as the body is immediate existence [*Dasein*] it is not commensurate with the spirit; before it can be the spirit's willing organ and soul-inspired instrument, it must first be *taken possession of* by the spirit (see § 57). – But *for others*, I am essentially a free entity within my body while I am in immediate possession of it.

It is only because I am alive as a free entity within my body that this living existence [*Dasein*] may not be misused as a beast of burden. In so far as I am alive, my soul (the concept and, on a higher level, the free entity) and my body are not separated; my body is the existence [*Dasein*] of freedom, and I feel through it. It is therefore only a sophistical understanding, devoid of any Idea, which can make a distinction whereby the *thing-in-itself* [*Ding an sich*], the soul, is neither touched nor affected if the *body* is abused and the *existence* [*Existenz*] of the person is subjected to the power of another.[1] I can withdraw into myself from my existence [*Existenz*] and make it external to me – I can keep particular feelings outside myself and be free even if I am in chains. But this is *my* will; *for others*, I am in my body. I am *free for the other* only in so far as I am free in my *existence* [*Dasein*]: this is an identical proposition (see my *Science of Logic*, Vol. 1 [first edition, 1812], pp. 49ff.).[2] Violence done to *my body* by others is violence done to me.

Because I feel, contact with or violence to my body touches me immediately as *actual* and *present*. This constitutes the difference between personal injury and infringement of my external property; for in the latter, my will does not have this immediate presence and actuality.

§ 49

In relation to external things, the *rational* aspect is that I possess property; the *particular* aspect, however, includes subjective ends, needs, arbitrariness, talents, external circumstances, etc. (see § 45). It is on these that mere possession as such depends, but this particular aspect, in this sphere of abstract personality, is not yet posited as identical with freedom. *What* and *how much* I possess is therefore purely contingent as far as right is concerned.

> If we may speak here of *more than one* person where no such distinction has yet been made, we may say that, in terms of personality, these persons are equal. But this is an empty and tautological proposition; for the person, as an abstraction, is precisely that which has not yet been particularized and posited in a determinate distinction. – *Equality* is the abstract identity of the understanding; it is the first thing which occurs to reflective thought, and hence to mediocrity of spirit in general, when it comes across the relation [*Beziehung*] of unity to a difference. Equality, in this case, can only be the equality of abstract persons as such, which thus *excludes* everything to do with possessions, this *basis of inequality.*[1] – The demand is sometimes made for *equality* in the distribution of land or even of other available resources. The understanding which makes this demand is all the more vacuous and superficial in that this particularity encompasses not only the external contingency of nature, but also the whole extent of spiritual nature in its infinite particularity and differentiation and in its organically developed reason. – One cannot speak of an *injustice of nature* in the unequal distribution of possessions and resources, for nature is not free and is therefore neither just nor unjust. That all human beings should have their livelihood [*Auskommen*] to meet their needs is, on the one hand, a moral *wish*; and when it is expressed in this indeterminate manner, it is indeed well intentioned, but like everything that is merely well intentioned, it has no objective being. On the other hand, a livelihood is something other than *possession* and belongs to another sphere, that of civil society.

Addition (H). The equality which one might wish to introduce, for example, with reference to the distribution of goods would in any case be destroyed again within a short time, because all resources are dependent on diligence. But if something is impracticable, it ought not to be put into practice either. For while human beings are certainly equal, they are equal only as persons, that is, in relation to the source of their possessions. Accordingly, everyone ought to have property.[2] If we therefore wish to speak of equality, it is this equality which we should consider. But this equality is distinct from the determination of particularity, from the question of how much I possess. In this context, it is false to maintain that justice requires everyone's property to be equal; for it requires only that everyone should have property. Particularity, in fact, is the very condition to which inequality is appropriate and in which equality would be contrary to right. It is perfectly correct that human beings often covet the goods of others; but this is precisely what is contrary to right, for right is that which remains indifferent to particularity.

§ 50

That a thing [*Sache*] belongs to the person who *happens to be the first* to take possession of it[1] is an immediately self-evident and superfluous determination, because a second party cannot take possession of what is already the property of someone else.

Addition (H). The above determinations have chiefly concerned the proposition that the personality must have existence [*Dasein*] in property. That the first person who takes possession of something is also its owner is, then, a consequence of what has been said. The first is not the rightful owner because he is the first, but because he is a free will, for it is only the fact that another comes after him which makes him the first.

§ 51

My *inner* idea [*Vorstellung*] and will that something should be *mine* is not enough to constitute property, which is the *existence* [*Dasein*] of personality; on the contrary, this requires that I should *take possession* of it. The *existence* which my willing thereby attains includes its ability to be recognized by others. – That a thing of which I can take possession should be *ownerless* is (see § 50) a self-evident negative condition; or rather, it refers to the anticipated relation to others.

Addition (H,G). The concept of property requires that a person should place his will in a thing [*Sache*], and the next stage is precisely the realization of this concept. My inner act of will which says that something is mine must also become recognizable by others. If I make a thing mine, I give it this predicate which must appear in it in an external form, and must not simply remain in my inner will. It often happens that children emphasize their prior volition when they oppose the appropriation of something by others; but for adults, this volition is not sufficient, for the form of subjectivity must be removed and must work its way out to objectivity.

§ 52

Taking possession of a thing [*Sache*] makes its *matter* my property, since matter in itself [*für sich*] does not own itself.

Matter offers resistance to me (and it consists solely in offering resistance to me). That is, it shows its abstract being-for-itself to me only in my quality as abstract spirit, namely as *sensuous* spirit. (Sensuous representation [*Vorstellen*] wrongly regards the sensuous being of the spirit as concrete and its rational being as abstract.) But in relation [*Beziehung*] to the will and to property, this being-for-itself of matter has no truth. Taking possession of something, as an *external activity* whereby the universal right to appropriate natural objects [*Naturdinge*] is actualized, falls under the conditions of physical strength, cunning, and skill – all of those means whereby we acquire physical ownership of things. Given the qualitative differences between natural objects, there are infinitely varied senses in which one can take control and possession of them, and doing so is subject to equally varied kinds of limitation and contingency. In any case, the generic and elemental aspects of something are not as such the *object* [*Gegenstand*] *of personal individuality* [*Einzelheit*]; in order to become such an object and be taken possession of, they must first be individualized (e.g. as a breath of air or a drink of water). With regard to the impossibility of taking possession of an external genus as such, or of the elemental, the ultimate consideration is not the external physical impossibility of doing so, but the fact that the person, as will, determines himself as an individual [*Einzelheit*] and, as a person, is at the same time immediate individuality; hence he is also related, as a person, to the external world as to individual things [*Einzelheiten*] (see my Remarks to § 13; also § 43). – The control and external possession [of things] thus becomes, in infinite ways, more or less indeterminate and incomplete. Matter, however, is never without an essential form, and it is only by virtue of this form

82

that it is something. The more I appropriate this form, the more I come into *actual* possession of the thing [*Sache*]. The consumption of foodstuffs is a penetration and alteration of their qualitative nature by virtue of which they were what they were before they were consumed. The training [*Ausbildung*] of my organic body in various skills, like the education of my spirit, is likewise a more or less complete penetration and taking possession thereof; the spirit is what I can appropriate most completely. But this *actuality of taking possession* is different from property as such, which is completed by the free will. In face of the free will, the thing does not retain any distinct property for itself, even if possession, as an external relationship, still retains an external aspect. The empty abstraction of a matter without attributes which, in the case of property, is supposed to remain external to me and the property of the thing itself, is something which thought must get the better of.

Addition (G). Fichte has raised the question of whether the matter also belongs to me if I give it form.[1] From what he says, it follows that, if I have made a cup out of gold, anyone else is at liberty to take the gold provided that he does not thereby damage my handiwork. However separable the two may be in terms of representation [*Vorstellung*], this distinction is in fact an empty piece of hair-splitting; for if I take possession of a field and cultivate it, not only the furrow is my property, but the rest as well, the earth which belongs to it. For I wish to take possession of this matter as a whole: it therefore does not remain ownerless or its own property. For even if the matter remains external to the form which I have given to the object [*Gegenstand*], the form itself is a sign that the thing is to be mine; the thing therefore does not remain external to my will or outside what I have willed. Thus, there is nothing there which could be taken possession of by someone else.

§ 53

The more precise determinations of property are to be found in the will's relationship to the thing [*Sache*]. This relationship is (α) in an immediate sense *taking possession*, in so far as the will has its existence [*Dasein*] in the thing as something *positive*; (β) in so far as the thing is negative in relation to the will, the will has its existence in it as in something to be negated – *use*; (γ) the reflection of the will from the thing back into itself – *alienation*; – *positive*, *negative*, and *infinite judgements* of the will upon the thing.[1]

A. Taking Possession

§ 54

Taking possession consists partly in the immediate *physical seizure* of something, partly in giving it form, and partly in merely *designating* its ownership.

Addition (G). These modes of taking possession contain the progression from the determination of individuality [*Einzelheit*] to that of universality. Physical seizure can occur only in the case of an individual thing [*Sache*], whereas the designation of ownership means taking possession in terms of representational thought [*Vorstellung*]. In the latter case, I have a representation of the thing and consider that the thing in its totality is mine, and not merely the part of which I can take possession physically.

§ 55

(α) From the point of view of the senses, *physical seizure* is the most complete mode of taking possession, because I am immediately present in this possession and my will is thus also discernible in it. But this mode in general is merely subjective, temporary, and extremely limited in scope, as well as by the qualitative nature of the objects [*Gegenstände*]. – The scope of this mode can be somewhat extended by other means – e.g. by the connection which I can establish between something and things [*Sachen*] which otherwise belong to me, or by a connection which may come about by chance.

> Mechanical forces, weapons, and instruments extend the range of my power. Connections between my property and something which abuts upon it may make it more easily *possible* for me than for another owner, or even exclusively so for me, to take possession of something or to make use of it; or the addition to my property may be regarded as a non-self-sufficient *accident of the thing* to which it has been added.[1] Such connections may include the fact that my land is beside

the sea or a river, that my fixed property borders on land suitable for hunting, pasture, or other uses, that stone or other mineral resources underlie my fields, that there may be treasure in or under the land which I own, and so on; or the connections may arise only in the course of time and as a result of chance, as with some so-called natural accessions, such as alluvial deposits and the like or items washed ashore. (The procreation of animals [*foetura*] is indeed also an accession to my resources; but as it is an organic relationship, no external thing is added to another thing which I already possess, so that this instance is quite different in kind from other accessions.)² All of these are *external* associations whose bond of union is neither the concept nor a living force [*Lebendigkeit*]. It is therefore the task of the understanding to adduce and weigh the reasons for and against them, and of positive legislation to reach a decision according to whether the relations [*Beziehungen*] between the things in question are more or less essential or inessential.

Addition (G). Taking possession is always incomplete in character. I take possession of no more than I can touch with my body, but it follows immediately that external objects [*Dinge*] extend further than I can grasp. Thus, when I have a specific thing in my possession, something else will be connected with it. I take possession of things with my hand, but its reach can be extended. The hand is a great organ which no animal possesses, and what I grasp with it can itself become a means of reaching out further. When I possess something, the understanding at once concludes that it is not just what I possess immediately that is mine, but also what is connected with it. Here, positive right must pronounce judgement, for nothing further can be deduced from the concept.

§ 56

(β) When I *give form* to something, its determinate character as mine receives *an independently* [*für sich*] *existing* [*bestehende*] externality and ceases to be limited to my presence in *this* time and space and to my present knowledge and volition.

To give form to something is the mode of taking possession most in keeping with the Idea, inasmuch as it combines the subjective and the objective. Otherwise, it varies infinitely according to the qualitative nature of the objects [*Gegenstände*] and the variety of subjective ends. – We must also include here the giving of form to the organic. The effects which I have on the latter do not remain merely external, but are assimilated by it, as in the tilling of the soil, the cultivation of plants, and the domestication, feeding, and conservation of animals; further examples are the measures we employ in order to utilize raw materials or the forces of nature, or the influence which we cause one substance [*Stoff*] to exert upon another, and so on.

Addition (H). In empirical contexts, this giving of form may assume the most varied shapes. The field which I cultivate is thereby given form. As far as the inorganic realm is concerned, I do not always give it form directly. If, for example, I build a windmill, I have not given form to the air, but I have constructed a form in order to utilize the air, which cannot be taken away from me just because I have not myself formed it [i.e. the air]. Even the fact that I conserve game may be regarded as a way of imparting form, for it is a mode of conduct calculated to preserve the object in question. The training of animals is, of course, a more direct way of giving them form, and I play a greater role in this process.

§ 57

The human being, in his *immediate* existence [*Existenz*] in himself, is a natural entity, external to his concept; it is only through the *development* [*Ausbildung*] of his own body and spirit, *essentially* by means of *his self-consciousness comprehending itself as free*, that he takes possession of himself and becomes his own property as distinct from that of others. Or to put it the other way round, this taking possession of oneself consists also in translating into *actuality* what one is in terms of one's concept (as *possibility*, capacity [*Vermögen*], or predisposition). By this means, what one is in concept is posited for the first time as one's own, and also as an object [*Gegenstand*] distinct from simple self-consciousness, and it thereby becomes capable of taking on the *form of the thing* [*Sache*] (cf. Remarks to § 43).

The alleged justification of *slavery* (with all its more specific explanations in terms of physical force, capture in time of war, the saving and preservation of life, sustenance, education [*Erziehung*], acts of benevolence, the slave's own acquiescence, etc.), as well as the justification of the *master's status* as simple lordship in general, and all *historical* views on the right of slavery and lordship, depend on regarding the human being simply as a *natural being [Naturwesen]* whose *existence [Existenz]* (of which the arbitrary will is also a part) is not in conformity with his concept. Conversely, the claim that slavery is absolutely contrary to right is firmly tied to the *concept* of the human being as spirit, as something free *in itself,* and is one-sided inasmuch as it regards the human being as *by nature* free, or (and this amounts to the same thing) takes the concept as such in its immediacy, not the Idea, as the truth. This *antinomy,* like all antinomies, is based on formal thinking, which fixes upon and asserts the two moments of an Idea in separation from each other, so that both are lacking in truth and do not conform to the Idea.[1] The free spirit consists precisely in not having its being as mere concept or *in itself* (see § 21), but in overcoming *[aufheben]* this formal phase of its being and hence also its immediate natural existence, and in giving itself an existence which is purely its own and free. That side of the antinomy which asserts the concept of freedom thus has the advantage that it contains the absolute *starting point* – though only the starting point – on the way to truth, whereas the other side, which goes no further than conceptless existence, does not contain the point of view of rationality and right at all. The point of view of the free will, with which right and the science of right begin, is already beyond that false *[unwahren]* point of view whereby the human being exists as a natural being and as a concept which has being only in itself, and is therefore capable of enslavement. This earlier and false appearance[2] *[Erscheinung]* is associated with the spirit which has not yet gone beyond the point of view of its consciousness; the dialectic of the concept and of the as yet only immediate consciousness of freedom gives rise at this stage to the *struggle for recognition* and the relationship of *lordship* and *servitude* (see *Phenomenology of Spirit,* pp. 115ff. and *Encyclopaedia of the Philosophical Sciences,* §§ 325ff.).[3] But that the objective spirit, the content of right, should no longer be apprehended merely in its subjective concept, and consequently that the ineligibility of the human being in and for himself for slavery should no longer be apprehended merely as something which *ought* to be [*als ein bloßes Sollen*], is an insight which comes only when we recognize that the Idea of freedom is truly present only as *the state.*

Addition (H). If we hold firmly to the view that the human being in and for himself is free, we thereby condemn slavery. But if someone is a slave, his own will is responsible, just as the responsibility lies with the will of a people if that people is subjugated. Thus the wrong of slavery is the fault not only of those who enslave or subjugate people, but of the slaves and the subjugated themselves. Slavery occurs in the transitional phase between natural human existence and the truly ethical condition; it occurs in a world where a wrong is still right. Here, the wrong *is valid*, so that the position it occupies is a necessary one.

§ 58

(γ) That mode of taking possession which is not actual in itself but merely *represents* my will occurs when I mark a thing [*Sache*] with a *sign* to indicate that I have placed my will in it. This mode of taking possession is highly indeterminate in its objective [*gegenständlichen*] scope and significance.

Addition (H). Taking possession by designation is the most complete mode of all, for the effect of the *sign* is more or less implicit [*an sich*] in the other ways of taking possession, too. If I seize a thing or give form to it, the ultimate significance is likewise a sign, a sign given to others in order to exclude them and to show that I have placed my will in the thing. For the concept of the sign is that the thing does not count as what it is, but as what it is meant to signify. A cockade, for example, signifies citizenship within a state, although the colour has no connection with the nation and represents not itself but the nation. It is precisely through the ability to make a sign and by so doing to acquire things [*Dinge*] that human beings display their mastery over the latter.

B. Use of the Thing [Sache]

§ 59

Through my taking possession of it, the thing [*Sache*] acquires the predicate of being *mine*, and the will has a *positive* relationship [*Bezie-*

hung] to it. Within this identity, the thing is equally posited as something *negative*, and my will in this determination is a *particular* will, need, preference, etc. But my need, as the particularity of *one* will, is the positive factor which finds satisfaction, and the thing, as negative in itself, exists only *for my need* and *serves* it. – *Use* is the realization of my need through the alteration, destruction, or consumption of the thing, whose selfless nature is thereby revealed and which thus fulfils its destiny [*Bestimmung*].

> That use is the *real* aspect and actuality of property is what representational thought [*Vorstellung*] has in mind when it regards disused property as dead and ownerless, and justifies its unlawful appropriation of it on the grounds that the owner did not use it. – But the will of the owner, in accordance with which a thing is his, is the primary substantial basis of property, and the further determination of use is merely the [outward] appearance and particular mode of this universal basis to which it is subordinate.

Addition (H,G). While I take complete possession of a thing in a universal way by designating it as mine, its use embodies an even more universal relation, because the thing is not then recognized in its particularity, but is negated by me. The thing is reduced to a means of satisfying my need. When I and the thing come together, one of the two must lose its [distinct] quality in order that we may become identical. But I am alive, a willing and truly affirmative agent; the thing, on the other hand, is a natural entity.[a] It must accordingly perish, and I survive, which is in general the prerogative and rationale [*Vernunft*] of the organic.

[a] *Translator's note: ist das Natürliche*; in Griesheim's notes, from which Gans derived this sentence, the phrase reads *ist das Negative* ('is the negative'): see VPR IV, 214.

§ 60

The *use* [*Benutzung*] of a thing [*Sache*] by immediate seizure is in itself an *individual* act of taking possession. But in so far as the use is based on a continuing need and entails the repeated use of a self-renewing product – perhaps even limiting itself with a view to safeguarding that renewal – these and other circumstances turn that immediate and individual seizure into a *sign* to indicate a universal act of taking possession, and hence that I take possession of the elemental or organic *basis* of such products or of any other conditions to which they are subject.

§ 61

Since the substance of the thing [*Sache*] for itself, which is my property, is its externality, i.e. its non-substantiality – for in relation to me, it is not an end in itself (see § 42) – and since this realized externality is the use or employment to which I subject it, it follows that *the whole use* or employment of it is *the thing in its entirety*. Thus, if I have the whole use of the thing, I am its owner; and beyond the whole extent of its use, nothing remains of the thing which could be the property of someone else.

Addition (G). The relation of use to property is the same as that of substance to accident, inner to outer, or force to its manifestation. A force exists only in so far as it manifests itself; the field is a field only in so far as it produces a crop.[1] Thus, he who has the use of a field is the owner of the whole, and it is an empty abstraction to recognize any further property in the object [*Gegenstand*] itself.[2]

§ 62

Only my entitlement to a *partial* or *temporary use* of something or to *partial* or *temporary possession* of it (a possession in the shape of the partial or temporary *possibility* of using it) is therefore to be *distinguished* from the *ownership* of the thing [*Sache*] itself. If the whole extent of the use of a thing were mine, but the abstract ownership were supposed to be someone else's, the thing as mine would be wholly penetrated by my will (see the previous paragraph and § 52), while it would at the same time contain something impenetrable by me, i.e. the will, in fact the empty will, of someone else. As positive will, I would thus be at the same time objective and not objective to myself in the thing – a relation of absolute contradiction. – Ownership is therefore essentially *free and complete* ownership.[1]

The distinction between the right to the *whole extent of the use* of a thing and *abstract ownership* is a product of the empty understanding, for which the Idea – here as the unity of ownership, or even of the personal will in general and its *reality* – is not the truth, but for which these two moments in their separation from one another count as something true. This distinction, therefore, as an actual relation, is one of an empty proprietorship which might be called a madness of personality (if the term 'madness' were used not just of a direct contradiction within a person between his merely subjective idea [*Vorstellung*] and his actuality), because the term 'mine', as applied to a *single* object, would have to mean both my exclusive individual will and another exclusive individual will, with no mediation between them.[2] – In the *Institutes*, Book II, Chapter 4, we are told: 'Ususfructus est ius *alienis* rebus utendifruendi salva rerum *substantia*.' And it is further stated: 'ne tamen in universum *inutiles* essent proprietates *semper* abscendente usufructu, *placuit*, certis modis extingui usumfructum et ad proprietatem reverti.'[a] 'The law *has decided*' – as if an initial preference or decision were needed to make sense of that empty distinction by a determination of this kind! A property which suffered 'the *permanent* cessation of usufruct' would not only be 'useless' but no longer a 'property' at all. – This is not the place to discuss other distinctions within property itself, such as those between *res mancipi* and *nec mancipi, dominium Quiritarium* and *Bonitarium*, and the like, since they are unconnected with any conceptual determination of property and are merely historical niceties associated with this [department of] right.[3] But on the one hand, the distinction discussed above is contained in the relations of *dominium directum* and *dominium utile*, in the *emphyteutic* contract and the further relations encountered in estates held in fief with their hereditary rents and other taxes, payments, feudal tributes, etc. in all their various determinations, where such burdens cannot be redeemed.[4] On the other hand, this distinction is not present in so far as *dominium utile* is associated with burdens as a result of which *dominium directum* becomes at the same time a *dominium utile*. If such

---

[a]*Translator's note:* 'Usufruct is the right to use and enjoy the fruits of *another's* property provided that its *substance* is conserved ... But in order that properties should not become *useless* through the *permanent* cessation of usufruct, the law *has decided* that, under certain circumstances, the right of usufruct should be annulled and the use should revert to the proprietor.'

relations contained nothing other than the above distinction in its strict abstraction, they would in fact imply not two *lords* (*domini*), but an *owner* on the one hand and a *lord* over nothing on the other. But on account of the burdens [on the property], what we have are *two owners* in a mutual relationship. Nevertheless, their relationship is not one of *common* ownership, although the transition from it to common ownership is very easy to make. This transition has already begun when, under *dominium directum*, the yield of the property is calculated and treated as its *essential aspect*, so that the incalculable aspect of proprietorship, which has perhaps been thought to lend it *nobility*, is subordinated to its *useful* [*utile*] aspect, which in this case is the rational element.

It must be nearly one and a half millennia since the *freedom of personality* began to flourish under Christianity and became a universal principle for part – if only a small part – of the human race.[5] But it is only since yesterday, so to speak, that the *freedom of property* has been recognized here and there as a principle – an example from world history of the length of time which the spirit requires in order to progress in its self-consciousness, and a caution against the impatience of opinion.

§ 63

A thing [*Sache*] in use is an individual thing, determined in quantity and quality and related to a specific need. But its specific utility, as *quantitatively* determined, is at the same time *comparable* with other things of the same utility, just as the specific need which it serves is at the same time *need in general* and thus likewise comparable in its particularity with other needs. Consequently, the thing is also comparable with things which serve other needs. This *universality*, whose simple determinacy arises out of the thing's particularity [*Partikularität*] in such a way that it is at the same time abstracted from this specific quality, is the thing's *value*, in which its true substantiality is *determined* and becomes an object [*Gegenstand*] of consciousness. As the full owner of the thing, I am the owner both of its *value* and of its use.

The property of the feudal tenant is distinguished by the fact
that the tenant is the owner only of the thing's *use*, not of its
value.

Addition (H). The qualitative disappears here in the form of the quantitative. For if I speak of 'need', this is a term which can encompass the most
diverse things [*Dinge*], and it is their common quality which makes them
commensurable.[1] Thus, the progression of thought here is from the
specific quality of the thing [*Sache*] to a stage at which this determinate
quality is indifferent, i.e. that of quantity. A similar situation arises in
mathematics. If, for example, I define a circle, an ellipse, or a parabola, it
can be seen that they are specifically different. Nevertheless, the distinction between these different curves is defined purely quantitatively, that
is, in such a way that the only relevant factor is a quantitative distinction
which relates to their coefficients alone, to their purely empirical dimen-
sions. In the case of property, the quantitative determination which
emerges from the qualitative is *value*. Here, the qualitative supplies the
quantum for the quantity, and is, as such, both preserved and superseded.
If one considers the concept of value, the thing [*Sache*] itself is regarded
merely as a sign, and it counts not as itself but as what it is worth. A bill of
exchange, for example, does not represent its quality as paper, but is
merely a sign representing another universal, namely value. The value of
a thing can vary greatly in relation [*Beziehung*] to need; but if one wishes to
express not the specific nature of its value but its value in the abstract, this
is expressed as *money*. Money can represent anything [*alle Dinge*], but
since it does not depict the need itself but is only a sign in place of it, it is
itself governed in turn by the specific value which it merely expresses in
the abstract. It is indeed possible to be the owner of a thing [*Sache*]
without at the same time being the owner of its value. A family which
cannot sell or mortgage its estate is not the proprietor of its value. But
since this form of property is out of keeping with the concept of property,
such limitations [of ownership] (feudal tenancies and entails) are now for
the most part disappearing.

§ 64

Without the subjective presence of the will, which alone constitutes
their significance and value, the form given to property and the sign
which denotes it are themselves mere externals. This presence,
however, which is use, employment, or some other expression of the
will, is located in *time*, in respect of which the *objective* factor is the
continuance of this expression. Without this, the thing [*Sache*] becomes

ownerless, because the actuality of will and possession has abandoned it. Consequently, I can gain or lose property by prescription.[1]

> Prescription, therefore, has not been introduced into right merely because of an external consideration at variance with right in its strict sense – that is, in order to terminate the disputes and confusions with which old claims would threaten the security of property, etc. On the contrary, prescription is based on the determination of the *reality* of property, of the will's need to express itself in order to possess something. – *Public memorials* are national property, or more precisely – like works of art in general without regard to their *use* [*Benutzung*] – it is their indwelling soul of remembrance and honour which gives them their validity as living and self-sufficient ends; but if this soul abandons them, they are then in this respect ownerless as far as the nation is concerned and become contingent private possessions, as, for example, the Greek and Egyptian works of art in Turkey. – The *right of private property* which an *author's* family has to his productions is subject to prescription for similar reasons; they become ownerless in the sense that, like public monuments (but in an opposite way), they become universal property and, according to the particular use that is made of the thing in question, contingent private possessions. – Mere *land*, consecrated as a place of burial or even dedicated in its own right [*für sich*] to perpetual *disuse*, embodies an empty and absent arbitrary will. An injury [*Verletzung*] to this will is not an injury to anything actual, and it cannot therefore be guaranteed that it will be respected.

Addition (H). Prescription is based on the assumption that I have ceased to regard the thing as mine. For if something is to remain mine, continuity of my will is required, and this is displayed in the use [*Gebrauch*] or conservation of the thing in question. – The loss of value which public memorials may suffer was often demonstrated at the time of the Reformation in the case of endowed Masses. The spirit of the old faith, that is, of the endowed Masses, had departed, and they could consequently be taken possession of as property.[2]

C. The Alienation[a] of Property

§ 65

It is possible for me to *alienate* my property, for it is mine only in so far as I embody my will in it. Thus, I may abandon (*derelinquiere*) as ownerless anything belonging to me or make it over to the will of someone else as his possession – but only in so far as the thing [*Sache*] is *external in nature*.[1]

Addition (H). While prescription is an alienation of property without a direct declaration on the part of the will, true alienation is a declaration by the will that I no longer wish to regard the thing as mine. The whole issue can also be viewed in such a way that alienation is regarded as a true mode of taking possession. The first moment in property is to take possession of something immediately; use is a further means of acquiring property; and the third moment is the unity of the first two, namely taking possession of something by alienating it.

§ 66

Those goods, or rather substantial determinations, which constitute my own distinct personality and the universal essence of my self-consciousness are therefore *inalienable*, and my right to them is *imprescriptible*. They include my personality in general, my universal freedom of will, ethical life, and religion.

> The idea that what spirit is in accordance with its concept or *in itself* should also have existence [*Dasein*] and being-for-itself (and hence that it should be a person, be capable of owning property, and have an ethical life and religion) – this Idea is itself the concept of spirit. (As *causa sui*, i.e. as a free

---

[a] *Translator's note:* Hegel's term *Entäußerung* and its synonym *Veräußerung* ('disposal' or 'alienation') are impossible to translate satisfactorily, as are the related forms *veräußern* and *sich entäußern* ('to dispose of' or 'to alienate'), *veräußerbar* ('disposable' or 'alienable') and *unveräußerlich* ('inalienable'). For the basic and original meaning of *entäußern* is 'to externalize', and Hegel, throughout the following section (§§ 65–71), repeatedly exploits this meaning by associating the terms in question with etymologically related words such as *äußerlich* ('external') and *Äußerung* ('expression' or 'utterance'). It is, of course, impossible to reproduce the resulting network of etymological associations in translation. Since the context is one of legal transactions, I have wherever possible used the English legal expression 'alienation' and its derivatives.

cause, spirit is that 'cuius natura non potest concipi nisi existens'[a] – Spinoza, *Ethics*, I, I).[1] In this very concept of spirit as that which is what it is *only through itself* and as *infinite return into itself* from the natural immediacy of its existence[2] lies the possibility of an opposition, in that what the spirit is only *in itself* may differ from what it is *for itself* (see § 57), or conversely, what it is only *for itself* – as with evil in the case of the will – may differ from what it is *in itself*. Herein lies the *possibility of the alienation of personality* and its substantial being, whether this alienation takes place in an unconscious or an explicit manner. – Examples of the alienation of personality include slavery, serfdom, disqualification from owning property, restrictions on freedom of ownership, etc. The alienation of intelligent rationality, of morality, ethical life, and religion is encountered in superstition, when power and authority are granted to others to determine and prescribe what actions I should perform (as when someone enters into an express agreement to commit robbery, murder, etc. or incurs the possibility of committing crimes) or how I should interpret the dictates of conscience, religious truth, etc. – The right to such inalienable things is imprescriptible, for the act whereby I take possession of my personality and substantial essence and make myself a responsible being with moral and religious values and capable of holding rights removes these determinations from that very externality which alone made them capable of becoming the possessions of someone else. When their externality is superseded in this way, the determination of time and all other reasons [*Gründe*] which can be derived from my previous consent or acceptance lose their validity. This return on my part into myself, whereby I make myself existent as Idea, as a person with rights and morality, supersedes the previous relationship and the wrong which I and the other party have done to my concept and reason [*Vernunft*] in treating the infinite existence [*Existenz*] of the self-consciousness as something external, and in allowing it to be so treated. – This return into myself reveals the contradiction inherent in handing over to others my capacity

---

[a]*Translator's note:* 'whose nature cannot be conceived other than as existing'.

for rights, my ethical life and religiosity; for I did not myself possess these things, and as soon as I do possess them, they exist essentially only as mine, and not as something external.

Addition (H). It is in the nature of the case [*Sache*] that the slave has an absolute right to free himself, and that, if someone has agreed to devote his ethical life to robbery and murder, this is null and void in and for itself, and anyone is entitled to revoke such a contract. The same applies if I put my religiosity at the disposal of a priest who is my confessor, for a human being must decide such inward matters entirely within himself. A religiosity which is in part controlled by someone else is not a genuine religiosity, for the spirit is only One and ought to dwell within me; the unification of being-in-and-for-itself is something which ought to belong to *me*.

§ 67

I can *alienate individual* products of *my particular physical and mental* [*geistigen*] *skills* and active capabilities to someone else*a* and allow him *to use them for a limited period*, because, provided they are subject to this limitation, they acquire an external relationship to my *totality* and *universality*. By alienating the *whole* of my time, as made concrete through work, and the totality of my production, I would be making the substantial quality of the latter, i.e. my *universal* activity and actuality or my personality itself, into someone else's property.

> It is the same relation as that discussed above (§ 61) between the substance of the *thing* [*Sache*] and its *use* [*Benutzung*]; just as use is distinct from substance only in so far as it is limited, so too does the use [*Gebrauch*] of my powers differ from the powers themselves – and hence also from me – only in so far as it is quantitatively limited; a power is the *totality* of its manifestations, just as substance is the totality of its accidents and the universal the totality of its particularizations.

Addition (H). The distinction discussed here is that between a slave and a modern servant or hired labourer. The Athenian slave perhaps had easier tasks and more intellectual [*geistigere*] work to perform than our servants

---

a Translator's note. I have chosen the reading 'an einen andern' ('to someone else'), as in Ilting's main text (VPR II, 278), in preference to 'von einem anderen' ('of someone else'), as in the first edition and the Suhrkamp edition (*Werke* VII, 144).

normally do, but he was nevertheless a slave, because the entire scope of his activity had been alienated to his master.

§ 68

The distinctive^a quality of intellectual [*geistigen*] production may, by virtue of the way in which it is expressed, be immediately transformed into the external quality of a thing [*Sache*], which may then in turn be produced by others. In acquiring it, the new owner may thus appropriate the thoughts which it communicates or the technical invention which it embodies, and it is this possibility which at times (as with literary works) constitutes the sole purpose [*Bestimmung*] of such things and their value as acquisitions; in addition, the new owner at the same time comes into possession of the *universal ways and means* of so expressing himself and of producing a multiplicity of such things.

In the case of works of art, the form which tangibly represents the thought in an external medium is, as an object [*Ding*], so distinctive a product of the individual artist that any copy of it is essentially the product of the intellectual [*geistigen*] and technical skill of the copyist. In the case of a literary work, the form which makes it an external thing [*Sache*], as with the invention of a technical device, is *of a mechanical kind*. For with a literary work, the thought is represented not in concrete depiction but only by a series of discrete and abstract *signs*, and with a technical device, the thought has a completely mechanical content; and the ways and means of producing such things [*Sachen*], *qua* things, belong to the category of ordinary skills. – Between the extremes of the work of art and the product of manual craftsmanship there are also transitional stages which share the character of one or other extreme to a greater or lesser extent.

^{a}*Translator's note.* Hegel uses the adjective *eigentümlich* ('distinctive', 'peculiar'), exploiting its close relationship with the noun *Eigentum* ('property', 'ownership') as on several other occasions in his discussion of property (§§ 41–71). It is not possible to preserve this formal association in English, since the only words which would adequately reflect it (the adjectives 'proper' and 'own') are rarely suitable as translations of *eigentümlich*.

§ 69

Since the person who acquires such a product possesses its entire use and value if he owns a *single* copy of it, he is the complete and free owner of it as an individual item. But the author of the book or the inventor of the technical device remains the owner of the *universal* ways and means of reproducing such products and things [*Sachen*], for he has not immediately alienated these universal ways and means as such but may reserve them for himself as his distinctive mode of expression.

The substance of an author's or inventor's right does not primarily consist in his arbitrarily imposing the *condition*, on alienating a single copy of his work, that the power which the other person thereby acquires to manufacture such products on his own account as things should not become the other's property, but should remain that of the inventor. The first question is whether such a separation between the ownership of the thing and the power which this confers to produce such things in turn is an admissible part of the concept, or whether it does not cancel [*aufhebt*] full and free ownership (see § 62) – so that it depends solely on the arbitrary will of the intellectual [*geistigen*] originator whether he retains the power to reproduce the things in question, or alienates this power as something of value, or places no value on it for his own part and relinquishes it along with the individual thing. For this power has the peculiar character of being that aspect of a thing which makes it not merely a possession but a *resource* (see below, §§ 170ff.), so that the latter quality lies in the particular kind of external use to which the thing is put, and is distinct and separable from the use to which the thing was immediately destined. (The use in question is not what is known as an *accessio naturalis* like the procreation of animals [*foetura*].)[1] Since, then, this distinction arises within that which is by nature divisible (that is, within external use), to retain one part of the use while alienating the other part is not to reserve a proprietorship without utility [*utile*]. – The purely negative, but most basic, means of furthering the sciences and arts is to protect those who work in them against *theft* and to provide them with security for their property, just as the earliest and most important means of furthering commerce and industry was to protect them against highway robbery. – Besides, the destiny [*Bestimmung*] of a product of the intellect [*Geistesprodukt*] is to be apprehended by other individuals and appropriated by their representational thinking, memory, thought, etc. Hence the mode of expression whereby these individuals in turn make *what they have learned* (for learning means not just memorizing or learning words by heart – the thoughts of others can be apprehended only by thinking, and this rethinking is also a kind of learning) into an *alienable thing* will always tend to have some distinctive *form*, so that they can regard the resources which flow from it as their property, and may assert their right to reproduce it. The propagation of the sciences in general, and the specific business of teaching in particular, in accordance with its determination and the duty associated with it (most specifically in the case of the positive sciences, Church doctrine, jurisprudence, etc.), consist in the *repetition* of established thoughts, all of which have already been expressed and acquired from external sources; the same is true of writings designed for teaching purposes and for the propagation and dissemination of the sciences. As for the extent to which the existing store of knowledge, and in particular the thoughts of other people who retain external ownership of their intellectual products, become, by virtue of the new *form* which they acquire through repeated expression, a special intellectual [*geistiges*] property of the individual who reproduces them and thereby give him (or fail to give him) the right to make them his external property in turn – the extent to which this is so cannot be precisely determined, nor therefore defined in terms of right and the law. The same is true of the extent to which such repetition in a written publication constitutes *plagiarism*. Plagiarism ought therefore to be a matter [*Sache*] of *honour*, and honour should deter people from committing it. – Thus laws against *breach of copyright* do attain their end of protecting the property rights of authors and publishers to the (albeit very limited) extent specified.[2] The ease with which one can deliberately alter the form of something or invent an insignificant modification to a major science or to a comprehensive theory which someone else has created, or even the impossibility of sticking to the words of the original author when expounding what one has learned – not to mention the particular ends which necessitate such repetition – in itself [*für sich*] introduces that endless multiplicity of alterations which give the property of others the more or less superficial imprint of being *one's own.* For example, the hundreds upon hundreds of compendia, excerpts, anthologies, etc., arithmetic books, geometries, devotional writings, etc., show how every new idea [*Einfall*] which appears in critical journals, poetry almanacs, encyclopaedias, etc. can also be immediately reported under the same or a different title, yet put forward as the writer's own property. This can easily have the effect that the profit which the author or inventive entrepreneur expected from his work or new idea is eliminated, reduced for both parties, or ruined for everyone.*a* – But as for the *effect of honour* in preventing plagiarism, it is remarkable that the expression 'plagiarism', or indeed 'literary theft', is no longer to be heard these days. This may be because honour has had its effect in suppressing plagiarism, or because plagiarism has ceased to be dishonourable and the revulsion against it has disappeared, or because an insignificant new idea and a change in outward form are rated so highly as originality and as the product of independent thought that it never occurs to anyone to suspect plagiarism.

---

a Translator's note. The Suhrkamp edition (*Werke* VII, 149) here reads *allein* ('alone'), which is undoubtedly an error. The correct reading is *allen* ('for everyone'), as in VPR II, 288 and other editions.

§ 70

The *comprehensive* totality of external activity, i.e. *life*, is not something external to personality, which is itself *this* personality and *immediate.* The disposal [*Entäußerung*] or sacrifice of life is, on the contrary, the opposite of the existence [*Dasein*] of *this* personality. I have therefore no *right* whatsoever to dispose of my life, and only an ethical Idea as something in which *this immediately* individual personality in itself has been submerged, and which is the *actual* power behind the latter, has such a right. Thus, just as life as such is *immediate*, so also is death at the same time its *immediate* negativity; death must consequently come from outside, either as a natural event [*Natursache*] or, in the service of the Idea, by the hand of an outsider [*von fremder Hand*].

Addition (H). It is certainly the case that the individual [*einzelne*] person is a subordinate entity who must dedicate himself to the ethical whole. Consequently, if the state demands his life, the individual [*Individuum*] must surrender it. But may a human being take his own life? One may regard suicide in the first instance as an act of bravery, albeit an inferior bravery of tailors and maidservants. On the other hand, it can also be seen as a misfortune, since it is the product of inner derangement. But the main question is: have I a right to commit suicide? The answer will be that, as *this* individual, I am not master of my life, for the comprehensive totality of activity, i.e. life, is not something external to personality, which is itself immediately *this*. Thus, it is a contradiction to speak of a person's right over his life, for this would mean that a person had a right over himself. But he has no such right, for he does not stand above himself and cannot pass judgement on himself. When Hercules burned himself to death or Brutus fell on his sword, this was a hero's behaviour in relation to his own personality; but if it is a question of a simple right to kill oneself, such a right may be denied even to heroes.[1]

Transition from Property to Contract

§ 71

Existence [*das Dasein*], as determinate being, is essentially being for another (see above, Remarks to § 48). Property, in view of its existence as an external thing [*Sache*], exists for other external things and within the context of their necessity and contingency. But as the existence of the *will*, its existence for another can only be *for the will* of another person. This relation [*Beziehung*] of will to will is the true distinctive ground in which freedom has its *existence*. This mediation whereby I no longer own property merely by means of a thing and my subjective will, but also by means of another will, and hence within the context of a common will, constitutes the sphere of *contract*.

Reason makes it just as necessary that human beings should enter into contractual relationships – giving, exchanging, trading, etc. – as that they should possess property (see Remarks to § 45). As far as their own consciousness is concerned, it is need in general – benevolence, utility, etc. – which leads them to make contracts; but implicitly [*an sich*], they are led by reason, that is, by the Idea of the real existence of free personality ('real' in the sense of 'present only within the will'). Contract presupposes that the contracting parties *recognize* each other as persons and owners of property; and since it is a relationship of objective spirit, the moment of recognition is already contained and presupposed within it (cf. § 35 and Remarks to § 57).[1]

Addition (H). In a contract, I have property by virtue of a common will: for it is the interest of reason that the subjective will should become more universal and raise itself to this actualization. Thus, my will retains its determination as *this* will in a contract, but in community with another will. The universal will, on the other hand, appears here as yet only in the form and shape of community.

SECTION 2
Contract

§ 72

That [kind of] property of which the *aspect* of existence [*Dasein*] or *externality* is no longer merely a thing [*Sache*] but contains the moment of a will (and hence the will of another person) comes into being through *contract*. This is the process in which the following contradiction is represented and mediated: I *am* and *remain* an owner of property, having being for myself and excluding the will of another, only in so far as, in identifying my will with that of another, I *cease* to be an owner of property.

§ 73

It is not only *possible* for me to dispose of an item of property as an external thing [*Sache*] (see § 65) – I am also *compelled* by the concept to dispose of it as property in order that *my* will, as *existent*, may become objective [*gegenständlich*] to me. But according to this moment, my will, as externalized,[a] is at the same time *another* will. Hence this moment, in which this necessity of the concept is real, is *the unity* of different wills, which therefore relinquish their difference and distinctiveness. Yet it is also implicit (at this stage) in this identity of different wills that each of them is and remains a will distinctive for itself and *not identical* with the other.

---

[a] *Translator's note.* The term Hegel uses is *entäußert* ('disposed of' or 'alienated'). Here, its original meaning of 'externalized' seems more appropriate (cf. translator's note to p. 95 above).

§ 74

This relationship is therefore the mediation of an identical will within the absolute distinction between owners of property who have being for themselves. It contains the implication that each party, in accordance with his own and the other party's will, *ceases* to be an owner of property, *remains* one, and *becomes* one. This is the mediation of the will to give up a property (an individual property) and the will to accept such a property (and hence the property of someone else). The context of this mediation is one of identity, in that the one volition comes to a decision only in so far as the other volition is present.

§ 75

Since the two contracting parties relate to each other as *immediate* self-sufficient persons, it follows that (α) the contract is the product of the *arbitrary will*; (β) the identical will which comes into existence [*Dasein*] through the contract is only *a will posited by the contracting parties*, hence only a *common* will,[1] not a will which is universal in and for itself; (γ) the object [*Gegenstand*] of the contract is an *individual external* thing [*Sache*], for only things of this kind are subject to the purely arbitrary will of the contracting parties to alienate them (see §§ 65ff.).

Marriage cannot therefore be subsumed under the concept of contract; this subsumption – which can only be described as disgraceful – is proposed in Kant's *Metaphysical Elements of the Theory of Right* [*Metaphysische Anfangsgründe der Rechtslehre*], pp. 106ff.[2] – The nature of the *state* has just as little to do with the relationship of contract, whether it is assumed that the state is a contract of all with all, or a contract of all with the sovereign and the government.[3] – The intrusion of this relationship, and of relationships concerning private property in general, into political relationships has created the greatest confusion in constitutional law [*Staatsrecht*] and in actuality. Just as in earlier times political rights and duties were regarded as, and declared to be, the immediate private property of particular individuals in opposition to the right of the sovereign and the state, so also in more recent times have the rights of the sovereign and the state been regarded as objects of contract and based on a contract, as the result merely of a *common* will and proceeding from the arbitrary will of those who have combined to form a state. – However different these two points of view may be in one respect, they do have this in common: they have transferred the determinations of private property to a sphere of a totally different and higher nature. (See below, 'Ethical Life' and 'The State'.)

Addition (H). In recent times, it has become very popular to regard the state as a contract of all with all. Everyone, we are told, makes a contract with the sovereign, and he in turn with the subjects. This view is the result of superficial thinking, which envisages only a *single* unity of different wills. But in a contract, there are two identical wills, both of which are persons and wish to remain owners of property; the contract accordingly originates in the arbitrary will of the person – an origin which marriage also has in common with contract.[4] But in the case of the state, this is different from the outset, for the arbitrary will of individuals [*Individuen*] is not in a position to break away from the state, because the individual is already by nature a citizen of it. It is the rational destiny [*Bestimmung*] of human beings to live within a state, and even if no state is yet present, reason requires that one be established. The state itself must give permission for individuals [*Einzelne*] to enter or leave it, so that this does not depend on the arbitrary will of the individuals concerned; consequently, the state is not based on contract, which presupposes an arbitrary will. It is false to say that the arbitrary will of everyone is capable of founding a state: on the contrary, it is absolutely necessary for each individual to live within the state. The great advance made by the state in modern times is that it remains an end in and for itself, and that each individual may no longer base his relationship [*Beziehung*] to it on his own private stipulation, as was the case in the Middle Ages.

§ 76

A contract is *formal* in so far as the two acts of consent whereby the common will comes into being – the negative moment of the alienation of a thing [*Sache*] and the positive moment of its acceptance – are performed separately by the two contracting parties: this is a *contract of gift*. – But a contract may be called *real* in so far as *each* of the *two* contracting wills is the totality of these mediating moments, and thereby both becomes and remains an owner of property in concluding it: this is a *contract of exchange*.

Addition (H). A contract requires two acts of consent in relation to two things: for I seek both to acquire property and to relinquish it. The contract is real when each party performs the entire action, both relinquishing and acquiring property and remaining an owner of property while relinquishing it; and it is formal when only one party acquires property or relinquishes it.

§ 77

Since each party, in a real contract, retains *the same* property with which he enters the contract and which he simultaneously relinquishes, that property which remains *identical* as having being *in itself* within the contract is distinct from the external things [*Sachen*] which change owners in the course of the transaction. The former is the *value*, in respect of which the objects of the contract [*Vertragsgegenstände*] are *equal* to each other, whatever qualitative external differences there may be between the things exchanged; it is their *universal* aspect (see § 63).

The determination that *laesio enormis*[a1] cancels [*aufhebe*] the contractual obligation consequently has its source in the concept of contract, and specifically in that moment whereby the contracting party, by alienating his property, *remains an owner of property* and, more precisely, remains quantitatively the same as he was before. But the damage is not just excessive (as it is considered to be if it exceeds one *half* of the value) but *infinite*, if a contract or stipulation of any kind has been entered into to alienate *inalienable* goods (see § 66). – Furthermore, a *stipulation*[2] differs from a contract first through its content, since it refers to a single part or moment of the whole contract, and secondly, since it is the *formal* settlement of the contract (of which more will be said later).[3] In respect of its content, the stipulation contains only the formal determination of the contract, the consent of one party to deliver something and the consent of the other to accept it; it has therefore been classed among so-called *unilateral* contracts. The distinction between unilateral and bilateral contracts,[4] and other classifications of contracts in Roman law, are in part superficial groupings based on a single and often external aspect such as the kind of formalities they are associated with; and in part they confuse (among other things) determinations which concern the nature of contract itself with others which concern only the administration of justice (*actiones*) and the legal [*rechtlichen*] consequences of positive law, and which often derive from wholly external circumstances and contravene the concept of right.

§ 78

The distinction between property and possession, the substantial and external aspects [of ownership] (see § 45), becomes, in contract, the distinction between the common will as *agreement* and its actualization through *performance*. An agreement which has been reached, considered by itself [*für sich*] without reference to its performance, is an idea of representational thought [*ein Vorgestelltes*], to which a particular *existence* [*Dasein*] must therefore be given in accordance with the distinctive manner in which *representational thoughts* [*Vorstellungen*] *have their existence in signs* (see *Encyclopaedia of the Philosophical Sciences*, §§ 379f.).[1] This is achieved by expressing the *stipulation* through formal *gestures* and other symbolic actions, and particularly by a specific declaration in *language*, the most appropriate medium [*Element*] of intellectual representation [*der geistigen Vorstellung*].

> According to this definition [*Bestimmung*], a stipulation is indeed the form through which the content of a contract, i.e. what is *concluded* in it, has its existence as something as yet only *represented*. But this representation is merely a form, and it does not mean that the content is still subjective in character, as something to be wished for or willed in such and such a way. On the contrary, the content is the decision which the will finally reaches on such matters.

Addition (H). Just as, in the theory [*Lehre*] of property, we had the distinction between property and possession, between the substantial and the merely external, so do we have in contract the difference [*Differenz*] between the common will as agreement and the particular will as performance. It lies in the nature of contract that both the common will and the particular will should be expressed, for a contract is a relationship between one will and another. The agreement, which manifests itself by means of a sign, and the performance are therefore kept separate among civilized [*gebildeten*] peoples, whereas they may coincide among the uncivilized. In the forests of Ceylon there is a nation of traders who lay out their property and peacefully wait until others come and put theirs down beside it; in this case, there is no difference between the mute declaration of will and its performance.

§ 79

The stipulation contains the aspect of will, and hence the *substantial* element of right in a contract. In contrast to this, the possession which remains in force so long as the contract is unfulfilled is in itself [*für sich*] merely the external aspect, which has its determination in the will alone. Through the stipulation, I have relinquished an item of property and my arbitrary will over it, and it has *already become the property of the other party*. In terms of right, I am thus immediately bound by the stipulation to *perform* what has been agreed.

The difference between a mere promise and a contract lies in the fact that, in a promise, whatever I intend to give, do, or perform is expressed as *something in the future*, and it still remains a *subjective* determination of my will, which I can therefore subsequently alter. The stipulation in a contract, on the other hand, is itself already the *existence* [*Dasein*] of my will's decision, in the sense that I have thereby alienated the thing [*Sache*] I own, that it has *now* ceased to be my property, and that I already recognize it as the property of the other party. The Roman distinction between *pactum* and *contractus* is a bad one.[1] – Fichte once maintained that my obligation to *observe* a contract *commences* only when the other party *begins* to perform [his side of the agreement], for until he does so, I do not know whether his original utterance was *seriously meant*; the obligation before the performance could therefore only be of a *moral* nature, rather than based on right.[2] But the utterance of a stipulation is not just an utterance in general; on the contrary, it embodies the *common will* which has come into being, and which has superseded the arbitrariness of [individual] *disposition* and its liability to change. It is not

therefore a question of whether the other party's attitude may
have differed *inwardly*, or subsequently become different, but
of whether he has any right to such different attitudes. Even if
the other party begins to perform [his side of the agreement], I
likewise retain the arbitrary will which enables me to do
wrong. The nullity of Fichte's view is at once apparent from
the fact that it would base contractual rights on the false
infinite,[3] on an infinite regress, on the infinite divisibility of
time, matter, action, etc. The *existence* which the *will* has in the
formality of gesture or in language which is determinate for
itself is already the complete existence of the will, as intellectual [*intellektuellen*] will, and the performance [of the agree-
ment] is merely its selfless consequence. – The fact that there
are also, in positive right, so-called *real contracts* as distinct
from so-called *consensual* contracts – in the sense that the
former are considered as fully valid only after the consent has
been followed by the actual performance (*res, traditio rei*) – is
of no consequence here.[4] For on the one hand, the former are
particular cases where it is only this transfer [of goods] which
enables me to perform my side [of the agreement], and where
my obligation to perform it refers to the thing in question only
in so far as it has come into my hands, as with loans, contracts
of lease, and deposits (and as may be the case with other
contracts, too) – a circumstance which concerns not the
nature of the relationship between stipulation and performance, but the manner of performance itself. And on the other
hand, the arbitrary will is always at liberty to stipulate in a
contract that the obligation of the one party to perform [his
side of the agreement] should not lie in the contract itself as
such, but should depend on the other party performing his
side first.

§ 80

The *classification* of contracts and a judicious analysis, in the light of
this classification, of their various kinds, should not be based on
external circumstances but on distinctions inherent in the nature of
contract itself. – These distinctions are those between formal contract
and real contract, between ownership and possession and use, and

between value and the specific thing [*Sache*]. They accordingly give rise to the *following kinds* of contract (the classification given here coincides on the whole with that of Kant's *Metaphysical Elements of the Theory of Right* [*Metaphysische Anfangsgründe der Rechtslehre*], pp. 120ff.,[1] and one might have expected that the old humdrum classification of contracts as real and consensual, named and unnamed, etc. would long since have been abandoned in favour of a rational classification):

A. *Contract of gift*, comprising
   1. Gift of a thing; so-called *gift* in the proper sense.
   2. *Loan* of a thing, i.e. the giving away of *part* of it or of the *limited enjoyment* and *use* of it; the lender here remains the *owner* of the thing (*mutuum* and *commodatum* without payment of interest).[2] The thing in this case is either a *specific* thing, or it may, even if it is a specific thing, nevertheless be regarded as universal, or it counts (like money) as a thing universal in itself [*für sich*].
   3. *Gift* of a *service* of any kind, e.g. the mere safe-keeping of an item of property (*depositum*).[3] *Testamentary* disposition, i.e. the gift of a thing with the particular condition that the other party should not become the owner until the *time of the donor's death* (at which time the latter in any case ceases to be the owner), has no place in the concept of contract, but presupposes civil society and a positive legislation.

B. *Contract of exchange*
   1. *Exchange* as such:
      (α) of a *thing* of any kind, i.e. of a *specific* thing for another of the same kind.
      (β) *purchase* or *sale* (*emtio, venditio*);[4] exchange of a *specific* thing for one designated [*bestimmt*] as universal and which counts only as *value*, without the other specific determination of utility – i.e. for *money*.
   2. *Letting or hiring* (*locatio, conductio*); alienation of the *temporary use* of a property in exchange for *rent*, viz.
      (α) of a *specific* thing, letting in the proper sense, or
      (β) of a *universal thing*, so that the lender remains only the owner of this universal, or in other words of the *value* – *loan* (*mutuum*, or *commodatum*, if a rent is payable).[5] The further empirical characteristics of the thing (whether it be a stick,

implement, house, etc., *res fungibilis* or *non fungibilis*[6] give rise to other particular determinations (as in A.2. above, loan as gift), but these are of no importance.[a]

3. *Wages contract (locatio operae);*[7] alienation of my *output [Produzierens]* or *services* (i.e. in so far as these are alienable) for a limited time or with some other limiting condition (see § 67).

Akin to this are *mandates* and other contracts whose performance depends on character and trust or on superior talents, and where an *incommensurability* arises between the performance and its external value (which in this case is not described as *wages*, but as an *honorarium*).

C. *Completion of a contract (cautio) by giving a pledge*
In those contracts whereby I alienate the use *[Benutzung]* of a thing, I am no longer in possession of it but am still its owner (as when I rent something out). Furthermore, in contracts of exchange, sale, and gift, I may have become the owner of something without yet being in possession of it, and the same disjunction arises with regard to any performance which does not follow *step by step.* Now the effect of the *pledge*[8] is that in the one case I remain, and in the other case I come into, actual *possession of the value* as that which is still, or has already become, my property, without being in possession of the *specific* thing which I am handing over or which I am to receive. The pledge is a specific thing, but it is my property only to the extent of the *value* of the property which I have handed over into someone else's possession or which is due to me. But as far as its specific character and any excess value it may have are concerned, it remains the property of the person giving the pledge. Consequently, giving a pledge is not itself a contract but only a stipulation (see § 77), i.e. the moment which completes a contract with regard to the possession of a property. – *Mortgage* and *surety* are particular forms of pledge.

Addition (H). In the case of contract, we made the following distinction: while I become the owner of an item of property through the agreement (stipulation), I do not yet have possession of it but gain possession only through the performance. Now if I already have full ownership of the

---

[a]*Translator's note:* Hegel's manuscript note adds the gloss 'i.e. of no importance for the universal determinations'.

thing, the purpose of the pledge is that I should at the same time gain possession of the value of the property, and that the performance should thereby be guaranteed within the agreement itself. Surety is a particular kind of pledge whereby someone tenders his promise or his credit as a guarantee of my performance. Here, a person assumes the role which, in the case of a pledge, is fulfilled by a mere thing.

§ 81

In any relationship of immediate persons to one another, their wills are not only *identical in themselves* and, in a contract, posited by them as *common*, but also *particular*. Since they are *immediate* persons, it is purely contingent whether their *particular* wills are in conformity with the will *which has being in itself*, and which has its existence [*Existenz*] solely through the former. If the particular will *for itself* is *different* from the universal, its attitude and volition are characterized by arbitrariness and contingency, and it enters into opposition to that which is right *in itself*; this is *wrong*.

> The transition to wrong is made by the logical higher necessity that the moments of the concept – here, that of right *in itself* or the will as *universal*, and that of right in its *existence*, which is simply the *particularity* of will – should be posited as *different for themselves*; this belongs to the *abstract reality* of the concept. – But this particularity of the will for itself is arbitrariness and contingency, and in contract, I have relinquished these only as arbitrariness in relation to an *individual* thing [*Sache*], not as the arbitrariness and contingency of the will itself.

Addition (H). In contract, we had the relationship of two wills as a common will. This identical will, however, is only relatively universal – a posited universal will – and is thereby still in opposition to the particular will. The contract or agreement nevertheless contains the right to require its performance; but this again is a matter [*Sache*] for the particular will, which may, as such, act in contravention of that right which has being in itself. Thus, there appears at this point the negation which was already present at an earlier stage in the will which has being in itself, and this negation is quite simply *wrong*. The overall progression is that the will is purged of its immediacy so that, from the common will, that particularity is evoked which then appears in opposition to it. In a contract, the consenting parties will retain their particular wills; thus, contract has not yet progressed beyond the stage of arbitrariness, and it therefore remains susceptible to wrong.

SECTION 3
Wrong [*Das Unrecht*]

§ 82

In contract, right *in itself* is present as something *posited*, and its inner universality is present as a *common factor* in the arbitrariness and particular wills of those concerned. This *appearance* of right, in which right itself and its essential *existence* [*Dasein*], the particular will, coincide immediately – i.e. in a contingent manner – goes on, in the case of *wrong*, to become a *semblance* – an opposition between right in itself and the particular will as that in which right becomes a *particular right*. But the truth of this semblance is that it is null and void, and that right re-establishes itself by negating this negation of itself.[1] Through this process of mediation whereby right returns to itself from its negation, it determines itself as *actual* and *valid*, whereas it was at first only *in itself* and something *immediate*.

Addition (H). Right in itself, the universal will, is essentially determined by the particular will, and thus stands in relation [*Beziehung*] to something inessential. This is the relationship [*Verhältnis*] of the essence to its appearance. Even if the appearance is in conformity with the essence, it is not in conformity with it from another point of view, for appearance is the stage of contingency, or essence in relation [*Beziehung*] to the inessential. But in the case of wrong, appearance goes on to become a semblance. A semblance is existence inappropriate to the essence, the empty detachment and positedness of the essence, so that in both [semblance and essence], their distinctness is [mere] difference. Semblance is therefore the untruth which disappears because it seeks to exist for itself, and in this disappearance, essence has shown itself as essence, that is, as the power over semblance. The essence has negated its own negation, and is thereby confirmed. Wrong is a semblance of this kind, and through its disappearance, right acquires the determination of something fixed and valid. What we have just referred to as essence is right in itself, in contrast to which the particular will is superseded [*sich aufhebt*] as untrue. Whereas right previously had only an immediate being, it now becomes *actual* as it returns out of its negation; for actuality is that which is effective[a] and sustains itself in its otherness, whereas the immediate still remains liable to negation.

[a] *Translator's note:* Hegel defines the term *Wirklichkeit* ('actuality') by exploiting its relationship with the verb *wirken* ('to be effective').

§ 83

Right, as something *particular* and therefore complex in contrast to the universality and simplicity of its being *in itself*, acquires the form of a *semblance*. It is this semblance either *in itself* or immediately, or it is posited by *the subject as semblance*, or it is posited by *the subject as completely null and void* – that is, it becomes *unintentional or civil wrong*, *deception*, or *crime*.

Addition (H). Wrong is thus the semblance of essence which posits itself as self-sufficient. If the semblance is present only in itself and not also for itself – that is, if the wrong is in my opinion right – the wrong is unintentional. Here, the semblance exists from the point of view of right, but not from my point of view. The second [kind of] wrong is deception. In this case, the wrong is not a semblance from the point of view of right in itself; instead, what happens is that I create a semblance in order to deceive another person. When I deceive someone, right is for me a semblance. In the first case, wrong was a semblance from the point of view of right. In the second case, right is only a semblance from my point of view, i.e. from the point of view of wrong. Finally, the third [kind of] wrong is crime. This is wrong both in itself and for me. But in this case, I will the wrong and do not employ even the semblance of right. The other person against whom the crime is committed is not expected to regard the wrong, which has being in and for itself, as right. The difference between crime and deception is that in the latter, a recognition of right is still present in the form of the action, and this is correspondingly absent in the case of crime.

A. *Unintentional Wrong*

§ 84

Taking possession (see § 54) and contract, for themselves and in their particular varieties, are in the first place different expressions and consequences of my will in general; but since the will is inherently [*in sich*] universal, they are also *legal claims* [*Rechtsgründe*] in respect of their recognition by others. By virtue of their multiplicity and mutual externality, they may be entertained by different persons with reference to one and the same thing [*Sache*], and each of these persons, on the strength of his particular claim, may regard the thing as his property. This gives rise to *collisions of rights*.

§ 85

Such a collision, in which *a legal claim* is made to a thing [*Sache*], and which constitutes the sphere of *civil actions*, involves the *recognition* of right as the universal and deciding factor, so that the thing may belong to the person who has a right to it. The action concerns merely the *subsumption* of the thing under the property of the one or the other party – a *completely negative* judgement whereby, in the predicate 'mine', only the particular is negated.

§ 86

For the parties involved, the recognition of right is bound up with their particular opposing interests and points of view. In opposition to this *semblance*,[1] yet at the same time *within the semblance itself* (see § 85), right *in itself* emerges as something represented [*vorgestellt*] and required. But it appears at first only as an *obligation*, because the will is not yet present as a will which has freed itself from the immediacy of interest in such a way that, as a particular will, it has the universal will as its end. Nor is it here determined as a recognized actuality of such a kind that, when confronted with it, the parties would have to renounce their particular points of view and interests.

Addition (H). What is right in itself has a determinate ground, and the wrong which I hold to be right I also defend on some ground or other. It is in the nature of the finite and particular that it leaves room for contingencies; collisions must therefore occur, for we are here at the level of the finite. This first kind of wrong negates only the particular will, while universal right is respected; it is consequently the least serious of all wrongs. If I say that a rose is not red, I nevertheless recognize that it has a colour. I therefore do not deny the genus, but only the particular colour, i.e. red. Right is also recognized in this case. Each person wills what is right, and each is supposed to receive only what is right; their wrong consists [*besteht*] solely in considering that what they will is right.

B. *Deception*

§ 87

Right *in itself*, as distinct from right as particular and existent, is indeed, as a *requirement*, determined as the essential; but as such, it is at the same time *only* a requirement and in this respect merely subjective, hence inessential and a mere semblance. When the universal is thus reduced by the particular will to a mere semblance, and, in the case of contract, is reduced in the first place to a purely external community of wills, this constitutes *deception*.

Addition (H). The particular will is respected at this second level of wrong, but universal right is not. In deception, the particular will is not infringed, because the deceived person is given the illusion that he is receiving his right. Thus, the right which is required is posited as something subjective, a mere semblance, and this constitutes deception.

§ 88

In a contract, I acquire an item of property on account of the particular nature of the thing [*Sache*] in question, and at the same time in the light of the inner universality which it possesses, partly through its *value* and partly through having been someone else's *property*. The arbitrary will of the other party may delude me with a false semblance as regards what I acquire, so that the contract may be perfectly in order as a free mutual agreement to exchange *this specific* thing in its *immediate* individuality [*Einzelheit*], although the aspect of what is universal *in itself* is lacking. (On the infinite judgement in its positive expression or as an identical proposition, see *Encyclopaedia of the Philosophical Sciences*, § 121.)[1]

§ 89

That the objective or universal element, as opposed to this acceptance of the thing [*Sache*] merely *as this thing* and to the mere opinions and arbitrariness of the will, should be recognizable as *value* and have validity as right, and that the subjective arbitrary will in its opposition to right should be superseded, is again in the first instance only a requirement.

Addition (H). No penalty attaches to civil and unintentional wrong, for in such cases I have willed nothing contrary to right. In the case of deception, however, penalties are introduced, because it is now a matter of infringements of right.

C. Coercion and Crime

§ 90

When I own property, my will is embodied in an *external thing* [*Sache*]. This means that my will, to the extent that it is reflected in the external thing, is also caught up in it and subjected to necessity. In this situation, it may either experience *force* in general, or it may be forced to sacrifice or do something as a condition of retaining some possession or positive being, thereby suffering *coercion*.

Addition (H). Wrong in the proper sense is crime, where neither right in itself nor [right] as it appears to me is respected – that is, where both sides, objective and subjective, are infringed.

§ 91

As a living being, the human being can certainly be *dominated* [*bezwungen*] – i.e. his physical side and other external attributes may be brought under the power of others. But the free will in and for itself cannot be *coerced* [*gezwungen*] (see § 5), except in so far as *it fails to withdraw itself from the external dimension* in which it is caught up, or from its idea [*Vorstellung*] of the latter (see § 7). Only he who *wills* to be *coerced* can be coerced into anything.[1]

§ 92

The will is Idea or actually free only in so far as it has existence [*Dasein*], and the existence in which it has embodied itself is the being of freedom. Consequently, force or coercion immediately destroys itself in its concept, since it is the expression of a will which cancels [*aufhebt*] the expression or existence of a will. Force or coercion, taken in the abstract, is therefore *contrary to right*.

§ 93

Because coercion destroys itself in its concept, it has its real expression [*Darstellung*] in the fact *that coercion is cancelled* [*aufgehoben*] *by coercion*; it is therefore not only conditionally right but necessary – namely as a *second* coercion which cancels an initial coercion.

> The violation of a contract through failure to perform what it stipulates or to fulfil rightful duties towards the family or state, whether by action or by default, is an initial coercion, or at least force, in so far as I withhold or withdraw from another person a property which belongs to him or a service which is due to him. – Pedagogical coercion, or coercion directed against savagery and barbarism [*Wildheit und Rohheit*], admittedly looks like a primary coercion rather than one which comes after a primary coercion which has already occurred. But the merely natural will is *in itself* a force directed against the Idea of freedom as that which has being in itself, which must be protected against this uncivilized [*ungebildeten*] will and given recognition within it. Either an ethical existence [*Dasein*] has already been posited in the family or state, in which case the natural condition referred to above is an act of violence against it, or there is nothing other than a state of nature, a state governed entirely by force, in which case the Idea sets up a *right of heroes*[1] against it.

Addition (H). Within the state, heroes are no longer possible: they occur only in the absence of civilization. The end they pursue is rightful, necessary, and political,^a and they put it into effect as a cause [*Sache*] of their own. The heroes who founded states and introduced marriage and agriculture admittedly did not do this as their recognized right, and these actions still appear as [a product of] their particular will. But as the higher right of the Idea against the state of nature, this coercion employed by heroes is a rightful coercion, for goodness alone can have little effect when confronted with the force of nature.

^a*Translator's note:* Instead of *staatlich* ('political'), the equivalent adjective in Hotho's notes (VPR III, 295), on which Gans based this Addition, is *sittlich* ('ethical').

§ 94

Abstract right is a *coercive right*, because a wrong committed against it is a force directed against the *existence* [*Dasein*] of my freedom in an *external* thing [*Sache*]. Consequently, the protection of this existence against such a force will itself appear as an external action and as a force which supersedes the original one.

> To define abstract right – or right in the strict sense – from the start as a *right* which justifies the use of coercion¹ is to interpret [*auffassen*] it in the light of a consequence which arises only indirectly by way of wrong.

Addition (H). Special attention must be paid here to the distinction between right and morality. In the moral sphere – that is, when I am reflected into myself – there is also a duality, for the good is my end and the Idea by which I should determine myself. The existence of the good is my decision, and I actualize it within myself; but this existence is wholly inward, so that coercion cannot be applied to it. Thus, the laws of the state cannot claim to extend to a person's disposition, for in the moral sphere, I exist [only] for myself, and force is meaningless in this context.

§ 95

The initial use of coercion, as force employed by a free agent in such a way as to infringe the existence [*Dasein*] of freedom in its *concrete* sense – i.e. to infringe right as right – is *crime*. This constitutes a *negatively infinite judgement* in its complete sense (see my [*Science of*] *Logic*, Vol. II, p. 99)¹ whereby not only the particular – i.e. the subsumption of a thing [*Sache*] under my will (see § 85) – is negated, but also the universal and infinite element in the predicate 'mine' – i.e. my *capacity for rights*. This does not involve the mediation of my opinion (as it does in deception; see § 88), but runs counter to it. This is the sphere of *penal law*.

> Right, whose infringement is crime, has admittedly appeared up till now only in those shapes which we have considered; hence crime likewise, for the moment, has only the more specific meaning associated with these determinations. But the substantial element within these forms is the universal, which remains the same in its further development and in the further shapes it assumes; thus its infringement, i.e. crime, also remains the same, in conformity with its concept. Hence the determination which will be considered in the following paragraph also applies to the particular and further determined content [of crime], e.g. in perjury, treason, counterfeiting, forgery, etc.

§ 96

It is only the *existent* will which can be infringed. But in its existence [*Dasein*], the will enters the sphere of quantitative extension and qualitative determinations, and therefore varies accordingly. Thus, it likewise makes a difference to the objective side of crime whether the will's existence and determinacy in general is infringed throughout its entire extent, and hence in that infinity which corresponds to its concept (as in murder, slavery, religious coercion, etc.) or only in one part, and if so, in which of its qualitative determinations.

> The Stoic view that there is only *one* virtue and *one* vice,[1] the laws of Draco[2] which punish every crime with death, and the barbarous code of formal honour which regards every infringement as an offence against the infinite personality, all have this in common: they go no further than the abstract thought of the free will and personality, and do not consider the latter in the concrete and determinate existence which it must have as Idea. – The distinction between *robbery* and *theft* is a qualitative one,[3] for in the case of robbery, [my] 'I' is also infringed as present consciousness and hence as *this subjective* infinity, and force is used against my person. – Various quali-

tative determinations [of crime], such as *danger to public security*, have their basis in more precisely determined circumstances, but they are often apprehended only indirectly in the light of other consequences rather than in terms of the concept of the thing [*Sache*]. Thus, the crime which is more dangerous in itself [*für sich*], in its immediate character, is a more serious infringement in its extent or quality. – The subjective, *moral* quality [of a crime] relates to the higher distinction regarding the extent to which an event or deed is in any sense an action, and concerns the latter's subjective nature itself (which will be discussed later).

Addition (H). Thought cannot specify how each crime should be punished; positive determinations are necessary for this purpose. With the progress of education, however, attitudes toward crime become more lenient, and punishments today are not nearly so harsh as they were a hundred years ago. It is not the crimes or punishments themselves which change, but the relation between the two.

§ 97

When an infringement of right as right occurs, it does have a *positive* external *existence* [*Existenz*], but this existence *within itself* is null and void. The *manifestation* of its nullity is that the nullification of the infringement likewise comes into existence; this is the actuality of right, as its necessity which mediates itself with itself through the cancellation [*Aufhebung*] of its infringement.

Addition (H). Through a crime, something is altered, and the thing [*Sache*] exists in this alteration; but this existence is the opposite of the thing itself, and is to that extent within itself [*in sich*] null and void. The nullity is [the presumption] that right as right has been cancelled [*aufgehoben*]. For right, as an absolute, cannot be cancelled, so that the expression of crime is within itself null and void, and this nullity is the essence of the effect of crime. But whatever is null and void must manifest itself as such – that is, it must itself appear as vulnerable. The criminal act is not an initial positive occurrence followed by the punishment as its negation, but is itself negative, so that the punishment is merely the negation of the negation. Actual right is thus the cancellation [*Aufhebung*] of this infringement, and it is in this very circumstance that it demonstrates its validity and proves itself as a necessary and mediated existence [*Dasein*].

§ 98

An infringement which affects only external existence [*Dasein*] or possessions is an evil [*Übel*] or *damage* done to some kind of property or resources; the cancellation [*Aufhebung*] of the infringement, where the latter has caused damage, is civil satisfaction in the form of *compensation* (in so far as any compensation is possible).

> With regard to this satisfaction, the *universal* character of the damage, as *value*, must in any case take the place of its specific qualitative character where the damage amounts to destruction and is altogether irreparable.

§ 99

But an injury [*Verletzung*] suffered by the will which has being *in itself* (and hence also by the will of the injuring party as well as by the injured and everyone else) has no *positive existence* [*Existenz*] in this will as such, no more than it has in the mere product [of the injury]. *For itself*, this will which has being in itself (i.e. right or law in itself) is rather something which has no external existence and is to that extent invulnerable. In the same way, the injury is a purely negative thing for the particular will of the injured party and of others. The *positive existence of the injury* consists solely in the *particular will of the criminal*. Thus, an injury to the latter as an existent will is the cancellation [*Aufheben*] of the crime, *which would otherwise be regarded as valid*, and the restoration of right.

> The theory of punishment is one of the topics which have come off worst in the positive jurisprudence [*Rechtswissenschaft*] of recent times; for in this theory, the understanding is inadequate, and the essential factor is the concept. – If the crime and its cancellation [*Aufhebung*], which is further determined as punishment, are regarded only as *evils* [*Übel*] in general, one may well consider it unreasonable to will an evil merely *because another evil is already present* (see Klein's *Elements of Penal Law* [*Grundsätze des peinlichen Rechts*], §§ 9f.).[1] This superficial character of an *evil* is the primary assumption in the various theories of punishment as prevention, as a deterrent, a threat, a corrective, etc.; and conversely, what is

124

supposed to result from it is just as superficially defined [*bestimmt*] as a *good*. But it is neither a question merely of an evil nor of this or that good; on the contrary, it is definitely [*bestimmt*] a matter of *wrong* and of *justice*. As a result of these superficial points of view, however, the objective consideration of *justice*, which is the primary and substantial point of view in relation to crime, is set aside; it automatically follows that the essential consideration is now the moral point of view, i.e. the subjective aspect of crime, intermixed with trivial psychological ideas [*Vorstellungen*] of stimuli and the strength of sensuous motives [*Triebfedern*] as opposed to reason, of psychological coercion and of psychological influences on representational thought [*die Vorstellung*] (as if such influences were not themselves reduced by freedom to something purely contingent). The various considerations which are relevant to punishment as a phenomenon [*Erscheinung*] and to its relation [*Beziehung*] to the particular consciousness, and which concern its effect on representational thought (as a deterrent, corrective, etc.), are of essential significance in their proper context, though primarily only in connection with the *modality* of punishment. But they take it for granted that punishment in and for itself is *just*. In the present discussion, we are solely concerned with the need to cancel [*aufzuheben*] crime – not as a source of *evil*, but as an infringement of right as right – and also with the kind of *existence* which crime possesses, which must also be cancelled. This existence is the true evil which must be removed, and the essential point is [to discover] where it lies. So long as the concepts relating to this have not been definitely [*bestimmt*] recognized, confusion must prevail in our views on punishment.

Addition (H). Feuerbach's theory[2] bases punishment on threat and maintains that, if anyone commits a crime in spite of the threat, the punishment must follow because the criminal knew about it in advance. But to what extent is the threat compatible with right? The threat presupposes that human beings are not free, and seeks to coerce them through the representation [*Vorstellung*] of an evil. But right and justice must have their seat in freedom and the will, and not in that lack of freedom at which the threat is directed. To justify punishment in this way is like raising one's stick at a dog; it means treating a human being like a dog instead of respecting his honour and freedom. But a threat, which may ultimately provoke someone into demonstrating his freedom in defiance of it, sets justice aside completely. Psychological coercion can refer only to qualitative and quantitative differences within crime, not to the nature of crime itself, and any legal codes which may have originated in this doctrine consequently have no proper foundation.

§ 100

The injury [*Verletzung*] which is inflicted on the criminal is not only just *in itself* (and since it is just, it is at the same time his will as it is *in itself*, an existence [*Dasein*] of his freedom, *his* right); it is also a *right for the criminal himself*, that is, a right *posited* in his *existent* will, in his action. For it is implicit in his action, as that of a *rational* being, that it is universal in character, and that, by performing it, he has set up a law which he has recognized for himself in his action, and under which he may therefore be subsumed as under *his* right.

> It is well known that Beccaria[1] questioned the right of the state to impose capital punishment, on the grounds that it could not be presumed that the social contract included the consent of individuals [*Individuen*] to allow themselves to be killed, and that we ought rather to assume the contrary. But the state is by no means a contract (see § 75), and its substantial essence does not consist unconditionally in the *protection* and *safeguarding* of the lives and property of individuals as such. The state is rather that higher instance which may even itself lay claim to the lives and property of individuals and require their sacrifice. – Furthermore, the *action* of the criminal involves not only the *concept* of crime, its rationality *in and for itself* which the state must enforce *with* or *without* the consent of individuals [*der Einzelnen*], but also the formal rationality of the *individual's* [*des Einzelnen*] *volition*. In so far as the punishment which this entails is seen as embodying *the criminal's own right*, the criminal is *honoured* as a rational being. – He is denied this honour if the concept and criterion of his punishment are not derived from his own act; and he is also denied it if he is regarded simply as a harmful animal which must be rendered harmless, or punished with a view to deterring or reforming him. – Besides, so far as the mode of

existence [*Existenz*] of justice is concerned, the form which it has within the state, namely that of *punishment*, is not its only form, and the state is not a necessary condition of justice in itself.

Addition (H,G). Beccaria is quite right to demand that human beings should give their consent to being punished, but the criminal gives this consent by his very act. Both the nature of crime and the criminal's own will require that the infringement for which he is responsible should be cancelled [*aufgehoben*]. Nevertheless, Beccaria's efforts to have capital punishment abolished [*aufheben zu lassen*] have had advantageous effects. Even if neither Joseph II nor the French have ever managed to secure its complete abolition,[2] people have begun to appreciate which crimes deserve the death penalty and which do not. The death penalty has consequently become less frequent, as indeed this ultimate form of punishment deserves to be.[3]

§ 101

The cancellation [*Aufheben*] of crime is *retribution* in so far as the latter, by its concept, is an infringement of an infringement, and in so far as crime, by its existence [*Dasein*], has a determinate qualitative and quantitative magnitude, so that its negation, as existent, also has a determinate magnitude. But this identity [of crime and retribution], which is based on the concept, is not an *equality* in the specific character of the infringement, but in its character *in itself* – i.e. in terms of its *value*.

It is usual in science for a determination – in this case, that of punishment – to be defined in terms of the *universal representations* [*Vorstellung*] of conscious psychological experience. In the present case, this experience would indicate that the universal feeling of peoples and individuals towards crime is, and always has been, that it *deserves* to be punished, and that *what the criminal has done should also happen to him*. It is incomprehensible how those sciences which derive their determinations from universal representations [*Vorstellung*] should on other occasions accept propositions which contradict such so-called universal *facts* of consciousness. – But the determination of *equality* has brought a major difficulty into the idea [*Vorstellung*] of retribution, although the justice (in terms of

127

their qualitative and quantitative character) of whatever punishments are determined is in any case a matter which arises later than the substance of the thing [*Sache*] itself. Even if, for this later determination of punishments, we had to look around for principles other than those which apply to the universal aspect of punishment, this universal aspect remains what it is. Yet the concept itself must always contain the basic principle, even for the particular instance. This determination of the concept, however, is precisely that necessary connection [which dictates] that crime, as the will which is null and void in itself, accordingly contains within itself its own nullification, and this appears in the form of punishment. It is this inner *identity* which, for the understanding, is reflected in external existence [*Dasein*] as *equality*. The qualitative and quantitative character of crime and its cancellation [*seines Aufhebens*] thus falls into the sphere of externality, in which no absolute determination is in any case possible (cf. § 49). *In the realm of finite things*, the absolute determination remains only a requirement, on which the understanding must impose increasing restrictions – and this is of the utmost importance – but which continues *ad infinitum* and admits in perpetuity of only an *approximate* fulfilment. – If we not only overlook this nature of the finite realm but also proceed no further than abstract and *specific equality*, an insuperable difficulty arises when we come to determine punishments (especially if psychology also invokes the strength of sensuous motives [*Triebfedern*] and, as a corollary, either the *correspondingly greater strength* of the evil will or – *if we prefer* – the *correspondingly lesser strength* and freedom of the will in general). Furthermore, it is very easy to portray the retributive aspect of punishment as an absurdity (theft as retribution for theft, robbery for robbery, an eye for an eye, and a tooth for a tooth,[1] so that one can even imagine the miscreant as one-eyed or toothless); but the concept has nothing to do with this absurdity, for which the introduction of that [idea of] *specific equality* is alone to blame. *Value*, as the *inner equality* of things [*Sachen*] which, in their existence [*Existenz*], are specifically quite different, is a determination which has already arisen in connection with contracts (see [§ 77] above) and with civil suits against crimes (see § 98),[a] and which raises our representation [*Vorstellung*] of a thing above its *immediate* character to the universal. In the case of crime, whose basic determination is the *infinite* aspect of the deed, that aspect which is only externally specific disappears all the more readily, and equality remains merely the basic measure of the criminal's *essential* deserts, but not of the specific external shape which the retribution should take. It is only in terms of this specific shape that theft and robbery [on the one hand] and fines and imprisonment etc. [on the other] are completely unequal, whereas in terms of their value, i.e. their universal character as injuries [*Verletzungen*], they are *comparable*. It is then, as already remarked, a matter [*Sache*] for the understanding to seek an approximate equivalence in this common value. If we do not grasp either the connection, as it is in itself, between crime and its nullification, or the thought of *value* and the comparability of crime and punishment in terms of value, we may reach the point (see Klein's *Elements of Penal Law*, § 9)[2] of regarding a proper punishment as a purely *arbitrary* association of an evil [*eines Übels*] with an illicit action.

Addition (H). Retribution is the inner connection and the identity of two determinations which are different in appearance and also have a different external existence [*Existenz*] in relation to one another. When the criminal meets with retribution, this has the appearance of an alien destiny [*Bestimmung*] which does not belong to him; yet as we have seen, the punishment is merely a manifestation of the crime, i.e. it is one half which is necessarily presupposed by the other. What is at first sight objectionable about retribution is that it looks like something immoral, like revenge, and may thus be interpreted as a personal matter. Yet it is not the personal element, but the concept itself which carries out retribution. 'Vengeance is mine' is the word of God in the Bible,[3] and if the word *re*tribution should evoke the idea [*Vorstellung*] of a particular caprice of the subjective will, it must be replied that it signifies merely the shape of the crime turned round against itself. The Eumenides[4] sleep, but crime awakens them; thus the deed brings its own retribution with it. But although retribution cannot aim to achieve specific equality, this is not the case with murder, which necessarily incurs the death penalty. For since life is the entire compass of existence [*Dasein*], the punishment [for

[a]*Translator's note:* The reference in all editions of Hegel's text is to § 95, which appears to be an error. I follow T. M. Knox in substituting § 98 as more appropriate.

murder] cannot consist [*bestehen*] in a *value* – since none is equivalent to life – but only in the taking of another life.

§ 102

In this sphere of the immediacy of right, the cancellation [*Aufheben*] of crime is primarily *revenge*, and its *content* is just so far as it constitutes retribution. But in its *form*, it is the action of a *subjective* will which can place *its infinity* in any infringement [of right] which occurs, and whose justice is therefore altogether contingent, just as it exists *for the other party* only as a *particular* will. Thus revenge, as the positive action of a *particular* will, becomes *a new infringement*; because of this contradiction, it becomes part of an infinite progression and is inherited indefinitely from generation to generation.

> Where the crimes are prosecuted and punished not as *crimina publica* but as *crimina privata* (as with theft and robbery among the Jews and Romans, and even today with certain offences in England, etc.) the punishment still has at least an element of revenge about it.[1] Private revenge is distinct from the revenge of heroes, knightly adventurers, etc., which belongs to the period when states first arose.

Addition (H). In a social condition in which there are neither magistrates nor laws, punishment always takes the form of revenge; this remains inadequate inasmuch as it is the action of a subjective will, and thus out of keeping with the content. It is true that the members of a tribunal are also persons, but their will is the universal will of the law, and they do not seek to include in the punishment anything but what is naturally present in the matter [*Sache*] in hand. On the other hand, the injured party does not perceive wrong in its quantitative and qualitative limitation [*Begrenzung*], but simply as wrong without qualification, and he may go too far in his retaliation, which will in turn lead to further wrong. Among uncivilized [*ungebildeten*] peoples, revenge is undying, as with the Arabs, where it can be suppressed only by superior force or by the impossibility of putting it into effect. There is still a residue of revenge in several legal codes in use today, as in those cases where it is left to individuals to decide whether they wish to bring an offence [*Verletzung*] to court or not.

§ 103

To require that this contradiction, which in the present case is to be found in the manner in which wrong is cancelled [*der Art und Weise des Aufhebens*], should be resolved in the same way as contradictions in other kinds of wrong (see §§ 86 and 89), is to require a justice freed from subjective interest and subjective shape and from the contingency of power – that is, a *punitive* rather than an *avenging justice*. *Primarily*, this constitutes a requirement for a will which, as a particular and *subjective* will, also wills the universal as such. But this concept of *morality* is not just a requirement; it has emerged in the course of this movement itself.

TRANSITION FROM RIGHT TO MORALITY

§ 104

Thus, crime and avenging justice represent the *shape* of the will's development when it has proceeded to the distinction between the *universal* will which has being *in itself*, and the *individual* [*einzelnen*] will which has being *for itself* in opposition to the universal. They also show how the will *which has being in itself*, by superseding this opposition, has returned into itself and thereby itself become *actual* and *for itself*. Having proved itself in opposition to the individual will *which has being only for itself*, right accordingly *is* and *is recognized* as *actual* by virtue of its necessity. – This shape [of the will's development] is also at the same time a further advance in the inner determination of the will by its concept. In accordance with its concept, the will's self-actualization is the process whereby it supersedes its being-in-itself and the form of immediacy in which it is initially present and which is its shape in the realm of abstract right (see § 21). Consequently, it first posits itself in the opposition between the universal will which has being *in itself* and the individual will which has being *for itself*; then, by superseding this opposition – the negation of the negation – it determines itself as will *in its existence* [*Dasein*], so that it is not only a free will in itself, but also *for itself*, as self-related [*sich auf sich beziehende*] negativity. Thus, it now has its *personality* – and in abstract right the will is no more than personality – as its *object* [*Gegenstand*]; the infinite subjectivity of freedom, which now has being *for itself*, constitutes the principle of the *moral point of view*.

> If we look again more closely at the moments through which the concept of freedom develops from the will's initially abstract determinacy to its self-related determinacy and hence to the *self-determination of subjectivity*, we see that they are as follows. In property, the will's determinacy is *abstract possession* [*das abstrakte Meinige*] and is therefore located in an external thing [*Sache*]; in contract, it is possession *mediated by will* and merely held *in common*; in wrong, the will of the sphere of right in its abstract being-in-itself or immediacy is posited as *contingency* by the individual will, which is itself *contingent*. In the moral point of view, it [i.e. the will's abstract determinacy] has been overcome to the extent that this contingency itself, as reflected *into itself* and *identical with itself*, is the infinite and inwardly present contingency of the will, i.e. its *subjectivity*.

Addition (H). It is [a necessary] part of the truth that the concept should exist, and that this existence should be in conformity with the concept. In right, the will has its existence in something external, but the next stage is for the will to have this existence in itself, in something internal. It must have being for itself, as subjectivity, and be confronted with itself. This relation to itself is that of *affirmation*, but it can attain this only by superseding its immediacy. The immediacy which is superseded in crime thus leads, through punishment – that is, through the nullity of this nullity – to affirmation, i.e. to *morality*.

PART TWO

Morality

§ 105

The moral point of view is the point of view of the will in so far as the latter is *infinite* not only *in itself* but also *for itself* (see § 104). This reflection of the will into itself and its identity for itself, as opposed to its being-in-itself and immediacy and the determinacies which develop within the latter, determine the *person* as a *subject*.

§ 106

Since subjectivity now constitutes the determinacy of the concept and is distinct from the concept as such (i.e. from the will which has being in itself), and more precisely since the will of the subject, as the individual [*des Einzelnen*] who has being for himself, at the same time *exists* (i.e. still has immediacy in it), it follows that subjectivity constitutes the *existence* [*Dasein*] of the concept. – A higher *ground* has thereby been determined for freedom; the Idea's aspect of *existence* [*Existenz*], its real moment, is now the *subjectivity* of the will. Only in the will as subjective will can freedom, or the will which has being *in itself*, be actual.

> The second sphere, i.e. morality, thus represents in its entirety the real aspect of the concept of freedom. The process within this sphere is such that the will which at first has being only for itself, and which is immediately identical only *in itself* with the will which has being *in itself* (i.e. with the universal will) is superseded; and leaving behind it this difference in which it has immersed itself in itself, it is posited for itself as *identical* with the will which has being in itself. This movement is accordingly the cultivation of the ground on which freedom is now established, i.e. subjectivity. The latter, which is at first *abstract* – i.e. distinct from the concept – becomes identical with the concept, so that the Idea thereby attains its true realization. Thus, the subjective will determines itself as correspondingly objective, and hence as truly concrete.

Addition (H). With right in the strict sense, it made no difference what my principle or intention was. This question of the self-determination and motive [*Triebfeder*] of the will and of its purpose now arises in connection with morality. Human beings expect to be judged in accordance with their self-determination, and are in this respect free, whatever external determinants may be at work. It is impossible to break into this inner conviction of human beings; it is inviolable, and the moral will is therefore inaccessible. The worth of a human being is measured by his inward actions, and hence the point of view of morality is that of freedom which has being for itself.

§ 107

The will's *self-determination* is at the same time a moment of its concept, and subjectivity is not just the aspect of its existence [*Dasein*], but its own determination (see § 104). The will which is determined as subjective and free for itself, though initially only concept, itself has *existence* in order to become *Idea*. The moral point of view therefore takes the shape of the *right of the subjective will*. In accordance with this right, the will can *recognize* something or *be* something only in so far as that thing is *its own*, and in so far as the will is present to itself in it as subjectivity.

> As far as this aspect is concerned, the process of the moral point of view referred to above (see Remarks to § 106) takes the following shape: it is the development of the *right* of the subjective will – or of its mode of existence – whereby this subjective will further determines what it recognizes as its own in its object [*Gegenstand*] so that this becomes the will's true concept – i.e. becomes objective in the sense of the will's own universality.

Addition (H). This entire determination of the subjectivity of the will is again a whole which, as subjectivity, must also have objectivity. Only in the subject can freedom be realized, for the subject is the true material for this realization. But this existence of the will which we have called subjectivity is different from the will which has being in and for itself. For in order to become the latter, the will must free itself from this second one-sidedness of mere subjectivity. In morality, it is the distinctive interest of the human being which comes into question, and the high value of this interest consists precisely in the fact that the human being knows himself as absolute and determines himself. The uncivilized [*ungebildete*] human being lets everything be dictated to him by brute force and by natural conditions; children have no moral will and allow themselves to be determined by their parents; but the cultivated [*gebildete*] and inwardly developing human being wills that he should himself be present in everything he does.

§ 108

The subjective will, as immediate for itself and distinct from that which has being in itself (see Remarks to § 106), is therefore abstract, circumscribed [*beschränkt*], and formal. But not only is subjectivity [itself] formal; as the infinite self-determination of the will, it also constitutes the *formal aspect* of the will [in general]. When it makes this first appearance in the individual [*einzelnen*] will, it has not yet been posited as identical with the concept of the will, so that the moral point of view is consequently the point of view of *relationship, obligation*, or *requirement*. – And since the difference [*Differenz*] of subjectivity likewise contains the determination whereby it is opposed to objectivity as external existence [*Dasein*], we also encounter here the point of view of *consciousness* (see § 8) – in general, the point of view of the difference, *finitude*, and *appearance* of the will.

The moral is not primarily defined [*bestimmt*] simply as the opposite of immoral, just as right is not in an immediate sense the opposite of wrong. On the contrary, the universal point of view of the moral and the immoral alike is based on the subjectivity of the will.

Addition (H). In morality, self-determination should be thought of as sheer restless activity which cannot yet arrive at something *that is*. Only in the ethical realm does the will become identical with the concept of the will and have the latter alone as its content. In the moral sphere, the will still relates to that which has being in itself; it is thus the point of view of *difference*, and the process associated with it is that whereby the subjective will achieves identity with its concept. The obligation which is therefore still present in morality is fulfilled only in the ethical realm. In addition, this 'other' to which the subjective will stands in relation is twofold: first, it is the substantial element of the concept, and secondly, it is that which exists externally. Even if the *good* were posited in the subjective will, this would not yet amount to its implementation.

§ 109

In accordance with its universal determination, this formal aspect [of the will] contains in the first place the opposition between subjectivity and objectivity and the activity associated with this opposition (see § 8). More precisely, its moments are as follows: *existence [Dasein]* and *determinacy* are identical in the concept (cf. § 104), and the will as subjective is itself this concept. The two sides [i.e. subjectivity and objectivity] must be distinguished – each as *independent [für sich]* – and posited as identical. In the self-determining will, determinacy is (α) initially posited *in the will* by the will itself – as its particularization within itself, a *content* which it gives to itself. This is the *first* negation, and the formal limitation [*Grenze*] of this negation is that it is merely something *posited* and subjective. As *infinite reflection* into itself this limitation is present *for the will itself*, and the will is (β) the aspiration [*Wollen*] to overcome [*aufzuheben*] this restriction [*Schranke*] – i.e. the *activity* of translating this content from subjectivity into objectivity in general, into an *immediate existence.*[1] (γ) The simple *identity* of the will with itself in this opposition is the *content* or *end* which remains constant in the two opposites and indifferent towards these differences of form.

§ 110

But this identity of content receives its more precise and distinctive determination within the moral point of view, in which freedom, this identity of the will with itself, is present *for* the will (see § 105).

(a) The content is determined for me as *mine* in such a way that, in its identity, it *contains* my subjectivity *for me* not only as my *inner* end, but also in so far as this end has achieved *external objectivity.*

Addition (H). The content of the subjective or moral will contains a determination of its own: even if it has attained the form of objectivity, it should nevertheless still contain my subjectivity, and my act should be recognized only in so far as it was inwardly determined by me as my purpose and intention. Only what was already present in my subjective will do I recognize as mine in that will's expression, and I expect to re-encounter my subjective consciousness in it.

§ 111

(b) Although the content does include something particular – regardless of where this may have come from – it nevertheless embodies, as the content of the will *reflected into itself* in its determinacy, and hence of the self-identical and universal will, (α) the inner determination of being in conformity with the will which has being in itself, or of possessing the *objectivity of the concept*; but (β) because the subjective will, in so far as it has being for itself, is at the same time still formal (see § 108), this is only a *requirement*, and it still includes the possibility of [the content] not being in conformity with the concept.

§ 112

(c) While I *preserve* my subjectivity in implementing my ends (see § 110), in the course of thus objectifying them I *at the same time* supersede this subjectivity in its *immediacy*, and hence in its character as my individual subjectivity. But the external subjectivity which is thus identical with me is the *will* of others (see § 73). – The basis of the will's *existence* [*Existenz*] is now *subjectivity* (see § 106), and the will of others is the existence [*Existenz*] which I give to my end, and which is for me at the same time an other. – The implementation of my end therefore has this identity of my will and the will of others within it – it has a *positive* reference to the will of others.

> The *objectivity* of the end, once it is implemented, therefore encompasses three meanings – or rather it contains as a unity the following three moments: it is (α) *external* immediate existence [*Dasein*] (see § 109), (β) in conformity with the *concept* (see § 112), and (γ) *universal* subjectivity. The *subjectivity* which is *preserved* in this objectivity is such that (α) the objective end is *my* end, so that I am preserved in it as *this* individual (see § 110); moments (β) and (γ) of subjectivity coincide with moments (β) and (γ) of objectivity (see above). – That these determinations, which from the point of view of morality are distinct from one another, are thus united only as a *contradiction* constitutes more precisely the *finitude* of this sphere, or its character as *appearance* (see § 108); and the development of this point of view is the development of these

contradictions and their resolutions (although such resolutions, within this sphere, can only be *relative*).

Addition (H). In connection with formal right, we noted that it contained only prohibitions, and that an action strictly in keeping with right consequently had a purely negative determination in respect of the will of others. In morality, on the other hand, the determination of my will with reference to the will of others is positive – that is, the will which has being in itself is inwardly present in what the subjective will realizes. This entails the production or alteration of something existent, which in turn has reference to the will of others. The concept of morality is the will's inner attitude [*Verhalten*] towards itself. But not just *one* will is present here. On the contrary, its objectivization also contains the determination whereby the individual will within it is superseded; and in consequence, since the determination of one-sidedness disappears, two wills with a positive reference to one another are now posited. In the context of right, any intentions which the will of others may have with reference to my will, which gives itself existence [*Dasein*] in property, are irrelevant. In the moral sphere, however, the welfare of others is also involved, and it is only at this point that this positive reference can come into play.

§ 113

The expression of the will as *subjective* or *moral* is *action*. Action contains the following determinations: (α) it must be known by me in its externality as mine; (β) its essential relation [*Beziehung*] to the concept is one of obligation; and (γ) it has an essential relation [*Beziehung*] to the will of others.

> Only with the expression of the moral will do we come to *action*. The *existence* [*Dasein*] which the will gives to itself in formal right is located in an *immediate thing* [*Sache*] and is itself immediate. Initially, it does not in itself [*für sich*] have any *explicit* reference to the concept, which is not yet opposed to or distinguished from the subjective will, nor does it have a *positive* reference to the will of others; in its basic determination, a commandment of right is merely a *prohibition* (see § 38). Contract and wrong do admittedly begin to have a reference to the will of others – but the *agreement* which is concluded in the former is based on arbitrariness; and its *essential* reference to the will of the other is, in terms of right, a

negative one, inasmuch as I retain my property (in terms of its value) and allow the other party to retain his. On the other hand, that aspect of crime which has its source in the *subjective will*, and the manner of its existence [*Existenz*] in that will, only now come into consideration. – The content of a legal [*gerichtliche*] action (*actio*), which is determined by rules, is not imputable to me; it thus contains only some of the moments of moral action proper, and these are only *externally* present. That aspect of action which makes it moral in the proper sense is therefore distinct from its legal [*gerichtliche*] side.

§ 114

The right of the moral will contains three aspects:

(a) The *abstract* or *formal* right of action, according to which the content of my action, as accomplished in *immediate* existence [*Dasein*], is entirely *mine*, so that the action is the *purpose* of the subjective will.

(b) The *particular* aspect of the action is its *inner* content, (α) i.e. the manner in which its universal character is determined *for me* – this constitutes the *value* of the action and the reason why I consider it valid, i.e. its *intention*; (β) its content, as the *particular* [*besonderer*] end of my particular [*partikulären*] and subjective existence, is *welfare*.

(c) This content, though *inward* in character, is at the same time raised to its *universality* and thus to that *objectivity* which has being in and for itself; as such, it is the absolute end of the will, i.e. the *good*, and its opposite, in the sphere of reflection, is *subjective* universality, either of *evil* or of the *conscience*.

Addition (H). For an action to be moral, it must in the first place correspond to my purpose, for it is the right of the moral will to recognize, in its existence, only what was inwardly present as purpose. Purpose concerns only the formal condition that the external will should also be present within me as an internal element. In the second moment, on the other hand, the question arises of the intention behind the action – that is, of the relative value of the action in relation [*Beziehung*] to me. And lastly, the third moment is not just the relative value of the action, but its universal value, the *good*. The first division in [moral] action is that between what is purposed and what is accomplished in the realm of existence; the second is between what is present externally as universal will and the particular inner determination which I give to it; and lastly, the third factor is that the intention should also be the universal content [of the action]. The good is the intention, raised to the concept of the will.

Purpose and Responsibility

§ 115

The *finitude* of the subjective will in the immediacy of action consists immediately in the fact that the action of the will *presupposes* an external object [*Gegenstand*] with various attendant circumstances. The *deed* posits an alteration to this given existence [*Dasein*], and the will is entirely *responsible* for it in so far as the abstract predicate '*mine*' attaches to the existence so altered.

> An event, or a situation which has arisen, is a *concrete* external actuality which accordingly has an indeterminable number of attendant circumstances. Every individual moment which is shown to have been a *condition*, *ground*, or *cause* of some such circumstance and has thereby contributed *its share* to it may be regarded as being *wholly*, or at least *partly*, *responsible* for it. In the case of a complex event (such as the French Revolution), the formal understanding can therefore choose which of a countless number of circumstances it wishes to make responsible for the event.

Addition (H). I can be made responsible for whatever was contained in my purpose, and this is the chief consideration as far as crime is concerned. But responsibility involves only the wholly external judgement as to whether I have done something or not; and the fact that I am responsible for something does not mean that the thing [*Sache*] can be imputed to me.

§ 116

It is admittedly not of my doing if damage is caused to others by things [*Dinge*] of which I am the owner and which, as external objects, exist and function within a varied context (as may even be the case with myself as a mechanical body or living entity). But the damage is *more* or *less* my fault, because the things which caused it are after all mine, although they are in turn only more or less subject to my control, supervision, etc., according to their own distinct nature.

§ 117

The autonomously acting will, in the ends which it pursues in relation to the existence [*Dasein*] it has before it, has an *idea* [*Vorstellung*] *of the circumstances which that existence involves.* But since, on account of this presupposition, the will is *finite*, the objective phenomenon [*gegenständliche Erscheinung*] is *contingent* for it, and may contain something other than what was present in the will's idea [*Vorstellung*] of it. It is, however, the right of the will to recognize as its *action*, and to accept *responsibility* for, only those aspects of its *deed* which it knew to be presupposed within its end, and which were present in its *purpose.* – I can be made *accountable* for a deed only if *my will was responsible* for it – *the right of knowledge.*

Addition (H). The will has before it an existence upon which it acts; but to be able to do this, it must have an idea [*Vorstellung*] of that existence. I am truly responsible only in so far as I had knowledge of the existence before me. Since the will has a presupposition of this kind, it is finite – or rather, since it is finite, it has a presupposition of this kind. In so far as my thinking and volition are rational, my point of view is not that of finitude, because the object [*Gegenstand*] upon which I act is not something other in relation to me. But limitation and restriction are always inherent in finitude. I am confronted with an other which is only contingent and only externally necessary, and which may either coincide with or be at variance with me. But I am only what has reference to my freedom, and my will is responsible for a deed only in so far as I have knowledge of it. Oedipus, who unwittingly killed his father, cannot be accused of parricide, although the legal codes of antiquity attached less importance to the subjective element, to responsibility [*Zurechnung*], than is the case today. This is why sanctuaries were established in antiquity, to receive and protect fugitives from vengeance.[1]

§ 118

Furthermore, action has multiple *consequences* in so far as it is translated into external existence [*Dasein*]; for the latter, by virtue of its context in external necessity, develops in all directions. These consequences, as the [outward] *shape* whose *soul* is the *end* to which the action is directed, belong to the action as an integral part of it. But the action, as the end translated into the *external world*, is at the same time exposed to external forces which attach to it things quite different from what it is for itself, and impel it on into remote and alien consequences. The will thus has the right *to accept responsibility* only for the first set of consequences, since they alone were part of its *purpose*.

The distinction between *contingent* and *necessary* consequences is indeterminate inasmuch as inner necessity comes into existence in the finite realm as *external* necessity, as a relationship between individual things [*Dingen*] which, as self-sufficient entities, come together in mutual indifference and in an external manner. The maxim [*Grundsatz*] which enjoins us to disregard the consequences of our actions, and the other which enjoins us to judge actions by their consequences and make the latter the yardstick of what is right and good, are in equal measure [products of the] abstract understanding. In so far as the consequences are the proper and *immanent* shape of the action, they manifest only its nature and are nothing other than the action itself; for this reason, the action cannot repudiate or disregard them.[1] But conversely, the consequences also include external interventions and contingent additions which have nothing to do with the nature of the action itself. – The development in the realm of existence of the contradiction which is contained in the *necessity of the finite* is simply the transformation of necessity into contingency and vice versa. From this point of view, to act therefore means *to submit oneself to this law*. – It follows from this that the criminal stands to benefit if his action has less adverse consequences, just as the good action must accept that it may have no consequences or relatively few; and it also follows that, once the consequences of a crime have developed more fully, the crime

itself is made responsible for them. – The *heroic* self-consciousness (as in ancient tragedies like that of Oedipus) has
not yet progressed from its unalloyed simplicity to reflect on
the distinction between *deed* and *action*, between the external
event and the purpose and knowledge of the circumstances, or
to analyse the consequences minutely, but accepts responsibility for the deed in its entirety.[2]

Addition (H). The fact that I recognize only what I had an idea [*Vorstellung*][a] of constitutes the transition to intention. For I can be made responsible only for what I knew of the circumstances. But necessary
consequences attach themselves to every action – even if what I initiate is
purely individual and immediate – and they are to that extent the universal element contained within it. It is true that I cannot foresee those
consequences which might be prevented, but I must be familiar with the
universal nature of the individual deed.[3] What is at issue here is not the
individual aspect but the whole, which concerns not the determinate
character of the particular action but its universal nature. The transition
from purpose to intention consists, then, in the fact that I ought to be
aware not only of my individual action, but also of the universal which is
associated with it. When it emerges in this manner, the universal is what I
have willed, i.e. my *intention*.

[a]*Translator's note:* In Hotho's notes (VPR III, 362), on which this Addition is based, the
equivalent word is in fact *Vorsatz* ('purpose'), which would yield the translation 'only
what was my purpose'.

Intention and Welfare

§ 119

The external existence [*Dasein*] of an action is a varied set of connections which may be regarded as infinitely divided into *individual units* [*Einzelheiten*], and the action itself can be thought of as having *touched only one of these units in the first instance*. But the truth of the *individual* [*des Einzelnen*] is the *universal*, and the determinate character of the action for itself is not an isolated content confined to one external unit, but a *universal* content containing within itself all its various connections. The purpose, as emanating from a *thinking* agent, contains not just the individual unit, but essentially that *universal aspect* already referred to – the *intention*.

[The word for] *intention* contains in its etymology [the idea of] *abstraction,*[a] either as the form of *universality* or as the selection of a *particular* aspect of the concrete thing [*Sache*]. To attempt to justify something in terms of its intention is to isolate an individual aspect completely and to maintain that it is the subjective essence of the action. – To judge an action as an external deed without first determining whether it is right or wrong is to apply a *universal* predicate to it, classifying it as arson, murder, or the like. – By its determination, external actuality consists of *individual units*, which shows that external *connections* are inherent in its *nature*. Actuality is touched in

[a] *Translator's note: Absicht* ('intention') is derived from the verb *absehen* ('to look away'), and Hegel associates it with the idea of abstraction as a 'looking away' from whatever is to be abstracted from.

the first instance only at one individual point (just as in arson, the flame is applied directly only to a small portion of the wood – this yields only a proposition, not a judgement), but the universal nature of this point implies its expansion. In living organisms, the individual [component] exists immediately not as a part, but as an organ in which the universal as such has its present existence. Hence in murder, it is not a piece of flesh as an individual entity which is injured, but the life itself within it. On the one hand, subjective reflection, ignorant of the logical nature of the individual and the universal, indulges in the minute analysis of individual units and consequences; and on the other hand, it is in the nature of the finite deed itself to contain such separable contingencies. – The notion of *dolus indirectus*[a1] was invented for the reason [*Grund*] just considered.

Addition (H). It is certainly the case that a greater or lesser number of circumstances may intervene in the course of an action. In a case of arson, for example, the fire may not take hold, or conversely, it may spread further than the culprit intended. Nevertheless, no distinction should be made here between good and ill fortune, for in their actions, human beings are necessarily involved in externality. An old proverb rightly says, 'The stone belongs to the devil when it leaves the hand that threw it.'[2] By acting, I expose myself to misfortune, which accordingly has a right over me and is an existence of my own volition.

[a]Translator's note: 'indirect wrong'.

§ 120

The *right of intention* is that the *universal* quality of the action shall have being not only *in itself*, but shall be *known* by the agent and thus have been present all along in his subjective will; and conversely, what we may call the right of the *objectivity* of the action is the right of the action to assert itself as known and willed by the subject as a *thinking agent*.

The right to such insight implies that the *responsibility* of children, imbeciles, lunatics, etc. for their actions is either totally *absent* or diminished. – But just as actions, in their external existence [*Dasein*], include contingent consequences, so also does *subjective* existence contain an indeterminacy as far as the power and strength of self-consciousness and presence of mind are concerned. This indeterminacy, however, can be taken into account only in connection with imbecility, lunacy, etc., and with childhood, because only such pronounced conditions as these can annul [*aufheben*] the character of thought and free will and allow us to deny the agent the dignity [*Ehre*] of being a thinking individual and a will.

§ 121

The universal quality of an action is the varied *content* of the action in general, reduced to the *simple form* of universality. But the subject, as reflected into itself and hence as a *particular* entity in relation to the particularity of the objective realm, has its own particular content in its end, and this is the soul and determinant of the action. The fact that this moment of the *particularity* of the agent is contained and implemented in the action constitutes *subjective freedom* in its more concrete determination, i.e. the *right* of the *subject* to find its *satisfaction* in the action.

Addition (H). I for myself, reflected into myself, am still a particular entity in relation to the externality of my action. My *end* constitutes the determining content of the action. Murder and arson, for example, as universals, do not constitute my positive content as a subject. If someone has perpetrated crimes of this kind, we ask why he committed them. The murder was not committed for the sake of murder; on the contrary, some particular positive end was also present. If we were to say, however, that the murder was committed for the pleasure of killing, then this pleasure would itself be the positive content of the subject as such, and the deed would then be the satisfaction of the subject's volition. Thus the *motive* [*Beweggrund*] of a deed is more precisely what we call the *moral* element, and this, in the present context, has two meanings – the universal which is inherent in the purpose, and the particular aspect of the intention. In recent times especially, it has become customary to enquire about the motives of actions, although the question used simply to be 'Is this man honest [*rechtschaffen*]? Does he do his duty?' Now, we seek to look into people's hearts, and thereby presuppose a gulf between the objective realm of actions and the inner, subjective realm of motives. The

determination of the subject must certainly be considered: it wills something whose ground lies within the subject itself; it wills the fulfilment of
its desire and the gratification of its passion. But the good and the right
are also a content – not just a natural content, but a content posited by my
rationality; and to make my freedom the content of my will is a pure
determination of my freedom itself. The higher moral viewpoint therefore
consists in finding satisfaction in one's action, not in stopping short at the
gulf between the self-consciousness of the human being and the objectivity of the deed – although the latter attitude does predominate in
certain periods of world history and of the lives of individuals.

§ 122

This particular aspect gives the action its subjective *value* and *interest*
for me. In contrast with this end – i.e. *the intention from the point of view
of its content* – the immediate character of the action in its further
content is reduced to a means. In so far as such an end is a finite one,
it may in turn be reduced to a means to some further intention, and so
on in an infinite progression.

§ 123

For the content of these ends, all that presents itself here is (α) formal
activity itself, inasmuch as the subject *actively* commits itself to
whatever it is to regard and promote as its end – for human beings
wish to act in support of whatever interests them, or should interest
them, as their own. (β) But the as yet abstract and formal freedom of
subjectivity has a more determinate content only in its *natural subjective existence* [*Dasein*] – its needs, inclinations, passions, opinions,
fancies, etc. The satisfaction of this content is *welfare* or *happiness*,
both in its particular determinations and in its universal aspect – the
ends of finitude in general.

> This is the point of view of *relationship* (see § 108), where the
> subject is determined in its differentiation and so counts as
> something *particular*, and where the content of the natural will
> makes its appearance (see § 11). But the will here is not as it is
> in its immediacy; instead, this content, belonging as it does to
> the will reflected into itself, is raised to a *universal* end, namely
> that of *welfare* or *happiness* (see *Encyclopaedia of the Philosophical*

Sciences, §§ 395ff.).¹ This is the point of view of thought which does not yet comprehend the will in its freedom, but *reflects* on its content as something natural and given – as, for example, in the days of Croesus and Solon.²

Addition (H). In so far as the determinations of happiness are present and given, they are not true determinations of freedom, which is not truly present for *itself* until it has adopted the good as an end in itself. We may ask at this point whether the human being has a right to set himself ends which are not based on freedom, but solely on the fact that the subject is a living being. The fact that he is a living being is not contingent, however, but in accordance with reason, and to that extent he has a right to make his needs his end. There is nothing degrading about being alive, and we do not have the alternative of existing in a higher spirituality. It is only by raising what is present and given to a self-creating process that the higher sphere of the good is attained (although this distinction does not imply that the two aspects are incompatible).

§ 124

Since the *subjective* satisfaction of the individual himself (including his recognition in the shape of honour and fame) is also to be found in the implementation of ends *which are valid in and for themselves*, it is an empty assertion of the abstract understanding to require that only an end of this kind shall appear willed and attained, and likewise to take the view that, in volition, objective and subjective ends are mutually exclusive. Indeed, such attitudes become even worse if they lead to the assertion that, because subjective satisfaction is present (as it *always* is when a task is completed), it constitutes the agent's *essential intention* to which the objective end was merely a *means*. – What the subject *is, is the series of its actions*. If these are a series of worthless productions, then the subjectivity of volition is likewise worthless; and conversely, if the series of the individual's deeds are of a substantial nature, then so also is his inner will.¹

> The right of the subject's *particularity* to find satisfaction, or – to put it differently – the right of *subjective freedom*, is the pivotal and focal point in the difference between *antiquity* and the *modern* age. This right, in its infinity, is expressed in Christianity, and it has become the universal and actual principle of a new form of the world. Its more specific shapes

include love, the romantic, the eternal salvation of the individual as an end, etc.; then there are morality and conscience, followed by the other forms, some of which will come into prominence below as the principle of civil society and as moments of the political constitution, while others appear within history at large, particularly in the history of art, the sciences, and philosophy. – Now this principle of particularity is admittedly a moment within an antithesis, and in the first instance at least, it is *just as much* identical with the universal as distinct from it. But abstract reflection fixes this moment in its difference from and opposition to the universal, and so produces a view of morality as a perennial and hostile struggle against one's own satisfaction, as in the injunction: 'Do with repugnance what duty commands.'*2* This same [use of the] understanding produces that psychological view of history which contrives to belittle and debase all great deeds and individuals by transforming into the main intention and effective spring [*Triebfeder*] of actions those inclinations and passions which were simultaneously satisfied by substantial activity, along with fame and honour and other consequences – indeed that whole particular aspect which it had declared in advance to be inherently inferior. The same attitude assures us that, since great actions and the activity associated with a series of these have accomplished great things in the world and have consequently brought power, honour, and fame to the *individual agent*, it is not the greatness itself which belongs to the individual, but only those particular and external consequences which accrued to him from it; and since this particular aspect is a consequence [of the individual's action], it is also supposed *for this reason* to have been the end, and indeed even the sole end in view. – Such reflection as this fixes upon the subjective side of great individuals – for its own basis is likewise subjective – and *overlooks* the substantial element in this edifice of vanity which it has itself constructed. This is the view of 'those psychological *valets de chambre* for whom there are no heroes, not because the latter are not heroes, but because the former are only *valets de chambre*' (see *Phenomenology of Spirit*, p. 616).*3*

Addition (H). 'In magnis voluisse sat est'ᵃ rightly signifies that we ought to will something great. But we must also be able to implement it, or else our willing is futile [*nichtig*]. The laurels of mere willing are dry leaves which have never been green.

ᵃ*Translator's note:* 'In great things, it is sufficient to have willed.'⁴

§ 125

Subjectivity, with its *particular* content of *welfare*, is reflected into itself and infinite, and consequently also has reference to the universal, to the will which has being in itself. This [universal] moment, initially posited within this particularity itself, includes *the welfare of others* – or in its complete, but wholly empty determination, the welfare of *all*. The welfare of *many other* particular beings in general is thus also an essential end and right of subjectivity. But since the *universal which has being in and for itself*, as distinct from such particular [kinds of] content, has not so far been determined beyond the stage of *right*, these ends of particularity, different as they are from the universal, may be in conformity with it – but alternatively, they may not.

§ 126

My particularity, however, like that of others, is only a right at all in so far as I am *free*. It cannot therefore assert itself in contradiction to this substantial basis on which it rests; and an intention to promote my welfare and that of others – and in the latter case in particular it is called a *moral intention* – cannot justify an *action which is wrong*.

> One of the most conspicuous among the corrupt maxims of our time is that we ought to interest ourselves in the so-called *moral intention* behind *wrong* actions, and to imagine [*vorzustellen*] inferior [*schlechte*] subjects with allegedly good hearts, i.e. hearts which will their own welfare and perhaps even the welfare of others. This maxim derives in part from the pre-Kantian period of sensibility [*guten Herzens*]¹ and constitutes, for example, the quintessence of familiar and affecting dramatic presentations.² But this doctrine has also been revived in a more extreme shape, and inner enthusiasm and

the emotions, i.e. the *form* of particularity as such, have been made the criterion of what is right, rational, and excellent. As a result, crimes and their guiding principles, even if these should be the most banal and empty fancies and foolish opinions, are presented as right, rational, and excellent on the grounds that they are based on the *emotions* and on *enthusiasm* (for further details, see Remarks to § 140 below). – In addition, we must bear in mind the point of view from which right and welfare are being examined here – namely as formal right and the particular welfare of the individual [*des Einzelnen*]. The so-called *common weal* or *welfare* of the state, i.e. the right of the actual and concrete spirit, is an altogether different sphere, in which formal right is just as much a subordinate moment as particular welfare and the happiness of the individual. We have already noted above [see § 29] that one of the commonest errors of abstraction is to insist on private rights and private welfare *as valid in and for themselves* in opposition to the universality of the state.

Addition (H). The famous answer 'je n'en vois pas la nécessité'*ᵃ* which was given to the libeller who excused himself by saying 'il faut donc que je vive'*ᵇ* is relevant here.³ For life, when confronted with the higher realm of freedom, is not necessary at all. When St Crispin stole leather to make shoes for the poor, his action was both moral and wrong, and hence invalid.⁴

> *ᵃTranslator's note:* 'I do not see the need for it.'
> *ᵇTranslator's note:* 'But I have to live.'

§ 127

The *particularity* of the interests of the natural will, taken together as a simple *totality*, is personal existence [*Dasein*] as *life*. *In extreme danger* and in collision with the rightful property of someone else, this life may claim (not in equity, but as a right) a *right of necessity*;¹ for the alternatives are an infinite injury [*Verletzung*] to existence with total loss of rights, and an injury only to an individual and limited existence of freedom, whereby right as such and the capacity for rights of the injured party, who has been injured only in *this* specific property, continue to be recognized.

From the right of necessity arises the benefit of competence, whereby a debtor is permitted to retain his tools, agricultural implements, clothes, and in general as much of his resources – i.e. of the property of his creditors – as is deemed necessary to support him, even in his accustomed station in society.

Addition (H). Life, as the totality of ends, has a right in opposition to abstract right. If, for example, it can be preserved by stealing a loaf, this certainly constitutes an infringement of someone's property, but it would be wrong to regard such an action as common theft. If someone whose life is in danger were not allowed to take measures to save himself, he would be destined to forfeit all his rights; and since he would be deprived of life, his entire freedom would be negated. There are certainly many prerequisites for the preservation of life, and if we look to the future, we must concern ourselves with such details. But the only thing that is necessary is to live *now*; the future is not absolute, and it remains exposed to contingency. Consequently, only the necessity [*Not*] of the immediate present can justify a wrong action, because its omission would in turn involve committing a wrong – indeed the ultimate wrong, namely the total negation of the existence of freedom. The *beneficium competentiae*² is of relevance here, because links of kinship and other close relationships entail the right to demand that no one should be sacrificed completely for the sake of right.

§ 128

Such necessity [*Not*] reveals the finitude and hence the contingency of both right and welfare – of the abstract existence [*Dasein*] of freedom as distinct from the existence [*Existenz*] of the particular person, and of the sphere of the particular will as distinct from the universality of right. Their one-sided and ideal character is thereby posited, just as it was already determined for them in their concept. Right has already (see § 106) determined its *existence* [*Dasein*] as the particular will; and subjectivity, in its comprehensive particularity, is itself the existence [*Dasein*] of freedom (see § 127), just as it is in itself, as the infinite self-reference of the will, the universal aspect of freedom. The two moments in right and subjectivity, thus integrated so as to attain their truth and identity – though initially still in a *relative* relation [*Beziehung*] to one another – are the *good* (as the *fulfilled* universal, determined in and for itself) and the *conscience* (as infinite and inwardly knowing [*wissende*]*ᵃ* subjectivity which determines its content within itself).

ᵃTranslator's note: Here, and throughout the following section (Section 3), Hegel exploits the etymological relationship between *Gewissen* ('conscience'), *Wissen* ('knowledge'), and *Gewißheit* ('certainty') to suggest an affinity between their meanings. It is, unfortunately, impossible to retain these associations in English translation.

The Good and the Conscience

§ 129

The *good* is the *Idea*, as the unity of the *concept* of the will and the *particular* will, in which abstract right, welfare, the subjectivity of knowing, and the contingency of external existence [*Dasein*], as *self-sufficient for themselves*, are superseded; but they are at the same time *essentially contained* and *preserved* within it. – [The good is] *realized freedom, the absolute and ultimate end of the world.*

Addition (H). Every stage is in fact the Idea, but the earlier stages contain it only in more abstract form. For example, even the 'I' as personality is already the Idea, but in its most abstract shape. The good is therefore the *Idea as further determined*, the unity of the concept of the will and the particular will. It does not belong to abstract right, but has a complete content whose import encompasses both right and welfare.

§ 130

Within this idea, welfare has no validity for itself as the existence [*Dasein*] of the individual and particular will, but only as *universal* welfare and essentially as *universal in itself*, i.e. in accordance with freedom; welfare is not a good without *right*. Similarly, right is not the good without welfare (*fiat iustitia* should not have *pereat mundus*[a1] as its consequence). Thus, since the good must necessarily be actualized through the particular will, and since it is at the same time the latter's

---

[a]*Translator's note:* The Latin saying which Hegel splits into two parts means roughly: 'Let justice be done, even if the world should perish.'

substance, it has an *absolute right* as distinct from the abstract right of property and the particular ends of welfare. In so far as either of the latter moments is distinguished from the good, it has validity only in so far as it is in conformity with it and subordinate to it.

§ 131

For the *subjective* will, the good is likewise absolutely essential, and the subjective will has worth and dignity only in so far as its insight and intention are in conformity with the good. In so far as the good is still at this point this *abstract Idea* of the good, the subjective will is not yet posited as assimilated to it and in conformity with it. It thus stands in a *relationship* to the good, a relationship whereby the good *ought* to be its substantial character, whereby it ought to make the good its end and fulfil it – just as it is only in the subjective will that the good for its part has the means of entering into actuality.

Addition (H). The good is the truth of the particular will, but the will is only what it commits itself to; it is not by nature good, but can become what it is only by its own efforts. On the other hand, the good itself, without the subjective will, is only an abstraction, devoid of that reality which it is destined to achieve only through the subjective will. The development of the good accordingly has three stages: (1) the good must be a particular will for me – since I am a will myself – and I must know it; (2) the nature of the good must be stated, and the particular determinations of the good must be developed; (3) and lastly, the good must be determined for itself and particularized as infinite subjectivity which has being for itself. This inward determination is conscience.

§ 132

The *right of the subjective will* is that whatever it is to recognize as valid should be *perceived* by it *as good*, and that it should be held responsible for an action – as its aim translated into external objectivity – as right or wrong, good or evil, legal or illegal, according to its cognizance [*Kenntnis*] of the value which that action has in this objectivity.

> The *good* is in general the essence of the will in its *substantiality* and *universality* – the will in its truth; the good therefore exists without exception only *in thought* and *through thought*. Consequently, the assertion that human beings cannot know

[*erkennen*] the truth, but have to do only with appearances, or that thought is harmful to the good will, and other similar notions [*Vorstellungen*], deprive the spirit both of intellectual and of all ethical worth and dignity. – The right to recognize nothing that I do not perceive as rational is the highest right of the subject, but by virtue of its subjective determination, it is at the same time *formal*; on the other hand, *the right of the rational* – as the objective – over the subject remains firmly established. – Because of its formal determination, insight is equally capable of being *true* and of being mere *opinion* and *error*. From the point of view of what is still the sphere of morality, the individual's attainment of this right of insight depends upon his particular subjective education. I may require of myself and regard it as an inner subjective right that my insight into an obligation should be based on *good* reasons and that I should be *convinced* by it, and in addition, that I should recognize it in terms of its concept and nature. But whatever I may require in order to satisfy my conviction that an action is good, permissible, or impermissible – and hence that the agent is in this respect responsible for it – in no way detracts from the *right of objectivity*. – This right of insight into the *good* is distinct from the right of insight with regard to *action* as such (see § 117). As far as the latter is concerned, the right of objectivity takes the following shape: since action is an alteration which must exist in an actual world and thus seeks recognition in it, it must in general conform to what is *recognized as valid* in that world. Whoever wills an action in the actual world has, *in so doing*, submitted himself to its laws and recognized the right of objectivity. – Similarly, in the *state*, as the *objectivity* of the concept of reason, *legal responsibility [die gerichtliche Zurechnung]* must not stop at what the individual considers to be in conformity with his reason or otherwise, or at his subjective insight into rightness or wrongness, good or evil, or at what he may require in order to satisfy his conviction. In this objective field, the right of insight applies to insight into *legality* or *illegality*, i.e. into what is *recognized* as right, and is confined to its primary meaning, namely *cognizance [Kenntnis]* in the sense of *familiarity* with what is legal and to that extent obligatory. Through the public nature of the laws and the universality of customs, the state takes away from the right of insight its formal aspect and that contingency which this right still has for the subject within the prevailing viewpoint [of morality]. The right of the subject to know [*kennen*] action in its determination of *good* or *evil*, legal or illegal, has the effect, in the case of children, imbeciles, and lunatics, of diminishing or annulling [*aufzuheben*] their responsibility in this respect, too; but it is impossible to impose a definite limit [*bestimmte Grenze*] on these conditions and the level of responsibility associated with them. But to make momentary blindness, the excitement of passion, intoxication, or in general what is described as the strength of sensuous motives [*Triebfedern*] (but excluding anything which gives grounds for a right of necessity – see § 127)ᵃ into grounds for attributing responsibility or determining the [nature of the] *crime* itself and its *culpability*, and to consider such circumstances as taking away the criminal's *guilt* [*Schuld*], is once again (cf. § 100 and Remarks to § 120)ᵇ to deny the criminal the right and dignity [*Ehre*] of a human being; for the nature of a human being consists precisely in the fact that he is essentially universal in character, not an abstraction of the moment and a single fragment of knowledge. – Just as what the arsonist sets on fire is not the isolated area of wood an inch wide to which he applies the flame, but the universal within it – i.e. the entire house – so, too, is the arsonist himself, as a subject, not just the individual aspect of *this* moment or this isolated passion for revenge. If he were so, he would be an animal which should be hit on the head because of its dangerousness and proneness to unpredictable fits of rage. – It is said that the criminal, at the moment of his action, must have a *clear representation* [*sich . . . müsse vorgestellt haben*] of its wrongfulness and culpability before he can be made responsible for it as a crime. This requirement, which appears to uphold his right of moral subjectivity, in fact denies his inherent nature as an intelligent being; for this nature, in

---

ᵃ*Translator's note:* The reference in most editions of Hegel's text is to § 120, which appears to be an error. I follow Iltings edition in substituting § 127 as more appropriate.
ᵇ*Translator's note:* I follow Ilting in substituting § 120 for § 119, which is given in most earlier editions, including the first.

its active presence, is not confined to the shape it assumes in Wolff's psychology – namely that of *clear representations* [*Vorstellungen*] – and only in cases of madness is it so deranged as to be divorced from the knowledge and performance of individual things [*Dinge*].¹ – The sphere in which the above circumstances come into consideration as grounds for relaxing the punishment is not the sphere of right, but the sphere of *clemency*.

§ 133

The relation of the good to the particular subject is that the good is the *essential* character of the subject's will, which thus has an unqualified *obligation* in this connection. Because *particularity* is distinct from the good and falls within the subjective will, the good is initially determined only as *universal abstract essentiality* – i.e. as *duty*. In view of this determination, *duty* should be done *for the sake of duty*.¹

Addition (H). The essential element of the will for me is duty. Now if I know nothing apart from the fact that the good is my duty, I do not go beyond duty in the abstract. I should do my duty for its own sake, and it is in the true sense my own objectivity that I bring to fulfilment in doing so. In doing my duty, I am with myself [*bei mir selbst*] and free. The merit and exalted viewpoint of Kant's moral philosophy are that it has emphasized this significance of duty.

§ 134

Since action for itself requires a particular content and a determinate end, whereas duty in the abstract contains nothing of the kind, the question arises: *what is duty?* For this definition [*Bestimmung*], all that is available so far is this: to do *right*, and to promote *welfare*, one's own welfare and welfare in its universal determination, the welfare of others (see § 119).

Addition (H). This is the very question which was put to Jesus when someone wished to know what to do in order to gain eternal life.¹ For the universal aspect of good, or good in the abstract, cannot be fulfilled as an abstraction; it must first acquire the further determination of particularity.

§ 135

These determinations, however, are not contained in the determination of duty itself. But since both of them are conditional and limited, they give rise to the transition to the higher sphere of the *unconditional*, the sphere of duty. Hence all that is left for duty itself, in so far as it is the essential or universal element in the moral self-consciousness as it is related within itself to itself alone, is abstract universality, whose determination is *identity without content* or the abstractly *positive*, i.e. the indeterminate.

However essential it may be to emphasize the pure and unconditional self-determination of the will as the root of duty – for knowledge [*Erkenntnis*] of the will first gained a firm foundation and point of departure in the philosophy of Kant, through the thought of its infinite autonomy (see § 133) – to cling on to a merely moral point of view without making the transition to the concept of ethics reduces this gain to an *empty formalism*, and moral science to an empty rhetoric of *duty for duty's sake*. From this point of view, no immanent theory of duties is possible. One may indeed bring in material *from outside* and thereby arrive at *particular* duties, but it is impossible to make the transition to the determination of particular duties from the above determination of duty as *absence of contradiction*, as *formal correspondence with itself*, which is no different from the specification of *abstract indeterminacy*; and even if such a particular content for action is taken into consideration, there is no criterion within that principle for deciding whether or not this content is a duty. On the contrary, it is possible to justify any wrong or immoral mode of action by this means. – Kant's further form – the capacity of an action to be envisaged as a *universal* maxim – does yield a more *concrete* representation [*Vorstellung*] of the situation in question, but it does not in itself [*für sich*] contain any principle apart from formal identity and that absence of contradiction already referred to. – The fact that *no property* is present is in itself [*für sich*] no more contradictory than is the non-existence of this or that individual people, family, etc., or the complete *absence of human life*. But if it is already established and presupposed that property and human life should exist and be respected, then it is a contradiction to commit theft or murder; a contradiction must be a contradiction with something, that is, with a content which is already fundamentally present as an established principle. Only to a principle of this kind does an action stand in a relation [*Beziehung*] of agreement or contradiction. But if a duty is to be willed merely as a duty and not because of its content, it is a *formal identity* which necessarily excludes every content and determination.

The further antinomies and shapes assumed by this perennial *obligation*, among which the merely moral point of view of *relationship* simply drifts to and fro without being able to resolve them and get beyond obligation, are developed in my *Phenomenology of Spirit*, pp. 550ff.; cf. *Encyclopaedia of the Philosophical Sciences*, §§ 420ff.[1]

Addition (H). Whereas we earlier emphasized that the point of view of Kant's philosophy is sublime inasmuch as it asserts the conformity of duty and reason, it must be pointed out here that this point of view is defective in that it lacks all articulation. For the proposition 'Consider whether your maxim can be asserted as a universal principle'[2] would be all very well if we already had determinate principles concerning how to act. In other words, if we demand of a principle that it should also be able to serve as the determinant of a universal legislation, this presupposes that it already has a content; and if this content were present, it would be easy to apply the principle. But in this case, the principle itself is not yet available, and the criterion that there should be no contradiction is non-productive – for where there is nothing, there can be no contradiction either.

§ 136

Because of the abstract character of the good, the other moment of the Idea, i.e. *particularity* in general, falls within subjectivity. Subjectivity, in its universality reflected into itself, is the absolute inward certainty of itself; it is that which posits particularity, and it is the determining and decisive factor – *the conscience*.[1]

Addition (H). One may speak of duty in a most sublime manner, and such talk glorifies the human being and fills his heart with pride. But if it leads to nothing determinate, it ultimately grows tedious, for the spirit requires that particularity to which it is entitled. Conscience, on the other hand, is that deepest inner solitude within oneself in which all externals and all limitation have disappeared – it is a total withdrawal into the self. As conscience, the human being is no longer bound by the ends of particularity, so that conscience represents an exalted point of view, a point of view of the modern world, which has for the first time attained this consciousness, this descent into the self. Earlier and more sensuous ages have before them something external and given, whether this be religion or right; but [my] conscience knows itself as thought, and that this thought of mine is my sole source of obligation.

<h1 style="text-align:center">§ 137</h1>

True conscience is the disposition to will what is good *in and for itself*; it therefore has fixed principles, and these have for it the character of determinacy and duties which are objective for themselves. In contrast to its content – i.e. truth – conscience is merely the *formal aspect* of the activity of the will, which, as *this* will, has no distinctive content of its own. But the objective system of these principles and duties and the union of subjective knowledge with this system are present only when the point of view of ethics has been reached. Here, within the formal point of view of morality, conscience lacks this objective content, and is thus for itself the infinite formal certainty of itself, which for this very reason is at the same time the certainty of *this* subject.

> *Conscience* expresses the absolute entitlement of subjective self-consciousness to know *in itself* and *from itself* what right and duty are, and to recognize only what it thus knows as the good; it also consists in the assertion that what it thus knows and wills is *truly* right and duty. As this unity of subjective knowledge and that which has being in and for itself, conscience is a sanctuary which it would be *sacrilege* to violate. But whether the conscience of a *specific individual* is in conformity with this Idea of conscience, and whether what it *considers* or declares *to be good* is also actually good, can be recognized only from the *content* of this supposed good. What constitutes right and duty, as the rationality in and for itself of the will's determinations, is essentially neither the *particular* property of an individual, nor is its *form* that of feeling [*Empfindung*] or any other individual – i.e. sensuous – kind of knowledge, but essentially that of *universal determinations of thought*, i.e. the

form of *laws* and *principles*. The conscience is therefore subject to judgement as to its *truth* or falsity, and its appeal solely *to itself* is directly opposed to what it seeks to be – that is, the rule for a rational and universal mode of action which is valid in and for itself. Consequently, the state cannot recognize the conscience in its distinctive form, i.e. as *subjective knowledge*, any more than science can grant any validity to subjective *opinion*, *assertion*, and the *appeal* to subjective opinion. What is not distinct within the true conscience is nevertheless distinguishable, and it is the determining subjectivity of knowledge and volition which can separate itself from the true content, posit itself for itself, and reduce the content to a *form* and *semblance*. The ambiguity associated with conscience therefore consists in the fact that conscience is assumed in advance to signify the identity of subjective knowledge and volition with the true good, and is thus declared and acknowledged to be sacrosanct, while it also claims, as the purely subjective reflection of self-consciousness into itself, the authority [*Berechtigung*] which belongs only to that identity itself by virtue of its rational content which is valid in and for itself. The point of view of morality, which is distinguished in this treatise from that of ethics, includes only the formal conscience; the true conscience has been mentioned only in order to indicate its different character, and to prevent the possible misunderstanding to the effect that we are here discussing the true conscience rather than the formal conscience, which is in fact our exclusive concern. The true conscience is contained in the ethical disposition, which will be considered only in the following section. The religious conscience, however, lies completely outside this sphere.[1]

Addition (H). When we speak of conscience, it may easily be thought that, because its form is that of abstract inwardness, it is already in and for itself the true conscience. But the true conscience is that which determines itself to will what is in and for itself the good and a duty. Here, however, we are dealing only with good in the abstract, and conscience still lacks this objective content and is as yet only the infinite certainty of itself.

§ 138

This subjectivity, as abstract self-determination and pure certainty of itself alone, *evaporates* into itself all *determinate* aspects of right, duty, and existence [*Dasein*], inasmuch as it is the power of *judgement* which determines solely from within itself what is good in relation to a given content, and at the same time the power to which the good, which is at first only an Idea [*vorgestellt*] and an *obligation*, owes its *actuality*.

> The self-consciousness which has managed to attain this absolute reflection into itself knows itself in this reflection as a consciousness which cannot and should not be compromised by any present and given determination. In the shapes which it more commonly assumes in history (as in the case of Socrates, the Stoics, etc.), the tendency to look *inwards* into the self and to know and determine from within the self what is right and good appears in epochs when what is recognized as right and good in actuality and custom is unable to satisfy the better will. When the existing world of freedom has become unfaithful to the better will, this will no longer finds itself in the duties recognized in this world and must seek to recover in ideal inwardness alone that harmony which it has lost in actuality. Once self-consciousness has grasped and acquired its formal right in this way, everything depends on the kind of content which it gives to itself.[1]

Addition (H). If we look more closely at this process of evaporation and observe how all determinations are absorbed into this simple concept and must again issue forth from it, we can see that the process depends primarily on the fact that everything which we recognize as right or duty can be shown by thought to be null and void, limited, and in no way absolute. Conversely, just as subjectivity evaporates every content into itself, it may also in turn develop it out of itself. Everything which arises in the ethical realm is produced by this activity of the spirit. On the other hand, this point of view is defective inasmuch as it is merely abstract. When I am aware of my freedom as the substance within me, I am inactive and do nothing. But if I proceed to act and look for principles, I reach out for determinations, and there is then a requirement that these should be deduced from the concept of the free will. Thus, while it is right to evaporate right or duty into subjectivity, it is on the other hand wrong if this abstract foundation is not in turn developed. Only in ages when the actual world is a hollow, spiritless, and unsettled existence [*Existenz*] may the individual be permitted to flee from actuality and retreat into his inner life. Socrates made his appearance at the time when Athenian democracy had fallen into ruin. He evaporated the existing world and retreated into himself in search of the right and the good. Even in our times it happens that reverence for the existing order is in varying degrees absent, and people seek to equate accepted values with their own will, with what they have recognized.

§ 139

Where all previously valid determinations have vanished and the will is in a state of pure inwardness, the self-consciousness is capable of making into its principle either *the universal in and for itself*, or the *arbitrariness* of its *own particularity*, giving the latter precedence over the universal and realizing it through its actions – i.e. it is capable of being *evil.*[1]

Conscience, as formal subjectivity, consists simply in the possibility of turning at any moment to *evil*; for both morality and evil have their common root in that self-certainty which has being for itself and knows and resolves for itself.

The *origin of evil* in general lies in the mystery – i.e. the speculative aspect – of freedom, in the necessity with which it emerges from the *natural* phase of the will and adopts a character of *inwardness* in relation to it. It is this natural phase of the will which comes into existence [*Existenz*] as self-contradiction, as incompatible with itself in this opposition, and thus it is this *particularity* of the will itself which further determines itself as evil. For particularity exists only as a *duality* – in the present case as the opposition between the will's natural phase and its inwardness. Within this opposition, the will's inwardness is only a *relative* and formal being-for-itself which can derive its content only from the determinations of the natural will, from desire, drive, inclination, etc. Now it is said of these desires, drives, etc. that they *may* be either good *or* evil. But when the will lets its content be determined by these desires etc. in the determination of *contingency* which they have as natural [forces], and hence also by the form which it [i.e. the will] has at this point, the form of particularity, it thereby becomes opposed to *universality* as inner objectivity, i.e. to the good, which, along with the will's internal self-reflection and the cognitive [*erkennenden*] consciousness, makes its appearance as the opposite extreme to immediate objectivity, to the merely natural. In this case, the inwardness of the will is evil. The human being is therefore evil both *in himself* or *by nature* and at the same time through his *reflection into himself*, so that neither nature as such (apart from the naturalness of the will which remains tied to its particular content) nor reflection *turned in upon itself*, i.e. in cognition in general (unless it remains attached to that opposition already referred to) is in itself [*für sich*] evil. – Absolutely united with this aspect of *the necessity of evil* is also the fact that this evil is determined as that which of necessity *ought not to be*, i.e. the fact that it ought to be cancelled [*aufgehoben*]. It is *not* that the point of view of division referred to above ought never to appear at all – on the contrary, it is this which constitutes the distinction between the unreasoning animal and the human being. But the will must not stop short at this point and cling on to particularity instead of the universal as the essential; the point of view of division should be overcome as null and void. In connection with this necessity of evil, [we should also note that] it is *subjectivity*, as the infinity of this reflection, which is faced with and present within this opposition; if it stops short at this juncture – i.e. if it is evil – it is consequently present *for itself*, retains its separate individuality, and is itself this arbitrary will. It is accordingly the individual *subject* as such which bears the entire *responsibility for its own evil.*[a]

Addition (H). The abstract certainty which knows itself as the basis of everything has within it the possibility of willing the universal of the concept, but also that of making a particular content into its principle and realizing this content. It follows that the abstraction of self-certainty is always a part of *evil*, which is the second of these alternatives, and that *only* the human being is good – but only in so far as he can also be evil. Good and evil are inseparable, and their inseparability derives from the

[a]*Translator's note:* I follow Ilting (VPR ii, 496) in reading *seines Bösen* ('its own evil') rather than *des Bösen* ('evil [in general]') as in the Suhrkamp edition of the text.

fact that the concept becomes its own object [*Gegenstand*] and, as object, immediately embodies the determination of difference. The evil will wills something opposed to the universality of the will, whereas the good acts in accordance with its true concept. The difficulty about the question of how the will can also be evil usually arises because we think of the will as having only a positive relationship to itself, and envisage it as something determinate which exists for itself, i.e. as the good. But the question of the origin of evil signifies more precisely this: 'How does the negative come into the positive?' If we presuppose that, at the creation of the world, God is the absolutely positive, it is impossible to recognize the negative within this positive, no matter which way we turn; for to assume that evil was permitted by God is to assume on his part a passive relationship which is unsatisfactory and meaningless. In the representational thought [*Vorstellung*] of religious myth, the origin of evil is not comprehended; that is, there is no recognition of the one in the other, but only a representation [*Vorstellung*] of succession and coexistence whereby the negative comes to the positive from outside. But this cannot satisfy thought, which demands a reason [*Grund*] and a necessity and seeks to apprehend the negative as itself rooted in the positive. The solution [of this problem], from the point of view of the concept, is contained in the concept itself, for the concept – or in more concrete terms, the Idea – has the essential characteristic of differentiating itself and positing itself negatively. If we merely stick to the positive, i.e. to the wholly good which is supposedly good in its origin, we have an empty determination of the understanding which clings to such one-sided abstractions and, by the mere act of asking the question, makes it into a difficult one. But from the point of view of the concept, positivity is apprehended as activity and self-differentiation. Thus, evil as well as good has its origin in the will, and the will in its concept is both good and evil. The natural will is in itself the contradiction of self-differentiation, of being [both] for itself and inward. To say then that evil contains the more precise determination that the human being is evil in so far as his will is natural would run counter to the common idea [*Vorstellung*] that it is precisely the natural will which is innocent and good. But the natural will is opposed to the content of freedom, and the child and uneducated man whose wills are natural are for that reason accountable for their actions only to a lesser degree. Thus, when we speak of human beings, we do not mean children but self-conscious individuals, and when we speak of the good, we mean knowledge of the good. Now it is true that the natural is in itself ingenuous, neither good nor evil; but in relation to the will as freedom and as knowledge of freedom, the natural contains the determination of the unfree, and is therefore evil. In so far as man wills the natural, it is no longer merely the natural but the negation of the good as the concept of the will. – But if it were now to be argued that, since evil is inherent in the concept and necessary, man would not be responsible if he committed it, it must be replied that the decision is man's own act, the product of his freedom and responsibility. Religious myth tells us that man is like God in his knowledge [*Erkenntnis*] of good and evil, and this likeness is indeed present in that the necessity here is not a natural necessity – on the contrary, the decision is in fact the cancellation [*Aufhebung*] of this duality of good and evil. Since I am confronted with both good and evil, I am able to choose between them; I can choose either of them and accept one or the other into my subjectivity. It is thus in the nature of evil that man may will it, but need not necessarily do so.

§ 140

The self-consciousness knows how to discover a *positive* aspect in its own end (see § 135); for this end, as part of the purpose of an *actual concrete* action, necessarily has a positive aspect. By virtue of this positive aspect, [which it regards] as a *duty and admirable intention*, the self-consciousness is able to assert that its action is good both *for others* and *for itself*. But because of its self-reflection and consequent awareness of the universal character of the will, it is also in a position to compare with this universal character the essentially *negative* content of its action, which is simultaneously present *within it*. To assert that this action is good for *others* is *hypocrisy*; and to assert that it is good for the self-consciousness *itself* is to go to the even greater extreme at which *subjectivity declares itself absolute*.

> This last and most abstruse form of evil, whereby evil is perverted into good and good into evil and the consciousness, knowing that it has the power to accomplish this reversal, consequently knows itself as absolute, is the greatest extreme of subjectivity from the point of view of morality. It is the form to which evil has advanced in our time – thanks to philosophy, i.e. to a shallowness of thought which has twisted a profound concept into this shape and has presumed to call itself philosophy, just as it has presumed to call evil good. In these present Remarks, I shall briefly indicate the principal shapes which this subjectivity commonly assumes.
>
> (a) *Hypocrisy* contains the following moments: (α) knowledge of the true universal, whether in the form merely of a

feeling of *right* and *duty* or of a more advanced knowledge [*Kenntnis*] and cognition of these; (β) a willing of the *particular* which is at odds with this universal; and (γ) a knowing *comparison* of these two moments so that the particular volition is determined, for the willing consciousness itself, as evil. These determinations signify *acting with a bad conscience*, but not yet hypocrisy as such. – It was at one time a question of great importance *whether an action was evil only in so far as it was done with a bad conscience*, i.e. with a *developed* consciousness of the moments indicated above. – Pascal (*Lettres provinciales*, 4) describes very well what follows from answering this question in the affirmative: 'Il seront tous damnés ces demi-pécheurs, qui ont quelque amour pour la vertu. Mais pour ces francs pécheurs, pécheurs endurcis, pécheurs sans mélange, pleins et achevés, l'enfer ne les tient pas: ils ont trompé le diable à force de s'y abandonner.'*ª†* – The subjective right of self-consciousness to *know* an action in its determination as either good or evil in and for itself must not be thought of as colliding with the absolute right of the *objectivity* of this determination in such a way that the two are represented as *separable*, and

---

ª Translator's note: 'They will all be damned, these half-sinners who retain some love of virtue. But as for those open sinners, hardened sinners, undiluted, complete, and consummate sinners, hell cannot hold them: they have deceived the devil by their complete surrender.'[1]

†Hegel's note: In the same context, Pascal also quotes Christ's intercession on the Cross for his enemies: 'Father, forgive them, for they know not what they do'[2] – a superfluous request if the fact that they did not know what they were doing removed the quality of evil from their action so that it did not require forgiveness. He likewise cites the opinion of Aristotle (*Nicomachean Ethics* III.2 [1110b27]), who distinguishes between acting οὐκ εἰδώς and acting ἀγνοῶν;*ᵇ³* in the former case of ignorance, the person concerned acts *involuntarily* (this ignorance relates to *external circumstances*; see § 117 above), and he cannot be held responsible for his action.[4] But of the latter instance, Aristotle says: 'All wicked men fail to recognize what they should do and refrain from doing, and it is this very defect (ἁμαρτία) which makes people unjust and in general evil. Ignorance of the choice between good and evil does not mean that an action is involuntary (i.e. that the agent cannot be held responsible for it), *but only that it is bad.*'[5] Aristotle, of course, had a deeper insight into the connection between cognition and volition than has become usual in that superficial philosophy which teaches that *emotion* and *enthusiasm, not cognition*, are the true principles of ethical action.[6]

ᵇTranslator's note: οὐκ εἰδώς ('without perception') is translated by both David Ross and Terence Irwin as 'in ignorance'; ἀγνοῶν ('from ignorance') is translated by Ross as 'by reason of ignorance' and by Irwin as 'caused by ignorance'.

indifferent and *contingent* towards one another; it was the latter relationship in particular which was regarded as fundamental in the old debates about *efficacious grace.*[7] In its formal aspect, evil is the individual's most distinctive property, because it is precisely his subjectivity positing itself entirely for itself, and is therefore entirely his responsibility (see § 139 and the appended Remarks); and on the objective side, man is *by his concept* spirit and rationality in general, and has the determination of self-knowing universality wholly within himself. It is therefore to deny him the honour due to his concept if his good side – and hence also the determination of his evil action as evil – is divorced from him and he is not made responsible for his evil action either. How determinate the consciousness of these moments in their respective differences is, what degree of clarity or obscurity it has attained as *developed cognition*, and to what extent the conscience associated with an evil action is more or less evil *in form* – all these are less important questions of a more empirical character.

(b) To act in an evil manner and with an evil conscience does not amount to *hypocrisy.*[8] Hypocrisy includes in addition the formal determination of untruthfulness, whereby *evil* is in the first place represented *for others* as *good* and the evildoer pretends in all external respects to be good, conscientious, pious, etc. – which in this case is merely a trick to deceive *others*. But secondly, the evil person may find in the good he does at other times, or in his piety, or in *good reasons* of any kind, a means of justifying *for himself* the evil he does, in that he can use these reasons to distort it into something he considers good. This possibility exists within subjectivity, for, as abstract negativity, it knows that all determinations are subordinate to it and emanate from it.

(c) We must in the first place include in this distortion that attitude [*Gestalt*] known as *probabilism.*[9] It adopts the principle that an action is permissible and can be done in good conscience if the consciousness can discover *any* good reason [*Grund*] for it – even if this is merely the *authority* of a single theologian, and even if other theologians are known to diverge very considerably from the former's judgement. Even in this notion [*Vorstellung*], there is still present the correct consciousness that a reason and authority of this kind affords only a *probability*, although this is regarded as sufficient to satisfy the conscience. It is at the same time conceded that a good reason is merely of such a kind that other reasons of at least equal merit may exist alongside it. A further trace of objectivity can be discerned in this attitude in so far as it assumes that a *reason* should be the determining factor. But since the decision between good and evil is made to depend upon many *good reasons*, including those authorities already referred to – despite the fact that these reasons are so numerous and discordant – it is also apparent that it is *not* this objectivity of the thing [*Sache*], but *subjectivity*, which is the decisive factor. As a result, [personal] preference and the arbitrary will are made the arbiters of good and evil, and both ethics and religiosity are undermined. But the fact that it is the agent's own subjectivity which makes the decision is not yet acknowledged as the [governing] principle – on the contrary (as already mentioned), it is claimed that a reason is the decisive factor. To this extent, probabilism is still a form of hypocrisy.

(d) The stage immediately above this is [the view] that the good will consists in *willing the good*; this willing of *good in the abstract* is supposed to be sufficient, indeed the sole prerequisite, for the goodness of the action itself. Since the action, as *determinate* volition, has a content, whereas *good in the abstract* determines nothing, it remains the task of particular subjectivity to give this abstraction its determination and fulfilment. Just as, in the case of probabilism, anyone who is not himself a learned *Révérend Père* relies on the authority of such a theologian in order to subsume a determinate content under the universal determination of the *good*, so in this case is every subject immediately accorded the honour [*Würde*] of providing the abstract good with a content, or – and this amounts to the same thing – of subsuming a content under a universal. This content is only one of the various aspects of a concrete action, some of which may even justify its description as criminal and bad. But that subjective determination which I give to the good is the good which I *know* in the action, i.e. my *good intention* (see § 114). There thus arises a conflict of determinations, for one of them suggests that an action is good, whereas others suggest that it is criminal.[10] It thus seems that the question also arises, in the case of an actual action, whether the *intention is actually good*. But it may not only be generally the case that the good is the *actual* intention; it must in fact always be so if we adopt the point of view that the abstract good is the determining ground of the subject. An injury done by a well-intentioned action whose determination is in other respects criminal and evil is, of course, also good, and all would seem to depend on which aspect of the action is the *most essential*. But this objective question is not applicable here – or rather, it is the subjectivity of consciousness itself whose decision alone constitutes the objective element. *Essential* and *good* are in any case synonymous; the former is just as much an abstraction as the latter; good is what is essential with regard to the will, and what should be essential in this respect is precisely that an action is determined as good for me. But this abstract good, being completely lacking in content, can be wholly reduced simply to meaning anything *positive* at all – anything, that is, which has any kind of validity and which, in its immediate determination, may even count as an essential end (such as doing good to the poor, or caring for myself, my life, my family, etc.). The immediate consequence of this for itself is that any content one pleases can be subsumed under the good. Furthermore, just as the good is an abstraction, so consequently is the bad likewise devoid of content, receiving its determination from my subjectivity; and this is also the source of the moral end of hating and eradicating the bad as an indeterminate quality. – Theft, cowardice, murder, etc., as actions – i.e. as products in general of a subjective will – have the immediate determination of being the *satisfaction*

of such a will, and hence of being something *positive*; and
in order to make the action into a good one, it is merely a
question of knowing this positive aspect as my *intention* in
performing the action, and this aspect is then the *essential*
factor in determining the action as good, because I know
it as the good in my intention. Theft in order to benefit
the poor, theft or desertion in battle for the sake of one's
duty to care for one's life or one's (perhaps even
impoverished) family, murder for hatred and revenge –
i.e. in order to satisfy a self-awareness of one's own rights
or of right in general, and one's sense of someone else's
wickedness, of wrong done by him to oneself or to others,
to the world or the *people* in general, by eliminating this
wicked individual who is wickedness personified, and
thereby contributing at least something towards the end of
eradicating the bad – all of these deeds, by virtue of the
positive aspect of their content, are in this way transformed into well-intentioned and consequently good
actions.[11] Even the *lowest degree* of understanding is
enough to discover, like those learned theologians, a positive aspect in every action and hence a good reason and
intention underlying it. Thus it has been said that there is
in fact no such thing as an *evil man*, for no one wills evil
for the sake of evil – i.e. the *purely negative* as such – but
always something *positive*, and hence, according to the
point of view in question, always something good. In this
abstract good, the distinction between *good* and *evil*, as
well as all actual duties, has vanished; consequently,
merely to will the good and to have a good intention in
one's action is more like evil than good, in that the good is
willed only in this abstract form so that its *determination* is
left to the arbitrary will of the subject.

   To this context there also belongs the notorious proposition that *the end justifies the means.*[12] – Taken on its own,
this expression is at first sight trivial and vacuous. It may
be replied in equally indeterminate fashion that a just end
doubtless justifies the means, whereas an unjust end does
not. [To say] that the means is right if the end is right is a
tautological statement inasmuch as the means is precisely

that which is nothing in itself [*für sich*] but exists for the sake of something else and has its determination and value in the latter as its end – *that is, if it is truly a means.* – But the meaning of the above proposition lies not just in its formal significance; it can also be understood in the more determinate sense that it is permissible, and perhaps even one's duty, to use as a means to a good end something which in itself is not a means at all, to violate something which is in itself sacrosanct, and thus to make a crime the means to a good end. In [those who follow] this proposition, there is on the one hand an indeterminate consciousness of the dialectic of the aforementioned *positive* element in isolated determinations of right or ethics, or of equally indeterminate general propositions such as 'Thou shalt not kill' or 'Care for your own welfare and that of your family'. Courts of law and soldiers have not only the right but also the duty to kill human beings; but in this case, there are *precise definitions* as to what kind of people and what circumstances make this permissible and obligatory. In the same way, my welfare and that of my family must also be subordinated to higher ends and thereby reduced to a means. But what we describe as a crime is not a general proposition of this kind, left indeterminate and still subject to a dialectic; on the contrary, it is already delimited in a determinate and objective manner. Now what is set up in opposition to this determination – namely that sacred end which is supposed to exonerate the crime – is nothing other than a *subjective opinion* of what is good or better. It is the same thing as happens when volition stops short at the abstract good, so that every determinate characteristic of good and evil or right and wrong which has being and validity in and for itself is cancelled [*aufgehoben*], and this determination is assigned instead to the feeling, imagination [*Vorstellen*], and caprice of the individual.

(e) *Subjective opinion* is at last expressly acknowledged as the criterion of right and duty when it is alleged that the ethical nature of an action is determined by *the conviction which holds something to be right.*[13] The good which is

willed does not yet have a content; and the principle of
conviction contains the further specification that the subsumption of an action under the determination of the
good is the responsibility of the *subject*. Under these
circumstances, any semblance of ethical objectivity has
completely disappeared. Such doctrines are intimately
connected with that self-styled philosophy, already
frequently referred to, which denies that *truth* – and the
truth of the spirit as will, its rationality in so far as it
actualizes itself, is to be found in the precepts of ethics –
can be recognized. Since such philosophizing maintains
that the knowledge [*Erkenntnis*] of truth is an empty vanity
which transcends the sphere of cognition [*Erkennen*], and
that the latter is a mere semblance, it must immediately
make this very semblance its principle as far as action is
concerned, and thereby equate the ethical with the *distinctive* outlook of the individual and his *particular conviction*.
The degradation into which philosophy has thus sunk
seems at first glance, in the eyes of the world, an utterly
indifferent happening which has affected only the idle talk
of academics; but such a view necessarily becomes part of
our view of ethics, which is an essential component of
philosophy, and only then do the implications of these
views become apparent in and for [the realm of] actuality.
– The dissemination of the view that subjective conviction
is the sole determinant of the ethical nature of an action
has had the effect that references to *hypocrisy*, which used
to be frequent, are nowadays uncommon; for to describe
evil as hypocrisy implies that certain actions are *in and for
themselves* misdemeanours, vices, and crimes, and that the
perpetrator is necessarily aware of them as such in so far
as he knows and acknowledges the principles and outward
acts of piety and integrity [*Rechtlichkeit*] even within the
pretence in whose interest he misuses them. Or in relation to evil in general, it used to be assumed that it is a
duty to recognize the good and to know how to distinguish
it from evil. But it was at all events an absolute requirement that human beings should not commit vicious and
criminal acts, and that they should be held responsible for

such acts in so far as they are human beings rather than animals. But if a good heart, good intentions, and subjective conviction are said to be the factors which give actions their value, there is no longer any hypocrisy or evil at all; for a person is able to transform whatever he does into something good by the reflection of good intentions and motives [*Bewegungsgründe*], and the element [*Moment*] of his *conviction* renders it good.† Thus, there is no longer such a thing as crime or vice in and for itself, and instead of those free and open, hardened and undiluted sinners referred to above we have a consciousness of complete justification by intention and conviction. My good intention in my action and my conviction of its goodness *make it good*. In so far as we speak of judging and pronouncing a verdict on an action, this principle requires that the agent should be judged only in terms of his intention and conviction, or of his *faith* – not in the sense in which Christ requires faith in *objective* truth (so that the judgement passed on a person of bad faith, i.e. on one whose conviction is bad in its *content*, must also be negative, in keeping with this evil content), but in the sense of loyalty to one's conviction (in so far as a person, in his action, remains *true to his conviction*), i.e. in the sense of formal, subjective loyalty, which is alone in keeping with duty. – Since this principle of conviction is at the same time *subjectively* determined, the thought of the possibility of *error* must also thrust itself upon us, and this in turn presupposes a law which has being in and for itself. But *the law [itself] does not act*; only an actual human being acts. And, according to the above principle, the sole criterion of the worth of human actions is the extent to which the individual

---

†*Hegel's note:* 'That he feels completely *convinced*, I do not doubt in the least. But how many people proceed from such felt conviction to commit the gravest misdeeds! Thus, if anything may be excused on such grounds, *no rational judgement of good and evil* or of *honourable and contemptible decisions* is any longer possible; *delusion* then has equal rights with reason, or rather, reason no longer has any rights or valid authority [*Ansehen*] whatsoever; its voice is an absurdity; *he who has no doubts is the possessor of truth!*

I tremble at the consequences of such toleration, which would be exclusively to the advantage of unreason.' (F. H. Jacobi to Count Holmer, Eutin, 5 August 1800, commenting on Count Stolberg's change of religion, in *Brennus* (Berlin, August 1802)).[14]

concerned has incorporated the law *into his own conviction*. But if, by this token, it is not actions which are to be judged by the law in question – i.e. to be measured by it in any way – it is impossible to tell what that law is for or what purpose it is to serve. Such a law is reduced to a purely *external letter*, indeed to an empty word, for it is only my conviction which *makes it a law* and a binding duty for me. – Such a law may have the authority of God and the state behind it, and the authority of the thousands of years for which it was the bond by which human beings and all their deeds and destinies were held together and sustained – authorities which encompass countless *individual convictions*. If *I* then set against all this the *authority* of my *individual* conviction – and as my subjective conviction its validity is merely [that of] authority – this may at first appear a monstrous presumption. But this appearance is refuted by the very principle which takes subjective conviction as its criterion. – If, however, the higher illogicality of reason and conscience – which shallow science and miserable sophistry can never entirely banish – admits the *possibility of error*, the very fact that crime and evil in general are classed as error reduces the fault to a minimum. For *to err is human*,[15] and who has not been mistaken about this or that circumstance, about whether there was cabbage or sauerkraut with yesterday's lunch, and about countless matters of greater and lesser importance? Yet the distinction between the important and the unimportant disappears if subjectivity of conviction and adherence to such conviction are the sole criterion. It is in the nature of the case that the higher illogicality already referred to should admit the possibility of error; but when it goes on to say that a bad conviction is merely an error, it in fact simply becomes another kind of illogicality, namely that of dishonesty. For in the first instance, conviction is supposed to be the basis of ethics and of man's supreme worth, and is thereby declared to be a supreme and sacred value; and in the second case, all that we are concerned with is error, and my conviction is insignificant and contingent, in fact a purely external circumstance which I may *encounter in one way or another.* And my conviction is indeed an extremely insignificant thing if I cannot recognize the truth; for then it is a matter of indifference *how* I think, and all that remains for me to think about is that empty good as an abstraction of the understanding. – It may also be remarked that, as far as the mode of action of other people in relation to my own action is concerned, it follows from this principle of justification on grounds of conviction that, if *their* faith and conviction make them regard my actions as *crimes*, they are *quite right* to do so – a consequence whereby I am not only denied all credit in advance, but am on the contrary simply reduced from a position of freedom and honour to a situation of unfreedom and dishonour. In the justice to which I am here subjected – and which in itself is also my own justice – I merely experience someone else's subjective conviction and, when it is implemented, I consider myself acted upon merely by an external force.

(f) Finally, the supreme form in which this subjectivity is completely comprehended and expressed is that to which the term 'irony', borrowed from Plato, has been applied.[16] Only the name is taken from Plato, however, for Plato used it of a method which Socrates employed in personal dialogue to defend the Idea of truth and justice against the complacency of the uneducated consciousness and that of the Sophists; but it was only this consciousness which he treated ironically, not the Idea itself. Irony concerns only a manner of speaking in relation to *people*; without this personal direction, the essential movement of thought is dialectic, and Plato was so far from treating the dialectic in itself [*für sich*], let alone irony, as the ultimate factor and as the Idea itself that, on the contrary, he ended the to and fro of thought, and particularly of subjective opinion, by submerging it in the substantiality of the Idea.† The only

†Hegel's note: My late colleague Professor Solger[17] did admittedly take over the expression 'irony' which Friedrich von Schlegel introduced during an earlier period of his literary career and whose meaning he extended to include that subjectivity which knows itself as supreme. But Solger's better judgement rejected this definition [*Bestimmung*], and his philosophical insight seized upon and retained only one aspect of it, namely the

possible culmination – and this must now be discussed –
of that subjectivity which regards itself as the ultimate
instance is reached when it *knows* itself as that power of
resolution and decision on [matters of] truth, right, and

dialectical element proper, the activating pulse of speculative reflection. But I do not find
his conclusions entirely clear, nor can I agree with the concepts which he develops in his
last, substantial work, his detailed *Critique of August Wilhelm von Schlegel's Lectures on
Dramatic Art and Literature* (*Wiener Jahrbuch*, Vol. VII, pp. 90ff.). 'True irony', says Solger
on that occasion (p. 92), 'starts from the point of view that, as long as human beings live
in this present world, it is only in this world that they can fulfil their destiny, even in the
highest sense of that word. Any means whereby we believe we can *transcend finite ends* is a
vain and *empty* fancy . . . Even the highest of things is present to our action only *in a
limited and finite shape.*' This, if understood correctly, is a Platonic view, very truly
expressed in opposition to that empty striving for the (*abstract*) infinite which Solger had
previously referred to. But to say that the highest of things is present in a limited and
finite shape, like the realm of ethics – and the ethical realm is essentially actuality and
action – is very different from saying that it is a *finite* end; the shape and form of finitude
do not deprive the content, i.e. the ethical realm, of any of its substantiality or of the
infinity which is inherent within it. Solger continues: 'And for this very reason, *it* [the
highest of things] is *as insignificant in us* as the lowest of things, and *necessarily perishes
with us and our insignificant intellects.* For it is truly present in God alone, and when it
perishes in us, it is transfigured as something divine, in which we would have no share if
there were not an immediate presence of this divinity which becomes manifest even as
our actuality disappears; but the state of mind to which this presence becomes immediately evident in human events themselves is tragic irony.' The arbitrary name 'irony'
would not in itself require comment, but there is an unclarity in the statement that it is
the highest of things which *perishes* with our insignificance, and that the divine is revealed
only when our actuality disappears, as when we are told on page 91: 'We see heroes lose
faith in the noblest and finest aspects of their dispositions and feelings, not only in
relation to what these lead to, but also in relation to *their source* and *their value*; indeed, we
are elevated by the *downfall of the best* itself.' The tragic downfall of figures of the highest
ethical worth can interest us, elevate us, and reconcile us to its occurrence only in so far
as such figures appear in mutual opposition, with equally justified but distinct ethical
powers which have unfortunately come into *collision*. (The just downfall of complete and
self-important rogues and criminals – as, for instance, the hero of the modern tragedy
Guilt [*Die Schuld*][18] – certainly has an interest for criminal law, but not for true art, with
which we are here concerned.) As a result of this opposition to an ethical principle, they
incur *guilt*, from which the right and wrong of both parties emerges, and with it the true
ethical Idea which, purified and triumphing over this *one-sidedness*, is thereby reconciled
in us. Accordingly, it is not the *highest* thing in us which perishes, and we are *elevated* not
by the downfall of the best but, on the contrary, by the triumph of the true. This is the true
and purely ethical interest of ancient tragedy, as I have explained more fully in my
Phenomenology of Spirit (pp. 404ff.; cf. pp. 683ff.).[19] (In romantic tragedy, this determination undergoes a further modification.) But the ethical Idea, *without such unfortunate
collisions* and the downfall of the individuals caught up in this misfortune, is *actual* and
present in the ethical world; and that this highest of things should *not appear insignificant
in its actuality* is what the real ethical existence [*Existenz*], the state, takes as its end and
puts into effect, and what the ethical self-consciousness possesses, intuits, and knows,
and thinking cognition comprehends, in *the state*.

duty which is already implicitly [*an sich*] present within the preceding forms. Thus, it does indeed consist in knowledge of the objective side of ethics, but without that self-forgetfulness and self-renunciation which seriously immerses itself in this objectivity and makes it the basis of its action. Although it has a relation [*Beziehung*] to this objectivity, it at the same time distances itself from it and knows *itself* as that which *wills* and *resolves in a particular way* but may *equally well* will and resolve otherwise. – 'You in fact honestly accept a law as existing in and for itself' [it says to others]; 'I do so, too, but I go further than you, for I am also beyond this law and can do *this or that* as I please. It is not the thing [*Sache*] which is excellent, it is I who am excellent and master of both law and thing; I *merely play* with them as with my own caprice, and in this ironic consciousness in which I let the highest of things perish, I *merely enjoy myself.*' – In this shape, subjectivity is not only *empty* of all ethical *content* [*die Eitelkeit alles sittlichen Inhalts*] in the way of rights, duties, and laws, and is accordingly evil (evil, in fact, of an inherently wholly universal kind); in addition, its form is that of *subjective* emptiness [*Eitelkeit*], in that it knows itself as this emptiness of all content and, in this knowledge, knows *itself* as the absolute. – The extent to which this absolute self-satisfaction does not simply remain a solitary worship of the self, but may even form a *community* whose bond and substance consist, for example, in mutual assurances of conscientiousness, good intentions, and enjoyment of this reciprocal purity, but above all in basking in the glory of this self-knowledge and self-expression and of cherishing and cultivating such pursuits; and the extent to which what has been called the 'beautiful soul' (i.e. that nobler kind of subjectivity which fades away inasmuch as it is empty of all objectivity and thus has no actuality of its own), and certain other phenomena [*Gestaltungen*] are related to the stage [of subjectivity] which we are here considering – these are questions which I have discussed in the *Phenomenology of Spirit* (pp. 605ff.). The whole of Section (c) of that work, 'The Conscience', should be compared with what is said here, especially in relation to the transition to a higher stage in general (although the latter is defined differently in the *Phenomenology*).[20]

Addition (H). Representational thought [*Vorstellung*] can go further and transform the evil will into a semblance of goodness. Even if it cannot alter the nature of evil, it can nevertheless make it appear to be good. For every action has a positive aspect, and since the determination of good as opposed to evil can likewise be reduced to the positive, I can maintain that my action is good with reference to my intention. Thus, evil is connected with good not only within the consciousness, but also in its positive aspect. If the self-consciousness passes its action off as good only for the benefit of other people, it takes the form of *hypocrisy*; but if it is able to assert that the deed is good in its own estimation, too, we have reached that even higher level of subjectivity which knows itself as absolute. For subjectivity of this kind, good and evil in and for themselves have disappeared, and it can pass off as good or evil whatever its wishes and its ability dictate. This is the point of view of absolute sophistry which sets itself up as a legislator and refers the distinction between good and evil to its own arbitrary will. As for hypocrisy, this includes above all those religious hypocrites (or Tartuffes) who comply with all ceremonial requirements and may even be pious in themselves [*für sich*], while at the same time doing whatever they please. Nowadays, there is no longer much talk of hypocrites, partly because this accusation appears too harsh, and partly because hypocrisy in its immediate shape has more or less disappeared. This barefaced lie and cloak of goodness has now become too transparent not to be seen through, and the distinction between doing good on the one hand and evil on the other is no longer present to the same extent since increasing education has made such antithetical determinations seem less clear-cut. Instead, hypocrisy has now assumed the subtler guise [*Gestalt*] of *probabilism*, which consists in the attempt to represent a transgression as something good from the point of view of one's own conscience. This can only occur where morality and goodness are determined by an authority, so that there are as many reasons as there are authorities for maintaining that evil is good. Casuistic theologians, especially Jesuits, have worked on these cases of conscience and endlessly multiplied them.

As these cases are refined to the highest pitch of subtlety, numerous collisions arise, and the antithesis of good and evil becomes so blurred that, in individual instances, the opposite poles prove interchangeable. All that is asked for is *probability*, that is, an approximation to goodness which can be substantiated by some reason or by some authority. Thus, this point of view has the peculiar determination of possessing only an abstract content; the concrete content is presented as inessential – or rather, it is allowed to depend on mere opinion. In this way, someone may have committed a crime while willing the good. If, for example, an evil man is murdered, the assertion that the murderer wished to resist evil and to diminish it can be passed off as the positive aspect [of the deed]. The next step beyond probabilism is that it is no longer someone else's authority or assertion that counts, but the subject itself, i.e. its *own* conviction, which can *alone* make something good. The inadequacy of this is that everything is made to refer solely to conviction, and that there is no longer any right which has being in and for itself, a right for which this conviction would merely be the form. It is not, of course, a matter of indifference whether I do something from habit or custom or because I am thoroughly persuaded of its truth. But objective truth is also different from my conviction, for the latter makes no distinction whatsoever between good and evil; conviction always remains conviction, and the bad can only be that of which I am not convinced. While this point of view is that of a supreme instance which obliterates good and evil, it at the same time acknowledges that it is subject to error, and to this extent, it is brought down from its exalted position and again becomes contingent and appears to deserve no respect. Now this form is *irony*, the consciousness that such a principle of conviction is of little value and that, within this supreme criterion, only arbitrariness prevails. This point of view was in fact a product of Fichte's philosophy, which maintains that the 'I' is absolute, i.e. that it is absolute certainty, the universal selfhood [*Ichheit*] whose further development leads to objectivity.[21] It cannot in fact be said of Fichte that he made the arbitrary will of the subject into a principle in the practical sphere, but this [principle of the] particular, in the sense of Friedrich von Schlegel's 'particular selfhood', was itself later elevated to divine status in relation to the good and the beautiful. This implies that objective goodness is merely something constructed by my conviction, sustained by me alone, and that I, as lord and master, can make it come and go [as I please]. As soon as I relate myself to something objective, it ceases to exist for me, and so I am poised above an immense void, conjuring up shapes and destroying them. This supremely subjective point of view can arise only in a highly cultivated age in which faith has lost its seriousness, which now exists essentially only in the vanity of all things.

TRANSITION FROM MORALITY TO ETHICAL LIFE

§ 141

For the *good* as the substantial universal of freedom, but still as something *abstract*, determinations of some kind are therefore *required*, as is a determining principle (although this principle is *identical* with the good itself). For the *conscience* likewise, as the purely abstract principle of determination, it is required that its determinations should be universal and objective. Both of them [i.e. the good and the conscience], if raised in this way to independent totalities [*für sich zur Totalität*], become the indeterminate which *ought* to be determined. – But the integration of these two relative totalities into absolute identity has already been accomplished *in itself*, since this very subjectivity of *pure self-certainty*, melting away for itself in its emptiness, is *identical* with the *abstract universality* of the good; the identity – which is accordingly *concrete* – of the good and the subjective will, the truth of them both, is *ethical life*.

A conceptual transition of this kind can be understood more fully with the help of logic. Here, it need only be said that the nature of the limited and the finite – which in this case are the abstract good which merely *ought to be*, and an equally abstract subjectivity which merely *ought to be good* – is for them to have their opposite present *within them*, the good its actuality, and subjectivity (the moment of the *actuality* of the ethical) the good; but since they are one-sided, they are not yet *posited* as what they are *in themselves*. They become posited in their negativity, for as they *one-sidedly* constitute themselves as independent totalities, both refusing to accept what is present *in itself* within them – the good lacking subjectivity and determination, and the determinant, i.e. subjectivity, lacking what has being in itself – they cancel themselves out [*sich aufheben*] and are thereby reduced to moments, to moments of the *concept* which becomes manifest as their unity and has attained *reality* through this very positing of its moments, so that it now exists as *Idea*; this is the concept which has developed its determinations to reality and which is simultaneously present in their identity as their essence *which has being in itself.* – That existence [*Dasein*] of freedom which was immediately present as *right* is determined in the reflection of self-consciousness as the *good*; the third stage, present here in its transition as the truth of this good and of subjectivity, is therefore also the truth of subjectivity and of right. – The *ethical* is a subjective disposition, but of that right which has being in itself. That this Idea is the *truth* of the concept of freedom cannot be assumed or derived from feeling or from any other source, but, in philosophy, can only be *proved*. Its deduction consists solely in the fact that right and the moral self-consciousness can be seen in themselves to return to this Idea as their own *result*. – Those who think they can dispense with proofs and deductions in philosophy show that they are still far from forming the least idea of what philosophy is; they may well speak on other matters, but those who wish to speak without the concept have no right to participate in philosophical discourse.

Addition (H). Both principles which we have so far considered, the abstract good and the conscience, lack their opposite: the abstract good evaporates into a complete powerlessness which I can endow with any content whatsoever, and subjectivity of spirit becomes no less impoverished in that it lacks any objective significance. A longing may therefore arise for an objective condition, a condition in which the human being gladly debases himself to servitude and total subjection simply in order to escape the torment of vacuity and negativity. If many Protestants have recently gone over to the Catholic Church,[¹] they have done so because they found that their inner life was impoverished, and they reached out for a fixed point, a support, and an authority, even if what they gained was not exactly the stability of thought. The unity of the subjective with the objective good which has being in and for itself is *ethical life*, and the reconciliation which takes place in it is in accord with the concept. For whereas morality is the form of the will in general in its subjective aspect, ethical life is not just the subjective form and self-determination of the will: it also has its own concept, namely freedom, as its content. The sphere of right and that of morality cannot exist independently [*für sich*]; they must have the ethical as their support and foundation. For right lacks the moment of subjectivity, which in turn belongs solely to morality, so that neither of the two moments has any independent actuality. Only the infinite, the Idea, is actual. Right exists only as a branch of a whole, or as a climbing plant attached to a tree which has firm roots in and for itself.

PART THREE

Ethical Life

§ 142

Ethical life is the *Idea of freedom* as the living good which has its knowledge and volition in self-consciousness, and its actuality through self-conscious action. Similarly, it is in ethical being that self-consciousness has its motivating end[1] and a foundation which has being in and for itself. Ethical life is accordingly the *concept of freedom which has become the existing [vorhandenen] world and the nature of self-consciousness.*

§ 143

Since this unity of the concept of the will with its existence [*Dasein*], i.e. with the particular will, is knowledge, consciousness of the difference between these moments of the Idea is present, but in such a way that each of these moments has become for itself the totality of the Idea and has the latter as its foundation and content.

§ 144

(α) The objective sphere of ethics, which takes the place of the abstract good, is substance made *concrete* by subjectivity *as infinite form*. It therefore posits *distinctions* within itself which are thus determined by the concept. These distinctions give the ethical a fixed *content* which is necessary for itself, and whose existence [*Bestehen*] is exalted above subjective opinions and preferences: they are *laws and institutions which have being in and for themselves.*

Addition (H). In ethical life as a whole, both objective and subjective moments are present, but these are merely its forms. Its substance is the good, that is, the fulfilment of the objective [united] with subjectivity. If we consider ethical life from the objective point of view, we may say that ethical man is unconscious of himself. In this sense, Antigone proclaims that no one knows where the laws come from: they are eternal.[1] That is, their determination has being in and for itself and issues from the nature of the thing [*Sache*]. But this substantial element is also endowed with consciousness, although the status of the latter is always only that of a moment.

§ 145

The fact that the ethical sphere is the *system* of these determinations of the Idea constitutes its *rationality*. In this way, the ethical sphere is freedom, or the will which has being in and for itself as objectivity, as a circle of necessity whose moments are the *ethical powers* which govern the lives of individuals. In these individuals – who are accidental to them – these powers have their representation [*Vorstellung*], phenomenal shape [*erscheinende Gestalt*], and actuality.

Addition (H). Since the determinations of ethics constitute the concept of freedom, they are the substantiality or universal essence of individuals, who are related to them merely as accidents. Whether the individual exists or not is a matter of indifference to objective ethical life, which alone has permanence and is the power by which the lives of individuals are governed. Ethical life has therefore been represented to nations as eternal justice, or as gods who have being in and for themselves, and in relation to whom the vain pursuits of individuals are merely a play of the waves.[a]

[a]*Translator's note: Ein anwogendes Spiel*, literally 'an upward-surging play'. The word *anwogendes*, perhaps a reminiscence of Goethe's poem 'Grenzen der Menschheit' ('Limitations of Mankind'),[1] which likens man, in contrast to the gods, to an evanescent phenomenon borne upwards by, then sinking beneath, the waves, is not found in Hotho's transcription of Hegel's lectures, from which Gans compiled this Addition (see VPR III, 485). It was therefore presumably added by Gans himself.

§ 146

(β) In this *actual self-consciousness* [which it now possesses], the substance knows itself and is thus an object [*Objekt*] of knowledge. In relation to the subject, the ethical substance and its laws and powers are on the one hand an object [*Gegenstand*], inasmuch as *they are*, in the supreme sense of self-sufficiency. They are thus an absolute authority and power, infinitely more firmly based than the being of nature.

The sun, moon, mountains, rivers, and all natural objects [*Naturobjekte*] around us *are*. They have, in relation to consciousness, the authority not only of *being* in the first place, but also of having a particular nature which the consciousness acknowledges, and by which it is guided in its behaviour towards them, its dealings with them, and its use of them. The authority of ethical laws is infinitely higher, because natural things [*Naturdinge*] display rationality only in a completely *external* and *fragmented* manner and conceal it under the guise [*Gestalt*] of contingency.

§ 147

On the other hand, they are not something *alien* to the subject. On the contrary, the subject bears *spiritual witness* to them as to *its own essence*, in which it has its *self-awareness* [*Selbstgefühl*] and lives as in its element which is not distinct from itself – a relationship which is immediate and closer to identity than even [a relationship of] *faith* or *trust.¹*

> Faith and trust arise with the emergence of reflection, and they presuppose representations and distinctions [*Vorstellung und Unterschied*]. For example, to believe in pagan religion and to be a pagan are two different things. That relationship – or rather, that relationless identity – in which the ethical is the actual living principle [*Lebendigkeit*] of self-consciousness, may indeed turn into a relationship of faith and conviction or a relationship mediated by *further reflection*, into insight grounded on reasons, which may also begin with certain particular ends, interests, and considerations, with hope or fear, or with historical presuppositions. But *adequate cognition* of this identity belongs to conceptual thought [*dem denkenden Begriffe*].

§ 148

All these substantial determinations are *duties* which are binding on the will of the individual; for the individual, as subjective and inherently undetermined – or determined in a particular way – is distinct from them and *consequently stands in a relationship to them* as to his own substantial being.

> The ethical *theory of duties* [*Pflichtenlehre*]¹ – i.e. in its *objective* sense, not as supposedly comprehended in the empty principle of moral subjectivity, which in fact determines

nothing (see § 134) – therefore consists in that systematic development of the circle of ethical necessity which follows here in *Part Three* of the work.[2] The difference between its presentation here and the form of a *theory of duties* lies solely in the fact that the following account merely shows that ethical determinations are necessary relations, and does not proceed to add in every case 'this determination is therefore a duty for human beings'. – A theory of duties, unless it forms part of philosophical science, will take its material from existing relations and show its connection with one's own ideas [*Vorstellungen*] and with commonly encountered principles and thoughts, ends, drives, feelings [*Empfindungen*], etc.; and as reasons in favour of each duty, it may also adduce the further consequences which this duty may have with reference to other ethical relations and to welfare and opinion. But an immanent and consistent theory of duties can be nothing other than the development of *those relations* which are necessitated by the Idea of freedom, and are therefore *actual* in their entirety, within the state.

§ 149

A binding duty can appear as a *limitation* only in relation to indeterminate subjectivity or abstract freedom, and to the drives of the natural will or of the moral will which arbitrarily determines its own indeterminate good. The individual, however, finds his *liberation* in duty. On the one hand, he is liberated from his dependence on mere natural drives, and from the burden he labours under as a particular subject in his moral reflections on obligation and desire; and on the other hand, he is liberated from that indeterminate subjectivity which does not attain existence [*Dasein*] or the objective determinacy of action, but remains *within itself* and has no actuality. In duty, the individual liberates himself so as to attain substantial freedom.

Addition (H). Duty places limits only on the arbitrary will of subjectivity and clashes only with that abstract good to which subjectivity clings. When people say that they want to be free, this means primarily only that they want to be free in an abstract sense, and every determination and division [*Gliederung*] within the state is regarded as a limitation of that freedom.[1] To this extent, duty is not a limitation of freedom, but only of freedom in the abstract, that is, of unfreedom: it is the attainment of essential being, the acquisition of affirmative freedom.

§ 150

The ethical, in so far as it is reflected in the naturally determined character of the individual as such, is *virtue*; and in so far as virtue represents nothing more than the simple adequacy of the individual to the duties of the circumstances [*Verhältnisse*] to which he belongs, it is *rectitude*.

In an ethical community, it is easy to say *what* someone must do and *what* the duties are which he has to fulfil in order to be virtuous. He must simply do what is prescribed, expressly stated, and known to him within his situation. Rectitude is the universal quality which may be required of him, partly by right and partly by ethics. But from the point of view of morality, rectitude can easily appear as something of a lower order, beyond which one must impose further demands on oneself and others. For the craving to be something *special [Besonderes]* is not satisfied with the universal, with what has being in and for itself; only in the *exceptional* does it attain consciousness of its distinctiveness. – The *different aspects* of rectitude may equally well be called *virtues*, because they are likewise properties of the *individual* – although not exclusive to him in comparison with other individuals. But talk of virtue *in general* can easily verge on empty declamation, because it refers only to something abstract and indeterminate; and such talk, with its reasons and descriptions [*Darstellungen*], is directed at the individual as arbitrary will and subjective caprice. Within a given ethical order whose relations are fully developed and actualized, *virtue in the proper sense* has its place and actuality only in extraordinary circumstances, or where the above relations come into collision. But such *collisions* must be genuine ones, for moral reflection can invent collisions for itself wherever it likes and so give itself a consciousness that something *special [Besonderem]* is involved and that *sacrifices* have been made.[1] This is why the form of virtue as such appears more frequently in uncivilized societies and communities, for in such cases, the ethical and its actualization depend more on individual discretion and on the distinctive natural genius of individuals. In this way, the ancients ascribed virtue to Hercules in particular.[2] And since, in the states of antiquity, ethical life had not yet evolved into this free system of self-sufficient development and objectivity, this deficiency had to be made good by the distinctive genius of individuals. – If the theory [*Lehre*] of virtues is not just a theory of duties and thus includes the particular aspects of character which are determined by nature, it will therefore be a *natural history of spirit*.

Since virtues are the ethical in its particular application, and since, in this subjective respect, they are indeterminate, the quantitative principle of more or less will play a part in their determination.[3] Discussion of them will therefore involve those defects or vices which are opposed to them, as in Aristotle, who judiciously defined each particular virtue as a mean between an *excess* and a *deficiency*. – The same content which assumes the form of *duties* and then of *virtues* also takes the form of *drives* (see Remarks to § 19). Their basic content is the same, but in drives, this content still belongs to the immediate will and to natural sensation and has not developed far enough to attain the determination of the ethical. Drives therefore have in common with the content of duties and virtues only their abstract object [*Gegenstand*], and since this is indeterminate in itself, it cannot serve to distinguish them as good or evil. Alternatively, if we abstract their positive aspect from them, they are *good*, and conversely, if we abstract their negative aspect, they are *evil* (see § 18).

Addition (H,G). If this or that particular action of a person is ethical, this does not exactly make him virtuous; it does so only if this mode of conduct is a constant feature of his character. Virtue consists rather in ethical virtuosity, and if we speak less about virtue nowadays than before, the reason [*Grund*] is that the ethical is no longer so much the form of a particular individual. The French, above all, are the people who speak most of virtue, because with them, the individual is characterized more by his distinctive qualities and by a natural mode of behaviour. The Germans, on the other hand, are more thoughtful, and in their case, the same content acquires the form of universality.

§ 151

But if it is simply *identical* with the actuality of individuals, the ethical [*das Sittliche*], as their general mode of behaviour, appears as *custom* [*Sitte*]; and the *habit* of the ethical appears as a *second nature¹* which takes the place of the original and purely natural will and is the all-pervading soul, significance, and actuality of individual existence [*Dasein*]. It is *spirit* living and present as a world, and only thus does the substance of spirit begin to exist as spirit.

Addition (H,G). Just as nature has its laws, and as animals, trees, and the sun obey their law, so is custom the law appropriate to the spirit of freedom. Custom is what right and morality have not yet reached, namely spirit. For in right, particularity is not yet that of the concept, but only of the natural will. Similarly, from the point of view of morality, self-consciousness is not yet spiritual consciousness. At this stage, it is merely a question of the value of the subject in itself – that is, the subject which determines itself in accordance with good as opposed to evil still has the form of arbitrary will. Here, on the other hand, at the level of ethics, the will is present as the will of spirit and has a substantial content which is in conformity with itself. Education [*Pädagogik*] is the art of making human beings ethical: it considers them as natural beings and shows them how they can be reborn, and how their original nature can be transformed into a second, spiritual nature so that this spirituality becomes *habitual* to them. In habit, the opposition between the natural and the subjective will disappears, and the resistance of the subject is broken; to this extent, habit is part of ethics, just as it is part of philosophical thought, since the latter requires that the mind [*der Geist*] should be trained to resist arbitrary fancies and that these should be destroyed and overcome to clear the way for rational thought. Human beings even die as a result of habit – that is, if they have become totally habituated to life and mentally [*geistig*] and physically blunted, and the opposition between subjective consciousness and mental activity has disappeared. For they are active only in so far as they have not yet attained something and wish to assert themselves and show what they can do in pursuit of it. Once this is accomplished, their activity and vitality disappear, and the loss of interest which ensues is mental or physical death.

§ 152

In this way, *ethical substantiality* has attained its *right*, and the latter has attained *validity*. That is, the self-will of the individual [*des Einzelnen*], and his own conscience in its attempt to exist for itself and in opposition to the ethical substantiality, have disappeared; for the ethical character knows that the end which moves it[1] is the universal which, though itself unmoved, has developed through its determinations into actual rationality, and it recognizes that its own dignity and the whole continued existence [*Bestehen*] of its particular ends are based upon and actualized within this universal. Subjectivity is itself the absolute form and existent actuality of substance, and the difference between the subject on the one hand and substance as its object [*Gegenstand*], end, and power on the other is the same as their difference in form, both of which differences have disappeared with equal immediacy.

> Subjectivity, which is the ground in which the concept of freedom has its existence [*Existenz*] (see § 106), and which, at the level of morality, is still distinct from this its own concept, is, in the ethical realm, that [mode of] existence of the concept which is adequate to it.

§ 153

The *right of individuals* to their *subjective determination to freedom* is fulfilled in so far as they belong to ethical actuality; for their *certainty* of their own freedom has its *truth* in such objectivity, and it is in the ethical realm that they *actually* possess *their own* essence and their *inner* universality (see § 147).

> When a father asked him for advice about the best way of educating his son in ethical matters, a Pythagorean replied: 'Make him the *citizen of a state with good laws*.' (This saying has also been attributed to others.)[1]

Addition (H). Those pedagogical experiments in removing people from the ordinary life of the present and bringing them up in the country (cf. Rousseau's *Emile*) have been futile, because one cannot successfully isolate people from the laws of the world.[2] Even if young people have to be educated in solitude, no one should imagine that the breath of the spiritual world will not eventually find its way into this solitude and that the power of the world spirit is too weak for it to gain control of such remote regions. The individual attains his right only by becoming the citizen of a good state.

§ 154

The right of individuals to their *particularity* is likewise contained in ethical substantiality, for particularity is the mode of outward appearance in which the ethical exists.

§ 155

Hence *duty* and *right* coincide in this identity of the universal and the particular will, and in the ethical realm, a human being has rights in so far as he has duties, and duties in so far as he has rights. In abstract right, I have the right and someone else has the corresponding duty; and in morality, it is merely an *obligation* that the right of my own knowledge and volition, and of my welfare, should be united with my duties and exist objectively.

Addition (H). The slave can have no duties; only the free human being has these. If all rights were on one side and all duties on the other, the whole would disintegrate, for their identity is the only basis we have to hold on to here.

§ 156

The ethical substance, as containing self-consciousness which has being for itself and is united with its concept, is the *actual spirit* of a family and a people.

Addition (H). The ethical is not abstract like the good, but is intensely actual. The spirit has actuality, and the individuals are its accidents. Thus, there are always only two possible viewpoints in the ethical realm: either one starts from substantiality, or one proceeds atomistically and moves upward from the basis of individuality [*Einzelheit*]. This latter viewpoint excludes spirit, because it leads only to an aggregation, whereas spirit is not something individual [*nichts Einzelnes*] but the unity of the individual and the universal.

§ 157

The concept of this Idea has being only as spirit, as self-knowledge and actuality, because it is the objectivization of itself, the movement through the form of its moments. It is therefore

A. immediate or *natural* ethical spirit – the *family*.
   This substantiality passes over into loss of unity, division, and the point of view of relativity, and is thus
B. *civil society*, i.e. an association of members as *self-sufficient individuals* [*Einzelner*] in what is therefore a *formal universality*, occasioned by their *needs* and by the *legal constitution* as a means of security for persons and property, and by an *external order* for their particular and common interests.
   This *external state*
C. withdraws and comes to a focus in the end and actuality of the substantial universal and of the public life which is dedicated to this – i.e. in the *constitution of the state*.

The Family

§ 158

The family, as the *immediate substantiality* of spirit, has as its determination the spirit's *feeling* [*Empfindung*] of its own unity, which is *love*. Thus, the disposition [appropriate to the family] is to have self-consciousness of one's individuality *within this unity* as essentiality which has being in and for itself, so that one is present in it not as an independent person [*eine Person für sich*] but as a *member*.

Addition (H,G). Love means in general the consciousness of my unity with another, so that I am not isolated on my own [*für mich*], but gain my self-consciousness only through the renunciation of my independent existence [*meines Fürsichseins*] and through knowing myself as the unity of myself with another and of the other with me. But love is a feeling [*Empfindung*], that is, ethical life in its natural form. In the state, it is no longer present. There, one is conscious of unity as law; there, the content must be rational, and I must know it. The first moment in love is that I do not wish to be an independent person in my own right [*für mich*] and that, if I were, I would feel deficient and incomplete. The second moment is that I find myself in another person, that I gain recognition in this person [*daß ich in ihr gelte*], who in turn gains recognition in me. Love is therefore the most immense contradiction; the understanding cannot resolve it, because there is nothing more intractable than this punctiliousness of the self-consciousness which is negated and which I ought nevertheless to possess as affirmative. Love is both the production and the resolution of this contradiction. As its resolution, it is ethical unity.

§ 159

The *right* which belongs to the *individual* [*dem Einzelnen*] by virtue of the family unit and which consists primarily in his life within this unit takes on *legal form* [*die Form Rechtens*], as the abstract moment of *determinate individuality* [*Einzelheit*], only when the family begins to dissolve. In this situation, those who ought to be members [of the family] become, in their disposition and actuality, like self-sufficient persons, and they now receive separately and in a purely external manner – [in the shape of] financial resources, food, costs of education [*Erziehung*], etc. – what was formerly their due as a determinate moment within the family.

Addition (G). The right of the family properly consists in the fact that its substantiality should have existence [*Dasein*]. It is thus a right against externality and against defection from the family unit. On the other hand, love is itself a feeling [*Empfindung*], subjective in character, and unity cannot assert itself against it. Thus, if unity is required, it can be required only with reference to those things [*Dinge*] which are by nature external and not conditioned by feeling.

§ 160

The family attains completion in these three respects:

(a) in the shape of its immediate concept, as *marriage*;
(b) in external existence [*Dasein*], as the *property* and *assets* of the family and their administration;
(c) in the *bringing up* of children and the dissolution of the family.

A. Marriage

§ 161

Marriage, as the *immediate ethical relationship*, contains *first* the moment of *natural* vitality; and since it is a substantial relationship, this involves life in its totality, namely as the actuality of the *species* [*Gattung*]ᵃ and its process (see *Encyclopaedia of the Philosophical*

ᵃ*Translator's note:* In this context of marriage and the family, the word *Gattung* (genus, species) carries with it strong overtones of the closely related word *Begattung* (mating, copulation). Hegel, who habitually exploits such etymological relationships, is doubtless aware of this affinity.

Sciences, §§ 167ff. and 288ff.).*¹* But *secondly*, in self-consciousness, the *union* of the natural sexes, which was merely *inward* (or had being only *in itself*) and whose existence [*Existenz*] was for this very reason merely external, is transformed into a *spiritual* union, into self-conscious love.

Addition (G). Marriage is essentially an ethical relationship. Formerly, especially under most systems of natural law, it was considered only in its physical aspect or natural character. It was accordingly regarded only as a sexual relationship, and its other determinations remained completely inaccessible.*²* But it is equally crude to interpret marriage merely as a civil contract, a notion [*Vorstellung*] which is still to be found even in Kant.*³* On this interpretation, marriage gives contractual form to the arbitrary relations between individuals, and is thus debased to a contract entitling the parties concerned to use one another. A third and equally unacceptable notion is that which simply equates marriage with love; for love, as a feeling [*Empfindung*], is open in all respects to contingency, and this is a shape which the ethical may not assume.*⁴* Marriage should therefore be defined more precisely as rightfully ethical [*rechtlich sittliche*] love, so that the transient, capricious, and purely subjective aspects of love are excluded from it.

§ 162

The subjective origin of marriage may lie to a greater extent in the *particular inclination* of the two persons who enter this relationship, or in the *foresight* and initiative of parents, etc. But its objective origin is the free consent of the persons concerned, and in particular their consent to *constitute a single person* and to give up their natural and individual personalities within this union. In this respect, their union is a self-limitation, but since they attain their substantial self-consciousness within it, it is in fact their liberation.

To enter the state of marriage is an objective determination, and hence an ethical duty. The external origin of a given marriage is by nature contingent, and depends in particular on the level of development [*Bildung*] of reflective thought [*Reflexion*]. At one extreme, the initial step is taken by well-intentioned parents, and when the persons destined to be united in love get to know each other as destined partners, a mutual inclination results. At the other extreme, it is the mutual inclination of the two persons, as *these* infinitely particularized individuals, which arises first. – The former extreme, or any way at all in which the decision to marry comes first and is followed by the inclination so that the two come together in the actual marital union, can itself be regarded as the more ethical course. – In the latter extreme, it is *infinitely particular* distinctness [*Eigentümlichkeit*] which asserts its claims; this is associated with the subjective principle of the modern world (see Remarks to § 124 above). – But in those modern dramas and other artistic presentations in which love between the sexes is the basic interest, we encounter a pervasive element of frostiness which is brought into the heat of the passion such works portray by the total *contingency* associated with it. For the whole interest is represented as resting solely upon *these* particular individuals. This may well be of infinite importance for *them*, but it is of no such importance *in itself*.[1]

Addition (H). Among those peoples who hold the female sex in little respect, the parents arrange marriages arbitrarily, without consulting the individuals concerned; the latter accept this arrangement, since the particularity of feeling [*Empfindung*] makes no claims for itself as yet. The girl's only concern is to find a husband, and the man's to find a wife. Under other circumstances, considerations of wealth [*des Vermögens*], connections, or political ends may determine the outcome. This may have very harsh effects, inasmuch as marriage is made a means to other ends. In modern times, on the other hand, the subjective origin [of marriage], the *state of being in love*, is regarded as the only important factor. Here, it is imagined that each must wait until his hour has struck, and that one can give one's love only to a specific individual.

§ 163

The *ethical* aspect of marriage consists in the consciousness of this union as a substantial end, and hence in love, trust, and the sharing of the whole of individual existence [*Existenz*]. When this disposition and actuality are present, the natural drive is reduced to the modality of a moment of nature which is destined to be extinguished in its very satisfaction, while the spiritual bond asserts *its rights* as the substantial factor and thereby stands out as indissoluble *in itself* and exalted above the contingency of the passions and of particular transient caprice.

It was noted above (§ 75) that marriage is not a contractual relationship as far as its essential basis is concerned. For the precise nature of marriage is to begin from the point of view of contract – i.e. that of individual personality as a self-sufficient unit – *in order to supersede it* [*ihn aufzuheben*]. That identification of personalities whereby the family is a *single person* and its members are its accidents (although substance is essentially the relationship of accidents to itself – see *Encyclopaedia of the Philosophical Sciences*, § 95)[1] is the ethical spirit. Taken by itself [*für sich*] – i.e. stripped of the many external features it possesses by virtue of its existence [*Dasein*] in *these* individuals and in those interests of [the realm of] appearance which are determined in time and in various different ways – and viewed in a shape appropriate to representational thought, this spirit has been venerated as the *Penates* etc.; and in general it is in this spirit that the *religious* character of marriage and the family, i.e. *piety*, is embodied.[2] It is a further abstraction if the divine and substantial is separated from its existence [*Dasein*] in such a way that feeling [*Empfindung*] and the consciousness of spiritual unity are categorized [*fixiert*] as what is falsely called *Platonic love*. This separation is associated with the monastic attitude which defines the moment of natural life [*Lebendigkeit*] as utterly *negative* and, by this very separation, endows it with infinite importance in itself [*für sich*].

Addition (H,G). Marriage differs from *concubinage* inasmuch as the latter is chiefly concerned with the satisfaction of the natural drive, whereas this drive is made subordinate within marriage. This is why, within marriage, one may speak unblushingly of natural functions which, in extra-marital relationships, would produce a feeling of shame. But this is also why marriage should be regarded as indissoluble *in itself*; for the end of marriage is the ethical end, which is so exalted that everything else appears powerless against it and subject to its authority. Marriage should not be disrupted by passion, for the latter is subordinate to it. But it is indissoluble only *in itself*, for as Christ says, divorce is permitted only 'because of the hardness of their hearts'.[3] Since marriage contains the moment of feeling [*Empfindung*], it is not absolute but unstable, and it has within it the possibility of dissolution. But all legislations must make such dissolution as difficult as possible and uphold the right of ethics against caprice.

§ 164

Just as the stipulation of a contract in itself [*für sich*] contains the genuine transfer of property (see § 79), so also do the solemn declaration of consent to the ethical bond of marriage and its recognition and confirmation by the family and community constitute the formal *conclusion* and *actuality* of marriage. (That the *church* plays a part in this connection is a further determination which cannot be discussed here.) It is accordingly only after this ceremony has *first taken place*, as the completion of the *substantial* [aspect of marriage] by means of the *sign* – i.e. by means of language as the most spiritual existence [*Dasein*] of the spiritual (see § 78) – that this bond has been ethically constituted. The sensuous moment which pertains to natural life [*Lebendigkeit*] is thereby put in its ethical context [*Verhältnis*] as an accidental consequence belonging to the external existence of the ethical bond, which may even consist exclusively in mutual love and support.

If, in order to establish or assess the legal determinations [of marriage], it is asked what the *chief end* of marriage is, this chief end will be understood to mean whatever individual aspect of its actuality is to be regarded as more essential than the others. But no one aspect on its own [*für sich*] constitutes the whole extent of its content which has being in and for itself – that is, of its ethical character – and one or other aspect of its existence [*Existenz*] may be absent, without prejudice to the essence of marriage. – If the *conclusion of marriage* as such – i.e. the ceremony whereby the essence of this bond is expressed and *confirmed* as an ethical quality exalted above the *contingency* of feeling [*Empfindung*] and *particular inclination* – is seen as an *external formality* and a so-called purely *civil precept*, nothing remains of this act except perhaps the purpose [*Zweck*] of edification and of attesting the civil relationship [of the marriage partners]. Or indeed, it is the merely positive, arbitrary enactment of a civil or ecclesiastical precept, which is not only indifferent to the nature of marriage, but also – in so far as the emotions are inclined by this precept to attach a value to the formal conclusion [of marriage] and to regard it as a condition which must be fulfilled before the partners can commit themselves totally to each other – brings disunity into[a] the disposition of love and, as an alien factor, runs counter to the inwardness of this union. Although such an opinion claims to impart the highest conception of the freedom, inwardness, and perfection of love, it in fact denies the ethical character of love, that higher suppression and subordination of mere natural drive which is already naturally present in *shame* and which the more determinate spiritual consciousness raises to *chastity* and *purity* [*Zucht*]. More particularly, the view just referred to casts aside the ethical determination [of marriage]. This consists in the fact that the consciousness emerges from its naturalness and subjectivity to concentrate on the thought of the substantial. Instead of further reserving to itself the contingency and arbitrariness of sensuous inclination, it removes the marriage bond from this arbitrariness and, pledging itself to the Penates, makes it over to the substantial; it thereby reduces the sensuous moment to a merely *conditional* one – conditioned, that is, by the true and ethical character of the relationship, and by the recognition of the marriage bond as an ethical one. – It is impertinence and its ally, the understanding, which cannot grasp the speculative nature of the substantial relationship; but both the uncorrupted ethical emotions [*Gemüt*] and the legislations of Christian peoples are in keeping with this speculative nature.

Addition (G). Friedrich von Schlegel in his *Lucinde* and a follower of his in the anonymous *Letters* (Lübeck and Leipzig, 1800) have argued that the marriage ceremony is superfluous and a formality which could be dispensed with, on the grounds that love is the substantial element and that its value may even be diminished by this celebration.[1] These writers represent the physical surrender as necessary in order to prove the freedom and intensity of love – an argument with which seducers are not unfamiliar. On the relations between man and woman, it should be noted that a girl loses her honour in [the act of] physical surrender, which is not so much the case with a man, who has another field of ethical activity apart from the family. A girl's vocation [*Bestimmung*] consists essentially only in the marital relationship; what is therefore required is that love

---

[a]*Translator's note:* Instead of *veruneinige*, which I have translated 'brings disunity into', Hoffmeister's edition has *verunreinige*, which means 'contaminates' or 'defiles'.

should assume the shape of marriage, and that the different moments which are present in love should attain their truly rational relation to each other.

§ 165

The *natural* determinacy of the two sexes acquires an *intellectual* and *ethical* significance by virtue of its rationality. This significance is determined by the difference into which the ethical substantiality, as the concept in itself, divides itself up in order that its vitality may thereby achieve a concrete unity.

§ 166

The *one* [sex] is therefore spirituality which divides itself up into personal self-sufficiency with being *for itself* and the knowledge and volition of *free universality*, i.e. into the self-consciousness of conceptual thought and the volition of the objective and ultimate end. And the *other* is spirituality which maintains itself in unity as knowledge and volition of the substantial in the form of concrete *individuality [Einzelheit]* and *feeling [Empfindung]*. In its external relations, the former is powerful and active, the latter passive and subjective. Man therefore has his actual substantial life in the state, in learning [*Wissenschaft*], etc., and otherwise in work and struggle with the external world and with himself, so that it is only through his division that he fights his way to self-sufficient unity with himself. In the family, he has a peaceful intuition of this unity, and an emotive [*empfindend*] and subjective ethical life. Woman, however, has her substantial vocation [*Bestimmung*] in the family, and her ethical disposition consists in this [family] *piety*.

> In one of the most sublime presentations of piety – the *Antigone* of Sophocles – this quality is therefore declared to be primarily the law of woman, and it is presented as the law of emotive [*empfindend*] and subjective substantiality, of inwardness which has not yet been fully actualized, as the law of the ancient gods and of the chthonic realm [*des Unterirdischen*] as an eternal law of which no one knows whence it came, and in opposition to the public law, the law of the state – an opposition of the highest order in ethics and therefore in tragedy,

and one which is individualized in femininity and masculinity in the same play; cf. *Phenomenology of Spirit*, pp. 383ff. and 417ff.[1]

Addition (H,G). Women may well be educated, but they are not made for the higher sciences, for philosophy and certain artistic productions which require a universal element.[2] Women may have insights [*Einfälle*], taste, and delicacy, but they do not possess the ideal. The difference between man and woman is the difference between animal and plant; the animal is closer in character to man, the plant to woman, for the latter is a more peaceful [process of] unfolding whose principle is the more indeterminate unity of feeling [*Empfindung*]. When women are in charge of government, the state is in danger, for their actions are based not on the demands of universality but on contingent inclination and opinion. The education of women takes place imperceptibly, as if through the atmosphere of representational thought, more through living than through the acquisition of knowledge [*Kenntnissen*], whereas man attains his position only through the attainment of thought and numerous technical exertions.

§ 167

Marriage is essentially *monogamy*, because it is personality or immediate exclusive *individuality* [*Einzelheit*] which enters into and surrenders itself to this relationship, whose truth and *inwardness* (*the subjective form of substantiality*) consequently arise only out of the mutual and *undivided* surrender of this personality.[1] The latter attains its right of being conscious of itself in the *other* only in so far as the other is present in this identity as a person, i.e. as atomic individuality.

> Marriage, and essentially monogamy, is one of the absolute principles on which the ethical life of a community is based; the institution of marriage is therefore included as one of the moments in the foundation of states by gods or heroes.

§ 168

Furthermore, since marriage arises out of the *free surrender* by both sexes of their personalities, which are infinitely unique [*eigen*] to themselves, it must not be concluded within the *naturally identical* circle of people who are acquainted and familiar with each other in every detail – a circle in which the individuals do not have a distinct personality of their own in relation to one another – but must take place [between people] from separate families and personalities of different origin. Marriage between *blood relations* is therefore at variance with the concept of marriage as an ethical act of freedom rather than an association based on immediate natural existence [*Natürlichkeit*] and its drives, and hence it is also at variance with genuine natural feeling [*Empfindung*].

> If marriage itself is regarded as an arbitrary contract and as grounded not in *natural law* but merely in the natural sexual drive, and if external reasons for monogamy have been derived even from the physical relation between numbers of men and women, and obscure feelings have been cited as the only reason for prohibiting marriage between blood relations, such arguments are based on the common notion [*Vorstellung*] of a state of nature and of the naturalness of right, and on the absence of the concept of rationality and freedom.

Addition (H). In the first place, marriage between blood relations runs counter even to the feeling [*Gefühl*] of shame, but this revulsion is justified by the concept of the thing [*Sache*]. In other words, what is already united cannot then be united only by means of marriage. As far as the purely natural relationship is concerned, it is well known that reproduction within a family of animals produces more feeble offspring, for what is to be united must first be separate; the power of procreation, like that of the spirit, increases with the magnitude of oppositions out of which it reconstitutes itself. Familiarity, acquaintance, and the habit of shared activity should not be present before marriage: they should be discovered only within it, and the value of this discovery is all the greater the richer it is and the more components it has.

§ 169

The family, as a person, has its external reality in *property*; and only in the latter, in the shape of *resources*, does its substantial personality have its existence [*Dasein*].

B. The Family's Resources

§ 170

Not only does the family have property; as a *universal* and *enduring* person, it also incurs the need for possessions which are determined as *permanent* and *secure*, i.e. it needs *resources*. Abstract property contains the arbitrary moment of the particular need of the *single individual* [*des bloß Einzelnen*]; this is here transformed, along with the selfishness of desire, into care and acquisition for a *communal purpose*, i.e. into an *ethical* quality.

> The introduction of permanent property appears, in conjunction with the institution of marriage, in the legends of the founding of states, or at least of civilized [*gesittet*] social life. But the precise nature of these resources and the true method of consolidating them become apparent within the sphere of civil society.

§ 171

The family as a legal [*rechtliche*] person in relation to others must be represented by the husband as its head. In addition, he is primarily responsible for external acquisition and for caring for the family's needs, as well as for the control and administration of the family's resources. These are common property, so that no member of the family has particular property, although each has a right to what is held in common. This right and the control of the resources by the head of the family may, however, come into collision, because the ethical disposition of the family is still immediate (see § 158) and exposed to particularization and contingency.

§ 172

When a marriage takes place, a *new family* is constituted, and this is *self-sufficient* for itself in relation to the *kinship groups* or houses from which it originated; its links with the latter are based on the natural blood relationship, but the new family is based on ethical love. The property of an individual is therefore also essentially connected with his marital relationship, and only more distantly connected with his kinship group or house.

> *Marriage settlements* which place a restriction on the common ownership by the partners of their goods, and measures which ensure that the wife will continue to receive legal support, etc., are significant inasmuch as they provide for the dissolution of the marriage in the event of natural death, divorce, etc., and attempt to guarantee that, in such an eventuality, the share of the various members of the family in the common property will be preserved.

Addition (H). Many legal codes relate to the family in the wider sense and regard it as the essential bond, whereas the other bond which unites each specific family appears less important in comparison. Thus, in older Roman law, the wife in the less binding variety of marriage had a closer relationship to her own kinsfolk than to her children and husband,[1] and in the era of feudal law, the maintenance of the *splendor familiae* made it necessary to count only the male members of the family as belonging to it and to regard the family in its entirety as the most important factor, whereas the newly constituted family disappeared from view. Nevertheless, every new family is more essential than the wider context of blood relationships, and marriage partners and children form the proper nucleus in opposition to what can also be described in a certain sense as the family. The financial circumstances [*Vermögensverhältnis*] of individuals must therefore have a more essential connection with their marriage than with the wider circle of their blood relations.

C. The Upbringing of Children and the Dissolution of the Family

§ 173

The *unity* of marriage, which in substance is merely *inwardness* and *disposition* but in existence [*als existierend*] is divided between the two subjects, *itself* becomes in the children *an existence* [*eine Existenz*] *which has being for itself*, and an *object* [*Gegenstand*] which they [i.e. the parents] love as their love and their substantial existence [*Dasein*]. – From the point of view of nature, the presupposition of persons existing *immediately* – as parents – here becomes the *result*, a process which runs on into the infinite progression of generations which produce and presuppose one another. This is the mode in which the simple spirit of the Penates reveals its existence [*Existenz*] as a species [*Gattung*]ᵃ in the finite realm of nature.

Addition (H). The relation of love between man and wife is not yet an objective one; for even if this feeling [*Empfindung*] is their substantial unity, this unity does not yet possess objectivity [*Gegenständlichkeit*]. The parents attain this unity only in their children, in whom they see the whole of their union before them. In the child, the mother loves her husband and he his wife; in it, they see their love before them. Whereas their unity is present in their [shared] resources only as in an external thing [*Sache*], it is present in their children in a spiritual form in which the parents are loved and which they love.

> ᵃ*Translator's note:* Compare note to § 161 above.

§ 174

Children have a right to be *brought up* and *supported* at the expense of the family. The right of the parents to their children's *services*, as services, is based on and limited to the common concern of caring for the family in general. In the same way, the right of the parents over the *arbitrary will* of the children is determined by the end of bringing them up and subjecting them to discipline. The end to which punishments are directed is not justice as such; it is rather of a subjective and moral nature, seeking to have a deterrent effect on a freedom which is still entrammelled in nature and to raise the universal into the children's consciousness and will.

Addition (H). Human beings do not arrive by instinct at what they are destined to become; on the contrary, they must attain this by their own efforts. This is the basis of the child's right to its upbringing. The same applies to peoples under paternal governments: they are fed out of central depots and are not regarded as self-sufficient adults. The services which may be required of children should therefore contribute solely to the end of their upbringing; they must not claim to be justified in their own right [*für sich*], for the most unethical of all relationships is that in which children are slaves.¹ One of the chief moments in a child's upbringing is discipline, the purpose of which is to break the child's self-will in order to eradicate the merely sensuous and natural. One should not imagine that kindness alone is sufficient for this purpose; for it is precisely the immediate will which acts according to immediate fancies and desires rather than reasons and representations [*Vorstellungen*]. If one presents children with reasons, it is left to them to decide whether to accept these or not, and thus everything is made to depend on their caprice.[2] The fact that the parents constitute the universal and essential element entails the need for obedience on the part of the children. Unless the feeling of subordination, which creates a longing to grow up, is nurtured in the children, they become forward and impertinent.[3]

§ 175

Children are free *in themselves*, and their life is merely the immediate existence [*Dasein*] of this freedom;[1] they therefore do not belong as things [*Sachen*] either to others or to their parents. As far as their relationship with the family is concerned, their *upbringing* has the *positive* determination that, in them, the ethical is given the form of immediate *feeling* [*Empfindung*] which is still without opposition, so that their early emotional life may be lived in this [context], as the *basis* of ethical life, in love, trust, and obedience. But in the same connection, their upbringing also has the *negative* determination of raising the children out of the natural immediacy in which they originally exist to self-sufficiency and freedom of personality, thereby enabling them to leave the natural unit of the family.

> The position of Roman children as slaves is one of the institutions which most tarnishes the Roman legal code, and this offence against the most vulnerable and innermost life of ethics is one of the most important moments which enable us to understand the world-historical character of the Romans and their tendency towards legal formalism. – The need for an upbringing is present in children as their own feeling of dissatisfaction within themselves at the way they are – as the drive to belong to the adult world whose superiority they sense, or as the desire to grow up. The method of education through play sees childishness itself as already inherently valuable, presents it in this light to the children, and debases serious things – and the method itself – to a childish form for which the children themselves have little respect.[2] By representing children, in the immature state which they feel they are in, as in fact mature, by endeavouring to make them

satisfied with the way they are, this method distorts and obscures the true need of the children themselves for something better; it creates in them on the one hand an indifference towards, and imperviousness to, the substantial relations of the spiritual world, and on the other a contempt for people inasmuch as they have presented themselves to them in a childish and contemptible light, and finally a vanity and self-importance which revels in its own excellence.

Addition (H,G). As a child, the human being must have lived with his parents in a circle of love and trust, and the rational must appear in him as his own most personal [*eigenste*] subjectivity. In the period of infancy, the mother's role in the child's upbringing is of primary importance, for [the principles of] ethics must be implanted in the child in the form of feeling [*Empfindung*]. It should be noted that, on the whole, children love their parents less than their parents love them, for the children are increasingly independent and gain in strength, thereby leaving their parents behind them, whereas the parents possess in their children the objective and concrete form [*die objektive Gegenständlichkeit*] of their union.

§ 176

Marriage is still only the immediate [form of the] ethical Idea and thus has its objective actuality in the inwardness of subjective disposition and feeling [*Empfindung*]. This accounts for the basic contingency of its existence [*Existenz*]. Just as there can be no compulsion to marry, so also can there be no merely legal [*rechtliches*] or positive bond which could keep the partners together once their dispositions and actions have become antagonistic and hostile. A third ethical authority is, however, required in order to uphold the right of marriage – i.e. of ethical substantiality – against the mere opinion that a hostile disposition is present, and against the contingency of merely transient moods, etc., to distinguish these from total estrangement, and to make sure that the partners are totally estranged before *divorce* is granted.

Addition (H). Since marriage is based only on subjective and contingent feeling, it may be dissolved. The state, on the other hand, is not subject to partition, for it is based on law. Marriage certainly *ought* to be indissoluble, but this indissolubility remains no more than an *obligation*. Since, however, marriage is an ethical institution, it cannot be dissolved by the arbitrary will but only by an ethical authority, whether this be the Church or a court of law. If a total estrangement has occurred – e.g. through adultery – then even the religious authority must permit divorce.

§ 177

The ethical dissolution of the family consists in the fact that the children are brought up to become free personalities and, when they have *come of age*, are recognized as legal [*rechtliche*] persons and as capable both of holding free property of their own and of founding their own families – the sons as heads of families and the daughters as wives. In this family they now have their substantial determination, and in relation to it, their original family recedes in importance as merely their original basis and point of departure, while the abstract category [*das Abstraktum*] of the kinship group has even fewer rights.

§ 178

The natural dissolution of the family through the death of the parents, particularly of the husband, results in *inheritance* of the family's resources. Inheritance is essentially a taking possession by the individual as his own property of what *in themselves* are common resources – an acquisition which, in the case of more distant relationships and with the increasing self-sufficiency of persons and families as a result of the dispersal of civil society, becomes more indeterminate as the disposition of unity declines and as every marriage leads to the renunciation of previous family relationships and the establishment of a new and self-sufficient family.

> The notion [*Einfall*] that inheritance is based on the fact that, by a person's death, his resources become *ownerless property* and as such accrue to the first person to take possession of them, and that, since it is *generally* the relatives of the deceased, as those who are *usually* closest at hand, who take possession in this way, this common occurrence is then made into a rule, for the sake of order, by positive legislation – this notion disregards the nature of the family relationship.[1]

§ 179

The disintegration [of the family] leaves the arbitrary will of the individual free either to expend his entire resources in accordance with his caprices, opinions, and individual ends [*Zwecke der Einzelheit*], or to regard a circle of friends, acquaintances, etc. so to speak as taking the place of a family and to make a pronouncement to that effect in a *testament* whereby they become his rightful heirs.

The formation [*Bildung*] of such a circle as would give the will an ethical justification for disposing of resources in this way – especially in so far as the very act of forming this circle has testamentary implications – involves so much contingency, arbitrariness, intent to pursue selfish ends, etc., that the ethical moment is extremely vague; and the recognition that the arbitrary will is entitled to make bequests is much more likely to lead to infringements of ethical relations and to base aspirations and equally base attachments, and to provide an opportunity and justification for foolish arbitrariness and for the insidious practice of attaching to so-called benefactions and gifts vain and oppressively vexatious conditions which come into effect after the benefactor's death, in which event his property in any case ceases to be his.

§ 180

The principle that the members of the family become self-sufficient and rightful persons (see § 177) allows something of this arbitrariness and discrimination to arise within the family circle among the natural heirs; but it must occur only on a very limited scale if the basic relationship is not to be damaged.

The simple direct arbitrariness of the deceased cannot be made the principle of the *right to make a will*, especially if it is opposed to the substantial right of the family; for the love and veneration of the family for its former member are primarily the only guarantee that his arbitrary will will be respected after his death. Such arbitrariness in itself contains nothing which deserves greater respect than the right of the family itself – on the contrary. Otherwise, the validity of a testamentary disposition would reside solely in its arbitrary recognition by others.[1] But a validity of this kind can be admitted primarily only when the family relationship of which the disposition forms an integral part grows more remote and ineffective. But ineffectiveness in a family relationship, when the latter is actually present, must be classed as unethical, and to extend the validity of arbitrary dispositions at the expense of family relationships is implicitly to weaken the latter's ethical standing. – To make this arbitrariness the main principle of inheritance within the family was, however, part of that harsh and unethical aspect of Roman law referred to above, whereby a son could even be sold by his father and, if he was given his freedom by others, again came under his father's authority [*Gewalt*] and did not actually become free until he had been given his freedom for the third time.[2] According to these laws, the son never attained his majority *de iure*, nor did he become a legal [*rechtliche*] person, and the spoils of war (*peculium castrense*) were the only property which he could own;[3] and if he escaped from his father's authority by being sold and liberated on three occasions in the manner described above, he could not inherit along with those who remained in servitude to the family unless he was expressly included in the will. In the same way, a wife (in so far as she entered marriage as a *matron*, and not as one who *in manum conveniret, in mancipio esset*,[a] as on entering a state of slavery) continued to belong to the family from which she came, rather than to the family which, by her marriage, she had in part founded and which was now actually *her own*; and she was therefore debarred from inheriting the resources of those who were *actually her family*, just as the latter could not inherit from their wife and mother.[4] – We have already noticed (see Remarks to § 3 above) how the unethical aspects of these and other such laws [*Rechte*] were circumvented in the administration of justice, e.g. with the help of the expression *bonorum possessio* instead of *hereditas*, and through the fiction of giving a *filia* the designation *filius* (the fact that *bonorum possessio* is in turn distinct from *possessio bonorum* belongs to that kind of knowledge

---

[a]*Translator's note:* 'entered into marriage and was thereby enslaved'.

[*Kenntnissen*] which characterizes the expert on legal matters).[5] This, as we noted, was the sad necessity to which the judge had to resort, in the face of bad laws, in order to smuggle rationality, *by artful means*, into at least some of their consequences. This was associated with the terrible instability of the main institutions [of the state], and with a frantic activity of legislation designed to counteract the outbreak of evils [*Übel*] which resulted from it. – The unethical consequences which this right of arbitrariness in testamentary dispositions had among the Romans are familiar enough from history, and from the accounts of Lucian and other writers.[6] – It lies in the nature of marriage itself, as the immediate [form of] ethical life, that it is a mixture of substantial relationship, natural contingency, and inner arbitrariness. If, then, arbitrariness is given precedence over the right of the substantial as a result of the servitude of children and the other determinations referred to above or associated with these, and not least because divorce was easy to obtain in Rome – so that even Cicero (and what fine things he has written about *honestum* and *decorum*[a] in his *De Officiis*[b] and everywhere else in his works!) could divorce his wife as a speculation in order to pay his debts out of his new wife's dowry – then a legal way is open to ethical corruption, or rather the laws make such corruption inevitable.[7]

That institution of the law of inheritance which, in order to *preserve* the *family* and to enhance its *renown* by means of *substitutions* and *family testamentary trusts*,[8] either favours the sons by excluding the daughters from inheritance or favours the eldest son by excluding the remaining children (or allows any other kind of inequality to arise) on the one hand infringes the principle of the freedom of property (see § 62), and on the other depends on an arbitrariness which in and for itself has no right to recognition – or more precisely, it depends on the intention to uphold not so much *this* family, as *this* kinship group or house. Not *this* house or kinship group, however, but the *family as such* is the Idea which has this right [to recognition], and freedom [to dispose] of resources and equality of

---

[a]*Translator's note:* 'morality' and 'propriety'.
[b]*Translator's note: Of Duties* (title of a work by Cicero).

inheritance are much more likely than their opposites to preserve both the shape [*Gestaltung*] of ethics and the *families* themselves. – Institutions like those of Rome totally misapprehend the right of marriage (see § 172), for marriage entails the complete foundation of a distinct and actual family, in comparison with which what is called the family in a general sense – i.e. the *stirps* or *gens* – becomes only an abstraction which grows ever more remote and less actual as one generation succeeds the other (see § 177). Love, the ethical moment in marriage, is, as love, a feeling [*Empfindung*] for actual individuals in the present, not for an abstraction. – On this abstraction of the understanding as the world-historical principle of the Roman Empire, see below (§ 356). – The higher sphere of politics brings with it a right of primogeniture and an inflexible entailment of resources – not, however, in an arbitrary manner, but as a necessary consequence of the Idea of the state; but this will be dealt with later (see § 306).

Addition (H,G). In Rome, the father in earlier times could disinherit his children, and could even kill them;[9] later, this was no longer permitted. Attempts were made to create a system out of this incongruity between the unethical and its ethical adaptations, and it is adherence to this system which constitutes the difficulty and inadequacy of our own law of inheritance. Wills may certainly be permitted; but in allowing them to be made, our point of view must be that this right of arbitrariness arises or increases with the disintegration of the family and the distance between its members; and the so-called *family of friendship* which a will brings into existence can arise only in the absence of the closer family of marriage and children. Wills in general have a disagreeable and unpleasant aspect, for in making my will, I identify those for whom I have an affection. But affection is arbitrary; it may be gained in various ways under false pretences or associated with various foolish reasons, and it may lead to a beneficiary being required to submit to the greatest indignities. In England, where all kinds of eccentricity are endemic,[a] innumerable foolish notions are associated with wills.

---

[a]*Translator's note:* The preceding seven words appear to be Gans's interpolation, since they have no counterpart in the sections of Hotho's and Griesheim's notes (VPR III, 558–562 and IV, 466–468) on which this Addition is based.

TRANSITION FROM THE FAMILY TO CIVIL SOCIETY

§ 181

The family disintegrates, in a natural manner and essentially through the principle of personality, into a *plurality* of families whose relation to one another is in general that of self-sufficient concrete persons and consequently of an external kind. In other words, the moments which are bound together in the unity of the family, as the ethical Idea which is still in its concept, must be released from the concept to [attain] self-sufficient reality. This is the stage of *difference* [*Differenz*]. To put it first in abstract terms, this gives the determination of *particularity* which is related to *universality*, but in such a way that the latter is its basis – though still only its *inner* basis; consequently, this universality is present only as a formal *appearance* in the particular [*auf formelle, in das Besondere nur scheinende Weise*]. This relation of reflection accordingly represents in the first instance the loss of ethical life; or, since the latter, as the essence, necessarily *appears* (see *Encyclopaedia of the Philosophical Sciences*, §§ 64ff. and 81ff.),[1] this relation constitutes the *world of appearance* of the ethical, i.e. *civil society*.

> The expansion of the family, as its transition to another principle, is, in [the realm of] existence [*Existenz*], either a peaceful expansion whereby it becomes a people or *nation*, which thus has a common natural origin, or a coming together of scattered family communities under the influence of a dominant power or in a voluntary union prompted by interdependent needs and their reciprocal satisfaction.

Addition (H). The point of departure of universality here is the self-sufficiency of the particular, so that ethical life appears to be lost at this level, for it is in fact the identity of the family which consciousness regards as the primary, divine, and obligating factor. But a relation now arises whereby the particular is to be my primary determining principle, and the ethical determination is thereby superseded. But I am in fact simply under a misapprehension, for while I believe that I am adhering to the particular, the universal and the necessity of the [wider] context nevertheless remain the primary and essential factor. I am thus entirely on the level of semblance, and while my particularity remains my determining principle – that is, my end – I am thereby serving the universal which in fact retains ultimate power over me.

SECTION 2

Civil Society

§ 182

The concrete person who, as a *particular* person, as a totality of needs and a mixture of natural necessity and arbitrariness, is his own end, is *one principle* of civil society. But this particular person stands essentially in *relation* [*Beziehung*] to other similar particulars, and their relation is such that each asserts itself and gains satisfaction through the others, and thus at the same time through the exclusive *mediation* of the form of *universality*, which is *the second principle*.

Addition (H,G). Civil society is the [stage of] difference [*Differenz*] which intervenes between the family and the state, even if its full development [*Ausbildung*] occurs later than that of the state; for as difference, it presupposes the state, which it must have before it as a self-sufficient entity in order to subsist [*bestehen*] itself. Besides, the creation of civil society belongs to the modern world, which for the first time allows all determinations of the Idea to attain their rights. If the state is represented as a unity of different persons, as a unity which is merely a community [of interests], this applies only to the determination of civil society. Many modern exponents of constitutional law have been unable to offer any view of the state but this. In civil society, each individual is his own end, and all else means nothing to him. But he cannot accomplish the full extent of his ends without reference to others; these others are therefore means to the end of the particular [person]. But through its reference to others, the particular end takes on the form of universality, and gains satisfaction by simultaneously satisfying the welfare of others. Since particularity is tied to the condition of universality, the whole [of civil society] is the sphere [*Boden*] of mediation in which all individual characteristics

[*Einzelheiten*], all aptitudes, and all accidents of birth and fortune are liberated, and where the waves of all passions surge forth, governed only by the reason which shines through them. Particularity, limited by universality, is the only standard by which each particular [person] promotes his welfare.

§ 183

The selfish end in its actualization, conditioned in this way by universality, establishes a system of all-round interdependence, so that the subsistence [*Subsistenz*] and welfare of the individual [*des Einzelnen*] and his rightful existence [*Dasein*] are interwoven with, and grounded on, the subsistence, welfare, and rights of all, and have actuality and security only in this context. – One may regard this system in the first instance as the *external state*, the *state of necessity*[1] and *of the understanding*.

§ 184

When it is divided in this way, the Idea gives a *distinct existence* [*Dasein*] to its *moments* – to *particularity* it gives the right to develop and express itself in all directions, and to universality the right to prove itself both as the ground and necessary form of particularity, and as the power behind it and its ultimate end. – It is the system of ethical life, lost in its extremes, which constitutes the abstract moment of the *reality* of the Idea, which is present here only as the *relative totality* and *inner necessity* of this external *appearance*.

Addition (H). Here, the ethical is lost in its extremes, and the immediate unity of the family has disintegrated into a plurality. Reality here is externality, the dissolution of the concept, the self-sufficiency of its liberated and existent moments. Although particularity and universality have become separated in civil society, they are nevertheless bound up with and conditioned by each other. Although each appears to do precisely the opposite of the other and imagines that it can exist only by keeping the other at a distance, each nevertheless has the other as its condition. Thus, most people regard the payment of taxes, for example, as an infringement of their particularity, as a hostile element prejudicial to their own ends; but however true this may *appear*, the particularity of their own ends cannot be satisfied without the universal,[a] and a country in

---

[a]*Translator's note:* The remainder of this sentence has no counterpart in the section of Hotho's notes (VPR III, 570–574) on which this Addition is based.

which no taxes were paid could scarcely distinguish itself in strengthening its particular interests [*Besonderheit*]. It might likewise appear that the universal would do better to absorb the strength of the particular, as described, for example, in Plato's *Republic*; but this again is only apparent, for the two exist solely through and for one another and are transformed into one another. In furthering my end, I further the universal, and this in turn furthers my end.[1]

§ 185

Particularity in itself [*für sich*], on the one hand indulging itself in all directions as it satisfies its needs, contingent arbitrariness, and subjective caprice, destroys itself and its substantial concept in the act of enjoyment; on the other hand, as infinitely agitated and continually dependent on external contingency and arbitrariness and at the same time limited by the power of universality, the satisfaction of both necessary and contingent needs is itself contingent. In these opposites and their complexity, civil society affords a spectacle of extravagance and misery as well as of the physical and ethical corruption common to both.

> The self-sufficient development of particularity (cf. Remarks to § 124) is the moment which appears in the states of the ancient world as an influx of ethical corruption and as the ultimate reason [*Grund*] for their downfall. These states, some of which were based on the patriarchal and religious principle and others on the principle of a more spiritual, though simpler, ethical life, but all of which were based on *original* natural intuition, could not withstand the division which arose within the latter as self-consciousness became infinitely reflected into itself. As this reflection began to emerge, first as a disposition and then in actuality, they succumbed to it, because the simple principle on which they were still based lacked the truly infinite power which resides solely in that unity which allows the *opposition* within reason [*Vernunft*] *to develop to its full strength*, and has overcome it so as to preserve itself within it and *wholly contain it within itself*. – Plato, in his *Republic*, presents the substance of ethical life in its ideal *beauty* and *truth*; but he cannot come to terms with the principle of self-sufficient particularity, which had suddenly

overtaken Greek ethical life in his time, except by setting up
his purely substantial state in opposition to it and completely
excluding it [from this state], from its very beginnings in
private property (see Remarks to § 46)[1] and the *family*[2] to its
subsequent development [*Ausbildung*] as the arbitrary will of
individuals and their choice of social position [*des Standes*],
etc.[3] This deficiency also explains why the great *substantial*
truth of his *Republic* is imperfectly understood, and why it is
usually regarded as a dream of abstract thought, as what is
indeed often called an *ideal*. The principle of the *self-sufficient
and inherently infinite personality* of the individual [*des
Einzelnen*], the principle of subjective freedom, which arose in
an inward form in the *Christian* religion and in an external
form (which was therefore linked with abstract universality) in
the *Roman* world, is denied its right in that merely substantial
form of the actual spirit [in Plato's *Republic*]. This principle is
historically later than the Greek world, and the philosophical
reflection which can fathom these depths is likewise later than
the substantial Idea of Greek philosophy.

Addition (H). Particularity in itself [*für sich*] is boundless [*maßlos*] extravagance, and the forms of this extravagance are themselves boundless.
Through their representations [*Vorstellungen*] and reflections, human
beings expand their desires, which do not form a closed circle like animal
instinct, and extend them to false [*schlechte*] infinity. But on the other
hand, deprivation and want are likewise boundless, and this confused
situation can be restored to harmony only through the forcible intervention of the state. Although Plato's state sought to exclude particularity,
this is of no help, because such help would contradict the infinite right of
the Idea to allow particularity its freedom. It was primarily in the
Christian religion that the right of subjectivity arose, along with the
infinity of being-for-itself; and in this situation, the totality must also be
endowed with sufficient strength to bring particularity into harmony with
the ethical unity.

§ 186

But in the very act of developing itself independently [*für sich*] to
totality, the principle of particularity passes over into *universality*, and
only in the latter does it have its truth and its right to positive actuality.
This unity is not that of ethical identity, because at this level of

division (see § 184), the two principles are self-sufficient; and for the same reason, it is present not as *freedom*, but as the *necessity* whereby the *particular* must rise to the *form of universality* and seek and find its subsistence in this form.

§ 187

Individuals, as citizens of this state, are *private persons* who have their own interest as their end. Since this end is mediated through the universal, which thus *appears* to the individuals as a *means*, they can attain their end only in so far as they themselves determine their knowledge, volition, and action in a universal way and make themselves *links* in the chain of this *continuum* [*Zusammenhang*]. In this situation, the interest of the Idea, which is not present in the consciousness of these members of civil society as such, is the *process* whereby their individuality [*Einzelheit*] and naturalness are raised, both by natural necessity and by their arbitrary needs, *to formal freedom* and formal *universality of knowledge and volition*, and subjectivity is *educated* in its particularity.

> The ideas [*Vorstellungen*] of the *innocence* of the state of nature and of the ethical simplicity of uncultured [*ungebildeter*] peoples imply that *education* [*Bildung*] will be regarded as something purely *external* and associated with corruption.[1] On the other hand, if one believes that needs, their satisfaction, the pleasures and comforts of individual [*partikularen*] life, etc. are *absolute* ends, education will be regarded as merely a *means* to these ends. Both of these views show a lack of familiarity with the nature of spirit and with the end of reason. Spirit attains its actuality only through internal division, by imposing this limitation and finitude upon itself in [the shape of] natural needs and the continuum [*Zusammenhang*] of this external necessity, and, *in the very process of adapting itself to these* limitations,[a] by overcoming them and gaining its *objective* existence [*Dasein*] within them. The end of reason is consequently

[a]*Translator's note: eben damit, daß er sich in sie hineinbildet.* In this section, Hegel plays repeatedly on various forms of the verb *bilden* (to educate, shape, or cultivate) in order to underline their semantic affinities. He exploits various forms of the verb *scheinen* (to appear) to similar effect in § 181.

neither the natural ethical simplicity referred to above, nor, as particularity develops, the pleasures as such which are attained through education. Its end is rather to work to eliminate *natural simplicity*, whether as passive selflessness or as barbarism of knowledge and volition – i.e. to eliminate the *immediacy* and *individuality* [*Einzelheit*] in which spirit is immersed, so that this externality may take on the rationality *of which it is capable*, namely the *form of universality or of the understanding*. Only in this way is the spirit *at home* and *with itself* in this *externality* as such. Its freedom thus has an existence [*Dasein*] within the latter; and, in this element which, *in itself*, is alien to its determination of freedom, the spirit becomes *for itself*, and has to do only with what it has impressed its seal upon and *produced* itself. – By this very means, the *form of universality* comes into existence [*Existenz*] for itself in thought, the only form which is a worthy element for the existence [*Existenz*] of the Idea. *Education*, in its absolute determination, is therefore *liberation* and *work* towards a higher liberation; it is the absolute transition to the infinitely subjective substantiality of ethical life, which is no longer immediate and natural, but spiritual and at the same time raised to the shape of universality. Within the subject, this liberation is the *hard work* of opposing mere subjectivity of conduct, of opposing the immediacy of desire as well as the subjective vanity of feeling [*Empfindung*] and the arbitrariness of caprice. The fact that it is such hard work accounts for some of the disfavour which it incurs. But it is through this work of education that the subjective will attains *objectivity* even within itself, that objectivity in which alone it is for its part worthy and capable of being the *actuality* of the Idea. – Furthermore, this form of universality to which particularity has worked its way upwards and cultivated [*heraufgebildet*] itself, i.e. the form of the understanding, ensures at the same time that particularity *becomes* the genuine *being-for-itself* of individuality [*Einzelheit*]; and, since it is from particularity that universality receives both the content which fills it and its infinite self-determination, particularity is itself present in ethical life as free subjectivity which has infinite being-for-itself. This is the level at which it becomes plain that *education* is an immanent moment of the absolute, and that it has infinite value.

Addition (H). By educated people, we may understand in the first place those who do everything as others do it[a] and who do not flaunt their particular characteristics [*Partikularität*], whereas it is precisely these characteristics which the uneducated display, since their behaviour is not guided by the universal aspects of its object [*Gegenstand*]. Similarly, in his relations with others, the uneducated man can easily cause offence, for he simply lets himself go and does not reflect on the feelings [*Empfindungen*] of others. He does not wish to hurt others, but his conduct is not in harmony with his will. Thus, education irons out particularity to make it act in accordance with the nature of the thing [*Sache*]. True originality, by which the [universal][b] thing is produced, requires true education, whereas false originality assumes tasteless forms which occur only to the uneducated.

[a] *Translator's note:* The text, as extracted by Gans from Hotho's notes, reads *solche . . . die alles machen können, was andere tun* ('those who can do everything that others do'). Hotho's notes in fact read *daß sie alles machen w[ie] Andere* ('that they do everything as others do it'; VPR III, 582). I have adopted the latter reading as more authentic and as giving a better sense, and have modified it to fit the structure of Gans's sentence.

[b] *Translator's note:* In Hotho's notes, on which this Addition is based, the term *Sache* is here defined as 'the universal in every form' (VPR III, 583). I have accordingly added 'universal' in brackets.

§ 188

Civil society contains the following three moments:

A. The mediation of *need* and the satisfaction of the *individual* [*des Einzelnen*] through his work and through the work and satisfaction of the needs of *all the others* – the system of *needs*.
B. The actuality of the universal of *freedom* contained therein, the protection of property through the *administration of justice*.
C. Provisions against the contingency which remains present in the above systems, and care for the particular interest as a *common* interest, by means of the *police* and the *corporation*.

A. The System of Needs

§ 189

Particularity, in its primary determination as that which is opposed to the universal of the will in general (see § 60),[a] is *subjective need*, which attains its objectivity, i.e. its *satisfaction*, by means of (α) external things [*Dinge*], which are likewise the *property* and product of the needs and *wills* of others and of (β) activity and work, as the mediation between the two aspects. The end of subjective need is the satisfaction of subjective *particularity*, but in the relation [*Beziehung*] between this and the needs and free arbitrary will of others, *universality* asserts itself, and the resultant manifestation [*Scheinen*] of rationality in the sphere of finitude is *the understanding*. This is the chief aspect which must be considered here, and which itself constitutes the conciliatory element within this sphere.

> *Political economy* is the science which begins with the above viewpoints but must go on to explain mass relationships and mass movements in their qualitative and quantitative determinacy and complexity. – This is one of the sciences which have originated in the modern age as their element [*Boden*]. The development of science is of interest in showing how *thought* extracts from the endless multitude of details with which it is initially confronted the simple principles of the thing [*Sache*], the understanding which works within it and controls it (see Smith, Say, and Ricardo).[1] – To recognize, in the sphere of needs, this manifestation [*Scheinen*] of rationality which is present in the thing [*Sache*] and active within it has, on the one hand, a conciliatory effect; but conversely, this is also the field in which the understanding, with its subjective ends and moral opinions, gives vent to its discontent and moral irritation.

Addition (H,G). There are certain universal needs, such as food, drink, clothing, etc., and how these are satisfied depends entirely on contingent circumstances. The soil is more or less fertile in different places, the years

---

[a] *Translator's note:* The first edition, and the Suhrkamp edition, refer to § 60, but Ilting's edition refers to § 6, which makes much better sense (VPR II, 640). T. M. Knox's suggestion of § 59 (Knox, p. 126) is less plausible.

are more or less productive, one man is industrious and the other lazy. But this proliferation of arbitrariness generates universal determinations from within itself, and this apparently scattered and thoughtless activity is subject to a necessity which arises of its own accord. To discover the necessity at work here is the object [*Gegenstand*] of political economy, a science which does credit to thought because it finds the laws underlying a mass of contingent occurrences. It is an interesting spectacle to observe here how all the interconnections have repercussions on others, how the particular spheres fall into groups, influence others, and are helped or hindered by these. This interaction, which is at first sight incredible since everything seems to depend on the arbitrary will of the individual [*des Einzelnen*], is particularly worthy of note; it bears a resemblance to the planetary system, which presents only irregular movements to the eye, yet whose laws can nevertheless be recognized.

a. The Nature of Needs and their Satisfaction

§ 190

The ways and means by which the *animal* can satisfy its needs are limited in scope, and its needs are likewise limited. Though sharing this dependence, the *human being* is at the same time able to transcend it and to show his universality, first by *multiplying* his needs and means [of satisfying them], and secondly by *dividing* and *differentiating* the concrete need into individual parts and aspects which then become different needs, *particularized* and hence *more abstract*.

> In right, the object [*Gegenstand*] is the *person*; at the level of morality, it is the *subject*, in the family, the *family-member*, and in civil society in general, the *citizen* (in the sense of *bourgeois*). Here, at the level of needs (cf. Remarks to § 123), it is that concretum *of representational thought* which we call *the human being*; this is the first, and in fact the only occasion on which we shall refer to *the human being* in this sense.

Addition (H). The animal is a particular entity [*ein Partikulares*] which has its instinct and the means of satisfying it, means whose bounds cannot be exceeded. There are insects which are tied to a specific plant, and other animals whose sphere is wider and which can live in different climates; but there is always a limiting factor in comparison with the sphere which is open to the human being. The need for food and clothing, the necessity of renouncing raw food and of making it fit to eat and destroying its natural immediacy, means that the human being's life is less comfortable than that of the animal – as indeed it ought to be, since man is a spiritual being. The understanding, which can grasp distinctions, brings multiplicity into these needs; and since taste and utility become criteria of judgement, the needs themselves are also affected by them. In the end, it is no longer need but opinion which has to be satisfied, and it is a distinctive feature of education that it resolves the concrete into its particulars. The very multiplication of needs has a restraining influence on desire, for if people make use of many things, the pressure to obtain any one of these which they might need is less strong, and this is a sign that necessity [*die Not*] in general is less powerful.

§ 191

In the same way, the *means* employed by particularized needs, and in general the ways in which these are satisfied, are *divided* and *multiplied* so that they in turn become relative ends and abstract needs. It is an infinite process of multiplication which is in equal measure a *differentiation* of these determinations and a *judgement* on the suitability of the means to their ends – i.e. [a process of] *refinement*.

Addition (H). What the English call 'comfortable'*ª* is something utterly inexhaustible; its ramifications are infinite, for every comfort in turn reveals its less comfortable side, and the resulting inventions are endless. A need is therefore created not so much by those who experience it directly as by those who seek to profit from its emergence.

ªTranslator's note: Hotho, on whose notes this Addition is based, cites this word in the French form *confortable*, and makes no reference to the English (VPR III, 593).

§ 192

Needs and means, as existing in reality [*als reelles Dasein*], become a *being* [*Sein*] for *others* by whose needs and work their satisfaction is mutually conditioned. That abstraction which becomes a quality of both needs and means (see § 191) also becomes a determination of the mutual relations [*Beziehung*] between individuals. This universality, as the *quality of being recognized*, is the moment which makes isolated and abstract needs, means, and modes of satisfaction into *concrete*, i.e. *social* ones.

Addition (H). The fact that I have to fit in with other people brings the form of universality into play at this point. I acquire my means of satisfaction from others and must accordingly accept their opinions. But at the same time, I am compelled to produce means whereby others can be satisfied. Thus, the one plays into the hands of the other and is connected with it. To this extent, everything particular [*alles Partikulare*] takes on a social character; in the manner of dress and times of meals, there are certain conventions which one must accept, for in such matters, it is not worth the trouble to seek to display one's own insight, and it is wisest to act as others do.

§ 193

This moment thus becomes a particular end-determinant for the means themselves and their ownership, and also for the way in which needs are satisfied. In addition, it immediately involves the requirement of *equality* in this respect with others. On the one hand, the need for this equality, together with *imitation* as the process whereby people make themselves like others, and on the other hand the need of *particularity* (which is likewise present here) to assert itself through some distinctive quality, themselves become an actual source of the multiplication and expansion of needs.

§ 194

Within social needs, as a combination of immediate or natural needs and the spiritual needs of *representational thought* [*Vorstellung*], the spiritual needs, as the universal, predominate. This social moment accordingly contains the aspect of *liberation*, because the strict natural necessity of need is concealed and man's relation is to *his own opinion*, which is universal, and to a necessity imposed by himself alone, instead of simply to an external necessity, to inner contingency, and to *arbitrariness*.

> The notion [*Vorstellung*] that, in relation to his needs, man lived in *freedom* in a so-called state of nature in which he had only so-called natural needs of a simple kind and in which, to satisfy these, he employed only those means with which a contingent nature immediately provided him[1] – this notion, even if we disregard the moment of liberation which is present

in work (and which will be discussed below), is mistaken. For a condition in which natural needs as such were immediately satisfied would merely be one in which spirituality was immersed in nature, and hence a condition of savagery and unfreedom; whereas freedom consists solely in the reflection of the spiritual into itself, its distinction from the natural, and its reflection upon the latter.

§ 195

This liberation is *formal*, because the particularity of the ends remains the basic content. The tendency of the social condition towards an indeterminate multiplication and specification of needs, means, and pleasures – i.e. *luxury* – a tendency which, like the distinction between natural and educated[a] needs, has no limits [*Grenzen*], involves an equally infinite increase in dependence and want. These are confronted with a material which offers infinite resistance, i.e. with external means whose particular character is that they are the property of the free will [of others] and are therefore absolutely unyielding.

Addition (H). Diogenes, in his whole character as a Cynic,[1] is in fact merely a product of the social life of Athens, and what determined him was the opinion against which his entire way of life reacted. His way of life was therefore not independent, but merely a consequence of these social conditions, and itself an unprepossessing product of luxury. Where, on the one hand, luxury is at its height, want and depravity are equally great on the other, and Cynicism is then evoked by the opposite extreme of refinement.

[a]*Translator's note:* The first edition, and the Suhrkamp edition, read *ungebildetem* ('uneducated'). I follow Ilting's edition (VPR II, 644), whose reading *gebildetem* ('educated') makes better sense.

b. The Nature of Work

§ 196

The mediation whereby appropriate and *particularized* means are acquired and prepared for similarly *particularized* needs is *work*. By the most diverse processes, work specifically applies to these numerous ends the material which is immediately provided by nature.

This process of formation gives the means their value and appropriateness, so that man, as a consumer, is chiefly concerned with *human* products, and it is human effort which he consumes.

Addition (H). There are few immediate materials which do not need to be processed: even air has to be earned – inasmuch as it has to be heated – and perhaps water is unique in that it can be drunk as it is found. It is by the sweat and labour of human beings that man obtains the means to satisfy his needs.

§ 197

The variety of determinations and objects [*Gegenstände*] which are worthy of interest is the basis from which *theoretical education* develops. This involves not only a variety of representations [*Vorstellungen*] and items of knowledge [*Kenntnissen*], but also an ability to form such representations [*des Vorstellens*] and pass from one to the other in a rapid and versatile manner, to grasp complex and general relations [*Beziehungen*], etc. – it is the education of the understanding in general, and therefore also includes language. – *Practical education* through work consists in the self-perpetuating need and *habit of being occupied* in one way or another, in the *limitation of one's activity* to suit both the nature of the material in question and, in particular, the arbitrary will of others, and in a habit, acquired through this discipline, of *objective* activity and *universally applicable* skills.

Addition (H). The barbarian is lazy and differs from the educated man in his dull and solitary brooding, for practical education consists precisely in the need and habit of being occupied. The clumsy man always produces something other than what he intended, because he is not in control of his own actions. But a worker can be described as skilled if he produces the thing [*Sache*] as it ought to be, and if, in his subjective actions, he encounters no resistance to the end he is pursuing.

§ 198

The universal and objective aspect of work consists, however, in that [process of] *abstraction* which confers a specific character on means and needs and hence also on production, so giving rise to the *division of labour*. Through this division, the work of the individual [*des Einzelnen*] becomes *simpler*, so that his skill at his abstract work becomes greater, as does the volume of his output. At the same time, this abstraction of skill and means makes the *dependence* and *reciprocity* of human beings in the satisfaction of their other needs complete and entirely necessary. Furthermore, the abstraction of production makes work increasingly *mechanical*, so that the human being is eventually able to step aside and let a *machine* take his place.[1]

c. Resources [and Estates]

§ 199

In this dependence and reciprocity of work and the satisfaction of needs, *subjective selfishness* turns into a *contribution towards the satisfaction of the needs of everyone else*. By a dialectical movement, the particular is mediated by the universal so that each individual, in earning, producing, and enjoying on his own account [*für sich*], thereby earns and produces for the enjoyment of others.[1] This necessity which is inherent in the interlinked dependence of each on all now appears to each individual in the form of *universal and permanent resources* (see § 170) in which, through his education and skill, he has an opportunity to share; he is thereby assured of his livelihood, just as the universal resources are maintained and augmented by the income which he earns through his work.

§ 200

The *possibility of sharing* in the universal resources – i.e. of holding *particular* resources – is, however, *conditional* upon one's own immediate basic assets (i.e. capital) on the one hand, and upon one's skill on the other; the latter in turn is itself conditioned by the former, but also by contingent circumstances whose variety gives rise to *differences* in the *development* of natural physical and mental [*geistigen*] aptitudes which are already unequal in themselves [*für sich*]. In this sphere of particularity, these differences manifest themselves in every direction and at every level, and, in conjunction with other contingent and arbitrary circumstances, necessarily result in *inequalities in the resources and skills* of individuals.

The spirit's objective *right of particularity*, which is contained within the Idea, does not cancel out [*nicht aufhebt*] the inequality of human beings in civil society – an inequality posited by nature, which is the element of inequality – but in fact produces it out of the spirit itself and raises it to an inequality of skills, resources, and even of intellectual and moral education. To oppose this right with a demand for *equality* is characteristic of the empty understanding, which mistakes this abstraction and *obligation* of its own for the real and the rational. This sphere of particularity imagines that it is universal, but in its merely relative identity with the universal, it retains both natural and arbitrary particularity, and hence the remnants of the state of nature. In addition, that reason which is immanent in the system of human needs and their movement articulates this system into an organic whole composed of different elements (see § 201).

§ 201

The infinitely varied means and their equally infinite and intertwined movements of reciprocal production and exchange *converge*, by virtue of the universality inherent in their content, and become *differentiated* into *universal masses*. In consequence, the whole complex [*Zusammenhang*] evolves into *particular systems* of needs, with their corresponding means, varieties of work, modes of satisfaction, and theoretical and practical education – into systems to which individuals are separately assigned, i.e. into different *estates*.

Addition (H). The manner in which the universal resources are shared depends on every particular characteristic of the individuals concerned; but the universal differences into which civil society is particularized are necessary in character. While the family is the primary basis of the state, the estates are the second. The latter are of special importance, because private persons, despite their selfishness, find it necessary to have recourse to others. This is accordingly the root which links selfishness with the universal, i.e. with the state, which must take care to ensure that this connection is a firm and solid one.

§ 202

The estates are determined, in accordance with *the concept*, as the *substantial* or immediate estate, the reflecting or *formal* estate, and lastly, the *universal* estate.

§ 203

(a) The *substantial* estate has its resources in the natural products of the *soil* which it cultivates – soil which is capable of being exclusively private property, and which requires not just indeterminate exploitation, but formation of an objective kind. Given the association of work and acquisition with fixed *individual* seasons, and the dependence of the yield on the varying character of natural processes, the end to which need is directed in this case becomes that of *provision* for the future. But because of the conditions to which it is subject, this provision retains the character of a [mode of] subsistence [*Subsistenz*] in which reflection and the will of the individual play a lesser role, and thus its substantial disposition in general is that of an immediate ethical life based on the family relationship and on trust.

The proper beginning and original foundation of states has rightly been equated with the introduction of *agriculture* and of *marriage*. For the former principle brings with it the cultivation of the soil, and in consequence exclusively private property (cf. Remarks to § 170), and it reduces the nomadic life of savages, who seek their livelihood in constant movement, to the tranquillity of civil law [*Privatrecht*] and the secure satisfaction of needs. This is accompanied by the restriction [*Beschränkung*] of sexual love to marriage, and the marriage bond is in turn extended to become a *lasting* and inherently [*in sich*] universal union, while need becomes *care for the family* and possession becomes *family property*. Security, consolidation, lasting satisfaction of needs, etc. – qualities by which these institutions primarily recommend themselves – are nothing but forms of universality and shapes assumed by rationality, the absolute and ultimate end, as it asserts itself in these objects [*Gegenständen*]. – What can be more interesting in this connection than the ingenious and learned *explanations* which my highly esteemed friend, Herr Creuzer, has given of the *agrarian* festivals, images, and shrines of the ancients (especially in the fourth volume of his *Mythology and Symbolism*)[1]? In the consciousness of the ancients, the introduction of agriculture and of the institutions associated with it were divine acts, and they were accordingly treated with religious veneration. A further consequence, which also occurs in the other estates, is that the substantial character of this estate entails modifications with regard to civil law – especially to the administration of justice – and likewise with regard to education and instruction and also to religion; these modifications do *not* affect the *substantial content*, but only its *form* and the *development of reflection*.

Addition (H). In our times, the [agricultural] economy, too, is run in a reflective manner, like a factory, and it accordingly takes on a character like that of the second estate and opposed to its own character of natural-ness. Nevertheless, this first estate will always retain the patriarchal way of life and the substantial disposition associated with it. The human being reacts here with immediate feeling [*Empfindung*] as he accepts what he receives; he thanks God for it and lives in faith and confidence that this goodness will continue. What he receives is enough for him; he uses it up, for it will be replenished. This is a simple disposition which is not concerned with the acquisition of wealth; it may also be described as that of the *old nobility*, which consumed whatever it had. In this estate, the main part is played by nature, and human industry is subordinate to it. In the second estate, however, it is the understanding itself which is essen-tial, and the products of nature can be regarded only as raw materials.

§ 204

(b) The *estate of trade and industry* [*Stand des Gewerbes*] has the task of *giving form* to natural products, and it relies for its livelihood on its *work*, on *reflection* and the understanding, and essentially on its medi-ation of the needs and work of others. What it produces and enjoys, it owes chiefly to *itself* and to its own activity. – Its business is in turn subdivided into work performed in a relatively concrete manner in re-sponse to individual [*einzelne*] needs and at the request of individuals [*Einzelner*] (*the estate of craftsmanship*); more abstract work of mass production which supplies individual needs but is more universally in demand (*the estate of manufacturers*); and the business of exchanging separate commodities [*Mittel*] for one another, chiefly through the universal means of exchange, namely money, in which the abstract value of all goods is actualized (*the estate of commerce*).

Addition (H). In the estate of trade and industry, the individual [*Individuum*] has to rely on himself, and this feeling of selfhood is intimately connected with the demand for a condition in which right is upheld. The sense of freedom and order has therefore arisen mainly in towns. The first estate, on the other hand, has little need to think for itself:[a] what it gains is an alien gift, a gift of nature. This feeling of dependence is fundamental to it, and may easily be coupled with a willingness to accept whatever may befall it at the hands of other people. The first estate is therefore more inclined to subservience, the second estate to freedom.

[a]*Translator's note: hat . . . wenig selbst zu denken*; this seems to be a misreading by Gans of the equivalent phrase in Hotho's notes (VPR III, 630), *hat wenig sich selbst zu danken* ('owes little to its own efforts').

§ 205

(c) The *universal estate* has *the universal interests* of society as its business. It must therefore be exempted from work for the direct satisfaction of its needs, either by having private resources, or by receiving an indemnity from the state which calls upon its services, so that the private interest is satisfied through working for the universal.

§ 206

On the one hand, the *estates*, as particularity become objective to itself, are divided in this way into different general categories in accordance with the concept. But on the other hand, the question of which particular estate the *individual* will belong to is influenced by his natural disposition, birth, and circumstances, although the ultimate and essential determinant is *subjective opinion* and the *particular arbitrary will*, which are accorded their right, their merit, and their honour in this sphere. Thus, *what* happens in this sphere through *inner necessity* is at the same time *mediated by the arbitrary will*, and for the subjective consciousness, it has the shape of being the product of its own will.[1]

> In this respect, too, in relation to the principle of particularity and subjective arbitrariness, a difference emerges between the political life of east and west, and of the ancient and modern worlds. In the former, the division of the whole into estates

came about *objectively and of its own accord*, because it is rational *in itself*; but the principle of subjective particularity was at the same time denied its rights, as when, for example, the allocation of individuals to specific estates was left to the rulers, as in Plato's *Republic* (Book III, p. 320, Zweibrücken edition, Vol. VI [415 a–d]), or to birth *alone*, as in the *Indian caste-system.*[2] Thus subjective particularity, excluded from the organization of the whole and not reconciled within it, consequently shows itself – since it likewise appears as an essential moment – as a hostile element, as a corruption of the social order (see Remarks to § 185). It either overthrows the latter, as in the Greek states and in the Roman Republic; or if the social order survives as a ruling power – or perhaps as a religious authority – it appears as inner corruption and complete degeneration, as was to some extent the case in *Sparta* and as is now entirely the case in *India*. – But if it is supported by the objective order, conforming to the latter and at the same time retaining its rights, subjective particularity becomes the sole animating principle of civil society and of the development of intellectual activity, merit, and honour. The recognition and right according to which all that is rationally necessary in civil society and in the state should at the same time come into effect *through the mediation of the arbitrary will* is the more precise definition [*Bestimmung*] of what is primarily meant by the universal idea [*Vorstellung*] of *freedom* (see § 121).

§ 207

The individual attains actuality only by entering into *existence* [*Dasein*] in general, and hence into *determinate particularity*; he must accordingly limit himself *exclusively* to one of the *particular* spheres of need. The ethical disposition within this system is therefore that of *rectitude* and the *honour of one's estate*, so that each individual, by a process of self-determination, makes himself a member of one of the moments of civil society through his activity, diligence, and skill, and supports himself in this capacity; and only through this mediation with the universal does he simultaneously provide for himself and gain *recognition* in his own eyes [*Vorstellung*] and in the eyes of others. – *Morality* has its proper place in this sphere, where reflection on one's own actions and the ends of welfare and of particular needs are dominant, and where contingency in the satisfaction of the latter makes even contingent and individual help into a duty.

Initially – i.e. especially in youth – the individual balks at the notion [*Vorstellung*] of committing himself to a particular estate, and regards this as a limitation imposed on his universal determination and as a purely *external* necessity. This is a consequence of abstract thinking, which stops short at the universal and so does not reach actuality; it does not recognize that the concept, in order *to exist*, must first of all enter into the distinction between the concept and its reality, and hence into determinacy and particularity (see § 7), and that only thus can abstract thinking attain actuality and ethical objectivity.

Addition (H). When we say that a human being must be *somebody* [*etwas*], we mean that he must belong to a particular estate; for being somebody means that he has substantial being. A human being with no estate is merely a private person and does not possess actual universality. On the other hand, the individual [*der Einzelne*] in his particularity may see himself as the universal and believe that he would be lowering himself if he became a member of an estate. This is the false notion [*Vorstellung*] that, if something attains an existence [*Dasein*] which is necessary to it, it is thereby limiting and surrendering itself.

§ 208

The principle of this system of needs, as that of the personal [*eigene*] particularity of knowledge and volition, contains within itself that universality which has being *in and for itself*, i.e. the universality of *freedom*, but only *abstractly* and hence as the *right of property*. Here, however, this right is present no longer merely *in itself*, but in its valid actuality as the *protection of property* through the *administration of justice*.

B. *The Administration of Justice*

§ 209

The *relativity* of the reciprocal relation between needs and work to satisfy these needs includes in the first place its *reflection into itself* as infinite personality in general, i.e. as (abstract) *right*. But it is this very sphere of relativity – as that of *education* – which gives right an *existence* [*Dasein*] in which it is *universally recognized, known*, and *willed*, and in which, through the mediation of this quality of being known and willed, it has validity and objective actuality.

> It is part of education, of *thinking* as consciousness of the individual [*des Einzelnen*] in the form of universality, that I am apprehended as a *universal* person, in which [respect] *all* are identical. A *human being counts as such because he is a human being*, not because he is a Jew, Catholic, Protestant, German, Italian, etc. This consciousness, which is the aim of *thought*, is of infinite importance, and it is inadequate only if it adopts a fixed position – for example, as *cosmopolitanism* – in opposition to the concrete life of the state.

Addition (H). On the one hand, it is through the system of particularity [*Partikularität*] that right becomes externally necessary as a protection for particular interests [*die Besonderheit*]. Even if its source is the concept, right comes into existence [*Existenz*] only because it is useful in relation to needs. In order to conceive of right in terms of thought, one must be educated in how to think, and not remain confined to the merely sensuous realm; one must adapt the form of universality to the objects [*Gegenständen*], and likewise regulate one's will according to a universal [principle]. Only after human beings have invented numerous needs for themselves, and the acquisition of these needs has become entwined with their satisfaction, is it possible for laws to be made.

§ 210

The objective actuality of right consists partly in its being present to the consciousness and being in some way *known*, and partly in its possessing the power of actuality, in having *validity* and hence also in becoming *known as universally valid*.

a. Right as Law

§ 211

When what is right *in itself* is *posited* in its objective existence [*Dasein*] – i.e. determined by thought for consciousness and *known* [*bekannt*] as what is right and valid – it becomes *law;*[a] and through this determination, right becomes *positive* right in general.

To posit something as *universal* – i.e. to bring it to the consciousness as a universal – is, as everyone knows, *to think* (cf. Remarks to §§ 13 and 21 above); when the content is reduced in this way to its simplest form, it is given its final *determinacy*. Only when it becomes law does what is right take on both the *form* of its universality and its true determinacy. Thus, the process of legislation should not be represented merely by that one of its moments whereby something is declared to be a rule of behaviour valid for everyone; more important than this is the inner and essential moment, namely *cognition of the content* in its *determinate universality*. Since only animals have their law as instinct, whereas only human beings have theirs as custom [*Gewohnheit*], *customary rights* contain the moment of being *thoughts* and of being *known* [*gewußt*]. The difference between these and laws consists [*besteht*] simply in the fact that the former are known in a subjective and contingent manner, so that they are less determinate for themselves and the universality of thought is more obscure; and in addition, cognizance [*die Kenntnis*] of this or that aspect of right, or of right in general, is the contingent property of only a few people. The view that such rights, since they take the form of *customs* [*Gewohnheiten*], are privileged in having become part of *life* is an illusion, for the valid laws of the nation do not cease to be its customs merely because they have been written down and collected. (Besides, it is precisely in those areas which involve the most lifeless material and the most lifeless thoughts that there is most talk nowadays of *life* and *becoming*

---

[a] *Translator's note:* Hegel is once again exploiting the etymological affinity of words to suggest a semantic affinity. In this case, the noun *Gesetz* ('law') echoes the verb *gesetzt* ('posited').

part of life.) When customary rights are eventually collected and put together – which must happen at an early stage among a people which has attained even some degree of education – this collection is a *legal code*; and since it is merely a collection, it will be characterized by *formlessness*, indeterminacy, and incompleteness. The main difference between this and a legal code in the proper sense is that in the latter, the principles of right in their *universality*, and hence in their determinacy, are apprehended and expressed in terms of thought. The *law of the land* (or common law) *of England* is contained, as everyone knows, in *statutes* (formal laws) and in so-called *unwritten law*; this unwritten law, incidentally, is likewise recorded in writing, and knowledge [*Kenntnis*] of it can and must be acquired solely through reading (of the many quarto volumes which it fills). The enormous confusion which prevails in England both in the administration of justice and in the matter [*Sache*] itself has, however, been described by those most familiar with it.[1] They note in particular the circumstance that, since this unwritten law is contained in the verdicts of courts of law and judges, the judges constantly act as *legislators*;[2] they are both dependent on the authority of their predecessors – since the latter merely gave expression to the unwritten law – and *independent* of it, because they themselves incorporate the unwritten law and are accordingly entitled to judge whether earlier decisions were compatible with the unwritten law or not. – A similar confusion which could have arisen in the administration of justice during the later Roman Empire because of the differing authorities of all the famous jurists was averted when an emperor devised the ingenious expedient, known as the *law of citations*,[3] which introduced a kind of college of *long-deceased* lawyers with a majority vote and a president (see Hugo's *History of Roman Law* [1799 edition], § 354). – To deny a civilized nation, or the legal profession [*dem juristischen Stande*] within it, the ability to draw up a legal code would be among the greatest insults one could offer to either;[4] for this does not require that a system of laws with a *new content* should be created, but only that the present content of the laws should be recognized in its determinate universality – i.e. grasped by means of *thought* – and subsequently applied to particular cases.

Addition (H,G). The sun and the planets also have their laws, but they are unaware of them. Barbarians are governed by drives, customs [*Sitten*], and feelings, but they have no consciousness of these. When right is posited and known [*gewußt*], all the contingencies of feeling [*Empfindung*] and opinion and the forms of revenge, compassion, and selfishness fall away, so that right only then attains its true determinacy and is duly honoured. Only through the discipline of being apprehended does it become capable of universality. Collisions arise in the application of the law, where the understanding of the judge has its place; this is entirely necessary, for the implementation of the law would otherwise be a completely mechanical process. But to go so far as to eliminate such collisions altogether by relying heavily on the discretion of the judge is a far worse solution, because collisions are also inherent in thought, in the thinking consciousness and its dialectic, whereas the mere decision of a judge would be arbitrary. It is usually argued in defence of customary right that it has a living quality, but this living quality, i.e. the identity of the determination with the subject, is not the whole essence of the matter [*Sache*]; right must be known by thought, it must be a system in itself, and only as such can it have any validity among civilized [*gebildeten*] nations. If it has lately been denied that nations have a vocation to legislate, this is not only offensive but also foolish, for it does not even credit individuals [*den Einzelnen*] with the skill to reduce the infinite mass of existing laws to a coherent system, despite the fact that the infinite urge of our times is precisely to systematize, i.e. to raise to the universal. It has likewise been held that collections of verdicts such as are found in the *corpus juris*[5] are much more valuable than a legal code worked out in the most general way, on the grounds that such verdicts always retain a certain particularity and association with history which people are reluctant to part with. But the practice of English law shows clearly enough how pernicious such collections are.

§ 212

In this identity of *being in itself* and *being posited*, only what is *law* has binding force as *right*. Since being posited constitutes the aspect of existence [*Dasein*] in which the contingency of self-will and of other particular factors may also intervene, what is law may differ in content from what is right in itself.

In positive right, what is *legal* [*gesetzmäßig*] is therefore the source of cognition of what is *right* [*Recht*], or more precisely, of what is *lawful* [*Rechtens*]; the positive science of right is to that extent a historical science whose principle is that of authority. Whatever else may arise is a matter [*Sache*] for the understanding and concerns the external classification, compilation, consequences, and further application etc. [of laws]. When the understanding becomes involved with the nature of the thing [*Sache*] itself, its theories (e.g. of criminal law) show what mischief it can do with its deductive reasoning [*Räsonnement aus Gründen*]. – On the one hand, positive science has not only the right, but also the necessary duty to deduce in every detail from its positive data both the historical developments and the applications and ramifications of the given determinations of right, and to follow up their consequences; but on the other hand, if it is then asked whether, after all these demonstrations, a determination of right is *rational*, those who occupy themselves with this science should at least not be absolutely astonished, even if they regard the question as *beside the point*. – On *understanding* [the law], cf. Remarks to § 3 above.

§ 213

While right comes into existence [*Dasein*] primarily in the form of being posited, it also comes into existence in terms of *content* when it is *applied* to the *material* of civil society – to its relationships and varieties of property and contracts in their endlessly increasing diversity and complexity – and to ethical relationships based on emotion, love and trust (but only in so far as these contain the aspect of abstract right – see § 159). Since morality and moral precepts concern the will in its most personal [*eigensten*] subjectivity and particularity, they cannot be the object [*Gegenstand*] of positive legislation. Further material [for the positive content of right] is furnished by the rights and duties which emanate from the administration of justice itself, from the state, etc.

Addition (G). In the higher relationships of marriage, love, religion, and the state, only those aspects which are by nature capable of having an external dimension can become the object of legislation. Nevertheless, the legislation of different peoples varies greatly in this respect. For example, the Chinese state has a law to the effect that a husband must love his first wife more than his other wives. If he is convicted of having done the opposite, he is subjected to corporal punishment. In older legislations, there are likewise numerous rules concerning loyalty and honesty which are out of keeping with the nature of law, because they apply entirely to the realm of inwardness. It is only in the case of oaths, where things [*Dinge*] are referred to the conscience, that honesty and loyalty must be taken into account as substantial issues.

§ 214

But apart from its application to the *particular*, the fact that right is posited also makes it *applicable* to the *individual* [*einzelnen*] *case*. It thereby enters the sphere of the *quantitative*, which is not determined by the concept (i.e. the quantitative in itself [*für sich*], or as the determination of value when one qualitative item is exchanged for another). Determination by the concept imposes only a general limit [*Grenze*] within which variations are also possible. But such variations must be eliminated if anything is to be actualized, at which point a contingent and arbitrary decision is arrived at within the limit referred to.

It is in this *focusing* of the universal, not just on the particular but on an individual case – i.e. in its *immediate application* – that the *purely positive* aspect of the law chiefly lies. It is impossible to determine by *reason*, or to decide by applying a determination derived from the concept, whether the just penalty for an offence is corporal punishment of forty lashes or thirty-nine,[1] a fine of five dollars [*Taler*] as distinct from four dollars and twenty-three groschen or less,[2] or imprisonment for a year or for 364 days or less, or for a year and one, two, or three days. And yet an injustice is done if there is even one lash too many, or one dollar or groschen, one week or one day in prison too many or too few. – It is reason itself which recognizes that contingency, contradiction, and semblance have their (*albeit limited*) sphere and right, and it does not attempt to reduce such contradictions to a just equivalence; here, the only interest present is that of *actualization*, the interest that some kind of determination and decision should

245

be reached, no matter how this is done (within given limits [*innerhalb einer Grenze*]). This decision belongs to formal self-certainty, to abstract subjectivity, which may rely either on its ability – *within the given limits* – to stop short and settle the matter simply in order that a settlement may be reached, or on such grounds for determination as the choice of a *round* number, or of the number forty minus one. – It makes no difference if the law does not specify this ultimate determination which actuality requires, but leaves it to the judge to decide and simply limits [*beschränkt*] him to a maximum and minimum; for the maximum and minimum will themselves be round numbers of this kind, and they do not remove [*hebt es nicht auf*] the need for the judge to arrive at a finite and purely positive determination of the kind referred to, but assign it to him as a necessary task.

Addition (H,G). There is essentially one aspect of law and the administration of justice which is subject to contingency, and this derives from the fact that the law is a universal determination which has to be applied to the individual case. If one were to object to this contingency, the objection would be merely abstract. For example, the magnitude of a punishment cannot be made to correspond with any conceptual definition [*Begriffsbestimmung*], and whatever is decided will in this respect always be arbitrary. But this contingency is itself necessary; and if one uses it as a general argument against a code of laws, for example, on the grounds that the latter is therefore imperfect, this overlooks the very aspect in which completeness is impossible to attain, and which must therefore be accepted as it stands.

b. The Existence [*Dasein*] of the Law

§ 215

For the law to have binding force, it is necessary, in view of the right of self-consciousness (see § 132 and its appended Remarks) that the laws should be made *universally known*.

To hang the laws at such a height that no citizen could read them, as Dionysius the Tyrant did,[1] is an injustice [*Unrecht*] of exactly the same kind as to bury them in an extensive apparatus of learned books and collections of verdicts based on divergent judgements, opinions, practices, etc., all expressed in a foreign language, so that knowledge [*Kenntnis*] of the laws currently in force is accessible only to those who have made them an object of scholarly study. – Those rulers who have given their peoples a collection of laws – if only a formless collection like that of Justinian, or better still, a *law of the land* embodied in an orderly and specific legal code[2] – were not only the greatest benefactors of their peoples, who duly praised and thanked them; what they did was at the same time a great *act of justice*.

Addition (G). The legal profession [*Juristenstand*], which has special knowledge of the laws, often regards this as its monopoly and no concern of those who are not among its members. Thus, the physicists took exception to Goethe's theory of colours[3] because he did not belong[a] to their profession and was a poet into the bargain. But just as one need not be a shoemaker to know whether one's shoes fit, so is there no need to belong to a specific profession in order to know about matters of universal interest. Right is concerned with freedom, the worthiest and most sacred possession of man, and man must know about it if it is to have binding force for him.

[a] *Translator's note:* The past tense is Gans's, for Griesheim's notes read 'does not belong to their profession and is even a poet' (VPR IV, 543); Goethe, who died in 1832, was still alive when Griesheim made his notes from Hegel's lectures.

§ 216

On the one hand, *simple* and universal determinations are required for the public legal code, but on the other, the nature of *the finite material* in question leads to endless further determinations. The scope of the law ought on the one hand to be that of a *complete* and self-contained whole, but on the other hand, there is a constant need for new legal determinations. But since this antinomy is merely a product of the *specialization* of universal principles which themselves remain unchanged, the right to a complete legal code remains intact, as does the right [which requires] that these simple and universal principles should be capable of comprehension and formulation without reference to, and in distinction from, their specialization.

One of the main sources of the complexity of legislation is that the rational, i.e. that which is rightful in and for itself, may gradually infiltrate primitive institutions which contain an unjust element [*ein Unrecht*] and are therefore of merely historical significance. This took place with Roman institutions, as already mentioned (see Remarks to § 180), and with the old feudal law, etc. But it is essential to realize that the very nature of the finite material entails an infinite progression when determinations which are universal in themselves and rational in and for themselves are applied to it. – It is therefore mistaken to demand that a legal code should be comprehensive in the sense of absolutely complete and incapable of any further determinations (this demand is a predominantly *German* affliction) and to refuse to accept, i.e. to actualize, something allegedly imperfect on the grounds that it is incapable of such completion. Both of these errors are based on a misapprehension of the nature of finite matters such as civil law [*Privatrecht*], whose so-called perfection is a *perennial approximation* to perfection, and on a misapprehension of the difference between the universal of reason and the universal of the understanding, and of the *application* of the latter to the material of finitude and individuality [*Einzelheit*], whose extent is infinite. – 'Le plus grand ennemi du bien c'est le mieux'[a] is an expression of true common sense, as opposed to the common sense of empty ratiocination and reflection.[1]

Addition (H,G). Completeness means the comprehensive collection of all individual items belonging to a given sphere, and no science or area of knowledge [*Kenntnis*] can be complete in this sense. Now if it is said that philosophy or any other science is incomplete, it is easy to conclude that one ought to wait for the remaining part to be added, for it may be that the best is yet to come. But this is not the way in which progress is made, whether in geometry, in which new determinations continue to emerge despite the fact that it appears to be a closed subject, or in philosophy, which is always capable of further specialization, even if it is concerned with the universal Idea. The universal law always used to be the Ten Commandments; and it is manifestly absurd not to promulgate the law 'Thou shalt not kill' on the grounds that a legal code cannot be complete.

[a]*Translator's note:* 'The greatest enemy of the good is the better.' I follow the Suhrkamp edition (*Werke* VII, 369) and VPR (II, 663) in reading '*mieux*', as against the first edition's '*meilleur*'.

Even idle reflection may conclude that every legal code is capable of improvement, for it is possible to imagine what is most glorious, exalted, and beautiful as being more glorious, exalted, and beautiful still. But a large and ancient tree puts out more and more branches without thereby becoming a new tree; yet it would be foolish to refuse to plant a tree just because it might produce new branches.

§ 217

Just as right *in itself* becomes law in civil society, so too does my individual [*einzelne*] right, whose existence [*Dasein*] was previously *immediate* and *abstract*, acquire a new significance when its existence is recognized as part of the existent [*existierenden*] universal will and knowledge. Acquisitions of property and transactions relating to it must therefore be undertaken and expressed in the *form* which that existence gives to them. Property is accordingly based on *contract* and on those *formalities* which make it capable of proof and valid before the law.

The original, i.e. immediate, modes of acquisition and titles (see §§ 54ff.) are in fact abandoned in civil society, and occur only as individual accidents or limited moments. – Both feeling, which remains confined to the subjective, and reflection, which clings to its abstract essences, reject such formalities, whereas the dead understanding may for its part hold on to them in preference to the thing [*Sache*] itself and multiply them indefinitely. – Besides, the process of development [*Bildung*] begins with a content whose form is sensuous and immediate and, by means of long and arduous work, arrives at the form of thought appropriate to this content and thereby gives it simple and adequate expression. It is in the nature of this process that, at the stage when the development of right is only just beginning, ceremonies and formalities are extremely elaborate, and count rather as the thing itself than as its symbol; this is why, even in Roman law, a multitude of determinations, and especially turns of phrase, was retained from earlier ceremonies instead of being replaced by determinations of thought and adequate means of expressing them.

Addition (H,G). When right is posited as what it is in itself, it is law. I possess something or own a property which I took over as ownerless; this property must now also be recognized and posited as mine. This is why there are *formalities* in society with reference to property: boundary stones are erected as symbols for others to recognize, and mortgage books and property registers are compiled. Most property in civil society is based on contract, whose formalities are fixed and determinate. One may well view such formalities with antipathy and believe that they exist only in order to bring in money for the authorities [*Obrigkeit*]; they may even be regarded as offensive and as a sign of mistrust, on the grounds that they invalidate the saying that a man's word is his bond; but the essential aspect of such forms is that what is right in itself should also be posited as right. My will is a rational will; it has validity, and this validity should be recognized by others. Here is the point at which my subjectivity and that of others must be put aside, and the will must attain a security, stability, and objectivity which form alone can give it.

§ 218

Since property and personality have legal recognition and validity in civil society, *crime* is no longer an injury [*Verletzung*] merely to a *subjective infinite*, but to the *universal* cause [*Sache*] whose existence [*Existenz*] is inherently [*in sich*] stable and strong. This gives rise to the viewpoint that an action may be a *danger* to society. On the one hand, this increases the magnitude of the crime; but on the other, the power of society has now become sure of itself, and this reduces the external *importance* of the injury and so leads to greater leniency in its punishment.

> The fact that an injury to *one* member of society is an injury to *all* the others does not alter the nature of crime in terms of its concept, but in terms of its outward existence [*Existenz*]; for the injury now affects the attitudes [*Vorstellung*] and consciousness of civil society, and not just the existence [*Dasein*] of the immediately injured party. In heroic ages – see the tragedies of the ancients – the citizens do not regard the crimes which members of royal houses commit against each other as injuries to themselves. – Crime *in itself* is an infinite injury, but as an *existence* [*Dasein*], it must be measured in terms of qualitative and quantitative differences (see § 96); and since its existence is essentially determined as a *represen-*

tation [*Vorstellung*] and *consciousness of the validity of the laws*, its *danger to civil society* is a determination of its magnitude, or even *one* of its qualitative determinations. – This quality or magnitude varies, however, according to the *condition* of civil society, and this is the justification both for attaching the death penalty to a theft of a few pence or of a turnip, and for imposing a lenient punishment for a theft of a hundred and more times these amounts. Although the view that they are a threat to civil society may appear to aggravate crimes, it has in fact been chiefly responsible for a reduction in punishments. A penal code is therefore primarily a product of its time and of the current condition of civil society.

Addition (H). That a crime committed in society should appear greater and yet be punished more leniently is an apparent contradiction. But whereas it would be impossible for society to leave a crime unpunished – since the crime would then be posited as right – the fact that society is sure of itself means that crime, in comparison, is always of a purely individual character, an unstable and isolated phenomenon. The very stability of society gives crime the status of something merely subjective, which seems the product not so much of the deliberate will as of natural impulse. This view makes crime appear in a milder light, so that its punishment also becomes milder. If society is still inwardly unstable, punishments must be made to set an example, for punishment is itself a counter-example to the example of crime. But in a society which is internally stable, the positedness of crime is so weak that the cancellation [*Aufhebung*] of this positedness must itself assume similar proportions. Thus, harsh punishments are not unjust in and for themselves, but are proportionate to the conditions of their time; a criminal code cannot be valid for every age, and crimes are semblances of existence [*Scheinexistenzen*] which can meet with greater or lesser degrees of repudiation.

c. The Court of Law

§ 219

When right has come into existence [*Dasein*] in the form of law, it has being for itself; as opposed to *particular volitions and opinions* with regard to right, it is self-sufficient and has to assert itself as *universal*. This *cognition* and *actualization* of right in the particular case, without the subjective feeling [*Empfindung*] of *particular* interest, is the responsibility of a public authority [*Macht*], namely the *court of law*.

The historical origin of judge and lawcourts may have taken the form of a patriarchal relationship, of coercion [*Gewalt*], or of free choice; but this is irrelevant as far as the concept of the thing [*Sache*] is concerned. To regard the introduction of jurisdiction by sovereign princes and governments as merely a matter [*Sache*] of *arbitrary grace and favour*, as Herr von Haller does (in his *Restoration of Political Science*),[1] is an example of that thoughtlessness which fails to realize that, since legal and political institutions in general are rational in character, they are necessary in and for themselves, and that the form in which they first arose and were introduced has no bearing on a discussion of their rational basis. – The opposite extreme to this view is the crude notion that the administration of justice, as in the days of the right of private warfare [*Faustrecht*], is an improper use of force, a suppression of freedom, and a rule of despotism.[2] The administration of justice should be regarded both as a duty and as a right on the part of the public authority, and as a right, it is not in the least dependent on whether individuals choose to entrust it to an authority or not.

§ 220

When the right against crime takes the form of *revenge* (see § 102), it is merely right *in itself*, not in a form that is lawful [*Rechtens*], i.e. it is not just [*gerecht*] in its existence [*Existenz*]. Instead of the injured party, the injured *universal* now makes its appearance, and it has its distinctive actuality in the court of law. It takes over the prosecution and penalization of crime, and these thereby cease to be the merely *subjective* and contingent retribution of revenge and are transformed into the genuine reconciliation of right with itself, i.e. into *punishment*. Objectively, this reconciliation applies to the *law*, which restores and thereby *actualizes itself as valid* through the cancellation [*Aufheben*] of the crime; and subjectively, it applies to the criminal in that *his law*, *which is known by him* and is *valid* for him and *for his protection*, is enforced upon him in such a way that he himself finds in it the satisfaction of justice and merely the enactment of *what is proper to him* [*des Seinigen*].

§ 221

A member of civil society has the *right to stand in a court of law* and also the *duty to submit to the court's authority* and to accept its decision alone when his own right is in dispute.

Addition (H). Since every individual has the right to stand in court, he must also know the laws, otherwise this entitlement would be of no use to him. But the individual also has the duty to submit to the court's authority. Under the feudal system, the powerful often refused to do so, challenging the court and treating it as an injustice [*Unrecht*] on the court's part if they were summoned before it. But conditions such as these contradict the purpose of a court. In more recent times, sovereign princes have had to recognize the authority of the courts in private matters, and in free states, they usually lose their cases.

§ 222

In the courts, right takes on the determination that it must be *capable of proof*. The *process of law* puts the parties in a position of having to substantiate their evidence and their legal arguments [*Rechtsgründe*], and to acquaint the judge and themselves with the matter [*Sache*] in question. These *steps are themselves rights*; their course must therefore be determined by law, and they also form an essential part of theoretical jurisprudence [*Rechtswissenschaft*].

Addition (H). It may be infuriating to know that one has a right and then be denied it on the grounds that it cannot be proved. But the right which I have must also be a posited right: I must be able to describe it and prove it, and a right which has being in itself cannot be recognized by society until it has also been posited.

§ 223

The fragmentation of these actions into more and more separate actions with their separate rights has no inherent limit [*Grenze*]. Through this fragmentation, the process of law, which *in itself* is already a means, stands out in opposition to its end as something external to it. – The parties have a right to go through these lengthy formalities, which are *their* right. But since these may also be turned into an evil [*Übel*] and even into an instrument of injustice [*Unrecht*], the parties must be obliged by law to submit themselves to a simple court (a court of arbitration or court of the first instance) in an attempt to settle their differences before they proceed any further. This is necessary in order to protect them – and right itself, as the substantial matter [*Sache*] at issue – against the process of law and its misuse.

> *Equity* involves a departure from formal right in the light of moral or other considerations, and relates primarily to the *content* of the legal action. The function of a *court of equity*, however, will be to reach a decision on the individual case, without adhering to the formalities of the legal process and in particular to the objective evidence as the law may interpret it; it will also reach its decision in the interests of the individual case in its *own* right, and not in the interests of making a universal legal disposition.[1]

§ 224

The rights of the subjective consciousness include not only that of making the laws publicly known (see § 215), but also the possibility of knowing [*zu kennen*] how the law is *actualized* in particular cases, i.e. of knowing the course of the external proceedings, legal arguments [*Rechtsgründe*], and so forth – *the publicity of the administration of justice*; for the course of law is in itself an occurrence of universal validity, and although the particular content of the case may be of interest only to the parties themselves, its universal content (i.e. the right within it and the decision on this right) is of interest to everyone.

> The deliberations of the members of the court among themselves on the judgement they are to deliver are expressions of opinions and views which are still *particular* and hence not of a public nature.

Addition (H). Straightforward common sense sees it as right and proper that the administration of justice should be public.[1] A major obstacle to this has always been the high station of those with powers of jurisdiction, since they are reluctant to appear before the general public, seeing themselves as guardians of a right to which the laity should not have access. But a primary characteristic of a right is that the citizens should have confidence in it, and it is this aspect which requires that justice should be dispensed in public. The right of publicity is based on the fact that the end of the court is right, which *as* a universal should also come *before* the universal, and also on the fact that the citizens are thereby convinced that justice [*Recht*] is actually being done.

§ 225

The dispensation of justice, as the application of the law to the *individual case*, involves *two distinct aspects*: *first*, a knowledge [*Erkenntnis*] of the nature of the case in its *immediate individuality* [*Einzelheit*] – e.g. whether a contract etc. has been made, whether an offence has been committed and who the culprit is, and in *criminal* law, whether the *substantial*, criminal character of the deed was determined by premeditation (see Remarks to § 119); and secondly, the subsumption of the case under the *law* of the restoration of right, which, in criminal cases, includes the punishment. The decisions on these two distinct aspects are also distinct functions.

> In the judicial system of Rome, the distinction between these two functions took the form that the praetor gave his decision *on the assumption* that the facts of the matter [*Sache*] were so and so, and then appointed a special *iudex* to inquire into these facts.[1] – In the English legal system, it is left to the insight or arbitrary will of the prosecutor to categorize an act in terms of its specific criminal character (e.g. as murder or manslaughter), and the court cannot determine otherwise if it finds his conclusion incorrect.[2]

§ 226

In the first place, the supervision of the whole course of the inquiry, and of the legal actions between the parties (which are themselves rights – see § 222), and in addition the second aspect of legal judgement (see § 225), are the proper task of the professional judge. Since he is the organ of the law, the case must be prepared for him to enable it to be subsumed [under the law in question]; that is, it must be raised out of its apparent empirical character to become a recognized fact of a universal kind.

§ 227

The first of these aspects – the *knowledge* [*Erkenntnis*] of the case in its *immediate* individuality [*Einzelheit*], and its categorization – does not in itself involve any legal dispensation. It is a knowledge to which *every educated person* may aspire. The essential factor in categorizing an action is the subjective moment of the agent's insight and intention (see Part Two above); besides, proof is concerned not with objects [*Gegenstände*] of reason or abstract objects of the understanding, but only with details, circumstances, and objects of sensuous intuition and subjective certainty, so that it does not involve any absolutely objective determination. For these reasons, the ultimate factors in such a decision are *subjective conviction* and conscience (*animi sententio*);[1] and in the case of the proof, which rests on the statements and affirmations of others, its ultimate (though subjective) guarantee is the *oath*.

> In dealing with this subject, it is of great importance to bear in mind the kind of *proof* here in question, and to distinguish it from other varieties of cognition and proof. To furnish a proof of a determination of reason like the concept of right – i.e. to recognize its necessity – requires a different method from that required to prove a theorem in geometry. Besides, in the latter case, the figure is determined by the understanding and already made abstract in accordance with a law. But with an empirical content such as a *fact* [*Tatsache*], the material of cognition is a given sensuous intuition and the subjective certainty of the senses, along with depositions and affirmations concerning such material; and from these statements, testimonies, circumstances, and the like, conclusions and inferences are subsequently drawn. The objective truth which emerges from such material and from the method appropriate to it leads, when the attempt is made to determine it objectively for itself, to *half-proofs* and also, as a perfectly logical consequence which at the same time contains a formal illogicality, to *extraordinary punishments*. This objective truth means something quite different from the truth of a determination of reason or of a proposition whose content the understanding has already determined abstractly for itself. To show that the recognition of this kind of empirical truth about an event lies

within the proper legal determination of a court, and that this determination also gives it a proper qualification, and hence an exclusive right *in itself*, to perform this task and makes it necessary for it to do so – this is an important factor in considering the extent to which judgements on facts [*das Faktum*], as well as on legal questions, should be assigned to formal courts of law.

Addition (H). There is no reason [*Grund*] to assume that the professional judge alone should establish the facts of the case [*Tatbestand*], for anyone with a general (as distinct from purely legal) education is competent in this matter [*Sache*]. An assessment of the facts of the case will be based on empirical circumstances, on testimonies concerning the deed [*Handlung*] in question and similar intuitive perceptions [*Anschauungen*], but also on facts [*Tatsachen*] from which conclusions can be drawn concerning the deed itself and which make it appear probable or improbable. The aim here is to attain *certainty*, not truth in the higher sense, which is invariably eternal in character. This certainty is subjective conviction or conscience, and the question here is: what form should this certainty assume in a court of law? The requirement commonly encountered in German law [*im deutschen Rechte*] that the criminal should confess his guilt has truth on its side inasmuch as the right of subjective self-consciousness is thereby satisfied; for what the judges pronounce must not differ from what is in the consciousness, and only when the criminal confesses does the judgement no longer contain anything alien to him. But the difficulty arises here that the criminal may deny his guilt, with the result that the interest of justice is prejudiced. If, on the other hand, the subjective conviction of the judge is to prevail, an element of harshness is again introduced, for the person in question is no longer treated as a free individual. The mediation [between these possibilities] is the requirement that the verdict of guilt or innocence should emanate from the soul of the criminal – as in *trial by jury*.

§ 228

When judgement is pronounced – in the sense that the case in question is thereby *subsumed* under the *law* – the right of self-consciousness of the [affected] party is preserved in relation to the *law*, inasmuch as the law is known and is consequently the law of the party concerned; and it is preserved in relation to the *subsumption*, inasmuch as the process of law is public. But as far as the decision on the *particular* subjective and external *content* of the matter [*Sache*] is concerned (knowledge [*Erkenntnis*] of which belongs to the first of the two aspects referred to in § 225 above), this right is satisfied by the *confidence* which can be placed in the subjectivity of those who arrive at the verdict. This confidence is based primarily on their equality with the party concerned in respect of their particularity – their social status [*Stand*] and the like.

The right of self-consciousness, the moment of *subjective freedom*, can be regarded as the substantial viewpoint when we consider the necessity for publicity in the administration of justice and for so-called *trials by jury*.[1] What may be said in favour of these institutions on the grounds of their *utility* is essentially reducible to this right. Other considerations and reasons concerning their various advantages and disadvantages may generate arguments and counter-arguments; but like all grounds for reasoning [*Räsonnement*], these are secondary and inconclusive, or else derived from other and possibly higher spheres. It is possible that the administration of justice in itself *could* be managed well by purely professional courts, perhaps better than by other institutions. But even if this possibility could be increased to probability – or indeed to necessity – it is of no relevance, for on the opposite side there is always the *right of self-consciousness* which retains its claims and finds that they are not satisfied. – Given the nature of the entire corpus of laws, knowledge [*Kenntnis*] of right and of the course of court proceedings, as well as the ability to pursue one's rights, may become the *property* of a class [*Stand*] which makes itself exclusive even by the terminology it uses, inasmuch as this terminology is a foreign language for those whose rights are at stake. In this situation, members of civil society, who depend for their livelihood on *their activity, their own knowledge* [*Wissen*] *and volition*, remain *alienated* not only from their own most personal interests but also from the substantial and rational basis of these, namely *right*, and they are reduced to a condition of *tutelage*, or even a kind of serfdom, in relation to the class [*Stand*] in question. Even if they have the right to be physically present in court, to have a *footing* in it (*in iudicio stare*), this counts for little if they are not to be present *in spirit* and with their own *knowledge* [*Wissen*], and the right which they receive will remain an external *fate* for them.

§ 229

In the administration of justice, civil society, in which the Idea has lost itself in particularity and split up into the division between inward and outward, returns to its *concept*, to the unity of the universal which has being in itself with subjective particularity (although the particularity in question is that of the individual case, and the universal is that of *abstract right*). The actualization of this unity in its extension to the entire range of particularity, first as a relative union, constitutes the determination of the *police*; and secondly, as a limited but concrete totality, it constitutes the *corporation*.

Addition (H). In civil society, universality is merely necessity. As far as needs are concerned, right as such is the only fixed point.[a] But this right, which is only a limited sphere, relates solely to the protection of what I possess; welfare is something external to right as such. Nevertheless, this welfare is an essential determination in the system of needs. Hence the universal, which in the first instance is merely right, has to be extended over the entire field of particularity. Justice is a major factor in civil society: good laws will cause the state to flourish, and free ownership is a fundamental condition of its success. But since I am completely involved in particularity, I have a right to demand that, within this context, my particular welfare should also be promoted. Account should be taken of my welfare, of my particularity, and this is the task of the police and the corporation.

---

[a]*Translator's note: ist nur das Recht als solches das Feste.* In Hotho's notes, the equivalent phrase reads *ist nur das Recht als solches das Erste* (VPR III, 689), i.e. 'right as such is alone primary'.

C. *The Police and the Corporation*

§ 230

In the *system of needs*, the livelihood and welfare of each individual [*jedes Einzelnen*] are a *possibility* whose actualization is conditioned by the individual's own arbitrary will and particular nature, as well as by the objective system of needs. Through the administration of justice, *infringements* of property or personality are annulled. But the right *which is actually present in particularity* means not only that *contingencies* which interfere with this or that end should be *cancelled* [*aufgehoben*] and that the *undisturbed security* of *persons* and *property* should be guaranteed, but also that the livelihood and welfare of individuals should be *secured* – i.e. that *particular welfare* should be *treated as a right* and duly *actualized*.

a. The Police[1]

§ 231

In so far as the principle by which this or that end is governed is still that of the particular will, that authority [*Macht*] of the universal which guarantees security remains, on the one hand, primarily limited to the sphere of *contingencies*, and on the other, it remains an *external order*.

§ 232

Apart from crimes which the universal authority [*Macht*] must prevent or bring to justice – i.e. contingency in the shape of arbitrary evil – the permissible arbitrariness of inherently [*für sich*] rightful actions and of the private use of property also has external relations [*Beziehungen*] with other individuals [*Einzelne*], as well as with other public arrangements designed to further a common end. Through this universal aspect, private actions become a contingent matter which passes out of my control [*Gewalt*] and which can wrong or harm other people or actually does so.

§ 233

There is admittedly *only* a *possibility* that harm may be done. But the fact that no harm is done is, as a contingency, likewise no more than that. This is the aspect of *wrong* which is inherent in such actions, and which is consequently the ultimate reason [*Grund*] for penal justice as implemented by the police.

§ 234

The relations [*Beziehungen*] of external existence [*Dasein*] fall within the infinite of the understanding; consequently, no boundary is present *in itself* between what is harmful and what is harmless (even with regard to crime), between what is suspicious and what is not suspicious, or between what should be prohibited or kept under surveillance and what should be exempted from prohibitions, surveillance and suspicion, inquiry and accountability. The more precise determinations will depend on custom, the spirit of the rest of the constitution, prevailing conditions, current emergencies, etc.

Addition (H). No fixed determinations are possible here, and no absolute boundaries can be drawn. Everything here is personal; subjective opinion comes into play, and the spirit of the constitution and current dangers will determine the more precise circumstances. In times of war, for example, various things which are otherwise harmless must be regarded as harmful. Because of these aspects of contingency and arbitrary personality, the police takes on a certain character of *maliciousness*. When reflection is highly developed, the police may tend to draw everything it can into its sphere of influence, for it is possible to discover some potentially harmful aspect in everything. On such occasions, the police may proceed very pedantically and disrupt the ordinary life of individuals. But however troublesome this may be, no objective boundary line can be drawn here.[1]

§ 235

In the indeterminate multiplication and interdependence of daily needs, the *procurement* and *exchange of means* to satisfy these (a process on whose unimpeded continuance everyone relies) and the need to make the requisite inquiries and negotiations as short as possible give rise to aspects of common interest in which the business *of one* is at the same time carried out on behalf of *all*; they also give rise to means and arrangements which may be of use to the community. These *universal functions* and arrangements *of public utility* require oversight and advance provision on the part of the public authority [*Macht*].

§ 236

The differing interests of producers and consumers may come into collision with each other, and even if, *on the whole*, their correct relationship re-establishes itself automatically, its adjustment also needs to be consciously regulated by an agency which stands above both sides. The right to regulate individual matters in this way (e.g. by deciding the value of the commonest necessities of life) is based on the fact that, when commodities in completely universal everyday use are publicly marketed, they are offered not so much to a particular individual [*Individuum*] as such, as to the individual in a universal sense, i.e. to the public; and the task of upholding the public's right not to be cheated and of inspecting market commodities may, as a common concern, be entrusted to a public authority [*Macht*]. – But the main reason why some universal provision and direction are necessary is that large branches of industry are dependent on external circumstances and remote combinations whose full implications cannot be grasped by the individuals [*Individuen*] who are tied to these spheres by their occupation.

> At the opposite extreme to freedom of trade and commerce in civil society are public arrangements to provide for and determine the work of everyone. These included, for example, the building of the pyramids in ancient times, and other enormous works in Egypt and Asia which were undertaken for public ends, and in which the work of the individual [*des Einzelnen*] was not mediated by his particular arbitrary will and particular interest. This interest invokes the freedom of trade and commerce against regulation from above; but the more blindly it immerses itself in its selfish ends, the more it requires such regulation to bring it back to the universal, and to moderate and shorten the duration of those dangerous convulsions to which its collisions give rise, and which should return to equilibrium by a process of unconscious necessity.

Addition (H). The aim of oversight and provisions on the part of the police is to mediate between the individual [*Individuum*] and the universal possibility which is available for the attainment of individual ends. The police should provide for street-lighting, bridge-building, the pricing of daily necessities, and public health. Two main views are prevalent on this subject. One maintains that the police should have oversight over everything,[1] and the other maintains that the police should have no say in such matters, since everyone will be guided in his actions by the needs of others. The individual [*der Einzelne*] must certainly have a right to earn his living in this way or that; but on the other hand, the public also has a right to expect that necessary tasks will be performed in the proper manner. Both viewpoints must be satisfied, and the freedom of trade should not be such as to prejudice the general good.

§ 237

Now even if the possibility exists for individuals to share in the universal resources, and even if this possibility is guaranteed by the public authority [*Macht*], it remains – apart from the fact that such a guarantee must always be incomplete – open to contingencies of a subjective kind. This is increasingly the case the more it takes such conditions as skill, health, capital, etc. for granted.

§ 238

Initially, the family is the substantial whole whose task it is to provide for this particular aspect of the individual, both by giving him the means and skills he requires in order to earn his living from the universal resources, and by supplying his livelihood and maintenance in the event of his incapacity to look after himself. But civil society tears the individual [*Individuum*] away from family ties, alienates the members of the family from one another, and recognizes them as self-sufficient persons. Furthermore, it substitutes its own soil for the external inorganic nature and paternal soil from which the individual [*der Einzelne*] gained his livelihood, and subjects the existence [*Bestehen*] of the whole family itself to dependence on civil society and to contingency. Thus, the individual [*Individuum*] becomes a *son of civil society*, which has as many claims upon him as he has rights in relation to it.

Addition (H). Admittedly, the family must provide food for its individual members [*Einzelnen*], but in civil society, the family is subordinate and merely lays the foundations; its effectiveness is no longer so comprehensive. Civil society, on the other hand, is the immense power which draws people to itself and requires them to work for it, to owe everything to it, and to do everything by its means. Thus, if a human being is to be a member of civil society, he has rights and claims in relation to it, just as he had in relation to his family. Civil society must protect its members and defend their rights, just as the individual [*der Einzelne*] owes a duty to the rights of civil society.

§ 239

In this character as a *universal family*, civil society has the duty and right, in the face of *arbitrariness* and contingency on the part of *the parents*, to supervise and influence the *education* [*Erziehung*] of children in so far as this has a bearing on their capacity to become members of society, and particularly if this education is to be completed not by the parents themselves, but by others. In so far as communal arrangements can be made for this purpose, it is likewise incumbent upon civil society to make them.

Addition (H,G). It is difficult to draw a boundary here between the rights of parents and those of civil society. As far as education is concerned, parents usually consider that they have complete freedom and can do whatever they please. With all public education, the main opposition usually comes from the parents, and it is they who protest and speak out about teachers and institutions because their own preference goes against them. Nevertheless, society has a right to follow its own tested views on such matters, and to compel parents to send their children to school, to have them vaccinated, etc. The controversies which have arisen in France between the demands for freedom of instruction (i.e. for parental choice) and for state supervision are relevant in this context.[a]

[a]*Translator's note:* This final sentence has no counterpart in the sections of Hotho's and Griesheim's notes on which this Addition is based (cf. *VPR* III, 701f. and IV, 602ff.).

§ 240

In the same way, society has the duty and right to act as guardian on behalf of those who destroy the security of their own and their family's livelihood by their extravagance, and to implement their end and that of society in their place.

Addition (G). In Athens, the law obliged every citizen to give an account of his means of support; the view nowadays is that this is a purely private matter.[1] On the one hand, it is true that every individual has an independent existence [*ist jedes Individuum für sich*]; but on the other, the individual is also a member of the system of civil society, and just as every human being has a right to demand a livelihood from society, so also must society protect him against himself. It is not just starvation which is at stake here; the wider viewpoint is the need to prevent a rabble from emerging. Since civil society is obliged to feed its members, it also has the right to urge them to provide for their own livelihood.

§ 241

Not only arbitrariness, however, but also contingent physical factors and circumstances based on external conditions (see § 200) may reduce individuals to *poverty*. In this condition, they are left with the needs of civil society and yet – since society has at the same time taken from them the natural means of acquisition (see § 217), and also dissolves [*aufhebt*] the bond of the family in its wider sense as a kinship group (see § 181) – they are more or less deprived of all the advantages of society, such as the ability to acquire skills and education in general, as well as of the administration of justice, health care, and often even of the consolation of religion. For the *poor*, the universal authority [*Macht*] takes over the role of the family with regard not only to their immediate deficiencies, but also to the disposition of laziness, viciousness, and the other vices to which their predicament and sense of wrong give rise.

§ 242

The subjective aspect of poverty, and in general of every kind of want to which all individuals are exposed, even in their natural environment, also requires *subjective* help, both with regard to the *particular* circumstances and with regard to *emotion* and *love*. This is a situation in which, notwithstanding all universal arrangements, *morality* finds plenty to do. But since this help, both in itself [*für sich*] and in its effects, is dependent on contingency, society endeavours to make it less necessary by identifying the universal aspects of want and taking steps to remedy them.

The contingent character of almsgiving and charitable donations (e.g. for burning lamps before the images of saints, etc.) is supplemented by public poorhouses, hospitals, streetlighting, etc. Charity still retains enough scope for action, and it is mistaken if it seeks to restrict the alleviation of want to the *particularity* of emotion and the *contingency* of its own disposition and knowledge [*Kenntnis*], and if it feels injured and offended by universal rulings and precepts of an *obligatory* kind. On the contrary, public conditions should be regarded as all the more perfect the less there is left for the individual to

265

do by himself [*für sich*] in the light of his own particular opinion (as compared with what is arranged in a universal manner).[1]

§ 243

When the activity of civil society is unrestricted, it is occupied internally with *expanding its population and industry*. – On the one hand, as the association [*Zusammenhang*] of human beings through their needs is *universalized*, and with it the ways in which means of satisfying these needs are devised and made available, the *accumulation of wealth* increases; for the greatest profit is derived from this twofold universality. But on the other hand, the *specialization* [*Vereinzelung*] and *limitation* of particular work also increase, as do likewise the *dependence* and *want* of the class[1] which is tied to such work; this in turn leads to an inability to feel and enjoy the wider freedoms, and particularly the spiritual advantages, of civil society.

§ 244

When a large mass of people sinks below the level of a certain standard of living – which automatically regulates itself at the level necessary for a member of the society in question – that feeling of right, integrity [*Rechtlichkeit*], and honour which comes from supporting oneself by one's own activity and work is lost. This leads to the creation of a *rabble*, which in turn makes it much easier for disproportionate wealth to be concentrated in a few hands.

Addition (G). The lowest level of subsistence [*Subsistenz*], that of the rabble, defines itself automatically, but this minimum varies greatly between different peoples. In England, even the poorest man believes he has his rights; this differs from what the poor are content with in other countries. Poverty in itself does not reduce people to a rabble; a rabble is created only by the disposition associated with poverty, by inward rebellion against the rich, against society, the government, etc. It also follows that those who are dependent on contingency become frivolous and lazy, like the *lazzaroni* of Naples, for example. This in turn gives rise to the evil that the rabble do not have sufficient honour to gain their livelihood through their own work, yet claim that they have a right to receive their livelihood. No one can assert a right against nature, but within the conditions of society hardship at once assumes the form of a wrong inflicted on this or that class. The important question of how poverty can be remedied is one which agitates and torments modern societies especially.[1]

§ 245

If the direct burden [of support] were to fall on the wealthier class, or if direct means were available in other public institutions (such as wealthy hospitals, foundations, or monasteries) to maintain the increasingly impoverished mass at its normal standard of living, the livelihood of the needy would be ensured without the mediation of work; this would be contrary to the principle of civil society and the feeling of self-sufficiency and honour among its individual members. Alternatively, their livelihood might be mediated by work (i.e. by the opportunity to work) which would increase the volume of production; but it is precisely in overproduction and the lack of a proportionate number of consumers who are themselves productive that the evil [*Übel*] consists [*besteht*], and this is merely exacerbated by the two expedients in question. This shows that, despite an *excess of wealth*, civil society is *not wealthy enough* – i.e. its own distinct resources are not sufficient – to prevent an excess of poverty and the formation of a rabble.

> The example of *England* permits us to study these phenomena [*Erscheinungen*] on a large scale, especially the results achieved by poor-rates, boundless donations, and equally limitless private charity, and above all by the abolition [*Aufheben*] of the corporations. There (especially in Scotland), it has emerged that the most direct means of dealing with poverty, and particularly with the renunciation of shame and honour as the subjective bases of society and with the laziness and extravagance which give rise to a rabble, is to leave the poor to their fate and direct them to beg from the public.

§ 246

This inner dialectic of society drives it – or in the first instance *this specific society* – to go beyond its own confines and look for consumers, and hence the means it requires for subsistence [*Subsistenz*], in other nations [*Völkern*] which lack those means of which it has a surplus or which generally lag behind it in creativity, etc.

§ 247

Just as the earth, the firm and *solid ground*, is a precondition of the principle of family life, so is the *sea* the natural element for industry, whose relations with the external world it enlivens. By exposing the pursuit of gain to danger, industry simultaneously rises above it; and for the ties of the soil and the limited circles of civil life with its pleasures and desires, it substitutes the element of fluidity, danger, and destruction. Through this supreme medium of communication, it also creates trading links between distant countries, a legal [*recht-lichen*] relationship which gives rise to contracts; and at the same time, such trade [*Verkehr*] is the greatest educational asset [*Bildungsmittel*] and the source from which commerce derives its world-historical significance.

Rivers are *not natural boundaries*, which they have been taken to represent in modern times. On the contrary, both they and the oceans link human beings together. It is also inaccurate on Horace's part to say:

> deus *abscidit*
> Prudens Oceano dissociabili
> Terras[a]

This can be seen not only from the fact that river basins are inhabited by a single tribe or people, but also, for example, from the relations which existed in former times between Greece, Ionia, and Magna Graecia, between Brittany and Britain, between Denmark and Norway, Sweden, Finland, Livonia, etc.; it is also particularly clear when we contrast this with the lesser degree of contact between the inhabitants of coastal territories and those of the interior. – But in order to appreciate what an educational asset is present in the link with the sea, one should compare the relationship to the sea of those nations in which creativity has flourished with those which have shunned navigation and which, like the Egyptians

---

[a] *Translator's note:* 'A prudent god *separated* the lands by the dividing ocean'.[1]

and Indians, have stagnated internally and sunk into the most appalling and miserable superstition; one should likewise note how all great and enterprising nations push their way to the sea.

§ 248

This extended link also supplies the means necessary for *colonization* – whether sporadic or systematic – to which the fully developed civil society is driven, and by which it provides part of its population with a return to the family principle in a new country, and itself with a new market and sphere of industrial activity.

Addition (G). Civil society is driven to establish colonies. The increase of population alone has this effect; but a particular factor is the emergence of a mass of people who cannot gain satisfaction for their needs by their work when production exceeds the needs of consumers. Sporadic colonization is found particularly in Germany. The colonists move to America or Russia and retain no links with their home country, to which they are consequently of no service. The second variety of colonization, quite different from the first, is systematic. It is initiated by the state, which is aware of the proper way of carrying it out and regulates it accordingly. This mode of colonization was frequently employed by the ancients, especially the Greeks. Hard work was not the concern [*Sache*] of the Greek citizen, whose activity was directed rather towards public affairs [*öffentlichen Dingen*]. Accordingly, whenever the population grew to a point at which it could become difficult to provide for it, the young people were sent off to a new region, which was either specifically chosen or left to be discovered by chance. In more recent times, colonies have not been granted the same rights as the inhabitants of the mother country, and this situation has resulted in wars and eventual independence, as the history of the English and Spanish colonies shows. The liberation of colonies itself proves to be of the greatest advantage to the mother state, just as the emancipation of slaves is of the greatest advantage to the master.[1]

§ 249

What the police provides for in the first instance is the actualization and preservation of the universal which is contained within the particularity of civil society, [and it does so] as *an external order and arrangement* for the protection and security of the masses of particular ends and interests which have their subsistence [*Bestehen*] in this universal; as the higher guiding authority, it also provides for those interests which extend beyond the society in question (see § 246). In accordance with the Idea, particularity itself makes this universal, which is present in its immanent interests, the end and object [*Gegenstand*] of its will and activity, with the result that *the ethical returns* to civil society as an immanent principle; this constitutes the determination of the *corporation*.

b. The Corporation

§ 250

The *agricultural estate*, in view of the substantiality of its natural and family life, has within itself, in immediate form, the concrete universal in which it lives. The *universal estate*, by definition [*in seiner Bestimmung*], has the universal for itself as its basis and as the end of its activity. The intermediate estate, i.e. the estate of trade and industry, is essentially concerned with the *particular*, and the corporation is therefore specially characteristic of it.[1]

§ 251

The work performed by civil society is divided into different branches according to its particular nature. Since the inherent likeness of such particulars, as the quality *common* to them all, comes into existence [*Existenz*] in the *association*, the *selfish* end which pursues its own particular interest comprehends [*faßt*] and expresses itself at the same time as a universal end; and the member of civil society, in accordance with his *particular skill*, is a member of a corporation whose universal end is therefore wholly *concrete*, and no wider in scope than the end inherent in the trade which is the corporation's proper business and interest.

§ 252

By this definition [*Bestimmung*], the corporation has the right, under the supervision of the public authority [*Macht*], to look after its own interests within its enclosed sphere, to admit members in accordance with their objective qualification of skill and rectitude and in numbers determined by the universal context, to protect its members against particular contingencies, and to educate others so as to make them eligible for membership. In short, it has the right to assume the role of a *second* family for its members, a role which must remain more indeterminate in the case of civil society in general, which is more remote from individuals and their particular requirements.

> The tradesman [*Gewerbsmann*] is distinct from the day labourer, as he is from someone who is prepared to perform an occasional [*einzelnen*] contingent service. The former, who is – or wishes to become – a *master*, is a member of an association not for occasional contingent gain, but for the *whole* range and universality of his particular livelihood. – *Privileges*, in the sense of rights of a branch of civil society which constitutes a corporation, are distinct from privileges proper in the etymological sense,[1] in that the latter are contingent exceptions to the universal law, whereas the former are no more than legally fixed determinations which lie in the *particular nature* of an essential branch of society itself.

§ 253

In the corporation, the family not only *has* its firm basis in that its livelihood is *guaranteed* – i.e. it has secure *resources* (see § 170) – on condition of its [possessing a certain] *capability*, but the two [i.e. livelihood and capability] are also *recognized*, so that the member of a corporation has no need to demonstrate his competence and his regular income and means of support – i.e. the fact that he *is somebody* – by any further *external evidence*. In this way, it is also recognized that he belongs to a whole which is itself a member of society in general, and that he has an interest in, and endeavours to promote, the less selfish end of this whole. Thus, he has *his honour in his estate*.

> As a guarantor of resources, the institution of the corporation corresponds to the introduction of agriculture and private property in another sphere (see Remarks to § 203). – When complaints are made about that luxury and love of extravagance of the professional [*gewerbetreibenden*] classes which is

associated with the creation of a rabble (see § 244), we must not overlook, in addition to the other causes [of this phenomenon] (e.g. the increasingly mechanical nature of work), its *ethical* basis as implied in what has been said above. If the individual [*der Einzelne*] is not a member of a legally recognized [*berechtigten*] corporation (and it is only through legal recognition that a community becomes a corporation), he is without the *honour of belonging to an estate*, his isolation reduces him to the selfish aspect of his trade, and his livelihood and satisfaction lack *stability*. He will accordingly try to gain *recognition* through the external manifestations of success in his trade, and these are without limit [*unbegrenzt*], because it is impossible for him to live in a way appropriate to his estate if his estate does not exist; for a community can *exist* in civil society only if it is legally constituted and recognized. Hence no way of life of a more general kind appropriate to such an estate can be devised. – Within the corporation, the help which poverty receives loses its contingent and unjustly [*mit Unrecht*] humiliating character, and wealth, in fulfilling the duty it owes to its association, loses the ability to provoke arrogance in its possessor and envy in others; rectitude also receives the true recognition and honour which are due to it.

§ 254

In the corporation, the so-called *natural right* to practise one's skill and thereby earn what there is to earn is limited only to the extent that, in this context, the skill is rationally determined. That is, it is freed from personal opinion and contingency, from its danger to oneself and others, and is recognized, guaranteed, and at the same time raised to a conscious activity for a common end.

§ 255

The *family* is the first *ethical* root of the state; the *corporation* is the second, and it is based in civil society. The former contains the moments of subjective particularity and objective universality in *substantial* unity; but in the latter, these moments, which in civil society are at first divided into the *internally reflected* particularity of need and satisfaction and abstract legal [*rechtlichen*] universality, are inwardly united in such a way that particular welfare is present as a right and is actualized within this union.

The sanctity of marriage and the honour attaching to the corporation are the two moments round which the dis-organization of civil society revolves.

Addition (H). When the corporations were abolished [*aufgehoben*] in recent times, it was with the intention that the individual [*der Einzelne*] should look after himself. But even if we accept this, the corporation does not affect the individual's obligation to earn his living. In our modern states, the citizens have only a limited share in the universal business of the state; but it is necessary to provide ethical man with a universal activity in addition to his private end. This universal [activity], which the modern state does not always offer him, can be found in the corporation. We saw earlier[1] that, in providing for himself, the individual [*das Individuum*] in civil society is also acting for others. But this unconscious necessity is not enough; only in the corporation does it become a knowing and thinking [part of] ethical life. The corporation, of course, must come under the higher supervision of the state, for it would otherwise become ossified and set in its ways, and decline into a miserable guild system.[2] But the corporation in and for itself is not an enclosed guild; it is rather a means of giving the isolated trade an ethical status, and of admitting it to a circle in which it gains strength and honour.

§ 256

The end of the corporation, which is limited and finite, has its truth in the *end which is universal* in and for itself and in the absolute actuality of this end. So likewise do the separation and relative identity which were present in the external organization of the police. The sphere of civil society thus passes over into the *state*.

The town is the seat of civil trade and industry, of self-absorbed and divisive [*vereinzelnden*] reflection, of individuals who mediate their own self-preservation in relation to other legal [*rechtlichen*] persons. The country is the seat of an ethical life based on nature and the family. Town and country – these constitute in general the two ideal moments from which the state *emerges* as their true *ground*. – This development of immediate ethical life through the division of civil society and on to the state, which is shown to be their true ground, is the *scientific proof* of the concept of the state, a proof which only a development of this kind can furnish. – Since the state appears as the *result* of the development of the scientific concept in that it turns out to be the *true* ground [of this development], the *mediation* and semblance already referred to are likewise *superseded* by *immediacy*. In actuality, therefore, the *state* in general is in fact the *primary* factor; only within the state does the family first develop into civil society, and it is the idea of the state itself which divides into these two moments. In the development of civil society, the ethical substance takes on its *infinite* form, which contains within itself the following two moments: (1) infinite *differentiation* to the point at which the *inward being* [*Insichsein*] of self-consciousness attains being-for-itself and (2) the form of *universality* which is present in education, the form of *thought* whereby the spirit is objective and actual to itself as an *organic* totality in *laws* and *institutions*, i.e. in its own will as *thought*.

The State

§ 257

The state is the actuality of the ethical Idea – the ethical spirit as substantial will, *manifest* and clear to itself, which thinks and knows itself and implements what it knows in so far as it knows it. It has its immediate existence [*Existenz*] in *custom* and its mediate existence in the *self-consciousness* of the individual [*des Einzelnen*], in the individual's knowledge and activity, just as self-consciousness, by virtue of its disposition, has its *substantial freedom* in the state as its essence, its end, and the product of its activity.

> The *Penates* are the inner and *lower* gods, and the *spirit of the nation* (Athene) is the divine which *knows* and *wills* itself. *Piety* is feeling [*Empfindung*] and ethical life governed by feeling, and *political virtue* is the willing of that thought end which has being in and for itself.

§ 258

The state is the actuality of the substantial *will*, an actuality which it possesses in the particular *self-consciousness* when this has been raised to its universality; as such, it is the *rational* in and for itself. This substantial unity is an absolute and unmoved end in itself, and in it, freedom enters into its highest right, just as this ultimate end possesses the highest right in relation to individuals [*die Einzelnen*], whose *highest duty* is to be members of the state.

If the state is confused with civil society and its determination is equated with the security and protection of property and personal freedom, *the interest of individuals [der Einzelnen] as such* becomes the ultimate end for which they are united; it also follows from this that membership of the state is an optional matter. – But the relationship of the state to the individual *[Individuum]* is of quite a different kind. Since the state is objective spirit, it is only through being a member of the state that the individual *[Individuum]* himself has objectivity, truth, and ethical life. *Union* as such is itself the true content and end, and the destiny *[Bestimmung]* of individuals *[Individuen]* is to lead a universal life; their further particular satisfaction, activity, and mode of conduct have this substantial and universally valid basis as their point of departure and result. – Considered in the abstract, rationality consists in general in the unity and interpenetration of universality and individuality *[Einzelheit]*. Here, in a concrete sense and in terms of its content, it consists in the unity of objective freedom (i.e. of the universal substantial will) and subjective freedom (as the freedom of individual *[individuellen]* knowledge and of the will in its pursuit of particular ends). And in terms of its form, it therefore consists in self-determining action in accordance with laws and principles based on *thought* and hence *universal*. – This Idea is the being of spirit as necessary and eternal in and for itself. – As far as the Idea of the state itself is concerned, it makes no difference what is or was the *historical* origin of the state in general (or rather of any particular state with its rights and determinations) – whether it first arose out of patriarchal conditions, out of fear or trust, out of corporations etc., or how the basis of its rights has been understood and fixed in the consciousness as divine and positive right or contract, habit, etc. In relation to scientific cognition, which is our sole concern here, these are questions of appearance, and consequently a matter *[Sache]* for history. In so far as the authority of any actual state concerns itself with the question of reasons, these will be derived from the forms of right which are valid within that state. – The philosophical approach deals only with the internal aspect of all this, with the *concept as thought [mit dem gedachten Begriffe]*. As far as the

search for this concept is concerned, it was the achievement of
Rousseau to put forward the *will* as the principle of the state, a
principle which has *thought* not only as its form (as with the
social instinct, for example, or divine authority) but also as its
content, and which is in fact *thinking* itself. But Rousseau
considered the will only in the determinate form of the
individual [einzelnen] will (as Fichte subsequently also did) and
regarded the universal will not as the will's rationality in and
for itself, but only as the *common element* arising out of this
individual *[einzelnen]* will *as a conscious will.*[1] The union of
individuals *[der Einzelnen]* within the state thus becomes a
contract, which is accordingly based on their arbitrary will and
opinions, and on their express consent given at their own
discretion; and the further consequences which follow from
this, and which relate merely to the understanding, destroy
the divine [element] which has being in and for itself and its
absolute authority and majesty. Consequently, when these
abstractions were invested with power, they afforded the
tremendous spectacle, for the first time we know of in human
history, of the overthrow of all existing and given conditions
within an actual major state and the revision of its constitution
from first principles and purely in terms of *thought*; the *intention* behind this was to give it what was *supposed* to be a purely
rational basis. On the other hand, since these were only
abstractions divorced from the Idea, they turned the attempt
into the most terrible and drastic event.[2] – In opposition to the
principle of the individual will, we should remember the
fundamental concept according to which the objective will is
rational in itself, i.e. in its *concept*, whether or not it is
recognized by individuals *[Einzelnen]* and willed by them at
their discretion – and that its opposite, knowledge and volition, the subjectivity of freedom[a] (which is the *sole* content of
the principle of the individual will) embodies only *one* (consequently one-sided) moment of the *Idea of the rational* will,
which is rational solely because it has being both *in itself* and
for itself. – Also at variance with the thought that the state may

---

[a]*Translator's note:* The word order in the first edition is 'the subjectivity of freedom,
knowledge and volition'; but since the following relative clause requires *Subjektivität* as
its antecedent, other editions have adopted the present word-order.

be apprehended by cognition as something rational for itself is [the practice of] taking the *externality* of appearance and the contingencies of want, need of protection, strength, wealth, etc. not as moments of historical development, but as the *substance* of the state. Here, the principle of cognition is once again that of separate individuality [*die Einzelheit der Individuen*], but not so much the *thought* of this individuality as the converse of this, namely empirical individuality with all its contingent qualities of strength and weakness, wealth and poverty, etc. This notion [*Einfall*] of ignoring the state's *infinity* and *rationality* in and for itself and of *banishing thought* from the apprehension of its inner nature has probably never appeared in so unadulterated a form as in Herr von Haller's *Restoration of Political Science.*[3] It is *unadulterated*, because in all other attempts to grasp the essence of the state, however one-sided or superficial their principles may be, this very intention of *comprehending* the state brings with it thoughts or universal determinations. Here, however, Herr von Haller not only consciously dispenses with the rational content of the state and with the form of thought, but fulminates with passionate zeal against them both. This *Restoration* doubtless owes part of what Herr von Haller assures us is the widespread influence of its principles to the fact that it has managed, in its presentation, to dispense with *all thoughts*, and has thereby managed to make the whole work as of *one* piece in its thoughtlessness. For in this way, it avoids the confusion and discontinuity which diminish the impact of a presentation in which references to the substantial are mixed in with the contingent, and reminders of the universal and rational are intermingled with the merely empirical and external, with the result that, in the sphere of the empty and insignificant, we are reminded of the higher realm of the infinite. – This presentation is equally *consistent* in one further respect. For since the sphere of contingency, rather than the substantial, is taken to be the essence of the state, the content of such a work is consistent precisely in the utter inconsistency of its thoughtlessness, in that it heedlessly goes its way and is soon just as much at home with the opposite of what it had approved a moment earlier.†

†*Hegel's note:* In view of the characteristics specified above, the book in question is of an

278

Addition (G). The state in and for itself is the ethical whole, the actualization of freedom, and it is the absolute end of reason that freedom should be actual. The state is the spirit which is present in the world and which *consciously* realizes itself therein, whereas in nature, it actualizes itself only as the other of itself, as dormant spirit. Only when it is present in consciousness, knowing itself as an existent object [*Gegenstand*], is it the state. Any discussion of freedom must begin not with individuality [*Einzelheit*] or the individual self-consciousness, but only with the essence of self-consciousness; for whether human beings know it or not, this essence realizes itself as a self-sufficient power of which single individuals [*die einzelnen Individuen*] are only moments. The state consists in the march of God in the world, and its basis is the power of reason actualizing itself as will. In considering the Idea of the state, we must not have any particular states or particular institutions in mind; instead, we should consider the Idea, this actual God, in its own right [*für sich*]. Any state, even if we pronounce it bad in the light of our own principles, and even if we discover this or that defect in it, invariably has the essential moments of its existence [*Existenz*] within itself (provided it is one of the more advanced states of our time). But since it is easier to discover deficiencies than to comprehend the affirmative, one may easily fall into the mistake of overlooking the inner organism of the state in favour of individual [*einzelne*] aspects. The state is not a work of art; it exists in the world, and hence in the sphere of arbitrariness, contingency, and error, and bad behaviour may disfigure it in many respects. But the ugliest man, the criminal, the invalid, or the cripple is still a living human being; the affirmative aspect – life – survives [*besteht*] in spite of such deficiencies, and it is with this affirmative aspect that we are here concerned.

original kind. In itself [*für sich*], the author's indignation could well have something noble about it, for it was sparked off by the false theories referred to above (which originated largely with Rousseau), and above all by attempts to put these theories into practice. But in order to escape from these, Herr von Haller has withdrawn to the opposite extreme, which is totally devoid of thought and therefore cannot claim to have any substance [*Gehalt*] – that is, the most virulent hatred of all *laws and legislation*, and of *all formally and legally determined right*. Hatred of *law*, of *legally* determined *right*, is the shibboleth whereby fanaticism, imbecility, and hypocritical good intentions manifestly and infallibly reveal themselves for what they are, no matter what disguise they may adopt. – Originality like that of Herr von Haller is always a remarkable phenomenon [*Erscheinung*], and I will cite some examples of it for those of my readers who are as yet unfamiliar with his book. Herr von Haller first puts forward his basic principle (Vol. i, pp. 342ff.), namely 'that just as, in the *inanimate* world, the larger displaces the smaller, the powerful the weak, etc., so also among the *animals*, and likewise among human beings, does the *same* law reappear in nobler (often surely also in ignoble?)[a] forms [*Gestalten*]', and 'that this is *accordingly the eternal and unalterable ordinance of God*, that the *more powerful* rules, must rule, and always shall rule'. It is evident even from this, as well as from what

[a]*Translator's note:* The words in parentheses are Hegel's own interjection.

follows, what is meant by *power* in this context: it is not the power of justice and ethics, but the contingent power of nature. In support of this, Herr von Haller further cites, among other reasons (pp. 365f.), the fact that nature, with admirable wisdom, has ordained that the very sense of one's *own superiority* irresistibly ennobles the character and favours the development of precisely those virtues which are most necessary to one's subordinates. He asks, with elaborate formal rhetoric, 'whether it is the strong or the weak in the realm of the sciences who more often abuse their authority and trust for base and selfish ends and to the detriment of credulous people, whether among jurists the masters of their science are the pettifoggers and cavilling lawyers who deceive the hopes of credulous clients, who call white black and black white, who misuse the laws as a vehicle of wrongdoing, who make beggars out of those who need their protection and who, like hungry *vultures*, tear the innocent *lamb* to pieces, etc.' Herr von Haller forgets at this point that he is employing such rhetoric precisely in order to defend the proposition that the *rule of the more powerful* is an eternal ordinance of God, the very ordinance whereby the vulture tears the innocent lamb to pieces, and that those whose knowledge [*Kenntnis*] of the law gives them greater power are therefore quite right to plunder the credulous people who need their protection, since they are the weak. But it would be expecting too much for two thoughts to be brought together where not a single thought is present. – It goes without saying that Herr von Haller is an enemy of *legal codes*. Civil laws, in his opinion, are on the one hand completely 'unnecessary, in that they follow *self-evidently from the law of nature*'. It would have saved much of the effort that has been expended on legislation and legal codes since states first began, and that is still expended on such matters and on the study of jurisprudence [*des gesetzlichen Rechts*], if people had always been content with the sound principle *that all this is self-evident*. 'On the other hand, laws are not in fact made for private persons, but as *instructions* for lesser magistrates to acquaint them with the will of the chief justice. *Jurisdiction* is not in any case a duty on the part of the state (Vol. I, pp. 297f. and *passim*), but a charitable act, a service provided by those with greater power and purely as an accessory. It is not the most perfect means of guaranteeing right, but is in fact *insecure* and *uncertain*. It is the only means with which our modern jurists have left us, for they have robbed us of the *other three means*, the very ones which *lead most quickly and reliably to the goal* and which, apart from the legal system, *friendly* nature has given to human beings in order *to secure their rightful freedom*.' And these three means are – what do you think? – '(1) *personal obedience* to, and *inculcation* of, the natural law; (2) *resistance* to injustice [*Unrecht*]; and (3) *flight*, when no other help is available.' (How unfriendly the jurists are in comparison with friendly nature!) 'The *natural* and *divine* law, however, which all-bountiful nature has given to everyone (Vol. I, p. 292), is: honour everyone as your equal' (on the author's own principles, this ought to read: 'honour him who is *not* your equal, but is more powerful than yourself'); 'give offence to no one *who gives no offence to you*; demand nothing but what he *owes* to you' (but what does he owe?); 'but more than this: love your neighbour and serve him where you can.' – The *implantation of this law* is supposed to render a legislation and constitution superfluous. It would be interesting to see how Herr von Haller interprets the fact that, despite the implantation of this law, legislations and constitutions have made their appearance in the world! In Volume III, pp. 362f., the author comes to the 'so-called national liberties', i.e. the juridical and constitutional laws of nations. (In this wider sense, every legally determined right may be described as a *liberty*.) He says of these laws, among other things, 'that their content is usually *very insignificant*, even if great value may be placed in *books* on such *documentary* liberties.' When we see then that the author is here referring to the national liberties of the German Imperial Estates,[4] of the English nation (such as the Magna Charta[5] '*which is little read, however, and even less understood* on account of its *archaic expressions*', the Bill of Rights[6] etc.), of the Hungarian nation, etc., we are amazed to discover that these once so highly prized possessions are of no significance, and that it is *only in books* that these nations place any value on their laws, which have had an effect on every garment the individual wears and every morsel of bread he eats, and whose effects are daily and hourly present in everything. – If we may also mention the *General Legal Code of Prussia*,[7] Herr von Haller speaks of it with particular disfavour (Vol. I, pp. 185ff.) because unphilosophical errors[a] (though not, at least, the Kantian philosophy, to which Herr von Haller reacts with particular bitterness) have exerted an *incredible* influence on it, and above all because it refers, among other things, to the *state*, the resources of the state, the end of the state, the head of state, the *duties* of the head of state, servants of the state, etc. Worst of all, in Herr von Haller's opinion, is 'the right to impose *taxes* on the private resources of individuals, their trade, their production, or their consumption in order *to pay for the needs of the state*; for this means that both the *king* himself (since the resources of the state are not the private property of the sovereign, but the resources of the state itself) and the *Prussian citizens have nothing of their own*, neither their persons nor their assets, and all subjects are *serfs in the eyes of the law*, because *they may not withdraw from the service of the state*'.

On top of all this incredible crudity, perhaps the most amusing touch is the emotion [*Rührung*] with which Herr von Haller describes his inexpressible pleasure at his discoveries (Vol. I, Preface [pp. xxiii–xxiv]) – 'a joy such as only the friend of truth can feel when, after honest enquiry, he attains the certainty that . . . he has, *so to speak* (yes, 'so to speak' indeed!), found the utterance of *nature*, the word of *God himself*'. (On the contrary, the word of God quite expressly distinguishes its revelations from the utterances of nature and of natural man.) He tells us 'how he could have fallen on his knees in sheer wonderment, how a flood of joyful tears poured from his eyes, and living religiosity arose from that moment within him'. – Herr von Haller's religiosity ought rather to have been bemoaned it as the harshest punishment imposed by God (for it is the harshest judgement human beings can experience) that he had strayed so far from thought and rationality, from respect for the laws, and from the knowledge [*Erkenntnis*] of how infinitely important and divine it is for the duties of the state and the rights of the citizens to be determined *by law* – that he had strayed so far from all this that absurdity was able to pass itself off in his eyes as the *word of God*.

[a]*Translator's note:* Haller's text reads *neuphilosophischen Irrtümer* ('errors of modern philosophy').

§ 259

The Idea of the state

(a) has *immediate* actuality and is the individual state as a self-related organism – the *constitution* or *constitutional law* [*inneres Staatsrecht*];

(b) passes over into the *relationship* of the individual state to other states – *international law* [*äußeres Staatsrecht*];

(c) is the universal Idea as a *genus* [*Gattung*] and as an absolute power in relation to individual states – the spirit which gives itself its actuality in the process of *world history*.

Addition (G). The state as actual is essentially an individual state, and beyond that a particular state. Individuality should be distinguished from

281

particularity; it is a moment within the very Idea of the state, whereas particularity belongs to history. States as such are independent of one another, and their relationship can consequently only be an external one, so that there must be a third factor above them to link them together. This third factor is in fact the spirit which gives itself actuality in world history and is the absolute judge of states. Admittedly, several states may form a league and sit in judgement, as it were, on other states, or they may enter into alliances (like the Holy Alliance,[1] for example), but these are always purely relative and limited, like [the ideal of] perpetual peace. The one and only absolute judge which always asserts its authority over the particular is the spirit which has being in and for itself, and which reveals itself as the universal and as the active genus in world history.

A. Constitutional Law

§ 260

The state is the actuality of concrete freedom. But *concrete freedom* requires that personal individuality [*Einzelheit*] and its particular interests should reach their full *development* and gain *recognition of their right* for itself (within the system of the family and of civil society), and also that they should, on the one hand, *pass over* of their own accord into the interest of the universal, and on the other, knowingly and willingly acknowledge this universal interest even as their own *substantial spirit*, and *actively pursue it* as their *ultimate end*. The effect of this is that the universal does not attain validity or fulfilment without the interest, knowledge, and volition of the particular, and that individuals do not live as private persons merely for these particular interests without at the same time directing their will to a universal end [*in und für das Allgemeine wollen*] and acting in conscious awareness of this end. The principle of modern states has enormous strength and depth because it allows the principle of subjectivity to attain fulfilment in the *self-sufficient extreme* of personal particularity, while at the same time *bringing it back to substantial unity* and so preserving this unity in the principle of subjectivity itself.

Addition (H,G). The Idea of the state in modern times has the distinctive characteristic that the state is the actualization of freedom not in accordance with subjective caprice, but in accordance with the concept of the will, i.e. in accordance with its universality and divinity. Imperfect states are those in which the Idea of the state is still invisible [*eingehüllt*] and where the particular determinations of this Idea have not yet reached free self-sufficiency. In the states of classical antiquity, universality was indeed already present, but particularity [*Partikularität*] had not yet been released and set at liberty and brought back to universality, i.e. to the universal end of the whole. The essence of the modern state is that the universal should be linked with the complete freedom of particularity [*Besonderheit*] and the well-being of individuals, and hence that the interest of the family and of civil society must become focused on the state; but the universality of the end cannot make further progress without the personal [*eigene*] knowledge and volition of the particular individuals [*der Besonderheit*], who must retain their rights. Thus, the universal must be activated, but subjectivity on the other hand must be developed as a living whole. Only when both moments are present [*bestehen*] in full measure can the state be regarded as articulated and truly organized.

§ 261

In relation to the spheres of civil law [*Privatrecht*] and private welfare, the spheres of the family and civil society, the state is on the one hand an *external* necessity and the higher power to whose nature their laws and interests are subordinate and on which they depend. But on the other hand, it is their *immanent* end, and its strength consists in the unity of its universal and ultimate end with the particular interest of individuals, in the fact that they have *duties* towards the state to the same extent as they also have rights (see § 155).

As has already been noted (in the Remarks to § 3 above), it was above all Montesquieu who, in his celebrated work *L'Esprit des Lois*, focused on and attempted to expound in detail both the thought that laws, including those of civil law in particular, are dependent on the specific character of the state, and the philosophical view that the part should be considered only with reference to the whole.[1] – *Duty* is primarily an attitude *towards* something which, for me, is *substantial* and universal in and for itself. Right, on the other hand, is in general the *existence [Dasein]* of this substantial element, and is consequently the latter's *particular* aspect and that of my own *particular* freedom.[2] Thus, on a formal level, right and duty appear to belong to different aspects or persons. In the state, as an ethical entity and as the interpenetration of the substantial and the particular, my obligation towards the substantial is at the same time the existence of my particular freedom; that is, duty and right are *united* within the state *in one and the same relation* [*Beziehung*]. But further, since the distinct moments also attain their *characteristic* shape and reality within the state, so that the distinction between right and duty again arises at this point, these moments, although identical *in themselves* (i.e. in a formal sense) are at the same time *different in content*. In the realms of civil law and morality, the relation [between right and duty] lacks *actual* necessity, so that only an *abstract* equality of content is present; in these abstract spheres, *what* is right for one person ought also to be right for another, and *what* is one person's duty ought also to be another person's duty. That absolute identity of duty and right [referred to above] occurs here only as an equivalent identity of *content*, in that the determination of the content is itself wholly universal; that is, there is a single principle for both duty and right, namely the personal freedom of human beings. Consequently, slaves have no duties because they have no rights, and vice versa. (Religious duties do not concern us here.)[3] – But in the internal development of the concrete Idea, its moments become differentiated, and their determinacy becomes at the same time a different content: in the family, the rights of the son are not *the same in content* as the son's duties towards his father, and the rights of the citizen are not *the same in content* as the citizen's duties towards the sovereign and government. – The above concept of the union of duty and right is a factor [*Bestimmung*] of the greatest importance, and the inner strength of states is embodied in it. – The abstract aspect of duty consists simply in disregarding and excluding particular interests as an inessential and even unworthy moment. But if we consider the concrete aspect, i.e. the Idea, we can see that the moment of particularity is also essential, and that its satisfaction is therefore entirely necessary; in the process of fulfilling his duty, the individual must somehow attain his own interest and satisfaction or settle his own account, and from his situation within the state, a right must accrue to him whereby the universal cause [*Sache*] becomes *his own particular* cause. Particular interests should certainly not be set aside, let alone suppressed; on the contrary, they should be harmonized with the universal, so that both they themselves and the universal are preserved. The individual, whose duties give him the status of a subject [*Untertan*], finds that, in fulfilling his duties as a citizen, he gains protection for his person and property, consideration for his particular welfare, satisfaction of his substantial essence, and the consciousness and self-awareness of being a member of a whole. And through his performance of his duties as services and tasks undertaken on behalf of the state, the state itself is preserved and secured. Viewed in the abstract, the sole interest of the universal would be [to ensure] that the tasks and services which it requires are performed as duties.

Addition (H). Everything depends on the unity of the universal and the particular within the state. In the states of antiquity, the subjective end was entirely identical with the will of the state; in modern times, however, we expect to have our own views, our own volition, and our own conscience. The ancients had none of these in the present sense; for them, the ultimate factor was the will of the state. Whereas, under the despotic regimes of Asia, the individual has no inner life and no justification within himself, in the modern world human beings expect their inner life to be respected. The association of duty and right has a dual aspect, in that what the state requires as a duty should also in an immediate sense be the right of individuals, for it is nothing more than the organization of the concept of freedom. The determinations of the will of the individual acquire an objective existence through the state, and it is only through the state that they attain their truth and actualization. The state is the sole precondition of the attainment of particular ends and welfare.

§ 262

The actual Idea is the spirit which divides itself up into the two ideal spheres of its concept – the family and civil society – as its finite mode, and thereby emerges from its ideality to become infinite and actual spirit for itself. In so doing, it allocates the material of its finite actuality, i.e. individuals as a *mass*, to these two spheres, and in such a way that, in each individual case [*am Einzelnen*], this allocation appears to be *mediated* by circumstances, by the individual's arbitrary will and personal [*eigene*] choice of vocation [*Bestimmung*] (see § 185 and the appended Remarks).[1]

Addition (H). In Plato's republic, subjective freedom is not yet recognized, because individuals still have their tasks assigned to them by the authorities [*Obrigkeit*].[2] In many oriental states, this assignment is governed by birth. But subjective freedom, which must be respected, requires freedom of choice on the part of individuals.

§ 263

In these spheres in which its moments, individuality [*Einzelheit*] and particularity, have their immediate and reflected reality, spirit is present as their objective universality which *manifests itself in them* [*als ihre in sie scheinende objektive Allgemeinheit*] as the power of the rational in necessity (see § 184), i.e. as the *institutions* considered above.[1]

Addition (H). The state, as spirit, is divided up into the particular determinations of its concept or mode of being. If we take an example from nature, the nervous system is, properly speaking, the system of sensation: it is the abstract moment of being with oneself [*bei sich*] and of thereby having one's own identity. But the analysis of sensation reveals two aspects, and these are divided in such a way that both of them appear as complete systems: the first is abstract feeling or self-containment, dull internal movement, reproduction, inner self-nutrition, growth [*Produzieren*], and digestion. The second moment is that this being-with-oneself stands in opposition to the moment of difference [*Differenz*] or outward movement. This is irritability, the outward movement of sensation, which constitutes a system of its own, and there are lower classes of animals which have developed this system exclusively as distinct from the soul-governed unity of inner sensation. If we compare these natural relations [*Naturbeziehungen*] with those of spirit, we must liken the family to sensibility and civil society to irritability. Then the third factor is the state, the nervous system itself [*für sich*], with its internal organization; but it is alive only in so far as both moments – in this case, the family and civil society – are developed within it. The laws which govern them are the institutions of that rationality which manifests itself within them [*des in sie scheinenden Vernünftigen*]. But the ground and ultimate truth of these institutions is the spirit, which is their universal end and known object [*Gegenstand*]. The family, too, is ethical, but its end is not a known end; in civil society, however, separation is the determining factor.

§ 264

Individuals as a mass are themselves spiritual natures, and they therefore embody a dual moment, namely the extreme of *individuality* [*Einzelheit*] which knows and wills *for itself*, and the extreme of *universality* which knows and wills the substantial. They can therefore attain their right in both of these respects only in so far as they have actuality both as private and as substantial persons. In the spheres in question [i.e. family and civil society], they attain their right in the first respect directly; and in the second respect, they attain it by discovering their essential self-consciousness in [social] institutions as that *universal* aspect of their particular interests which has being in itself, and by obtaining through these institutions an occupation and activity directed towards a universal end within a corporation.

§ 265

These institutions together form the *constitution* – that is, developed and actualized rationality – in the realm of *particularity*, and they are therefore the firm foundation of the state and of the trust and disposition of individuals towards it. They are the pillars on which public freedom rests, for it is within them that particular freedom is realized and rational; hence the union of freedom and necessity is present *in itself* within these institutions.

Addition (G). It has already been noted that the sanctity of marriage and the institutions in which civil society takes on an ethical appearance constitute the stability of the whole – that is, the universal is simultaneously the concern [*Sache*] of each [individual] as a particular [entity]. What matters most is that the law of reason should merge with the law of particular freedom, and that my particular end should become identical with the universal; otherwise, the state must hang in the air. It is the self-awareness of individuals which constitutes the actuality of the state, and its stability consists in the identity of the two aspects in question. It has often been said that the end of the state is the happiness of its citizens. This is certainly true, for if their welfare is deficient, if their subjective ends are not satisfied, and if they do not find that the state as such is the means to this satisfaction, the state itself stands on an insecure footing.

§ 266

But the spirit is objective and actual to itself not only as this necessity and as a realm of appearance, but also as the *ideality* and inner dimension of these. Thus, this substantial universality becomes *its own object* [*Gegenstand*] and end, with the result that the necessity in question similarly becomes its own object and end in the *shape* of freedom.

§ 267

The *necessity* in ideality is the *development* of the Idea within itself; as *subjective* substantiality, it is the [individual's] political *disposition*, and as *objective* substantiality – in contrast with the former – it is the *organism* of the state, the *political* state proper and *its constitution*.

Addition (G). The unity of freedom which wills and knows itself is present in the first instance as necessity. Here, the substantial is present as the subjective existence [*Existenz*] of individuals; but the other mode of necessity is the organism, i.e. the spirit is a process within itself which is internally articulated, and which posits differences within itself through which it completes its cycle.

§ 268

The political *disposition*, i.e. *patriotism* in general, is certainty based on *truth* (whereas merely subjective certainty does not originate in *truth*, but is only opinion) and a volition which has become *habitual*. As such, it is merely a consequence of the institutions within the state, a consequence in which rationality is *actually* present, just as rationality receives its practical application through action in conformity with the state's institutions. – This disposition is in general one of *trust* (which may pass over into more or less educated insight), or the consciousness that my substantial and particular interest is preserved and contained in the interest and end of an other (in this case, the state), and in the latter's relation to me as an individual [*als Einzelnem*]. As a result, this other immediately ceases to be an other for me, and in my consciousness of this, I am free.

Patriotism is frequently understood to mean only a willingness to perform *extraordinary* sacrifices and actions. But in essence, it is that disposition which, in the normal conditions and circumstances of life, habitually knows that the community is the substantial basis and end. It is this same consciousness, tried and tested in all circumstances of ordinary life, which underlies the willingness to make extraordinary efforts. But just as human beings often prefer to be guided by magnanimity instead of by right, so also do they readily convince themselves that they possess this extraordinary patriotism in order to exempt themselves from the genuine disposition, or to excuse their lack of it. – Furthermore, if we take this *disposition* to be something which can originate independently [*für sich*] and arise out of subjective representations [*Vorstellungen*] and thoughts, we are confusing it with opinion; for in this interpretation, it is deprived of its true ground, i.e. objective reality.

Addition (H). Uneducated people delight in argument [*Räsonieren*] and fault-finding, for it is easy to find fault, but difficult to recognize the good and its inner necessity. Education in its early stages always begins with fault-finding, but when it is complete, it sees the positive element in everything. In religion, it is equally easy to say that this or that is superstition, but it is infinitely more difficult to comprehend the truth which it contains. Thus people's apparent political disposition should be distinguished from what they genuinely will; for inwardly, they in fact will the thing [*Sache*], but they fasten on to details and delight in the vanity of claiming superior insight. They trust that the state*a* will continue to exist [*bestehen*] and that particular interests can be fulfilled within it alone; but habit blinds us to the basis of our entire existence [*Existenz*]. It does not occur to someone who walks the streets in safety at night that this might be otherwise, for this habit of [living in] safety has become second nature, and we scarcely stop to think that it is solely the effect of particular institutions. Representational thought often imagines that the state is held together by force; but what holds it together is simply the basic sense of order which everyone possesses.

---

a Translator's note: The equivalent term in Hotho's notes (VPR III, 725) is not *der Staat* ('the state'), as in Gans's version here, but *die Sache* ('the thing').

§ 269

The [*political*] disposition takes its particularly determined *content* from the various aspects of the organism of the state. This *organism* is the development of the Idea in its differences and their objective actuality. These different aspects are accordingly the *various powers* [within the state] with their corresponding tasks and functions, through which the universal continually *produces* itself. It does so in a *necessary* way, because these various powers are determined by the *nature of the concept*; and it *preserves* itself in so doing, because it is itself the presupposition of its own production. This organism is the *political constitution*.

Addition (G). The state is an organism, i.e. the development of the Idea in its differences. These different aspects are accordingly the various powers with their corresponding tasks and functions, through which the universal continually produces itself in a necessary way and thereby preserves itself, because it is itself the presupposition of its own production. This organism is the political constitution; it proceeds perpetually from the state, just as it is the means by which the state preserves itself. If the two diverge and the different aspects break free, the unity which the constitution produces is no longer established. The fable of the belly and the other members is relevant here.[1] It is in the nature of an organism that all its parts must perish if they do not achieve identity and if one of them seeks independence. Predicates, principles, and the like get us nowhere in assessing the state, which must be apprehended as an organism, just as predicates are of no help in comprehending the nature of God, whose life must instead be intuited as it is in itself.[2]

§ 270

The fact that the end of the state is both the universal interest as such and the conservation of particular interests within the universal interest as the substance of these constitutes (1) the *abstract actuality* or substantiality of the state. But this substantiality is (2) the *necessity* of the state, for it divides itself up into the conceptual *differences* within the state's functions; and these differences, by virtue of this substantiality, are likewise actual and *fixed* determinations or powers. (3) But this very substantiality is the spirit which knows and wills itself as having *passed through the form of education*. The state therefore *knows* what it wills, and knows it in its *universality* as something *thought*. Consequently, it acts and functions in accordance with known ends and recognized principles, and with laws which are laws not only *in themselves* but also for the consciousness; and it likewise acts in determinate knowledge [*Kenntnis*] of existing circumstances and relations in so far as its actions have relevance to these.

This is the point at which we must touch on *the state's relation to religion,*[1] because it has repeatedly been maintained in recent times that religion is the foundation of the state, and has even been presumed that this assertion constitutes the whole of political science. No assertion is more apt to produce so much confusion, or indeed to set up confusion itself as the political constitution and the form which cognition ought to take. – It may at first seem suspicious that people recommend and resort to religion above all in times of public distress, disruption, and oppression, and that they are referred to it for consolation in the face of *wrong* and for hope as a compensation for *loss*. When it is further regarded as a precept of religion that we ought to treat worldly interests and the course of actual events with indifference, despite the fact that the state is the spirit *which is present in the world*, this religious advice does not seem calculated to promote the interest and business of the state as an essential and serious end. On the contrary, it seems to represent the entire political regime as a matter [*Sache*] of indifference and arbitrariness, either because it is formulated in such a way as to suggest that the state is dominated by the ends of passion, unjust [*unrechtlicher*] force, and the like, or because such religious advice attempts to retain exclusive validity and claims authority to determine and administer [the process of] right. Although it may seem derisive to dismiss all resentment towards tyranny by declaring that the oppressed find consolation in religion, it should not be forgotten that religion can take on a form which leads to the harshest servitude within the fetters of superstition and to the debasement of human beings to a level below that of the animals (as among the Egyptians and Indians, who venerate animals as higher beings).[2] This phenomenon [*Erscheinung*] may at least draw our attention to the fact that we ought not to speak of religion in wholly general terms, and that we instead require a power to rescue us from it in some of the shapes it assumes and to champion the rights of reason and self-consciousness. – But the essential determinant of the relationship between religion and the state can be discovered only if we recall the concept of religion. The content of religion is absolute truth, and it is therefore associated with a disposition of the most exalted kind. As intuition, feeling, and representational cognition [*vorstellende Erkenntnis*] whose concern is with God as the unlimited foundation and cause on which everything depends, it contains the requirement that everything else should be seen in relation [*Beziehung*] to this and should receive confirmation, justification, and the assurance of certainty from this source. It is within this relationship that the state, laws, and duties all receive their highest endorsement as far as the consciousness is concerned, and become supremely binding upon it; for even the state, laws, and duties are in their actuality something determinate which passes over into the higher sphere as that in which its foundation lies (see *Encyclopaedia of the Philosophical Sciences*, § 453).³ Religion therefore also contains that point which, in spite of all change, failure of actual ends and interests, and loss of possessions, affords a consciousness of immutability and of the highest freedom and satisfaction.† If, then, religion constitutes the *foundation* which embodies the ethical realm in general, and, more specifically, the nature of the state as the divine will, it is at the same time only a *foundation*; and this is where the two [i.e. the state and religion] diverge. The state is the divine will as present spirit, *unfolding* as the actual shape and *organization of a world*. – Those who refuse to go beyond the form of religion when confronted by the state behave like those who,

---

†*Hegel's note: Religion*, like *cognition* and *science*, has as its principle a distinct form which is different from that of the state. All of these therefore enter into the state, partly as *means* to education and the [appropriate] disposition, and partly in so far as they are essentially *ends in themselves* inasmuch as they have an external existence [*Dasein*]. In both respects, the principles of the state are *applicable* to them. A comprehensively concrete treatise on the state would also have to consider these spheres, as well as art, purely natural circumstances, etc., in their relevance [*Beziehung*] to and position within the state. In the present treatise, however, in which it is the principle of the state which is expounded in its *own distinct* sphere and in accordance with its Idea, the principles of these other areas and the *application* of the right of the state to them can be mentioned only in passing.

in the cognitive realm, claim to be right even if they invariably stop at the *essence* instead of proceeding beyond this abstraction to existence [*Dasein*], or like those who (see Remarks to § 140 above) will only the *abstract good* and leave it to the arbitrary will to determine *what* is good. Religion is the relation to the absolute *in the form of feeling, representational thought, and faith*, and within its all-embracing centre, everything is merely accidental and transient. If, then, we also adhere to this form in relation [*Beziehung*] to the state and act as if it were the essentially valid and determining factor in this [political] context, too, we thereby expose the state, as an organism within which lasting [*bestehende*] differences, laws, and institutions have developed, to instability, insecurity, and disruption. The laws, as the objective and universal element [within the state], no longer have a lasting and valid determination, but take on a negative determination in relation to that form [of religion] which veils over everything determinate and thereby assumes a subjective character. The consequence for human behaviour is [such advice as] 'To the righteous, no law is given', 'Be pious, and you may otherwise do as you please', or 'You may abandon yourselves to your own arbitrariness and passion, and refer others who thereby suffer wrong to the solace and hope of religion, or (even worse) dismiss and condemn them as irreligious'.[4] If, however, this negative attitude does not simply remain an inward disposition and viewpoint, but turns instead to the actual world and asserts itself within it, it leads to religious *fanaticism* which, like political fanaticism, repudiates all political institutions and legal order as restrictive limitations [*Schranken*] on the inner emotions and as incommensurate with the infinity of these, and hence also rejects private property, marriage, the relationships and tasks of civil society, etc. as unworthy of love and the freedom of feeling. Since, however, decisions still have to be made in relation to actual existence [*Dasein*] and action, the same thing happens as in the case of that subjectivity of the will in general which knows itself to be absolute (see § 140), namely that the decisions are made on the basis of subjective representations [*Vorstellung*], i.e. of *opinion* and the *caprice of the arbitrary will*. – The truth, however – as opposed to this truth which veils itself in the subjectivity of feeling and representational thinking – is the momentous transition of the inner to the outer, that incorporation [*Einbildung*] of reason into reality which the whole of world history has worked to achieve. Through this work, educated humanity has actualized and become conscious of rational existence [*Dasein*], political institutions, and laws. Those who 'seek the Lord' and assure themselves, in their uneducated opinion, that they possess everything *immediately* instead of undertaking the work of raising their subjectivity to cognition of the truth and knowledge of objective right and duty, can produce nothing but folly, outrage, and the destruction of all ethical relations. These are necessary consequences of that religious disposition which insists exclusively on its form, and so turns against actuality and the truth which is present in universal form within the laws. But this disposition need not necessarily proceed to actualize itself in this way. With its negative point of view, it may well retain its inward character, conform to [social] institutions and laws, and simply resign itself to these with sighs, or with contempt and longing. It is not strength but weakness which, in our times, has turned religiosity into a *polemical* kind of piety, whether this is associated with a genuine need or merely with unsatisfied vanity. Instead of mastering one's opinions by the labour of study and subjecting one's volition to discipline so as to elevate it to free obedience, the easiest course is to renounce cognition of objective truth, to nurse a sense of grievance and hence also of self-conceit, and to find in one's own godliness all that is required in order to see through the nature of the laws and of political institutions, to pass judgement on them, and to lay down what their character should and must be. And indeed, since these are the findings of a pious heart, they must be infallible and indisputable; for if we make religion the basis of our intentions and assertions, these cannot be faulted on account of either their shallowness or their injustice [*Unrechtlichkeit*].[5]

But if the religion in question is of a genuine kind and does not have this negative and polemical attitude towards the state, but acknowledges and endorses it, it will also have a *status* [*Zustand*] and *expression* of its own [*für sich*]. The business of its worship consists in *actions* and in *doctrine*; for these, it requires *possessions* and *property*, as well as *individuals* dedicated to the *service* of the community. A relationship thus arises between the state and the religious community, and its determination is a simple one. It is in the nature of the case [*Sache*] that the state fulfils a duty by giving the [religious] community every assistance and protection in the pursuit of its religious end. Indeed, since religion is that moment which integrates the state at the deepest level of the disposition [of its citizens], the state ought even to require all its citizens to belong to such a community – but to any community they please, for the state can have no say in the content [of religious belief] in so far as this relates to the internal dimension of representational thought. A state which is strong because its organization is fully developed can adopt a more liberal attitude in this respect, and may completely overlook individual matters [*Einzelheiten*] which might affect it, or even tolerate communities whose religion does not recognize even their direct duties towards the state (although this naturally depends on the numbers concerned). It is able to do this by entrusting the members of such communities to civil society and its laws, and is content if they fulfil their direct duties towards it passively, for example by commutation or substitution [of an alternative service].† But in so far as the religious

† *Hegel's note:* Of Quakers, Anabaptists, etc., it may be said that they are active members only of civil society and that, as private persons, they have purely private relations with other people. Even in this context, they have been exempted from taking oaths; they fulfil their direct duties towards the state in a passive manner, and although they reject outright one of the most important of these, namely the defence of the state against its enemies, they may even be allowed to fulfil this duty by substituting another service instead.[6] Towards such sects, the state practises *toleration* in the proper sense of the word; for since they do not recognize their duties towards it, they cannot claim the right to belong to it. When, on one occasion, there was a strong movement in the American Congress to abolish negro slavery, a member from the southern states aptly retorted: 'Leave us our negroes and you can keep your Quakers.' – Only if the state is strong in other respects can it overlook and tolerate such anomalies, relying above all on the power of custom and the inner rationality of its institutions to reduce and overcome the discrepancy if the state does not strictly enforce its rights in this respect. For example, although it may well have been contrary to formal right to grant even civil rights to the *Jews*, on the grounds that the latter should be regarded not just as a particular religious group but also as members of a foreign nation [*Volk*], the outcry which this viewpoint and others produced overlooked the fact that the Jews are primarily *human beings*; this is not just a neutral and abstract quality (see Remarks to § 209), for its consequence is that the

community owns *property* and otherwise performs *acts* of worship with the help of individuals employed for this purpose, it emerges from the inner realm into that of worldly affairs and hence into the province of the state, thereby placing itself *immediately* under its laws. It is true that the oath and the ethical realm in general, including the marriage relationship, involve that inner penetration and elevation of the *disposition* which is confirmed at the profoundest level by religion. [But] since ethical relations are essentially relations of *actual rationality*, the rights of this rationality must first be asserted within them, and the confirmation of the Church is then added to these rights as their purely inward and more abstract aspect. – As for the other ways in which the Church community expresses itself, the inward [dimension] predominates over the outward to a greater extent in matters of *doctrine* than in *acts* of worship and other related kinds of behaviour, in which it is at once apparent that the *legal* [*rechtliche*] aspect at least is in itself [*für sich*] a matter [*Sache*] for the state. (Admittedly, Churches have also contrived to exempt their servants and property from the authority [*Macht*] and jurisdiction of the state, and have even acquired jurisdiction over laymen in matters such as divorce proceedings, the taking of oaths, etc., in which religion plays a part.) – The role of the *police* with regard to such actions is, of course, more indeterminate, but this lies in the nature of their function and applies equally to other purely civil activities (see § 234 above). Whenever individuals of the same religious persuasion join together to form a community or corporation, the latter will in general be subject to the policing and supervision of the state. – *Doctrine* itself, however, has its province within the conscience, and

granting of civil rights gives those who receive them a *self-awareness* as recognized *legal* [*rechtliche*] persons in civil society, and it is from this root, infinite and free from all other influences, that the desired assimilation in terms of attitude and disposition arises.[7] [If they had not been granted civil rights,] the Jews would have remained in that isolation with which they have been reproached, and this would rightly have brought blame [*Schuld*] and reproach upon the state which excluded them; for the state would thereby have failed to recognize its own principle as an objective institution with a power of its own (cf. the end of the Remarks to § 268). While the demand for the exclusion of the Jews claimed to be based on the highest right, it has proved in practice to be the height of folly, whereas the way in which governments have acted has proved wise and honourable.[8]

enjoys the right of the subjective freedom of self-consciousness, that sphere of inwardness which is not, as such, the
province of the state. Nevertheless, the state, too, has its
doctrine, for its institutions and whatever it recognizes as valid
in relation to right, to the constitution, etc. are present essentially in the form of *thought* as law. And since the state is not a
mechanism but the rational life of self-conscious freedom and
the system of the ethical world, the *disposition* [of its citizens],
and so also the[ir] consciousness of this disposition in
principles, is an essential moment in the actual state. But the
doctrine of the Church is in turn not just an internal matter
for the conscience; as doctrine, it is in fact an *expression*,
indeed the expression of a content which is intimately connected, or even directly concerned, with ethical principles and
with the laws of the state. Thus, state and Church are at this
point either in direct *agreement* or in direct *opposition*. The
Church may go so far as to present the difference between
their respective provinces as an abrupt opposition, for it may
take the view that, since the Church embodies the absolute
content of religion, the *spiritual* in general and hence also the
ethical element are part of its concern, whereas the state is a
mechanical framework serving non-spiritual and external
ends. The Church may look on itself as the kingdom of God,
or at least as the road and forecourt which lead to it, yet regard
the state as the kingdom of the world, i.e. of the transitory and
finite; in other words, it may see itself as an end in itself, but
the state purely as a *means*. And as far as *doctrinal instruction* is
concerned, these claims may be coupled with the demand that
the state should not only grant the Church complete freedom
in such matters, but should also treat its teachings, as doctrines, with unconditional respect, regardless of what they
may contain, on the grounds that the Church is alone responsible for determining them. But while the Church bases these
claims on the far-reaching argument [*Gründe*] that the
spiritual element in general is its property, *science* and cognition in general are also represented in this province and, like a
Church, develop into a totality with its own distinct principle
which may consider itself as occupying the same position as
the Church, but with even greater justification. Thus, science

297

may also demand the same independence from the state, and treat the latter simply as a means which should provide for it as an end in itself. – Furthermore, it makes no difference to this relationship [between Church and state] whether the individuals and heads of congregations who devote themselves to the service of the religious community have gone so far as to lead an existence [*Existenz*] separate from the state, so that only the other members of their community are subject to its control, or whether they remain in other respects within the state and regard their ecclesiastical vocation [*Bestimmung*] merely as one aspect of their social status [*Stand*] which they keep separate from the state. It should in the first place be noted that such a relationship is associated with that view [*Vorstellung*] of the state according to which its sole function [*Bestimmung*] is to protect and secure the life, property, and arbitrary will of everyone, in so far as the latter does not infringe the life, property, and arbitrary will of others; in this view, the state is merely an arrangement dictated by necessity [*Not*]. In this way, the higher spiritual element of what is true in and for itself is placed, as subjective religiosity or theoretical science, beyond the [confines of the] state which, as the *laity* in and for itself, should merely show respect [for this element] and is thus completely deprived of its proper ethical character. We do indeed know from history that there have in the past been periods and conditions of barbarism in which all higher spirituality had its seat in the Church, while the state was merely a secular regime of violence, arbitrariness, and passion and the abstract opposition [of Church and state] referred to above was the main principle of actuality (see § 358).[9] But to claim that this situation is the one which truly corresponds to the Idea is to proceed too blindly and superficially. On the contrary, the development of this Idea has established the truth [of the proposition] that spirit, as free and rational, is inherently [*an sich*] ethical, that the true Idea is *actual* rationality, and that it is this rationality which exists as the state. It has further emerged just as plainly from this Idea that the ethical *truth* which it embodies is present for *thinking* consciousness as a *content* on which the form of *universality* has been conferred – i.e. as *law* – and that the state in general *knows* its ends, and recognizes and implements them with a determinate consciousness and in accordance with principles. Now religion, as already remarked, has the truth as its universal object [*Gegenstand*], but as a *given* content whose basic determinations have not been recognized in terms of concepts and thought. In the same way, the relation of the individual to this object is an obligation based on authority, and the *witness* of his *own* spirit and heart, as that in which the moment of freedom is contained, is *faith* and *feeling* [*Empfindung*]. It is philosophical insight which recognizes that Church and state are not opposed to each other as far as their *content* is concerned, which is truth and rationality, but merely differ in form. Thus, when the Church proceeds to put forward *doctrines* (although there are and have been Churches which confine themselves to worship, and others in which worship is the principal concern, and doctrine and a more educated consciousness are merely secondary), and its doctrines relate to *objective principles*, to ethical and rational thoughts, its expression of these doctrines immediately brings it into the province of the state. In contrast with the *faith* and *authority* of the Church in relation to ethics, right, laws, and institutions, and with its *subjective conviction*, the state possesses *knowledge*. Within its principle, the content is no longer essentially confined to the form of feeling and faith, but belongs to determinate thought. When the content which has being in and for itself appears in the shape of religion as a particular content, as the doctrines peculiar to the Church as a religious community, they remain outside the domain of the state. (In Protestantism, there is no *laity*, so that there is likewise no clergy to act as an exclusive depositary of Church doctrine.) Since ethical principles and the organization of the state in general may be drawn into the province of religion and not only may, but also should, be framed with reference to the latter, this reference gives the state itself its religious accreditation. On the other hand, the state retains the right and form of self-conscious, objective rationality, the right to enforce the latter and to defend it against assertions based on the *subjective* variety [*Gestalt*] of truth, no matter what *assurances* and *authority* this truth may carry with it. Since the essential principle of the form of the state as a universal is thought, it was in fact *from the state* that *freedom of thought and science* first emerged (whereas it was a Church which burned Giordano Bruno[10] and forced Galileo to recant on his knees for *expounding* the *Copernican* theory of the solar system,[11] etc.).† Thus, *science*, too, is to be found on the side of the state, for it has the same element of form as the state, and its end is *cognition*, by means of thought, of *objective* truth and rationality. Thinking cognition may admittedly fall from [the level of] science to [that of] opinion and deductive reasoning [*Räsonieren aus Gründen*] and, turning its attention to ethical subjects and the organization of the state, set itself up in contradiction to their principles. And it may in so doing make the same pretensions as the Church makes for its own distinctive sphere, namely by presenting its *opinions* as reason, and as the right of the subjective self-consciousness to freedom of opinion and convic-

†*Hegel's note.* See Laplace, *Exposition of the System of the World* [*Exposition du Système du monde* (Paris, 1796)], Book v, Chapter 4: 'When Galileo announced the discoveries he had made with the telescope (the phases of Venus, etc.), he showed at the same time that they proved beyond doubt the movement of the earth itself. But the idea [*Vorstellung*] of this movement was pronounced heretical by an assembly of cardinals, and Galileo, its most famous advocate, was summoned before the court of the Inquisition and compelled to recant it in order to escape a harsh prison sentence. In a man of intellect [*Geist*], one of the strongest passions is the passion for truth. Galileo, convinced of the earth's movement by his own observations, reflected for a long time over a new work in which he intended to develop all the proofs in its favour. But in order to avoid that persecution to which he would otherwise certainly have fallen victim, he adopted the stratagem of presenting these proofs in the form of dialogues between three individuals. It is obvious enough that the advocate of the Copernican system has the advantage; but since Galileo did not pronounce a verdict, and since he gave as much weight as possible to the objections advanced by the adherents of Ptolemy, he was entitled to expect that he would be left to enjoy unmolested that peace which his advanced years and labours had earned for him. In his seventieth year, he was again summoned before the tribunal of the Inquisition; he was put in prison, and there required to recant his opinions for a second time, under threat of the penalty laid down for relapsed heretics. He was made to sign the following formula of abjuration: "I, Galileo, having appeared in person before the court in my seventieth year, on bended knee and with the holy Gospels before my eyes and in my hands, abjure, damn, and curse, with sincere heart and true belief, the absurdity, falsity, and heresy of the doctrine of the earth's movement", etc. What a spectacle, to see a venerable old man, famed throughout a long life devoted solely to the study of nature, abjuring on his knees and against the testimony of his own conscience that truth which he had convincingly demonstrated! A judgement of the Inquisition condemned him to imprisonment in perpetuity. A year later, on the intercession of the Grand Duke of Florence, he was set at liberty. He died in 1642. His loss was mourned throughout Europe, which his labours had enlightened and which was incensed at the judgement passed by a hated tribunal on so great a man.'

tion. The principle of this subjectivity of knowledge has already been discussed above (see Remarks to § 140). All that need be mentioned here is that the attitude of the state towards *opinion* – in so far as it is merely opinion, a subjective content which therefore has no true inner force and power, however grandiose its claims – is on the one hand one of infinite indifference, like that of the painters who stick to the three primary colours on their palettes, regardless of the *wisdom of the schools* which tells them that there are seven. But on the other hand, when these opinions based on bad principles give themselves a universal existence [*Dasein*] which undermines actuality, the state must protect objective truth and the principles of ethical life; and it must do the same if the formalism of unconditional subjectivity should seek to make science its basis and starting-point, and to turn the state's own educational establishments against it by inciting them to make pretensions akin to those of a Church. And conversely, when confronted with a Church which claims unlimited and unconditional *authority*, the state must on the whole assert the formal right of self-consciousness to its own insight and conviction, and in general to thoughts concerning what should count as objective truth.

The *unity of state and Church*, a subject [*Bestimmung*] which has likewise been much discussed and held up as an ultimate ideal in recent times, may also be mentioned here.[12] Although their essential unity lies in the truth of principles and disposition, it is just as essential that, along with this unity, the *difference* between their forms of consciousness should attain *particular existence* [*Existenz*]. That unity of Church and state which has so often been wished for is to be found in oriental despotism – but in this case, there is no state in the sense of that self-conscious configuration [*Gestaltung*] of right, of free ethical life, and of organic development which is alone worthy of the spirit. – Furthermore, if the state is to attain existence [*Dasein*] as the *self-knowing* ethical actuality of spirit, its form must become distinct from that of authority and faith. But this distinction emerges only in so far as the Church for its part becomes divided within itself. Only then, [when it stands] above the *particular* Churches, can the state attain *universality* of thought as its formal principle and bring it into existence [*Existenz*]; but in order to recognize this, one must know not only what universality is *in itself*, but also what its *existence* [*Existenz*] is. Consequently, far from it being, or ever having been, a misfortune for the state if the Church is divided, it is *through this division alone* that the state has been able to fulfil its destiny [*Bestimmung*] as self-conscious rationality and ethical life. This division is likewise the most fortunate thing which could have happened to the Church and to thought as far as their freedom and rationality are concerned.

Addition (H). The state is actual, and its actuality consists in the fact that the interest of the whole realizes itself through the particular ends. Actuality is always the unity of universality and particularity, the resolution of universality into particularity; the latter then appears to be self-sufficient, although it is sustained and supported only by the whole. If this unity is not present, nothing can be *actual*, even if it may be assumed to have *existence* [*Existenz*]. A bad state is one which merely exists; a sick body also exists, but it has no true reality. A hand which has been cut off still looks like a hand and exists, but it has no actuality.[13] True actuality is necessity: what is actual is necessary in itself. Necessity consists [*besteht*] in the division of the whole into the distinctions within the concept, and in the fact that this divided whole exhibits a fixed and enduring determinacy which is not dead and unchanging but continues to produce itself in its dissolution. An essential part of the fully developed state is consciousness or thought; the state accordingly knows what it wills and knows this as an object of thought [*ein Gedachtes*]. Since, then, the seat of knowledge is within the state, science also has its seat *here* and not within the Church. This notwithstanding, there has been much talk in recent times to the effect that the state should grow out of religion. The state is [fully] developed spirit and it displays its moments in the light of consciousness; and the fact that what lies within the Idea emerges into [the sphere of] objectivity [*Gegenständlichkeit*] means that the state appears as a finite entity and is thereby shown to be a secular realm [*Gebiet*], whereas religion presents itself as a realm of infinity. The state consequently seems subordinate, and since the finite cannot exist on its own [*für sich bestehen*], it allegedly requires the Church as its basis. As a finite entity, it is said to lack justification, and only through religion can it be sanctified and belong to the infinite. But this view of the matter [*Sache*] is extremely one-sided. The state is indeed essentially secular and finite, and has particular ends and particular powers; but its secularity is only one of its aspects, and only a spiritless perception can regard it as merely finite. For the state has a soul which animates it, and this animating soul is subjectivity, which creates distinctions on the one hand but preserves their unity on the other. In the realm [*Reich*] of religion, distinctions and finite elements are also present. God, it is said, is three in one; there are accordingly three determinations, and it is only the unity of these which constitutes the spirit. Consequently, if we apprehend the divine nature in concrete terms, this can be done only by means of distinctions. Thus, finite elements are to be found in the divine realm as well as in the secular, and [to contend] that the secular spirit, i.e. the state, is purely finite is a one-sided view, for actuality is not irrational. A bad state, of course, is purely secular and finite, but the rational state is infinite within itself. Secondly, it is argued that the state should derive its justification from religion. The Idea, within [the context of] religion, is spirit internalized in emotion, but it is this same Idea which gives itself secular expression in the state and secures an existence [*Dasein*] and actuality for itself in knowledge and volition. Thus, to say that the state must be founded on religion may mean that it should be based on and grow out of rationality. But the same proposition can also be misunderstood to mean that those human beings whose spirit is fettered by an unfree religion are best equipped to obey. The Christian religion, however, is the religion of freedom – although it may come about that this freedom is perverted into unfreedom under the influence of superstition. If, then, the above proposition means that individuals must have religion in order that their fettered spirit can be more effectively oppressed within the state, its sense is a bad one; but if it is meant that human beings should have respect for the state as that whole of which they are the branches, the best way of achieving this is, of course, through philosophical insight into its essence. But if this insight is lacking, the religious disposition may lead to the same result. Consequently, the state may have need of religion and faith. But the state remains essentially different from religion, for what it requires has the shape of a legal [*rechtlichen*] duty, and it is indifferent to the emotional attitude with which this duty is performed. The field of religion, on the other hand, is inwardness; and just as the state would prejudice the right of inwardness if it imposed its requirements in a religious manner, so also does the Church, if it acts like a state and imposes penalties, degenerate into a tyrannical religion. A third difference, connected with that just mentioned, is that the content of religion is and remains latent [*eingehüllt*], so that emotion, feeling [*Empfindung*], and representational thought are the ground on which it rests. On this ground, everything has the form of subjectivity, whereas the state actualizes itself and gives its determinations a stable existence [*Dasein*]. Thus, if religiosity sought to assert itself in the state in the manner which it usually adopts on its own ground, it would subvert the organization of the state; for the differences within the state are far apart, whereas everything in religion invariably has reference to the totality. And if this totality sought to take over all the relations [*Beziehungen*] of the state, it would become fanaticism; it would wish to find the whole in every particular, and could accomplish this only by destroying the particular, for fanaticism is simply the refusal to admit particular differences. If we may so put it, the saying 'Laws are not made for the pious' is no more than an expression of this fanaticism. For when piety adopts the role of the state, it cannot endure anything determinate, but simply destroys it. It is also in keeping with this if piety leaves decisions to the conscience, to inwardness, and is not determined by *reasons*; for inwardness does not develop reasons and is not accountable to itself. Thus, if piety is to count as the actuality of the state, all laws are swept aside and it is subjective feeling which legislates. This feeling may be pure arbitrariness, and it is only by its actions that we can tell whether or not this is so. But in so far as they are actions or precepts, they assume the shape of laws, and this is in direct contradiction to the subjective feeling referred to. God, as the object [*Gegenstand*] of this feeling, might also be made the determinant; but God is the universal Idea which remains indeterminate within this feeling, and which is not sufficiently mature to determine what exists in developed form within the state. The very fact that everything in the state is stable and secure is a defence against arbitrariness and positive opinion. Thus, religion as such should not hold the reins of government.

§ 271

The political constitution is, *first*, the organization of the state and the process of its organic life *with reference to itself*, in which it differentiates its moments within itself and develops them to *established existence* [*zum Bestehen*].

Secondly, the state in its individuality is an *exclusive* unit which accordingly has relations with *others*; it thereby turns its differentiation *outwards* and, in accordance with this determination, posits its existing [*bestehenden*] differences within itself in their *ideality*.

Addition (H). Just as irritability in the living organism is itself in one respect an inward quality which belongs to the organism as such, so also in the present case is the outward reference directed towards inwardness. The inward aspect of the state as such is the civil power, and its outward direction is the military power, although the latter is also a specific aspect within the state itself. The equilibrium of these two aspects is an important factor in the history*ᵃ* of the state. Sometimes the civil power is completely defunct and based exclusively on the military power, as at the time of the Roman emperors*ᵇ* and the praetorians;*¹* and at other times – as in the modern period – the military power is solely a product of the civil power, as when all citizens are eligible for conscription.*²*

ᵃTranslator's note: The word *Gesinnung* ('disposition'), which appears at this point in all of those editions of the *Rechtsphilosophie* which include Gans's Additions, should read *Geschichte* ('history') as in Hotho's notes, used by Gans as the basis of this Addition (see VPR III, 742). The error is presumably a misreading by Gans.

ᵇTranslator's note: The remainder of this sentence appears to be Gans's own interpolation, as it has no counterpart in either Hotho's or Griesheim's notes.

I *The Internal Constitution*ᶜ

§ 272

The constitution is rational in so far as the state *differentiates* and determines its activity within itself *in accordance with the nature of the concept*. It does so in such a way that *each* of the *powers* in question is in itself the *totality*, since each contains the other moments and has them active within it, and since all of them, as expressions of the differentiation [*Unterschied*] of the concept, remain wholly within its ideality and constitute nothing but *a single individual* whole.

In recent times, we have heard an endless amount of empty talk both about the constitution and about reason itself. The most vapid of this has come from those in Germany who have persuaded themselves that they have a better understanding than anyone else – especially governments – of what a constitution is, and who believe that all their superficialities are irrefutably justified because they are allegedly based on religion and piety. It is no wonder that such talk has made reasonable men [*Männer*] sick of the words 'reason', 'enlightenment', 'right', etc., and likewise of the words 'constitution' and 'freedom', and that one is almost ashamed to enter into any further discussion of political constitutions.*¹* But it may at least be hoped that such excesses will lead to a more widespread conviction that philosophical *cognition* of such subjects cannot come from ratiocination or from [the

ᶜ *Translator's note:* Literally: 'The Internal Constitution for Itself [*für sich*]' – i.e. the internal aspects will be considered here in their own right.

consideration of] ends, grounds, and utilities – let alone from emotionality, love, and enthusiasm – but only from the concept; and it is also to be hoped that those who believe that the divine is incomprehensible and that cognition of the truth is a futile [*nichtiges*] enterprise will take no further part in the discussion. At any rate, neither the undigested chatter nor the edifying sentiments which their emotions and enthusiasm generate can claim to merit the attention of philosophy.

Among ideas [*Vorstellungen*] now in currency, that of the *necessary division* [*Teilung*] *of powers* within the state calls for mention (with reference to § 269).[2] This is a highly important determination which, if understood in its true sense, could rightly be regarded as the guarantee of public freedom; but it is also an idea [*Vorstellung*] of which those very people who believe that they speak out of love and enthusiasm know nothing and wish to know nothing, for it is in this very idea that the moment of *rational determinacy* lies. In other words, the principle of the division of powers contains the essential moment of *difference*, of *real* rationality; but such is the view of the abstract understanding that, on the one hand, it attributes to this principle the false determination of the *absolute self-sufficiency* of each power in relation to the others, and on the other hand, it one-sidedly interprets [*auffassen*] the relation of these powers to one another as negative, as one of mutual *limitation*. In this view, the reaction of each power to the others is one of hostility and fear, as if to an evil [*Übel*], and their determination [*Bestimmung*] is such that they oppose one another and produce, by means of this counterpoise, a general equilibrium rather than a living unity. It is only the *self-determination* of the concept within itself, not any other ends or utilities, which contains the absolute origin of the different powers, and it is solely because of this that the organization of the state is inherently [*in sich*] rational and the image of eternal reason. – How the *concept* and subsequently, in concrete fashion, the Idea, become determined in themselves and thereby posit their moments – universality, particularity, and individuality [*Einzelheit*] – in abstraction can be learned from logic (though not, of course, from the logic commonly in use).[3] At any rate, to take the negative as a starting-point and to make malevolence and distrust of malevolence the primary factor, and then, on this assumption, to devise ingenious defences whose efficiency depends merely on corresponding counter-defences is, as far as thought is concerned, characteristic of the *negative understanding* and, as far as the disposition is concerned, characteristic of the outlook of the rabble (see § 244 above). – If the powers – e.g. what have been called the *executive* and *legislative* powers – attain *self-sufficiency*, the destruction of the state, as has been witnessed on a grand scale[d] [in our times], is immediately posited; or if the state is essentially preserved, a unity of one kind or another is established for the time being by means of a conflict whereby one power subjugates the others, and it is by this means alone that the essential [object], the survival [*Bestehen*] of the state, is achieved.

Addition (H). One should expect nothing from the state except what is an expression of rationality. The state is the world which the spirit has created for itself; it therefore follows a determinate course which has being in and for itself. How often do we hear talk of the wisdom of God in nature! But we must not for a moment imagine that the physical world of nature is of a higher order than the world of the spirit; for the state is as far above physical life as spirit is above nature. We should therefore venerate the state as an earthly divinity[a] and realize that, if it is difficult to comprehend nature, it is an infinitely more arduous task to understand the state. It is of the utmost significance that, in recent times, we have attained specific[b] intuitions concerning the state in general and have been so much occupied with discussing and framing constitutions. But this still does not resolve the problem; it is also necessary to bring to a rational matter [*Sache*] the reason of intuition,[c] to know what its essence is, and [to realize] that its most conspicuous aspect is not always the essential. Thus, while the powers of the state must certainly be distinguished, each must form a whole in itself and contain the other moments within it. When we speak of the distinct activities of these powers, we must not fall into the monumental error of taking this to mean that each power should exist independently [*für sich*] and in abstraction; on the contrary, the powers should be distinguished only as moments of the concept. On the other

[a]*Translator's note: als ein Irdisch-Göttliches*; Hotho's notes, on which Gans based this Addition, read simply *als ein Göttliches* ('as something divine'): see VPR III, 744.
[b]*Translator's note:* Hotho's notes read *bestimmtere* ('more specific'): see VPR III, 744.
[c]*Translator's note:* Hotho's notes read (in translation): 'One must also bring reason to a rational intuition' (VPR III, 744).

hand, if these differences do exist [*bestehen*] independently and in abstraction, it is plain to see that two self-sufficient entities cannot constitute a unity, but must certainly give rise to a conflict whereby either the whole is destroyed or unity is restored by force. Thus, during the French Revolution, the legislative power at times engulfed the so-called executive, and at other times the executive power engulfed the legislative, so that it remains an absurdity in this context to raise, for example, the moral demand for harmony. For if we refer the matter [*Sache*] to the emotions, we admittedly save ourselves all the trouble; but although ethical feeling may be necessary, it is not qualified to determine the powers of the state on its own. Thus, the main point to note is that, just as the determinations of the powers are in themselves the whole, so too do all of them, in their existence [*Existenz*], constitute the entire concept. We usually speak of three powers – the legislative, the executive, and the judiciary. The first of these corresponds to universality and the second to particularity; but the judiciary is not the third constituent of the concept, because its [i.e. the judiciary's] individuality [*Einzelheit*] lies outside the above spheres.

§ 273

The political state is therefore divided into three substantial elements:[1]

(a) the power to determine and establish the universal – the *legislative* power;

(b) the subsumption of *particular* spheres and individual cases under the universal – the *executive power*;

(c) subjectivity as the ultimate decision of the will – *the power of the sovereign*, in which the different powers are united in an individual unity which is thus the apex and beginning of the whole, i.e. of *constitutional monarchy*.

The development [*Ausbildung*] of the state to constitutional monarchy is the achievement of the modern world, in which the substantial Idea has attained infinite form. The *history* of this immersion of the world spirit in itself or – and this amounts to the same thing – this free development in which the Idea releases its moments (and they are only its moments) from itself as totalities, and in so doing contains them in that ideal unity of the concept in which real rationality consists [*besteht*] – the history of this true formation [*Gestaltung*] of ethical life is the concern [*Sache*] of universal world history.

The old classification of constitutions into *monarchy, aristocracy,* and *democracy* presupposes a *still undivided and substantial unity* which has not yet attained its *inner differentiation* (as an organization developed within itself) and which consequently still lacks *depth* and *concrete rationality.*[2] From the point of view of the ancient world, therefore, this classification is the true and correct one; for in the case of a unity which is still substantial and has not yet progressed to its absolute development [*Entfaltung*] within itself, the difference is essentially *external* and appears primarily as a difference in the *number* of those in whom that substantial unity is supposed to be immanent (see *Encyclopaedia of the Philosophical Sciences,* § 52).[a] These forms, which in this instance belong to different wholes, are reduced, in constitutional monarchy, to [the status of] moments. The monarch is *one* [individual]; *several* participate in the executive power, and the *many* at large participate in the legislative power. But as already mentioned, such purely quantitative differences are merely superficial and do not convey the concept of the thing [*Sache*]. There has been much talk in recent times of the democratic and aristocratic elements *in monarchy,* but this is equally beside the point; for in so far as the determinations in question do occur *in monarchy,* they have lost their democratic and aristocratic character. – Some representations [*Vorstellungen*] of constitutions merely set up the state as an *abstraction* which governs and issues commands, and leave it undecided – or regard it as immaterial – whether this state is headed by *one* or *several* or *all.* – 'All these forms', says Fichte in his *Natural Law* (Part I, p. 196), 'are right and proper provided that there is an *ephorate*'[4] (an institution devised by Fichte as a counterweight to the supreme power), 'and may promote and preserve universal right within the state'. – Such a view (like the device of an ephorate) is a product of that superficial conception of the state referred to above. If social conditions are quite simple, these differences are admittedly of little or no significance;

<hr>

[a]*Translator's note:* The first edition refers to § 82 of the *Encyclopaedia* (first edition); I follow Knox (p. 367) and VPR II, 730 in preferring § 52[3] as more plausible.

thus Moses, for example, made no provision in his legislation for institutional changes in the event of the people requiring a king, but merely added the commandment that the king should not possess large quantities of horses, wives, and silver and gold (Deuteronomy 17:16ff.). – Furthermore, it is certainly possible in one sense to say that the Idea is likewise indifferent to the three forms in question (including that of *monarchy*, at least in its limited meaning as an *alternative* to *aristocracy* and *democracy*); but it is indifferent to them in the opposite sense [to that of Fichte], because all three are out of keeping with the Idea in its rational development [*Entwicklung*] (see § 272), and the latter could not attain its right and actuality in any of them. For this reason, it has become utterly pointless to ask which of the three is most commendable; such forms can be discussed only in a historical context. – Nevertheless, in this as in so many other instances, we must acknowledge Montesquieu's depth of insight in his famous account of the principles of these forms of government. But while acknowledging the accuracy of his account, we must not misunderstand it. It is common knowledge that he specified *virtue* as the principle of *democracy*;[5] and such a constitution does indeed depend on the *disposition* [of the citizens] as the purely substantial form in which the rationality of the will which has being in and for itself still exists under this constitution. But Montesquieu[6] adds that *England*, in the seventeenth century, afforded a fine spectacle of how efforts to establish a democracy were rendered impotent by a lack of virtue on the part of the leaders, and further observes that, when virtue disappears from the republic, ambition takes hold of those whose hearts [*Gemüt*] are susceptible to it and greed takes possession of everyone, so that the state falls prey to universal exploitation and its strength resides solely in the power of a few individuals and the unruliness of everyone. To these remarks, it must be replied that, as the condition of society grows more advanced and the powers of *particularity* are developed and liberated, it is not enough for the heads of state to be virtuous; another form of rational law is required apart from that of the [individual] disposition if the whole is to have the strength to maintain its unity and to grant the forces of developed particularity their positive as well as negative rights. In the same way, we must avoid the misunderstanding of imagining that, since the disposition of virtue is the substantial form in a democratic republic, this disposition thereby becomes superfluous, or may even be totally absent, in a monarchy; and still less should we imagine that virtue and the *legally determined* activity of an *articulated* organization are mutually opposed and incompatible. – The view that *moderation* is the principle of *aristocracy*[7] entails an incipient divergence between public power and private interest, which at the same time affect each other so directly that this constitution is intrinsically liable at any moment to turn immediately into the harshest condition of tyranny or anarchy – as witness the history of Rome – and so to destroy itself. – The fact that Montesquieu recognizes *honour* as the principle of *monarchy*[8] is enough to indicate that the monarchy he has in mind is neither the patriarchal or ancient variety nor that which has developed an objective constitution, but *feudal monarchy* as that in which the relationships covered by its constitutional law [*inneren Staatsrecht*] have become firmly established as rights of private property and privileges of individuals and corporations. Since the life of the state is based, under this constitution, on privileged personalities to whose discretion a large part of what has to be done for the preservation [*Bestehen*] of the state is entrusted, the objective aspect of their services consists not in *duties* but in *representations* [*Vorstellung*] and *opinions*; consequently, the state is held together not by duty but merely by *honour*.

Another question naturally presents itself here: *who is to draw up the constitution?* This question seems clear enough, but closer inspection at once shows that it is nonsensical. For it presupposes that no constitution as yet exists, so that only an atomistic *aggregate* of individuals is present. How such an aggregate could arrive at a constitution, whether by its own devices or with outside help, through altruism [*Güte*], thought, or force, would have to be left to it to decide, for the concept is not applicable to an aggregate. – But if the above question presupposes that a constitution is already present, *to draw up* a constitution can only mean to change it, and the very fact that a constitution is presupposed at once implies that this change could take place only in a constitutional manner. – But it is at any rate utterly essential that the constitution should *not* be regarded as *something made*, even if it does have an origin in time. On the contrary, it is quite simply that which has being in and for itself, and should therefore be regarded as divine and enduring, and as exalted above the sphere of all manufactured things.[9]

Addition (H). The principle of the modern world at large is freedom of subjectivity, according to which all essential aspects present in the spiritual totality develop and enter into their right. If we begin with this point of view, we can scarcely raise the idle question of which form, monarchy or democracy, is superior. We can only say that the forms of all[a] political constitutions are one-sided if they cannot sustain within themselves the principle of free subjectivity and are unable to conform to fully developed reason.

[a]*Translator's note:* In Hotho's notes, on which this Addition is based, this word is not *aller* ('all') but *alter* ('ancient'), so that Hegel's observation, which then reads 'the forms of ancient political constitutions are one-sided and cannot sustain [etc.]', applies only to the constitutions of antiquity. Gans has removed the sentence from its context in the notes and given it a more general application.

§ 274

Since spirit is actual only as that which it knows itself to be, and since the state, as the spirit of a nation [*Volk*], is both the law which *permeates all relations within it* and also the customs and consciousness of the individuals who belong to it, the constitution of a specific nation will in general depend on the nature and development [*Bildung*] of its self-consciousness; it is in this self-consciousness that its subjective freedom and hence also the actuality of the constitution lie.

The wish to give a nation a constitution *a priori*, even if its content were more or less rational, is an idea [*Einfall*] which overlooks the very moment by virtue of which a constitution is more than a product of thought. Each nation accordingly has the constitution appropriate and proper to it.

Addition (H,G). The constitution of a state must permeate all relations within it. Napoleon, for example, tried to give the Spanish a constitution *a priori*, but the consequences were bad enough. For a constitution is not simply made: it is the work of centuries, the Idea and consciousness of the rational (in so far as that consciousness has developed in a nation). No constitution can therefore be created purely subjectively [*von Subjekten*]. What Napoleon gave to the Spanish was more rational than what they had before, and yet they rejected it as something alien, because they were not yet sufficiently cultivated [*gebildet*].*[1]* The constitution of a nation must embody the nation's feeling for its rights and [present] condition; otherwise it will have no meaning or value, even if it is present in an external sense. Admittedly, the need and longing for a better constitution may often be present in individuals [*Einzelnen*], but for the entire mass [of people] to be filled with such an idea [*Vorstellung*] is quite another matter, and this does not occur until later. Socrates' principle of morality or inwardness was a necessary product of his age, but it took time for this to become [part of] the universal self-consciousness.

a. The Power of the Sovereign

§ 275

The power of the sovereign itself contains the three moments of the totality within itself (see § 272), namely the *universality* of the constitution and laws,*[1]* consultation as the reference of the *particular* to the universal, and the moment of ultimate *decision* as the *self-determination* to which everything else reverts and from which its actuality originates. This absolute self-determination constitutes the distinguishing principle of the power of the sovereign as such, and will accordingly be dealt with first.

Addition (H). We begin with the power of the sovereign, i.e. with the moment of individuality [*Einzelheit*], for it contains within itself the three moments of the state as a totality. In other words, the 'I' is simultaneously the most individual*[a]* and the most universal [element]. On the face of it, nature, too, is individual in character, but reality – i.e. non-ideality or mutual externality – is not that which has being with itself [*das Beisichseiende*]; for in reality, the various individual units [*Einzelheiten*] subsist side by side. In the spirit, on the other hand, all the various elements are present only ideally and as a unity. Thus, the state, as spiritual in character, is the exposition of all its moments, but individuality*[b]* is at the same

[a]Translator's note: Hotho's notes read simply 'the individual' (*das Einzelne*; VPR III, 756).
[b]Translator's note: Hotho reads 'ideality' (*die Idealität*; VPR III, 757).

time its inner soul and animating principle, [and this takes the form of] sovereignty, which contains all differences within itself.

§ 276

1. The basic determination of the political state is the substantial unity or *ideality* of its moments. (α) In this unity, the particular powers and functions of the state are both dissolved and preserved. But they are preserved only in the sense that they are justified not as independent entities, but only in such a way and to such an extent as is determined by the Idea of the whole; their source is the latter's authority [*Macht*] and they are its fluid members, just as it is their simple self.

Addition (G). This ideality of the moments [in the state] is like life in an organic body: it is present at every point, there is only one life in all of them, and there is no resistance to it. Separated from it, each point must die. The same applies to the ideality of all the individual estates, powers, and corporations, however much their impulse may be to subsist and have being for themselves. In this respect, they resemble the stomach of an organism which also posits itself as independent [*für sich*] but is at the same time superseded and sacrificed and passes over into the whole.[1]

§ 277

(β) The particular functions and activities of the state *belong to it* as its own essential moments, and the *individuals* who perform and implement them are associated with them not by virtue of their immediate personalities, but only by virtue of their universal and objective qualities. Consequently, the link between these functions and particular personalities as such is external and contingent in character. For this reason, the functions and powers of the state cannot be *private property*.[1]

Addition (G). The activity of the state is associated with individuals. The latter, however, are not entitled by nature to perform these tasks, but [only] by virtue of their objective qualities. Ability, skill, and character are *particular* qualities of an individual, who must be trained and educated for a particular occupation. For this reason, an office can neither be sold nor inherited. In France, seats in parliament were formerly sold, as are officers' commissions up to a certain rank in the English army to this day; but this practice was (or still is) connected with the medieval constitutions of certain states, and these constitutions are now gradually disappearing.*

"Translator's note: The second half of this sentence is an extremely free paraphrase of much fuller reflections in Griesheim's notes on the conflict in England between nobility and crown (VPR IV, 668).

§ 278

The above two determinations – i.e. that the particular functions and powers of the state are not self-sufficient and fixed, either on their own account [*für sich*] or in the particular will of individuals, but are ultimately rooted in the unity of the state as their simple self – constitute the *sovereignty of the state.*

> This is *internal* sovereignty. The second aspect is *external* sovereignty (see below). – In the *feudal monarchy* of earlier times, the state certainly had external sovereignty, but internally, neither the monarch himself nor the state was sovereign. On the one hand (cf. Remarks to § 273), the particular functions and powers of the state and civil society were vested in independent corporations and communities, so that the whole was more of an aggregate than an organism; and on the other hand, they [i.e. these functions and powers] were the private property of individuals, so that what the latter had to do in relation to the whole was left to their own opinion and discretion. – The *idealism* which constitutes sovereignty is the same determination as that according to which the so-called *parts* of an animal organism are not parts, but members or organic moments whose isolation and separate existence [*Für-sich-Bestehen*] constitute disease (see *Encyclopaedia of the Philosophical Sciences*, § 293).[1] It is the same principle which we encountered (see § 7) in the abstract concept of the will (see Remarks to § 279) as self-referring negativity, and hence as universality *determining itself to individuality* [*Einzelheit*], in which all particularity and determinacy are superseded – i.e. the absolute and self-determining ground. In order to grasp this, one must first have understood the whole conception of the substance and true subjectivity of the concept. – Since sovereignty is the ideality of every particular authority [*Berech-*

tigung], it is easy to fall into the very common misunderstanding of regarding this ideality as mere power and empty arbitrariness, and of equating sovereignty with despotism. But despotism signifies the condition of lawlessness in general, in which the particular will as such, whether of a monarch or of the people (ochlocracy), counts as law (or rather replaces law), whereas sovereignty is to be found specifically under lawful and constitutional conditions as the moment of ideality of the particular spheres and functions [within the state]. In other words, these spheres are not independent or self-sufficient in their ends and modes of operation, nor are they solely immersed in themselves; on the contrary, in these same ends and modes of operation, they are determined by and dependent on *the end of the whole* (to which the indeterminate expression 'the *welfare of the state*' has in general been applied). This ideality manifests itself in two different ways. – In times of *peace*, the particular spheres and functions [within the state] pursue the course of satisfying themselves and their ends, and it is in part only as a result of the unconscious *necessity* of the thing [*Sache*] that their selfishness is *transformed* into a contribution to mutual preservation, and to the preservation of the whole (see § 183). But it is also in part a *direct influence* from above which constantly brings them back to the end of the whole and limits them accordingly (see 'The Executive Power', § 289), and at the same time urges them to perform direct services for the preservation of the whole. – But in a *situation of crisis* [*Not*] – whether in internal or external affairs – it is around the simple concept of sovereignty that the organism and all the particular spheres of which it formerly consisted rally, and it is to this sovereignty that the salvation of the state is entrusted, while previously legitimate functions [*dieses sonst Berechtigte*] are sacrificed; and this is where that idealism already referred to attains its distinct actuality (see § 321 below).

§ 279

2. Sovereignty, which is initially only the *universal* thought of this ideality, can *exist* only as *subjectivity* which is certain of itself, and as

the will's abstract – and to that extent ungrounded – *self-determination* in which the ultimate decision is vested. This is the individual aspect of the state as such, and it is in this respect alone that the state itself is *one*. But subjectivity attains its truth only as a *subject*, and personality only as a *person*, and in a constitution which has progressed to real rationality, each of the three moments of the concept has its distinctive [*ausgesonderte*] shape which is *actual for itself*. This absolutely decisive moment of the whole, therefore, is not individuality in general, but *one* individual, the *monarch*.

The immanent development of a science, the *derivation of its entire content* from the simple *concept* – and without such a derivation it certainly does not deserve the name of a philosophical science – has the following distinctive feature. One and the same concept – in this case the will – which begins by being abstract (because it is itself the beginning), retains its character yet [at the same time] consolidates its determinations, again through its own exclusive agency, and thereby acquires a concrete content. Thus, it is the basic moment of personality, initially abstract in [the sphere of] immediate right, which has continued to develop through its various forms of subjectivity until at this point, in [the sphere of] absolute right, in the state, and in the completely concrete objectivity of the will, it becomes the *personality of the state*, its *certainty of itself*. This last [instance], whose simple self supersedes all particularities, cuts short the weighing of arguments [*Gründe*] and counter-arguments (between which vacillations in either direction are always possible) and *resolves* them by its 'I will', thereby initiating all activity and actuality. – But personality (and subjectivity in general), as infinite and self-referring, has its *truth* – and indeed its proximate and immediate truth – simply and solely as a person, i.e. as a subject which has being for itself; and that which has being for itself is also simply *one*. The personality of the state has actuality only as a *person*, as *the monarch*. – Personality expresses the concept as such, whereas the person also embodies the actuality of the concept, and only when it is determined in this way [i.e. as a person] is the concept *Idea* or truth. – A so-called *moral person*, [such as] a society, community, or family, however concrete it may be in itself, contains personality only abstractly as one of its moments. In such a person, personality has not yet reached the truth of its existence [*Existenz*]. The state, however, is precisely this totality in which the moments of the concept attain actuality in accordance with their distinctive truth. – All these determinations, both in themselves [*für sich*] and in the [particular] shapes which they assume, have been discussed throughout this entire treatise; but they are repeated here because, although they are readily accepted when they assume a particular shape, they are no longer recognized and apprehended precisely when they reappear in their true position, i.e. no longer in isolation, but in their truth as *moments* of the Idea. – The concept of the monarch is therefore extremely difficult for ratiocination – i.e. the reflective approach of the understanding – to grasp, because such ratiocination stops short at isolated determinations, and consequently knows only [individual] reasons [*Gründe*], finite viewpoints, and *deduction* from such reasons. It accordingly presents the dignity of the monarch as *derivative*, not only in its form but also in its determination, whereas the very concept of monarchy is that it is not deduced from something else but *entirely self-originating*. The idea [*Vorstellung*] that the right of the monarch is based on divine authority is therefore the closest approximation to this concept, because it conveys the unconditional aspect of the right in question. But the misunderstandings associated with this idea are familiar enough, and the task of philosophical enquiry consists precisely in comprehending this divine quality.

The term *'popular sovereignty'* may be used to indicate that a people is self-sufficient for all *external* purposes and constitutes a state of its own, like the people of Great Britain – as distinct from the peoples of England, Scotland, or Ireland, or of Venice, Genoa, Ceylon, etc., who are now no longer sovereign because they have ceased to have sovereign princes or supreme governments of their own. – We may also say that *internal sovereignty* lies with the *people*, but only if we are speaking of the *whole* [state] in general, in keeping with the above demonstration (see §§ 277 and 278) that sovereignty belongs to the *state*. But the usual sense in which the term 'popular sovereignty' has begun to be used in recent times is to denote *the opposite of that sovereignty which exists in the monarch.* In this oppositional sense, popular sovereignty is one of those confused thoughts which are based on a *garbled* notion [*Vorstellung*] of the *people. Without* its monarch and that *articulation* of the whole which is necessarily and immediately associated with monarchy, *the* people is a formless mass. The latter is no longer a state, and *none* of those determinations which are encountered only in an *internally organized* whole (such as sovereignty, government, courts of law, public authorities [*Obrigkeit*], estates, etc.) is applicable to it. It is only when moments such as these which refer to an organization, to political life, emerge in a people that it ceases to be that indeterminate abstraction which the purely general idea [*Vorstellung*] of the *people* denotes. – If 'popular sovereignty' is taken to mean a *republican* form [of government], or more specifically democracy (for the term 'republic' covers many other empirical combinations which are in any case irrelevant in a philosophical discussion), then all that needs to be said has already been said above (see Remarks to § 273), apart from which there can be no further discussion of such a notion [*Vorstellung*] in face of the developed Idea. – If a people is represented neither as a patriarchal *tribe* [*Stamm*], nor as existing in an undeveloped condition in which democratic or aristocratic forms are possible (see Remarks to § 273) – or indeed in any other arbitrary and inorganic condition – but is envisaged as an internally developed and truly organic totality, its sovereignty will consist in the personality of the whole, which will in turn consist in the reality appropriate to its concept, i.e. the *person of the monarch.*

At that stage referred to above at which constitutions were divided into democracy, aristocracy, and monarchy – i.e. the point of view of substantial unity which remains within itself and which has not yet attained its infinite differentiation and immersion in itself – the moment of the *ultimate and self-determining decision of the will* does not emerge for itself in its *own distinct actuality* as an *immanent* organic moment of the state. Admittedly, even when the state assumes these less advanced shapes, there must always be an individual at its head. This individual is either already present as such [*für sich*], as in monarchies of the type in question, or, as in aristocracies and more particularly in democracies, he may rise up from among the statesmen or generals in a contingent manner and as *particular circumstances* require; for all actions and all actuality are initiated and implemented by a leader as the decisive unit. But enclosed in a union of powers which is still undifferentiated, this subjectivity of decision must either be contingent in its origin and emergence or occupy an altogether subordinate position. So long as heads of state were subject to such conditions, it was only in a sphere beyond their own that a pure and unalloyed decision could be found in the shape of a fate which determined [events] from without. As a moment within the Idea, this decision had to come into existence [*Existenz*], but its roots lay outside the circle of human freedom which the state encompasses. – This is the origin of the need to derive the *ultimate* decision on major issues and important concerns [*Momente*] of the state from *oracles*, a *daemon* (in the case of Socrates), the entrails of animals, the feeding and flight of birds, etc.;[1] for when human beings had not yet fathomed the depths of self-consciousness or emerged from the undifferentiated condition of substantial unity to attain being for themselves, they were not yet strong enough to perceive this decision *within* their own being. – In the *daemon* of Socrates (cf. [Remarks to] § 138 above), we can see how the will which in the past had simply projected itself *beyond* itself began to turn in upon itself and to recognize itself from within, which is the beginning of a *self-knowing* and hence genuine freedom. Since this real freedom of the Idea consists precisely in giving each of the moments of rationality its own present and *self-conscious* actuality, it is through its agency that the ultimate self-determining certainty which constitutes the apex of the concept of the will is allotted the function of a[n individual] consciousness. But this ultimate self-determination can fall within the sphere of human freedom only in so far as it occupies this supreme position, *isolated for itself* and exalted *above everything particular and conditional*; for only thus does its actuality accord with its concept.

Addition (G). In the organization of the state (which in this case means constitutional monarchy), the one thing which we must bear in mind is the internal necessity of the Idea; all other considerations are irrelevant. The state must be regarded as a great architectonic edifice, a hieroglyph of reason which becomes manifest in actuality. All considerations of mere utility, externality, and the like must therefore be excluded from a philosophical treatment [of this subject]. Representational thought can easily comprehend that the state is the self-determining and completely sovereign will, the ultimate source of decisions. But it is more difficult to grasp this 'I will' as a person, for this [formula] does not imply that the monarch may act arbitrarily: on the contrary, he is bound by the concrete content of the advice he receives, and if the constitution is firmly established, he often has nothing more to do than to sign his name. But this *name* is important: it is the ultimate instance and *non plus ultra*. It could be said that an organic articulation was already present in the beautiful democracy of Athens, but we can see at once that the Greeks based the ultimate decision on completely external phenomena [*Erscheinungen*] such as oracles, the entrails of sacrificial animals, and the flight of birds, and that they regarded nature as a power which proclaimed and expressed by these means what was good for human beings. At that time, self-consciousness had not yet arrived at the abstraction of subjectivity, nor had it yet realized that an 'I will' must be pronounced by man himself on the issue to be decided. This 'I will' constitutes the great difference between ancient and modern worlds, so that it must have its own distinct existence [*Existenz*] in the great edifice of the state. Unfortunately, however, this determination is regarded[a] as merely external and discretionary.

[a] *Translator's note:* Griesheim's notes, from which this Addition is extracted, read 'frequently regarded' (*häufig . . . angesehen*; VPR IV, 676).

§ 280

3. Seen in abstraction, this ultimate self of the will of the state is simple and therefore an *immediate* individuality [*Einzelheit*], so that the determination of *naturalness* is inherent in its very concept. The monarch, therefore, is essentially determined as *this* individual, in abstraction from every other content, and this individual is destined [*bestimmt*] in an immediate and natural way, i.e. by his natural *birth*, to hold the dignity of the monarch.

This transition from the concept of pure self-determination to the immediacy of being, and hence to the natural realm, is of a purely speculative nature, and its cognition accordingly belongs to logical philosophy. Furthermore, it is, on the whole, the same transition as that which is already familiar to us from the nature of the will in general, as the process which translates a content from subjectivity (as an end in view [*als vorgestellten Zweck*]) into existence [*Dasein*] (see § 8). But the distinctive form of the Idea and of the transition here in question is the *immediate transformation* of the pure self-determination of the will (i.e. of the simple concept itself) into *this* [specific entity], into natural existence, without the mediation of a *particular* content (such as the end of an action). – In the so-called *ontological proof* of the *existence of God*, it is this same transformation of the absolute concept into being which has given the Idea its profundity in the modern age. But this has recently been declared *incomprehensible*, which amounts to renouncing all cognition of the *truth*, for truth is simply the unity of the concept and existence (see § 23).[1] Since this unity is not to be found in the consciousness of the understanding, which continues to regard these two moments of the truth as *separate*, this consciousness may perhaps, in the present [religious] context, concede the possibility of a *faith* in this unity. But since the idea [*Vorstellung*] of the monarch is regarded as entirely within the scope of ordinary consciousness, the understanding insists all the more firmly on its separation [of the two moments] and on the consequences which its astute reasoning can deduce from this. It accordingly denies that the moment of ultimate decision in the state is linked *in and for itself* (i.e. in the concept of reason) with the immediate and natural, and concludes from this first, that this link is *contingent*, and secondly – since it equates rationality with the absolute distinctness of the two moments – that such a link is irrational. From this, further devastating consequences ensue for the Idea of the state.

Addition (H). A frequent objection to monarchy is that it makes the affairs of the state subject to contingency – since the monarch may be ill-educated or unworthy of holding the highest office – and that it is absurd for such a situation to be regarded as rational. But this objection is based on the invalid assumption that the monarch's particular character is of vital importance. In a fully organized state, it is only a question of the highest instance of formal decision, and all that is required in a monarch is someone to say 'yes' and to dot the 'i'; for the supreme office should be such that the particular character of its occupant is of no significance. Whatever other qualities the monarch has in addition to his role of ultimate decision belong to [the sphere of] particularity [*Partikularität*], which must not be allowed to affect the issue. There may indeed be circumstances in which this particularity plays an exclusive part, but in that case the state is either not yet fully developed, or it is poorly constructed. In a well-ordered monarchy, the objective aspect is solely the concern of the law, to which the monarch merely has to add his subjective 'I will'.[2]

§ 281

The two moments in their undivided unity – i.e. the ultimate ungrounded self of the will, and its existence [*Existenz*] which is consequently also ungrounded (and which belongs by definition [*Bestimmung*] to *nature*) – constitute the Idea of something *unmoved* by arbitrary will, i.e. the *majesty* of the monarch. In this unity lies the *actual unity* of the state, and it is only by virtue of its inward and *outward immediacy* that this unity is saved from being dragged down into the sphere of *particularity* with its arbitrariness, ends, and attitudes, from the strife of factions round the throne, and from the enervation and destruction of the power of the state.

The rights of birth and inheritance constitute the basis [*Grund*] of *legitimacy*, i.e. the basis not just of a purely positive right but also [of a right contained] in the Idea. – If the mode of succession is clearly defined – i.e. if the throne is inherited – the formation of factions is prevented when the throne falls vacant; this circumstance has long been cited, and rightly so, in support of hereditary succession. Nevertheless, this aspect is merely a consequence, and if it is made into a *ground* [*Grund*], it debases [the monarch's] majesty to the sphere of ratiocination and, regardless of its character of ungrounded immediacy and ultimate inward being, grounds it not upon the Idea of the state which is immanent within it, but on something *outside it*, on some thought of a different character such as the welfare *of the state or of the people*. From a determination of this kind, it is indeed possible, by using middle terms [*medios terminos*], to deduce [the need for] hereditary succession; but other middle terms, and hence other consequences, are equally possible, and the consequences which have been drawn from this *welfare* of the people (*salut du peuple*) are only too familiar. – For these reasons, *philosophy alone* is in a position to consider this majesty [of the monarch] by means of thought, for every method of enquiry other than the speculative method of the infinite and self-grounded Idea annuls [*aufhebt*] the nature of majesty in and for itself. – *Elective monarchy[1]* may well seem the most *natural* idea [*Vorstellung*], i.e. the one most obvious to superficial thinking; for since it is the concerns and interests of the people that the monarch must look after, it can be argued that the people must also be left to choose whom they wish to entrust their welfare to, and that it is from this trust alone that the right to rule arises. This view, like the ideas [*Vorstellungen*] of the monarch as the first servant of the state,[2] of a contractual relationship between monarch and people, etc., bases itself on the will in the sense of the *caprice*, opinion, and arbitrariness *of the many* – a determination which, as we noticed some time ago,[a3] is of primary importance in civil society (or merely seeks to assert itself as such), but is not the [basic] principle of the family, let alone of the state, and is completely opposed to the Idea of ethical life. – Indeed, it is even possible for ratiocination to deduce from the *consequences* of elective monarchy that it is the worst of institutions. But these consequences appear to ratiocination only as a *possibility* or *probability*, although they are in fact an essential concomitant of this institution. That is to say, the nature of the situation in an elective monarchy whereby the *particular* will is made the ultimate source of decisions means that the constitution becomes an *electoral contract* [*Wahlkapitulation*], i.e. a surrender of the power of the state at the discretion of the particular [*partikularen*] will; as a result, the particular [*besonderen*] powers of the state are turned into private property, the sovereignty of the state is weakened and lost, and the state is dissolved from within and destroyed from without.[4]

---

[a]*Translator's note:* See, for example, §§ 182–189 above.

Addition (G). In order to grasp the Idea of the monarch, it is not enough to say that kings are appointed by God, for God has made everything, including the worst [of things].[5] The point of view of utility does not get us far either, for it is always possible to point to disadvantages. And it is of just as little help to regard monarchy as a positive right. The fact that I have property is necessary, but this [or that] particular possession is contingent, and the right whereby one individual must occupy the highest office appears in a similar light if it is taken in an abstract and positive sense. But this right is present as a felt need and as a need of the thing [*Sache*] in and for itself. Monarchs are not exactly distinguished by their physical powers or intellect [*Geist*], yet millions accept them as their rulers. But it is absurd to say that people allow themselves to be ruled in defiance of their own interests, ends, and intentions, for they are not as stupid as that; it is their need, the inner power of the Idea, which compels them to accept such rule and keeps them in this situation, even if they appear to be consciously opposed to it. Thus, whereas the monarch functions as head of state and as part of the constitution, it has to be said that a conquered people is not constitutionally identical with its sovereign. If a rebellion occurs in a province conquered in war, this is not the same thing as a revolt in a well-organized state. The conquered people are not rebelling against their sovereign prince, and they are not committing a political crime, for they are not linked with their master in terms of the Idea or through the inner necessity of the constitution. There is only a contract, but not a political association. 'Je ne suis pas votre prince, je suis votre maître'[a] was Napoleon's reply to the delegates at Erfurt.[6]

[a] *Translator's note:* 'I am not your prince, I am your master.'

§ 282

The sovereignty of the monarch is the source of the *right to pardon* criminals, for only the sovereign is entitled to actualize the power of the spirit to undo what has been done and to nullify crime by forgiving and forgetting.

The right of pardon is one of the highest acknowledgements of the majesty of the spirit. – Furthermore, this right is one of those instances in which a determination from a higher sphere is applied to, or reflected in, a lower one. – But such applications are the concern of particular science, which must deal with the entire empirical range of its subject (cf. [the first] footnote to the Remarks to § 270). – Another example of such applications is the subsumption under the concept of crime (which we encountered in an earlier context – see §§ 95–102) of injuries [*Verletzungen*] to the state in general, or to the sovereignty, majesty, and personality of the sovereign prince; such injuries are in fact classed as crimes of the *highest order*, and a particular procedure etc. [is applied to them].

Addition (H). Pardon is the remission of punishment, but it is not a cancellation of right [*die aber das Recht nicht aufhebt*]. On the contrary, right continues to apply, and the pardoned individual still remains a criminal; the pardon does not state that he has not committed a crime. This cancellation [*Aufhebung*] of punishment may be effected by religion, for what has been done can be undone in spirit by spirit itself.[1] But in so far as it is accomplished in this world, it is to be found only in the majesty [of the sovereign] and is the prerogative of [the sovereign's] ungrounded decision.

§ 283

The *second* moment contained in the power of the sovereign is that of *particularity* or of determinate content and its subsumption under the universal. In so far as this moment attains a particular existence [*Existenz*], it does so in the highest advisory offices and in the individuals who hold them; these individuals submit to the monarch for his decision the content of current affairs of state, or the legal determinations made necessary by present needs, along with their *objective* aspects, grounds for decision, relevant laws, circumstances, etc. The appointment of *individuals* for this purpose and their dismissal from office fall within the [competence of the] unrestricted arbitrary will of the monarch, since the individuals in question are in immediate personal contact with him.[1]

§ 284

The only factors for which people can be made *accountable* – i.e. those which are capable of objective proof and on which advice distinct from the personal will of the monarch as such can appropriately be sought – are the *objective* aspects of decision such as knowledge [*Kenntnis*] of the content and circumstances, and the legal and other grounds for determination. It is only for matters such as these that the advisory offices and their incumbents can be held accountable.[1] But the distinctive majesty of the monarch, as the ultimate subjectivity of decision, is raised above all accountability for the acts of government.

§ 285

The *third* moment in the power of the sovereign concerns the universal in and for itself, which is present subjectively in the *conscience* of the *monarch* and objectively in the *constitution* and *laws* as a *whole*. To this extent, the power of the sovereign presupposes the other moments, just as it is presupposed by each of them.

§ 286

The *objective guarantee* of the power of the sovereign and of rightful succession to the throne by way of inheritance, etc., lies in the fact that, just as this sphere has its own actuality distinct from that of other rationally determined moments, so also do these other moments have their own distinct rights and duties in accordance with their determination. Each member [of the whole], in maintaining itself independently [*für sich*], thereby also maintains the others in their own distinct character within the rational organism.

One of the more recent achievements of history has been to develop the monarchic constitution to the point where hereditary succession to the throne is firmly based on primogeniture. Monarchy has thereby reverted to the patriarchal principle in which it had its historical origin, although it now has the higher determination whereby the monarch is the absolute apex of an organically developed state. This achievement is of the greatest importance for public freedom and for a rational constitution, although it is often very poorly understood – as we earlier noticed – even if it is treated with respect. Thus, the history of despotisms and of the purely feudal monarchies of earlier times represents a succession of rebellions, acts of violence by rulers, civil wars, the downfall of sovereign princes and dynasties, and in consequence, general devastation and destruction on both internal and external fronts. The reason for this is that, in conditions such as these, the division [*Teilung*] of political business is purely mechanical, with its different parts distributed among vassals, pashas, etc., so that the difference [between these elements] is not one of determination and form, but merely of greater or lesser power. Thus, each part maintains *itself alone*, and in so doing, it promotes only itself and not the others along with it, and has within itself the complete set of moments which it requires for independence and self-sufficiency. In an organic relationship, the units in question are not parts but members, and each maintains the others while fulfilling *its own* function; the substantial end and product of each is to maintain the *other* members while simultaneously maintaining *itself.* Such guarantees as are required, whether for the continuity of the succession and of the power of the sovereign in general, or for justice, public freedom, etc., are secured by means of *institutions.* Such factors as the love of the people, character, oaths, coercion, etc. may be regarded as *subjective* guarantees; but when we are dealing with the *constitution*, we are concerned solely with *objective* guarantees or institutions, i.e. with organically linked and mutually conditioning moments. Thus, public freedom in general and a hereditary succession guarantee each other reciprocally, and their association [*Zusammenhang*] is absolute, because public freedom is the rational constitution, and the hereditary character of the power of the sovereign is, as has already been shown, the moment inherent in its concept.

b. The Executive Power

§ 287

The execution and application of the sovereign's decisions, and in general the continued implementation and upholding of earlier decisions, existing laws, institutions, and arrangements to promote common ends, etc., are distinct from the decisions themselves. This task of *subsumption* in general belongs to the *executive power*, which also includes the powers of the *judiciary* and the *police*; these have more immediate reference to the particular affairs of civil society, and they assert the universal interest within these [particular] ends.

§ 288

The *particular* common interests which fall within civil society, and which lie outside the universal interest of the state as the interest which has being in and for itself (see § 256), are administered by the corporations (see § 251) which represent the communities and the various professions [*Gewerbe*] and estates, with their authorities [*Obrigkeit*], supervisors, administrators, etc. On the one hand, the business of these administrators is to look after the *private property* and *interests* of these *particular* spheres, and in this respect, their authority [*Autorität*] is based in part on the trust of their fellow-citizens and equals. On the other hand, these circles must be subordinated to the higher interests of the state. Thus, the filling of such offices will in general involve a mixture of popular election by the interested parties, and confirmation and determination by a higher authority.[1]

§ 289

The task of *upholding*, within these particular rights, *legality* and the *universal interest of the state*, and that of bringing these rights back to the universal, need to be performed by delegates of the executive power, i.e. the executive *civil servants* and the higher consultative bodies. The latter necessarily work together in groups, and they converge in their supreme heads who are in touch with the monarch himself.[1]

Just as civil society is the field of conflict in which the private interest of each individual comes up against that of everyone else,[2] so do we here encounter the conflict between private interests and particular concerns of the community, and between both of these together and the higher viewpoints and ordinances of the state. The spirit of the corporation, which arises when the particular spheres gain legal recognition [*Berechtigung*], is now at the same time inwardly transformed into the spirit of the state, because it finds in the state the means of sustaining its particular ends. This is the secret of the patriotism of the citizens in the sense that they know the state as their substance, for it is the state which supports their particular spheres and the legal recognition, authority, and welfare of these. In so far as the *rooting of the particular in the universal* is contained *immediately* in the spirit of the corporation, it is in this spirit that such depth and strength of *disposition* as the state possesses are to be found.

The administration of a corporation's affairs by its own supervisors will often be inept, for although they know [*kennen*] and have before them their own distinct interests and affairs, they have a less complete grasp of the connection between these and more remote conditions and universal points of view. Besides, further circumstances have a similar effect, e.g. the close personal contact and other kinds of equality between the supervisors and those who should be subordinate to them, the various ways in which they are dependent on others, etc. But this personal [*eigene*] sphere may be seen as belonging to the moment of *formal freedom*, which provides an arena in which personal cognition and personal decisions and their execution, as well as petty passions and imaginings, may indulge themselves. This is all the more acceptable in proportion to the triviality of the business which is thereby vitiated or conducted less efficiently, more laboriously, etc., and to its relative unimportance for the more general concerns of the state; and the same applies the more directly the laborious or foolish conduct of such trifling business is related to the satisfaction and self-esteem [*Meinung von sich*] which are derived from it.

§ 290

The *division* [*Teilung*] *of labour* (see § 198) likewise makes its appearance in the business of the executive. The *organization* of official bodies accordingly faces the formal but difficult task of ensuring that civil life shall be governed in a *concrete* manner from below, where it is concrete, but that the business in question shall be divided into its *abstract* branches and dealt with by distinct bodies; the latter should function as separate centres whose activities should again converge both at the lowest level and in a concrete overview on the part of the supreme executive.[1]

Addition (G). The most important issue for the executive power is the division of functions. The executive power is concerned with the transition from the universal to the particular and individual, and its functions must be divided in accordance with its different branches. The difficulty, however, is [that of ensuring] that they also come together again at upper and lower levels. For although the power of the police and that of the judiciary, for example, are divergent, they do converge in every particular case [*Geschäft*]. The expedient which is often employed in these circumstances is to appoint a State Chancellor, Prime Minister, or Cabinet Council in order to simplify the highest level of government. But this may have the result that everything is again controlled from above by ministerial power, and that functions are, to use the common expression, centralized.[2] This is associated with a high degree of facility, speed, and effectiveness in measures adopted for the universal interest of the state. A regime of this kind was introduced by the French Revolution and further developed by Napoleon, and it still exists [*besteht*] in France today. On the other hand, France lacks corporations and communal associations [*Kommunen*] – that is, circles in which particular and universal interests come together. Admittedly, these circles gained too great a degree of self-sufficiency in the Middle Ages, when they became states within the state and behaved in an obdurate manner like independently established bodies.[a] But although this ought not to happen, it can still be argued that the proper strength of states resides in their [internal] communities [*Gemeinden*]. In these, the executive encounters legitimate [*berechtigte*] interests which it must respect; and since the administration can only encourage such interests – although it must also supervise them – the individual finds protection for the exercise of his rights, so that his particular [*partikulares*] interest is bound up with the preservation of the whole. For some time now, organization has always been directed from above, and efforts have been devoted for the most part to this kind of organization, despite the fact that the lower level of the masses as a whole can easily be left in a more or less disorganized state. Yet it is extremely important that the masses should be organized, because only then do they constitute a power or force; otherwise, they are merely an aggregate, a collection of scattered atoms. Legitimate power is to be found only when the particular spheres are organized.

---

[a]*Translator's note:* Gans's version, as translated by the nine preceding words, reads *gerierten sich auf harte Weise als für sich bestehende Körperschaften*. Griesheim's original, of which Gans's text is a paraphrase, reads *genirten auf eine harte Weise die Ausübung allgemeiner Zwecke*, i.e. 'obstructed the implementation of universal ends in an obdurate manner' (VPR IV, 691). Gans appears to have misread *genirten* as *geri(e)rten*.

§ 291

The functions of the executive are *objective* in character; as such [*für sich*], they have already been substantially decided in advance (see § 287), and they must be fulfilled and actualized by *individuals*. Individuals are not destined by birth or personal nature to hold a particular office, for there is no immediate and natural link between the two. The objective moment in their vocation [*Bestimmung*] is knowledge [*Erkenntnis*] and proof of ability; this proof guarantees that the needs of the state will be met, and, as the sole condition [of appointment], at the same time guarantees every citizen the possibility of joining the universal estate.[1]

§ 292

There is necessarily an *indeterminate number* of candidates for public office, because their objective qualification does not consist in genius (as it does in art, for example), and their relative merits cannot be determined with absolute certainty. The selection of *this* particular individual for a given post, his appointment, and his authorization to conduct public business are subjective decisions, in that they link together an individual and an office as two factors whose mutual relation must always be contingent. This subjective aspect pertains to the sovereign as the supreme [*souveränen*] and decisive power within the state.

§ 293

The particular tasks within the state which the monarch assigns to the official bodies form part of the *objective* aspect of sovereignty which is inherent in him. The specific *differences* between these tasks are likewise given in the nature of the thing [*Sache*]; and just as the activity of the official bodies is the fulfilment of a duty, so also does their business constitute a right which is exempt from contingency.

§ 294

The individual who has been appointed to his professional office by an act of the sovereign (see § 292) must fulfil his duties, which are the substantial aspect of his position [*Verhältnis*], as a condition of his appointment. *As a consequence* of this substantial position, his appointment provides him with resources, guarantees the satisfaction of his particularity (see § 264), and frees his external situation and official activity from other kinds of subjective dependence and influence.¹

The state does not count on arbitrary and discretionary services (for example, the administration of justice by knights errant), precisely because such services are discretionary and arbitrary, and because those who perform them reserve the right to do so in accordance with their subjective views, or not to perform them at all if they so wish and to pursue subjective ends instead. As regards the service of the state, the opposite extreme to the knight errant would be a *civil servant* who performed his work purely out of necessity [*Not*] without any genuine duty and likewise without any right. – In fact, the service of the state requires those who perform it to sacrifice the independent and discretionary satisfaction of their subjective ends, and thereby gives them the right to find their satisfaction in the performance of their duties, and in this alone. It is here that, in the present context, that link is to be found between universal and particular interests which constitutes the concept of the state and its internal stability (see § 260). – Similarly, the [civil servant's] relationship to his office is not one of *contract* (see § 75), although the parties in question both give their consent and render a service. The civil servant is not employed, like an agent, to perform a single contingent task, but makes this relationship [to his work] the main interest of his spiritual and particular existence [*Existenz*]. Likewise, the task which he has to perform and with which he is entrusted is not a purely particular thing [*Sache*] of an external character; the *value* of such a thing is an inward quality which is therefore distinct from its external nature, so that it is not impaired [*verletzt*] if what has been stipulated is not delivered (see § 77). But the task which the civil servant has to perform is, in its immediate character, a value in and for itself. The wrong which is done by non-performance or positive infringement (i.e. by an action in violation of one's duty, which applies in both of these cases) is therefore an infringement of the universal content itself, i.e. a negatively infinite judgement (cf. § 95), and hence a misdemeanour or even a crime. – The guaranteed satisfaction of particular needs removes that external necessity [*Not*] which may induce someone to seek the means of satisfying them at the expense of his official activities and duty. Those who are entrusted with the business of the state find protection in its universal power against another subjective factor, namely the private passions of the governed, whose private interests etc. are prejudiced when the universal is asserted against them.

§ 295

The protection of the state and the governed against the misuse of power on the part of the official bodies and their members is, on the one hand, the direct responsibility [*Verantwortlichkeit*] of their own hierarchy; on the other hand, it lies with the legal recognition [*Berechtigung*] accorded to communities and corporations, for this prevents subjective arbitrariness from interfering on its own account [*für sich*] with the power entrusted to officials, and supplements from below that control from above which does not extend as far as individual conduct.

The conduct and education of the officials is the point at which the laws and decisions of the executive come into contact with individuals [*die Einzelheit*] and are translated into actuality. This is accordingly the factor on which the satisfaction and confidence of the citizens in relation to the executive depend, as does the execution (or dilution and frustration) of the government's intentions – in the sense that the *manner* in which these intentions are executed may well be rated as highly by the feelings [*Empfindung*] and disposition [of the citizens] as the *content* of the intention to be implemented, even though this content may itself be of a burdensome nature. Because of the immediate and personal character of such contact, control from above can attain its end in this respect only partially, and this end may also encounter obstacles in the shape of the common interest of the officials in maintaining solidarity amongst themselves in opposition to their subordinates and superiors. The need to remove such obstacles, especially in cases where the institutions in question may still be relatively imperfect in other respects also, calls for and justifies the higher intervention of the sovereign (as, for example, of Frederick the Great in the notorious case [*Sache*] of the miller Arnold).[1]

§ 296

Whether or not dispassionateness, integrity [*Rechtlichkeit*], and polite behaviour become *customary* will depend in part on direct *education in ethics and in thought*, for this provides a spiritual counterweight to the mechanical exercises and the like which are inherent in learning the so-called sciences appropriate to these [administrative] spheres, in the required business training, in the actual work itself, etc. But the *size* of the state is also an important consideration, for it both reduces the burden of family ties and other private commitments and lessens the power – and thereby takes the edge off – such passions as revenge, hatred, etc. These subjective aspects disappear of their own accord in those who are occupied with the larger interests of a major state, for they become accustomed to dealing with universal interests, views, and functions.

§ 297

Members of the executive and civil servants constitute the bulk of the middle class [*des Mittelstandes*], which embodies the educated intelligence and legal [*rechtliche*] consciousness of the mass of the people. The institutions which prevent this class from adopting the isolated position of an aristocracy and from using its education and skill as arbitrary means of domination are the sovereign, who acts upon it from above, and the rights of the corporations, which act upon it from below.

> It was in this way that the administration of justice, whose object is the proper interests of all individuals, was at one time transformed into an instrument of profit and domination, because knowledge [*Kenntnis*] of right hid behind scholarship and a foreign language, and knowledge of the legal process hid behind complicated formalities.

Addition (H,G). The middle class, to which the civil servants belong, has a political consciousness and is the most conspicuously educated class. For this reason, it is the mainstay of the state as far as integrity [*Rechtlichkeit*] and intelligence are concerned. Consequently, the level of a state which has no middle class cannot be high. This is true of Russia, for example, which has a mass of serfs and another mass of rulers. It is central to the interests of the state that this middle class should develop, but this can occur only in an organization like the one we have just considered, i.e. in which legal recognition [*Berechtigung*] is given to particular bodies which are relatively independent, and in which the arbitrariness of officialdom is broken down by institutions of this kind. Action in accordance with universal right and the habit of such action are consequences of the opposition offered by bodies which are self-sufficient in themselves.

c. The Legislative Power

§ 298

The *legislative power* has to do with the laws as such, in so far as they are in need of new and further determination, and with those internal concerns of the state whose content is wholly universal. This power is itself a part of the constitution, which it presupposes and which to that extent lies in and for itself outside the sphere which the legislative power can determine directly; but the constitution does undergo further development through the further evolution of the laws and the progressive character of the universal concerns of government.

Addition (H). The constitution must be in and for itself the firm and recognized ground on which the legislative power is based, so that it does not first have to be constructed. Thus, the constitution *is*, but it just as essentially *becomes*, i.e. it undergoes progressive development. This progression is a change which takes place imperceptibly and without possessing the form of change. If, for example, the resources of the German princes and their families were originally private property but were then transformed, without conflict or opposition, into crown domains, i.e. into resources of the state, this occurred because the princes felt the need to maintain their possessions intact and demanded guarantees to this effect from their country and its Estates.[1] Thus, the latter became involved in the way in which the resources in question were conserved, so that the princes no longer had exclusive control over them. Similarly, the Emperor was at one time a judge who travelled round the Empire dispensing justice. Then, the (merely apparent) progress of culture [*Bildung*] made it outwardly necessary for the Emperor to delegate this judicial office increasingly to others, which led to the transfer of judicial power from the person of the sovereign to [judicial] colleges.[2] Thus, conditions evolve in an apparently peaceful and imperceptible manner, with the result that a constitution changes its character completely over a long period of time.

§ 299

These matters are more precisely determined, as far as individuals are concerned, in the following two respects: (α) in relation to the benefits which the state enables them to enjoy, and (β) in relation to the services which they must perform for the state. The former include the laws of civil right [*die privatrechtlichen Gesetze*] in general, the rights of communities and corporations, all arrangements of a wholly universal character, and indirectly (see § 298), the constitution as a whole. But as for services to the state, it is only when these are expressed in terms of *money*, as the existing and universal *value* of things [*Dinge*] and services, that they can be determined justly and at the same time in such a way that the *particular* work and services which the individual can perform are mediated by his own arbitrary will.

It is possible to distinguish in general terms between what is the object [*Gegenstand*] of universal legislation and what should be left to the direction [*Bestimmung*] of administrative bodies or to any kind of government regulation, in that the former includes only what is wholly universal in content – i.e. legal determinations – whereas the latter includes the particular and the ways and means whereby measures are *implemented*. This distinction is not entirely determinate, however, if only because a law, in order to be a law, must be more than just a commandment in general (such as 'Thou shalt not kill' – cf. Remarks to § 140, p. 144[*a*]), i.e. it must be *determinate* in itself; but the more determinate it is, the more nearly capable its content will be of being implemented as it stands. At the same time, however, so far-reaching a determination as this would give the laws an empirical aspect which would necessarily be subject to alteration when they were actually

---

[*a*]*Translator's note:* p. 176 in this edition (Hegel's reference is to the first edition).

implemented, and this would detract from their character as laws. It is implicit in the organic unity of the powers of the state itself that *one* and the same spirit decrees the universal and brings it to determinate actuality in implementing it. – It may at first seem remarkable that the state requires no direct services from the numerous skills, possessions, activities, and talents [of its citizens] and from the infinitely varied living *resources* which these embody and which are at the same time associated with the disposition [of those who possess them], but lays claim only to the *one* resource which assumes the shape of *money*. (Services associated with the defence of the state against its enemies belong to those duties which will be considered in the following section.) But money is not in fact one *particular* resource among others; on the contrary, it is the universal aspect of all of them, in so far as they express themselves in an external existence [*Dasein*] in which they can be apprehended as *things* [*als eine Sache*]. Only at this extreme point of externality is it possible to determine services *quantitatively* and so in a just and equitable manner. – In Plato's *Republic*, it is the task of the guardians to allot individuals to their particular estates and to specify what *particular* services they have to perform (cf. Remarks to § 185). In feudal monarchies, the services required of vassals were equally indeterminate, but these vassals also had to serve in their *particular* capacity, e.g. as judges.[1] Services imposed in the Orient and in Egypt in connection with immense architectural enterprises etc. are likewise of a *particular* character. In these circumstances, what is lacking is the principle of *subjective freedom* whereby the individual's substantial activity (whose content is in any case of a particular nature in the services in question) is mediated by his own *particular will*. This right cannot be enjoyed until the demand for services is expressed in terms of the universal value, and it is itself the reason [*Grund*] why this change was introduced.

Addition (H). The two aspects of the constitution relate respectively to the rights and services of individuals. As far as services are concerned, nearly all of them have now been reduced to money. Military duties are now almost the only personal service required. In earlier times, far more claims were made on individuals in a concrete sense, and they were called upon to work according to their skills. In our times, the state *purchases* what it needs. This may at first seem an abstract, lifeless, and soulless procedure, and it may also look as if the state has become decadent if it is satisfied with abstract services. But it is inherent in the principle of the modern state that all of an individual's actions should be mediated by his will. The justice of equality, however, can be achieved far more effectively by means of money. Otherwise, if the criterion were concrete ability, the talented individual would be taxed much more heavily than the untalented. But the very fact that people are now required to deliver only what they are able to deliver is a sign that public freedom is respected.

§ 300

In the legislative power as a whole, the other two moments have a primary part to play, namely the *monarchy* as the power of ultimate decision, and the *executive power* as the advisory moment which has concrete knowledge [*Kenntnis*] and oversight of the whole with its numerous aspects and the actual principles which have become established within it, and knowledge of the needs of the power of the state in particular. The final element [in the legislature] is the *Estates*.

Addition (H,G). One of the misconceptions concerning the state is the view that members of the executive should be excluded from the legislative bodies, as happened, for example, in the Constituent Assembly [of France].[1] In England, ministers must be Members of Parliament, and rightly so, since those who participate in government should be associated with, rather than opposed to, the legislative power. The idea [*Vorstellung*] of the so-called independence of powers contains the basic error [of supposing] that the powers should be independent yet mutually limiting. If they are independent, however, the unity of the state, which is the supreme requirement, is destroyed [*aufgehoben*].[2]

§ 301

The role [*Bestimmung*] of the Estates is to bring the universal interest [*Angelegenheit*] into existence [*Existenz*] not only *in itself* but also *for itself*, i.e. to bring into existence the moment of subjective *formal freedom*, the public consciousness as the *empirical universality* of the views and thoughts of the *many*.

The expression '*the many*' (οἱ πολλοί) denotes empirical universality more accurately than the usual term '*all*'. For if it is said to be obvious that the term '*all*' excludes from the start at least children, women, etc., it is by the same token even more obvious that the entirely specific expression '*all*' ought not to be used with reference to something else which is entirely unspecific.[1] – In fact, such untold numbers of warped and erroneous ideas [*Vorstellungen*] and turns of phrase concerning 'the people', 'the constitution', and 'the Estates' have passed into current opinion that it would be a futile endeavour to try to enumerate, discuss, and rectify them. The idea with which the ordinary consciousness usually begins when it considers the necessity or usefulness of a convention of the Estates will generally be, for example, that delegates of the people, or indeed the people themselves, *must know best* what is in their own best interest, and that their own will is undoubtedly the one best equipped to pursue the latter. As for the first of these propositions, the reverse is in fact the case, for if the term 'the people' denotes a particular category of members of the state, it refers to that category of citizens *who do not know their own will*. To know what one wills, and even more, to know what the will which has being in and for itself – i.e. reason – wills, is the fruit of profound cognition and insight, and this is the very thing [*Sache*] which 'the people' lack. – It can be seen with a little reflection that the guarantee which the Estates provide for universal welfare and public freedom does not lie in any particular insight they may possess. For the highest officials within the state necessarily have a more profound and comprehensive insight into the nature of the state's institutions and needs, and are more familiar with its functions and more skilled in dealing with them, so that they *are able* to do what is best even without the Estates, just as they must continue to do what is best when the Estates are in session. The guarantee doubtless lies rather in the extra insight which the delegates have, first of all into the activities of those officials who are less visible to their superiors, and in particular into the more urgent and specialized needs and deficiencies which they [the delegates] see in concrete form before their eyes; and secondly, it lies in the effect which the expectation of criticism, indeed of public criticism, at the hands of the many has in compelling the officials to apply their best insights, even before they start, to their functions and to the plans they intend to submit, and to put these into effect only in accordance with the purest of motives. (This compulsion is equally effective for the members of the Estates themselves.) But as for the [belief that there is] particular *good will* on the part of the Estates towards the universal welfare, we have already noted (see Remarks to § 272) that it is characteristic of the rabble, and of the negative viewpoint in general, to assume ill will, or less good will, on the part of the government. If this assumption were to be answered in kind, it would invite the counter-accusation that, since the Estates have their origin in individuality [*Einzelheit*], in the private point of view and in particular interests, they are inclined to direct their efforts towards these at the expense of the universal interest, whereas the other moments in the power of the state are by their very nature [*schon für sich*] dedicated to the universal end and disposed to adopt the point of view of the state. As for that general guarantee which is supposed to lie in the Estates in particular, each of the other institutions within the state shares with them the quality of being a guarantee of public welfare and rational freedom; and in some of these institutions – such as the sovereignty of the monarch, hereditary succession, the constitution of the courts, etc. – this guarantee is present to a much greater degree. The proper conceptual definition [*Begriffsbestimmung*] of the Estates should therefore be sought in the fact that, in them, the subjective moment of universal freedom – the personal [*eigene*] insight and personal will of that sphere which has been described in this work as civil society – comes *into existence in relation* [*Beziehung*] *to the state*. As in every other case, the philosophical viewpoint here enables us to conclude that this moment is a determination of the Idea when the latter has reached its total development, and the inner necessity of this moment should not be confused with *external necessities* and *utilities*.

Addition (H). The attitude of the government towards the Estates should not be essentially hostile, and the belief that this relationship is necessarily a hostile one is a sad mistake. The government is not a party opposed to another party in such a way that both have to fight for major concessions from each other; and if a state does get into a predicament of this kind, this cannot be described as health but only as a misfortune.[2] Besides, the taxes which the estates approve should not be regarded as a gift presented to the state; on the contrary, they are approved for the benefit of those who approve them. The proper significance of the Estates is that it is through them that the state enters into the subjective consciousness of the people, and that the people begins to participate in the state.

§ 302

Viewed as a *mediating* organ, the Estates stand between the government at large on the one hand and the people in their division into particular spheres and individuals [*Individuen*] on the other. Their determination requires that they should embody in equal measure both the *sense* and *disposition* of the *state* and *government* and the *interests* of *particular* circles and *individuals* [*Einzelnen*]. At the same time, this position means that they share the mediating function of the organized power of the executive, ensuring on the one hand that the power of the sovereign does not appear as an isolated *extreme* – and hence simply as an arbitrary power of domination – and on the other, that the particular interests of communities, corporations, and individuals [*Individuen*] do not become isolated either. Or more important still, they ensure that individuals do not present themselves as a *crowd* or *aggregate*, unorganized in their opinions and volition, and do not become a massive power in opposition to the organic state.[1]

It is one of the most important insights of logic that a specific moment which, when it stands in opposition, has the position of an extreme, loses this quality and becomes an *organic* moment by being simultaneously a *mean*.[2] It is all the more important to stress this aspect in the present context, because it is a common but highly dangerous prejudice to represent [*vorzustellen*] the Estates chiefly from the point of view of their opposition to the government, as if this were their essential position. It is only through their mediating function that the Estates display their organic quality, i.e. their incorporation in the totality. In consequence, their opposition is itself reduced to a [mere] semblance. If this opposition does make its appearance, and if it is not just superficial but actually takes on a substantial character, the state is close to destruction. – It is evident from the nature of the thing [*Sache*] that the conflict is not of this kind if the matters in dispute are not the essential elements of the political organism but more specialized and trivial things [*Dinge*], and if the passion with which even this content is associated consists of factional rivalry over merely subjective interests such as the higher offices of state.

Addition (H). The constitution is essentially a system of mediation. In despotic states, where there are only rulers [*Fürsten*] and people, the people function – if they function at all – merely as a destructive mass opposed to all organization. But when it becomes part of the organism, the mass attains its interests in a legitimate and orderly manner. If, however, such means are not available, the masses will always express themselves in a barbarous manner. This is why, in despotic states, the despot always treats the people with indulgence and vents his wrath only on his immediate circle. In the same way, the people in such states pay only modest taxes, whereas in constitutional states, the taxes become higher as a result of the people's own consciousness. In fact, in no country are so many taxes paid as in England.

§ 303

It is integral to the definition [*Bestimmung*] of the *universal* estate – or more precisely, the estate which devotes itself to the *service of the government* – that the universal is the end of its essential activity; and in the *Estates*, as an element of the legislative power, the *private estate* attains a *political significance* and function. In this capacity, the private estate cannot appear either as a simple undifferentiated mass or as a crowd split up into atomic units. It appears rather as *what it already is*, namely as an *estate* consisting of two distinct parts, the one based on the substantial relation, and the other on particular needs and the work through which these are mediated (see §§ 201 ff.). Only in this respect is there a genuine link between the *particular* which has actuality in the state and the universal.

This runs counter to another prevalent idea [*Vorstellung*] according to which, if the private estate is raised to the level of participating in the universal interest [*Sache*] via the legislative power, it must appear therein in the form of *individuals*, whether representatives are elected to fulfil this function or whether every individual is in fact to have a vote himself.[1] This atomistic and abstract view ceases to apply even within the family, as well as in civil society, where the individual makes his appearance only as a member of a universal. But the state is essentially an organization whose members constitute *circles in their own right* [*für sich*], and no moment within it should appear as an unorganized crowd. *The many* as single individuals – and this is a favourite interpretation of [the term] 'the people' – do indeed live *together*, but only as a *crowd*, i.e. a formless mass whose movement and activity can consequently only be elemental, irrational, barbarous, and terrifying. If we hear any further talk of 'the people' as an unorganized whole, we know in advance that we can expect only generalities and one-sided declamations. – The idea [*Vorstellung*] that those communities which are already present in the circles referred to above can be split up again into a collection of individuals as soon as they enter the sphere of politics – i.e. the sphere of the *highest concrete universality* – involves separating civil and political life from each other and leaves political life hanging, so to speak, in the air; for its basis is then merely the abstract individuality of arbitrary will and opinion, and is thus grounded only on contingency rather than on a foundation which is *stable* and *legitimate* [*berechtigt*] in and for itself. – Although the *estates* of *civil* society in general and the *Estates* in the *political* sense are represented, in so-called [political] theories, as remote from each other, linguistic usage still preserves the unity which they certainly possessed in earlier times.

§ 304

The Estates in their political capacity still retain within their own determination those distinctions between different estates which were already present in the preceding spheres. Their initially abstract position – namely as the *extreme* of *empirical universality* as opposed to the *principle of the sovereign* or *monarch* in general – contains only the *possibility of agreement*, and hence also the *possibility of hostile* opposition. This abstract position becomes a rational relation (i.e. a [logical] *conclusion* – cf. Remarks to § 302) only when its *mediation* comes into existence [*Existenz*]. Just as, in the case of the power of the sovereign, this function [*Bestimmung*] is already fulfilled by the executive power

344

(see § 300), so in the case of the estates must one of their moments be given the function of existing essentially as a moment of mediation.

§ 305

One of the estates of civil society contains the principle which is in itself capable of being adapted to this political relation [*Beziehung*], namely the estate of natural ethical life; its basis is the life of the family and, as far as its livelihood is concerned, landed property. Thus, in its particular aspect, this estate shares that independent volition and natural determination which is also contained in the moment [*Element*] of sovereignty.

§ 306

This estate is better equipped for its political role and significance inasmuch as its resources are equally independent of the resources of the state and of the uncertainty of trade, the quest for profit, and all variations in property. It is likewise independent of the favour of the executive power and of the masses, and is even protected *against its own arbitrariness* by the fact that those members of this estate who are called to this vocation [*Bestimmung*] do not have the same right as other citizens either to dispose freely of their entire property or to know that it will pass on to their children in proportion to the equal degree of love that they feel for them. Thus, their resources become *inalienable inherited property*, burdened with primogeniture.

Addition (H). This estate has a more independent [*für sich bestehend*] volition. On the whole, the estate of landowners can be divided into the educated section and the estate of farmers. Distinct from both of these, however, are the estate of trade and industry, which is dependent on needs and their satisfaction, and the universal estate, which is essentially dependent on the state. The security and stability of this [landowning] estate can be further enhanced by the institution of primogeniture, but this is desirable only in a political sense, for it involves a sacrifice for the political end of enabling the eldest son to live independently. The justification of primogeniture lies in the fact that the state should be able to count on a disposition [to political service] not just as a possibility, but as necessarily present. Now it is true that such a disposition is not tied to the possession of resources; but the relatively necessary connection between the two consists in the fact that someone of independent means is not limited by external circumstances, and is accordingly able to play his part without encumbrance, and to act in the interests of the state. But where no political institutions are present, the foundation and furtherance of primogeniture are merely fetters on the freedom of civil right, and they must either acquire a political significance, or face eventual extinction.[a]

[a] *Translator's note:* This final sentence appears to be Gans's own addition, since it has no counterpart in either Hotho's or Griesheim's notes, on which Gans's Additions are based.

§ 307

In this way, the right of this section of the substantial estate is indeed based on the natural principle of the family; but at the same time, this principle is given a new direction by stringent sacrifices for the *political end*, so that this estate is essentially eligible for activities connected with the latter. Consequently, it is likewise called and *entitled* to such a career by *birth*, without the contingency of an election. It accordingly occupies a firm and substantial position between the subjective arbitrariness and contingency of the two extremes; and just as it itself contains a counterpart to the moment of the power of the sovereign (see § 305),[a] so also does it share the otherwise identical needs and rights of the other extreme, so that it becomes a support both of the throne and of [civil] society.

[a] *Translator's note:* Hegel actually writes 'see the preceding paragraph' (i.e. § 306), but must in fact have § 305 in mind.

§ 308

The second section of the Estates encompasses the *changing* element in *civil* society, which can play its part only by means of *deputies*; the external reason for this is the sheer number of its members, but the essential reason lies in the nature of its determination and activity. In so far as these deputies are elected by civil society, it is immediately evident that, in electing them, society acts *as what it is*. That is, it is not split up into individual atomic units which are merely assembled for a moment to perform a single temporary act and have no further cohesion; on the contrary, it is articulated into its associations, communities, and corporations which, although they are already in being, acquire in this way a political connotation. In the entitlement of this estate to elect deputies at the request of the sovereign power, and in the entitlement of the first estate to appear [in person] (see § 307), the existence [*Existenz*] of the Estates and of their assembly acquires its own constitutional guarantee.

The idea [*Vorstellung*] that *all* individuals ought to participate in deliberations and decisions on the universal concerns of the state – on the grounds that they are all members of the state and that the concerns of the state are the concerns of *everyone*, so that everyone has a *right* to share in them with his own knowledge and volition – seeks to implant in the organism of the state a *democratic* element *devoid of rational form*, although it is only by virtue of its rational form that the state is an organism. This idea [*Vorstellung*] appears plausible precisely because it stops short at the *abstract* determination of membership of the state and because superficial thinking sticks to abstractions. Rational deliberation or the consciousness of the Idea [*Idee*] is *concrete*, and it coincides to that extent with true *practical* sense, which is itself nothing other than rational sense or the sense of the Idea; it must not, however, be confused with the mere routine of business and the horizon of a limited sphere. The concrete state is *the whole, articulated into its particular circles*. Each member of the state is a *member* of an *estate* of this kind, and only in this objective determination can he be considered in relation to the state. His universal determination in general includes two moments, for he is a *private person* and at the same time a *thinking* being with consciousness and volition of the *universal*. But this consciousness and volition remain empty and lack *fulfilment* and actual *life* until they are filled with particularity, and this is [to be found in] a particular estate and determination. Otherwise, the individual remains a *generic category* [*Gattung*], but only within the *next* generic category does he attain his *immanent* universal *actuality*. – Consequently, it is within the sphere of his corporation, community, etc. (see § 251) that the individual first attains his actual and living determination as *universal*, and it remains open to him to enter any sphere, including the universal estate, for which his aptitude qualifies him. The idea

[*Vorstellung*] that *everyone* should participate in the concerns of the state entails the further assumption that *everyone is an expert on such matters*; this is also absurd, notwithstanding the frequency with which we hear it asserted. In public opinion, however (see § 316), the way is open for everyone to express and give effect to his subjective opinions on the universal.

§ 309

Since deputies are elected to deliberate and decide on matters of *universal* concern, the aim of such elections is to appoint individuals who are credited by those who elect them with a better understanding of such matters than they themselves possess. It is also the intention that these individuals will not subordinate the universal interest to the particular interest of a community or corporation, but will give it their essential support. Their position is accordingly not that of commissioned or mandated agents, especially since the purpose [*Bestimmung*] of their assembly is to provide a forum for live exchanges and collective deliberations in which the participants instruct and convince one another.

Addition (G). The introduction of representation [*Repräsentation*] means that consent is not given directly by everyone but only by authorized deputies, for the individual [*der Einzelne*] is no longer involved as an infinite person. Representation is based on trust, but trust is not the same thing as giving my vote *in person*. Majority decisions are also at variance with the principle that I should be personally present in anything which imposes an obligation on me. I can trust a person if I believe that he has sufficient insight to treat my cause [*Sache*] as if it were his own, and to deal with it in the light of his own best knowledge and conscience. Thus, the principle of the individual subjective will is no longer applicable, for the trust is vested in a cause, in the principles of a human being and his conduct, actions, and concrete sense in general. It is therefore desirable that anyone who becomes a member of the Estates should possess a character, insight, and will consistent with his task of participating in universal concerns. For it is not essential that the individual [*Individuum*] should have a say as an abstract individual entity; on the contrary, all that matters is that his interests should be upheld in an assembly which deals with universal issues. The electors require a guarantee that the elected deputy will promote and accomplish this end.

§ 310

In the second section of the Estates, whose members are drawn from the changing and variable element in civil society, the guarantee that the deputies will have the qualities and disposition required for this end – for independent means have already claimed their right in the first section – consists above all in the disposition, skill, and knowledge [*Kenntnis*] of the institutions and interests of the state and civil society which they have acquired through the *actual* conduct of business in *positions of authority* or *political office*, and which have proved their worth *in practice*; it further consists in the *sense of authority* and *political sense* which they have developed and put to the test in the process.

The subjective opinion which individuals have of themselves may well find the demand for such guarantees, if it is made with explicit reference to 'the people', superfluous and perhaps even insulting. But the determination of the state is objectivity, not subjective opinion and the self-confidence which accompanies it. The state is concerned only with those aspects of individuals which are objectively recognizable and which have been tried and tested, and it must pay all the more attention to such aspects in the case of the second section of the Estates, because this section is rooted in interests and activities which are directed towards the particular, and in which contingency, mutability, and arbitrary will have the right to express themselves. – Taken on its own, the external qualification of possessing a certain amount of property has the appearance of a one-sided extreme of externality in contrast to the other, equally one-sided, extreme of the purely subjective trust and opinion of the electorate. Both of these extremes contrast, in their abstraction, with those concrete qualities which are necessary for deliberations on political business, and which are contained within the specifications [*Bestimmungen*] indicated in § 302. – Nevertheless, the selection of individuals for positions of authority and other offices within corporations [*Genossenschaften*] and communities does constitute a sphere in which the property qualification has been able to operate effectively, particularly if some of these tasks are performed without remuneration; and it is directly relevant to the business of the Estates if the members do not receive a salary.[1]

§ 311

In view of the fact that the deputies are elected by civil society, it is also desirable that they should be familiar with and party to its special needs, frustrations, and particular interests. Given the nature of civil society, the deputies are elected by the various corporations (see § 308), and this simple mode of procedure is not impaired by abstractions and atomistic notions [*Vorstellungen*] [of society]. Consequently, it directly fulfils the requirement referred to above, and the election itself is either completely superfluous or can be reduced to an insignificant play of arbitrary opinion.

It is clearly in the general interest that the deputies should include individuals who are thoroughly familiar with, and personally involved in, each particular major branch of society (e.g. commerce, manufacturing industries, etc.) – an important consideration which the idea [*Vorstellung*] of loose and indeterminate elections leaves entirely to chance. Each of these branches of society, however, has the same right as the others to be represented. If the deputies are regarded as *representatives*, this term cannot be applied to them in an organic and rational sense unless they are *representatives* not of *individuals* as a crowd, but of one of the essential *spheres* of society, i.e. of its major interests. Thus, representation no longer means the *replacement* of one individual *by another*; on the contrary, the interest itself is *actually present* in its representative, and the latter is there to represent the objective element he himself embodies. – As for mass elections, it may also be noted that, in large states in particular, the electorate inevitably becomes *indifferent* in view of the fact that a single vote has little effect when numbers are so large; and however highly they are urged to value the right to vote, those who enjoy this right will simply fail to make use of it. As a result, an institution of this kind achieves the opposite of its intended purpose [*Bestimmung*], and the election comes under the control of a few people, of a faction, and hence of that particular and contingent interest which it was specifically designed to neutralize.

§ 312

Each of the two sections of the Estates (see §§ 305 and 308) introduces a particular modification to the process of deliberation; and since one of the moments in question also has the characteristic function of mediation within this sphere – mediation between two existents – this moment must likewise take on a separate existence [*Existenz*]. The assembly of the Estates will therefore be divided into *two houses*.[1]

§ 313

This division, by creating a plurality of *instances*, not only provides an increased guarantee of mature decisions and eliminates the contingent quality which the mood of the moment[a] possesses and which decisions by majority vote may acquire. Above all, it ensures that the Estates are less likely to come into direct opposition to the government; and if the mediating moment also happens to take the side of the second Estate, the latter's view will carry all the more weight, for it will appear more impartial and its opposition will appear to be neutralized.

[a]*Translator's note:* Hegel's phrase 'Stimmung des Augenblicks' is (perhaps intentionally) ambiguous: it may mean either 'mood of the moment' or possibly 'instantaneous vote' (although present-day German would use the term *Abstimmung* in the latter context).

§ 314

The determination of the Estates as an institution does not require them to achieve optimum results in their deliberations and decisions on the business of the state *in itself*, for their role in this respect is purely accessory (see § 301). On the contrary , they have the distinctive function [*Bestimmung*] of ensuring that, through their participation in [the government's] knowledge, deliberations, and decisions on matters of universal concern, the moment of *formal* freedom attains its right in relation to those members of civil society who have no share in the government. In this way, it is first and foremost the moment of *universal* knowledge [*Kenntnis*] which is extended by the *publicity* with which the proceedings of the Estates are conducted.

§ 315

The provision of this opportunity of [acquiring] knowledge [*Kenntnissen*] has the more universal aspect of permitting *public opinion* to arrive for the first time at *true thoughts* and *insight* with regard to the condition and concept of the state and its affairs, thereby *enabling it to form more rational judgements on the latter*. In this way, the public also becomes familiar with, and learns to respect, the functions, abilities, virtues, and skills of the official bodies and civil servants. And just as such publicity provides a signal opportunity for these abilities to develop, and offers them a platform on which they may attain high honours, so also does it constitute a remedy for the self-conceit of individuals and of the mass, and a means – indeed one of the most important means – of educating them.

Addition (H,G). If the Estates hold their assemblies in public, they afford a great spectacle of outstanding educational value to the citizens, and it is from this above all that the people can learn the true nature of their interests. As a rule, it is accepted that everyone already knows what is good for the state, and that the assembly of the Estates merely discusses this knowledge. But in fact, precisely the opposite is the case, for it is only in such assemblies that those virtues, abilities, and skills are developed which must serve as models [for others]. These assemblies are, of course, tiresome for ministers, who must themselves be armed with wit and eloquence if they are to counter the attacks which are here directed against them. Nevertheless, such publicity is the most important means of education as far as the interests of the state in general are concerned. In a nation where this publicity exists, there is a much more lively attitude towards the state than in one where the Estates have no assembly or where such assemblies are not held in public. It is only by informing the public of every move they make that the two houses remain in touch with the wider implications of *public opinion*. It then becomes evident that a man's imaginings at home in the company of his wife or friends are very different from events in a great assembly, where one ingenious idea [*Gescheitheit*] devours another.

§ 316

Formal subjective freedom, whereby individuals as such entertain and express their *own* judgements, opinions, and counsels on matters of universal concern, makes its collective appearance in what is known as *public opinion*. In the latter, the universal in and for itself, the *substantial* and the *true*, is linked with its opposite, with what is *distinct* in itself [*dem für sich Eigentümlichen*] as the *particular opinions* of the many. This existence [*Existenz*] [of public opinion] is therefore a manifest self-contradiction, an *appearance* of cognition; in it, the essential is just as immediately present as the inessential.

Addition (G). Public opinion is the unorganized way in which the will and opinions of the people make themselves known. Whatever actually gains recognition within the state must, of course, perform an organic function, as is the case with the constitution. But public opinion has been a major force in all ages, and this is particularly so in our own times, in which the principle of subjective freedom has such importance and significance. Whatever is to achieve recognition today no longer achieves it by force, and only to a small extent through habit and custom, but mainly through insight and reasoned argument.

§ 317

Public opinion therefore embodies not only the eternal and substantial principles of justice – the true content and product of the entire constitution and legislation and of the universal condition in general – in the form of *common sense* [*des gesunden Menschenverstandes*] (the ethical foundation which is present in everyone in the shape of prejudices), but also the true needs and legitimate [*richtigen*] tendencies of actuality. – As soon as this inner content attains consciousness and is represented [*zur Vorstellung kommt*] in general propositions (either in its own right [*für sich*] or for the purpose of concrete reasoning [*Räsonnieren*] on felt needs and on events, dispensations, and circumstances within the state), all the contingencies of opinion, with its ignorance and perverseness, its false information and its errors of judgement, come on the scene. Since what is at issue here is the consciousness of the *distinctive nature* [*Eigentümlichkeit*] of the views and knowledge [*Kenntnis*] [of individuals], the worse the content of an opinion is, the more distinctive it will be; for the bad is that whose content is entirely particular and distinctive, whereas the rational is that which is universal in and for itself, and the *distinctive* is that on which opinion *prides itself.*

It must therefore not be regarded as a subjective difference of views if we are told on the one hand that the voice of the people is the voice of God [*Vox populi, vox dei*], and on the other (by Ariosto, for example):†

> Che'l Volgare ignorante ogn' un riprenda
> E parli più di quel che meno intenda.*a1*

Public opinion contains these two qualities simultaneously, and if truth and endless error are so closely united within it, it cannot be genuinely *serious* about them both. It may seem difficult to decide which to take seriously, and this will in fact be the case even if we stick to the *immediate expression* of public opinion. But since the substantial is its inner content, only this can be taken completely seriously. The substantial cannot be known [*erkannt*] from public opinion itself, however; its very substantiality means that it can be recognized only in and from itself [*aus und für sich*]. No matter how passionately an opinion is held or how seriously it is asserted or attacked or contested, this is no criterion of what is really at issue; but the last thing which this opinion can be made to realize is that its seriousness is not serious at all. – A leading spirit [*ein großer Geist*] set as the theme of an essay competition the question 'whether it is permissible to deceive a people'*3* The only possible answer was that it is impossible to deceive a people about its substantial basis, about the *essence* and specific character of its spirit, but that the people is deceived *by itself* about the way in which this character is known to it and in which it consequently passes judgement on events, its own actions, etc.

---

†*Hegel's note:* Or as Goethe puts it:
Zuschlagen kann die Masse
Da ist sie respektabel;
*Urteilen gelingt ihr miserabel.*b2
*a*Translator's note: 'That the ignorant mass finds fault with everyone and talks most of what it understands least'.
*b*Translator's note: 'The masses can fight respectably, *but their judgements are miserable.*'

Addition (H). The principle of the modern world requires that whatever is to be recognized by everyone must be seen by everyone as entitled to such recognition. But in addition, each individual wishes to be consulted and to be given a hearing. Once he has fulfilled this responsibility and had his say, his subjectivity is satisfied and he will put up with a great deal. In France, freedom of speech was always*ᵃ* regarded as less dangerous than silence, for if people remained silent, it was feared that they were keeping their opposition to something to themselves, whereas argument [*Räsonnement*] gives them an outlet and some degree of satisfaction, which also facilitates the progress of the matter [*Sache*] in question.

ᵃTranslator's note: The word *immer* ('always') does not appear in Hotho's notes, from which Gans compiled this Addition.

§ 318

Public opinion therefore deserves to be *respected* as well as *despised* – despised for its concrete consciousness and expression, and respected for its essential basis, which appears in that concrete consciousness only in a more or less obscure manner. Since it contains no criterion of discrimination and lacks the ability to raise its own substantial aspect to [the level of] determinate knowledge, the first formal condition of achieving anything great or rational, either in actuality or in science, is to be independent of public opinion. Great achievement may in turn be assured that public opinion will subsequently accept it, recognize it, and adopt it as one of its prejudices.

Addition (H). Every kind of falsehood and truth is present in public opinion, but it is the prerogative [*Sache*] of the great man to discover the truth within it. He who expresses the will of his age, tells it what its will is, and accomplishes this will,*ᵇ* is the great man of the age.*¹* What he does is the essence and inner content of the age, and he gives the latter actuality; and no one can achieve anything great, unless he is able to despise public opinion as he here and there encounters it.

ᵇTranslator's note: I translate directly from Hotho's notes (VPR III, 821) which, in Gans's (inaccurate) transcription, would yield the translation 'He who tells his age, and accomplishes, what it wills and expresses'.

§ 319

Freedom of public communication (of whose two modes the *press* has a wider range of contact than the spoken word, although it lacks the latter's vitality), the satisfaction of the burning urge to express one's opinion and to have expressed it, is directly guaranteed by those laws and ordinances, as upheld by the police, which prevent or punish its excesses. It is indirectly guaranteed, however, by its innocuous character, which it owes chiefly to the rationality of the constitution and the stability of the government, but also to the publicity of the assemblies of the Estates. It is rendered innocuous by the latter because these assemblies give expression to sound [*gediegene*] and educated insights concerning the interests of the state, leaving little of significance for others to say, and above all denying them the opinion that what they have to say is of distinctive importance and effectiveness. But it is also guaranteed by the indifference and scorn which shallow and malicious talk quickly and inevitably brings down upon itself.

To define freedom of the press as freedom to say and write *whatever one pleases* is equivalent to declaring that freedom in general means freedom *to do whatever one pleases.* – Such talk is the product of completely uneducated, crude, and superficial thinking [*Vorstellens*]. Besides, it is in the nature of the case [*Sache*] that formalistic thinking [*Formalismus*] is nowhere so stubborn and uncompromising as it is with this matter, for the subject in question is the most fleeting, contingent, and particular aspect of opinion in the infinite variety of its content and modulations. Beyond direct incitement to theft, murder, rebellion, etc. lie the art and cultivation [*Bildung*] of its expression, which seems in itself [*für sich*] quite general and indeterminate yet at the same time conceals another quite specific meaning, or leads to consequences which are not actually expressed and of which it is impossible to determine whether they follow legitimately [*richtig*] from it and whether they were meant to be drawn from it or not. This indeterminacy of the material and its form makes it impossible for laws on such matters to attain that determinacy which the law requires; and since any misdemeanour, wrong, or injury [*Verletzung*] here assumes the most particular and *subjective* shape, judgement on it likewise becomes a wholly *subjective* decision. Besides, such an injury will be directed at the thoughts, opinion, and will of others, and they are the element in which it attains actuality. But this element is part of the freedom of others, and it will therefore depend on them whether or not the injurious action constitutes an actual deed. – Laws in this area are therefore open to criticism on account of their indeterminacy, and also because turns of phrase and forms of expression can be devised in order to circumvent the law or to maintain that the judicial decision is a subjective judgement. It can further be argued, if the [offending] expression is treated as an *injurious act*, that it is not an act at all, but only *opinion* and *thought* on the one hand and *talk* on the other. Thus, it is argued in one breath that mere opinion and talk should be *exempt from punishment* because their form and content are purely subjective and because they are *insignificant* and *unimportant*, and that this same opinion and talk should be *highly respected* and *esteemed* on the grounds that the former is personal property of the *most spiritual kind*, and that the latter is the expression and use of this personal property. – But the substantial [issue here] is and remains the fact that all injuries to the honour of individuals, slander, abuse, vilification of the government, of its official bodies and civil servants, and in particular of the sovereign in person, contempt for the laws, incitement to rebellion, etc., are crimes and misdemeanours of widely varying degrees of gravity. The fact that such actions become more indeterminable as a result of the element in which they are expressed does not annul [*hebt nicht auf*] this substantial character, and its effect is therefore simply [to ensure] that the *subjective* sphere [*Boden*] in which they are committed also determines the *nature* and *shape* of the *reaction*. It is this very sphere in which the misdemeanour is committed which necessarily leads to subjectivity of view, contingency, etc., in the reaction to it, whether this reaction consists of measures taken by the police to prevent crime, or of punishment proper. Here as always, formalistic thinking [*Formalismus*] endeavours to rationalize away [*wegzuräsonnieren*] the substantial and concrete nature of the thing [*Sache*] in favour of *individual* aspects which belong to its external appearance and of abstractions which it derives from these. – The *sciences*, however – that is, if they really are sciences – have no place at all in the sphere of opinion and subjective views, nor does their presentation consist in the art of allusions, turns of phrase, half-utterances and semi-concealment, but in the unambiguous, determinate, and open expression of their meaning and sense. Consequently, they do not come under the category of public opinion (see § 316).[1] – Besides, as I have already pointed out, the element in which views and their modes of expression as such become *completed actions* and attain actual existence [*Existenz*] is the intelligence, principles, and opinions of *others*. Consequently, this aspect of actions – i.e. their proper effect and the *danger* they hold for individuals, society, and the state (cf. § 218) – likewise depends on the nature of this element [*Boden*], just as a spark thrown on to a powderkeg is far more dangerous than if it falls on solid ground, where it disappears without trace. – Thus, just as scientific utterances have their right and safeguard in their material and content, so also is there a safeguard, or at least [an element of] toleration, for wrongful utterances in the contempt which they bring upon themselves. Some misdemeanours of this kind, which may even be legally punishable in themselves, are attributable to that variety of *nemesis* which inner impotence, when it feels oppressed by superior talents and virtues, is impelled to exact in order to reassert itself in the face of such superiority and to give renewed self-consciousness to its own nullity. Thus, the Roman soldiers used to inflict a relatively harmless nemesis on their emperors by singing satirical songs during triumphal processions in order to compensate for their arduous service and obedience, and especially for the fact that their names were not included in the roll of honour; in this way, the balance was to some extent redressed.[2] The former base and spiteful variety of nemesis is rendered ineffectual by the contempt which it incurs, and, like the public which may provide an audience for such activities, it is confined to empty malice and to the self-condemnation which is implicit within it.

§ 320

Subjectivity, whose *most external* manifestation is the dissolution of the existing life of the state by opinion and ratiocination as they seek to

assert their contingent character and thereby destroy themselves, has
its true actuality in its own opposite, i.e. in *subjectivity* as identical with
the substantial will, the subjectivity which constitutes the concept of
the power of the sovereign and which, as the *ideality* of the whole, has
not up till now attained its right and its existence [*Dasein*].

Addition (H). We have considered subjectivity once already in connection
with the monarch as the apex of the state. Its other aspect is its arbitrary
appearance in public opinion as its most external[a] manifestation. The
subjectivity of the monarch is in itself abstract, but it should be concrete
in character as the ideality which pervades the whole. The peaceful state
is that in which all branches of civil life subsist, while their collective and
separate subsistence proceeds from the Idea of the whole. This process
[*Hervorgehen*] must also make its *appearance* as the ideality of the whole.

---

[a]*Translator's note:* Gans here uses the adjective *äußersten* ('most extreme'), which should
in fact be *äußerlichsten* ('most external'), as in Hotho's original notes (VPR III, 826) and
in § 320 itself.

II *External Sovereignty*

§ 321

Internal sovereignty (see § 278) is this ideality in so far as the moments
of the spirit and of its actuality, the state, have *developed* in their
necessity and *subsist* as *members* of the state. But the spirit, which in its
freedom is *infinitely negative* reference *to itself*, is just as essentially
being-for-itself which has *incorporated* the subsistent differences *into
itself* and is accordingly exclusive. In this determination, the state has
individuality, which is [present] essentially as an individual and, in the
sovereign [*Souverän*], as an actual and immediate individual (see
§ 279).

§ 322

Individuality, as exclusive being-for-itself, appears *as the relation* [of
the state] *to other states*, each of which is independent [*selbständig*] in
relation to the others. Since the *being-for-itself* of the actual spirit has
its *existence [Dasein]* in this independence, the latter is the primary
freedom and supreme dignity of a nation [*eines Volkes*].

Those who speak of the wishes of a totality [*Gesamtheit*] which constitutes a more or less independent state with its own centre to abandon this focal point and its own independence in order to form a whole with another state know little of the nature of a totality and of the self-awareness which an autonomous nation possesses.[1] – Hence, the primary authority [*Gewalt*] which states possess when they make their appearance in history is quite simply this independence, even if it is completely abstract and without any inner development. It is therefore in keeping with this original appearance that the head of state should be an individual, such as a patriarch or a tribal chief.

§ 323

In *existence [Dasein]* this *negative* relation [*Beziehung*] of the state to itself thus appears as the relation of *another* to *another*, as if the negative were something *external*. The existence [*Existenz*] of this negative relation therefore assumes the shape of an event, of an involvement with contingent occurrences coming *from without*. Nevertheless, this negative relation is the state's *own* highest moment – its actual infinity as the ideality of everything finite within it. It is that aspect whereby the substance, as the state's absolute power over everything individual and particular, over life, property, and the latter's rights, and over the wider circles within it, gives the nullity of such things an existence [*Dasein*] and makes it present to the consciousness.

§ 324

This determination whereby the interests and rights of individuals [*der Einzelnen*] are posited as a transient moment is at the same time their *positive* aspect, i.e. that aspect of their individuality [*Individualität*] which is not contingent and variable, but has *being in and for itself*. This relation and its recognition are therefore the substantial duty of individuals – their duty to preserve this substantial individuality – i.e. the independence and sovereignty of the state – even if their own life and property, as well as their opinions and all that naturally falls within the province of life, are endangered or sacrificed.

It is a grave miscalculation if the state, when it requires this sacrifice, is simply equated with civil society, and if its ultimate end is seen merely as the *security of the life and property* of individuals [*Individuen*]. For this security cannot be achieved by the sacrifice of what is supposed to be *secured* – on the contrary. – The ethical *moment of war* is implicit in what was stated above. For war should not be regarded as an absolute evil [*Übel*] and as a purely external contingency whose cause [*Grund*] is therefore itself contingent, whether this cause lies in the passions of rulers or nations [*Völker*], in injustices etc., or in anything else which is not as it should be. Whatever is by nature contingent is subject to contingencies, and this fate is therefore itself a necessity – just as, in all such cases, philosophy and the concept overcome the point of view of mere contingency and recognize it as a *semblance* whose essence is necessity. It is *necessary* that the finite – such as property and life – should be *posited* as contingent, because contingency is the concept of the finite. On the one hand, this necessity assumes the shape of a natural power, and everything finite is mortal and transient. But in the ethical essence, i.e. the state, nature is deprived of this power, and necessity is elevated to a work of freedom, to something ethical in character. The transience of the finite now becomes a *willed* evanescence, and the negativity which underlies it becomes the substantial individuality proper to the ethical essence. – War is that condition in which the vanity of temporal things [*Dinge*] and temporal goods – which tends at other times to be merely a pious phrase – takes on a serious significance, and it is accordingly the moment in which the ideality of *the particular attains its right* and becomes actuality. The higher significance of war is that, through its agency (as I have put it on another occasion), 'the ethical health of nations [*Völker*] is preserved in their indifference towards the permanence of finite determinacies, just as the movement of the winds preserves the sea from that stagnation which a lasting calm would produce – a stagnation which a lasting, not to say perpetual, peace would also produce among nations'.[1] Of the allegation that this is *only* a philosophical Idea or – to use another common expression – a justification of *providence*, and that actual wars require a further justification as well, more will be said below.[2] – The ideality which makes its appearance in war in the shape of a contingent external relationship is the same as the ideality whereby the internal powers of the state are organic moments of the whole. This is apparent in various occurrences in history, as when successful wars have averted internal unrest and consolidated the internal power of the state.[3] Other phenomena [*Erscheinungen*] of the same kind include the following: nations which are reluctant or afraid to accept internal sovereignty may be subjugated by others, and their failure to attain honour and success in their struggles for independence has been proportionate to their initial failure to organize the power of the state from within (i.e. their freedom has died from the fear of dying); and states whose independence is guaranteed not by their armed strength but by other factors (as in those states which are disproportionately small in relation to their neighbours) have been able to survive [*bestehen*] with an internal constitution which would not on its own have secured either internal or external peace.

Addition (G). In peace, the bounds of civil life are extended, all its spheres become firmly established, and in the long run, people become stuck in their ways. Their particular characteristics [*Partikularitäten*] become increasingly rigid and ossified. But the unity of the body is essential to the health, and if its parts grow internally hard, the result is death. Perpetual peace is often demanded as an ideal to which mankind should approximate. Thus, Kant proposed a league of sovereigns to settle disputes between states, and the Holy Alliance was meant to be an institution more or less of this kind.[4] But the state is an individual, and negation is an essential component of individuality. Thus, even if a number of states join together as a family, this league, in its individuality, must generate opposition and create an enemy. Not only do peoples emerge from wars with added strength, but nations [*Nationen*] troubled by civil dissension gain internal peace as a result of wars with their external enemies. Admittedly, war makes property insecure, but this *real* insecurity is no more than a necessary movement. We hear numerous sermons on the insecurity, vanity, and instability of temporal things, but all who hear them, however moved they may be, believe that they will none the less retain what is theirs. But if this insecurity should then actually become a serious proposition in the shape of hussars with sabres drawn, the edifying sentiments which predicted all this turn into imprecations against the conquerors.

But wars will nevertheless occur whenever they lie in the nature of the case [*Sache*]; the seeds germinate once more, and talk falls silent in face of the solemn recurrences of history.[a]

[a]*Translator's note:* This sentence has no counterpart in the corresponding section of Griesheim's notes (VPR IV, 733ff.), on which Gans based this Addition.

§ 325

Since sacrifice for the individuality of the state is the substantial relation of everyone and therefore a *universal duty*, it itself becomes, as *one* aspect of the ideality (as distinct from the reality) of particular subsistence [*Bestehen*], at the same time a particular relation with an estate of its own – the *estate of valour* – attached to it.

§ 326

Disputes between states may have any *particular* aspect of their mutual relations as their object [*Gegenstand*], and therein lies the chief vocation [*Bestimmung*] of the *particular* group to which the defence of the state is entrusted. But in so far as the state as such and its independence are at risk, duty requires all citizens to rally to its defence.[1] If the entire state has thus become an armed power and is wrenched away from its own internal life to act on an external front, the war of defence becomes a war of conquest.

> The fact that the armed power of the state becomes a *standing army* and that the vocation [*Bestimmung*] for the particular task of defending it becomes an *estate* is [a result of] the same necessity whereby its other particular moments, interests, and functions become estates such as those of marriage, trade and industry, the civil service, business, etc. Ratiocination, which goes back and forth over the reasons in question, indulges in reflections on the greater advantages or disadvantages of employing standing armies, and opinion readily comes down on the side of the disadvantages, because the concept of a thing [*Sache*] is more difficult to grasp than its individual and external aspects, and also because the interests and ends of particularity (the costs involved and their consequences, higher taxes, etc.) are rated more highly in the consciousness

of civil society than what is necessary in and for itself, which is accordingly regarded only as a means to particular ends.

§ 327

Valour is in itself a *formal* virtue, because it is the highest abstraction of freedom from all particular ends, possessions, pleasure, and life (although the way in which it negates these is *external and actual*), and because the alienation [*Entäußerung*] of these, as the *enactment* of valour, is not in itself of a spiritual nature; besides, the inner disposition [associated with it] may be [the product of] this or that [particular] reason [*Grund*], and its actual result may exist [*sein*] only for others and not *for itself*.

Addition (G). The military estate is the universal estate to which the defence of the realm is entrusted, and its duty is to give existence [*Existenz*] to the ideality within itself, i.e. to sacrifice itself. There are, of course, various kinds of valour. The courage of an animal or a robber, valour for the sake of honour, and knightly valour are not its true forms. The true valour of civilized nations [*Völker*] is their readiness for sacrifice in the service of the state, so that the individual merely counts as one among many. Not personal courage but integration with the universal is the important factor here. In India, five hundred men defeated twenty thousand who were not cowards, but who simply lacked the disposition to act in close association with others.[1]

§ 328

The significance [*Gehalt*] of valour as a disposition lies in the true, absolute, and ultimate end, the *sovereignty* of the state. The *actuality* of this ultimate end, as the product of valour, is mediated by the surrender of personal actuality. This phenomenon [*Gestalt*] therefore embodies the harshness of extreme opposites: *alienation* [*Entäußerung*] itself, but as the *existence* [*Existenz*] of freedom; the supreme *self-sufficiency* of *being-for-itself*, which at the same time exists in the mechanical *service* of an *external order*; total obedience and renunciation of personal [*eigenen*] opinion and reasoning [*Räsonieren*], and hence personal *absence* of mind [*des Geistes*], along with the most intense and comprehensive *presence* of mind and decisiveness at a given moment; the most hostile and hence most personal action

against individuals, along with a completely indifferent or even bene-
volent attitude [*Gesinnung*] towards them as individuals.

> To risk one's life is certainly superior to simply fearing death,
> but it is also purely negative and therefore indeterminate and
> valueless in itself. Only a positive end and content can give
> significance to such courage. Robbers and murderers whose
> end is crime, adventurers whose end is a product of their own
> opinion, etc. also have the courage to risk their lives. – The
> principle of the modern world – *thought* and the *universal* – has
> given a higher form [*Gestalt*] to valour, in that its expression
> seems to be more mechanical and not so much the deed of a
> *particular* person as that of a *member* of a whole. It likewise
> appears to be directed not against individual persons, but
> against a hostile whole in general, so that personal courage
> appears impersonal. This is why the principle of thought has
> invented the *gun*, and this invention, which did not come
> about by chance, has turned the purely personal form of
> valour into a more abstract form.[1]

§ 329

The outward orientation of the state derives from the fact that it is an
individual subject. Its relationship with other states therefore comes
under the *power of the sovereign*, who therefore has direct and sole
responsibility for the command of the armed forces, for the conduct
of relations with other states through ambassadors etc., and for making war and peace and concluding treaties of other kinds.

Addition (G). In almost all European countries, the supreme individual
authority is the power of the sovereign, who has control of external
relations. Where the Estates form part of the constitution, the question
may arise whether they should not be responsible for making war and
peace, and they will in any case retain their influence on the provision of
financial means in particular. In England, for example, no unpopular war
can be waged. But if it is imagined that sovereign princes and cabinets are
more subject to passion than parliaments are, and if the attempt is accordingly made to transfer responsibility for war and peace into the hands of
the latter, it must be replied that whole nations are often more prone to
enthusiasms and subject to passion than their rulers are.[1] In England, the
entire people has pressed for war on several occasions and has in a sense

compelled the ministers to wage it. The popularity of Pitt arose from the fact that he knew how to comply with the nation's current wishes.*^a* Only later, when emotions had cooled, did people realize that the war was useless and unnecessary, and that it had been entered into without calculating the cost.[2] Besides, the state has relations not just with *one* other state, but with several; and the complexities of these relations become so delicate that they can be handled only by the supreme authority.

^aTranslator's note: The preceding sentence has no equivalent in Griesheim's notes, on which this Addition is based (see VPR IV, 738f.).

B. International Law [Das äußere Staatsrecht]

§ 330

International law [*das äußere Staatsrecht*] applies to the *relations* between independent states. What it contains *in and for itself* therefore assumes the form of an *obligation*, because its actuality depends on *distinct and sovereign wills*.

Addition (H). States are not private persons but completely independent totalities in themselves, so that the relations between them are not the same as purely moral relations or relations of private right. Attempts have often been made to apply private right and morality to states, but the position of private persons is that they are subject to the authority of a court which implements what is right in itself. Now a relationship between states ought also to be inherently governed by right, but in worldly affairs, that which has being in itself ought also to possess power. But since no power is present to decide what is right in itself in relation to the state and to actualize such decisions, this relation [*Beziehung*] must always remain one of obligation. The relationship between states is a relationship of independent units which make mutual stipulations but at the same time stand above these stipulations.

§ 331

The nation state [*das Volk als Staat*] is the spirit in its substantial rationality and immediate actuality, and is therefore the absolute power on *earth*; each state is consequently a sovereign and independent entity in relation to others. The state has a primary and absolute entitlement to be a sovereign and independent power *in the eyes of others*, i.e. *to be recognized* by them. At the same time, however, this entitlement is purely formal, and the requirement that the state should be recognized simply because it is a state is abstract. Whether the state does in fact have being in and for itself depends on its content – on its constitution and [present] condition; and recognition, which implies that the two [i.e. form and content] are identical, also depends on the perception and will of the other state.

> Without relations [*Verhältnis*] with other states, the state can no more be an actual individual [*Individuum*] than an individual [*der Einzelne*] can be an actual person without a relationship [*Relation*] with other persons (see § 322). On the other hand, the legitimacy of a state, and more precisely – in so far as it has external relations – of the power of its sovereign, is a purely *internal* matter (one state should not interfere in the internal affairs of another). On the other hand, it is equally essential that this legitimacy should be *supplemented* by recognition on the part of other states. But this recognition requires a guarantee that the state will likewise recognize those other states which are supposed to recognize it, i.e. that it will respect their independence; accordingly, these other states cannot be indifferent to its internal affairs. – In the case of a nomadic people, for example, or any people at a low level of culture, the question even arises of how far this people can be regarded as a state. The religious viewpoint (as in former times with the Jewish and Mohammedan nations [*Völkern*]) may further entail a higher opposition which precludes that universal identity that recognition requires.

Addition (G). When Napoleon said before the Peace of Campo Formio 'the French Republic is no more in need of recognition than the sun is',[a] his words conveyed no more than that strength of existence [*Existenz*] which itself carries with it a guarantee of recognition, even if this is not expressly formulated.

---

[a]*Translator's note:* The remainder of this sentence has no equivalent in Griesheim's notes, on which this Addition is based (see VPR IV, 741).

§ 332

The immediate actuality in which states coexist is particularized into various relations which are determined by the independent arbitrary wills of both parties, and which accordingly possess the formal nature of *contracts* in general. The subject-matter [*Stoff*] of these contracts, however, is infinitely less varied than it is in civil society, in which individuals [*die Einzelnen*] are mutually interdependent in innumerable respects, whereas independent states are primarily wholes which can satisfy their own needs internally.

§ 333

The principle of *international law* [*Völkerrecht*], as that *universal* right which ought to have international validity in and for itself (as distinct from the particular content of positive treaties), is that *treaties*, on which the mutual obligations of states depend, *should be observed.* But since the sovereignty of states is the principle governing their mutual relations, they exist to that extent in a state of nature in relation to one another, and their rights are *actualized* not in a universal will with constitutional powers over them, but in their own particular wills. Consequently, the universal determination of international law remains only an *obligation*, and the [normal] condition will be for relations governed by treaties to alternate with the suspension [*Aufhebung*] of such relations.

> There is no praetor to adjudicate between states, but at most arbitrators and mediators, and even the presence of these will be contingent, i.e. determined by particular wills. Kant's idea [*Vorstellung*] of a *perpetual peace* guaranteed by a federation of states which would settle all disputes and which, as a power recognized by each individual state, would resolve all disagreements so as to make it impossible for these to be settled by war presupposes an *agreement* between states. But this agreement, whether based on moral, religious, or other grounds and considerations, would always be dependent on particular sovereign wills, and would therefore continue to be tainted with contingency.

§ 334

Consequently, if no agreement can be reached between particular wills, conflicts between states can be settled only by *war*. Since the sphere of the state is extensive and its relations [*Beziehungen*] through its citizens are extremely varied, it may easily suffer injuries [*Verletzungen*] on many occasions. But which of these injuries should be regarded as a specific breach of treaties or as an injury to the recognition and honour of the state remains *inherently* [*an sich*] indeterminable; for a state may associate its infinity and honour with any one of its individual interests, and it will be all the more inclined to take offence if it possesses a strong individuality which is encouraged, as a result of a long period of internal peace, to seek and create an occasion [*Stoff*] for action abroad.

§ 335

Furthermore, the state, as a wholly spiritual entity, cannot confine itself simply to noting that an *injury* has actually taken place. On the contrary, a further cause of discord arises in the *idea* [*Vorstellung*] of such an injury as a *danger* threatening from another state, in changing estimates of greater and lesser degrees of probability, in conjectures as to the other state's intentions, etc.

§ 336

The relationship of states to one another is a relationship between independent entities and hence between *particular* wills, and it is on this that the very validity of treaties depends. But the *particular will* of the whole, *as far as its content is concerned*, is its own *welfare* in general. Consequently, this welfare is the supreme law for a state in its relations with others, especially since the Idea of the state is precisely that the opposition between right as abstract freedom and the particular content which fills it, i.e. the state's own welfare, should be superseded within it, and it is on this Idea as a *concrete* whole that the initial recognition of states is based (see § 331).

§ 337

The substantial welfare of the state is its welfare as a *particular* state in its specific interest and condition and in its equally distinctive external circumstances in conjunction with the particular treaties which govern them. Its government is accordingly a matter of *particular wisdom*, not of universal providence (cf. Remarks to § 324), just as its end in relation to other states and its principle for justifying wars and treaties is not a universal (philanthropic) thought, but its actually offended or threatened welfare in *its specific particularity*.

> There was at one time a great deal of talk about the opposition between morality and politics and the demand that the latter should conform to the former.¹ In the present context, we need only remark in general that the welfare of a state has quite a different justification from the welfare of the individual [*des Einzelnen*]. The immediate existence [*Dasein*] of the state as the ethical substance, i.e. its right, is directly embodied not in abstract but in concrete existence [*Existenz*], and only this concrete existence, rather than any of those many universal thoughts which are held to be moral commandments, can be the principle of its action and behaviour. The allegation that, within this alleged opposition, politics is always wrong is in fact based on superficial notions [*Vorstellungen*] of morality, the nature of the state, and the state's relation to the moral point of view.

§ 338

The fact that states reciprocally recognize each other as such remains, *even in war* – as the condition of rightlessness [*Rechtlosigkeit*], force, and contingency – a *bond* whereby they retain their validity for each other in their being in and for themselves, so that even in wartime, the determination of war is that of something which ought to come to an end. War accordingly entails the determination of international law [*Völkerrecht*] that it should preserve the possibility of peace¹ – so that, for example, ambassadors should be respected and war should on no account be waged either on internal institutions and the peace of private and family life, or on private individuals.

Addition (G). Modern wars are accordingly waged in a humane manner, and persons do not confront each other in hatred. At most, personal enmities will arise at military outposts, but in the army as such, hostility is something indeterminate which takes second place to the duty which each respects in the other.

§ 339

Otherwise, the conduct of states towards one another in wartime (e.g. in the taking of prisoners), and concessions of rights in peacetime to the citizens of another state for the purpose of private contacts, etc. will depend primarily on national *customs*, for these are the universal aspect of behaviour which is preserved under all circumstances.

Addition (G). The European nations [*Nationen*] form a family with respect to the universal principle of their legislation, customs, and culture [*Bildung*], so that their conduct in terms of international law is modified accordingly in a situation which is otherwise dominated by the mutual infliction of evils [*Übeln*]. The relations between states are unstable, and there is no praetor to settle disputes; the higher praetor is simply the universal spirit which has being in and for itself, i.e. the world spirit.

§ 340

Since states function as *particular* entities in their mutual relations, the broadest view of these relations will encompass the ceaseless turmoil not just of external contingency, but also of passions, interests, ends, talents and virtues, violence [*Gewalt*], wrongdoing, and vices in their inner particularity. In this turmoil, the ethical whole itself – the independence of the state – is exposed to contingency. The principles of the *spirits of nations* [*Volksgeister*] are in general of a limited nature because of that particularity in which they have their objective actuality and self-consciousness as *existent* individuals, and their deeds and destinies in their mutual relations are the manifest [*erscheinende*] dialectic of the finitude of these spirits. It is through this dialectic that the *universal* spirit, *the spirit of the world*, produces itself in its freedom from all limits, and it is this spirit which exercises its right – which is the highest right of all – over finite spirits in *world history* as the *world's court of judgement* [*Weltgericht*].[1]

C. World History

§ 341

The *element* of the *universal spirit's* existence [*Dasein*] is intuition and image in art, feeling and representational thought in religion, and pure and free thought in philosophy. In *world history*, it is spiritual actuality in its entire range of inwardness and externality. World history is a court of judgement [*Gericht*] because, in its *universality* which has being in and for itself, the *particular* – i.e. the Penates, civil society, and the spirits of nations [*Völkergeister*] in their multifarious actuality – is present only as *ideal*, and the movement of spirit within this element is the demonstration of this fact.

§ 342

Furthermore, it is not just the *power* of spirit which passes judgement in world history – i.e. it is not the abstract and irrational necessity of a blind fate. On the contrary, since spirit in and for itself is *reason*, and since the being-for-itself of reason in spirit is knowledge, world history is the necessary development, from the *concept* of the freedom of spirit alone, of the *moments* of reason and hence of spirit's self-consciousness and freedom. It is the exposition and the *actualization of the universal spirit*.

§ 343

The history of spirit is its own *deed*; for spirit is only what it does, and its deed is to make itself – in this case as spirit – the object of its own consciousness, and to comprehend itself in its interpretation of itself to itself. This comprehension is its being and principle, and the *completion* of an act of comprehension is at the same time its alienation [*Entäußerung*] and transition. To put it in formal terms, the spirit which comprehends this comprehension *anew* and which – and this amounts to the same thing – returns into itself from its alienation, is the spirit at a stage higher than that at which it stood in its earlier [phase of] comprehension.

The question of *perfectibility*[1] and of the *education of the human race* arises here.² Those who have proclaimed this perfectibility have had some inkling of the nature of spirit, which is to have Γνῶϑι σεαυτόν^a as the law of its *being*,³ and, as it comprehends what *it is*, to assume a higher shape than that in which its being originally consisted. But for those who reject this thought, spirit has remained an empty word, and history has remained a superficial play of *contingent* and allegedly 'merely human' aspirations and passions. Even if they at the same time profess their faith in a higher power by references to *providence* and a providential *plan*, these remain empty ideas [*Vorstellungen*], for they also declare explicitly that the plan of providence is beyond their cognition and comprehension.

^a*Translator's note:* 'Know thyself'.

§ 344

The states, nations [*Völker*], and individuals involved in this business of the world spirit emerge with their own *particular and determinate principle*, which has its interpretation and actuality in their *constitution* and throughout the whole *extent* of their *condition*. In their consciousness of this actuality and in their preoccupation with its interests, they are at the same time the unconscious instruments and organs of that inner activity in which the shapes which they themselves assume pass away, while the spirit in and for itself prepares and works its way towards the transition to its next and higher stage.

§ 345

Justice and virtue, wrongdoing, violence [*Gewalt*], and vice, talents and their [expression in] deeds, the small passions and the great, guilt and innocence, the splendour of individual and national life [*Volkslebens*], the independence, fortune, and misfortune of states and individuals [*der Einzelnen*] – all of these have their determinate significance and value in the sphere of conscious actuality, in which judgement and justice – albeit imperfect justice – are meted out to them. World history falls outside these points of view; in it, that necessary moment of the Idea of the world spirit which constitutes *its* current stage attains its *absolute right*, and the nation [*Volk*] which lives at this point, and the deeds of that nation, achieve fulfilment, fortune, and fame.*¹*

§ 346

Since history is the process whereby the spirit assumes the shape of events and of immediate natural actuality, the stages of its development are present as *immediate natural principles*; and since these are natural, they constitute a plurality of separate entities [*eine Vielheit außereinander*] such that *one of them is allotted to each nation* [*Volke*] in its *geographical* and *anthropological* existence [*Existenz*].

§ 347

The nation [*Volk*] to which such a moment is allotted as a *natural* principle is given the task of implementing this principle in the course of the self-development of the world spirit's self-consciousness. This nation is the *dominant* one in world history for this epoch, *and only once in history can it have this epoch-making role* (see § 346). In contrast with this absolute right which it possesses as bearer of the present stage of the world spirit's development, the spirits of other nations are without rights, and they, like those whose epoch has passed, no longer count in world history.

The particular history of a world-historical nation contains, on the one hand, the development of its principle from its latent [*eingehüllten*] childhood phase until it blossoms out in free ethical self-consciousness and makes its mark in universal history, and on the other, the period of its decline and fall – for these denote the emergence within it of a higher principle which is simply the negative of its own.*¹* This signifies the spirit's transition to the higher principle and hence the transition of world history to *another* nation. From this period onwards, the previous nation has lost its absolute interest, and although it will also positively absorb the higher principle and incorporate it in its own development, it will react to it as to an extraneous element rather than with immanent vitality and vigour. It will perhaps lose its independence, or it may survive or eke out its existence as a particular state or group of states

374

and struggle on in a contingent manner with all kinds of internal experiments and external conflicts.

§ 348

At the forefront of all actions, including world-historical actions, are *individuals* as the subjectivities by which the substantial is actualized (see Remarks to § 279).[1] Since these individuals are the living expressions of the substantial deed of the world spirit and are thus immediately identical with it, they cannot themselves perceive it and it is not their object [*Objekt*] and end (see § 344). They receive no *honour* or thanks on its account, either from their contemporaries (see § 344) or from the public opinion of subsequent generations; all that they are accorded by this opinion is *undying fame* [in their role] as formal subjectivities.[2]

§ 349

In its initial stage, a nation [*Volk*] is not a state, and the transition of a family, tribe, kinship group, mass [of people], etc. to the condition of a state constitutes the *formal* realization of the Idea in general within it. If the nation, as ethical substance – and this is what it is *in itself* – does not have this form, it lacks the objectivity of possessing a universal and universally valid existence [*Dasein*] for itself and others in [the shape of] laws as determinations of thought, and is therefore not recognized; since its independence has no objective legality or firmly established rationality for itself, it is merely formal and does not amount to sovereignty.

Even in the context of ordinary ideas [*Vorstellung*], we do not describe a patriarchal condition as a constitution, nor do we describe a people living in this condition as a state, or its independence as sovereignty. Consequently, the actual beginning of history is preceded on the one hand by dull innocence which lacks all interest, and on the other by the valour of the formal struggle for recognition and revenge (cf. § 331 and Remarks to § 57).

§ 350

It is the absolute right of the Idea to make its appearance in legal determinations and objective institutions, beginning with marriage and agriculture (see Remarks to § 203), whether the form in which it is actualized appears as divine legislation of a beneficial kind, or as violence [*Gewalt*] and wrong. This right is the *right of heroes* to establish states.[1]

§ 351

The same determination entitles civilized nations [*Nationen*] to regard and treat as barbarians other nations which are less advanced than they are in the substantial moments of the state (as with pastoralists in relation to hunters, and agriculturalists in relation to both of these), in the consciousness that the rights of these other nations are not equal to theirs and that their independence is merely formal.

Consequently, in the wars and conflicts which arise in these circumstances, the feature which lends them significance for world history is the fact [*Moment*] that they are struggles for recognition with reference to a specific content [*Gehalt*].

§ 352

The concrete Ideas of national spirits [*Völkergeister*] have their truth and destiny [*Bestimmung*] in the concrete Idea as *absolute universality*, i.e. in the world spirit, around whose throne they stand as the agents of its actualization and as witnesses and ornaments of its splendour. As spirit, it is simply the movement of its own activity in gaining absolute knowledge of itself and thereby freeing its consciousness from the form of natural immediacy and so coming to itself. The *principles* behind the configurations [*Gestaltungen*] which this self-consciousness assumes in the course of its liberation – i.e. the world-historical realms – are accordingly *four* in number.

§ 353

In its *first* and *immediate* revelation, the spirit has as its principle the shape of the *substantial* spirit as the identity in which individuality

[*Einzelheit*] is submerged in its essence, and in which it does not yet have legitimacy for itself.

The *second* principle is *knowledge* on the part of this substantial spirit, so that the latter becomes a positive content and fulfilment of spirit and its *being-for itself* as its own living *form* – i.e. *beautiful* ethical individuality [*Individualität*].

The *third* principle is the self-absorption of this knowing being-for-itself to the point of *abstract universality*; it thereby becomes the infinite *opposite* of the objective world which has at the same time likewise been abandoned by the spirit.

The principle of the *fourth* configuration [*Gestaltung*] is the transformation of this spiritual opposition in such a way that the spirit attains its truth and concrete essence in its own inwardness, and becomes at home in and reconciled with the objective world; and since this spirit, having reverted to its original substantiality, is the spirit which has *returned from infinite opposition*, it produces and knows its own truth as thought and as a world of legal actuality.

§ 354

In accordance with these four principles, the world-historical realms are four in number: 1. the Oriental, 2. the Greek, 3. the Roman, 4. the Germanic.

§ 355

1. The Oriental Realm

The world-view of this first realm is inwardly undivided and substantial, and it originates in the natural whole of patriarchal society. According to this view, the secular government is a theocracy, the ruler is also a high priest or a god, the constitution and legislation are at the same time religion, and religious and moral commandments – or rather usages – are also laws of right and of the state. Within this magnificent whole, the individual personality has no rights and disappears altogether, external nature is immediately divine or an adornment of the god, and the history of the actual world is poetry. The distinctions which develop between the various aspects of customs, government, and the state take the place of laws, and even where customs are simple, these distinctions become ponderous, elaborate, and superstitious ceremonies – the accidents [*Zufälligkeiten*] of personal power and arbitrary rule – and the divisions of social estates harden into a natural system of castes. Consequently, the Oriental state lives only in its movement, and since nothing in it is stable and what is firmly established is fossilized, this movement turns outwards and becomes an elemental rage and devastation. The inner calm [of such a state] is that of private life and of submersion in weakness and exhaustion.

> The moment in the state's development [*Staatsbildung*] at which *spirituality* is still *substantial and natural* constitutes, *as a form*, the absolute beginning of every state's history. This has been emphasized and demonstrated with learning and profound perception, and with reference to the history of particular states, by Dr Stuhr in his work *The Downfall of Natural States* (Berlin, 1812), which has cleared the way for a rational view of constitutional history and of history in general.[1] The author has likewise shown that the principle of subjectivity and self-conscious freedom is present in the Germanic nation; but since his treatise goes no further than the downfall of natural states, this principle is followed only up to the point where it either appears as restless mobility, human arbitrariness, and corruption, or assumes the particular shape of *emotion* without having developed to the objectivity of *self-conscious* substantiality or to organized *legality*.

§ 356

2. The Greek Realm

In this realm, the substantial unity of the finite and the infinite is present, but only as a mysterious substratum, banished as a dim recollection into the recesses [*Höhlen*][a] and images of tradition. Reborn from the self-differentiating spirit into individual spirituality and the daylight of knowledge, this substratum is modified and transfigured to become beauty and a free and serene ethical life. Within this determination, the principle of personal individuality accordingly emerges, though it is not yet engrossed in itself [*in sich selbst befangen*] but still retains its ideal unity. Consequently, the whole

---

[a]*Translator's note:* Literally 'caves'.

splits up into a series of particular national spirits [*Volksgeister*], and on the one hand, the ultimate decision of the will is not yet assigned to the subjectivity of self-consciousness which has being for itself, but to a power which stands above and outside it (see Remarks to § 279), while on the other, the particularity associated with needs has not yet become part of [the realm of] freedom, but is confined to a class of slaves [*Sklavenstand*].

§ 357

3. The Roman Realm

In this realm, [the process of] differentiation comes to an end with the infinite diremption [*Zerreißung*] of ethical life into the extremes of *personal* or private self-consciousness and *abstract universality*. This opposition, which begins with a collision between the substantial intuition of an aristocracy and the principle of free personality in democratic form, develops into superstition and the assertion of cold and acquisitive power on the one hand, and into a corrupt rabble on the other. The dissolution of the whole ends in universal misfortune and the demise of ethical life, in which the individualities of nations [*Völker*] perish in the unity of a pantheon, and all individuals [*Einzelnen*] sink to the level of private persons with an *equal* status and with formal rights, who are accordingly held together only by an abstract and arbitrary will of increasingly monstrous proportions.

§ 358

4. The Germanic Realm

Having suffered this loss of itself and its world and the infinite pain which this entails (and for which a particular people, namely the *Jews*,[1] was held in readiness), the spirit is pressed back upon itself at the extreme of its absolute *negativity*. This is the *turning point* which has being in and for itself. The spirit now grasps the *infinite positivity* of its own inwardness, the principle of the unity of divine and human nature and the reconciliation of the objective truth and freedom which have appeared within self-consciousness and subjectivity. The task of accomplishing this reconciliation is assigned to the Nordic principle of the *Germanic peoples*.[2]

379

§ 359

The inwardness of this principle is the – as yet abstract – reconciliation and resolution of all opposition, and it exists in feeling
[*Empfindung*] as faith, love, and hope. It reveals its content in order to
raise it to actuality and self-conscious rationality, to [make it into] a
secular realm based on the emotions, loyalty, and companionship of
free individuals – although it is also, in this subjectivity, a realm of
ethical barbarism and of crude arbitrariness which has being for itself.
This stands in opposition to an otherworldly and *intellectual* realm
whose content, although it is indeed the truth of the spirit within it,
has not yet been *thought* and is therefore still veiled in the barbarism
of representational thinking; as a spiritual power set over the actual
emotions, this realm adopts the role of an unfree and terrible force in
relation to these.[1]

§ 360

In the hard struggle between these two realms – whose difference has
now reached the stage of absolute opposition, despite the fact that
both are rooted in a *single* unity and Idea – the spiritual realm brings
the existence [*Existenz*] of its heaven down to earth in this world,[1] to
the ordinary secularity of actuality and representational thought. The
secular realm, on the other hand, develops its abstract being-for-itself
to the level of thought and to the principle of rational being and
knowing, i.e. to the rationality of right and law. As a result, their
opposition has faded away *in itself* and become an insubstantial shape.
The present has cast off its barbarism and unjust [*unrechtliche*]
arbitrariness, and truth has cast off its otherworldliness and contingent force, so that the true reconciliation, which reveals the *state* as
the image and actuality of reason, has become objective. In the *state*,
the self-consciousness finds the actuality of its substantial knowledge
and volition in organic development; in *religion*, it finds the feeling and
representation [*Vorstellung*] of this truth as ideal essentiality; but in
science, it finds the free and comprehended cognition of this truth as
one and the same in all its complementary manifestations, i.e. in the
state, in *nature*, and in the *ideal world*.

Editorial notes

Preface

1 Hegel lectured on the topics in *The Philosophy of Right* seven times:

1 Heidelberg, 1817–1818. Text: EH (see note 2 below). Transcription: P. Wannenmann, a law student VPR17 35–202).

2 Berlin, 1818–1819. Text: EH. Transcription: C. G. Homeyer, VPR I, 217–352; cf. VPR17 203–285). By this time Hegel probably had completed a manuscript version of PR, which the sudden imposition of censorship (see note 18 below) caused him to withdraw and revise.

3 Berlin, 1819–1820. Text: EH. Transcription: anonymous (VPR19). PR was completed in 1820 and appeared early in 1821.

4 Berlin, 1821–1822. Text: PR. Transcription: None extant.

5 Berlin, 1822–1823. Text: PR. Transcription: H. G. Hotho (VPR III, 87–841).

6 Berlin, 1824–1825. Text: PR. Transcription: K. G. von Griesheim (VPR IV, 67–752).

7 Berlin, 1831. Text: PR. Transcription: David Friedrich Strauss (the Young Hegelian theologian) (VPR IV, 905–925). (Hegel had barely begun this series of lectures on PR when he was stricken with cholera and died on 14 November 1831.)

Throughout most of the 1820s, Hegel preferred not to lecture on PR himself, leaving this task to his younger colleague Eduard Gans (1798–1839). The transcriptions by Hotho (1822–1823) and Griesheim (1824–1825) were used by Gans as the basis for the 'Additions' to PR, first published with the 1833 edition; cf. Eduard

Gans, *Naturrecht und Universalrechtsgeschichte* (*Natural Right and the Universal History of Law*) (1827–1833), ed. Manfred Riedel (Stuttgart: Klett-Cotta, 1981).

2 Hegel first published his *Encyclopaedia of the Philosophical Sciences* in Heidelberg in 1817. The topics dealt with in P R are covered (but much more briefly and sketchily) under the heading of 'Objective Spirit' (E H §§ 400–452). This discussion is expanded in subsequent (3-volume) editions of the *Encyclopaedia* (second edition 1827, third edition 1830) (E G §§ 483–552).

3 Penelope, wife of Odysseus, promised the suitors who beset her in her husband's long absence from Ithaca that she would marry one of them as soon as she completed weaving a shroud for her father-in-law, Laertes. But each night she secretly undid the day's weaving, so that the task would never be completed (Homer, *Odyssey* 19.137–155).

4 Hegel regards the 'speculative mode of cognition' as the distinguishing mark of his philosophy. His fullest introductory exposition of the differences between speculation and other philosophical approaches is to be found in the introduction which he later wrote for his *Encyclopaedia* in 1827 (E L §§ 1–83).

5 Hegel's best brief exposition of his speculative method before 1820 is to be found in the Prefaces and Introduction of *The Science of Logic* (W L v, 13–56/25–59).

6 Cf. Jacob Friedrich Fries (1773–1843):

> To us Germans the splendour of the virtues of patriotism and piety has recently appeared in our life, and their significance for the life of every individual has become clearer. May the German people grow stronger in the healthy spirit of the virtues of public life: so we will and believe! For this great work I think I can do my part by further developing the scientific presentation of ethical truths in the German language. (Fries, H P P vi)

Hegel and Fries were long-time personal rivals. Both held the position of Privatdozent at the University of Jena from 1801 to 1805, when Fries was promoted to professor of philosophy at the University of Heidelberg. Hegel bitterly resented Fries's advancement, and Fries continued to do everything he could to hinder Hegel's career. In 1811 Hegel wrote the following to his friend Niethammer:

> I have known Fries for a long time. I know that he has gone beyond the Kantian philosophy by interpreting it in the most superficial manner, by earnestly watering it down ever more, making it ever more superficial ... The first volume [of Fries's

System of Logic] is spiritless, completely superficial, threadbare, trivial, devoid of the least intimation of scientific coherence. The explanations [in the second volume] are . . . the most slovenly disconnected explanatory lecture-hall twaddle, such as only a truly empty-headed individual in his hour of digestion could come up with. I prefer to say nothing more specific about his miserable thoughts. (B I, 338–339/257)

Fries remained professor in Heidelberg for eleven years; during most of this time Hegel languished as headmaster of a Nuremberg gymnasium (secondary school). When Fries moved to a professorship at Jena in 1816, Hegel returned to university life by becoming his successor. In 1818, however, Hegel was promoted to the prestigious chair of philosophy at Berlin. In 1820, as part of the so-called 'demagogue persecutions' (carried out by the newly ascendant reactionaries in the Prussian government (see note 18 below)) Fries was deprived of his professorship at Jena for his participation in the Wartburg Festival (see notes 11–12 below). (The professorship was restored to Fries in 1824.)

In 1819, several of Hegel's students and assistants (including Gustav Asverus (1798–1843), Friedrich Wilhelm Carové (1789–1852), Friedrich Christoph Förster (1791–1868), and Leopold von Henning (1791–1866)) were subject to these same persecutions. Hegel intervened on their behalf, not always with success (he put up 500 imperial dollars – nearly three months' pay – as bail for Asverus, who was nevertheless not released until 1826). Hegel had some reason to fear both for his own position and for the fate of PR in the hands of the censorship. In the Preface of PR, Hegel wants to reassure the censors that his philosophy of the state contains nothing dangerous or subversive; Hegel's unattractive perpetuation of his old vendetta against a victim of political persecution is thus also being used to serve the end of self-protection.

7 Cf. Luke 16:29.
8 In this passage, Hegel once again has mainly Fries in mind. Fries's DBS was dedicated 'To Germany's Youth' (DBS 3).

Religious convictions of the holy origin of all things, of the existence of God and eternal life, should not be scientifically supported and proved, nor should they be applied scientifically as principles of proof; rather, they are properly the immediate fundamental thoughts of those living feelings of presentiment (*Ahndung*) which recognize eternal truth through inspiration and devotion to the beauty of natural appearances and above all to the spiritual beauty of human life. (Fries, HPP 6–7)

More generally, he probably intends to refer to the anti-rationalistic philosophy of the Romantics, and especially those influenced by *Christendom or Europe* (1799) (often attributed to Friedrich von Hardenberg ('Novalis') (1772–1801)), and by the later political thought of Johann Gottlieb Fichte (1762–1814), such as his posthumously published *Theory of the State* (1813). See Reinhold Aris, *History of Political Thought in Germany 1789–1815* (London: Allen & Unwin, 1936), especially Chapters 6–12; and H. S. Reiss (ed.), *The Political Thought of the German Romantics* (Oxford: Blackwell, 1955).

9 Cf. Psalms 127:2: 'It is vain for you to rise up early, to sit up late, to eat the bread of sorrows: for so he giveth his beloved sleep.' A literal translation of Luther's German version of the last clause (which Hegel typically quotes imperfectly, from memory) would be: 'To his friends he gives it [bread] in sleep.'

10 Compare the following footnote from Hegel's *Science of Logic*:

> The latest treatment of [the science of logic] which has recently appeared, the *System of Logic* by Fries, reverts to anthropological foundations. The superficiality of the notion (*Vorstellung*) or opinion on which it is based, both in and for itself and in its execution, relieves me of the trouble of taking any notice whatever of this insignificant publication.   (WL v, 47/52)

> Fries tried to prevent the first volume of Hegel's *Science of Logic* (containing this footnote) from being reviewed at all; finally, he reviewed it himself in 1814 – at greater length than Hegel's comment just quoted, but with no greater respect (cf. B ii, 381–382).

11 Hegel is referring to the Wartburg Festival of October 1817. On 18 and 19 October, the student fraternities (*Burschenschaften*) held a festival at the Wartburg, in the town of Eisenach, to celebrate both the tricentennial of the Lutheran Reformation and the fourth anniversary of the victory over Napoleonic troops at the Battle of Leipzig. About five hundred students from about a dozen universities took part, as did a few of their professorial mentors. Prominent among the latter were Lorenz Oken (1779–1851) and Fries. The festival was one of the earliest expressions of 'student dissent' in the German universities. It founded a 'General German Student Fraternity' whose 'Principles' favoured German unity, national representation and constitutional government, opposing feudal social organization and the police state. Their spirit was an emotional combination (not always coherent) of the ideals of the French Revolution with German nationalism, Romantic organicism and Christian piety. At the end of the first day, there was a burning of 'un-German' books, including the

Napoleonic Code, the Prussian Police Laws, and the writings of reactionaries such as Karl Ludwig von Haller (1768–1854) (see note 15 below) and August von Kotzebue (1761–1819) (see note 18 below). See Thomas Nipperdey, *Deutsche Geschichte 1800–1866* (Munich: C. H. Beck, 1983), p. 280. The German authorities perceived the Wartburg Festival as a direct threat to them. Hegel's reference here to the 'notorious' Wartburg Festival is apparently hostile. But on closer inspection we see that it is his enemy Fries who absorbs all the hostility. Hegel was himself a professorial sponsor of the *Burschenschaften* both in Heidelberg and Berlin. Though he was not present at the Wartburg Festival, he had numerous ties to those who were. He was a close friend of Oken, and several of his students were active in the *Burschenschaften*, as were Hegel's brother-in-law, Gottlieb von Tücher, and also Robert and Wilhelm Wesselhöft, with whose family Hegel's illegitimate son lived for some time (see Jacques d'Hondt, *Hegel in His Time*, tr. J. Burbidge (Lewiston, NY: Broadview, 1988), pp. 113–114). Hegel's publisher and friend Karl Friedrich Ernst Frommann (1765–1837) had a son who was also present at the festival, and published a glowing account of the proceedings (Friedrich Johannes Frommann, *Das Burschenfest auf der Wartburg* (Jena: Friedrich Frommann, 1818)).

Carové spoke prominently at the Wartburg Festival and was founder of the 'General German Student Fraternity'. (Hegel later tried to have Carové appointed his assistant at Berlin, but failed owing to Carové's unacceptable political activities.) Within the German student movement, Hegel and Fries represent conflicting tendencies. Fries is a republican, and a proponent of German unity and German nationalism. Hegel is a supporter of constitutional monarchy (cf. PR §§ 273, 278R) and representative institutions (cf. PR §§ 302–314), and a consistent opponent of feudal institutions (cf. PR §§ 46, 62R, 64, 75R, 172A, 180R, 273R, 278R, 286R). He attacks the reactionary Haller (cf. PR §§ 258R) but admires the Prussian and Napoleonic Codes (cf. PR §§ 211,R, 216, 258R; VPR19 172). Hegel's attitude toward German nationalism and German unity is less than enthusiastic: as a south German from the Duchy of Württemberg with indigenous traditions of representative government, he is wary of the absorption of the smaller German states into a 'German nation' (cf. PR § 322R and note 1); Hegel's contemptuous pun on the German nationalist watchword *Deutschtum* ('Teutonism') is *Deutschdumm* ('German stupidity') (B II, 43/312).

12 Hegel is apparently referring to the following remarks from Fries's speech:

But if the spirit of a people were to attain to a genuinely common spirit, then justice, chastity and self-sacrificing patriotism would rule in this people; then life in this people would come from beneath, from the people, in every business of public concern. Not only the form of law and authority, not only the private compulsion of official duty, but also the spirit of subordination would drive the individual; the desire for knowledge and the striving of the student would drive the teacher to enthusiasm, the spirit of the people would drive the judge to justice. And in this people living societies would dedicate themselves to every individual work of popular education and service of the people, unbreakably united through the holy chain of friendship.

(Fries, FDB; cf. HPP 328–329)

Hegel's attacks on Fries have often been cited as evidence of his 'conservatism', in opposition to Fries's 'liberalism'. Hegel's defenders, in response, have often contrasted Hegel's defence of equal civil rights for Jews (PR §§ 209R, 270R) with Fries's vicious anti-Semitism (Walter Kaufmann, 'The Hegel Myth and Its Method', in Kaufmann (ed.) *Hegel's Political Philosophy* (New York: Atherton, 1970), pp. 145–147; see PR § 270, note 6). Nevertheless, whatever it may do to our moral sensibilities, anti-Semitism (or lack of it) is not, in this period, a reliable barometer of a person's general political position. More to the point is the judgement of the French liberal Victor Cousin (1792–1867):

In politics, M. Hegel is the only man from Germany with whom I was always on the best of terms. He was, like me, infused with the new spirit; he considered the French Revolution to be the greatest step forward taken by humankind since Christianity and he never ceased questioning me about the issues and men of this great epoch. He was profoundly liberal without being the least bit republican.
(Victor Cousin, 'Souvenirs d'Allemagne', *Revue des deux mondes*, August 1866, pp. 616–617)

In the Preface to PR, Hegel emphasizes his (quite real) philosophical differences with Fries, but probably gives the impression of a much greater disagreement between them on political issues than really exists. For instance, Hegel quotes with apparent disapproval Fries's opinion that public business should gain its life 'from below', but Hegel himself asserts that 'civil life should be governed in a *concrete* manner from below, where it is concrete' (PR § 290). Fries, like Hegel, favours 'gradual change of the constitution' (Fries, DBS 1,

165) as a way of realizing the modern spirit without the terrible effects of the French Revolution (toward which Fries's attitude, unlike Hegel's, is unreservedly hostile) (Fries, DBS 1, 41–56); both men advocate a constitutional government with Estates assemblies with representatives of both the nobility and the bourgeoisie (cf. PR §§ 289–320 and Fries, DBS 1, 146–162). Philosophical differences cannot fully account for Hegel's attitude toward Fries; Hegel was on good terms with the aging F. H. Jacobi (1743–1819), whose philosophical position was in many ways quite close to Fries's. The differences between Hegel and Fries were more philosophical than political, but more personal than philosophical.

13 The Greek philosopher Epicurus (*c.* 341–271 B.C.) believed that nothing exists in nature except atoms and the void, but he tried to reconcile this with incompatibilist-indeterminist views about freedom of the will, which led him to postulate a degree of randomness in nature. His extant writings do not contain the doctrine articulated by the Roman Epicurean Lucretius (*c.* 99–55 B.C.) that in their motion atoms swerve randomly into parallel paths, but this doctrine is widely enough attributed to Epicurus himself to make it probable that he held it. Hegel may also have in mind Epicurus' denial of any natural teleology. Cf. A. A. Long and D. N. Sedley, *The Hellenistic Philosophers* I (Cambridge: Cambridge University Press, 1987), pp. 52, 57, 72, 102–112.

14 Hegel's quotation from Goethe, which contains minor inaccuracies, runs together several lines of Mephistopheles' speech: *Faust*, Part I, lines 1851–1855:

> Do but despise reason and science
> Highest of all the human powers,
> Let yourself, through magic and delusion,
> Grow strong through the spirit of deception,
> Then it's certain I will get you!

and lines 1866–1867:

> And even if he hadn't given himself over to the devil
> He would perish just the same!

Goethe, *Werke* III, ed. Erich Trunz (Munich: Beck, 1982), p. 61

The same passage was (mis)quoted by Hegel at PhG ¶ 360.

15 Cf. PR § 258R. The remark was made, however, in the course of criticizing the views of the reactionary Romantic Karl Ludwig von Haller (1768–1854), whose *Restoration of Political Science, or Theory of the Natural-Social Condition, Opposed to the Chimaera of the Artificial-Civil Condition* (Winterthur: Steiner, 1816–1820) was one of the

books burnt at the Wartburg Festival (see PR § 258, note 3). Hegel's defenders sometimes point to this as an example of Hegel's even-handedness – balancing his attack on the liberal Fries with an attack on the conservative Haller. But there is something craftier than even-handedness going on here. Hegel is trying to portray his scathing critique of the authoritarian reactionary Haller (who, at the time the Preface was written, was still something of a favourite at the Prussian court) as if it were a rejection of Fries's views. (The favourable attitude of the Prussian reactionaries toward Haller changed suddenly in 1821 when it was revealed to them that Haller had secretly converted to Roman Catholicism, on the ground that he had come to regard the spirit of the Lutheran Reformation as leading inevitably to the French Revolution, from which he felt he must distance himself as far as possible.)

16 Cf. Plato, *Gorgias* 463a–465d; *Republic* 493a–495e; *Sophist* 217a–218a and *passim*.

17 'Wer ein Amt erhält im Land, der erhält auch den Verstand' ('Whoever receives an office in the land, also receives understanding') (*Deutsches Sprichwörter-Lexikon* I (Darmstadt: Wissenschaftliche Buchgesellschaft, 1977), p. 71.70; cf. Leonhard Winkler, *Deutsches Recht im Spiegel deutscher Sprichwörter* (Leipzig: Quelle & Meyer, 1927), p. 205). The proverb is usually meant ironically, as it is in Hegel's use of it here.

18 This refers to the Carlsbad Decrees of 1819 and to the consequent censorship to which publications like PR had recently become subject. The decrees were a prominent part of a movement of political reaction which took place quite suddenly in the summer of 1819. After the defeat of Prussia at the hands of Napoleon in 1808, an era of reform had been initiated by Heinrich Karl vom Stein (1757–1831). It achieved the abolition of serfdom, administrative reorganization of the government and the army, and the partial emancipation of a capitalist economy from feudal and guild encumbrances. Stein's idealism, refusal to compromise, and unbending nationalistic hostility to Napoleon led to his dismissal in 1810. But many of his reforms, which (despite his attitude toward Napoleon) imitated French examples, were continued after 1811 by Karl August von Hardenberg (1750–1822).

On 23 March 1819, the reactionary poet August von Kotzebue (1761–1819) was assassinated by a student, Karl Ludwig Sand (1795–1820), who believed (very likely correctly) that Kotzebue was a Russian (Tsarist) agent. Sand was an associate of Karl Follen (1795–1840), a student of Fries, who advocated a 'theory of individual terror', according to which such an assassination was a noble deed, if carried out from political motives, 'a war of individuals, a war of one individual against another' (K. G. Faber, 'Student und Politik in der ersten deutschen Burschenschaft', *Geschichte in Wissenschaft und Unterricht* 21 (1970); cf. Karl Alexander von Müller, *Karl Ludwig Sand* (Munich: C. H. Beck, 1925), and Richard Preziger, *Die politischen Ideen des Karl Follen* (Tübingen: Mohr, 1912)).

The murder of Kotzebue became a *cause célèbre* for Prussian reactionaries, who used it as a rallying point for the nobility's reaction against the entire reform movement. It was equally an opportunity for Metternich and the forces of continental reaction outside Prussia, who looked askance at the liberal direction in which affairs were moving there. In August 1819, a meeting of continental powers was convened in Carlsbad (now in Czechoslovakia), resulting in the Carlsbad Decrees, which resolved on the institution, throughout the states belonging to the federation there convened, of statutes providing for the dismissal of all university teachers deemed to have 'an influence on the minds of the young through the propagation of corrupt doctrines, hostile to public order and peace or subversive of the principles of the existing political institutions'; imposed censorship on academics and academic publications; and established a commission for the investigation of 'revolutionary activities and demagogical associations' (quoted in Theodor Schieder, *Vom deutschen Bund zum deutschen Reich 1815–1871* (Stuttgart: Klett, 1970), pp. 30–31). Hegel had completed a draft of PR, but withdrew and revised it in the light of these new circumstances. As we have already seen, the Preface in particular is designed to quiet any possible suspicions the censors might have concerning Hegel's political opinions.

19 Johannes von Müller, *Sämmtliche Werke* XXXII, ed. Johann Georg Müller (Stuttgart and Tübingen: J. G. Cotta, 1835), p. 240. Johannes von Müller (1752–1809) was a Swiss historian and diplomat, political progressive and associate of Goethe, Schiller and Herder. He served the Elector of Mainz, Joseph II of Austria and, in his last years, Napoleon Bonaparte. The quoted remark is from a graphic description of the dismal and demoralized conditions prevailing in Rome under French occupation.

20 Cf. PhG ¶ 482; VPG 380–385/314–318.

21 Hegel is apparently referring to the passage two paragraphs earlier, where he claimed that in the modern world philosophy has a public existence, in contrast to its existence as a private art among the Greeks.

22 In his later expositions of this famous (or infamous) saying, Hegel is at

pains to point out that it does *not* mean that everything is as it ought to be, or (more particularly) that the existing political order is always rational:

> But if I have spoken of *actuality*, then it is self-evident that you are to think of the sense in which I use this expression, since I have treated of actuality in a worked-out *Logic*, distinguishing it precisely not only from the contingent, which has existence, but also from [two senses of] existence (*Existenz, Dasein*) and other determinations ... When [the understanding] with its 'ought' turns to trivial, external and transitory objects, institutions, conditions, etc., which perhaps may have a great relative actuality for a certain time and in a certain sphere, it may be right and in such cases it may find much which does not correspond to universally correct determinations. For who is not clever enough to see much in his environment which is not in fact as it ought to be? But this cleverness is wrong to imagine that such objects and their 'ought' have any place within the interests of philosophical science. For science has to do only with the Idea, which is not so impotent that it only ought to be without actually being; hence philosophy has to do with an actuality of which those objects, institutions, conditions, etc. are only the superficial exterior.
> (EL § 6; for Hegel's discussion of 'actuality' in his logic see EL §§ 142–147 and WL VI, 186–213/541–550; cf. also VGP II, 110–111/95–96 and VPR IV, 923–924)

Far from hallowing the status quo, Hegel's formulations of the rationality of the actual in his lectures of 1817–1820 emphasize the dynamic and progressive aspect of the reason which is at work actualizing itself in the world: 'What is actual becomes rational, and the rational becomes actual' (VPR19 51); 'What is rational must happen, since on the whole the constitution is only its development' (VPR17 157); cf. also PR § 258A.

23 Cf. Plato, *Laws* 789b–790a; Fichte, GNR § 21, 295/379.

24 'Here is Rhodes, jump here.' This saying is drawn from one of Aesop's fables:

The Braggart

An athlete who had always been criticized by his fellow townsmen for not being much of a man once went away and came back after a time boasting that besides performing many feats of valour in other cities, at Rhodes he had made such a jump that none of the Olympic victors could equal it. Moreover, he claimed that he would offer people who were there as witnesses if any of

them ever came to town. One of the bystanders spoke up and said to him, 'Well, my friend, if what you say is true, you don't need any witnesses. Here is Rhodes, [jump here].'
(Lloyd W. Daly (tr.), *Aesop Without Morals* (New York: Thomas Yoseloff, 1961), p. 107)

25 Hegel now apparently means: to leap over the city of Rhodes, or over its harbour, which was straddled by the Colossus of Rhodes, a huge statue of Apollo erected about 300 B.C. after Rhodes had withstood siege by the navy of Antigonus I, King of Macedonia.

26 In Greek, *Rhodos* means either 'Rhodes' or 'rose', and in Latin, *salta* means either 'jump' or 'dance'. The pun suggests to Hegel that to meet the challenge of comprehending the rationality of the actual is also to find a way of rejoicing in the present.

27 Compare the following from Hegel's hand-written lecture notes: 'The present appears to reflection, and especially to self-conceit, as a cross (indeed, of necessity) – and philosophy teaches [us] to recognize the rose – i.e. reason – in this cross' (VPR II, 89, cf. also VR I, 272/I, 284–285). The image of the rose in the cross was apparently suggested to Hegel by the name (and the visual emblem) of the 'Rosicrucians', the secret religious society, apparently begun in the seventeenth century, and prominently represented by Michael Maier (1568–1622) and Robert Fludd (1574–1637). The name 'Rosicrucian' was based on that of the (alleged) founder of the society, Christian Rosencreutz (fourteenth century). But the name itself also has doctrinal significance for Rosicrucians, associated with their proverb 'No cross, no crown': i.e., one reaches the 'rose' (the divine), only through the 'cross' (earthly suffering) (see Harry Wells Fogarty, 'Rosicrucians', *The Encyclopedia of Religion* XII (New York: Macmillan, 1987), pp. 476–477).

28 'A little taste of philosophy perhaps moves one to atheism, but more of it leads back to religion' (Francis Bacon, *The Advancement of Learning*, *Works* I, ed. Spedding, Ellis, and Heath (London: Longman, 1857–1874), p. 436; cf. *The Essayes or Counsels, Civill and Morall*, ed. Michael Kiernan (Cambridge, MA: Harvard Press, 1985), Number 16: 'Of Atheisme', p. 51).

29 'So then because thou art lukewarm, and neither cold nor hot, I will spue thee out of my mouth' (Revelation 3:16).

30 Compare also the following, from Hegel's lectures of 1819–1820:

The modern age has determined what is in itself rational and perfect through thought, and simultaneously removed the cloak of dust and rust from the positive. This is nothing but the fundamental principle of philosophy, of the free cognition of truth, no longer cloaked by contingency. The age has at present nothing to do except to cognize what is at hand, and thus to make it accord with thought. This is the path of philosophy.

(VPR19 290)

31 The owl is the sacred bird of Minerva (Greek: Athena), goddess of wisdom. The apparent meaning of this famous saying is that a culture's philosophical understanding reaches its peak only when the culture enters its decline (cf. VG 66/58, 178–180/145–147).

§ *1*

1 Ordinary thinking identifies a 'concept' (*Begriff*) with something general abstracted from particulars. Hegel's name for this is a 'representation' (*Vorstellung*) or 'determination of the understanding'. For Hegel, the 'concept' is 'the free', 'the principle of life and so at the same time the absolutely concrete' (EL § 160,A); 'the concept, in so far as it has attained to a [developed] existence [*Existenz*] which is free, is nothing other than the "I" or pure self-consciousness' (WL VI, 253/583). The concept strives to give itself actual objective existence, and then it is called the 'Idea' (*Idee*): 'the Idea is the adequate concept' (WL VI, 462/755), 'the Idea is the true in and for itself, the absolute unity of the concept and objectivity' (EL § 213).

§ *2*

1 The development or 'proof' of the concept of right was given in the *Encyclopaedia* (cf. EG §§ 485–487). PR is an expansion of the part of Hegel's system presented in EG §§ 488–552.
2 The thesis that philosophy forms a circle seems to lie behind Hegel's choice of the title 'Encyclopaedia' for the complete exposition of his system (EL §§ 15–18).
3 'In civil law all definitions are hazardous' (Justinian, *Digest* 50.17.202; see PR § 3, note 2). The proposition is usually attributed to the Roman jurist Iavolenus, first century A.D.
4 The phrase 'facts of consciousness' recalls Fichte's *The Facts of Consciousness* (1813) (FW II, 537–691), but Hegel's remarks seem to be aimed especially at Fries's psychologizing of Kantian transcendental philosophy:

Kant committed the great mistake of holding transcendental cognition to be a kind of a priori cognition, and he thus missed its empirical psychological nature. This mistake is an unavoidable consequence of the other one, which we have already reproved, of confusing a philosophical deduction with a kind of proof, which he called a transcendental proof.

(Fries, AKV, Introduction, I, 29; cf. HPP 367–370; cf. Hegel, VGP III, 418–419/510–511)

In the mid-1790s, the phrase 'facts of consciousness' was also closely associated with the Kantian epistemological theories of the Jena philosopher Christian Erhard Schmid (1761–1812), who was the object of a contemptuous attack by Fichte (FW II, 421–458). (See Preface, notes 7, 9–11, 18.)

§3

1 See 'The geographical basis of world history' (VPG 105–132/79–102) and 'The natural context or the geographical basis of world history' (VG 198–241/152–239).
2 The *Institutes* and *Pandects* (Latin title: *Digest*) were the first two of four parts of the legal code (later given the collective name *Corpus iuris civilis*) compiled and promulgated in A.D. 529 by the Roman Emperor Justinian (reigned 527–565). The *Corpus iuris civilis* consists of:

1 The *Institutes*: a general and comprehensive textbook of Roman law. It was based on the *Institutes* of Gaius (c. A.D. 110–180), a jurist of the reigns of Antoninus Pius and Marcus Aurelius. (Justinian destroyed the sources of his codification, but the main text of Gaius' *Institutes* was discovered in a palimpsest in 1816 by the legal historian Barthold Georg Niebuhr (1776–1831).)
2 The *Pandects* (from *pan dechesthai* – 'taking in all'): a lengthier compilation of earlier legal sources, organized under headings.
3 The *Codex*, a collection of enactments by past emperors.
4 The *Novels*, new laws enacted by Justinian himself.

On account of its reception by the eleventh century revival (chiefly at the great law school of Bologna), the *Corpus iuris civilis* was later to become the basis for all modern continental European systems of law. The standard edition of the *Corpus iuris civilis* was edited by Mommsen and Krueger (1895). Cf. also *Corpus iuris civilis: The Institutes*, translated by Thomas C. Sandars (Westport, CT: Greenwood Press, 1970). The standard edition of the *Institutes* of Gaius is by F. de Zulueta (2 volumes, 1946, 1953). The standard reference work on Roman law in English is W. W. Buckland, *Textbook of Roman Law from Augustus to Justinian*, 3rd ed. (Cambridge: Cambridge University Press, 1963).

3 Compare the following passage from Montesquieu:

> The government most conformable to nature is that which best agrees with the humor and disposition of the people in whose favor it is established ... Law in general is human reason, inasmuch as it governs all the inhabitants of the earth: the political and civil laws of each nation ought to be only the particular cases in which human reason is applied. They should be adapted in such a manner to the people for whom they are framed that it should be a great chance if those of one nation should suit another. They should be in relation to the nature and principle of each government: whether they form it, as may be said of political laws, or whether they support it, as in the case of civil institutions. They should be in relation to the climate of each country, to the quality of its soil, to its situation and extent, to the principal occupation of the natives ... They should have relation to the degree of liberty which the constitution will bear; to the religion of the inhabitants, to their inclinations, riches, numbers, commerce, manners and customs. In fine, they have relations to each other, as also to their origin, to the intent of the legislator, and to the order of things on which they are established; in all of which different lights they ought to be considered.
> (Charles Louis de Secondat, Baron de Montesquieu, *The Spirit of the Laws*, tr. by T. Nugent (New York: Hafner, 1962) I, 1.3, pp. 6–7)

4 These remarks are directed against the historical school of law, whose chief representative was Hegel's colleague in Berlin, Friedrich Karl von Savigny (1779–1861) (see § 211, note 4). The historical school reacted against Enlightenment attempts to interpret law in terms of an ahistorical reason, approaching it instead by grasping it historically, in terms of the original meaning legal provisions had within the social context in which they arose. This approach represented a genuine respect for the empirical history of law, but also a Romantic reverence for tradition and national heritage and a rejection of the claims of human reason in the social and political sphere, which went along with the Romantic rejection of the Enlightenment and the ideals of the French Revolution. It is this latter aspect of the historical school which draws Hegel's criticisms. Savigny was a leading academic representative of Prussian conservatism; he and Hegel did not get along well, either philosophically or personally. Hegel never mentions Savigny by name in P R (cf., however, V P R 17 54), but he is doubtless a target here and again in P R §§ 211R, 212R.

5 Gustav Ritter von Hugo (1764–1844), a member of the historical

school of law, was professor of law at Göttingen. Hegel refers to his *Lehrbuch des römischen Rechts* (*Textbook of Roman Law*), 5th ed. (Berlin: A. Mylius, 1815).

6 The Twelve Tables was the early Roman legal code, promulgated about 450 B.C. The reference is to the following passage from Marcus Tullius Cicero (106–43 B.C.): 'Truly it seems to me that all the collections of philosophical books are outweighed, both in their importance and in the wealth of their utility, by the one little book which contains the Twelve Tables of Law' (Cicero, *De oratore* 1.44).

7 Aulus Gellius lived in the second century A.D. His *Noctes Atticae* (*Attic Nights*) are twenty books of essays on a wide variety of subjects, which is a valuable source of anecdotes, quotations, and observations on life in classical Rome. Favorinus was a second-century philosopher, born at Arles in Gaul, whom Aulus Gellius admired. Sextus Caecilius was a jurist from Africa. Both Favorinus and Sextus Caecilius belonged to the court of the Emperor Hadrian (A.D. 117–138). The conversation between them serves Hugo's purpose (see notes 4 and 5 above) because in it a jurist learned in the history of the law corrects the philosopher's criticisms of traditional statutes by showing them to be based on misunderstandings caused by ignorance of the historical circumstances in which the laws were made.

8 In 376 B.C., under the Roman Republic, the tribunes P. Licinius Stolo and L. Sextius Lateranus proposed certain measures (commonly called the 'Licinian Rogations') which were aimed at agrarian reforms, at reducing political inequalities between patricians and plebeians, and at remedying the distress of the poor (especially debtors). The law of Stolo limited each citizen's ownership of land to 500 jugera. Over patrician objections, they were adopted in 367 B.C. with great success, but by A.D. 100 they were considered antiquated (see Livy, *History of Rome* 2.6.35–38).

9 The *lex Voconia* (promulgated 169 B.C.) regulated the inheritances of women (see Cicero, *De re publica* 3.10).

10 As Aulus Gellius makes clear, the 'Licinian Law' intended here was a sumptuary law, which prosperity had since rendered obsolete (*Noctes Atticae* 20.1.25).

11 Shylock lends 3,000 ducats to Bassanio, on condition that if he fails to repay, Shylock may take a pound of flesh from Antonio, who, out of friendship to Bassanio, generously agrees to the bargain (*Merchant of Venice* I.iii). Shylock is prevented from enforcing the bond by the precise interpretation placed on it by Portia.

12 This is what Aulus Gellius reports as Sextus Caecilius' opinion (*Noctes Atticae* 20.1.41–50).

13 By A.D. 100 *iumentum* meant a draft animal; when the law was made, it

referred to a vehicle drawn by yoked animals (*Noctes Atticae* 20.1.28–30). An *arcera* is a covered vehicle; Favorinus thinks it extravagant to specify it as a conveyance for bringing sick witnesses to court (*Noctes Atticae* 20.1.29–31).

14 Hugo cites Leibniz's authority for the claim that jurists are generally superior to metaphysicians in drawing rigorous deductive inferences from principles: 'Jurisprudence itself is a science having very much to do with reasoning, and among the ancients I find nothing which approaches the style of the geometers as much as that of the pandects' (Philip Wiener (ed.) *Leibniz: Selections* (New York: Scribner, 1951), p. 580). But Hegel regards deductive inference as only a superficial side of philosophy (EL §§ 181, 231), characteristic of the dogmatic metaphysics of the understanding (cf. EL §§ 26–36).

15 The Twelve Tables did not permit children emancipated from their father's authority (*patria potestas*, see § 172, note 1 and § 180, notes 2, 3, 9) to inherit from their father's estate; rather than revoke this outright, praetorian edicts permitted emancipated children to share in the estate by a legal fiction under the name *bonorum possessio* – 'possession of goods'. This device is recorded in Gaius, *Institutes* 3.25–28.

16 This legal device is mentioned by one of Hegel's main sources for the history of Roman law: Johann Christian Gottlieb Heineccius (1681–1741), *Antiquitatum Romanarum iurisprudentiam illustrantium syntagma* (*Illustrated Treatise on Ancient Roman Jurisprudence*) (1st ed., Halae de Magdeburg: Novi Bibliopolli, 1719).

§ 4

1 Cf. Genesis 2:22–23.

2 This is a reference to the Kantian position on freedom of the will, and specifically to the position of Fries (VPG III, 419/511). Kant sometimes regards freedom of the will, along with the existence of God and the immortality of the soul, as objects of moral faith or belief (*Critique of Pure Reason*, B xxx); but he rejected the view that we have any immediate consciousness of freedom (KpV 4/4). Fries, on the other hand, thinks that 'for the human being basic ethical truths are valid with immediate, irrefutable necessity, hence he is conscious of his freedom'; sometimes he infers from this that we do not need to believe (*glauben*) in it, as we do need to believe in God and immortality; but in other places he does speak of the 'belief' or 'faith' (*Glaube*) which we have in our freedom on the basis of moral consciousness (Fries, AKV I, xvii–xviii; II, 259; III, 251).

3 EG §§ 440–482.

4 EG § 444.

§5

1 From Hegel's lectures of 1822–1823: 'Freedom is just thinking itself. Whoever rejects thinking and speaks of freedom, does not know what he is talking about' (VGP III, 308/402). From what Hegel says elsewhere, the intended target of these remarks seems to be Wolffian rationalism (EL § 28,A; cf. VGP III, 312/407, EG § 468; cf. below § 15, note 1).

2 Cf. VR I, 345–350/II, 31–40.

3 In PR, Hegel has few good words to say about the French Revolution, but this is uncharacteristic of him (perhaps a concession to the Prussian censors, see Preface, note 6). Compare, however, his remark in § 258R, which alludes to it as 'the overthrow of all existing and given conditions within an actual major state *and the revision of its constitution from first principles and purely in terms of thought*' (emphasis added). Hegel regards the Terror as resulting from the first, merely abstract form in which the principle of freedom was applied to the state, but he regards the Revolution as having accomplished the overcoming of spirit's self-alienation, bringing the other-worldly aspirations of Christianity to actuality in the here and now (PhG ¶¶ 584–593). Though never a Jacobin, Hegel always regarded the Revolution as a colossal and progressive world-historical event (VPG 531–535/449–452). In 1807, after the army of Napoleon had conquered Prussia, he wrote:

> Thanks to the bath of her revolution, the French nation has freed herself of many institutions which the human spirit had outgrown like the shoes of a child. These institutions accordingly once oppressed her, and they now continue to oppress other nations as so many fetters devoid of spirit. What is even more, however, is that the individual as well has shed the fear of death along with the life of habit – which, with the change of scenery, is no longer self-supporting. This is what gives this nation the great power she displays against others. She weighs down upon the impassiveness and dullness of these other nations, which, finally forced to give up their indolence in order to step out into actuality, will perhaps . . . surpass their teachers.   (B I,85/123)

A student reported that in 1826 Hegel still drank a toast to the Revolution on Bastille day: 'He explained its significance and said that a year never passed without his celebrating the anniversary in this way' (quoted by T. M. Knox, 'Hegel and Prussianism', in Walter Kaufmann (ed.) *Hegel's Political Philosophy* (New York: Atherton, 1970), p. 20). See also Jean Hyppolite, *Studies in Hegel and Marx* (New York:

Harper, 1969), pp. 35–69; and Joachim Ritter, *Hegel and the French Revolution* (Cambridge, MA: MIT Press, 1975).

4 Compare the following, from Hegel's lectures of 1824–1825: 'The human being can abstract from every content, make himself free of it, whatever is in my representation I can let it go, I can make myself entirely empty . . . The human being has the self-consciousness of being able to take up any content, or of letting it go, he can let go of all bonds of friendship, love, whatever they may be' (VPR IV, 111–112).

§ 6

1 In Fichte's *Science of Knowledge* (*Wissenschaftslehre*), the first principle is the identity of the 'I' with itself (W § 1, 91–101/93–102). The second principle is that of opposition, in which the 'I', in order to form a determinate conception of itself, must posit a not-'I' (W § 2, 101–105/102–105). Hegel's position is that self-consciousness and consciousness of a not-self are not two successive principles, but are inseparable from one another (EG §§ 449–450), cf. Hegel, VGP III, 388–396/481–489.

§ 7

1 EL §§ 163–165.
2 Cf. EG § 471.

§ 8

1 Cf. EG § 440.

§ 10

1 The target here seems to be Wolffian rationalism, cf. EL § 35,A. (See § 15, note 1.)

§ 11

1 Compare the following, from Hegel's lectures of 1824–1825:

Not all drives are rational, but all rational determinations of the will also exist as drives. As natural, the will can also be irrational, partly against reason, partly contingent . . . Irrational drives, drives of envy, wicked drives, have no substantial content, none determined through the concept, they are contingent, irrational, and so they are not our concern here.   (VPR IV, 128)

§ 13

1 Descartes, *Meditations* IV, locates the possibility of error in the fact that the freedom of the human will is infinite, while the human intellect is finite.

2 A reference to the ideal of the 'beautiful soul' put forward by Goethe, Schiller, and the Romantics (cf. PhG ¶ 668). See § 140, note 19.

3 As usual, Hegel's quotation is not quite accurate. It is drawn from the last three lines of Goethe's sonnet 'Nature and Art':

Whoever wills something great must collect himself
It is only in limitation that mastery shows itself
And only law can give us freedom.
  Goethe, *Werke* I, ed. Erich Trunz (Munich: Beck, 1982), p. 245

§ 14

1 Cf. EG §§ 476–478.

§ 15

1 Christian Wolff (1679–1754), a follower of Leibniz, was the most important German philosopher in the first half of the eighteenth century. In 1723 he was dismissed from his professorship at the University of Halle at the instigation of the pietists (he was restored to his position at Halle in 1740, upon the accession of Frederick the Great). One of the points of controversy was the allegation that Wolff denied freedom of the will because he held that every volition is determined by a sufficient reason (VGP III, 256–257/350–351; cf. EL § 35,A).

2 Kant does maintain that only *Willkür*, and not *Wille*, is free (TL 212–213/9–10). But he does not mean by this that we act most freely when we act arbitrarily. Rather, he means that our freedom consists in our capacity to choose which maxim we adopt (the faculty of *Willkür*, Lat. *arbitrium*) rather than in the faculty of *Wille* (Lat. *voluntas*), which rationally legislates to our capacity to choose. Hegel also attributes this view to Fries, on equally dubious grounds (VGP III, 419/511). But the view that freedom consists in arbitrariness was held by some of the Romantics, such as Friedrich Schlegel (see following note).

3 Phidias (*c.* 500–430 B.C.), a friend of Pericles, was one of the greatest of Athenian artists, creator of three statues of Athene on the Acropolis, and sculptor, or at least supervisor, of the frieze of the Parthenon. Hegel's remark here is a critical reference to Romantic

theories of art, which locate the superiority of modern poetry (*Poesie*) to ancient poetry in the fact that among the moderns the work expresses the personal peculiarities and arbitrariness of the artist. In particular, it seems to be a response to the contrast of 'Romantic' to 'Classical' poetry formulated by Friedrich Schlegel (1767–1829):

> Romantic poetry is a progressive universal poetry. It can lose itself so completely in its subject matter that one may consider its supreme purpose to be the characterization of poetic individuals of every kind; and yet there is no form better suited to the complete self-expression of the spirit of the author, so that many an artist who merely wanted to write a novel [*Roman*] willy nilly portrayed himself . . . The Romantic genre . . . alone is infinite, as it alone is free; its supreme law is that the arbitrariness [*Willkür*] of the author shall be subject to no law. The Romantic genre is the only one that is more than a genre, but is, as it were, poetry itself; for in a certain sense, all poetry is or should be Romantic. (Friedrich Schlegel, 'Athenäums-Fragment' 116 (1798), *Kritische Friedrich Schlegel Ausgabe* II, *Charakteristiken und Kritiken I*, ed. Hans Eichner (Munich: Paderborn, 1966).

§ 17

1 The 'tedious platitudes' are probably what Kant calls 'counsels of prudence', 'e.g. those of diet, economy, courtesy, restraint, which are shown by experience best to promote well-being on the average' (Kant, G 418/36). Like Kant, Hegel thinks that because human desires and circumstances are so variable, there are no universal principles which lead, always and without exception, to human happiness.

§ 18

1 The idea that human nature was fundamentally good was in Hegel's day commonly associated with the name of Rousseau. Kant had, to the chagrin of Goethe, defended the Christian idea that human nature had a fundamental propensity to evil. But Kant's position was not that natural human drives and inclinations were evil, only that the human will, which is free to subject natural desires to the law of reason, has a propensity to do the reverse (R 26/21, 36/31).

§ 19

1 This is probably a snide reference to Fries's discussion of 'The Drives of Human Reason', A K V III, Part 3, §§ 178–183, which treats our intellectual and moral aspirations to formative education (*Bildung*) as 'drives' found in us empirically: 'It is a matter of experience what can contribute to my education (*Bildung*), and even that I am interested in this education is for me only a fact of inner perception; hence I cognize (*erkennen*) here the impulse (*Antrieb*) only in empirical judgments and not with a priori necessity' (A K V III, 72, § 182).

2 Cf. P R §§ 133, 148.

§ 20

1 Compare the following, from Hegel's lectures of 1822–1823:

We start with the question: What should a human being do? To this the answer is that we have to get to know human nature. A human being has such and such drives. When they are summarized as a single end, then this gives rise to the theory of happiness. In what should a human being seek satisfaction? In drives, but not in individual ones; instead we should calculate to what extent the one must take precedence over the other.

(V P R III, 143–144; cf. E G §§ 479–480)

2 Cf. § 123, note 2.

§ 21

1 Cf. E L §§ 158–159.

§ 22

1 Cf. E L § 54A.

§ 23

1 Hegel speaks of freedom in the abstract as being 'with oneself': 'I can make myself entirely empty. Only I am I, with myself' (V P R IV, 111; cf. P R § 5, note 4 and PhG ¶ 197). But he speaks of concrete or absolute freedom as 'being with oneself *in an other*' (P R § 4A; E G §§ 382,A and 469; E L § 24A). I am absolutely free when even that which I oppose to myself as an object is also me. 'That in which I am free, is to be I myself' (V P R III, 180). I am 'present in it' (V P R IV,

124), when it is 'posited by me' (VPR IV, 106), when it is 'mine' (VPR IV, 102), or when I am 'at home' in it (VPR IV, 105). Here 'the subject is in its homeland [*Heimat*], in its element' (VPR19 122). Hegel's claim that the state is the actuality of concrete freedom (PR § 260) is the claim that it is in the state that the individual self is most fully at home or 'with itself', or at least that those objects in which the self is at home require the institutions of the state for their actuality.

§ 24

1 Cf. EL §§ 168–179.

§ 26

1 Compare the following, from Hegel's lectures of 1824–1825:

> The ethical will is [the will's] most universal existence [*Existenz*]. In so far as the subjective will is sunk into custom [*Sitte*], it is ethical, but only objectively, universally. This will can be ethical, but it can have an unethical content, in so far as it is only objective in general. Subjective freedom is lacking in it and this is cognized in our time as an essential moment.
>
> (VPR IV, 146; cf. VPR III, 161)

§ 27

1 Cf. EG § 469A.

§ 29

1 Compare the following, from Hegel's lectures of 1824–1825:

> Right is grounded on freedom, which must be Idea, must have existence [*Dasein*], reality; and this is what right is. Right also often has the significance of a *recta linea* [straight line], something which conforms to an other, to a rule, but here right is the existence of the free will . . . We do not begin with the representation of right, with what people take right to be; our vocation [*Bestimmung*] is freedom, which must realize itself, and this realization is right. But further, we now say that the other representations of right are false, for only this one is necessary, that freedom gives itself existence; this is the necessary content, this definition will be elucidated by examples, and the entire treatise is such an example. (VPR IV, 149)

2 Kant's fundamental principle of right is: 'Act externally in such a way that the free employment of your power of choice [*Willkür*] could exist together with the freedom of everyone according to a universal law' (Kant, RL § C, 230/35).

3 Cf. PR § 261A.

4 Hegel is probably referring to the French Revolution and the Terror. Cf. PR § 5 and note 3.

§ 30

1 Compare the following from Hegel's Heidelberg lectures of 1817–1818: '*Right* expresses in general a relation which is constituted by freedom of the will and its realization. *Duty* is such a relation in so far as it is to count for me as essential, I have to recognize, respect or produce it' (VPR17 40; cf. PR §§ 148–149).

§ 31

1 Cf. VGP II, 62–86/49–71. But in the *Encyclopaedia* Hegel himself describes dialectic as having a purely negative result, contrasting it with the speculative stage of reason, whose function it is to apprehend the dialectical opposites in their unity (EL §§ 81–82).

2 Cf. Hegel's 1802 essay, 'Relation of Scepticism to Philosophy, Exposition of its Different Modifications and Comparison of the Latest Form with the Ancient One' (SP); cf. PhG ¶¶ 202–206, VGP II, 358–402/328–373. See also Michael Forster, *Hegel and Skepticism* (Cambridge, MA: Harvard University Press, 1989).

§ 33

1 Hegel intends the PR to be structured according to the speculative method, whose stages are moments of the absolute idea (EL §§ 236–242). These moments correspond to the structure of speculative logic: (1) immediate being (EL § 240), (2) essence (EL § 241), (3) the concept, and (4) the Idea (EL § 242). Abstract right apparently corresponds to the stage of immediate being (cf. PR § 34), morality to the stage of essence or reflection (cf. PR § 105), and ethical life to the sphere of the concept; and this implies that the state, as ethical life fully developed, would correspond to the Idea. But Hegel describes ethical life as the Idea (PR § 142) and the state as the actuality of the ethical Idea (PR § 257).

2 Compare the following, from Hegel's Heidelberg lectures of 1817–1818:

Here there is a distinction between morality [*Moralität*] and ethics [*Sittlichkeit*]. Morality is the reflected; but ethics is the interpenetration of the subjective and the objective. (Although it is to be wished that we could express everything in our language, philosophy has made it so that we use a foreign [Latin] name for the more distant, the reflected – as with being [*Sein*] and existence [*Existenz*]. Right and morality are only ideal moments; their existence is only in ethical life. The actual morality is only the morality of the whole in ethical life. (VPR17 89)

'Morality' refers to the subjective life of the individual agent, in so far as it abstracts itself from its social and historical situation and reflects critically on them, or considers its moral predicament without taking them explicitly into account; Hegel tends to identify morality with the standpoint of Kantian moral philosophy (cf. PR §§ 105–108, PhG ¶¶ 596–598, EG §§ 503–512). 'Ethics' or 'ethical life' (*Sittlichkeit*) means something like 'customary morality'. Hegel uses it to refer simultaneously to a system of social institutions (PR § 144) and to the moral attitude of the individual who identifies with and lives them (PR §§ 146–147). Ethical life is supposed to harmonize or reunite what is separated by morality (PR § 141; cf. PR §§ 142–157; PhG ¶¶ 347–357, 438–445; EG §§ 513–516).

§ 35

1 Cf. PR § 5.
2 Cf. PhG ¶¶ 166–167; EG § 424.
3 PhG ¶ 480.

§ 36

1 Cf. the following remark from the *Encyclopaedia*: 'It is a *duty* to possess things as *property*, i.e. to be as a person; which, in the relation of appearance, positing the reference to another person, develops itself into the duty of the *other* to respect my right' (EG § 486R).

§ 37

1 Cf. PR §§ 127–128.

§ 38

1 Compare the following remarks from Hegel's lectures: '"Permitted" means "possible according to right"' (VPR17 45); 'That is permitted

which does not violate my free will; a warrant [*Befugnis*] is that others have to recognize this' (VPR 1, 255).

2 'All commands of right are only prohibitions (except the command "Be a person")' (VPR17 45; cf. PR § 36 and note 1).

§ 40

1 For the traditional division of right into the rights of persons, things, and actions in Roman law, see Justinian, *Institutes* 1.2.12; Justinian, *Digest* 1.5.1, and Gaius, *Institutes* 1.8.

2 Kant, RL § 10, 260. 'Right of things' is the right of ownership over them (RL §§ 11–17); 'right of persons' is the right to a voluntary performance of actions by some person or persons, acquired by contract (RL §§ 18–21); 'personal rights of a real kind' (RL § 22) are rights involved in family relationships: the right of spouses over one another (RL §§ 24–27) and the right of parents over children (RL §§ 28–29).

3 According to one of Hegel's main sources for Roman law: 'In law, man and person are quite distinct. A man is a being who possesses a human body and a mind endowed with reason; a person is a man regarded as having a certain status' (J. G. Heineccius, *Elementa iuris civilis* (*Elements of Civil Law*) (Amstelodami [Amsterdam], 1726), § 75.

4 *Caput* refers to the possession of a certain legal status; a person undergoes *capitis diminutio* when this status is changed or lost, as by being sold into slavery (Justinian, *Institutes* 1.16.1–2; cf. Gaius, *Institutes* 1.160).

5 Perhaps the basis for identifying the right of persons with family law is that in Roman law three things were required for someone to be a 'person': (1) *caput*, or status (see above, note 4), (2) *libertas*, or the capacity to be subject to the rights and obligations of a Roman citizen, and (3) *familia*, or the capacity to be subject to the rights and obligations of membership in a Roman family (Justinian, *Digest* 1.5). But as Hegel was aware, 'person' was sometimes used in a looser sense in Roman law, so that even a slave could sometimes be called a 'person' (PhG ¶ 477; VPG 383/316).

6 Kant, RL §§ 22–30.

7 Kant, RL §§ 18–21.

§ 41

1 Cf. Fichte, GNR 41–44/63–68.

§ 42

1 Cf. PR § 26.

§ 43

1 This is an allusion to Kant's Antinomy of Pure Reason, in which it is argued, for example, that matter is *neither* finitely nor infinitely divisible (A524–532/B552–560). Hegel argues, on the contrary, that matter can be seen as *both* finitely divisible and infinitely divisible in so far as the concept of quantity contains both the determination of discreteness and the determination of continuity (WL v, 216–227/190–199; cf. EL § 100).

§ 44

1 An allusion to Kant's thesis that we can think, but cannot know, things as they are in themselves; cf. PhG ¶ 74, EL § 44.
2 Cf. PhG ¶ 109.

§ 45

1 In other places, Hegel follows Fichte (GNR 130/182) in holding that what turns possession into property is the *recognition* of my possession by other persons (NP 237; VPR17 56–57; EG § 490; cf. PR § 71R).

§ 46

1 An allusion to the struggle over the land reforms carried out by Tiberius Sempronius Gracchus and his brother Gaius Gracchus during the second century B.C. The reforms had to do with the *ager publicus*, or lands obtained by Rome through conquests, and the appropriation of these lands by individuals. Legislation instituted in 133 B.C. by Tiberius Gracchus limited the amount of land an individual could own, providing for the confiscation of excess holdings and their distribution to smaller landholders. The large landed interests arranged for the assassination of Tiberius Gracchus in 133, but the laws were enacted by Gaius Gracchus in 124 (in 121 he was

also murdered). In 111 B.C. the *lex Thoria* annulled many of the Gracchan reforms. Hegel apparently views the Gracchi as asserting the right of the community over the *ager publicus* and their opponents as asserting the right of individuals to appropriate land.

2 An entailment (*fideicommissa*) limits the rights of heirs to dispose of inherited property, requiring them to keep it in the family: 'When it is required, pertaining to a certain parcel of land or to a certain capital, that it should remain in a family either perpetually or for a specified number of generations, this is called a family entailment [*Fideicommiß*]' (*Prussian General Legal Code* of 1794, Part 2, Title 4.2, § 23; cf. Justinian, *Institutes* 2.23, Gaius, *Institutes* 2.246–247). Hegel regards such provisions as undue limitations on the right of private property (cf. PR § 180). But he argues, too, that family property is really common property, with the father acting merely as administrator; this means that Hegel also limits a father's right to bequeath property outside the family, since it is held in common by the family and is not his private property in the first place (PR §§ 178–180).

3 Plato's *Republic* specifies that the guardians' life-style should be governed by the proverb 'all things in common among friends', including wives, children, and property (*Republic* 424a, 449c). The most specific provisions, however, require of the guardians that they live in state-owned quarters, that they possess no money, and that they hold private property 'only if it is necessary' (*Republic* 416e). Later it is claimed, perhaps hyperbolically, that the guardians will own nothing but their own bodies (*Republic* 464d–e). These strictures, however, apply only to the guardians, not to the most numerous class in Plato's state, who have no share in political rule, but are owners of property: 'of land, grand and beautiful houses, and furnishings appropriate to them, gold and silver and all the possessions which are thought to make men happy' (*Republic* 417b). But compare the comments of the Athenian stranger in *Laws* 739b–d:

> You'll find the ideal society and state, and the best code of laws, where the old saying 'friends' property is genuinely shared' is put into practice as widely as possible throughout the entire state. Now I don't know whether in fact this situation – community of wives, children and all property – exists anywhere today, or will ever exist, but at any rate in such a state the notion of 'private property' will have been by hook or by crook completely eliminated from life.
> (Plato, *Laws* 739b–d, tr. T. J. Saunders (Harmondsworth:
> Penguin, 1970), p. 207)

§ 47

1 Cf. EN §§ 337–352; EL §§ 213, 216 and EN § 376; EG § 399.

§ 48

1 T. M. Knox points out that the 'sophistry' condemned here can be found in Luther's treatise *On Christian Liberty* (*Hegel's Philosophy of Right* (Oxford: Oxford University Press, new edition 1967), p. 376). But Hegel's lectures make it plain that he was thinking not of Luther but of August von Rehberg, a critic of the French Revolution (VPR17 55; VPR IV, 196).

2 Cf. WL V, 125–131/117–122.

§ 49

1 Compare the following remarks from Hegel's Heidelberg lectures of 1817–1818:

> The person has one body by nature; human beings have only in the abstract sense *equal right* to the totality of other external things, the earth . . . Each has really an equal right to the whole earth, as some say. Such a distribution has colossal difficulties, and with each newborn [person] the division would have to be taken up once again. Equality is an attribute which expresses an external reference. All have an equal right to the world; but abstract right must realize itself, and in its realization right steps into the sphere of contingency, e.g. of preference, need, and hence into the sphere of inequality. (VPR17 47)

Cf. 'Equal right is a right of inequality in its content, like every right' (Karl Marx, 'Critique of the Gotha Program', *Marx Engels Selected Works* (New York: International Publishers, 1968), p. 324).

2 This requirement is derived from Fichte, for whom its consequences are far from trivial. Fichte maintains that if anyone is propertyless, then he has a right to the property of others: 'Each possesses his civil property only in so far, and on the condition that, all citizens of the state can live from what is theirs; and in so far as they cannot live, it becomes their property' (GNR 213/293; cf. SL 295/311–312). In Fichte's view, the state has both the right and the responsibility to redistribute property so that all its members can carry on a productive life on the basis of what they possess.

§ 50

1 The rule of Roman law is *res nullius occupanti cedit* 'A thing belonging to no one is ceded to the occupant' (Gaius, *Institutes* 2.66). Hegel probably has in mind Fichte's version of the saying: *Res nullius cedit primo occupanti* (GNR 133/185). In Roman law a *res nullius* was not necessarily something which had not yet been appropriated by anyone; it could also be a sacred object, consecrated by pontiffs or by the Church: such objects were regarded as not properly subject to human ownership, and their sale or mortgage was forbidden (Justinian, *Institutes* 2.1.8). Like Kant and Fichte, Hegel rejects the possibility of the latter sort of *res nullius* (Kant, RL § 2, 246–247/52–53; Fichte, GNR 133/185; Hegel, PR § 44; cf. Hegel's views on endowments, § 64A and note 2).

§ 52

1 Cf. Fichte, GNR § 19, 217–219/299–300. Fichte's principal application of the idea is to the ownership of land, implying state dominion over land, along with redistributive responsibilities (see § 49, note 2). At one point, Hegel suggests that it is Fichte's view that the matter of a formed object belongs to God (VPR17 48). But this idea would have been as repugnant to Fichte as to Hegel himself (see § 50, note 1).

§ 53

1 A positive judgement is of the form 'x is F' (e.g. 'the rose is red'); a negative judgement is of the form 'x is not F' (e.g. 'the rose is not red'); an infinite judgement is of the form 'x is non-F', i.e. x has a property which complements F (e.g. 'the rose is some colour other than red') (cf. Kant, *Critique of Pure Reason* A71–73/B97–98). This distinction might be employed, for example, by someone who wants to preserve the law of the excluded middle while denying both the (positive) judgement that the number 7 is blue and the (infinite) judgement that the number 7 is *non*-blue. Such a person could still assert the (negative) judgement that the number 7 is *not* blue, because this does not imply that it is any other colour. Hegel discusses these forms of judgement in WL VI, 311–326/630–643, cf. EL §§ 172–173. Apparently, Hegel thinks that the will's positive judgement on a thing consists in declaring it mine, the will's negative judgement consumes the thing or uses it up, and the will's infinite judgement declares it to be someone else's (cf. § 65A).

§ 55

1 Cf. Fichte, GNR § 19C, 219/306.
2 Both Roman law and the *Prussian General Legal Code* of 1794 provide that the owner of a piece of land becomes proprietor of alluvial deposits, and the owner of an animal becomes proprietor of its off-spring. In Roman law the name for this is *accessio* (Justinian, *Institutes* 2.1.18–37; cf. Gaius, *Institutes* 2.66–79; *Prussian General Legal Code*, Part 1, Title 1; Title 9).

§ 57

1 WL v, 216/190.
2 An 'appearance' for Hegel is an existence (*Existenz*) which issues forth from a ground (WL 124/499; EL § 131). An 'untrue appearance' or 'semblance' (*Schein*) is not something unreal or imaginary, but rather something defective or imperfect, which does not adequately cor-respond to its concept (WL vi, 19–24/395–399). An injustice is in that sense a mere 'untrue appearance' because it is the act of a free person in which the person's particular will is opposed to what is right in itself, and thus at odds with its own concept (PR § 82). In the same way, a slave is the 'untrue appearance' of a human being, since the status of slavery is opposed to the concept of a human being as a free person.
3 PhG ¶¶ 178–196; EG §§ 430–436.

§ 61

1 Cf. PhG ¶¶ 136–139; WL vi, 172–185/518–528; EL §§ 136–141.
2 Cf. Fichte, GNR § 19, 217–219/299–300.

§ 62

1 This paragraph is directed against the feudal conception of 'divided property' which distinguishes the 'supreme proprietor' (the overlord) from the 'utilizing proprietor' (the vassal) (*Prussian General Legal Code*, Part 1, Title 18, § 14).
2 Cf. EG § 408.
3 In Roman law, *res mancipi* are things whose ownership is supposed to be transferred by a formal ceremony of 'mancipation' (included in this category were: land within Italy, slaves, and beasts of burden); *res nec mancipi* are things whose ownership is transferred by simply handing them over to the new owner (Gaius, *Institutes* 2.15–17). *Dominium*

Quiritarium was originally the only type of property formally recognized by Roman law; later it was treated as a higher status of ownership, attributable only to Roman citizens; it was distinguished from *dominium Bonitarium*, an ownership recognized by law despite certain formal defects in the owner's legal title to it (Gaius, *Institutes* 2.40). (Both the distinction between *res mancipi* and *res nec mancipi* and the distinction between quiritarian and bonitarian ownership were abolished by Justinian.) Hegel regards these distinctions as merely matters of positive law, irrelevant to the philosophical science of right.

4 *Dominium directum* is a landlord's ownership of land, while *dominium utile* is the ownership pertaining to the tenant who uses the property. From Kant Hegel derives both the notion of 'co-ownership' (*condominium*) and the distinction between the 'direct owner' (*dominus directus*) and the 'owner for use' (*dominus utilis*) (RL § 17, 270). An emphyteutic contract grants the proprietor the full and unconditional use of a piece of land, either perpetually or for a long period of time, in return for a tithe or rent (Justinian, *Novels* 7.3.1–2; *Digest* 13.7.16.2). Unlike the conceptions of property discussed in note 3, Hegel finds these (feudal) conceptions quite relevant to the philosophical science of right, because he thinks they violate the very concept of property as free and full ownership (see note 1 above).

5 Cf. VPG 31/18; VGP II, 507/III, 10.

§ 63

1 Cf. Hegel's conception of 'measure' (WL V, 387–394/327–332; EL § 107), which seems to be the basis for his treatment of value in this paragraph. Hegel was, however, a student of Adam Smith's *Wealth of Nations*; in his lectures of 1819–1820 he endorses Smith's labour theory of value: 'Manual labour in general, a day's wages, these are the final elements of the price of things in relation to each other' (VPR19 162).

§ 64

1 For some legal rights, a statute of limitations is specified ('prescribed') by law, and the right expires or lapses (*verjährt*) at that time (Justinian, *Digest* 18.1.76). A 'prescriptible' right is one which will be lost after a certain length of time unless it is renewed, especially a right which will be lost if it is not used for a long time. Hegel holds that the fundamental abstract right of persons (which others call 'natural rights' or 'human rights') are 'imprescriptible' (they cannot expire or be lost through disuse or the passage of time) just as they are 'inalienable' (they cannot be given up or bartered away) (see PR § 66).

2 In the Middle Ages, an endowed mass (*missa fundata*) was one common form of 'pious legacy' (*legatum pium*), by which a sum was set aside in perpetuity for the purpose of having masses said regularly on behalf of the soul of the departed. During the English Reformation, and on the continent after the French Revolution, the abolition of such endowments and their appropriation by secular authorities was a prominent feature of anti-ecclesiastical legislation and the secularization of Church property. In Germany, for instance, it was provided for by Article 55 of the Resolutions of the Deputation of the Empire (1803) (see 'Endowment', *The Catholic Encyclopedia* v (New York: Appleton, 1910) pp. 421–422).

§ 65

1 According to Roman law, an owner might abandon (*derelinquiere*) a piece of property by displaying the intention no longer to own it; such a thing then becomes a *res nullius* and can be appropriated by someone else. Such things were distinguished from items thrown overboard in a storm to lighten the vessel, where no intention of abandonment is present (Justinian, *Institutes* 2.1.47–48).

§ 66

1 This is Spinoza's definition of 'substance', or God, with which Hegel wants to equate his conception of the ultimate reality, spirit (cf. PhG ¶ 17).
2 Cf. PhG ¶ 18; EG §§ 381–384.

§ 69

1 Cf. PR § 55R and note 1.
2 Issues concerning the ethics of copyrights were discussed in several places by Kant (RL § 31, 289–291; 'On the Unjust Printing of Books' (1785), GS IX, 77–88; 'On Publishing' (1798), GS IX, 431–438).

§ 70

1 Philosophers of Hegel's time were often troubled by the case of pagan heroes who committed suicide in defiance of Christianity's absolute prohibition against it. According to Greek legend, Heracles, the greatest of all Greek heroes, was given a robe poisoned with the blood of a hydra. It clung to his flesh and caused horrible and incurable

suffering. To escape this Heracles had himself carried to the summit
of Mount Oeta and burned to death on a pyre. After the death of
Pompey, Marcus Porcius Cato (95–46 B.C.) chose to take his own life
rather than be captured by Julius Caesar. Marcus Junius Brutus,
adopted son of Julius Caesar, conspired to murder Caesar and then,
with Cassius, attempted to resist the triumvirs. Defeated by the
armies of Marcus Antonius and Octavianus at the battle of Philippi,
Brutus preferred death to capture, and took his own life by falling on
his sword. In the last analysis, however, Hegel and his contemporaries
generally sided with Christianity even when confronting these cases
(cf. Kant, TL 421–423/84–86 and Fichte, SL 261–267/279–284).
Fichte, however, held that although suicide is contrary to moral duty,
persons have a right over their own lives and the state has no right to
forbid suicide by law (GNR 331/425). Once in his lectures, Kant
appears to admit that in the case of Cato, 'suicide is a virtue', but he
hastens to add that 'this is the only example which has given the world
the opportunity of defending suicide' (Kant, VE 187/149).

§ 71

1 The basis of personhood for Hegel, as for Fichte, is the mutuality of
recognition between free self-consciousnesses (cf. PhG ¶¶ 178–200;
EG §§ 430–437; Fichte, GNR §§ 3–4, 30–56/48–83).

§ 75

1 Roman law treats a contract as an accord of two wills (Justinian, *Digest*
1.12.3), as does Kant (RL § 18, 271). It is from Fichte that Hegel
derives the idea that a contract establishes a 'common will' (GNR
193/211).
2 Hegel alludes to Kant's notorious remark that 'the contract of marriage [is one in which] man and woman will the reciprocal enjoyment
of one another's sexual attributes' (Kant RL § 24, 277–278).
3 Cf. § 258R and note 1. The contractarian tradition in modern political thought includes Hobbes, Locke, and Rousseau, but its most
immediate representative for Hegel was Fichte, GNR § 17, 191–
209/209–233. It is interesting that what Hegel finds most objectionable about this tradition is that it intends to found the state on relations of abstract right, in particular on property relations. This is at
the same time his objection to reactionary absolutism, which treats the
state as the monarch's private property (cf. PR § 258R). Hegel credits

Frederick the Great with overcoming the idea that the state is the monarch's private property (VPR iv, 253).

4 Cf. PR § 162.

§ 77

1 In Roman law, a contract of sale could be voided on the grounds of 'excessive damage' if an item was found to have been sold for less than half its true value (Justinian, *Codex* 4.44.2).

2 In Roman law, a *stipulatio* was a solemn formal promise to perform (Justinian, *Institutes* 3.15; Gaius, *Institutes* 3.92).

3 See PR § 217.

4 Following Justinian, (*Institutes* 3.13), Kant distinguishes 'unilateral contracts' (gifts, A in Hegel's table in § 80) from 'bilateral contracts' (exchanges, B in the table) (Kant, RL § 31, 285).

§ 78

1 Cf. EG §§ 458–459.

§ 79

1 In Roman law a *pactum* (or *pactum nudum*) was an agreement which could be the basis of a legal obligation, but which did not take the form of a legal contract, while a *contractus* was a formal contract (Justinian, *Digest* 2.14). Hegel seems to regard a *pactum* as a declaration of an intention to alienate a thing or put oneself under an obligation in the future, as distinct from a contractual agreement which actually alienates or obligates as of the time of the contract. Only the latter sort of agreement, he thinks, should create an obligation.

2 Fichte's theory of right is based on a sharp distinction between right and morality, involving a strict interpretation of the idea that relations of right have to do only with external actions, and not at all with inner intentions. Hegel interprets this idea as implying that I am obligated only by the external performance of the other. What Fichte actually held in 1793, however, was the highly paradoxical view that not even the performance of a contract by one party obligates the other party to perform, since the performance would rather ground a right of restitution or reparation for losses incurred by the performance, at least until the second party's performance had been completed (Fichte, FR 114). Later Fichte argued on similar grounds that no contract can obligate if it is made simply between the two parties involved in it, because neither can have a sufficient reason to judge

that the other intends to perform, and each has the right to withhold performance indefinitely until such a reason is present (GNR 195/220). This argument forms part of his transcendental deduction of the necessity of a 'union contract' (*Vereinigungsvertrag*), through which individuals establish a real common whole uniting them; only through such a union, he argues, do valid contracts in general become possible (GNR 198–207/223–231).

3 Concerning the 'false infinite', see WL v, 166–171/150–154; EL §§ 94–95.

4 Roman law distinguishes four kinds of contracts, in descending order of explicitness:

  1 *Contractus re*, involving an actual performance, such as the handing over of a thing (*traditio rei*).
  2 *Contractus litteris*, in which the agreement was written down.
  3 *Contractus verbis*, through an explicit oral agreement, such as a stipulation (see § 77, note 2).
  4 *Contractus consensu*, involving a tacit sign of agreement, such as the acceptance of some benefit (e.g. the taking possession of something bought or rented).
    (Justinian, *Institutes* 3.13.2; cf. *Digest* 44.7.1, Gaius, *Institutes* 3.88–89)

§ 80

1 Hegel does indeed follow Kant's table of contracts (RL § 31, 285–286) quite closely. In Kant's taxonomy, Hegel's A1 and A3 are in reverse order; Kant draws no distinction between Hegel's B2α and B2β; but Kant distinguishes *mandatum* as B2γ, instead of leaving it as an afterthought; and under C, Kant distinguishes between (a) a pledge (*pignus*), (b) vouching for the promise of another (*fideiussio*), and (c) giving a personal guarantee for another (*praestatio obsidis*).

2 Under real contracts (*contractus re*, § 79, note 4), Roman law in turn distinguishes four kinds:

  1 *Mutuum*, or loan for consumption, to be repaid in kind (Justinian, *Institutes* 3.14.1). E.g. I borrow a bushel of grain from you, eat it, and give you a different bushel of grain in return. Here the grain was called a *res fungibilis*, because it was a thing on which a claim to a different thing could be founded (see note 6 below.) A *mutuum* was supposed to be a loan without charge (see note 5 below).

2 *Commodatum*, or loan for use only, where the loaned item itself was to be returned (Justinian, *Institutes* 3.14.2). E.g. I borrow your plough, use it, and return the very same plough to you. Here the plough was called a *res non fungibilis* (see note 6 below). Again, the loan was supposed to be free of charge (see note 5 below).

3 *Depositum*, a deposit or bailment, a thing left with someone for safe-keeping (Justinian, *Institutes* 3.14.3).

4 *Pignus*, pledge. A pledge (Lat. *pignus*, Ger. *Pfand*; cf. the English word 'pawn') is a thing used as collateral for a loan, especially when the thing is turned over to the creditor until the loan is repaid. A *pignus* is also a kind of contract, viz. one establishing a certain thing as a pledge (Justinian, *Institutes* 3.14.4). See note 8 below.

3 See note 2 above.

4 Sale (*emptio, venditio*) refers to the transfer of a thing for a specified monetary price (Justinian, *Institutes* 3.23).

5 Strictly speaking, *mutuum* and *commodatum* were supposed to be gratuitous loans; if rent was to be paid, then the loan was called a 'letting' or 'hiring' (*locatio et conductio*) (Justinian, *Institutes* 3.24).

6 A *res fungibilis* is a thing to be returned in kind, as in a *mutuum*, where the thing loaned is intended to be consumed; a *res non fungibilis* is a thing which is to be returned itself, as in a *commodatum* (Justinian, *Digest* 12.1.6) (see note 2 above).

7 Roman law distinguishes three kinds of *locatio*: (a) *locatio conductio rerum*, 'letting for hire of a thing', (b) *locatio conductio operarum*, 'letting for hire of labour', and (c) *locatio conductio operis faciendi*, 'letting for hire of a labour to be done' (Justinian, *Institutes* 3.24, cf. *Digest* 19.2.2). In (b), a person hires out services without reference to the particular labour to be performed, while in (c) the person is hired to perform a specified task.

8 See note 2 above. Hegel, however, treats the pledge not as a specific kind of contract, but as a 'moment which completes a [certain kind of] contract', e.g. a loan.

§ 82

1 See § 57, note 2.

§ 86

1 Again, see § 57, note 2.

§ 88

1 Cf. EL § 173, and PR § 53, note 1. A 'positively infinite judgement' is a judgement which asserts the abstract identity of subject and predicate, e.g. 'a lion is a lion'. A 'negatively infinite judgement' asserts the incompatibility of subject and predicate, e.g. 'the mind is no elephant', 'a lion is no table'. This apparently differs from a simple negative judgement in that it asserts the incompatibility of the subject not merely with a certain specific predicate, but with all predicates of a certain kind. Hegel also compares disease to a negative judgement, because it negates a particular life-function of the organism; but death is like a negatively infinite judgement because it negates the organism's life in its entirety. Hegel regards a civil suit (or unintentional wrong) as like a simple negative judgement which denies a person's right to a particular thing; he says that this is parallel to a judgement such as 'This rose is not red'; a crime, on the other hand, attacks the right of the person in general, and is parallel to the (false) judgement 'This rose has no colour at all' (or, presumably, to the (true) judgement 'The number 7 has no colour at all' (EL § 173A)). Cf. also WL VI, 324–326/641–643.

§ 91

1 Cf. NR 476–480/88–92.

§ 93

1 Cf. VG 100–105/83–89.

§ 94

1 An allusion to Kant's equation of 'right' with 'warrant to use coercion' (RL 232/37).

§ 95

1 WL VI, 324–326/641–643; cf. § 88, note 1.

§ 96

1 There seems little foundation for the claim that the Stoics believed there is only one virtue and one vice. They apparently did hold (with Plato) that the virtues are inseparable from one another:

> Zeno [founder of the Stoic school] admits several virtues, as Plato does, namely prudence, courage, moderation and justice, on the grounds that although inseparable they are distinct and different from one another . . . [The Stoics] say that the virtues are inter-entailing, not only because he who has one has them all but also because he who does any action in accordance with one does so in accordance with them all.
> (Plutarch, *On Stoic Self-Contradictions* 1034C–F, in A. A. Long and D. N. Sedley, *The Hellenistic Philosophers* I
> (Cambridge University Press, 1987), pp. 378–379)

If Hegel is alluding to a Stoic doctrine which might be compared with the notion that all crimes are of equal gravity, then he may be thinking of the Stoic rejection of Aristotle's view that virtue and vice admit of degrees: 'It is their [the Stoics'] doctrine that nothing is in between virtue and vice, though the Peripatetics say that progress is in between these. For as, they say, a stick must be either straight or crooked, so a man must be either just or unjust but not either more just or more unjust, and likewise with the other virtues' (Diogenes Laertius 7.127, in *The Hellenistic Philosophers* I, p. 380).

2 Draco recodified Athenian laws in 621 B.C., with the aim of replacing private vengeance with public justice. The proverbial rigidity and severity of his punishments is probably exaggerated in most accounts, such as Plutarch's description of Solon's reforms of them in 594 B.C.: 'Being once asked why he made death the punishment of most offences, [Draco] replied, "Small ones deserve that, and I have no higher for the greater crimes"' (Plutarch, *Life of Solon* in *Plutarch's Lives*, tr. John Dryden (New York: Random House, 1960), p. 107; cf. Aristotle, *Politics* 2.12.1274b).

3 Roman law distinguishes 'theft' (*furtum*) from 'robbery' (*rapina, vi bona rapta*) which involves the taking of a thing by force (Justinian, *Institutes* 4.1–2). *Furtum*, however, has a much broader meaning than the English 'theft', and includes embezzlement and conversion (*Institutes* 4.1.6), the application of a borrowed item to a use not intended by the lender (*Institutes* 4.1.7) and even the use of one's own property if it has been pledged to another (*Institutes* 4.1.10).

§ 99

1 Hegel may be alluding to the following passage: 'By punishment in the most universal sense is understood an evil [*Übel*] which follows upon an illegal action as such. In so far as such an evil is used for the effecting of future lawful actions or omissions, a punishment in the usual signification is present. A genuine punishment in the usual signification presupposes that the evil is voluntarily [*willkürlich*] combined with the unallowed action toward the end specified' (Ernst Ferdinand Klein (1744–1810), *Grundsätze des gemeinen deutschen und preußischen peinlichen Rechts* (*Principles of Common German and Prussian Penal Law*) (Halle: Hemmende & Schmetzke, 1799), p. 6). Klein was one of the co-authors of the *Prussian General Legal Code* of 1794. Hegel thinks that it is an error to build consequentialist considerations into the very concept of punishment, as Klein suggests here. Instead, Hegel insists that the concept of punishment involves retributive considerations ('wrong and justice'), even if punishment is also used to achieve desirable consequences (such as preventing future violations of law).

2 Paul Johann Anselm Ritter von Feuerbach (1775–1833), father of the Young Hegelian philosopher Ludwig Feuerbach (1804–1872), was author of the influential *Lehrbuch des gemeinen in Deutschland gültigen peinlichen Rechts* (*Textbook of the Penal Law Commonly Valid in Germany*) (1801). He was a proponent of penal reform, best known for successfully implementing the rule *nullum crimen, nulla poena sine lege* ('no crime, no punishment without law') – which restricted the power of courts to administer punishment unless there was a crime and a corresponding punishment for it provided by legal statute. He was also author of the *Bavarian Penal Code* (1813) which, along with the Napoleonic Code, formed the basis of continental penal legislation throughout most of the nineteenth century. His philosophical theory of punishment, based on the idea of a threat published in advance, is found in his *Textbook*: Book 1 ('Philosophical or Universal Part of Penal Law') (5th ed., Giessen: G.F. Heyer, 1812), pp. 13–18.

§ 100

1 Cesare Beccaria (1738–1794), often considered the father of modern criminology, is the most important theorist of penal reform in the eighteenth century. His influence is based almost entirely on his *Dei delitti e delle pene* (*On Crimes and Punishments*) (1764), which was best known in the French translation of the Abbé Morellet (1766). It influenced enlightened sovereigns throughout Europe, including the

Grand Duke Leopold of Tuscany, Frederick the Great of Prussia, Catherine the Great of Russia (who invited Beccaria to reside at her court), and Maria Theresa and Joseph II of Austria. Jeremy Bentham and John Adams were among Beccaria's admirers. Beccaria opposed capital punishment, both on the contractarian ground that citizens cannot be understood to have alienated to the state their right not to be killed, and on the consequentialist ground that life imprisonment is a more effective deterrent than the death penalty. See Beccaria, *On Crimes and Punishments*, tr. Henry Paolucci (Indianapolis: Bobbs-Merrill, 1963), pp. 10–14, 45–53, 62–64.

2 The Emperor Joseph II of Austria (reigned 1765–1790) promulgated a new penal law in 1787 which substituted life imprisonment for the death penalty, but the death penalty was reinstituted in 1795. The death penalty was retained in the French Penal Code of 1791, but only with restrictions and after a long and searching debate.

3 Hegel criticizes the English practice of using the death penalty to punish theft (VPR III, 304–305).

§ 101

1 'Eye for eye, tooth for tooth, hand for hand, foot for foot, burning for burning, wound for wound, stripe for stripe' (Exodus 21:24).

2 See above § 99, note 1.

3 'Dearly beloved, avenge not yourselves, but rather give place unto wrath: for it is written, "Vengeance is mine; I will repay", saith the Lord' (Romans 12:19); cf. 'To me belongeth vengeance, and recompense' (Deuteronomy 32:35).

4 According to Hesiod, the Erinyes (the Furies) were primeval beings, born from the blood of Uranus, who was mutilated by his son Zeus. Their office it was to avenge crime, especially crimes against ties of kinship. ('Eumenides' is a propitiatory name for them, meaning 'the kindly ones'.) They are represented as three winged women, sometimes with snakes about them. Their vengeance against the matricide of Orestes, and their appeasement at the court of Athens through the intercession of Apollo on Orestes' behalf and the final verdict of acquittal by Athena, are the focus of Aeschylus' tragedy *The Eumenides*.

§ 102

1 In Roman law, both theft (*furta*) and robbery (*rapina*) are classed as *crimina privata*, as distinct from *crimina publica* or crimes against the

state (Gaius, *Institutes* 3.182). A civil action for damages could be brought against a thief (Justinian, *Institutes* 4.1.11–15, 4.2, cf. *Digest* 44.7.4, Gaius, *Institutes* 3.182, 4.8). In Jewish law, thefts are punishable by restoration to the victim of more than was stolen; the victim of a theft is permitted to wound or even kill the thief, if the theft occurs at night (if such a killing occurs during the day, it is murder and punishable by death) (Exodus 22:1–4). Blackstone also draws the distinction between private and public crimes (*Commentaries on the Laws of England* III (Chicago: University of Chicago Press, 1979) p. 2).

§ 109

1 The distinction between 'limit' (*Grenze*) and 'restriction' (*Schranke*) occurs as part of Hegel's development of the determination of true infinity out of finitude. See WL v, 142–150/131–138, EL §§ 91–94.

§ 117

1 Without knowing it, Oedipus fulfilled the prophecy that he would kill his father and marry his mother. When he discovered the truth, he blinded himself and left Thebes, arriving at Colonus, near Athens. There he took refuge in the sacred grove of the Furies, under the protection of Theseus, the ruler of Athens (Sophocles, *Oedipus at Colonus*, lines 17–18, 36–45, 920–923). Similarly, after killing his mother, Orestes followed the advice of Apollo and fled from the avenging Eumenides, taking refuge on the Areopagus (or Hill of Ares) in Athens, where he was acquitted in a trial presided over by Athena (Aeschylus, *The Eumenides*, lines 79–84, 235–240, 287–289, 680–710).

§ 118

1 In general, the 'nature' of anything for Hegel is what we grasp from rational reflection upon it and its connection with other things (EL § 23). Accordingly, the nature of an action includes those consequences which rational reflection might have anticipated. 'In general it is important to think about the consequences of an action because in this way one does not stop with the immediate standpoint but goes beyond it. Through a many-sided consideration of the action, one will be led to the nature of the action' (NP 230).

2 Oedipus killed his father and married his mother, but did not believe (and had no reason to believe) that he was committing parricide in the first case or incest in the second; yet he regarded himself as a criminal. Hegel regards this as indicative of the naive simplicity (*Gediegenheit*) of the attitude of Greek ethical life, in which the concept of moral subjectivity had yet to develop (cf. PhG ¶¶ 468–470). Hegel has similar remarks concerning the ancient Greeks' view of responsibility for acts done in madness: 'e.g. Ajax, when he killed the Greeks' cattle and sheep in an insane fury because he had not received the arms of Achilles; he did not attribute the guilt to his insanity, as though in it he were another being, but took the whole action upon himself as its perpetrator and did away with himself from shame' (NP 224).

3 See note 1 above.

§ 119

1 'The distinction between *dolus directus* and *indirectus*, in the sense that, in the latter case, the intention of the agent was not to commit the wrong which resulted, but only a slighter one, is now quite obsolete, though it still obtains in Austria' (Franz Joachim Wilhelm Philipp von Holtzendorff, *Enzyklopädie der Rechtswissenschaft in systematischer und alphabetischer Bearbeitung* 1 (Leipzig: Duncker & Humblot, 1875), p. 402).

2 'Wenn der Stein aus der Hand ist, so ist er des Teufels' (When the stone is out of the hand, it is the devil's); the upper Austrian version of the proverb is: 'Der Stein aus der Hand, ist des Teufels Pfand' (The stone out of the hand is the devil's pawn), see *Deutsches Sprichwörter-Lexicon* IV (Darmstadt: Wissenschaftliche Buchgesellschaft, 1977), pp. 810.151, 809.20, cf. 809.201.

§ 123

1 Cf. EG §§ 478–480.

2 According to Herodotus (whose account cannot be true, since it is chronologically impossible), the Lydian King Croesus asked the Greek sage Solon: 'Who is the happiest man you have ever seen?' The question was rhetorical, since Croesus expected to be told that he himself was the happiest. Solon, however, denied that he could estimate Croesus' happiness until he had seen the end of his life. Life is such a chancy thing, said Solon, that we should call no man happy until he is dead. Solon's caution was confirmed when Croesus was defeated by the Persian King Cyrus. According to Herodotus, Cyrus

was about to have Croesus burned alive, when he was told of Solon's remarks, and (reflecting on his own possible fate) he set Croesus free (Herodotus, *The Histories* 1.30, tr. A. de Sélincourt (Harmondsworth: Penguin, 1954) pp. 23–25; cf. Aristotle, *Nicomachean Ethics* 1.10,1100a10–b7). Compare the following remark from Hegel's lectures of 1822–1823:

> If we consider the history of Greek philosophy, then we find that an [idea of] universal happiness occurred to Solon when he spoke to Croesus. With such a theory of happiness milder mores [*Sitten*] naturally supervene, since you strive after a universal and the power of human nature is broken. Solon also demands of Croesus that happiness is not constituted by what one has right now, but rather by one's whole way of life and death. Solon's thought did not go beyond this happiness.
>
> (VPR III, 144; cf. E G §§ 395A, 396A)

§ 124

1 Compare the following remarks from Hegel's *Encyclopaedia* and the lectures on it:

> A human being – as he is externally, i.e. in his actions (obviously, not in his merely bodily externality), so he is inwardly; and when he is virtuous, moral, etc. *only* inwardly, i.e. *only* in intentions, dispositions, and when his externals are not identical with this, then the one is as hollow and empty as the other.
>
> (EL § 140)

> We are accustomed to say of human beings that everything depends on their essence [*Wesen*] and not on their deeds and conduct. Now in this lies the correct thought that what a human being does should be considered not in its immediacy, but only by means of his inwardness and as a manifestation of that inwardness. But with that thought we must not overlook the point that the essence and also the inward only prove themselves as such by stepping forth into appearance. On the other hand, the appeal which human beings make to inwardness as an essence distinct from the content of their deeds often has the intention of validating their mere subjectivity and in this way of escaping what is valid in and for itself. (EL § 112A)

2 As usual, Hegel's quotation from Schiller is from memory, and not precisely accurate:

Scruples of Conscience
I like to serve my friends, but unfortunately I do it by inclination
And so I am often bothered by the thought that I am not virtuous.

Decision
There is no other way out but this! You must seek to despise
    them
And to do with repugnance what duty bids you.
(Schiller, *Xenien*: 'The Philosophers', see Goethe, *Werke* I, ed.
        Erich Trunz (Munich: Beck, 1982), p. 221; the *Xenien* were
            published jointly by Goethe and Schiller)

3 The French *bon mot* 'No man is a hero to his *valet de chambre*' is usually attributed to Marie de Rabutin-Chantal, Marquise de Sévigné (1626–1696). But the best evidence, a letter by Charlotte Elisabeth Aissé (1695–1733), attributes it to Mme Cornuel (1605–1694): 'I remind you of what Mme Cornuel said, that there is no hero at all for his *valet de chambre*, and no Fathers of the Church for their contemporaries' (*Lettres de Mlle Aissé à Mme Calendrini* (Paris: Stock, Delamain & Boutelleau, 1943), letter of 13 August 1728. The idea, however, was much older: 'Few men have been admired by their domestics' (Montaigne (1533–1592), *Essays* III, 2); when the Macedonian general Antigonus (*c.* 382–301 B.C.), was described by Hermodotus as 'Son of the Sun', he replied: 'My servant is not aware of it' (quoted by Plutarch, *Apothegms*, 'Antigonus'). Hegel was the first to add: 'Yet not because the former is no hero, but rather because the latter is only a *valet de chambre*' (PhG ¶ 665). Goethe used the saying (with a slightly different version of Hegel's wry addition) two years later in the novel *Die Wahlverwandtschaften* (*Elective Affinities*): 'There is, it is said, no hero for his chamber servant. That is only because a hero can be recognized only by a hero. The servant will probably know how to evaluate only his equals' (*Elective Affinities*, Part 5, Chapter 2, Ottilie's diary, Goethe, *Werke* VI, ed. Erich Trunz (Munich: Beck, 1982), p. 398; cf. VG 104/87). The attitude targeted by Hegel's remarks in PR was expressed by Fries in the following passage:

Reflective, living strength of soul gives a human being character; but not yet morality of character . . . Morality of character consists in the will's subjecting itself to the higher law with pure respect. Someone might show reflectiveness, patience and tranquillity, valour and moderation, yet without being led by any idea of the good. Rather, such a reflective steadfastness will be proper to the most dangerous characters in history, who are ruled by crude ambition and lust for power. (Fries, HPP 242)

4 The quotation is from Propertius, *Elegies* 2.10.6. Sextus Aurelius Propertius (*c.* 50–10 B.C.) wrote lyric verse pervaded by a spirit of melancholy, self-absorption, and self-pity, original in its time but later common in Latin elegiac poetry.

§ 126

1 Cf. 'The Law of the Heart', PhG ¶¶ 367–380.
2 Possibly an allusion to Schiller's play *The Robbers* (1781) (Schiller, *Werke* I (Frankfurt: Insel, 1966), pp. 5–130), in which Franz Moor, a young man unjustly deprived of his inheritance, organizes a band of robbers with the aim of fighting tyranny and rectifying injustices. Schiller's play, however, is only the best known example of the type; the motif of the noble-hearted criminal was common in the drama of the German *Sturm und Drang* in the 1770s.
3 According to the story, a scandalmonger attempted to excuse himself to Cardinal Richelieu with this plea, and got this often quoted pithy rejoinder.
4 St Crispin and St Crispinian (third century A.D.) were brothers, converts to Christianity from a noble Roman family. They are the patron saints of cobblers and other leather workers. Hegel's reference here, however, is either obscure or in error; I am unable to locate any source which says anything about their stealing leather for their noble labours. See Sabine Baring-Gould, *Lives of the Saints* (Edinburgh: John Grant, 1914), October, Part 2, pp. 628–630.

§ 127

1 Cf. Kant, RL 235–236/41–42.
2 *Beneficium competentiae* or 'beneficence of need': Under certain provisions deriving from Roman law, a debtor or unsuccessful defendant in a civil action could not be required to pay more than his means permitted (*quantum facere potest*); for example, he could not be deprived of the tools necessary to ply his trade. Cf. Justinian, *Institutes* 4.6.29, 37–38.

§ 130

1 *Fiat justitia, pereat mundus* is attributed to the Holy Roman Emperor Ferdinand I (1503–1564, reigned 1556–1564) (Manlius, *Loci Communes* 2.290). The saying is quoted (with approval) by Kant (EF 378/123); cf. also Kant's infamous remark about the justice of capital punishment for murder: 'If justice should perish, it would no longer be worthwhile for men to remain alive on earth . . . Even if a civil society were to dissolve itself by common agreement of all its members . . . the last murderer remaining in prison must first be executed . . . for if they fail to do so, then they may be regarded as accomplices in this public violation of legal justice' (Kant, RL 332–333/100–102).

§ 132

1 The explicit reference here is to Christian Wolff (see above, § 15, note 1) and his theory of clear and obscure ideas (see Wolff, *Psychologica empirica, Gesammelte Werke* II.5 (Halle, 1962), § 220). Hegel's actual target is probably Fries's account of moral imputability (HPP §§ 48–52). Fries distinguishes between legal and moral imputability (HPP pp. 186–203). Regarding the former, the question is simply whether the agent did the deed intentionally (HPP pp. 189–190); regarding moral responsibility, however, Fries argues that we must distinguish within the agent's character between what comes from nature and what is due to the agent's freedom (HPP pp. 190–191). Fries argues that acts must be judged morally by nothing but the degree to which the decision to perform them is motivated by duty. This motive may sometimes arise from moral *feeling*, which Fries characterizes (in Leibnizian-Wolffian terminology) as 'obscure thought', that is, thought which has not been logically resolved into its rational grounds (HPP pp. 207–208). For Fries, the educability (*Bildungsfähigkeit*) of conscience consists in developing one's thoughts about duty toward clarity, possibly with consequent revisions in what one understands the content of one's duty to be (HPP pp. 208, 210–211, 213–215). Fries does not say that people are responsible only for acts accompanied by such 'clear thoughts', but he apparently does hold that we are not to be blamed for following our sincerely held moral convictions, even if clarification of our moral thoughts would reveal them to be objectively wrong. See below, § 140, note 13.

§ 133

1 Cf. Kant, G 397–400/13–16. Kant's usual expression, however, is 'from duty' [*aus Pflicht*] rather than 'for duty's sake' [*um der Pflicht willen*]. Note also that while Hegel says that duty should be done for duty's sake, he does not insist, as Kant does, that it should be done *only* for duty's sake.

§ 134

1 'Jesus said unto him, "If thou wilt be perfect, go and sell that thou hast, and give to the poor and thou shalt have treasure in heaven: and come and follow me." But when the young man heard that saying, he went away sorrowful: for he had great possessions.' (Matthew 19:20–22; cf. Luke 10:25).

§ 135

1 Cf. PhG ¶¶ 596–631, EG §§ 503–512. Hegel's most extensive critique of Kantian ethics and the alleged 'emptiness' and 'formalism' of its standpoint is NR 459–468/75–83. The same criticisms are presented again in summary form here in PR § 135R and also in PhG ¶¶ 429–437, EL § 54,A and VGP III, 367–369/458–461.

2 'Act only according to that maxim by which you can at the same time will that it should become a universal law' (G 421/39). Kant formulates the same principle in a number of other ways, but never in exactly the words Hegel uses.

§ 136

1 Cf. PhG ¶¶ 632–671.

§ 137

1 Hegel's principal discussion of religious conscience is EG § 552.

§ 138

1 Hegel often ties the rise of moral subjectivity to the decline of ethical life in the ancient world, especially in imperial Rome. He connects it with the rise of Stoicism and the social alienation involved in life under the Roman Imperium (PhG ¶¶ 197–199; VPG 384–385/317–318). But he also suggests that the decline of an ethical life founded

on custom is inevitable, because subjective reflection on the ethical life of custom is inevitable and because such reflection inevitably finds this ethical life limited and hence unsatisfactory (VG 177–180, 71–72/145–147, 62; VPG ii, 286/267).

§ *139*

1 See Genesis 2:8–17, 3:1–19. For Hegel's exegesis of the myth of the Fall, see EL § 24A3; cf. PhG ¶ 775–778.

§ *140*

1 Pascal's *Provincial Letters* (1656) are a polemical contribution to disputes in Catholic moral theology between the Jesuits (members of the Society of Jesus) and the Jansenists (followers of Cornelius Jansenius (1585–1638), Bishop of Ypres in Flanders). Specifically, they are a defence of Antoine Arnauld (1611–1694), who was censured in 1655 for his adherence to certain Jansenist doctrines. The passage quoted by Hegel is an ironic comment on the views expressed in the following excerpts from the writings of various Jesuits:

> For someone to sin and incur guilt before God, he must know that what he intends to do is no good, or at least have doubts or fears on that score.
> [quoted from Father Étienne Beauny, *Summary of Sins* (1633)]

> Anyone with no thought of God, or his sins, or any apprehension of an obligation to perform acts of love toward God, or acts of contrition, has no actual grace to perform these acts; but it is also true that he commits no sin if he omits them.
> [quoted from François Annat, *The Good Faith of the Jansenists* (1655)]

> 1. On the one hand God imparts to the soul a certain love which inclines it toward the thing commanded, and on the other rebellious concupiscence invites it to do the opposite. 2. God inspires the soul with a knowledge of its weakness. 3. God inspires it with knowledge of the physician who is to cure it. 4. God inspires it with the desire to be cured. 5. God inspires it with the desire to pray and implore his help. And unless all these things take place in the soul, the action is not strictly sinful, and cannot be imputed.
> [quoted from Pierre LeMoine, a close associate of Cardinal Richelieu]

Pascal's comment on these views immediately precedes the passage quoted by Hegel:

> Oh Father, what a blessing for some of the people I know! I must bring them along to you. You can hardly have met people with fewer sins, for they never think of God; vice has warped their reason: They have never known their infirmity nor the physician who can cure it. They have never thought of desiring spiritual health, still less of praying God to grant it, so that they are in a state of baptismal innocence according to M. LeMoine. The thought of loving God has never entered their heads, nor that of being contrite for their sins; thus, according to Fr. Annat, they have committed no sin through being without charity or repentance; their life is a continual search for pleasure of every kind, uninterrupted by the slightest twinge of remorse. Such excesses had led me to believe that their damnation was assured; but I learn from you, Father, that these same excesses ensure their salvation . . . I had always thought that the less one thought of God the more sinful one was. But, from what I can see, once one has managed to stop thinking of him altogether the purity of all one's future conduct becomes assured. They will all be damned, these half-sinners . . .
>
> (Blaise Pascal, *The Provincial Letters*, tr. A. J. Krailsheimer (Harmondsworth: Penguin, 1967), pp. 62–65)

2 Luke 23: 34.

3 Aristotle distinguishes actions done 'in ignorance', including those done in rage or drunkenness, from cases of actions 'done by reason of ignorance' or 'caused by ignorance' (of particular circumstances). The latter sort of action is involuntary, but the former is not a case of involuntariness, and the agent is to blame.

4 Aristotle, *Nicomachean Ethics* 3.1.1110b30–1111a21.

5 Aristotle, *Nicomachean Ethics* 3.1.1110b28–30.

6 This is a reference to Fries (see note 13 below and § 132, note 1 above).

7 This is a theological topic also discussed in Pascal's *Provincial Letters*. Catholic and Lutheran theology customarily distinguish 'prevenient grace', which makes the human will free, from 'co-operating grace', which assists in the salvation of those who seek it. Co-operating grace may be either 'efficacious grace' which is so strong that the soul cannot resist it, or it may be of lesser strength and resistible (if accepted, however, the latter is called 'sufficient grace'). The controversy is whether grace is ever 'efficacious', in other words, whether the will retains the freedom to reject co-operating grace. Jesuits were

inclined to answer this question in the affirmative, Jansenists to answer it in the negative. Hegel apparently interprets the issue in terms of the relationship between objective knowledge of the good and subjective conscience; siding with Pascal's Jansenist position (as he has reinterpreted it) Hegel wants to deny that the relation between objective knowledge and subjective conscience is one of separability, indifference and contingency.

8 Cf. PhG ¶¶ 660–666.

9 Probabilism is a Jesuit doctrine, for which Hegel's source is once again Pascal. According to probabilism, we incur no guilt even if we do wrong, so long as the moral opinion according to which we act is 'probable'. Pascal's attack on the doctrine is part of the Jansenist charge that the Jesuits have acquired secular and ecclesiastical influence by sycophancy, adapting their theological and moral advice to the desires and interests of the rich and powerful. To this end, Pascal quotes from various Jesuit fathers the following account of what the 'probability' of a moral opinion consists in:

> An opinion is called probable when it is founded on reasons of some importance. Whence it sometimes happens that one really grave doctor can make an opinion probable . . . You may perhaps doubt whether the authority of one good and learned doctor makes an opinion probable . . . I reply that . . . a probable opinion is one with a basis of some importance. Now the authority of a pious and learned doctor is of no small importance, but rather of great importance . . . Very often [learned doctors] do have different opinions; but that does not matter. Each one makes his own opinion probable and safe . . . One may even do what one thinks lawful according to a probable opinion, although the contrary is more certain . . . It is even lawful to follow the least probable opinion, although it is the least certain . . . A doctor, when consulted, may give advice not merely probable according to his opinion, if it is considered probable by others, but contrary to his opinion, when this view, contrary to his own, happens to prove more favourable and attractive to the person consulting him.   (*Provincial Letters*, pp. 82–84)

10 Cf. GW 426/184–185; PhG ¶ 635.

11 This is probably a reference to Sand's assassination of Kotzebue, see Preface, note 18.

12 The saying 'The end must justify the means' is usually attributed to the English poet Matthew Prior (1664–1721), but cf. ' . . . the line often adopted by strong men in controversy, of justifying the means by the end' (St Jerome (*c.* 342–420), *Epistle* 48).

13 The target of these remarks is Fries. 'The command of duties of virtue commands: to act from respect for the law according to one's conviction of what the duty of virtue requires' (Fries, NKV III, 189). The 'immediate command of virtue' is: 'Give allegiance to your own conviction of duty!' (Fries, HPP 243, cf. HPP 158, 164). Fries distinguishes 'conviction' (*Überzeugung*) from mere 'opinion' (*Meinung*). Conviction is formed by a process of moral education and experience, yet 'not by learning rules but by the exercise of the moral sentiment' (Fries, NKV III, 206–208; cf. Fries, JE 55/23). In fact, Fries insists that to be morally genuine, my conviction must be 'pure' (*lauter*): 'By the virtue of purity I understand a man's truthfulness and sincerity toward himself and in himself' (HPP 344); self-deceiving moral beliefs and rationalizations do not count for Fries as 'pure convictions'. Fries allows us no faculty for the infallible knowledge of our duty. Conscience, he insists, is 'educable' (*bildungsfähig*) (HPP 214); but he still maintains (as did Kant and Fichte before him) that conscience is 'infallible':

> It can easily appear that the doctrine of the infallibility of conscience stands opposed to this doctrine of the educability of conscience. The following should clear this up. For the man who has attained to purity (*Lauterkeit*), conscience is *infallible* according to an identical proposition; for no more can be demanded of any man than that he faithfully follow his *pure* conviction. Now since conscience expresses this conviction, it is always right for every individual man at the given moment. (HPP 214–215)

Cf. also:

> The first law of the philosophical theory of virtue is the good disposition of character: respect for the practical spirit. Correctness of conviction in respect of the command is by contrast only the second law. Hence the first rule by which I should compare the actions of others with the duty of virtue must be distinguished from the rule which tells me what duties are imposed on me. For each can be judged only according to his own conviction, and what it would be wrong to do according to a correct conviction can for the individual be precisely what accords with duty.
> (Fries, NKV III, 190)

> If we wish to pass judgement upon the true worth of someone else's life, we must remember that virtue is not the law. What is important is not the fact that an externally virtuous action has been performed but that virtue has been internally willed and practised . . . If we now ask, 'What then is the good?' only the

431

educated understanding could give a correct reply. The decision is no longer a matter of the will but of insight, so that here even the purest and the best in earthly life could err and be mistaken.

(Fries, JES 49/20, 55/23)

14 Friedrich Heinrich Jacobi (1743–1819) was an influential figure in late eighteenth-century German philosophy. He was a critic of both Enlightenment and German idealist rationalism, advocating a philosophy of faith or intuition which had much in common with the views of Fries which are under attack in PR § 140 (cf. VPG III, 419/511). For this very reason, however, Hegel is anxious to quote Jacobi against Fries. Hegel criticized Jacobi in the 1802 essay *Faith and Knowledge*, but in later years he and Jacobi were on good terms, and Hegel's discussions of Jacobi in his later writings are generally favourable (cf. EL §§ 61–78, VGP 315–329/410–423). Jacobi's remarks refer to the conversion to Roman Catholicism of the poet Count Friedrich Leopold von Stolberg (1750–1819), see § 141, note 1.

15 The most familiar form of this saying is: 'To err is human, to forgive divine' (Alexander Pope, *Essay on Criticism* 2.325). But Pope was alluding either to the anonymous Latin proverb: *Errare humanum est*, or to Plutarch: 'For to err in opinion, though it be not the part of wise men, is at least human' (*Morals: Of Man's Progress in Virtue. Against Colotes*).

16 Hegel is referring to the theory of irony put forward by Friedrich Schlegel (1772–1829), chiefly in the *Lyceum Fragments* (Schlegel, *Kritische Ausgabe*, ed. Ernst Behler, Jean-Jacques Anstett, and Hans Eichner (Munich: Ferdinand Schöningh, 1957ff.), Volume II: Characteristiken und Kritiken I (1966)). The classical definition of irony is that of the Roman rhetorician Quintilian (*c.* A.D. 35–95): a figure of speech in which 'what is to be understood is something contrary to what is said' (Quintilian, *Institutiones oratoriae* 9.22.44). Originally, the Greek term εἰρωνία meant 'dissemblance' or 'deception'; but through the life and image of Socrates, the consummate ironist, its meaning was subtly transformed until 'irony' came to signify (as in Quintilian's later definition) not a dissemblance of one's thought but a special way of expressing it by saying the opposite (see Gregory Vlastos, 'Socratic Irony', *Classical Quarterly* 37 (1987)). As Schlegel understands it, Socratic irony is the essence of artistic communication: '[In irony] everything should be both playful and serious, both frank and obvious and yet deeply hidden' (Schlegel, *Lyceum Fragment* 108). Irony for Schlegel is the form of communication best suited to express a (pantheistic) religious consciousness of 'the infinitely full chaos' whose ineffability makes its adequate expression

impossible in finite terms (*Ideen* § 69, *Kritische Ausgabe* II). 'Irony is, as it were, the ostension (*epideixis*) of infinity, of universality, of the feeling for the universe' (*Kritische Ausgabe* XVIII, 128). '[Socratic irony] contains and arouses a feeling of the irresolvable conflict of the limit-less and the limited, of the impossibility and the necessity of complete communication' (*Lyceum Fragment* 108). '[In irony there is] the mood which surveys everything and rises infinitely above everything that is limited, even above one's own art, virtue or genius' (*Lyceum Fragment* 42).

Hegel insists that Romantic irony is fundamentally different from Socratic irony; he interprets Schlegel's concept of irony not as an expression of the paradoxical human situation confronting the opposi-tion of finite and infinite, but rather (invidiously) as an expression of an extravagant, self-indulgent (even self-deifying) subjectivism. He regards it as one of the (irrational, unserious, unphilosophical) developments of Fichte's philosophy of the abstract subjective 'I' (VGP III, 415–416/507–508). It was this Hegelian image of Schlegel which Kierkegaard was both attacking in *The Concept of Irony* and unfavourably portraying in *Either/Or* I; Schlegel's actual theory of irony, however, seems quite close to the conception of 'indirect com-munication' which Kierkegaard (through the pseudonym of Johannes Climacus) advocated in the *Concluding Unscientific Postscript*. Hegel locates Schlegel at the extreme point where moral subjectivity is transformed into evil; Hegel's and Kierkegaard's images of Schlegel as libertine were always coloured by the associations of his scandalous novel *Lucinde* (see below § 164, note 1). However, Schlegel's portrait of Hegelian philosophy was equally invidious, virtually the mirror image of Hegel's portrait of him. For Schlegel, the Hegelian dialectic was the self-deification of 'the spirit of denial': (see Ernst Behler, 'Friedrich Schlegel und Hegel', *Hegel-Studien* II (1963), p. 243. 'The spirit of denial' (*der Geist, der stets verneint*) is of course Mephistopheles' self-description, in Goethe, *Faust*, Part I, line 1338.)

17 According to Hegel's aesthetics lectures: 'It was Solger and Ludwig Tieck who accepted irony as the highest principle of art' (VA I, 98/93). Karl Wilhelm Ferdinand Solger (1780–1819) was Hegel's colleague in philosophy in Berlin, whose speciality was the philosophy of fine art, especially literature (though he also lectured on ethics and political philosophy). Solger published a lengthy review of Schlegel's reflections on irony in two parts, the first appearing in 1809, the second in 1811. (The text from which Hegel quotes has been photographically reproduced in K. W. F. Solger, *Erwin*, ed. Wolfhart Henckmann (Munich: Wilhelm Funk, 1971) (for the quoted pass-ages, see pp. 407–409).) Ludwig Tieck (1773–1853) was a leading

Romantic poet, novelist, dramatist, and critic; together with Friedrich Schlegel's brother August Wilhelm Schlegel (1767–1845) he produced the definitive German translation of Shakespeare's works.

18 Adolf Müllner (1774–1829), *Die Schuld* (*Guilt*) (1813), a popular melodrama in which the central character murders a man with whose wife he is in love, only to commit suicide when he finds out that the man was his brother (cf. VA III, 537/IV, 311).

19 PhG ¶¶ 733–743.

20 PhG ¶¶ 632–671. The notion of the 'beautiful soul' was common among the Romantics (see § 13, note 2). It was derived from Schiller's treatise *On Grace and Dignity* (1793) and used by Goethe to refer to the aunt of Natalie in *Wilhelm Meister's Apprenticeship* (1795) ('Confessions of a Beautiful Soul', Goethe, *Werke* VII, ed. Erich Trunz (Munich: Beck, 1982), pp. 350, 358; cf. *Iphigenie in Tauris* IV, ii, *Werke* V, p. 48). In his manuscripts of 1797, Hegel himself applies the term (with wholly favourable connotations) to Christ (TJ 349–351/ETW 234– 236). In PhG ¶ 658, it is usually thought to refer to the poet Friedrich von Hardenberg ('Novalis') (1772–1801). In Goethe, Novalis, and PhG ¶ 658 (but not in Schiller or in Hegel's early writings), the term signifies a personality who shuns the active life, since that might defile its inward purity. 'Beauty of soul' (but once again without quietistic connotations) was later to be Fries's term for the chief object of the moral life (HPP § 19). See J. Hyppolite, *Genesis and Structure of Hegel's Phenomenology of Spirit* (Evanston: Northwestern University Press, 1974), pp. 512–517; and E. Hirsch, 'Die Beisetzung der Romantiker in Hegels Phänomenologie', *Deutsche Vierteljahrsschrift für Literaturwissenschaft und Geistesgeschichte* 2 (1924), pp. 510–532. In PhG as in PR, the dialectical inversion of conscience into evil marks the limit of the moral sphere, and its transition into a higher one. In PR this leads to (modern) ethical life as the foundation on which moral subjectivity rests. But in PhG, ethical life was treated as the immediate stage of spirit and identified with ancient Greek culture; morality was the outcome of the historical development which began with ethical life. The discussion of conscience and evil thus led instead to forgiveness and the reconciliation of spirit with itself in the form of religion (PhG ¶¶ 672–683).

21 Hegel regards the Romantics generally as followers of Fichte, carrying a one-sided subjectivistic interpretation of his philosophy to its final extreme (see note 15 above). Under this heading, Hegel includes Friedrich Schlegel (1772–1829), Friedrich Schleiermacher (1768–1834), Friedrich von Hardenberg ('Novalis') (1772–1801), J. F. Fries (1773–1843), Friedrich Bouterwek (1766–1828), and Wilhelm Trau-

gott Krug (1770–1842). In Hegel's opinion, however, these Romantics were not genuine philosophers at all; the first to make a genuine advance beyond Fichte was F. W. J. Schelling (1775–1854) (VGP 415–420/506–512). The definitive discussion of Hegel's relation to the Romantics is Otto Pöggeler, *Hegels Kritik der Romantik* (Bonn: Bouvier, 1956).

§ *141*

1 One convert to Catholicism who caused consternation in Protestant intellectual circles was Count Friedrich Leopold zu Stolberg (see § 140, note 14). Several prominent German Romantics also converted to Roman Catholicism; perhaps the most famous was Friedrich Schlegel (see § 140, notes 16 and 21). The chief motivations of such converts were a hostility to the Protestant de-sacralization of the natural and social worlds, and a rejection of the rationalist ideals of the French Revolution in favour of the security of a faith rooted in institutional tradition and authority. According to some, Hegel himself may have briefly considered converting to Catholicism in 1804 for such reasons (see Clark Butler (ed.), *Hegel: The Letters* (Bloomington: Indiana University Press, 1984), p. 8), but the outcome of this consideration was apparently a reaffirmation of the very things from which the converts to Catholicism wanted to flee.

§ *142*

1 This appears to be an allusion to Aristotle's conception of the unmoved mover, which moves as an object of desire does: 'There is a mover which moves without being moved, being eternal, substance and actuality. And the object of desire and the object of thought move in this way; they move without being moved' (Aristotle, *Metaphysics* 12.7.1072a25). Cf. §§ 152, 258.

§ *144*

1 Antigone justifies her defiance of Creon by appealing to the laws of the gods:

> 'Your edict, King, was strong,
> But all your strength is weakness itself against
> The immortal unrecorded laws of God.

They are not merely now: they were, and shall be,
Operative for ever, beyond man utterly.'

(Sophocles, Antigone, lines 453–457)

Hegel cites the same lines in PhG ¶ 437, VPG 56/38–39.

§ 145

1 The reference to 'waves' may be an allusion to the penultimate stanza of Goethe's poem 'Limitations of Mankind' (Goethe, *Werke* I, ed. Erich Trunz (Munich: Beck, 1982), pp. 146–147).

§ 147

1 Cf. 'He that believeth on the Son of God hath the witness in himself' (1 John 5:10).

§ 148

1 In TL, Kant provides a taxonomy of moral duties under the title *Ethische Elementarlehre* ('ethical theory of elements'); Section Three of Fichte's SL is entitled *Die eigentliche Pflichtenlehre* ('the genuine theory of duties'); Fries introduces Part Two ('The Theory of Virtue') of HPP by referring to its contents also as *Die allgemeine Pflichtenlehre* ('the universal theory of duties').
2 Cf. § 2, note 2.

§ 149

1 Another reference to the French Revolution as the natural outcome of the idea of negative freedom, cf. § 5, note 3.

§ 150

1 Hegel wants to distinguish genuine tragic ethical collisions (PhG ¶¶ 464–475, VA I, 266–283/272–288) from the artificial collisions manufactured by moralizing reflection (PhG ¶ 635, D 89/150, GW 427/184–185).
2 Compare the following comments from Hegel's lectures on aesthetics:

The Greek heroes step forth in a pre-legal age, or they are themselves the founders of states, so that right and social order, law and custom [*Sitte*], proceed from them, and actualize them-

selves as their individual work, remaining connected to them ...
We may add that he was not strictly a moral [*moralisch*] hero, as is
shown by the story about him and the fifty daughters of Thespius,
who were all received by him in one night ... Instead, he appears
as an image of this perfect, self-dependent force and strength of
right and justice, for whose actualization he undertakes countless
tribulations and labours by free choice and his own arbitrary will.

(VA I, 240–241/250)

3 See Aristotle, *Nicomachean Ethics* 1.13.1102a–1103a, 2.6.1106a–
1107b. In his lectures on the history of philosophy, Hegel has the
following to say about Aristotle's conception of virtue:

> Aristotle determines the concept of virtue more precisely by
> distinguishing a rational aspect of the soul from an irrational one;
> in the latter *nous* [reason] is only *dynamei* [potentially] – sensa-
> tions, inclinations, passions, emotions apply to it. In the rational
> side, understanding, wisdom, reflectiveness, knowledge
> [*Kenntnis*] all have their place. But they do not constitute virtue,
> which consists only in the unity of the rational with the irrational
> side. We call it virtue when the passions (inclinations) are so
> related to reason that they do what reason commands. If insight
> (*logos*) is bad or not present at all but passion (inclination, the
> heart) conducts itself well, then goodness of heart [*Gutmütigkeit*]
> may exist, but not virtue, because the ground (*logos*, reason) or
> *nous* is lacking, which is necessary to virtue ... Because the
> virtues, considered as the unity of the desiring, actualizing ele-
> ment with the rational element, have an alogical moment in them,
> [Aristotle] posits their *logos* as a *mean*, so that virtue is a mean
> between two extremes. (VGP II, 222–224/204–206)

§ *151*

1 Cf. 'Custom is almost a second nature' (Plutarch, *Rules for the
Preservation of Health* 18).

§ *152*

1 See § 142, note 1.

§ *153*

1 Elsewhere Hegel attributes this saying to Socrates (VPR II, 568) on
the basis of Xenophon, *Memorabilia* 1.3.1. Diogenes Laertius (8.1.15)
attributes it to Xenophilius the Pythagorean.

2 Rousseau proposes to educate Émile 'as a man' by separating him from the corrupting influences of (modern) society. He distinguishes this from educating someone 'as a citizen' in conformity with the laws of a good state, as could have been done in the ancient world (Rousseau, *Emile*, tr. B. Foxley (New York: Dutton, 1969), p. 8).

§ *161*

1 Cf. EN §§ 367–370.
2 Perhaps an allusion to Samuel Pufendorf, *The Law of Nature and Nations* XVI, ch. 1. Also: 'The chief end of marriage is the generation and bringing up of children' (*Prussian General Legal Code*, Part 2, Title 1, § 1).
3 Cf. § 75, note 2.
4 Cf. below, § 164, note 1.

§ *162*

1 Cf. the following remarks from Hegel's lectures on aesthetics: 'What matters primarily in ancient drama, tragedy and comedy, is what is universal and essential in the end which the individuals achieve . . . In *modern*, Romantic poetry, on the other hand, the primary object is personal passion, whose satisfaction can deal only with a subjective end, and in general the fate of a particular individual and character in special relationships' (VA III, 535–536/IV, 309–310).

§ *163*

1 Cf. EL § 151.
2 In Roman religion, the *penates* were spirits of the cupboard (*penus*); together with the *lares* (spirits of the hearth) they were worshipped as guardians of the house, in rites which focused on the family meal. There were also state *Penates*, however, regarded as protectors of Rome, to whom state officials had to swear an oath.
3 '[Christ] saith unto them, Moses because of the hardness of your hearts suffered you to put away your wives' (Matthew 19:8).

§ *164*

1 In 1798, Friedrich Schlegel began an affair with Dorothea Veit, daughter of the philosopher Moses Mendelssohn and wife of Berlin banker Simon Veit. Late in that year, Dorothea left her husband,

obtaining a divorce in 1799. In the summer of that year, Schlegel published a novel *Lucinde*, chronicling the illicit relationship between Lucinde and her lover Julius. The novel, especially in Julius' somewhat didactic prologue, contains an attack on traditional sexual mores, which condemns marriage without love as mere concubinage, insists on the priority of personal love over public standards of social respectability, blasts the unnatural hypocrisy of the prudery women are expected to show in good society, and, perhaps most significantly, criticizes the one-sidedness of prevailing moral ideals of masculinity and femininity, insisting that for either sex a healthy personality and successful love relationships are possible only if there is a harmonious balance between the active impulses commonly attributed to the masculine and the passive tendencies associated with the feminine. Julius' attack on hypocrisy involves an explicit defence of his own 'effrontery' or 'impertinence' *(Frechheit)*. (See Hans Eichner, *Friedrich Schlegel* (New York: Twayne, 1970), Chapter 4.) Schlegel's views were defended by the anonymous *Letters on Schlegel's 'Lucinde'* (1800), whose real author was the philosopher and theologian Friedrich Schleiermacher. The real-life identities of Lucinde and Julius were well known, and *Lucinde* was widely regarded as obscene; its notoriety followed Schlegel through life (even after he had become grotesquely obese and reactionary). *Lucinde* was a work far ahead of its time, though by the standards of our day, *Lucinde* is not sexually explicit and Schlegel's ideas about love and sex no longer appear radical.

§ 166

1 Cf. PhG ¶¶ 464–468, 473–475 and VA II, 60/II, 215, III, 550/IV, 318. 'Antigone is the most beautiful description of femininity; she holds fast to the bond of the family against the law' (VPR I, 301).

2 Compare the following remarks from Hegel's lectures of 1822–1823:

> The man's dominion is scientific universal cognition, and so art is also the object of the man, for although it is presented in individuality, it is a universal, a universal idea, the imagination inspired by reason, the Idea of a universal. These are the man's provinces. There can be exceptions for individual women, but the exception is not the rule. Women, when they trespass into these provinces, put the provinces themselves in danger.
>
> (VPR III, 525–526)

§ 167

1 Compare the following, from Hegel's lectures of 1818–1819: 'The woman must come into her right just as much as the man. Where [there is] polygamy, [there is] slavery of women' (VPR I, 301).

§ 172

1 In the earliest times, the chief consequence of Roman marriage was that the wife passed *in manum viri* ('into the man's hands'), falling under her husband's *patria potestas* and becoming in effect his property. (This provision seems to have applied to the patrician class only, not to the plebeians.) By the time of the Twelve Tables (*c.* 450 B.C.), if a wife was absent from her husband for three nights in a year, she could avoid becoming an *uxor in manu* by remaining technically a part of her birth family, remaining under her own father's *patria potestas*. Her husband then acquired no right over her property and she was termed a *matrona* rather than a *materfamilias*. Both modes of marriage were considered legal, and coexisted into the era of later Roman law (see Gaius, *Institutes* 1.136). The children of a *matrona* as well as a *materfamilias* were, however, under the *patria potestas* of their father (Justinian, *Digest* 1.16.195.5).

§ 174

1 See § 3, note 15, and § 180, notes 2 and 9.
2 Educating children by teaching them to reason was advocated by John Locke, *Some Thoughts Concerning Education* (1693); this characterization seems to be an allusion to Rousseau's criticism of Locke, in *Emile* tr. B. Foxley (New York: Dutton, 1969), pp. 53–55.
3 Rousseau opposes the policy of making children feel confined by their condition of immaturity and so creating in them a desire to grow up (*Emile*, pp. 42–43).

§ 175

1 Cf. PR § 57.
2 The chief German proponents of the 'play theory' of education were Johann Bernhard Basedow (1723–1790) and Joachim Heinrich Campe (1746–1818). Both are criticized by name elsewhere in Hegel's writings (*Werke* XI, 283, VA I, 384/II, 404, TJ 26/TE 43, VPR I, 306; EG § 396A). Kant endorsed Basedow's methods in his

essays on Basedow's academy, the *Philanthropin* (see GS II, 445–452).

§ 178

1 The 'notion' in question is apparently Fichte's (GNR 367/467). Contrary to what Hegel implies, however, it is not Fichte's doctrine that a deceased person's children usually inherit because they happen to be near by the property when it falls ownerless. Rather, Fichte regards the state as 'the first proprietor' of such things (GNR 257/341); his aim is to give the state maximal discretion to determine matters of inheritance as it sees fit.

§ 180

1 This seems to be a reference to Fichte's actual doctrine, which does indeed hold that the validity of a testamentary disposition is contingent on its recognition by the state (GNR 256–257/340–341).
2 According to the Twelve Tables 4.2, a father has the right to sell his children into slavery, and if they are manumitted, he has the power to sell them again. However, after they are freed for a third time, they cease to be under his *patria potestas*.
3 According to Justinian, *Codex* 12.36, a father has no right over spoils taken by his son in war.
4 See § 172, note 1.
5 See § 3, note 15.
6 Lucian of Samosata (c. A.D. 115–200) was an author of satiric dialogues, including a speech in a law-court by a son who had been twice disinherited by his father (Lucian, 'The Disinherited', *Works* II, tr. H. W. Fowler and F. G. Fowler (Oxford: Clarendon, 1905), pp. 183–201). Similar cases appear in the *Controversiae* of Lucius Annaeus Seneca (called Seneca 'the Elder' or 'the Rhetorician'), father of Seneca the Roman philosopher.
7 In 46 B.C. Marcus Tullius Cicero divorced his wife Terentia and married Publilia, who had been his ward, acquiring her considerable inheritance in the process. His grief upon the death of his beloved daughter Tullia one year later led to a falling out, and the marriage to Publilia also ended in divorce.
8 See § 46, note 2.
9 The *patria potestas* of a Roman father did indeed include the right of life and death (*ius vitae necisque*) over his children. The most famous case of its exercise occurred in 507 B.C. when Lucius Junius Brutus, consul and founder of the Roman Republic, ordered his two sons

Titus and Tiberius to be beheaded before his eyes on account of their conspiracy to restore the Tarquins to power (Livy, *History of Rome* 2.5). This right was affirmed in the Twelve Tables about fifty years later. But it was modified in later Roman law, where the father was permitted to inflict only moderate chastisement (Justinian, *Codex* 4.43.1); following a judgement of Constantine, a father who killed his child could even be sentenced to the same punishment as a parricide (Justinian, *Codex* 9.17.1).

§ 181

1 See EL §§ 131 ff., 142 ff.

§ 183

1 Schiller appears to equate the 'state of necessity' (*Staat der Not*) with the 'natural state', which is 'based on force and not on laws'; this is contrasted with the 'state of reason' or 'state of freedom', founded on a 'moral unity'; the task of humanity is to exchange the state of necessity for the state of freedom (Schiller *Werke* IV (Frankfurt: Insel, 1966), p. 202; Friedrich Schiller, *Letters on the Aesthetic Education of Man*, tr. Reginald Snell (New York: Ungar, 1965), Third and Fourth Letters, pp. 29–34). Like Schiller, Fichte identifies the 'state of necessity' with the existing state, and looks for a gradual progress from it toward the 'rational state' (Fichte, SL 238–239/251–252). Hegel is perhaps implying that these thinkers have viewed the existing state only in its relation to civil society, missing altogether the rational state as it actually is.

§ 184

1 Plato, *Republic* 462a–e, argues that the ideal state should be like an organism; when any one part is pleased or pained, the other parts should share in it, and when one member of the state suffers or rejoices, the whole should suffer or rejoice with him. Hegel rejects *this* application of the organic conception of the state, because it does not provide for the principle of modernity, the principle of subjective freedom, that each individual should have a separate and self-determined life. See above, § 46, note 3, and below, § 185, notes 1–3.

§ 185

1 Concerning property in Plato's state, see § 46, note 3.
2 Along with little or no private property, Plato's guardians are sup-

posed to share wives and children (*Republic* 424a, 449c). Again, it is only the guardian class about which Plato says this; neither private property nor the family are excluded for the majority in Plato's state.

3 Plato's state is founded on the principle that all should do what they are best fitted by nature to do (*Republic* 453b). This principle lies behind the division of the state into rulers, auxiliaries, and farmers or artisans. Within the guardian class, rulers are to be carefully selected and trained from an early age (*Republic* 535a–537d); further, the rulers are responsible for determining in which of the three classes a child should be placed (*Republic* 415a–d). Beyond that, however, Plato does not say how people are supposed to find the particular jobs they are best suited to do, and he neither affirms nor denies that a person's occupation should be a matter of choice for that person.

§ 187

1 A reference to ideas put forward by Jean-Jacques Rousseau in *Discourse on the Arts and Sciences* (1750), *Discourse on the Origin of Inequality* (1755), *Emile* (1762), and other writings.

§ 189

1 Adam Smith (1723–1790), author of *An Inquiry into the Nature and Causes of the Wealth of Nations* (1776); Jean-Baptiste Say (1767–1832), author of *Traité d'économie politique* (1803); David Ricardo (1772–1823), author of *Principles of Political Economy and Taxation* (1817).

§ 194

1 Once again a reference to Rousseau, especially to his account of the innocence, freedom, and contentment of 'natural man' in the first part of *Discourse on the Origin of Inequality* (1755).

§ 195

1 The Cynic school of philosophy was founded in Athens by Antisthenes (born *c.* 440 B.C.), a pupil of Socrates. He taught that happiness consists in virtue and in freedom from excessive desires. The school's most famous representative was Antisthenes' pupil Diogenes of Sinope (4th century B.C.), who lived for a time at Athens but was buried in Corinth. He advocated, and practised, an extreme simplicity in his manner of life; this, along with his blunt, witty contempt for his fellow citizens, as well as for civilized life generally, made him the subject of many amusing anecdotes. Cf. VGP I, 551–560/479–487.

§ *198*

1 Compare the following remarks from Hegel's Jena lectures:

> In the machine, man abolishes his own formal activity and makes [nature] work for him. But this deception, which he perpetrates on nature, takes vengeance on him. The more he takes from nature, the more he subjugates it, the baser he becomes himself. By processing nature through a multitude of machines, he does not abolish the necessity of his own labour; he only pushes it further on, removes it from nature and ceases to relate to it in a living way. Instead he flees from negative life, and that work which is left to him becomes itself machine-like. The amount of labour decreases only for the whole, not for the individual; on the contrary, it is being increased, since the more mechanized labour becomes, the less value it possesses, and the more the individual must toil. (JR I, 237)

> Through the work of the machine, the human being becomes more and more machine-like, dull, spiritless. The spiritual element, the self-conscious plenitude of life, becomes empty activity. The power of the self resides in rich comprehension: this being lost. He can leave some work to the machine; his own doing thus becomes even more formal. His dull work limits him to one point, and labour is the more perfect, the more one-sided it is. (JR I, 232)

§ *199*

1 Perhaps an allusion to the well-known doctrine of Adam Smith that we most successfully procure help from others when we offer them a bargain, enlisting their self-love in our favour (*The Wealth of Nations* I.2 (New York: Random House, 1937), p. 14).

§ *203*

1 Georg Friedrich Creuzer (1771–1858), *Symbolik und Mythologie der alten Völker, besonders der Griechen* (*Symbolism and Mythology of Ancient Peoples, especially the Greeks*) (Leipzig: Leske, 1810–1812), 4 volumes. During Creuzer's lifetime, there was a second edition of this work (1819–1823) and a third (1836–1843).

§ 206

1 When Hegel wrote this, the legal freedom to choose one's occupation was only a little over a decade old in Prussia, and was still a matter of controversy. The *Prussian General Legal Code* of 1794 still provided that people were to belong to the estate into which they were born (Part 1, Title 1, § 6). This was altered through Stein's economic reforms of 1808, many of which were introduced by Theodor von Schön (1773–1856). Motivated by the free-trade doctrines of Adam Smith and the German political economist Christian Jakob Kraus (1753–1807), these reforms abolished serfdom and other hereditary occupational restrictions, together with most guild monopolies. See Friedrich Meinecke, *The Age of German Liberation, 1795–1815* (1906), tr. Peter Paret (Berkeley: University of California Press, 1977), Chapter 5.

2 See above, § 185, note 3. The Indian caste system was codified in the Law of Manu (*c.* 200 A.D.). It regulated the relations between the hereditary castes: the priestly (*brahmin*) caste, the warrior and ruler (*ksatriya*) caste, the agricultural, craftsmanship and trade (*vaisiya*) caste, the labouring (*sudra*) caste, and the 'untouchable' (*chandala*) caste. Cf. VPG 180–185/144–148.

§ 211

1 The most famous treatment of this theme is Sir William Blackstone (1723–1780), *Commentaries on the Laws of England* (1765–1769) (Chicago: Chicago University Press, 1979), 4 volumes. For the relation of *lex scripta* (statute law) to *lex non scripta* (laws given by judicial precedent), see *Commentaries* 1, 63.

2 Compare the following remarks of Francis Bacon concerning the authority of judges to make law:

> Judges ought to remember, that their Office is *Jus dicere* [to pronounce law], and not *Jus dare* [to give law]; to *Interpret Law*, and not to *Make Law*, or *Give Law*. Else it will be like the Authority, claimed by the *Church* of *Rome*; which under pretext of Exposition of Scripture, doth not sticke to Adde and Alter; And to Pronounce that, which they doe not Finde; and by *Shew* of *Antiquitie*, to introduce *Noveltie*.

Francis Bacon, *The Essayes* ed. M. Kiernan, 56: Of Judicature, p. 165

3 The 'law of citations' was promulgated in A.D. 446 by the Emperor Valentinian III (reigned 425–455) and included in the Theodosian Code 1.4.3. According to it, cases were to be decided by citing the five great Roman jurists: Papinian, Paul, Gaius, Ulpian, and Modestin. When these authorities disagreed, the majority was to be favoured; when the authorities were evenly divided, Papinian's opinion was to be preferred to the others.

4 It was the principal thesis of Karl Friedrich von Savigny, *Vom Beruf unserer Zeit für Gesetzgebung und Rechtswissenschaft* (1815) (English translation by Abraham Hayward: *Of the Vocation of our Age for Legislation and Jurisprudence* (New York: Argo, 1975)) that Germans should not follow the French example and codify their law. Savigny was replying to *Über die Notwendigkeit eines allgemeinen bürgerlichen Rechts für Deutschland* (*On the Necessity of a Universal Civil Law for Germany*) (1814) by Hegel's friend Anton Friedrich Justus Thibaut (1772–1840). See § 3, note 4.

5 Cf. § 3, note 2.

§ 214

1 Perhaps an allusion to Deuteronomy 25:1–3.
2 In the German currency of Hegel's time, there were 24 groschen in one dollar (*Reichsthaler*).

§ 215

1 Dionysius I (430–367 B.C.), a man of low birth, commanded the army of the Syracusan republic against the Carthaginian invaders of Sicily in 406. His campaign to drive them out was unsuccessful, but he managed to make an unfavourable peace with them, and in 405 he used his military command to establish himself as tyrant, ruling 405–367. His son, Dionysius II (*c.* 395–343), ruled as tyrant from 367 until 357, when he was deposed by Dion, his uncle and his father's sometime advisor. Dion hoped to re-establish a constitutional government, but he was assassinated in 353, and Dionysius II ruled again until 344. Plato's friendly relations with Dion – and his unsuccessful attempts to reform the rule of Dionysius I and educate Dionysius II – are the main subject of Plato's Epistles 3, 7, and 8. Hegel's reference to 'hanging the laws at such a height that no citizen could read them' is, however, either obscure or misinformed; it is not even clear whether he intends to refer to the father or the son.

2 Hegel may be referring to the *Prussian General Legal Code* of 1794; but his model for 'an orderly and specific legal code' was the Napoleonic Code, which he greatly admired and desired to see imitated in German states. Compare the following remark from Hegel's lectures of 1819–1820:

> Where it was introduced, the Code Napoleon is still recognized as a deed of beneficence. It is at least Napoleon's work that this legal code is complete, even if its material content does not belong to him. It is the bad habit of Germans never to be able to complete anything . . . The Code Napoleon contains those great principles of the freedom of property and the abolition of everything arising from the age of feudalism. (VPR19 172–173)

3 Goethe's *Farbenlehre* (1810), Goethe, *Werke* XIII, ed. Erich Trunz (Munich: Beck, 1982), pp. 314–523; Goethe, *Theory of Colors*, tr. Charles Locke Eastlake (1840) (Cambridge: MIT Press, 1976) was widely read and discussed in Hegel's day, and it attracted some prominent admirers, including both Hegel and Schopenhauer; but it was generally dismissed by the scientific community in its own day and has usually been treated in the same way since then.

§ 216

1 This proverb is best known from its use by Voltaire ('La Begueule, conte morale' (1772), *Œuvres complètes* X (Paris: Garnier, 1877), p. 50):

> Dans ses écrits, un sage Italien
> Dit que le mieux est l'ennemi du bien.
>
> In his writings, a wise Italian
> Says that the better is the enemy of the good.

In his lectures, Hegel uses another proverb to rebut Savigny's argument (see above, § 211, note 4): 'It is the bad habit of Germans never to be able to complete anything. Bad weather is always better than no weather at all' (VPR19 172).

§ 219

1 See above, Preface, note 15; and below PR § 258, note 3.
2 It was only since the time of Stein's reforms (see Preface, note 18) that the system of justice was unified under state control. Before

447

1807, much of Prussia was under the feudal system of 'patrimonial justice'; landowning nobles were empowered to do justice to the peasants who lived on their lands. See Walter Simon, *The Failure of the Prussian Reform Movement, 1807–1819* (Ithaca: Cornell University Press, 1955), pp. 27–29, 94–95.

§ 223

1 The following account of the 'equity court' is given by one legal historian: 'Equity refers to the power of a judge to mitigate the harshness of a statute . . . Equity is, in other words, a limited grant of power to the court to apply principles of fairness in resolving a dispute tried before it' (J. H. Merryman, *The Civil Law Tradition* (Stanford: Stanford University Press, 1985), p. 49). Courts of equity, or 'chancery courts' were an institution in English common law. Unlike Hegel, Kant denied the legitimacy of such courts, on the ground that they violate the republican principle of the separation of powers. It seemed to him that a judge empowered to overrule the provisions of strict justice according to the law was empowered to trespass on the proper functions of the legislator (RL 233–235/39–41). Within the continental law tradition, the majority position on this issue was clearly Kant's:

> German law – like other continental laws – knows no parallel to the two distinctions which are paramount in importance in English law, i.e. the distinction between common law and equity law and between case law and statute law. German has always been one unified system of law in which there was and is neither need nor room for a separate system of equity.
>
> (E. J. Cohn, *Manual of German Law* III (London: British Institute
> of Comparative Law, 1968), p. 3)

Thus Hegel's admission of courts of equity constitutes an (uncharacteristic) preference on his part for British legal institutions over continental ones.

§ 224

1 In the Prussia of Hegel's time, trials were not held in public.

§ 225

1 In the system of Roman law, there were two officials present at a trial: the *magistratus* or magistrate, and the *iudex* or judge. A magistrate was

a legal expert, whose task it was to prepare the *actio*, or formulate the legal question posed by the case. The judge was generally not an expert in the law; it was his job to examine witnesses, determine the facts, and rule on the case in accordance with the legal formula. The pronouncement of a magistrate was called *ius*, while the decision of the *iudex* was called the *iudicium*. After 367 B.C., legal proceedings were under the control of a new class of magistrates, called *praetors*. In early Roman law, only a senator was eligible to be a *iudex*; but with the Gracchan reforms (see § 46, note 1), the task of being a judge passed to the Equestrian Order, a somewhat more numerous body of the Roman nobility. (The Equestrians were so called because they derived from an order of cavalrymen; but in later times they generally had no military connections and were often merchants or financiers.) After the demise of the Republic, eligibility to be a *iudex* was even wider, extending even to some plebeians. The *iudex* was usually selected by mutual agreement of the parties to a case; if they could not agree, the *iudex* was chosen by lot from those eligible. Although in legal matters the *iudex* was to act under the guidance of the magistrate, Hegel is mistaken when he suggests that the authority of the *iudex* was restricted to determining the facts of a case. Hegel's depiction of the two roles is designed to provide a defence of his recommendation that a trial should be presided over by a professional judge, who leaves issues of fact to be decided by a jury.

2 See Blackstone, *Commentaries* IV, p. 333.

§ 227

1 The formula in which a Roman *iudex* pronounced judgement was *ex animi sententia*, meaning (in substance, if not literally) 'upon my conscience and to the best of my belief'.

§ 228

1 Just as trials were not public in Hegel's Prussia (see § 224, note 1) so verdicts were always given by an appointed magistrate or judge. Trial by jury was never part of the Prussian judicial system in Hegel's lifetime. The jury system had earlier been advocated by Anselm Feuerbach (see § 99, note 2), in *Considerations Concerning Jury Courts* (1812). Under Napoleon's rule, jury courts were established in Magdeburg, Hanover, and Westphalia; but they were later abolished (see Eduard Gans, *Naturrecht und Universalrechtsgeschichte*, ed. Manfred Riedel (Stuttgart: Klett-Cotta, 1981), p. 89).

a. The Police

1 Hegel uses the term 'police' (*Polizei*) in what seems to us a very broad sense, defining the term as 'the state, in so far as it relates [*sich bezieht*] to civil society' (VPR19 187); '"Police" is here the most suitable name, even though in ordinary use it has a more limited significance' (VPR iv, 587). The 'police' in this sense includes all the functions of the state which support and regulate the activities of civil society with a view to the welfare of individuals. Thus it includes public works (e.g. highways, harbours, and waterways (VPR iv, 595)), all economic regulatory agencies, and also what we would call the 'welfare' system. In 1820, however, this broad meaning of *Polizei* was not in the least technical or idiosyncratic. The word in German originally had the broad meaning Hegel gives it, and in the *Prussian General Legal Code* of 1794, *Polizei* includes building regulation, fire protection, public health, and relief for the poor. As a consequence, the term *Polizeistaat* was used by Fichte with no derogatory connotations whatever (also occasionally by Hegel with positive connotations). (For Germans of Hegel's day, the meaning of *Polizeistaat* was perhaps closer to our term 'welfare state' than to our term 'police state'.) Only later in the nineteenth century was the meaning of *Polizei* limited to the maintenance of peace and order, 'law enforcement' in a narrower sense (see G. C. von Unruh, 'Polizei, Polizeiwissenschaft und Kameralistik', in K. G. A. Jeserich, Hans Pohl, and G. C. von Unruh (eds.) *Deutsche Verwaltungsgeschichte* i (Stuttgart: Deutsche Verlagsanstalt, 1983), pp. 388–427). In several places, Hegel emphasizes the derivation of the word *Polizei* from the Greek *politeia* ('constitution') along with differences between ancient Greek and modern constitutions which derive from the modern principle of subjective freedom (VPR17 iii, 259, 266, VPR iv, 587; cf. also Fichte, GNR 292–303/374–387, and Hegel's criticisms of him in VPR19 152, VPR iv, 190–191, 617, VPR17 139).

§ 234

1 Obviously, Hegel's view that no sharp line can be drawn between legitimate and illegitimate state interference with individuals is not equivalent to the view that any form of state interference can be justified. Hegel insists that individual freedom from state interference (which he calls 'civil freedom'), along with the freedom to participate in the state (which he calls 'political freedom') are both essential to the health of the economy and the state (VPR17 140–141). For this

reason, he attacks Fichte's insistence that the police should have a right to know at all times who each person on the public street is, and what business he is about (GNR 298/378):

> Fichte's whole state is police ... The police should know of each citizen what he is doing every moment, where he is, but of course his inner life is not to be inspected. If someone buys a knife, the police have to know why, and then follow him around to prevent his stabbing someone to death. A traveller is immediately suspicious, and it is not enough to legitimate him that he have a pass or a mere identity card, the pass has to be his portrait.
>
> (VPR iv, 617)

Hegel insists that, to be consistent, in Fichte's state the police themselves would have to be overseen, leading to an infinite regress of police spies. The only solution, he says, is that 'the universal should be essentially not external but an inward, immanent end, the activity of individuals themselves' (VPR iv, 617). Both Fichte and Hegel insist that the police have no right to enter private dwellings without a special order 'for the internal doings of the family should be unobserved' (VPR17 138; cf. Fichte, GNR 240–242/322–324). Hegel thinks that the police ought not to make its presence obvious: 'It is something equally obnoxious when one sees police officers everywhere ... But [even] the hidden [activities] of the police must have the end that public life should be free' (VPR17 139). Again agreeing with Fichte (GNR 303/386–387), Hegel criticizes the British institution of police spies (VPR17 139).

§ 236

1 Probably an allusion to Fichte. See above § 231, note 1 and § 234, note 1.

§ 240

1 'Amasis [of Egypt] established an admirable custom, which Solon borrowed and introduced at Athens, where it is still preserved; this was that every man once a year should declare before the Nomarch, or provincial governor, the source of his livelihood; failure to do this, or inability to prove that the source was an honest one, was punishable by death' (Herodotus, *The Histories* 2.177, tr. Aubrey de Sélincourt (Harmondsworth: Penguin, 1954), pp. 171–172). Even before 600 B.C., an Athenian citizen was enfranchised at maturity by being

admitted either to a 'clan' (*gene*) or a 'guild' (*orgeones*). Clan membership involved his family's (inalienable) property rights over land, and
signified that the citizen lived by agriculture. Guild membership
signified the citizen's admission to a definite trade or handicraft.
These economic provisions formed the basis of the legal and constitutional reforms of Solon and Cleisthenes (see N. G. L. Hammond, *A
History of Greece* (Oxford: Clarendon Press, 1967), pp. 153–154). In
Fichte's political theory, all citizens are also required to give an
account of their livelihood to the state (GNR § 18,
210–215/289–295).

§ 242

1 Compare the following remark from Hegel's Heidelberg lectures of
1817–1818:

> The beneficent person has the intention of helping others, and
> this depends on his arbitrary will. But in this system of mediation,
> those who care for themselves also care for others. He who pays
> out his money for his needs, gives others his money, but makes it
> a condition of this that they do their duty, that they be
> industrious, and so he gives them a more correct feeling of self
> than the one who gives his money to the poor; for the poor man
> who receives alms does not have a feeling of independence . . . In
> general, the state must prevent general distress through its
> arrangements. A subjective distress can arise, whereby a person's
> disposition is helped through advice and deed; but it is better if
> the state cares for the needs of the individual . . . Subjective
> helping of the poor must be minimized as much as possible,
> because giving subjective help, instead of being useful, can do
> harm. (VPR17 125)

§ 243

1 Hegel distinguishes an 'estate' (*Stand*) from a 'class' (*Klasse*):

> The different *estates* of a state are in general concrete distinc-
> tions, according to which the individuals are divided into classes;
> classes rest chiefly on the *inequality* of wealth, upbringing, and
> education, just as these again rest on inequality of birth, through
> which some individuals receive a kind of activity which is more
> useful for the state than that received by others. (NP 63)

§ 244

1 The problem of poverty in modern civil society plainly disturbed Hegel greatly, and led to thoughts which are not easily reconciled with his generally optimistic attitude toward the ethical prospects of modern civil society. Consider the following remarks from his lectures of 1819–1820:

> The emergence of poverty is in general a consequence of civil society, and on the whole it arises necessarily out of it . . . Poverty is a condition in civil society which is unhappy and forsaken on all sides. The poor are burdened not only by external distress, but also by moral degradation. The poor are for the most part deprived of the consolation of religion; they cannot visit church often, because they have no suitable clothing or must work on Sundays. Further, they must participate in a worship which is chiefly designed for an educated audience. In this connection, Christ said that the Gospel is preached for the poor . . . Equally, the enjoyment of the administration of justice is often made very difficult for them. Their medical care is usually very bad. Even if they receive treatment for actual illnesses, they lack the means necessary for the preservation and care of their health . . .
>
> The poor are subject to yet another division, a division of emotion [*Gemüt*] between them and civil society. The poor man feels excluded and mocked by everyone, and this necessarily gives rise to an inner indignation. He is conscious of himself as an infinite, free being, and thus arises the demand that his external existence should correspond to this consciousness. In civil society it is not only natural distress against which the poor man has to struggle. The poor man is opposed not only by nature, a mere being, but also by my will. The poor man feels as if he were related to an arbitrary will, to human contingency, and in the last analysis what makes him indignant is that he is put into this state of division through an arbitrary will. Self-consciousness appears driven to the point where it no longer has any rights, where freedom has no existence. In this position, where the existence of freedom becomes something wholly contingent, inner indignation is necessary. Because the individual's freedom has no existence, the recognition of universal freedom disappears. From this condition arises that shamelessness that we find in the rabble. A rabble arises chiefly in a developed civil society . . .
>
> Earlier we considered the right of distress [PR § 127] as something referring to a momentary need. Here distress no longer has merely this momentary character. In the emergence of poverty,

the power of particularity comes into existence in opposition to the reality of freedom. That can produce the negatively infinite judgement of the criminal. Of course crime can be punished, but this punishment is only contingent . . . On the one hand, poverty is the ground of the rabble-mentality, the non-recognition of right; on the other hand, the rabble disposition also appears where there is wealth. The rich man thinks that he can buy anything, because he knows himself as the power of the particularity of self-consciousness. Thus wealth can lead to the same mockery and shamelessness that we find in the poor rabble. The disposition of the master over the slave is the same as that of the slave . . . These two sides, poverty and wealth, thus constitute the corruption of civil society.   (VPR19 194–196; cf. VPR I, 322)

§ 247

1 Horace, *Odes* 1.3.

§ 248

1 About thirty years after the independence from Britain of a large part of North America in 1776, Spanish and Portuguese colonies in the New World began a drive for independence, led by Simon Bolivár (1783–1830). These movements achieved success in the years immediately preceding the composition of *The Philosophy of Right*: Ecuador declared its independence from Spain in 1809, followed by Venezuela in 1810, Paraguay in 1811, Mexico in 1813, Argentina in 1816, and Chile in 1818; Brazil declared its independence from Portugal in 1815.

§ 250

1 'Corporation' for Hegel includes not only a society of people sharing the same trade or profession, but any society which is officially recognized by the state but is not itself a part of the political state. Thus Churches (PR § 270R, p. 296) and municipal governments (PR § 288) are also called 'corporations'.

§ 252

1 'Privilege' is a thirteenth-century derivation from the latin *privus* (private, special, particular, or exceptional) and *lex* (law, legal statute):

it originally referred to a legal statute conferring some special right or benefit on a designated individual or individuals.

§ 255

1 See § 199, perhaps also § 184.

2 On the basis of their firm belief in the principle of freedom of enterprise, Stein proposed, and Hardenberg carried into effect (through the edicts of 2 November 1810 and 7 September 1812), the abolition of guild monopolies (see Meinecke, *The Age of German Liberation*, pp. 86–88, and Max Braubach, *Von der französischen Revolution bis zum Wiener Kongreß* (Stuttgart: Klett, 1974), Chapter 17). Though he approves of the abolition of 'the miserable guild system', Hegel plainly has mixed feelings about this development:

> The natural difference between social estates [*Stände*] must not remain merely natural, but must also exist as a universal, so that it can be recognized as a universal. Each in his civil existence (as *bourgeois*) must belong to a determinate estate [*Stand*]. But it must first be determined whether he has the skill and resources for it. These estates, which at first refer only to needs, must become firm corporations. The rational aspect of corporations is that the common interest, this universal, actually exists in a determinate form. According to the principle of atomicity, each cares merely for himself and does not concern himself about anything in common; it is left to each whether he is destined for a certain social estate, without considering the utility of his choice from a political point of view; since, according to those who want it this way, someone whose work no one approves will go into another trade on his own. This principle [of atomicity] gives such a person over to contingency. Our standpoint of reflection, this spirit of atomicity, this spirit of finding your honour in your individuality and not in what is common – this is destructive, and has caused the corporations to fall to pieces.   (VPR17 142–143)

§ 258

1 Jean-Jacques Rousseau, *The Social Contract* (1762); for Fichte's somewhat complex version of social contract theory, see GNR § 17, 191–209/209–233.

2 The French Revolution, see § 5, note 3.
3 Karl Ludwig von Haller (1768–1854), *Restoration of Political Science* (1816–1820; 2nd ed., 1834), 6 volumes. See Preface, note 15. For an account of Haller's political thought, see Robert M. Berdahl, *The Politics of the Prussian Nobility: The Development of a Conservative Ideology, 1770–1848* (Princeton: Princeton University Press, 1988), Chapter 7.
4 In the Holy Roman Empire there evolved during the Middle Ages the institution of the *Reichstag* or Imperial Diet, a council composed exclusively of the nobility, whose function was to advise the emperor. In the thirteenth century it contained two houses, the Council of Electors and the Council of Greater Princes. The so-called Golden Bull of 1356 empowered the Archbishop of Mainz to call the Estates. In 1489 the Imperial Diet came to include representatives of the free imperial cities. It was now organized into three colleges or *curiae*, known as the 'imperial Estates' (*Reichsstände*): (1) the six electors (who chose the emperor); (2) the princes, including prelates, counts, and lords; and (3) municipal representatives of the free cities. See J. Zophy (ed.) *The Holy Roman Empire* (Westport, CT: Greenwood Press, 1980), pp. 108–109. During the eighteenth century there were such Estates assemblies or diets in many of the German states. Like the Imperial Estates they were composed not of elected representatives but of certain members of the nobility and officials from the larger municipalities. Hegel is attempting to see such institutions as precedents for a modern system of representation; in fact, the diets were usually anything but progressive institutions. They often defended their members' own entrenched privileges simultaneously against the centralized sovereign power and against the aspirations of the wider population for political participation. In Hegel's home state of Württemberg, it was such an assembly that in 1816 turned down the king's proposal for a new and comparatively progressive constitution, including genuine representative institutions. Hegel, who favoured the king's proposal, was highly critical of the diet and its fixation on the 'good old law' (L W 493–508/271–284).
5 At Runnymede in 1215 the English barons compelled King John to sign a document guaranteeing baronial privileges against royal incursion. Later, after concluding favourable negotiations with the papal legate Cardinal Pandulph, John succeeded, with papal support, in repudiating the agreement. Subsequent tradition, however, has viewed the Magna Charta as one of the most important documents in English constitutional history, establishing the principle of the supremacy of constitution over king.
6 The English Bill of Rights of 1689, issued by William and Mary after

the expulsion of the Stuart monarchy, recognized certain civil and political rights of British citizens, and established the political supremacy of Parliament.

7 The *Prussian General Legal Code* of 1794 was viewed by many, including Hegel, as an important part of the legacy of Frederick the Great and the Enlightenment: 'Frederick II deserves special mention here, because he grasped in thought the universal end of the state . . . His immortal work was the domestic legal code – the [Prussian] General Code' (VPG 523/441). (Though Frederick died in 1786, the project of legal codification had been initiated by him.) For the same reason, the *General Code* was a common object of attack by Romantic reactionaries, including Haller and Savigny.

§ 259

1 The Holy Alliance was concluded in September 1815 by the three main continental opponents of Napoleonic France: Austria, Russia, and Prussia. It was seen by its enthusiastic supporters, especially Tsar Alexander I, as a pact for the maintenance of permanent peace under Christian principles, as well as for the protection of traditional Christian values against the impious and subversive tendencies of modern times, such as those leading to the French Revolution and the Napoleonic empire.

§ 261

1 See § 3, note 3.
2 See § 30, note 1.
3 See § 137, note 1.

§ 262

1 See also § 206, note 1.
2 See § 185, note 3.

§ 263

1 On the basis of § 256A, the institutions in question are apparently marriage and the corporation. But elsewhere Hegel says that 'the guarantee and actuality of the free whole lies in the institutions of the freedom of the person and property, public laws, a system of justice involving equality, trial by jury, and public trials' (VPR17 271).

§ 269

1 In 503 B.C., a section of the Roman plebeians seceded from the city in protest against patrician privileges. Menenius Agrippa, consul of Rome, is supposed to have persuaded them to return, by telling them a fable: All the members of the body rebel against the belly, accusing it of living idly off their labours; the belly replies that they receive their food only through it. Menenius Agrippa likens the Roman Senate to the belly, and the rebellious plebeians to the members. The original source for this fable is Livy, *History of Rome* 1.2.32, but it is probably best known in Shakespeare's version, *Coriolanus* 1.i.93–151. Hegel also refers to this fable elsewhere (VPG 15/5; VA III, 368/IV, 148).

2 Cf. EL §§ 28–29; VR II, 224/III, 13–14.

§ 270

1 Cf. VR I, 236–246/246–257.
2 Cf. VR I, 373/II, 63, II, 417/II, 94, I, 433/II, 112.
3 Cf. EG §§ 553–555.
4 None of these appear to be direct quotations from anyone. The best known saying expressing a similar idea is St Augustine's *Dilige et quod vis fac*, 'Love and do what you want to' (St Augustine, *In epistolam Ioannis tractatus* 7.8). Hegel himself, in the manuscripts of his Frankfurt period, maintained (in opposition to what he regarded as the spirit of both Judaism and Kantian morality) that Jesus' religion of love transcends and abolishes both duty and the law (TJ 324–326/ETW 213–215).
5 This is another polemic against Fries, whose ethics of conviction (see § 140, note 12) was often given a religious setting.
6 In Hegel's time there was no military conscription in Prussia (see below § 271, note 2). But after it was introduced later in the nineteenth century, religious objections to military service were recognized there, until the time of the Franco-Prussian War.
7 After 1815, there was a resurgence of anti-Semitism in many quarters (not least among the liberal German nationalist wing of the student *Burschenschaften*). More specifically, the 'viewpoint' criticized here is probably that of Hegel's enemy Fries, in his vicious pamphlet of 1816:

> Jews can be *subjects* of our government, but as Jews they can never become *citizens* of our people, for as Jews they want to be a distinct people, and so they necessarily separate themselves from our German national community. Indeed, they form not merely a people, but at the same time they form a *state*. The basic laws of Jewish religion are at the same time the basic laws of their state,

their rabbis are at the same time their chiefs, to whom the people owe the highest reverence and the most blind obedience . . .

Their nationality signifies in itself only their physical origin from a distinct people. Here we have to judge them as favourably as possible. No man who loves justice wants to stand by the proposition that black is the colour of slaves, or any other proposition of that kind. In every civilized state, the same innate rights of a free man, equal protection and equal civil rights, pertain to everyone, whether by origin a Saxon, Wend, or Jew. But let us observe that we may not concede these same innate rights to anyone if he is not ready to fulfil to the state in full measure all the duties of a free man and a citizen. And here, even disregarding religion, state, and trade, and considering their mere derivation, we encounter the first great failing of Jewishness. They have existed for millennia between all other peoples on the earth, and they have cultivated themselves only in becoming rich through bargaining and haggling; they teach this to one another and that is how they preserve the purity of their race . . .

It is not against the *Jews*, our brothers, but against *Jewishness*, that we declare war . . . *Jewishness* is a relic of an earlier, uncivilized age, which must not be merely limited, but wholly extirpated. To improve the civil condition of the *Jews* would be precisely to extirpate *Jewry*, to destroy the society of conniving second-hand street peddlers and tradesmen . . . For the Jews themselves it is of the greatest importance that Jewishness should be made an end of as soon as possible . . .

So the Jewish caste, wherever it has been admitted, has always had over the whole people, above and below, from the highest to the lowest, a frightful demoralizing power. Here is the most important moment of this whole affair: *that this caste should be extirpated root and branch, since of all societies and states, secret or public, it is plainly the most dangerous to the state.*

(Fries, GDJ 3, 12, 10–11, 18)

8 This is a reference to Chancellor Hardenberg's 'Edict Concerning the Civil Relations of the Jews' (11 March 1812), which declared that Jews were to enjoy full equality of civil and political rights in Prussia.

9 Hegel takes this to be the condition of the Christian Middle Ages, cf. PhG ¶¶ 484–487, VPG 385–406/318–336.

10 Giordano Bruno (1548–1600) was an Italian philosopher, condemned by the Church for pantheism and the denial of Church authority. He was declared a heretic and burned at the stake in Rome.

11 Galileo Galilei (1564–1642) defended the Copernican theory that the

earth moves about the sun in his *Dialogue on the Two Chief World Systems* (1632). In 1634 he was called before the Court of the Inquisition and compelled to abjure his doctrine that the earth moves, which had been declared heretical in 1616. With all due deliberate speed in righting the Church's past wrongs, Pope John Paul II reversed the Church's condemnation of the Copernican theory in 1979, admitting that the Church had done Galileo an injustice. Hegel's mention of the cases of Bruno and Galileo may have been occasioned in part by the Roman Church's re-establishment of the Inquisition in both Italy and Spain in 1814.

12 In the concluding section of his treatise *Signatur des Zeitalters* (*Signature of the Age*) (1820–1823), Friedrich Schlegel praises the thinkers of his age who have variously propounded and defended the idea of a 'Christian state, with an absolute monarchical constitution, founded on the institution of the Church' (*Friedrich Schlegel Kritische Ausgabe* VII, p. 561); this seems to be the idea of the 'unification of Church and state' which Hegel has in mind. Schlegel gives chief credit for developing this idea to Adam Müller (1779–1829), *Elemente der Staatskunst* (Berlin: Sander, 1809); others he especially credits are: Louis Gabriel Ambroise, Vicomte Bonald (1754–1840), Karl Ludwig von Haller, Joseph Görres (1776–1848), and Joseph deMaistre (1753–1821).

13 Cf. Aristotle, *Politics* 1.2. 1253a: 'The city has priority over the household and over any individual, for the whole must be prior to the parts. Separate a hand or foot from the whole body and they will no longer be a hand or a foot – except in name, as one might speak of a hand or foot sculptured in stone.'

§ 271

1 Under the Roman Republic, it was customary for a general to have a personal bodyguard, made up of his friends and clients, called his 'praetorians' (from *praetorium*, a Roman army headquarters). Later these private armies grew in size and consisted largely of mercenaries. The resulting system of private armies turned the de facto government of Rome more and more into a military dictatorship, leading to the fall of the Republic and the transition to the Empire, whose rulers often became emperor through their positions of military command.

2 After its humiliating defeat by the French in 1806, the Prussian army was reorganized under Stein's reforms. The directors of the military reforms were August Graf Neidhart von Gneisenau (1760–1831) and Gerhard von Scharnhorst (1755–1813). The plan of the reformers was to end the nobility's exclusive privileges in the officer corps, and

replace an army of mercenaries with a 'citizen army' for which all adult males would be eligible. A system of conscription was to be instituted, and at least minimal military training was to be provided (as Scharnhorst colourfully put it) for 'anyone who can piss against a wall'. The conservative nobility prevented these plans from being carried out, but the political values which lay behind them would naturally be endorsed by those (such as Hegel and Gans) who shared the goals of the reform era. (See Friedrich Meinecke, *The Age of German Liberation 1795–1815* (1906), tr. Peter Paret (Berkeley: University of California Press, 1977), Chapter 5; and Constantin de Grunwald, *Baron Stein: Enemy of Napoleon*, tr. C. F. Atkinson (London: Cape, 1940), Chapter 8, especially pp. 124–131.)

§ 272

1 This is evidently another reference to Fries, whose treatise *The German Federation and German Constitution* advocated 'a pure German Federal state' in the form of 'a republican union' of all German-speaking peoples (Fries, DBS I, 167–168, cf. II, 112).

2 Kant (RL § 49, 316–318/81–84) regarded the separation of executive and legislative powers as the fundamental principle of a republican form of government. The originator of the idea of separation of powers, however, was the constitutional monarchist Montesquieu (see *The Spirit of the Laws* I, 11.6).

3 Universality, particularity, and individuality are the three moments of the concept in Hegel's speculative logic (WL VI, 273–300/600–621; EL §§ 163–165).

4 The French Revolution of 1789, as well as the English Civil War of 1640, involved conflicts between the Crown (the executive) and the Parliament or Estates (the legislative).

§ 273

1 In place of Montesquieu's division of governmental powers into executive, legislative, and judiciary, Hegel constructs his division on the three moments of the concept (see above § 272, notes 2 and 3).

2 For this taxonomy of constitutions, see Aristotle, *Politics* 3.7.1279a and Montesquieu, *The Spirit of the Laws* I, 3.

3 Cf. EL § 99.

4 Fichte firmly believes that there must be a check on the power of the government, but he is equally opposed to any division of powers

within the state. His solution to this dilemma is to devise an institution which he called the 'ephorate'. The ephors ('overseers') are to be a group of the oldest and wisest citizens, chosen by the people. They are to have no governmental power themselves, but they are empowered to dissolve the government at any time and call a convention of the people to sit in judgement on those who had been in charge of it (Fichte GNR 166–178/253–271).

5 Montesquieu, *The Spirit of the Laws* I, 3.3, I, 5.1–7.

6 Montesquieu, *The Spirit of the Laws* I, 11.6.

7 Montesquieu, *The Spirit of the Laws* I, 3.4, I, 5.8.

8 Montesquieu, *The Spirit of the Laws* I, 3.7–10, I, 5.9–12. For Hegel's discussion of 'honour' as the principle of early modern feudal monarchy, see PhG ¶¶ 505–510.

9 Despite his general advocacy of written, codified laws (see PR §§ 211–218), in PR Hegel is silent on the question of whether the constitution should be written. In 1817 Hegel was a supporter of the king's plan for a written constitution in his home state of Württemberg, and criticized those who prevented the plan from being adopted (see LW). In Prussia, too, the issue of a written constitution had been raised. In 1810, and again in 1815, Friedrich Wilhelm III promised in writing that he would draw up a written constitution. In 1819 both Hardenberg and Humboldt drew up constitutional plans (which, especially in their provisions for representative government, both follow the earlier plans devised by Stein and bear a striking resemblance to the political system described in PR). In 1819 conservatives gained ascendancy over the reformers (see Preface, note 18), Humboldt was dismissed and the king's promises for a written constitution (which were opposed by the conservatives) were never fulfilled. Hegel's pronouncements in his lectures on the relation of the constitution to written law and to the legislative power are various and not easily reconciled with each other. Some suggest that the constitution is something beyond written law, and which must always remain so: 'The constitution itself lies outside the legislative power; but in the development of the laws lies also the development of the constitution' (VPR19 259). In other places, however, the constitution is spoken of along with the laws, as one moment of the state:

> In the concept of the state three moments are contained: [1] the universal, rational will, partly as the constitution and the laws of the constitution, partly as the laws in the genuine sense – the constitution itself and the legislative power; [2] . . . the governmental power; [3] . . . the sovereign power. (VPR17 151)

§ 274

1 Napoleon expelled the Bourbons from Spain in 1808 and established his brother Joseph Bonaparte as Spanish monarch under the Constitution of Bayonne. Devised according to Jacobin principles, this constitution gave the king very little power, completely disenfranchised the clergy, and invested chief authority in the Cortes (or Estates), from which the royal ministers were barred (see § 300, note 1). The Constitution of Bayonne was extremely unpopular: the Spaniards had no experience with representative institutions, and no politically educated middle class; they resented the imposition of French ideas on them; they were disoriented by the absence of royal authority in their political life and outraged by the exclusion of the Church from all political influence. Largely through British naval power, the French were driven out of Spain in 1812–1813; the Cortes formulated the equally liberal Constitution of Cadiz, but it was no more favourably received than the Constitution of Bayonne had been, and never really took effect. When the Bourbon King Ferdinand VII was restored in 1814, the people are said to have greeted the event with cries of 'Long live the absolute King!' and 'Down with the Constitution!' It is revealing of Hegel's general political orientation that he regards the Constitution of Bayonne as inherently rational and ascribes its failure solely to the political immaturity of the Spanish nation.

§ 275

1 'The constitution and laws comprise the foundation of the sovereign power, and the sovereign must govern according to them' (VPR17 162).

§ 276

1 See § 269, note 1.

§ 277

1 Under feudal institutions, which still existed in many German states at the end of the eighteenth century, some state functions (e.g. a military command, a magistracy or local administrative authority over a certain territory) were the hereditary property of a noble family. The administrative and military reorganization of the Prussian state under

Stein abolished such functions, replacing them with civil servants appointed by the king. This was achieved chiefly by doing away with the system in which the departments of government were divided along regional lines, and put in the hands of local administrators, replacing it with a system of ministries with nationwide responsibility for specific departments of government (see § 289). The idea that all offices in the state, including that of the sovereign, are private property, was one of the basic principles of Haller's theory of the state (see Preface, note 15 and § 258, note 3). He maintained that the fundamental error of the *Prussian General Legal Code* of 1794 was Frederick the Great's erroneous Enlightenment notion that state officials are 'servants of the state' whose functions are public rather than private property (Haller, *Restauration* I, pp. 181–185).

§ 278

1 Cf. EN § 371.

§ 279

1 Regarding Socrates' *daimon*, see Plato, *Apology* 31. The Greeks sometimes made political decisions based on the advice of oracles (e.g. the oracle of Apollo at Delphi) or on the results of divination, using the entrails of animals or the flight of birds.

§ 280

1 For Hegel's defence of the ontological proof of God's existence against Kant's objections, see EL § 52, VR II, 518–529/III, 416–430.
2 Compare the following remarks from Hegel's Heidelberg lectures of 1817–1818 and his Berlin lectures of 1819–1820: 'The monarch acts only as a subject, and only what is objective in an action can be justified. Hence he is not [to be held] responsible' (VPR17 164).

> Laws and institutions are something in and for themselves, and the monarch does not decide them . . . The responsibility can fall only on the ministers. To be responsible means that actions must be according to the constitution and so on. This objective side pertains to the ministers. The majesty of the monarch is not at all to be held responsible for the actions of the government . . . It is the government which must always finally take up [the people's] thoughts about improving things.   (VPR19 252–253, 246)

These quotations echo the words of Article 13 of the French 'Charte constitutionelle' of 1815: 'The person of the king is inviolable and sacred. His ministers are responsible' (J. Godechot, *Les Constitutions de la France depuis 1789* (Paris: Garnier-Flammarion, 1970), p. 219). This provision was understood in one way by the ultra-royalists and in another by constitutionalists. The ultras took it to mean that the ministers are responsible *to the king*, and the king is utterly inviolable, responsible to no one (but God). Constitutionalists, such as Benjamin Constant (1767–1830), Victor Cousin (1792–1867), Pierre Royer-Collard (1763–1845), and François Guizot (1787–1874), interpreted it as meaning that the ministers are responsible *to the people*, and that since they are, the substantive decision-making powers ought to lie with them; that, in their view, is the price the royalists must pay for the inviolability of the king. Here Hegel is expressing agreement with the constitutionalist interpretation of the principle of sovereign-inviolability and executive-responsibility.

§ 281

1 In Hegel's time, the notion of elective monarchy was associated with the institution of the Holy Roman Emperor, who was chosen by a college of six electors, whose positions were hereditary. Hegel is probably also thinking of the elective monarchy in Poland (VPR19 247; VPG 517/427).

2 The motto of Fries's *The German Federation and German Constitution* (1816) was: 'Frederick [the Great] alone appeared and from the throne declared the sovereign to be the first servant of the state' (Fries, DBS 2). Fries was quoting from August Ludwig Schlözer (1735–1809), *Allgemeine Staatsrechts- und Staatsverfassungslehre* (Göttingen: Vandenhoek & Ruprecht, 1793), p. 29, but Frederick's remark was famous and often quoted (e.g. by Kant, EF 352/101). Hegel denies that 'first servant' is an appropriate title for the sovereign (VPR19 248).

3 See, for example, above PR §§ 182–189.

4 The weakness of the Holy Roman Empire was treated by Hegel in his early untitled manuscript now customarily called 'The German Constitution' (DV). The 'Golden Bull' of 1356 established the system of electors for the Holy Roman Empire. From the time of the election of Charles V in 1519, the emperor had to agree to an 'electoral contract', which involved recognizing the electors' proprietary right in certain offices.

5 Cf. Rousseau's remark: 'I admit that all power comes from God. But all disease also comes from him. Does that mean that it is forbidden to call for a doctor?' (Rousseau, *The Social Contract* I, Ch. 3).

6 After his victories over Prussia and Austria, Napoleon met Tsar Alexander I at Erfurt in October 1808. Representatives of a number of the conquered German states attended, in the hope of gaining concessions from him by adopting the position of dutiful subjects petitioning their sovereign. The quoted remark indicates the manner in which Napoleon rebuffed them.

§ 282

1 Compare the following remark from Hegel's *Phenomenology of Spirit*: 'Spirit, in the absolute certainty of itself, is master over every deed and actuality, and can cast them off, and make them as if they had never happened' (PhG ¶ 667).

§ 283

1 Compare the following remarks from Hegel's Heidelberg lectures of 1817–1818:

> The ministers must be chosen by the sovereign, and he also has to choose all the other officials, but he can arbitrarily dismiss only the former . . . [But] the guarantee of the Estates of the realm in particular requires the monarch to take up suitable subjects, and requires that the ministers be chosen on the basis of talent, virtue, rectitude, and diligence. The Prince Regent [of England, later King George IV, governing during the incompetency of his father George III] who had his friends in the opposition party and his enemies in the ministry, could not, when he took up the regency, make his friends into ministers. Hence the French ministry [in 1817 under King Louis XVIII] is made up of enemies of the royal family, the ultra-royalists. These examples show that the choice of ministers in a well-constituted monarchy is not a matter of the mere arbitrary will of the regent.
>
> (VPR17 166–167)

§ 284

1 Regarding the accountability of executive officials, see above § 280, note 2.

§ 288

1 Here Hegel follows Stein's reforms of 1807–1808, which created local government by municipal councils:

> Local administration was to be the sphere of self-government and elected officials. This innovation could be based on the existing administration of the rural district [*Landkreis*]; [that administrator] was a representative of – and nominated by – the county Estates, and [was] simultaneously a state official by royal appointment.
>
> (Friedrich Meinecke, *The Age of German Liberation, 1795–1815* (1906), p. 74 [English translation amended])

§ 289

1 Again, Hegel's executive is structured according to Stein's reforms:

> Stein demanded the replacement of cabinet government by a ministerial system. He wanted the Council of Ministers to work directly with the king so that major decisions were no longer made in the monarch's office but in council. It is no exaggeration to regard Stein's proposals as a revolt of the senior bureaucracy against the autocratic absolutism in power until then, as a preparation for the eventual transition from absolute to constitutional monarchy . . . He introduced another fundamental change in the position of the ministers: they no longer administered separate provinces but were now responsible for departments that covered the entire state . . . Departmental ministries were established for interior affairs, finance, foreign affairs, war and justice. (Meinecke, *The Age of German Liberation*, pp. 70–72)

2 This is an allusion to Hobbes's description of the state of nature as a 'war of all against all' (Leviathan I, Ch. 13; *De cive*, Preface).

§ 290

1 See § 288, note 1 and § 289, note 1.
2 Elsewhere Hegel also criticizes the French system in which local officials are appointed by the central government (VPG 537/454).

§ 291

1 During Hegel's lifetime, the ministry and highest levels of the civil service and the military were open only to the nobility. Hegel appears to have accepted this situation in some of his early writings (cf. NR 489/99–100). Stein attempted to reform this system, making everyone legally eligible for all state offices; but his proposals were successfully resisted by the nobility. In PR, Hegel evidently favours Stein's plan. In his lectures, Hegel indicates that the 'objective qualifications' are to be determined by examinations: 'The only condition of entry into the universal estate is the proof of one's capacity. Hence examinations must be arranged, in order to prove this capacity' (VPR17 171).

§ 294

1 This closely follows the *Prussian General Legal Code*'s provisions for the rights and duties of civil servants (Part 2, Title 10).

§ 295

1 This is an allusion to the celebrated legal battle involving Arnold the Miller of Züllichau. The Miller was unable to pay his rent after the Count von Schmettau cut off the water to his mill in order to build a fish pond. For several years the Miller was denied justice, until Frederick the Great himself heard his case. He found in the Miller's favour and dismissed three magistrates who had earlier ruled against the Miller.

§ 298

1 This change was effected in the *Prussian General Legal Code*, Part 2, Title 14, § 11. Through an executive order of 1820 the lands were used as collateral for state debt.
2 Before 1495, the Holy Roman Emperor dispensed justice personally through the Imperial Court of Justice (*Reichshofgericht*). In that year the imperial reform movement, led by Archbishop Berthold von Henneberg of Mainz (1484–1504) created the Imperial Cameral Court (*Reichskammergericht*), controlled not by the Emperor Maximilian I (reigned 1493–1519) but by the Imperial Estates (see § 258, note 4). The emperor appointed the chief justice and two presidents, but sixteen associate justices were nominated by the Imperial Estates. By

1648 these associate justices had grown to over fifty in number (see J. Zophy (ed.) *The Holy Roman Empire*, pp. 232–234).

§ 299

1 Such provisions were still included in the *Prussian General Legal Code* of 1794: 'Through investiture the vassal assumes the duty of fealty to the chief proprietor, and the services or other obligations bound up with the possession of the fief' (Part 1, Title 18, § 143).

§ 300

1 Members of the executive were excluded from all legislative functions according to Section 3, § 4 of the French revolutionary constitution of 1791. The rationale for this was Rousseau's insistence that the government, or executive power, which applies the laws to particular cases, should be distinct from the sovereign – the people (or, as the revolutionaries interpreted it, their representatives) – who makes the laws (*Social Contract* III, Ch. 1). Hegel intends the executive to have a share in legislation, not by themselves being members of the Estates (after the English model), but instead by advising on and proposing laws. The Estates, on the other hand, are to be the legislative province exclusively of the private estate (see § 303). In the constitutional proposals for Württemberg, which Hegel favoured, the Crown (through the executive) was to initiate all legislative proposals, but the Estates were to have the power of veto over all legislation affecting personal freedom or property or the constitution; the Estates might, however, submit legislative proposals to the Crown, and if the proposals were rejected, the Crown would have to give reasons for the rejection (LW 470/253). In Wilhelm von Humboldt's 1819 constitutional plan for Prussia, it was similarly provided that only the Crown could initiate legislation, but the Estates were to have the power of veto over legislation generally; there were special provisions regarding consent to taxation by the Estates and for the rejection of a governmental administration by the Estates (cf. below, § 301, note 2) (Wilhelm von Humboldt, 'Denkschrift über Preußens ständische Verfassung (1819)', *Gesammelte Schriften* XII.1, ed. Bruno Gebhardt (Berlin: Behr, 1904), §§ 23–42, pp. 236–243).

2 Cf. § 272R,A.

§ 301

1 In Hegel's day, the voting franchise throughout Europe (where it existed at all) was not only limited to males, but further restricted by

property or occupational qualifications. Among those (such as Hegel) who advocated the introduction of representative institutions where they had not previously existed, all but the most radical favoured such electoral qualifications. In the proposed constitution for Württemberg, for instance, voters had to be twenty-five years of age and have an income of at least 200 guilders from real property (LW 470/253). Hegel supported this provision, regarding the property qualification as 'insignificant' (LW 481/262). Kant argues that eligibility for 'active' citizenship should be restricted to those who are, by occupation, 'their own masters'; this is intended to exclude not only all women and children, but also all servants, wage labourers and tenant farmers (RL § 46, 313–315/78–80). The main reason for all such restrictions on the franchise was the idea that those who are economically dependent on others would therefore be obliged to vote in a manner prescribed by their patrons, and so there would be no point in extending the franchise to them.

2 In his Heidelberg lectures of 1817–1818, Hegel maintains that the government must always have the support of the majority party in the Estates, and that there must also be an opposition party (apparently after the English model):

> Hence there must always be an opposition within the Estates assembly; the ministry must be in the majority in an Estates assembly, but the existence of an opposition is equally necessary . . . If in general the ministry is in the minority, then another ministry must step into the place of this ministry, and it can hold its place only as long as it in general has the majority for it.
>
> (VPR17 187)

§ 302

1 Compare the following remarks from Hegel's *Encyclopaedia*:

> The aggregate of private persons is often spoken of as the 'people': but as such an aggregate it is *vulgus*, not *populus*: and in this regard the principal aim of the state should be that the people should not exist or come to power and action, *as such an aggregate*. That condition of the people is a condition of lawlessness, unethicality, brutishness: in it the people is only a shapeless, wild, blind force.   (EG § 544)

2 Cf. EL § 192.

§ 303

1 In the constitutional projects of Stein, and the later proposal of Wilhelm von Humboldt, representatives were to be deputies of corporations, not of geographical districts (Humboldt, 'Denkschrift', *Gesammelte Schriften* XII.1, §§ 61–62, pp. 252–253). In Hardenberg's constitutional proposal, the deputies to the general Estates were to be chosen from and by the provincial Estates assemblies, but the latter were representatives of corporations (Hardenberg, 'Verfassungsentwurf für Preußen vom 3. Mai 1819 in Form eines Kgl. Kabinetsbefehles', printed in Alfred Stern, *Geschichte Europas 1815–1871* 1 (Berlin: Hertz, 1894), pp. 649–653.) One of Hegel's criticisms of the English system of representation generally, and of the English Reform Bill of 1831 in particular, was the fact that Members of Parliament were elected from geographical districts; there was nothing to ensure that voters would have social or economic solidarity with their representatives. Under these circumstances, Hegel thought, extension of the franchise has chiefly the effect of alienating voters from the political process by making each individual vote that much less significant (RB 113/318).

§ 310

1 In the constitutional proposal for Württemberg, there were no property qualifications for deputies, but eligibility was restricted by age (thirty years minimum) and religion (deputies had to be members of either the Catholic, Lutheran, or Calvinist Churches). Further, Crown officials, clergy, physicians, and lawyers were all barred from serving as deputies (LW 469/252). Hegel does not comment on the age or religious qualifications, but he endorses the occupational restrictions, especially the prohibition against lawyers. He quotes Napoleon's remark that lawyers are 'the people most unfitted to advise on and transact public business' (LW 473/256). Hegel's advocacy of these restrictions and of property qualifications reflects the opinion that deputies to the Estates should be genuine representatives of the people (that is, members of the specific professions and corporations they represent); they should not be professional politicians.

§ 312

1 Like Hegel's theory of representation here, both Hardenberg's and Humboldt's constitutional plans called for a bicameral Estates assembly, with an 'upper house' (analogous to the British House of Lords)

composed of the hereditary nobility (Humboldt, 'Denkschrift', *Gesammelte Schriften* XII.1, 60, p. 252; Hardenberg, 'Verfassungsentwurf', Stern, *Geschichte Europas* I, p. 650). The constitutional proposal for Württemberg, however, was unicameral; it provided fifty-three seats for the nobility and seventy-three for elected representatives (LW 471/254).

§ 317

1 Ariosto, *Orlando furioso* 28.1.
2 The quotation is from Goethe, 'Sprichwörtlich', *Goethes poetische Werke* I (Stuttgart: Cotta, 1959), p. 441:

> What should I say?
> The masses can fight, anyway.
> At that, at least, they are respectable.
> But at judging, they are miserable.

3 In 1780, Frederick the Great proposed as the theme of an essay competition whether it could ever be *useful* for a ruler to deceive the people.

§ 318

1 Compare the following remarks from Hegel's lectures on world history:

> The spirit's inward development has outgrown the world it inhabits, and it is about to progress beyond it. Its self-consciousness no longer finds satisfaction in the present, but its dissatisfaction has not yet enabled it to discover what it wants . . . World-historical individuals are those who were the first to formulate the desires of their fellows explicitly. (VG 97/84)

§ 319

1 When P R was published, it was subject (under the Carlsbad Decrees) to the censorship from which it here declares that scientific works should be exempt (see Preface, note 18).
2 After a Roman victory, it became customary to hold a 'triumph' (a triumphal procession celebrating the conquest and honouring the general). The most prominent example of what Hegel refers to is Suetonius' description of the behaviour of Julius Caesar's soldiers during his triumph after his victories over Gaul. Caesar had recently given preferments to a man named Nicomedes in gratitude for his sexual favours. During Caesar's triumph, his soldiers are supposed to

have followed his chariot, chanting irreverent verses which comically juxtapose Caesar's glorious conquest with the rather less glorious conquest of Caesar himself by Nicomedes:

Caesar did subdue the Gauls, and him did Nicomedes subdue.
Behold how Caesar triumphs, who did the Gauls subdue.
But Nicomedes does not triumph, though he Caesar did subdue.

(Suetonius, *Gaius Julius Caesar* 49)

§ 322

1 Hegel's high praise for the modern nation state has given him the reputation of being a cultural nationalist. But from what Hegel says here in § 322R, it is clear that despite what both some of his Prussian interpreters and liberal enemies have maintained, he would not have looked favourably on the swallowing up of the smaller German states (including his own homeland of Württemberg) by Prussia, as occurred later in the nineteenth century. Unlike Fries, he did not advocate that the various German nations should form a political union; in fact, he was generally opposed to this. See Franz Rosenzweig, *Hegel und der Staat* II (Berlin: Oldenburg, 1920), p. 168 and Shlomo Avineri, *Hegel's Theory of the Modern State* (Cambridge University Press, 1972), pp. 45–46, 79–80, 240–241. Nevertheless, Hegel's views about the relationship between the cultural and political realms were not inflexible: 'Small states can be united into a larger one, if this larger state formed out of them is well organized' (VPR IV, 732).

§ 324

1 Cf. NR 481/93. The reference to 'perpetual peace' is an allusion to Kant, EF. Hegel's metaphor of the winds over the sea seems also to be an allusion to a remark by the French statesman, economist, and philosopher of history Anne-Robert-Jacques Turgot (1727–1781), whose views concerning the effects of war on human progress were well-known:

War desolates only the frontier of empires; [in war], towns and country places continue to breathe in the bosom of peace; the ties of society unite a greater number of men; the communication of ideas becomes more prompt and further spread; the arts, sciences, and manners make progress at a more rapid rate. Thus like the storm which agitates the waves of the sea, the evils inseparable from revolutions disappear, the good remains and humanity perfects itself.

473

('Discourse at the Sorbonne on the Successive Advancements of the Human Mind' (1750), *Œuvres de Turgot* i, ed. Gustave Schelle (Paris: Alcan, 1913), p. 218)

2 Cf. §§ 334, 337.

3 Perhaps an allusion to the dying words of Shakespeare's King Henry IV, *King Henry IV, Part Two*, iv.v.181–213.

4 See above, § 259, note 1.

§ 326

1 See above, § 271, note 2.

§ 327

1 In 1751, Lord Robert Clive (1725–1774) was besieged in the citadel of Arcot in India. At twenty-six, he was not an experienced officer and he had only 500 soldiers to defend the citadel against 18,000 men, led by Raja Chandra Sahib, nawab of Carnatic. After fifty days, Clive had only about 320 men left and Raja Sahib decided to storm the fort. After one hour, the attackers retreated, having lost over 400 men, while Clive had lost only six. The siege was then lifted, and Clive had begun making his legendary reputation as a British military hero in India.

§ 328

1 Cf. Hegel's earlier description of war, and the effect of the introduction of firearms on the attitude of soldiers:

> The military estate and war are the actual sacrifice of the self – the danger of death for the individual, his looking at his abstract immediate negativity, just as he is his immediate positive self . . . The end is the maintenance of the totality, against the enemy who is out to destroy it. This externalization must have this same abstract form, must be without individuality – death, coldly received and given, not in a standing fight where each individual looks his opponent in the eye and kills him out of immediate hatred, but instead by giving and receiving death emptily, *impersonally*, out of the smoke of gunpowder. (JR 261–262/171)

§ 329

1 This is probably intended as a rebuttal of Kant's contention that republican governments are most conducive to peace (EF 351/100).

2 William Pitt 'the Younger' (1759–1806) became Prime Minister of England in 1783. Personally, Pitt was initially disposed toward peace with the French Republic, but in 1793, after the execution of Louis XVI, he yielded to popular sentiment (and the urgings of such foes of the Revolution as Edmund Burke). Organizing a coalition of states (including Holland, Spain, and Portugal), he attempted to bring down the revolutionary Republic ('War of the First Coalition'). The coalition soon dissolved, and the war was effectively ended by the Peace of Campo Formio in April 1797 (to which, however, the British were not a party). In 1798 Pitt attempted to assemble a new coalition, enlisting Russia and Austria as allies ('War of the Second Coalition'). But once again the effort was unsuccessful; Russia withdrew in 1799 and Austria agreed to a separate peace at Lunéville in 1801. By that time, Pitt's war policy had become extremely unpopular in England, and he resigned as Prime Minister in 1801.

§ 331

1 On the Peace of Campo Formio, see § 329, note 2.

§ 337

1 For example, by Kant, EF 370–386/116–130, who was himself alluding to Christian Garve, *Abhandlung über die Verbindung der Moral mit der Politik* (*Treatise on the Connection of Morality with Politics*) (1788).

§ 338

1 On this point, Hegel is apparently agreeing with Kant:

No state at war with another shall permit such acts of hostility as would make mutual confidence impossible during a future time of peace. Such acts would include the employment of *assassins* (*percussores*) *or poisoners* (*venefici*), *breach of agreements, the instigation of treason* (*perduellio*) within the enemy state, etc.

(Kant, EF 346/96)

§ 340

1 The dictum *Die Weltgeschichte ist das Weltgericht* ('World history is the world's court of judgement') is often attributed to Hegel himself; but

he is actually quoting it from the penultimate stanza of Schiller's poem 'Resignation' (1794) (Schiller, *Werke* III (Frankfurt: Insel, 1966), pp. 61–62).

§ 343

1 Cf. The following famous passage from Rousseau's second discourse:

> [It is] the faculty of self-perfection, which, by the help of circumstances, gradually develops all the rest of our faculties, and is inherent as much in the species as in the individual. It would be melancholy were we forced to admit that this distinctive and almost unlimited faculty is the source of all human misfortunes; that it is this which, in time, draws man out of his original state, in which he would have spent his days insensibly in peace and innocence; that it is this faculty, which, successively producing in different ages his discoveries and his errors, his vices and his virtues, makes him at length a tyrant both over himself and over nature.
>
> (Rousseau, *Discourse on the Origin of Inequality*, in *The Social Contract and Discourses*, tr. G. D. H. Cole (New York: Dutton, 1950), pp. 208–209)

A less pessimistic estimate of the same trait was provided by a number of thinkers between Rousseau and Hegel. See, for instance, Herder's discussion of the same quality under the name '*Humanität*' – 'the end of human nature [through which] God has put the fate of our race in its own hands' (*Ideas Toward the Philosophy of History of Mankind, Herders Sämtliche Werke*, ed. B. Suphan (Berlin: Weidmann, 1877–1913), XIII, pp. 115–166, XIV, pp. 204–252).

2 Gotthold Ephraim Lessing (1729–1781), 'The Education of the Human Race' (1780), *Lessing's Theological Writings*, tr. Henry Chadwick (Stanford: Stanford University Press, 1967), pp. 82–98.

3 Compare the following remarks from Hegel's lectures on the philosophy of world history and on the *Encyclopaedia*:

> The business of spirit is to produce itself, to make itself its own object, and to gain knowledge of itself; in this way, it exists for itself . . . The spirit produces and realizes itself in the light of its knowledge of itself; it acts in such a way that all its knowledge of itself is also realized. Thus everything depends on spirit's self-awareness; if the spirit knows that it is free, it is altogether different from what it would be without this knowledge . . . The aim of world history, therefore, is that spirit should attain knowledge

of its own true nature, that it should objectivize this knowledge and transform it into a real world, and give itself an objective existence. (VG 56, 74/48, 64)

Know thyself, this absolute commandment, considered either in itself or where its expression first occurred historically, does not have the significance merely of a self-knowledge in respect of the *particular self's* capacities, character, inclinations and weaknesses; rather, its significance is the knowledge of the truth of humanity and the true in and for itself, of the *essence* of spirit . . . The demand for self-knowledge made by the Delphic Apollo on the Greeks thus does not have the meaning of a law imposed on the human spirit externally by an alien power; on the contrary, the god who impels us to self-knowledge is nothing other than the absolute law of spirit itself. (EG § 377,A)

'Know thyself' was the Delphic oracle's injunction to Socrates.

§ 345

1 Compare the following remarks from Hegel's lectures on the philosophy of world history:

World history moves on a higher plane than that to which morality properly belongs, for the sphere of morality is that of private convictions, the conscience of individuals, and their own particular will and mode of action; and the latter have their value, imputation and reward or punishment within themselves. Whatever is required and accomplished by the ultimate end of the spirit, which exists in and for itself, and whatever providence does, transcends the obligations, liability and responsibility which attach to individuality by virtue of its ethical existence. Those who, on ethical grounds (and hence with a noble intention), have resisted what the progress of the Idea of the spirit required, stand higher in moral worth than those whose crimes have been transformed by a higher order into the instruments of realizing its will. But in revolutions of this kind, both parties alike stand within the same circle of corruptible existence, so that it is merely a formal kind of justice, abandoned by the living spirit and by God, which those who have the existing law on their side defend. The deeds of the great men who are the individuals of world history thus appear justified not only in their inner significance (of which the individuals in question are unconscious) but also in a secular sense. But from this latter point of view, no representations should be made against world historical deeds and those who perform them by moral circles to which such individuals do not belong. The litany of private virtues – modesty, humility, charity, liberality, etc. – must not be raised against them. (VG 171/141)

§ 347

1 Compare the following remarks from Hegel's lectures on the philosophy of world history:

The nation must know the universal on which its ethical life is based and before which the particular vanishes away, and it must therefore know the determinations which underlie its justice and religion . . . This spiritual self-consciousness is the nation's supreme achievement . . . The nation now has both a real and an ideal existence. At such a time, we shall therefore find that the nation derives satisfaction from the idea of virtue and from discussion of it – discussion which may either coexist with virtue itself or become a substitute for it. All this is the work of the spirit, which knows how to bring the unreflected – i.e. the merely factual – to the point of reflecting on itself. It thereby becomes conscious to some degree of the limitation of such determinate things as belief, trust and custom, so that the consciousness now has reasons for renouncing the latter and the laws which they impose. This is indeed the inevitable result of any search for reasons . . . This dissolving activity of thought also inevitably gives rise to a new principle . . . Spirit, in its new inward determination, has new interests and ends beyond those which it formerly possessed. (VG 178–180/145–147)

§ 348

1 Cf. VG 96–98/82–84 and § 318, note 1.
2 Compare the following remarks from Hegel's lectures on the philosophy of world history:

[World-historical individuals] cannot be said to have enjoyed what is commonly called happiness . . . It was not happiness that they chose, but exertion, conflict, and labour in the service of their end. And even when they reached their goal, peaceful enjoyment and happiness were not their lot. Their actions are their entire being, and their whole nature and character are determined by their ruling passion. When their end is attained, they fall aside like empty husks . . . They die early like Alexander, are murdered like Caesar, or deported like Napoleon. One may well ask what they gained for themselves. What they gained was that concept or end which they succeeded in realizing. Other kinds of gain, such as peaceful enjoyment, were denied them.

(VG 99/85)

§ 350

1 Cf. § 150, note 2.

§ 355

1 Peter Feddersen Stuhr (1787–1851), under the pseudonym Feodor Eggo, wrote *Untergang der Naturstaaten* (*The Downfall of Natural States*) (Berlin: Salfeld, 1812). This work was a discussion, in the form of letters, of Barthold Georg Niebuhr (1776–1831), *Critical History of Rome* (1811).

§ 358

1 Compare the following remarks from Hegel's lectures on the philosophy of world history:

> External unhappiness has to become a sorrow of the human being within himself: he has to feel himself as the negative of himself, he has to see that his unhappiness is an unhappiness of his nature, that he is within himself a separated and divided being. This vocation of self-chastisement, sorrowing over one's own nothingness, one's own wretchedness, the longing to go beyond this condition of inwardness, is to be sought elsewhere than in the Roman world. This vocation is what gives the *Jewish people* its world-historical significance and importance. For from it the higher [spirit] has arisen, spirit has come to absolute self-consciousness, since it is reflected out of its otherness, which is its division and sorrow.   (VPG 388/321)

2 Hegel's use of 'Germanic' (*germanisch*) is very broad in its reference: it includes 'Germany proper' (*das eigentliche Deutschland*) – which Hegel understands to include the Franks, the Normans, and the peoples of England and Scandinavia (VPG 421/349). But it also encompasses the 'Romanic' peoples of France, Italy, Spain, and Portugal (in which he includes not only the Lombards and Burgundians, but also the Visigoths and Ostrogoths) (VPG 420/348). The Germanic world even includes the Magyars and the Slavs of Eastern Europe (VPG

422/350). But the prominence he gives both to Tacitus' image of the Teutonic character and to the Lutheran Reformation indicates that Hegel gives a prominent role in the development of the modern spirit to German culture in a narrower sense (cf. Tacitus, *Germany* in *Agricola, Germany, Dialogue on Orators*, ed. Herbert W. Benario (Indianapolis: Bobbs-Merrill, 1967), pp. 37–65; DV 465–467/146–150, 532–533/202–203; VPG 494/414).

§ 359

1 Hegel sees the Christian Middle Ages as a time of self-alienation, whose deepest form consists in the sense of separation between the social realm, which is seen as belonging to a fallen world of finitude and evil, and the individual human personality, which is destined for an otherworldly spiritual realm (cf. PhG ¶¶ 487).

§ 360

1 Elsewhere Hegel identifies the French Revolution as the event which 'brings heaven down to earth' (PhG ¶ 581). See § 5, note 3.

Glossary

An asterisk denotes those English terms which are followed, in the text, by the original German term in square brackets. Where the English term in question occurs more than once in any one of Hegel's numbered paragraphs (including its appendages) or in the Preface, the German original is normally supplied only on the first occurrence, unless the interval between occurrences is so long as to justify its repetition.

For further comments on the scope and function of the glossary see p. xli.

Absicht	intention
Aktion	action* [cf. *Handlung*]
allgemein	universal; general
anerkennen	to recognize [cf. *erkennen*]; to acknowledge
Anmerkung	Remarks [Hegel's designation for the indented comments which he appends to many of the numbered paragraphs of his work]
Anschauung	intuition; perception*
Ansehen	authority* [in the sense of 'standing' or 'reputation'; cf. *Autorität, Berechtigung, Macht, Obrigkeit*]
an sich	in itself, in themselves [cf. *für sich, in sich*]; implicitly*; inherently* [cf. *in sich*]
Ansichsein	being-in-itself [cf. *Insichsein*]

481

Arbeit	work; labour
auffassen	to apprehend [cf. *fassen*]; to interpret*
aufheben	to supersede; to cancel*; to annul*; to dissolve*; to overcome* [cf. also comments on p. xlii]
Aufsicht	oversight; supervision
Ausbildung	training*; development* [cf. *Bildung, Entfaltung, Entwicklung*]; construction*
Auskommen	livelihood* [cf. *Subsistenz*]
äußeres Staatsrecht	international law*
Autorität	authority [frequently used by Hegel in general contexts; cf. *Ansehen, Berechtigung, Macht, Obrigkeit*]
Beamte	official; civil servant
Bedeutung	significance [cf. *Gehalt*]; meaning
Bedürfnis	need
begreifen	to comprehend [cf. *erfassen*]; to conceive
Begriff	concept
Behörde	official body
bei sich	with itself, with themselves
Belieben	caprice; discretion; preference
Benutzung	use* [cf. *Gebrauch*]; employment
berechtigt	entitled, authorized; legally recognized*; legitimate* [cf. *richtig*]
Berechtigung	justification [cf. *Rechtfertigung*]; entitlement; authority* [cf. *Ansehen, Autorität, Macht, Obrigkeit*]; legal recognition*; right* [cf. *Recht*]
beschließen	to resolve
beschränkt	limited; circumscribed*
Beschränkung	limitation [cf. *Grenze*]; restriction* [cf. *Schranke*]
Besitz	possession(s)
besonder	particular [cf. *partikular*]; special*
Besonderheit	particularity [cf. *Partikularität*]
bestehen	to subsist; to (continue to) exist* [cf. *existieren, sein*]; to survive*; to consist*
Bestehen	subsistence [cf. *Subsistenz*]; (lasting or

	continued) existence* [cf. *Dasein, Existenz*]; survival*
bestimmen	to determine
bestimmt	determinate; specific; definite
Bestimmtheit	determinacy, determinateness; determinate character
Bestimmung	determination; specification*; definition* [cf. *Definition*]; destiny*; vocation*; purpose* [cf. *Vorsatz*]; function*; role*; factor* [cf. also comment on pp. xxxviii–xxxix]
Beweggrund, Bewegungsgrund	motive* [cf. *Motiv, Trieb, Triebfeder*]
Bewußtsein	consciousness
Beziehung	reference; relation(ship)* [cf. *Relation, Verhältnis*]; relevance*
Bildung	education [cf. *Erziehung*]; culture* [cf. *Kultur*]; development* [cf. *Ausbildung, Entfaltung, Entwicklung*]; formation* [cf. *Gestaltung*]
Boden	soil, land; ground, basis [cf. *Grund*]; sphere* [cf. *Sphäre*]; element* [cf. *Element, Moment*]
böse	evil [adjective]
Böse	evil [noun, of evil in general; cf. *Übel*]
Bürger	citizen
bürgerlich	civil
darstellen	to portray, to depict; to (re)present; to display
Darstellung	description; presentation; expression*
Dasein	existence* [rendered by some translators as 'determinate being'; cf. *Bestehen, Existenz*]
Definition	definition [cf. *Bestimmung*]
Differenz	difference* [cf. *Unterschied, Verschiedenheit*]
Ding	thing* [cf. *Sache*]; object* [cf. *Gegenstand, Objekt*]
Ehre	honour; dignity* [cf. *Würde*]

eigen	own; inherent*; personal*; unique*
eigentlich	proper [usually after noun]; properly; in fact
Eigentum	property; ownership
eigentümlich	distinct(ive), distinguishing; characteristic; peculiar; proper [usually before noun]
Einfall	fancy; notion* [cf. *Vorstellung*]; insight*; (good) idea* [cf. *Idee*]
eingehüllt	[past participle of *einhüllen*, q.v.] invisible*; latent*
Einheit	unit; unity, union
einhüllen	to veil [see also *eingehüllt*]
Einteilung	classification; subdivision(s); division [cf. *Entzweiung, Teilung, Trennung*]
Einzelheit	detail, individuality* [cf. *Individualität*]; individual characteristic*; individual unit*
einzeln	individual [cf. *individuell*]; single; occasional*
(*der*) *Einzelne*	individual* [noun; cf. *Individuum*]
eitel	vain
Eitelkeit	vanity; emptiness*
Element	element [cf. *Boden, Moment*]
Empfindung	sensation; feeling* [cf. *Gefühl*]
entäußern	to alienate [as applied to goods or property], to dispose of [cf. *veräußern*]
Entfalten, Entfaltung	development* [cf. *Ausbildung, Bildung, Entwicklung*]; unfolding
entschließen	[reflexive verb] to decide
Entwicklung	development [cf. *Ausbildung, Bildung, Entfaltung*]
Entzweiung	division [in the sense of splitting asunder or into two opposing parts; cf. *Einteilung, Teilung, Trennung*]
erfassen	to grasp [cf. *fassen*]; to comprehend [cf. *begreifen*]
erkennen	to recognize [cf. *anerkennen*]; to know* [cf. *kennen, wissen*]

Erkennen, Erkenntnis	cognition; recognition; knowledge* [cf. *Kenntnis, Wissen*]
erscheinen	to appear; to seem [cf. *scheinen*]
Erscheinung	appearance; phenomenon* [cf. *Phänomen*]
Erziehung	upbringing; education* [cf. *Bildung*]
Existenz	existence* [cf. *Bestehen, Dasein*]
existieren	to exist [cf. *bestehen, sein*]
Faktum	fact* [cf. *Moment, Tatsache*]
falsch	false [cf. *unwahr*]
Familienrecht	family law
fassen	to grasp [cf. *erfassen*]; to apprehend [cf. *auffassen*]; to understand [cf. *verstehen*]
fordern	to require; to demand
Forderung	requirement; demand
Form	form [cf. *Gestalt*]
formal, formell, förmlich	formal [cf. note to § 8, p. 43]
für sich	for itself, for themselves; in itself, in themselves* [cf. *an sich, in sich*]; independent(ly)*; on its own, on their own*
Fürsichsein	being-for-itself
Fürst	sovereign [cf. *Souverän*]; (sovereign) prince; ruler*
Gattung	genus; generic character*; species* [cf. note to § 161, p. 200]
Gebiet	province; realm* [cf. *Reich*]
gebildet	educated; cultivated*; refined*; civilized*
Gebot	precept; commandment
Gebrauch	use [cf. *Benutzung*]
gediegen	unalloyed; undifferentiated; sound*
Gefühl	feeling [cf. *Empfindung*]
Gegensatz	antithesis; opposite [cf. *Gegenteil*]; opposition; discrepancy
Gegenstand	subject [cf. *Subjekt, Untertan*]; (subject-)

	matter [cf. *Materie, Sache, Stoff*]; object* [cf. *Objekt* and comments on p. xl]
gegenständlich	objective* [cf. *objektiv*]
Gegenteil	opposite [cf. *Gegensatz*]; (the) contrary
Gehalt	import, significance [cf. *Bedeutung*]; content [cf. *Inhalt*]; substance* [cf. *Stoff, Substanz*]
Geist	spirit; intellect*; mind*
geistig	spiritual; intellectual* [cf. *intellektuell*]; mental*
gelten	to be valid, to have validity; to count; to be recognized
Gemeinde	(religious) community
Gemeinschaft, Gemeinwesen	community
Gemüt	emotion(s), emotionality [cf. *Rührung*]; disposition* [cf. *Gesinnung*]; heart* [cf. *Herz*]
Genossenschaft	association; corporation* [cf. *Korporation*]
gerecht	just
Gerechtigkeit	justice [cf. *Recht*]
Gericht	court (of law), lawcourt [cf. *Gerichtshof*]; tribunal; court of judgement*
gerichtlich	court-; legal* [cf. *gesetzlich, gesetzmäßig, rechtlich*]
Gerichtsbarkeit	[power of] jurisdiction [cf. *Rechtsprechen*]
Gerichtshof	court of law, lawcourt [cf. *Gericht*]
Geschäft	business, occupation; function; task
Gesetz	law [cf. *Recht*]
Gesetzbuch	legal code [cf. *Gesetzgebung*]
Gesetzgebung	legislation, legislature; legal code* [cf. *Gesetzbuch*]
gesetzlich	legal [cf. *gerichtlich, gesetzmäßig, rechtlich*]
gesetzmäßig	legal* [cf. *gerichtlich, gesetzlich, rechtlich*]
Gesetztsein	positedness
Gesichtspunkt	viewpoint; point of view [cf. *Standpunkt*]
Gesinnung	disposition [cf. *Gemüt*]; attitude* [cf. *Verhalten*]

Gestalt	shape; figure; form* [cf. *Form*]; guise*; manifestation* [cf. *Manifestation, Scheinen*]
Gestaltung	shape; formation* [cf. *Bildung*]; configuration*
Gewalt	force; power [cf. *Macht*]; violence* [cf. *Gewalttätigkeit*]; coercion* [cf. *Zwang*]
Gewalttätigkeit	violence [cf. *Gewalt*]
Gewerbe	trade (and industry) [cf. *Verkehr*]; profession*
Gewissen	conscience
Gewißheit	certainty
Gewohnheit	habit; practice; custom* [cf. *Sitte*]
Gewohnheitsrecht	customary right, right of custom
Gliederung	articulation
Grenze	bound(ary); limit(ation)* [cf. *Beschränkung, Schranke*]
Grund	ground [cf. *Boden*]; basis [cf. *Boden*]; reason* [as a specific ground or cause; cf. *Vernunft*]; cause* [in the sense of ground or reason; cf. *Sache*]
Gründe	[plural of *Grund*] reasons
Grundlinien	[in title of Hegel's work] elements
Grundsatz	principle [cf. *Prinzip*]; maxim* [cf. *Maxime*]
gültig	valid
Gültigkeit	validity
Handel	commerce [cf. *Verkehr*]
handeln	to act
Handlung	action; act [cf. *Tat*]; deed* [cf. *Tat*]; transaction
Haufen	aggregate; mob
Herz	heart [cf. *Gemüt*]
Ich	(the) 'I'
Ichheit	selfhood
ideal, ideell	ideal
Idee	Idea

Individualität	individuality [cf. *Einzelheit*]
individuell	individual [adjective; cf. *einzeln*]
Individuum	individual [noun; cf. *Einzelne*]
Inhalt	content(s) [cf. *Gehalt*]
inneres Staatsrecht	constitutional law*
Innerlichkeit	inwardness [cf. *Innigkeit*]
Innigkeit	inwardness [cf. *Innerlichkeit*]; intensity [of feeling]
in sich	(with)in itself, (with)in themselves [cf. *an sich, für sich*]; into itself, into themselves; inherently* [cf. *an sich*]
Insichsein	inward being; being-in-itself* [cf. *Ansichsein*]
intellektuell	intellectual [cf. *geistig*]
Jurisprudenz	jurisprudence [cf. *Rechtswissenschaft*]
Jurist	jurist [cf. *Rechtsgelehrte*]
Juristenstand	legal profession
Kammer	house [of parliament]
Kapital	capital
kennen	to be familiar with; to know* [cf. *erkennen, wissen*]
Kennen	knowing [in the sense of being familiar or acquainted with]
Kenntnis, Kenntnisse	knowledge* [cf. *Erkennen, Wissen*]; cognizance*
Klasse	[socio-economic] class [cf. *Stand*]
Korporation	corporation [cf. *Genossenschaft*]
Kraft	force [cf. *Gewalt*]; strength; power [cf. *Gewalt, Macht*]
Kultur	culture [cf. *Bildung*]
Landrecht	law of the land
Lebendigkeit	vitality; life; living principle*
Lehre	doctrine; theory* [cf. *Theorie*]
Macht	power [cf. *Gewalt, Kraft*]; authority* [cf. *Ansehen, Autorität, Berechtigung, Obrigkeit*]
Manifestation	manifestation [cf. *Gestalt, Scheinen*]
Material	(raw) material [cf. *Stoff*]; medium

Materie	matter [as physical substance; cf. *Gegenstand*, *Sache*]; topic [cf. *Stoff*]
Maxime	maxim [cf. *Grundsatz*]
Mensch	human being; man(kind) [cf. also comments on p. xliv]
Mittel	means [cf. *Vermittlung*]; commodity*
Mittelstand	middle class* [cf. *Stand* and comments on p. xliii]
Moment	moment [in the sense of 'essential component']; element* [cf. *Boden*, *Element*]; fact* [cf. *Faktum*, *Tatsache*]; concern*
Moral, *Moralität*	morality
Motiv	motive [cf. *Beweggrund*, *Trieb*, *Triebfeder*]
Mut	courage
Nation	nation [cf. *Volk*]
Naturrecht	natural law
nichtig	null and void; insignificant; futile*
Nichtigkeit	nullity; insignificance
Not	want [cf. *Notdurft*]; necessity* [cf. *Notwendigkeit*]
Notdurft	requirements; want [cf. *Not*]
Notrecht	right of necessity
Notstaat	state of necessity
Notwendigkeit	necessity [cf. *Not*]
Objekt	object [cf. *Ding*, *Gegenstand*]
objektiv	objective [cf. *gegenständlich*]
Obrigkeit	authority, authorities* [of publicly constituted bodies within the state; cf. *Ansehen*, *Autorität*, *Berechtigung*, *Macht*]
partikular, *partikulär*	particular* [cf. *besonder*]
Partikularität	particularity* [cf. *Besonderheit*]
Person	person
Phänomen	phenomenon [cf. *Erscheinung*]
Pöbel	rabble
Polizei	police [cf. comments on pp. xlii–xliii and 450]
Prinzip	principle [cf. *Grundsatz*]
Privatrecht	civil law*

Räsonieren, Räsonnement	ratiocination; reasoning*; argument*
real	real [cf. *reell*]
Realität	reality
Recht	right [cf. *Berechtigung*]; law* [cf. *Gesetz, Naturrecht, römisches Recht*]; justice* [cf. *Gerechtigkeit*] [see also comments on p. xxxviii]
Rechtens	lawful*
Rechtfertigung	justification [cf. *Berechtigung*]
rechtlich	rightful; legal* [cf. *gerichtlich, gesetzlich, gesetzmäßig*]; right-minded*
Rechtlichkeit	rightness; integrity*
rechtschaffen	upright; honest
Rechtschaffenheit	rectitude
Rechtsgang	process of law, legal process
Rechtsgelehrte	jurist [cf. *Jurist*]; lawyer
Rechtsgrund	legal claim*; legal argument*
Rechtspflege	administration of justice
Rechtsprechen	dispensation of justice; legal dispensation; [act of] jurisdiction* [cf. *Gerichtsbarkeit*]
Rechtswissenschaft	science of right; jurisprudence* [cf. *Jurisprudenz*]
reell	real [cf. *real*]
Regierung	government; executive
Regierungsgewalt	executive power
Reich	realm [cf. *Gebiet*]
Reichtum	wealth [cf. *Vermögen*]
Relation	relationship* [cf. *Beziehung, Verhältnis*]
Repräsentation	representation [cf. *Vorstellung*]
Richter	judge; magistrate
richterlich	judicial
richtig	correct; accurate; legitimate* [cf. *berechtigt*]
römisches Recht	Roman law
Rührung	emotion* [cf. *Gemüt*]
Sache	thing* [cf. *Ding*]; matter* [cf. *Gegenstand,*

	Materie]; cause* [as a principle espoused; cf. *Grund*]; concern*; case*
Schein	semblance; pretence*
scheinen	to seem; to appear [cf. *erscheinen*]; to manifest itself*
Scheinen	manifestation* [cf. *Gestalt, Manifestation*]
schlecht	bad; wicked; inferior*
schlechte Unendlichkeit	false infinity
Schlechtigkeit	wickedness
Schranke	limit [cf. *Grenze*]; restriction* [cf. *Beschränkung*]
Schuld	responsibility [cf. *Verantwortung*]; guilt
sein	to be; to exist [cf. *bestehen, existieren*]; to be present; to have being [cf. also comment on pp. xliii–xliv]
Sein	being [cf. *Wesen*]
selbständig	self-sufficient; independent [cf. *unabhängig*]
Selbständigkeit	self-sufficiency; independence
Selbstgefühl	self-awareness; self-esteem*
Setzen	to posit
Sitte	ethics [cf. *Sittlichkeit*]; custom [cf. *Gewohnheit*]
sittlich	ethical
Sittlichkeit	ethics [cf. *Sitte*]; ethical life
Sollen	obligation; something which ought to be*
souverän	sovereign [adjective]; supreme*
Souverän	sovereign [noun; cf. *Fürst*]
Souveränität	sovereignty
Sphäre	sphere [cf. *Boden*]
Spitze	apex; culmination; supreme office, supreme position; head (of state)
Staat	state
Staatsrecht	see *äußeres Staatsrecht, inneres Staatsrecht*
Staatswissenschaft	political science
Stamm	kinship group; tribe*
Stand	estate; class* [cf. *Klasse*]; status* [cf. also comment on p. xliii]

Stände	[plural of *Stand*] Estates [as a parliamentary institution]; estates [as social groupings or classes; cf. also comments on p. xliii]
Standpunkt	point of view; viewpoint [cf. *Gesichtspunkt*]; position [doctrinal or ideological]; level [cf. *Stufe*]
Stoff	material [cf. *Material*]; substance* [in the sense of 'material'; cf. *Gehalt, Substanz*]; topic [cf. *Materie*]; subject-matter* [cf. *Gegenstand*]
Stufe	stage; level [cf. *Standpunkt*]; phase
Subjekt	subject [cf. *Gegenstand, Untertan*; see also comments on p. xli]
Subsistenz	livelihood [cf. *Auskommen*]; subsistence* [cf. *Bestehen*]
substantiell	substantial
Substanz	substance [in the metaphysical sense; cf. *Stoff*]
Tapferkeit	valour; bravery
Tat	deed [cf. *Handlung*]; act [cf. *Handlung*]
Tatbestand	facts of the case*
Tätigkeit	activity [cf. *Wirksamkeit*]
Tatsache	fact [cf. *Faktum, Moment*]
Teil	part; component; section
Teilung	division* [in the sense of 'partition'; cf. *Einteilung, Entzweiung, Trennung*]
Theorie	theory [cf. *Lehre*]
trennen	to separate; to divide
Trennung	separation; division [cf. *Einteilung, Entzweiung, Teilung*]; disjunction
Trieb	drive; urge; motive* [cf. *Beweggrund, Motiv, Triebfeder*]
Triebfeder	motive* [cf. *Beweggrund, Motiv, Trieb*]; spring [of action]*
Übel	evil* [usually of a specific evil; cf. *Böse*]

Umstand	circumstance [cf. *Verhältnisse*]
unabhängig	independent [cf. *selbständig*]
unbefangen	ingenuous; unintentional [of a wrong committed in good faith]
unbegrenzt	unbounded
unbeschränkt	unlimited; unrestricted
ungebildet	uneducated; uncivilized*
ungerecht	unjust [cf. *unrechtlich*]
Ungerechtigkeit	injustice [cf. *Unrecht*]
unmittelbar	immediate(ly); direct(ly)
Unrecht	wrong, wrongdoing; violation of right, something contrary to right; injustice* [cf. *Ungerechtigkeit*]
unrechtlich	contrary to right; wrong; unjust* [cf. *ungerecht*]
unrechtmäßig	unlawful
Unterschied	distinction; difference [cf. *Differenz, Verschiedenheit*]; differentiation* [cf. *Verschiedenheit*]
Untertan	subject* [of a state or sovereign; cf. *Gegenstand, Subjekt*]
unveräußerlich	inalienable
unwahr	untrue; false* [cf. *falsch*]
unzweckmäßig	inappropriate
Veranstaltung	arrangement
Verantwortung, Verantwortlichkeit	accountability; responsibility* [cf. *Schuld*]
veräußerlich	alienable
veräußern	to alienate [as applied to goods or property], to dispose of [cf. *entäußern*]
Veräußerung	alienation [of goods or property], disposal
Verbrechen	crime
Verfassung	constitution
Vergehen	misdemeanour; offence [cf. *Verletzung*]
Verhalten	conduct; attitude [cf. *Gesinnung*]
Verhältnis	relation(ship) [cf. *Beziehung, Relation*]; situation [cf. *Zustand*]

Verhältnisse	[plural of *Verhältnis*] relation(ship)s; circumstances [cf. *Umstand*]
Verjährung	prescription
Verkehr	trade* [cf. *Gewerbe*]; commerce* [cf. *Handel*]
Verletzung	infringement, violation; injury*; offence* [cf. *Vergehen*]
vermitteln	to mediate
Vermittlung	mediation; means [cf. *Mittel*]
Vermögen	capacity; faculty; resource(s); wealth* [cf. *Reichtum*]
Vernichtung	nullification; annihilation; destruction
Vernunft	reason [i.e. rationality in a universal sense; cf. *Grund*]
vernünftig	rational
Verschiedenheit	difference [cf. *Differenz*, *Unterschied*]; diversity; variety; differentiation [cf. *Unterschied*]
Verstand	understanding
verstehen	to understand [cf. *fassen*]
Vertrag	contract [cf. *Wahlkapitulation*]
verwirklichen	to actualize
Verwirklichung	actualization
Volk	people; nation* [cf. *Nation*]
Völkerrecht	international law*
Volksgeist	national spirit, spirit of the nation
Vorsatz	purpose [cf. *Zweck*]
Vorsorge	provision(s); foresight
vorstellen	[reflexive verb] to represent to oneself; to imagine; to envisage
Vorstellen	representational thinking; imagination*
Vorstellung	representational thought; representational thinking; representation* [cf. *Repräsentation*]; (common) idea*; notion* [cf. *Einfall*; see also comments on p. xlii]
Wahlkapitulation	electoral contract* [cf. *Vertrag*]
wahr	true
wahrhaft(ig)	true; genuine

Wahrheit	truth
Weltgeist	world spirit
Wert	value; worth
Wesen	essence; essential being; being* [cf. *Sein*]
Wille(n)	will
Willkür	arbitrariness; arbitrary will
willkürlich	arbitrary
wirklich	actual
Wirklichkeit	actuality
Wirksamkeit	activity [cf. *Tätigkeit*]; effectiveness
wissen	to know [cf. *kennen, erkennen*]
Wissen	knowledge [cf. *Erkennen, Kenntnis*]
Wissenschaft	science; learning*
Wohl	welfare
Wollen	volition; willing
Würde	dignity [cf. *Ehre*]
Zeichen	sign; symbol
Zufall, Zufälligkeit	contingency; chance; eventuality*
zufällig	contingent
zurechnen	to hold responsible for
Zurechnung	imputation*; making (or holding) responsible (or accountable) for*
zurechnungsfähig	responsible (for one's actions)
Zusammenhang	context; link, connection(s); association*; continuum*; complex*
Zustand	condition; situation [cf. *Verhältnis*]
Zwang	coercion [cf. *Gewalt*]
Zweck	end [in the sense of 'aim' or 'purpose']; purpose* [cf. *Vorsatz*]
zweckmäßig	appropriate; expedient

Selected bibliography

For references to Hegel's own writings, see key to abbreviations, pp. xlv–xlix. For a thorough bibliography of secondary sources on Hegel to 1980, see Kurt Steinhauer (ed.) *Hegel Bibliographie: Materialien zur Geschichte der internationalen Hegel-Rezeption und zur Philosophie-Geschichte* (Munich: K. G. Sauer, 1980). For a good bibliography of secondary sources on Hegel's PR before 1957, see the appendix (by Hans-Martin Saß) to Joachim Ritter, *Hegel und die französische Revolution* (Cologne: Westdeutscher Verlag, 1957). The following is a selected bibliography of secondary sources in English, French and German on PR and topics in Hegel's philosophy related to it.

Albrecht, Reinhart. *Hegel und die Demokratie.* Bonn: Bouvier, 1978.

Althusser, Louis. *Politics and History,* tr. B. Brewster. London: New Left Books, 1972.

Angehrn, Emil. *Freiheit und System bei Hegel.* Berlin: W. de Gruyter, 1976.

Avineri, Shlomo. *Hegel's Theory of the Modern State.* Cambridge University Press, 1972.

Barion, Jakob. *Hegel und die marxistische Staatslehre,* 2nd ed. Bonn: Bouvier, 1970.

Benhabib, Seyla. 'The Logic of Civil Society: A Re-consideration of Hegel and Marx', *Philosophy and Social Theory* (1972).

Berry, Christopher J. *Hume, Hegel and Human Nature.* The Hague: Nijhoff, 1982.

Bitsch, Brigitte. *Sollensbegriff und Moralitätskritik bei Hegel.* Bonn: Bouvier, 1977.

Bloch, Ernst. *Subjekt–Objekt: Erläuterungen zu Hegel* (1951). Bloch, *Werkausgabe.* Frankfurt: Suhrkamp, 1985. Volume VIII.

Bülow, Friedrich. *Die Entwicklung der Hegelschen Sozialphilosophie.* Leipzig: Meiner, 1920.

Cassirer, Ernst. *The Myth of the State* (1946). Garden City, NY: Doubleday, 1955.

Chamley, Paul. *Economie politique et philosophie chez Steuart et Hegel.* Paris: Dalloz, 1963.

Colletti, Lucio. *Marxism and Hegel*, tr. L. Garner. London: Verso, 1979.
Cullen, Bernard. *Hegel's Social and Political Thought*. New York: St Martin's, 1979.
Fackenheim, Emil L. 'On the Actuality of the Rational and the Rationality of the Actual', *Review of Metaphysics* 13 (1970).
Fleischmann, Eugène. *La Philosophie politique de Hegel*. Paris: Plon, 1964.
Foster, Michael B. *The Political Philosophies of Plato and Hegel* (1935). New York: Garland, 1984.
Fulda, Hans-Friedrich. *Das Recht der Philosophie in Hegels Philosophie des Rechts*. Frankfurt: Klostermann, 1968.
Garaudy, Roger. *La Pensée de Hegel*. Paris: Bordas, 1966.
Habermas, Jürgen. *Theory and Praxis*, tr. J. Viertel. Boston: Beacon, 1974.
Harris, H. S. *Hegel's Development: Toward the Sunlight 1770–1801*. Oxford: Clarendon Press, 1972.
Hegel's Development: Night Thoughts (Jena, 1801–1806). Oxford: Clarendon Press, 1983.
Haym, Rudolf. *Hegel und seine Zeit*. Berlin: Gaertner, 1857.
Henrich, Dieter. *Hegel im Kontext*. Frankfurt: Suhrkamp, 1971.
Henrich, Dieter and Horstmann, Rolf-Peter (eds.) *Hegels Philosophie des Rechts: Die Theorie der Rechtsformen und ihre Logik*. Stuttgart: Klett-Cotta, 1983.
Hinchman, Lew. *Hegel's Critique of the Enlightenment*. Tampa: University of Florida Press, 1984.
Hočevar, Rolf K. *Stände und Repräsentation beim jungen Hegel*. Munich: Beck, 1968.
Hegel und der preußische Staat. Munich: Beck, 1973.
d'Hondt, Jacques. *Hegel in his Time* (1968), tr. J. Burbidge. Lewiston, NY: Broadview, 1988.
Hyppolite, Jean. *Studies on Marx and Hegel*, tr. J. O'Neill. New York: Harper & Row, 1969.
Kaufmann, Walter (ed.). *Hegel's Political Philosophy*. New York: Atherton, 1970.
Kelly, George Armstrong. *Idealism, Politics and History: Sources of Hegelian Thought*. Cambridge University Press, 1969.
Hegel's Retreat from Eleusis. Princeton: Princeton University Press, 1978.
Knox, T. M. 'Hegel and Prussianism', *Philosophy* (1940).
Kojève, Alexander. *Introduction to the Reading of Hegel*, tr. J. H. Nichols. New York: Basic Books, 1969.
Löwith, Karl. *From Hegel to Nietzsche*, tr. David F. Green. New York: Doubleday, 1967.
Lukács, György. *The Young Hegel*, tr. Rodney Livingstone. Cambridge, MA: MIT Press, 1975.
MacGregor, David. *The Communist Ideal in Hegel and Marx*. Toronto: University of Toronto Press, 1984.
MacIntyre, Alasdair (ed.) *Hegel: A Collection of Critical Essays*. Garden City, NY: Doubleday, 1972.

Select bibliography

Marcuse, Herbert. *Reason and Revolution: Hegel and the Rise of Social Theory* (1941, 2nd ed. 1955). Boston: Beacon, 1960.

Marx, Karl. *Critique of Hegel's Philosophy of Right*, tr. J. O'Malley. Cambridge University Press, 1970.

Miskell, Thomas. *Hegels Lehre vom abstrakten Recht*. Freiburg i.B.: Albert-Ludwigs-Universität, 1972.

Mitias, Michael. *The Moral Foundation of the State in Hegel's 'Philosophy of Right'*. Amsterdam: Rodopi, 1984.

Moran, Philip. *Hegel and the Fundamental Problems of Philosophy*. Amsterdam: Gruner, 1988.

Mure, G. R. G. 'The Organic State', *Philosophy* (1949).

Nicolin, Friedhelm. *Hegels Bildungstheorie*. Bonn: Bouvier, 1955.
'Hegel über konstitutionelle Monarchie', *Hegel-Studien* 10 (1975).

Nusser, Karl-Heinz. *Hegels Dialektik und das Prinzip der Revolution*. Munich: Pustet, 1973.

O'Brien, George Dennis. *Hegel on Reason and History*. Chicago: University of Chicago Press, 1975.

O'Hagan, T. 'On Hegel's Critique of Kant's Moral and Political Philosophy', in Stephen Priest (ed.) *Hegel's Critique of Kant*. Oxford: Clarendon Press, 1987.

Ottmann, Henning. *Individuum und Gemeinschaft bei Hegel*. Berlin: W. de Gruyter, 1977.

Parkinson, G.H.R. 'Hegel's Concept of Freedom', in M. Inwood (ed.) *Hegel*. Oxford University Press, 1985.

Pelczynski, Z. (ed.) *Hegel's Political Philosophy: Problems and Perspectives*. Cambridge University Press, 1971.

(ed.) *The State and Civil Society: Studies in Hegel's Political Philosophy*. Cambridge University Press, 1984.

Pippin, Robert. 'Hegel's Political Argument and the Problem of *Verwirklichung*', *Political Theory* 9 (1981).

Plamenatz, John. *Man and Society*, Volume II. New York: McGraw-Hill, 1963.

Plant, Raymond. *Hegel: An Introduction*, 2nd ed. Oxford: Blackwell, 1983.

Pöggeler, Otto. *Hegels Kritik der Romantik*. Bonn: Bouvier, 1956.

Pöggeler, Otto (ed.) *Hegel: Einführung in seine Philosophie*. Freiburg/Munich: Alber, 1977.

Prior, Andrew. *Revolution and Philosophy: The Significance of the French Revolution for Hegel and Marx*. Capetown: D. Philip, 1972.

Reyburn, Hugh A. *The Ethical Theory of Hegel*. Oxford: Clarendon Press, 1921.

Riedel, Manfred. *Bürgerliche Gesellschaft und Staat bei Hegel*. Neuwied: Luchterhand, 1970.

System und Geschichte. Frankfurt: Suhrkamp, 1973.

(ed.) *Materialien zu Hegels Rechtsphilosophie*, 2 volumes. Frankfurt: Suhrkamp, 1975.

Between Tradition and Revolution. Cambridge University Press, 1984.

Ritter, Joachim. *Hegel and the French Revolution* (1957; 2nd ed., 1965). Cambridge, MA: MIT Press, 1982.

'Person und Eigentum: Zu Hegels "Grundlinien der Philosophie des Rechts"', *Marxismusstudien* 4 (1962).

Metaphysik und Politik: Studien zu Aristoteles und Hegel. Frankfurt: Suhrkamp, 1969.

Rose, Gillian R. *Hegel Contra Sociology.* Atlantic Highlands, NJ: Humanities Press, 1981.

Rosenkranz, Karl. *Hegels Leben.* Berlin: Duncker & Humblot, 1844.

Rosenzweig, Franz. *Hegel und der Staat*, 2 volumes. Munich and Berlin: Oldenbourg, 1920.

Rothe, Klaus. *Selbstsein und bürgerliche Gesellschaft: Hegels Theorie der konkreten Freiheit.* Bonn: Bouvier, 1976.

Shklar, Judith. *Freedom and Independence: A Study of the Political Ideas of Hegel's 'Phenomenology of Mind'.* Cambridge University Press, 1976.

Singer, Peter. *Hegel.* Oxford: Oxford University Press, 1983.

Smith, Steven B. *Hegel's Critique of Liberalism: Rights in Context.* Chicago: University of Chicago Press, 1989.

Steinberger, Peter. *Logic and Politics: Hegel's Philosophy of Right.* New Haven: Yale University Press, 1988.

Stepelevich, L. S. and Lamb, D. (eds.) *Hegel's Philosophy of Action.* Atlantic Highlands, NJ: Humanities Press, 1983.

Stillman, Peter. 'Hegel's Critique of Liberal Theories of Right', *American Political Science Review* 68 (1974).

'Property, Freedom and Individuality in Hegel's and Marx's Political Thought', *Nomos* 22 (1980).

Taylor, Charles. *Hegel.* Cambridge University Press, 1975.

Hegel and Modern Society. Cambridge University Press, 1979.

Theunissen, Michael. *Hegels Lehre vom absoluten Geist als theologisch-politischer Traktat.* Berlin: W. de Gruyter, 1970.

Die Verwirklichung der Vernunft: zur Theorie-Praxis-Diskussion in Anschluß an Hegel. Tübingen: Mohr, 1970.

Toews, John Edward. *Hegelianism.* Cambridge University Press, 1980.

Tugendhat, Ernst. *Self-Consciousness and Self-Determination*, tr. Paul Stern. Cambridge, MA: MIT Press, 1986.

Verene, Donald P. (ed.) *Hegel's Social and Political Thought.* Atlantic Highlands, NJ: Humanities Press, 1980.

Walsh, W. H. *Hegelian Ethics.* New York: Garland, 1984.

Weil, Eric. *Hegel et l'état*, 2nd ed. Paris: Vrin, 1966.

Wildt, Andreas. *Autonomie und Anerkennung.* Stuttgart: Klett-Cotta, 1982.

Wilkins, Burleigh T. *Hegel's Philosophy of History.* Ithaca: Cornell University Press, 1974.

Wood, Allen W. 'Hegel's Concept of Morality', in I. Patoluoto (ed.), *J. V. Snellmanin Filosofia ja sen Hegelilainen Tausta.* Helsinki, 1984.

'The Emptiness of the Moral Will', *Monist* 72 (1989).

Hegel's Ethical Thought. Cambridge University Press, 1990.

'Does Hegel Have an Ethics?' *Monist* 74 (1991).

Index of subjects

Index of subjects

education [*Bildung*], xix, 52, 61, 136–
137, 159, 212–213, 224–226, 230–
234, 240, 264, 290–291, 376–377,
401, 426, 438, 440; ethical, 195–
196; play theory of, 212–213, 440;
see also upbringing
education [*Pädagogik*], 195
elections, 348–351
embezzlement, 418
emptiness of moral standpoint, 162–
163, 427
end [*Zweck*], xxiv–xxvi, 42–43, 149,
157, 189; subjective, 43
end justifies the means, 175–176, 430
endowments, 94, 412
English law, *see* law, English
ephorate, 309, 461–462
equality, 39, 80–81, 128, 230, 234,
240, 408, 457
error, 399; moral, 171–172, 178–180,
432
Erscheinung, see appearance
estate [*Stand*], xix–xxii, xliii, 71, 233–
239, 347; choice of an, 237–238;
formal (business), 234, 236–237,
270–271; honour of, 271; middle,
335–336; military, 363–365; private,
343; substantial (agricultural), xx-
xxi, 234–236, 270; universal (civil
service), 234, 237, 270, 328–336
Estates [*Stände*], x, xxiii–xxiv, xliii,
339–353, 469–470; as mediating
organ, 342–343; bicameral system,
345–352; lower house, 346–348;
publicity of debate in, 352, 356;
upper house, 345–346
ethical life [*Sittlichkeit*], xii, xv–xvi,
xxxix, 12, 53, 59, 62–63, 137, 185–
186, 189–198, 402, 404; as custom,
195; objective side, 189–190;
subjective side, 190–191
ethics, 10–11, 20
evil, 51, 167–184, 194, 428; origin of,
167–170
excessive damage, 107, 414
executive power, 316, 328–336;
accountability of, 326, 334, 464–
465; role in legislation, 339
existence [*Dasein, Existenz*], 20–22, 25,
138, 390, 410

facts of consciousness, 27, 51, 392–
393

family, xxiii, 33–34, 62, 64, 71, 77,
198–219, 272, 283–286, 377–378,
396, 405, 407, 451; feudal, 209–
210
family-member, 199–200, 228
feudalism, xvii, 77, 106, 388, 407,
410–411, 469
fiat iustitia, pereat mundus, 157, 426
fideicommissa, 77, 407
finitude, 39–40, 46–47, 137, 139, 399
foetura, 85, 99, 410
foreign trade, 268
form-giving, as mode of appropriation,
83, 85–86
fraternities [*Burschenschaften*], 383–385
free will, development of, 35–45
freedom [*Freiheit*], xi–xvii, xxvii–xxix,
35–58, 119–120, 189, 230–231,
288, 396–397; absolute, 52–55;
abstract, 37–38, 67–68, 119–120,
192–193, 398; affirmative, 193; as
arbitrariness, 48–50, 399–400; as
contingency, 49; as its own object,
57; civil, 261, 450–451; concrete,
401–402; external, 79; formal, 37–
38, 224–226, 330, 351; negative,
38–39, 398, 436; objective, 275–
282; of commerce, 262; of public
communication, 355–358; personal,
68, 284; subjective, xiv–xxii, 20, 22,
149–152, 166–167, 196, 201–202,
221–226, 230–231, 237–238, 246,
256, 258, 282–288, 338, 353, 355–
359, 402, 442–443; substantial, 192,
275

Geist, see spirit
genius, ethical, 193–194
German nationalism, *see* nationalism,
German
Gesinnung, see disposition
gnothi seauton [Γνῶθι σεαυτόν],
373, 477
God, 18, 22, 168–170, 279–281, 290,
325, 354, 465, 476–477; ontological
proof of, 322, 464
good, 62, 64, 141, 157–161
good will, 158, 173–176
grace, efficacious, 172, 429
guilds, xx–xxi, 445, 452; *see also*
corporations

habit, 194–195

503

Index of subjects

logic, formal 34
logic, speculative, 10, 27–28, 42, 382
lord and servant, 87
love, 199–202, 209–211; illicit, 438–439; parental, 210–211; Platonic, 203
luck, its role in morality, 148

magistrate (*magistratus*), 255, 448–449
Magna Charta, *see* index of names
mandatum, 110, 415
manufacture, 237
many, the [*hoi polloi*; οἱ πολλοί], 339, 353, 472
marking, as mode of appropriation, 88
marriage, 200–208, 457; arranged, 201–202; as contract, 201, 203; ceremony of, 201–202, 205; monogamous, 207; Roman, 209, 440
Marxism, ix, xxxi
masses, endowed, 94, 412
mathematics, 34
method, philosophical, 10, 59
military, x, 305, 338–339, 361–365, 460–461, 474; conscription, 295, 305, 460–461
monarch, xxiii, 313–328; as first servant of the state, 324, 465; inviolability of, 464–465; right to appoint ministers, 326; role in legislation, 339
monarchy, constitutional, xxiii–xxiv, 308, 313–328; elective, 324, 465; feudal, 310, 315, 463–464; hereditary, 321–325
monasticism, 78, 203
money, 93, 337–338, 343
monogamy, 207
morality, xi, xxvii–xxix, 53, 59, 62–64, 131–132, 135–186, 404, 421–435
morality and politics, 370, 475
mortgage, 112
motive, 149–150, 152, 160, 178
mutuum, 110, 415

Napoleonic Code, 419, 447
nation [*Volk*], xxxii, 28, 88, 359–369, 375–376; principle of, 374–377, 478
National Socialism, viii, xxx–xxxi
nationalism, 360; German, viii–ix, 383, 385, 461, 473

natural states, 378, 479
nature, 12, 190–191; does no injustice, 80, 266–267; laws of, 13
nature of an action, 145–148, 421
necessity, right of, 154–156
needs, 226–240, 259; natural, 228–229; refinement of, 229, 231; social, 229–230
negation of negation, 115–116, 131
negativity, 37–40
nobility, feudal, 235–236, 345–346, 460–461, 468
nullum crimen, nulla poena sine lege, 419

objectivity, 42–43, 55–56, 138–142, 159
obligation, 117, 137, 197
office, he who gets one gets understanding, 18, 388
opinion [*Meinung*], 11–12, 16; *see also* public opinion
Oriental Realm, *see* index of names
'ought', 22, 88, 158, 390
ouk eidos [οὐκ εἰδώς], 171
owl of Minerva, 23, 392
ownerlessness, 81, 94, 409, 412

pactum, 109, 414
pardon, 161, 325–326, 466
particularity, 39–40, 69, 219–224, 282–288; *see also* freedom, subjective
parties, political, 470
passion, 202–203
patria potestas, 29, 75, 211–213, 218, 396, 440
patriotism, xxv–xxvi, 288–289
peace, perpetual, 362, 368, 473
peasantry, 235–237
people, the, 15–17, 318–321, 339–342, 349–355, 465, 472
perfectibility, 376–377, 476–477
permission [*Erlaubnis*], 69–70, 404–405
person, xiii–xvii, 67–69, 71, 199, 207, 224–226, 228, 379, 404–407, 457
philosophy, 15–16, 21–23, 25–28, 34, 40, 391–392; as a circle, 26–27
philosophy and jurisprudence, 28–34, 395
piety, 16, 275, 293
plagiarism, 100–101
pledge [*Pfand*], 112–113, 415–416

Index of subjects

Twelve Tables, 31–32, 34, 395–396, 440–442

understanding [*Verstand*], 10, 30–34, 38–39, 392
unintentional wrong [*unbefangenes Unrecht*], 116–119
universality, xii, 37–38, 54–55, 67, 140–141, 146–148, 157, 219–220, 224–226, 276; formal, 52; self-determining, 52–53
unmoved mover, 189, 275, 435
Unrecht, see wrong
use of property, 83, 88–94

valet, no man a hero to his, 152, 424
valour [*Tapferkeit*], 363–365
value [*Wert*], 92–93, 107, 127–128, 411
Vernunft, see reason
Versöhnung, see reconciliation
Verstand, see understanding
virtue [*Tugend*], 122, 194–195, 418; as mean, 194, 437
Volk, see people; nation
Vorsatz, see purpose
Vorstellung, see representation
voting franchise, 469–470

wages, contract of, 98–99, 112, 416
Wahl, see choice
war, xxvi–xxvii, 101–102, 360–365, 369; modern, 365, 474; prisoners of, 371; rules of, 370–371, 475
warrant [*Befugnis*], 69–70, 404–405
welfare [*Wohl*], xvii–xviii, xxiv–xxv, 141, 150–158, 197, 220–221, 283–288, 369
will [*Wille*], 35–58, 78–79; common, 104–106; freedom of, 35–37, 396–397; immediate, 44–45; natural, 167; subjective, 135–142
Willkür, see arbitrariness
women, 206–207, 439–440
work [*Arbeit*], 231–233, 444
world-historical individual, 375, 477–479
world history, xxv, 62–63, 281, 371–380; its right is absolute, 63–64, 373–374, 477–478
world spirit, *see* spirit
wrong [*Unrecht*], xxi, 70, 113, 115–131, 260; civil, 116–119

youth, 15, 383

Zwang, see coercion
Zweck, see end

Index of names

Index of names

CAMBRIDGE TEXTS IN THE HISTORY OF POLITICAL THOUGHT

Titles published in the series thus far:

Aristotle   *The Politics* (edited by Stephen Everson)

Bakunin   *Statism and Anarchy* (edited by Marshall Shatz)

Bentham   *A Fragment on Government* (introduction by Ross Harrison)

Bossuet   *Politics Drawn from the Very Word of Holy Scripture* (edited by Patrick Riley)

Cicero   *On Duties* (edited by M.T. Griffin and E.M. Atkins)

Constant   *Political Writings* (edited by Biancamaria Fontana)

Filmer   *Patriarcha and Other Writings* (edited by Johann P. Sommerville)

Hegel   *Elements of the Philosophy of Right* (edited by Allen W. Wood and H.B. Nisbet)

Hobbes   *Leviathan* (edited by Richard Tuck)

Hooker   *Of the Laws of Ecclesiastical Polity* (edited by A.S. McGrade)

John of Salisbury   *Policraticus* (edited by Cary Nederman)

Kant   *Political Writings* (edited by H.S. Reiss and H.B. Nisbet)

Leibniz   *Political Writings* (edited by Patrick Riley)

Locke   *Two Treatises of Government* (edited by Peter Laslett)

Luther   *On Secular Authority* and Calvin   *On Civil Government* (edited by Harro Höpfl)

Machiavelli   *The Prince* (edited by Quentin Skinner and Russell Price)

J.S. Mill   *On Liberty*, with *The Subjection of Women* and *Chapters on Socialism* (edited by Stefan Collini)

Milton   *Political Writings* (edited by Martin Dzelzainis)

Montesquieu   *The Spirit of the Laws* (edited by Anne M. Cohler, Basia Carolyn Miller and Harold Samuel Stone)

More   *Utopia* (edited by George M. Logan and Robert M. Adams)

Nicholas of Cusa   *The Catholic Concordance* (edited by Paul E. Sigmund)

Paine   *Political Writings* (edited by Bruce Kuklick)

Pufendorf   *On the Duty of Man and Citizen according to Natural Law* (edited by James Tully)

The Radical Reformation (edited by Michael G. Baylor)

Vitoria   *Political Writings* (edited by Anthony Pagden)